The Blackwell Guide to

Philosophy of Mind

—— Blackwell Philosophy Guides ——

Series Editor: Steven M. Cahn, City University of New York Graduate School

Written by an international assembly of distinguished philosophers, the *Blackwell Philosophy Guides* create a groundbreaking student resource – a complete critical survey of the central themes and issues of philosophy today. Focusing and advancing key arguments throughout, each essay incorporates essential background material serving to clarify the history and logic of the relevant topic. Accordingly, these volumes will be a valuable resource for a broad range of students and readers, including professional philosophers.

The Blackwell Guide to
Philosophy of Mind

Edited by

Stephen P. Stich and Ted A. Warfield

Blackwell
Publishing

350 Main Street, Malden, MA 02148–5018, USA
108 Cowley Road, Oxford OX4 1JF, UK
550 Swanston Street, Carlton South, Melbourne, Victoria 3053, Australia
Kurfürstendamm 57, 10707 Berlin, Germany

First published 2003 by Blackwell Publishing Ltd

Library of Congress Cataloging-in-Publication Data
The Blackwell guide to philosophy of mind/edited by Stephen P. Stich and Ted A. Warfield.
p. cm. – (Blackwell philosophy guides ; 9)
Includes bibliographical references and index.
ISBN 0-631-21774-6 (alk. paper) – ISBN 0-631-21775-4 (pbk. : alk. paper)
1. Philosophy of mind. I. Stich, Stephen P. II. Warfield, Ted A., 1969– III. Series.

BD418.3 .B57 2003
128′2–dc21   2002071221

A catalogue record for this title is available from the British Library.

Set in 10/13pt Galliard
by Graphicraft Limited, Hong Kong
Printed and bound in the United Kingdom
by MPG Books Ltd, Bodmin, Cornwall

For further information on
Blackwell Publishing, visit our website:
http://www.blackwellpublishing.com

Contents

Contents

Contributors

Fred Adams is Professor of Philosophy at the University of Delaware.

Kenneth Aizawa is Charles T. Beaird Professor of Philosophy at Centenary College of Louisiana.

John Bickle is Professor of Philosophy and Professor in the Graduate Neuroscience Program at the University of Cincinnati.

David J. Chalmers is Professor of Philosophy at the University of Arizona.

Andy Clark is Professor of Philosophy and Director of the Cognitive Sciences Program at Indiana University.

Randolph Clarke is Associate Professor of Philosophy at the University of Georgia.

Paul E. Griffiths is Professor of History and Philosophy of Science at the University of Pittsburgh.

John Heil is Paul B. Freeland Professor of Philosophy at Davidson College.

Stephen Laurence is a Senior Lecturer in Philosophy at the University of Sheffield.

Kirk Ludwig is Associate Professor of Philosophy at the University of Florida.

William G. Lycan is William Rand Kenan Jr. Professor of Philosophy at the University of North Carolina.

Eric Margolis is Associate Professor of Philosophy at Rice University.

Andrew Melnyk is Associate Professor of Philosophy at the University of Missouri.

Shaun Nichols is Associate Professor of Philosophy at the College of Charleston.

Eric T. Olson is University Lecturer in Philosophy and Fellow of Churchill College, University of Cambridge.

Howard Robinson is Professor of Philosophy at Central European University.

Stephen P. Stich is Board of Governors Professor of Philosophy and Cognitive Science at Rutgers University.

Ted A. Warfield is Associate Professor of Philosophy at the University of Notre Dame.

Robert A. Wilson is Professor of Philosophy at the University of Alberta.

Introduction

This volume is another in the series of Blackwell Philosophy Guides.[1] It contains 16 new essays covering a wide range of issues in contemporary philosophy of mind. Authors were invited to provide opinionated overviews of their topic and to cover the topic in any way they saw fit. This allowed them the freedom to make individual scholarly contributions to the issues under discussion, while simultaneously introducing their assigned topic. I hope that the finished product proves suitable for use in philosophy of mind courses at various levels. The volume should be a good resource for specialists and non-specialists seeking overviews of central issues in contemporary philosophy of mind. In this brief introduction I will try to explain some of the reasons why philosophy of mind seems to be such an important sub-field of philosophy. I will also explain my view of the source of the great diversity one finds within philosophy of mind. This discussion will lead to some commentary on methodological issues facing philosophers of mind and philosophers generally.[2]

Few philosophers would disagree with the claim that philosophy of mind is one of the most active and important sub-fields in contemporary philosophy. Philosophy of mind seems to have held this status since at least the late 1970s. Many would make and defend the stronger claim that philosophy of mind is unequivocally *the* most important sub-field in contemporary philosophy. Its status can be attributed to at least two related factors: the importance of the subject matter and the diversity of the field.

Mental phenomena are certainly of great importance in most, if not all, human activities. Our hopes, dreams, fears, thoughts, and desires, to give just some examples, all figure in the most important parts of our lives. Some maintain that mentality is essential to human nature: that at least some sort of mental life is necessary for being human or for being fully human. Others maintain that specific features of human mentality (perhaps human rationality) distinguish humans from other creatures with minds. Whether or not these ambitious claims are correct, the mental is at least of great importance to our lives. Who would deny that thoughts, emotions, and other mental phenomena are centrally involved in almost everything important about us? This obvious truth only partly explains the importance of philosophy of mind. The size and diversity of the field also deserve some credit for this standing.[3]

A quick glance at this volume's table of contents will give some indication of the breadth of the field.[4] In addition to essays on topics central to contemporary philosophy of mind, such as mental content, mental causation, and consciousness, we find essays connecting the philosophy of mind with broadly empirical work of various kinds. This empirically oriented work covers areas in which philosophers make contact with broad empirical psychological work on, for example, the emotions and concepts. The intersections of philosophy with both neuroscience and artificial intelligence are also topics of serious contemporary interest. In contrast to this empirically oriented work, we also see essays on traditional philosophical topics such as the mind–body problem, personal identity, and freedom of the will. These topics (especially the latter two) are often classified as a part of contemporary metaphysics but they are, traditionally, a part of philosophy of mind and so they are included in this volume.

Despite these initial classifications of work as either "traditional" or "empirically oriented," one should not assume that this distinction marks a sharp divide. It is possible to work on traditional topics while being sensitive to relevant empirical work; and making use of traditional philosophical tools, such as some kind of conceptual analysis, is probably *necessary* when doing empirically oriented philosophy of mind. What one finds in the field are not perfectly precise methodological divisions. Rather, one finds differences in the degree to which various philosophers believe empirical work is relevant to philosophy of mind and differences in the degree to which philosophers try to avoid traditional philosophical analysis.[5]

The breadth and diversity of philosophy of mind is not fully captured in a survey of topics arising in the field and in highlighting different approaches that are taken to those projects. In addition to a wide range of topics and different approaches to these topics, we also find a somewhat surprising list of different explanatory targets within this field. A philosopher doing philosophy of mind might be primarily interested in understanding or explaining the *human* mind or, more modestly, some features of the human mind. Alternatively, one might be interested in examining the broader abstract nature of "mentality" or "mindedness" (human or otherwise). One might also focus on *our concept* of the human mind, or *our concept* of minds generally, with or without any particular view of how our concept of these things relates to the reality of the subject matter.[6] These different possible targets of inquiry at least appear to lead to very different kinds of questions. Despite the apparent differences, however, this large variety of project falls quite comfortably under the umbrella heading of "philosophy of mind."

The diversity of philosophy of mind becomes even clearer when one realizes that one can mix and match the various targets of inquiry and the different methodologies. One might be interested in a largely empirical inquiry into our concept of the human mind. Alternatively, one might be interested in a broadly conceptual inquiry into the exact same subject matter. The different methodologies (and again, recall that these differences are best thought of as differences of degree not kind) can also be applied in investigations of the nature of the human mind or the nature of mentality.

We might expect methodological disputes to break out as philosophers take different approaches to different topics within philosophy of mind. For example, those favoring traditional a priori methodology might challenge empirically oriented philosophers who claim to reach conclusions about the nature of the human mind primarily through empirical work to explain how they bridge the apparent gap between the way human minds are and the way they must be. Similarly, empirically oriented philosophers of mind might challenge those favoring a priori methods to explain why they think such methods can reach conclusions about anything other than the concepts of those doing the analysis. Why, for example, should we think that an analysis of our concept of the mind is going to reveal anything about the mind? Perhaps, the criticism might continue, our concept of mind does not accurately reflect the nature of the mind. Unfortunately and surprisingly, however, discussions of these methodological issues are not common.[7] Fortunately these and related methodological issues also arise in other areas of philosophy, and there seems to be a growing interest in understanding and commenting upon various approaches to philosophical inquiry inside and outside of philosophy of mind.[8]

Contributors to this volume were not asked to comment on methodological issues in philosophy of mind. They were simply invited to introduce and discuss their assigned topic in whatever way they saw fit, using whatever methodology they chose to bring to the task. In addition to thinking about the first-order philosophical issues under discussion in these outstanding essays, readers are invited to reflect on the methodological and metaphilosophical issues relevant to the discussions. Perhaps such reflection will help us better understand some or all of the topics we encounter in the philosophy of mind.

Ted A. Warfield

Notes

1   A volume of this sort does not come together easily. I thank the contributors for their varying degrees of patience and support as we confronted difficulties at various stages of this project. I especially thank my co-editor for his unwavering support and guidance. For helpful discussion of some of the issues arising in this brief introduction, I thank my colleagues Leopold Stubenberg and William Ramsey. I do not thank my employer, the University of Notre Dame, though it did kindly allow me the use of a computer and printer while at work on this project.

2   The volume contains two distinct opening essays on the mind–body problem. In introducing the volume, I resist the temptation to write a third such essay and instead focus on a few organizational and methodological issues.

3 These partial explanations together still do not fully explain the status of philosophy of mind within contemporary philosophy. Ethics, for example, is tremendously important and is also a large and diverse field. I am unable to fully explain the status of philosophy of mind. Though now a bit dated, Tyler Burge's important essay "Philosophy of Language and Mind: 1950–1990" (*Philosophical Review*, 101 (1992), pp. 3–51) contains some helpful ideas about this matter.

4 But no one volume could really cover this entire field. One helpful additional resource, a good supplemental resource to this volume, is *The Blackwell Companion to Philosophy of Mind*, edited by Samuel Guttenplan (Blackwell, 1994).

5 The same philosopher might even take different general methodological approaches to different problems or even to the same problem at different times.

6 One can easily imagine how one might conclude, for example, that our concept of mind is in some sense a "dualistic" concept, but not think it follows from this that dualism is the correct position on the mind–body problem.

7 Some recent debates about consciousness have included, at a very high level of sophistication, some methodological discussion along these lines (see, for example, David J. Chalmers and Frank Jackson's "Conceptual Analysis and Reductive Explanation," *Philosophical Review*, 110 (2001), 315–60.

8 Anyone wishing to explore these issues could profitably begin with Michael R. DePaul and William Ramsey (eds.), *Rethinking Intuition* (Rowman and Littlefield, 1998).

Chapter 1

The Mind–Body Problem: An Overview

Kirk Ludwig

I have said that the soul is not more than the body,
And I have said that the body is not more than the soul,
And nothing, not God, is greater to one than one's self is.
                                        Walt Whitman

1.1 Introduction

Understanding the place of thought and feeling in the natural world is central to that general comprehension of nature, as well as that special self-understanding, which are the primary goals of science and philosophy. The general form of the project, which has exercised scientists and philosophers since the ancient world, is given by the question, 'What is the relation, in general, between mental and physical phenomena?' There is no settled agreement on the correct answer. This is the single most important gap in our understanding of the natural world. The trouble is that the question presents us with a problem: each *possible* answer to it has consequences that appear unacceptable. This problem has traditionally gone under the heading 'The Mind–Body Problem.'[1] My primary aim in this chapter is to explain in what this traditional mind–body problem consists, what its possible solutions are, and what obstacles lie in the way of a resolution.

The discussion will develop in two phases. The first phase, sections 1.2–1.4, will be concerned to get clearer about the import of our initial question as a precondition of developing an account of possible responses to it. The second phase, sections 1.5–1.6, explains how a problem arises in our attempts to answer the question we have characterized, and surveys the various solutions that can be and have been offered.

More specifically, sections 1.2–1.4 are concerned with how to understand the basic elements of our initial question – how we should identify the mental, on the one hand, and the physical, on the other – and with what sorts of relations between them we are concerned. Section 1.2 identifies and explains the two traditional marks of the mental, consciousness and intentionality, and discusses how they are related. Section 1.3 gives an account of how we should understand 'physical' in our initial question so as not to foreclose any of the traditional positions on the mind–body problem. Section 1.4 then addresses the third element in our initial question, mapping out the basic sorts of relations that may hold between mental and physical phenomena, and identifying some for special attention.

Sections 1.5–1.6 are concerned with explaining the source of the difficulty in answering our initial question, and the kinds of solutions that have been offered to it. Section 1.5 explains why our initial question gives rise to a problem, and gives a precise form to the mind–body problem, which is presented as a set of four propositions, each of which, when presented independently, seems compelling, but which are jointly inconsistent. Section 1.6 classifies responses to the mind–body problem on the basis of which of the propositions in our inconsistent set they reject, and provides a brief overview of the main varieties in each category, together with some of the difficulties that arise for each. Section 1.7 is a brief conclusion about the source of our difficulties in understanding the place of mind in the natural world.[2]

1.2   Marks of the Mental

The suggestion that consciousness is a mark of the mental traces back at least to Descartes.[3] Consciousness is the most salient feature of our mental lives. As William James put it, "The first and foremost concrete fact which every one will affirm to belong to his inner experience is the fact that *consciousness of some sort goes on*" (James 1910: 71). A state or event (a change of state of an object[4]) is mental, on this view, if it is *conscious*. States, in turn, are individuated by the properties the having of which by objects constitutes their being in them.

Identifying consciousness as a mark of the mental only pushes our question one step back. We must now say what it is for something to be conscious. This is not easy to do. There are two immediate difficulties. First, in G. E. Moore's words, "the moment we try to fix our attention upon consciousness and to see *what*, distinctly, it is, it seems to vanish: it seems as if we had before us a mere emptiness . . . as if it were diaphanous" (1903: 25). Second, it is not clear that consciousness, even if we get a fix on it, is understandable in other terms. To say something substantive about it is to say something contentious as well. For present purposes, however, it will be enough to indicate what we are interested in in a way that everyone will be able to agree upon. What I say now then is not intended to provide an analysis of consciousness, but rather to draw attention to, and to describe, the phenomenon, in much the same way a naturalist would draw attention to a certain species of insect or plant by pointing one out, or describing conditions under which it is observed, and describing its features, features which anyone in an appropriate position can himself confirm to be features of it.

First, then, *we* are conscious when we are awake rather than in dreamless sleep, and, in sleep, *when* we dream. When we are conscious, we have conscious states, which we can discriminate, and remember as well as forget. Each conscious mental state is a mode, or way, of being conscious. Knowledge of our conscious mental states, even when connected in perceptual experiences with knowledge of the world, is yet distinct from it, as is shown by the possibility of indistinguishable yet non-veridical perceptual experiences. Conscious mental states include paradigmatically perceptual experiences, somatic sensations, proprioception, pains and itches, feeling sad or angry, or hunger or thirst, and occurrent thoughts and desires. In Thomas Nagel's evocative phrase, an organism has conscious mental states if and only if "there is something it is like to be that organism" (1979b: 166). There is, in contrast, nothing it is like in the relevant sense, it is usually thought, to be a toenail, or a chair, or a blade of grass.

In trying to capture the kinds of discrimination we make between modes of consciousness (or ways of being conscious), it is said that conscious states have a phenomenal or qualitative character; the phenomenal qualities of conscious mental states are often called 'qualia'. Sometimes qualia are reified and treated as if they were objects of awareness in the way tables and chairs are objects of perception. But this is a mistake. When one is aware of one's own conscious mental states or their phenomenal qualities, the only object in question is oneself: what one is aware of is a particular modification of that object, a way it is conscious. Similarly, when we see a red apple, we see just the apple, and not the redness as another thing alongside it: rather, we represent the apple we see *as* red.

A striking feature of our conscious mental states is that we have non-inferential knowledge of them. When we are conscious, we know that we are, and we know *how* we are conscious, that is, our modes of consciousness, but we do not infer, when we are conscious, that we are, or how we are, from anything of which we are more directly aware, or know independently.[5] It is notoriously difficult to say what this kind of non-inferential knowledge comes to. It is difficult to see how to separate it from what we think of as the qualitative character of conscious mental states.[6] Arguably this "first-person" knowledge is *sui generis.* There is a related *asymmetry* in our relation to our own and others' conscious mental states. We do not have to *infer* that we are conscious, but others must do so, typically from our behavior, and cannot know non-inferentially. Others have, at best, "third-person" knowledge of our mental states. These special features of conscious states are connected with some of the puzzles that arise from the attempt to answer our opening question. Consciousness has often been seen as the central mystery in the mind–body problem, and the primary obstacle to an adequate physicalist understanding of the mental.[7]

The other traditional mark of the mental, first articulated clearly by Franz Brentano (1955 [1874], bk 2, ch. 1), is called 'intentionality'.[8] The adjectival form is 'intentional'. But this is a technical term, and does not just involve those states that in English are called 'intentions' (such as my intention to have another cup of coffee). Intentionality, rather, is the feature of a state or event that makes it *about* or *directed at* something. The best way to make this clearer is to give some examples. Unlike the chair that I am sitting in as I write, I have various beliefs *about* myself, my surroundings, and my past and future. I believe that I will have another cup of coffee before the day is out. My chair has no corresponding belief, nor any other. Beliefs are paradigmatically intentional states. They represent the world as being a certain way. They can be true or false. This is their particular form of *satisfaction* condition. In John Searle's apt phrase, they have mind-to-world direction of fit (1983: ch. 1). They are supposed to fit the world. Any state with mind-to-world direction of fit, any representational state, or attitude, is an intentional state (in the technical sense). False beliefs are just as much intentional states as true ones, even if there is nothing in the world for them to be about of the sort they represent. I can think *about* unicorns, though there are none. The representation can exist without what it represents. It is this sense of 'aboutness' or 'directedness' that is at issue in thinking about intentionality.

There are intentional states with mind-to-world direction of fit in addition to beliefs, such as expectations, suppositions, convictions, opinions, doubts, and so on. Not all intentional states have mind-to-world direction of fit, however. Another important class is exemplified by desires or wants. I believe I will, but also want to have another cup of coffee soon. This desire is also directed at or about the world, and even more obviously than in the case of belief, there need not be anything in the world corresponding. But in contrast to belief, its aim is not to get its content (that I have another cup of coffee soon) to match the world, but *to get the world to match its content*. It has world-to-mind direction of fit. A desire may be satisfied or fail to be satisfied, just as a belief can be true or false. This is its particular form of satisfaction condition. Any state with world-to-mind direction of fit is likewise an intentional state.

Clearly there can be something in common between beliefs and desires. I believe that *I will have another cup of coffee soon*, and I desire that *I will have another cup of coffee soon*. These have in common their content, and it is in virtue of their content that each is an intentional state. (Elements in common between contents, which would be expressed using a general term, are typically called 'concepts'; thus, the concept of *coffee* is said to be a constituent of the content of the belief *that coffee is a beverage* and of the belief *that coffee contains caffeine*.) The content in each matches or fails to match the world. The difference between beliefs and desires lies in their role in our mental economy: whether their purpose is to change so that their content matches the world (beliefs) or to get the world to change to match their content (desires). States like these with contents that we can express using sentences are called 'propositional attitudes' (a term introduced by Bertrand Russell, after the supposed objects of the attitudes, propositions, named or denoted by phrases of the form 'that p', where 'p' is replaced by a sentence). Propositional attitudes are individuated by their psychological mode (belief, supposition, doubt, desire, aspiration, etc.) and content. States with world-to-mind direction of fit are *pro* or, if negative, *con attitudes.* There are many varieties besides desires and wants, such as hopes, fears, likes, dislikes, and so on.

It is not clear that all representational content is fully propositional. Our perceptual experiences, e.g., our visual, auditory, and tactile experiences, represent our environments as being a certain way. They can be *veridical* (correctly represent) or *non-veridical* (incorrectly represent), as beliefs can be true or false. They have mind-to-world direction of fit, hence, representational contents, and intentionality. But it is not clear that all that they represent could be captured propositionally. Attitudes and perceptual experiences might be said to be different currencies for which there is no precise standard of exchange.

Can there be states directed at or about something which do not have full contents? Someone could have a fear of spiders without having any desires directed at particular spiders, though the fear is in a sense directed at or about spiders. Yet a fear of spiders does entail a desire to avoid contact with, or proximity to, spiders: and it is this together with a particular emotional aura which thinking of or perceiving spiders evokes which we think of as the fear of spiders. In any case, we will call this class of states intentional states as well, though their intentionality seems to be grounded in the intentionality of representational, or pro or con attitudes, which underlie them, or, as we can say, on which they depend.

We may, then, say that an intentional state is a state with a content (in the sense we've characterized) or which depends (in the sense just indicated) on such a state.[9]

A state then is a mental state (or event) if and only if (iff) it is either a conscious or an intentional state (or event). An object is a thinking thing iff it has mental states.

What is the relation between conscious states and intentional states? If the two sorts are independent, then our initial question breaks down into two subquestions, one about the relation of consciousness, and one about that of intentionality, to the physical. If the two sorts are not independent of one another, any answer to the general question must tackle both subquestions at once.

Some intentional states are clearly not conscious states. Your belief that Australia lies in the Antipodes was not a conscious belief (or an *occurrent* belief) just a moment ago. You were not *thinking* that, though you believed it. It was a *dispositional*, as opposed to an occurrent, belief. The distinction generalizes to all attitude types. A desire can be occurrent, my present desire for a cup of coffee, for example, or dispositional, my desire to buy a certain book when I am not thinking about it.[10] This does not, however, settle the question whether intentional and conscious mental states are independent. It may be a necessary condition on our conceiving of dispositional mental states as intentional attitudes that among their manifestation properties are occurrent attitudes with the same mode and content. In this case, the strategy of *divide and conquer* will be unavailable: we will not be able to separate the projects of understanding the intentional and the conscious, and proceed to tackle each independently.[11]

Some conscious mental states seem to lack intentionality, for example, certain episodes of euphoria or anxiety. Though typically caused by our beliefs and desires, it is not clear that they are themselves about anything. Likewise, somatic sensations such as itches and pains seem to have non-representational elements. Typically somatic sensations represent something's occurring in one's body. A headache is represented as in the head, a toe ache as in the toe. But the quality of pain itself, though it be taken to be a biological indicator of, say, damage to the body, in the way that smoke indicates combustion, seems not to have any associated representational content. Pain does not *represent* (as opposed to indicate) damage. And, though we usually wish pain we experience to cease, the desire that one's pain cease, which has representational content, is not the pain itself, any more than a desire for a larger house is itself a house.[12]

1.3   The Physical

Characterizing physical phenomena in a way that captures the intention of our initial question is not as easy as it may appear. We cannot say that physical phenomena consist in what our current physics talks about. Physical theory changes constantly; current physical theory may undergo radical revision, as past physical theory has. The mind–body problem doesn't change with passing physical theory. There are at least three other options.

The first is to characterize physical phenomena as what the ultimately correct physical theory talks about, where we think of physical theory as the theory that tells us about the basic constituents of things and their properties. The second is to treat physical phenomena as by definition non-mental. There are reasons to think that neither of these captures the sense of our initial question.

One response to the mind–body problem is that the basic constituents of things have irreducible mental properties. On the first interpretation, such a position would be classified as a version of physicalism (we will give a precise characterization of this at the end of section 1.4), since it holds that mental properties are, in the relevant sense, physical properties. But this position, that the basic constituents of things have irreducible mental properties, is usually thought to be incompatible with physicalism.

The second interpretation in its turn does not leave open the option of seeing mental phenomena as conceptually reducible to physical phenomena. If the physical is non-mental per se, then showing that mental properties are really properties that fall in category *F* would just show that a subcategory of properties in category *F* were not physical properties. But we want the terms in which our initial question is stated to leave it open whether mental properties are conceptually reducible to physical properties. (We will return to what this could come to below.)

A third option is to take physical phenomena to be of a general type exemplified by our current physics. Here we would aim to characterize a class of properties that subsumes those appealed to by past and current physical theories, from the scientific revolution to the present, but which is broad enough to cover properties appealed to in any extension of our current approach to explaining the dynamics of material objects. This interpretation leaves open the options foreclosed by our first two interpretations, and comports well with the development of concerns about the relation of mental to physical phenomena from the early modern period to the present. It is not easy to say how to characterize the intended class of properties. The core conception of them is given by those qualities classed as *primary qualities* in the seventeenth and eighteenth centuries: size, shape, motion, number, solidity, texture, logical constructions of these, and properties characterized essentially in terms of their *effects* on these (mass and charge, e.g., arguably fall in the last category).[13] It is not clear that this is adequate to cover everything we might wish to include. But it is fair to say that, typically, philosophers have in mind this conception of the physical in posing the question we began with, without having a detailed conception of how to delineate the relevant class of properties.[14]

1.4   Mind–Body Relations

The question of the relation between the mental and the physical can be posed equivalently as about mental and physical properties, concepts, or predicates. A property is a feature of an object, such as being round, or being three feet from the earth's surface. A concept, as we have said, is a common element in different thought contents expressed by a general term. We deploy concepts in thinking about a thing's properties. So, corresponding to the property of being round is the concept of being round, or of roundness. When I think that this ball is round, and so think of it as having the property of being round, I have a thought that involves the concept of being round. I am said to bring the ball under the concept of roundness. Predicates express concepts, and are used to attribute properties to objects.[15] Thus, 'is round' expresses (in English) the concept of roundness, and is used to attribute the property of being round. We may say it picks out that property. For every property there is a unique concept that is about it, and vice versa. More than one predicate can express the same concept, and pick out the same property, but then they must be synonymous.[16] Corresponding to each property category (mental or physical, e.g.) is a category of concepts and predicates. Thus, any question we ask about the relation of mental and physical properties can be recast as about concepts or predicates, and vice versa.

The basic options in thinking about the relation of mental and physical properties can be explained in terms of the following three sentence forms, where 'is M' represents a mental predicate, and 'is P' represents a physical predicate (this is generalizable straightforwardly to relational terms).

[A]   For all x, if x is P, then x is M
[B]   For all x, if x is M, then x is P
[C]   For all x, x is M if and only if (iff) x is P

Though [C] is equivalent to the conjunction of [A] and [B], it will be useful to state it separately. The relation of the mental to the physical is determined by which instances of [A]–[C] are true or false, and on what grounds. One could hold each to be necessarily true or necessarily false, in one of three senses of "necessity": conceptual, metaphysical (*so*-called), and nomological.

Two notions that figure prominently in discussions of the mind–body problem can be characterized in this framework. The first is that of reduction, and the second that of supervenience. Each can be conceptual, metaphysical, or nomological. I begin with conceptual reduction and supervenience.

Conceptual necessities are truths grounded in the concepts used to express them. This is the strongest sort of necessity. What is conceptually necessary is so in every metaphysically and nomologically possible world, though not vice versa. Knowledge of conceptual truths can be obtained from reflection on the concepts involved, and need not rest on experience (traditionally, knowledge of one's own conscious mental states is counted as experiential knowledge). They are thus said to be knowable a priori. Knowledge obtained in this way is a priori knowledge. A proposition known on the basis of experience is known a posteriori, or empirically. Knowledge so based is a posteriori or empirical knowledge. Conceptual truths are not refutable by the contents of any experiences. A sentence expressing (in a language L) a conceptual truth is *analytically true (in L)*, or, equivalently, *analytic (in L)* (henceforth I omit the relativization). A sentence is analytic iff its truth is entailed by true meaning-statements about its constituents.[17] For example, 'None of the inhabitants of Dublin resides elsewhere', or 'There is no greatest prime number' would typically be regarded as analytic.[18]

Conceptual reduction of mental to physical properties, or vice versa, is the strongest connection that can obtain between them. (We say equivalently, in this case, that mental concepts/predicates can be analyzed in terms of physical concepts/predicates, or vice versa.) If a mental property is conceptually reducible to a physical property, then two conditions are met: (a) the instance of [C], in which 'is *M*' is replaced by a predicate that picks out the mental property, and 'is *P*' by a (possibly complex) predicate that picks out the physical property, is conceptually necessary, and (b) the concepts expressed by 'is *P*' are conceptually prior to those expressed by 'is *M*', which is to say that we have to have the concepts expressed by 'is *P*' in order to understand those expressed by 'is *M*', but not vice versa (think of the order in which we construct geometrical concepts as an example). The second clause gives content to the idea that we have effected a reduction, for it requires the physical concepts to be more basic than the mental concepts. A conceptual reduction of a mental property to a physical property shows the mental property to be a species of physical property. This amounts to the identification of a mental property with a physical property. Similarly for the reduction of a physical property to a mental property.

One could hold that instances of [C] were conceptually necessary without holding that either the mental or the physical was conceptually reducible to the other. In this case, their necessary correlation would be explained by appeal to another set of concepts neither physical nor mental, in terms of which each could be understood. For example, it is conceptually necessary that every triangle is a trilateral, but neither of these notions provides a conceptual reduction of the other.

'Supervenience' is a term of art used in much current philosophical literature on the mind–body problem. It may be doubted that it is needed in order to discuss the mind–body problem, but given its current widespread use, no contemporary survey of the mind–body problem should omit its mention. A variety of related notions has been expressed using it. Though varying in strength among themselves, they are generally intended to express theses weaker than reductionism, invoking only sufficiency conditions, rather than conditions that are both necessary and sufficient.[19] Supervenience claims are not supposed to provide explanations, but rather to place constraints on the *form* of an explanation of one sort of properties in terms of another. I introduce here a definition of one family of properties supervening on another, which will be useful for formulating a position we will call 'physicalism', and which will be useful later in our discussion of a position on the relation of mental to physical properties known as 'functionalism'. I begin with 'conceptual supervenience'.

> F-properties *conceptually supervene* on G-properties iff for any x, if x has a property f from F, then there is a property g from G, such that x has g and it is *conceptually* necessary that if x has g, then x has f.[20]

Conceptual reduction of one family of properties to another implies mutual conceptual supervenience. But the supervenience of one family of properties on another does not imply their reducibility to them.

I will characterize 'physicalism' as the position according to which, *whatever mental properties objects have, they conceptually supervene on the physical properties objects have, and whatever psychological laws there are, the physical laws entail them.*[21] This allows someone who thinks that nothing has mental properties, and that there are no mental laws, to count as a physicalist, whatever his view about the conceptual relations between mental and physical properties.[22] The definition here is stipulative, though it is intended to track a widespread (though not universal) usage in the philosophical literature on the mind–body problem.[23] The question whether physicalism is true, so understood, marks a fundamental divide in positions on the mind–body problem.

Nomological necessity we can explain in terms of conceptual necessity and the notion of a natural law. A statement that p is nomologically necessary iff it is conceptually necessary that if L, it is the case that p, where "L" stands in for a sentence expressing all the laws of nature, whether physical or not (adding "boundary conditions" to "L" yields more restrictive notions). I offer only a negative characterization of metaphysical necessity, which has received considerable attention in contemporary discussion of the mind–body problem. I will argue in section 1.6 that no concept corresponds to the expression "metaphysical necessity" in these contexts, despite its widespread use. For now, we can say that metaphysical necessity is supposed to be of a sort that cannot be discovered a priori, but which is stronger than nomological necessity, and weaker than conceptual necessity. To obtain corresponding notions of *metaphysical* and *nomological* supervenience, we substitute 'metaphysically' or 'nomologically' for 'conceptually' in our characterization above.

Metaphysical and nomological reduction require that biconditionals of the form [C] are metaphysically or nomologically necessary (but nothing stronger), respectively. But reduction is asymmetric. So we must also give a sense to the idea that one side of the biconditional expresses properties that are more basic. In practice, the question is how to make sense of the asymmetry for metaphysical or nomological reduction of the mental to the physical. There is nothing in the case of metaphysical or nomological necessity that corresponds to conceptual priority. It looks as if the best we can do is to ground the desired asymmetry in physical properties being basic in our general explanatory scheme. This is usually understood to mean that the physical constitutes an explanatorily closed system, while the mental does not. This means that every event can be explained by invoking physical antecedents, but not by invoking mental antecedents.

1.5 The Mind–Body Problem

A philosophical problem is a knot in our thinking about some fundamental matter that we have difficulty unraveling. Usually, this involves conceptual issues that are particularly difficult to sort through. Because philosophical problems involve foundational issues, how we resolve them has significant import for our understanding of an entire field of inquiry. Often, a philosophical problem can be presented as a set of propositions all of which seem true on an initial survey, or for all of which there are powerful reasons, but which are jointly inconsistent. This is the form in which the problem of freedom of the will and skepticism about the external world present themselves. It is a significant advance if we can put a problem in this way. For the ways in which consistency can be restored to our views determines the logical space of solutions to it. The mind–body problem can be posed in this way. Historical and contemporary positions on the relation of the mental to the physical can then be classified in terms of which of the propositions they choose to reject to restore consistency.

The problem arises from the appeal of the following four theses.

1   *Realism.* Some things have mental properties.
2   *Conceptual autonomy.* Mental properties are not conceptually reducible to non-mental properties, and, consequently, no non-mental proposition entails any mental proposition.[24]
3   *Constituent explanatory sufficiency.* A complete description of a thing in terms of its basic constituents, their non-relational properties,[25] and relations to

one another[26] and to other basic constituents of things, similarly described (the constituent description) entails a complete description of it, i.e., an account of all of a thing's properties follows from its constituent description.

4   *Constituent non-mentalism.* The basic constituents of things do not have mental properties as such.[27]

The logical difficulty can now be precisely stated. Theses (2)–(4) entail the negation of (1). For if the correct fundamental physics invokes no mental properties, (4), and every natural phenomenon (i.e., every phenomenon) is deducible from a description of a thing in terms of its basic constituents and their arrangements, (3), then given that no non-mental propositions entail any mental propositions, (2), we can deduce that *there are no things with mental properties,* which is the negation of (1).

The logical difficulty would be easy to resolve were it not for the fact that each of (1)–(4) has a powerful appeal for us.

Thesis (1) seems *obviously* true. We seem to have direct, non-inferential knowledge of our own conscious mental states. We attribute to one another mental states in explaining what we do, and base our predictions on what others will do in part on our beliefs about what attitudes they have and what their conscious states are. Relinquishing (1) seems unimaginable.

Proposition (2) is strongly supported by the prima facie intelligibility of a body whose behavior is like that of a thinking being but which has no mental life of the sort we are aware of from our own point of view. We imagine that our mental states cause our behavior. It seems conceivable that such behavior results from other causes. Indeed, it seems conceivable that it be caused from exactly the physical states of our bodies that we have independent reasons to think animate them without the accompanying choir of consciousness. It is likewise supported by the prima facie intelligibility of non-material thinking beings (such as God and His angels, whom even atheists have typically taken to be conceivable). Thus, it seems, prima facie, that having a material body is neither conceptually necessary nor sufficient for having the sorts of mental lives we do.

Thought experiments ask us to imagine a possibly contrary to fact situation and ask ourselves whether it appears barely to make sense (not just whether it is compatible with natural law) that a certain state of affairs could then obtain. We typically test conceptual connections in this way. For example, we can ask ourselves whether we can conceive of an object that is red but not extended. The answer is 'no'. We can likewise ask whether we can conceive of an object that is red and shaped like a penguin. The answer is 'yes'. This provides evidence that the first is conceptually impossible – ruled out by the concepts involved in its description – and that the second is conceptually possible – not ruled out by the concepts involved. No one is likely to dispute the results here.[28] But we can be misled. For example, it may seem easy to conceive of a set that contains all and only sets which do not contain themselves (the Russell set). For it is easy to conceive a set which contains no sets, and a set which contains sets only, and so it can seem easy to conceive of a special set of sets whose members are just those sets not containing themselves. But it is possible to show that this leads to a contradiction. Call the set of all sets that do not contain themselves 'R'. If R is a member of R, it fails to meet the membership condition for R, and so is not a member of itself. But if it is not a member of itself, then it meets the membership condition and so is a member of itself. So, it is a member of itself iff it is *not*, which is a contradiction, and necessarily false. There cannot be such a set.[29] Thus, something can seem conceivable to us even when it is not. In light of this, it is open for someone to object that despite the apparent intelligibility of the thought experiments that support (2), we have made some mistake in thinking them through.[30]

Proposition (3) is supported by the success of science in explaining the behavior of complex systems in terms of laws governing their constituents. While there are still many things we do not understand about the relation of micro to macro phenomena, it looks as if the techniques so far applied with success can be extended to those features of complex systems we don't yet understand fully in terms of their constituents' properties – with the possible exception of psychological phenomena. Proposition (3) expresses a thought that has had a powerful ideological hold on our the scientific worldview, that nature is ultimately intelligible as a kind of vast machine, a complex system a complete understanding of which can be obtained by analyzing its structure and the laws governing the properties of its parts. "It has been," in E. O. Wilson's words, "tested in acid baths of experiment and logic and enjoyed repeated vindication" (1998: 5). This thought motivates much scientific research, and to give it up even with respect to a part of the natural world would be to give up a central methodological tenet of our current scientific worldview. It would be to admit that nature contains some basic element of arbitrariness, in the sense that there would be features of objects that were not explicable as arising from their manner of construction.

Finally, proposition (4) is supported also by the success of physics (so far) in accounting for the phenomena that fall in its domain without appeal to any mental properties. In the catalog of properties of particle physics, we find mass, charge, velocity, position, size, spin, and the like, but nothing that bears the least hint of the mental, and nothing of that sort looks to be required to explain the interaction and dynamics of the smallest bits of matter.[31] It can seem difficult even to understand what it would be to attribute mental properties to the smallest constituents of matter, which are incapable of any of the outward signs of mental activity.

This then is the mind–body problem. Propositions (1)–(4) all seem to be true. But they cannot all be, for they are jointly inconsistent. That is why our initial question, "What is the relation, in general, between mental and physical phenomena?," gives rise to a philosophical problem. Each answer we might like to give will involve rejecting one of our propositions (1)–(4); yet, considered independently, each of these propositions seems to be one we have good reasons to accept.

1.6   The Logical Space of Solutions

Proposed solutions to the mind–body problem can be classified according to which of (1)–(4) they reject to restore consistency. There are only four basic positions, since we seek a minimal revision. To reject (1) is to adopt *irrealism* or *eliminativism* about the mental. To reject (2) is to adopt *conceptual reductionism* for the mental. This includes neutral monism, psychophysical identity theories, functionalism, and functionalism-cum-externalism. To reject (3) is to adopt *conceptual anti-reductionism*, but not ontological anti-reductionism. Neutral emergentism and emergent materialism fall into this category. To reject (4) is to adopt *ontological anti-reductionism* in addition to conceptual anti-reductionism. This subsumes varieties of what might be called 'mental particle theories', and includes substance dualism, idealism, panpsychism, double (or dual) aspect theories (on a certain conception), and what I will call 'special particle theories'.

We take up each in reverse order, since this represents their historical development. I primarily discuss views on the mind–body problem from the beginning of the modern period to the present, though in fact all the basic positions except eliminativism were anticipated in antiquity.[32]

1.6.1   Ontological anti-reductionism

Rejecting proposition (4), the non-mental character of the basic constituents of things, has been historically the most popular position. The generic view, according to which some *basic* constituents of things *as such* have mental properties, may be called 'the mental particle theory'. These may be further divided into *pure* and *mixed* mental particle theories, according to whether the mental particles are thought to have only mental, or to have mental and physical properties, and then, divided again according to whether all or only some things have mental properties (*universal* vs. *restricted*).

The most prominent, and historically important, view of this sort is substance dualism, which traces back to the ancient view of the soul as a simple substance.[33] Substance dualism holds that there are both material substances and mental substances: the former have only physical properties, and none mental, the latter only mental properties, and none physical. This is a restricted pure mental particle theory. Descartes (1985 [1641]) is the most prominent of the early modern defenders of dualism. The appeal of dualism lies in part in its ability to find a place for irreducible mental properties in a world that seems largely to be explainable as a mechanical system reducible to parts which themselves are exhaustively characterized in terms of their primary qualities. Descartes wrote at the beginning of the scientific revolution, and was himself a major proponent of the new 'mechanical philosophy', whose fundamental assumptions provide those for modern physics.

Dualism was Descartes's answer to the problem the mechanical philosophy presents for finding a place for mind in the natural world.

Descartes has had such an enormous influence on the development of the western tradition in philosophy that it will be useful to review briefly his official arguments for dualism. This sets the stage for subsequent discussions of the mind–body problem. To explain Descartes's arguments, however, we must first get clearer about the notion of a substance. This notion, central to philosophical discussion in the seventeenth and eighteenth centuries,[34] traces back to Aristotle's characterization of it as "that which is neither said of a subject nor in a subject" (*Categories* (*Cat*) 1b2–5; in 1984: 4). This is the conception of a substance as a property bearer, something that undergoes and persists through change: "A substance . . . numerically one and the same, is able to receive contraries . . . pale at one time and dark at another" (*Cat* 4a19–21; in 1984: 7). This gave rise in medieval philosophy (in scholasticism, the tradition to which the recovery of Aristotle's works gave rise) to the view of substances as independent existents, because of the contrast with properties, which were thought to exist only in a subject, not independently. Descartes gives two characterizations of substance. One is as that which is absolutely independent of everything else. This generalizes the scholastic notion. Descartes held that, on this conception, God is the only substance, since everything depends on God for its existence. But Descartes admits substances as property bearers in a subsidiary sense, and allows two fundamentally different kinds in addition to God: thinking and corporeal substances (*Princ.* 1644, I.51–2; in 1985, vol. I: 210). Henceforth I restrict attention to the latter sort. A central feature of Descartes's theory of substance kinds is that each different substance kind has a principal individuating attribute, of which every other property of a substance of the kind is a modification: *extension*, for corporeal substances, and *thought*, for thinking substances (*Princ.* 1644, I.53–4; in 1985, vol. I: 210–11). This feature of the theory, often overlooked in introductory discussions, is essential for a correct understanding of the force of Descartes's arguments for substance dualism.

The doctrine that each substance has a principal attribute forces the individuating and essential property of a substance kind to be a fundamental way of being something, or a categorical property. A categorical property is a determinable but not a determinate. A determinable is a property an object can have in different ways, and must have in some particular way, as, e.g., being colored. Something can be colored by being blue, or green, or red, and so on, and if colored must be colored in some determinate way (hence the terminology, 'determinable', 'determinate'). Extension and thought Descartes conceived as determinables, and they are not themselves apparently determinates of any other determinable property.[35]

With this theory in place, there is an easy argument to mind–body dualism. If there are two most general ways of being, and things that have them, it follows immediately that there are two kinds of substance. Descartes argued that he had a clear and distinct conception of himself as a thinking thing, a thing that at least can exist independently of his body, and likewise a clear and distinct conception of a corporeal object as a solely extended thing, a thing that can at least exist without thinking, and, moreover, that these conceptions are complete and not in need of appeal to any more general conception of a kind.[36] From this, it follows that thinking and extension are categorical properties. From the theory of substances, it follows that thinking and extended substances are necessarily distinct.

The argument is unquestionably valid: necessarily, if its premises are true, so is its conclusion. Whether we should accept its premises (and so whether it is sound, i.e., has true premises in addition to being valid) is less clear. Its weakest premise is the assumption that distinct kinds of substance must have only one categorical attribute. It is unclear why Descartes held this. The thought that substances are property bearers provides insufficient support. Even Spinoza, who was heavily influenced by Descartes, objected that precisely because mental and corporeal properties are conceptually independent, there can be no barrier to one substance possessing both attributes (*Ethics* IP10 Scholium; in Spinoza 1994: 90). And, as P. F. Strawson (1958) has observed, we routinely attribute to the very same thing, persons, both material and mental properties: I walk, and sleep, as well as think and feel.

Descartes endorsed causal interactionism between mental and material substance to explain why our limbs move in accordance with what we want to do, and how we are able to correctly perceive things in our bodies' physical surroundings. Some philosophers, including many of Descartes's contemporaries, have objected that we cannot conceive of causal interaction between such fundamentally different kinds of substance as mind and body, the latter in space, the former not. (Though it is hard to see this as a *conceptual* difficulty; see Bedau 1986.) This gives rise to a version of epiphenomenalism, according to which the mental is not causally relevant to the physical. The rejection of causal interactionism together with the obvious correlations between mental and physical events gave rise to parallelism, according to which mental and physical events evolve independently but in a way that gives rise to non-causal correlations, as the hands of two clocks, set independently a minute apart, may appear to be causally interacting because of the correlations in their positions, though they are not.[37] Parallelism is usually explained by reference to God's arranging things originally so that the mental and the physical develop in parallel (pre-established harmony), or through His constant intervention in bringing about what events, both physical and mental, give rise to the appearance of interaction (occasionalism).

Barring a reason to think that a property bearer cannot possess both irreducibly mental and physical properties, at most Descartes's arguments establish that there *could* be things which have only mental properties, as well as things which have only physical properties, not that there are or must be. If we can establish a priori at most that dualism could be true, whether it is true is to be determined, insofar as it can be, by empirical investigation. So far, there seems to be no very good empirical reason to suppose dualism is true.[38]

Idealism is the historical successor to dualism. It is dualism without material substance. Thus, it is a universal, pure mental particle theory. The classical position is laid out in George Berkeley's *A Treatise Concerning the Principles of Human Knowledge* (1710). More sophisticated modern versions are called 'phenomenalism'.[39] Idealism is often motivated by a concern to understand the possibility of knowledge of objects of ordinary perception: forests and meadows, mountains and rain, stars and windowpanes. The Cartesian view of the relation of mind to world leaves it mysterious how we can have knowledge of it: if we know in the first instance only our conscious mental states, and whatever we can know by reason alone, yet the mental and material are conceptually independent, it looks as if we have no reason to believe that there is a material world causing our conscious experiences. Berkeley solved the problem by denying that objects of perception were material, and identifying them instead with collections of ideas (hence *idealism*). More recent treatments identify ordinary objects of common-sense knowledge with logical constructions out of phenomenal states. Berkeley denied also that we could even make sense of material substance. Leibniz (1714) likewise held that the basic constituents of things, monads (*unit*, from the Greek *monos*), were a sort of mind – though he did not hold that all were conscious – and that talk of ordinary things was to be understood in terms of monads and their states (as David Armstrong has put it, on Leibniz's view, "material objects are colonies of rudimentary souls" (1968, p. 5)). Kant (1781) is sometimes also interpreted as a phenomenalist. This view is not now widely embraced. It seems to be part of our conception of the world of which we think we have knowledge that it is independent of the existence of thinking beings, who are contingent players on the world stage.

Panpsychism holds that everything is a primary bearer of mental properties (not simply by being related to a primary bearer – as my chair has the property of being occupied by someone thinking about the mind–body problem). Panpsychism comes in reductive and non-reductive varieties. Its root can be traced back to antiquity (Annas 1992: 43–7). Panpsychists are represented among the Renaissance philosophers, and among prominent nineteenth-century philosophers, including Schopenhauer, W. K. Clifford, William James (at one time), and C. S. Peirce.[40] Panpsychism is associated often with (what seems to be) a revisionary metaphysics, with special motivations, as in the case of idealism, which is a reductive version of panpsychism. However, non-reductive panpsychism, which accepts a basic materialist ontology, is motivated by the thought that otherwise it would be inexplicable (a species of magic) that complex objects have mental properties. William James, in his monumental *Principles of Psychology* (1890), lays out this argument explicitly in chapter VI, "Evolutionary Psychology demands a Mind-dust." Thomas Nagel (1979a) has more recently revived the argument (see also Menzies 1988).[41] Panpsychism is a universal mental particle theory, and may be pure or mixed.

The double aspect theory should be thought of as a family of theories, rather than a single doctrine. What unifies the family is their affinity for being expressed with the slogan that the mental and the physical are different aspects by which we comprehend one and the same thing, though the slogan may be understood differently on different "versions" of the theory. Spinoza's doctrine of the parallelism of thought and extension is the original of the double aspect theory, though he did not himself so describe his position.[42] Spinoza held that there was a single, infinite, eternal, and necessary substance, which had every possible categorical attribute, and so both extension and thought. Ordinary things were to be (re)conceived as modes (modifications) of the world substance. Thinking and extension were related in accordance with the parallelism thesis: "The order and connection of ideas is the same as the order and connection of things" (*Ethics*, IIP7; in 1994: 119–20). As Spinoza further explains it in the Scholium: "the thinking substance and the extended substance are one and the same substance, which is now comprehended under this attribute, now under that. So also a mode of extension and the idea of that mode are one and the same thing, but expressed in two ways" (ibid: 119). This is not an entirely pellucid doctrine. We understand it only to the extent that we understand Spinoza's metaphysics, itself a matter of interpretive difficulty. The idea that the mental and the physical are two ways of comprehending one thing, however, can survive the rejection of Spinoza's metaphysics, and has inspired a number of views which appeal to similar language.

If we allow a multitude of substances, the double aspect theory holds that every object, or some, can be viewed as mental or physical, depending on how we take it. In G. H. Lewes's image (1877; repr. in Vesey 1964: 155), to comprehend a thing as mental or physical is like seeing a line as concave or convex: "The curve has at every point this contrast of convex and concave, and yet is the identical line throughout." The double aspect theory is not currently popular. Partly this is due to its unclarity. It is intended to be more than the claim that there are objects that have mental and physical properties, neither being conceptually reducible to the other (though sometimes it has been used in this broader sense), or even that there are systematic correlations between everything physical and something mental.[43] But there seems to be nothing more in general to say about what it comes to, and we must rather look to particular theories to give it content. Its lack of popularity is partly due to factors independent of the details, and, in particular, to the dominance of our current scientific worldview, according to which the world once contained no thinking things, and has evolved to its present state by natural law.

Double aspect theories may be either universal or restricted, mixed mental particle theories. Some double aspect theories are versions of panpsychism, then, as in the case of Spinoza, since he does maintain that everything has mental properties. Compatibly with the guiding idea, however, one might also maintain that some objects have two aspects, two ways of comprehending them, mental and physical, though not all do.[44]

Finally, there is what I call the special particle theory, which holds that some basic constituents of things, which are at least spatially located, have mental properties, but not all. This counts as a restricted, mixed mental particle theory, counting spatial location as a broadly physical property. So far as I know, this is not a view that has been represented among traditional responses to the mind–body problem.[45]

1.6.2   Conceptual anti-reductionism

Rejecting proposition (3) leads to emergentism. There are in principle two varieties, neutral emergentism and emergent materialism, according to whether basic constituents are conceived as physical or neither physical nor mental. Most emergentists are materialists, and I concentrate therefore on emergent materialism. Emergent materialists hold that there are only material things, but that some complex material things, though no simple ones considered independently of complexes in which they participate, have mental properties, and that those mental properties are not conceptually reducible to any of the physical properties of the complexes that have them. Emergentism historically was a response to the rejection of forms of dualism and idealism in favor of a materialist ontology. It is associated with the rise of science generally in the nineteenth century, and the development of the theory of evolution in particular. It dispenses with the ontological, but retains the conceptual anti-reductionism of Cartesian dualism. Late nineteenth- and early twentieth-century emergentists included T. H. Huxley ("Darwin's bulldog"; 1901), Samuel Alexander (1920), C. Lloyd Morgan (1923), and C. D. Broad (1925). The term "emergent" was pressed into service because the universe was thought to have once not contained any objects that had any mental properties. Since all its objects are material objects, once they had no mental properties, but now some do, and those properties are not conceptually reducible to physical properties, mental properties must emerge from, in some way, certain organizations of matter, though this cannot be deduced from a complete description of the objects that have mental properties in terms of their physical properties.[46] Emergentists take seriously the evidence that at least some aspects of the mental are not in any sense physical phenomena. This was the traditional view, and is undeniably an initially attractive position. Once we have extricated ourselves from the confusions that lead to the view that there must be mental substances distinct from material substances to bear irreducible mental properties, the view that we are latecomers to the physical world – natural objects that arose by natural processes from materials themselves falling wholly within the realm of mechanics – leads naturally to emergent materialism.

Varieties of emergentism arise from different views about the relation between fundamental properties and mental properties. Traditional emergent materialists held that there were type-type nomic correlations between physical and mental states. This is to hold that for every mental property some sentence of the form [C] obtains with the force of nomological necessity. One may hold that mental properties merely nomically supervene on physical properties, and that there are no type-type correlations.[47] Finally, one might hold a version of what is called 'anomalous monism'. Anomalous monism was originally proposed as a thesis about the relation of mental and physical events (Davidson 1980). It holds that every mental event is token identical[48] with a physical event, but there are no strict psychophysical laws, and so no strict bridge laws.[49] This still allows loose, *non-strict*, nomic supervenience or nomic type correlation. A stronger version denies even that there are loose nomic relations between mental and physical event types. The idea can be adapted to objects as the view that though some complex objects have mental properties, there are no strict nomic correlations or supervenience relations between physical and mental properties, or, in the stronger version, none at all.

Emergentism is often (nowadays especially) associated with epiphenomenalism.[50] Epiphenomenalism holds that mental properties are not causally relevant to anything (or, at least, to anything physical). Among late nineteenth- and early twentieth-century emergentists there was disagreement about the causal efficacy of the mental. Some (e.g. Morgan and Broad) held that there were not only emergent properties, but also emergent laws governing systems at the level of the emergent properties which could then affect the course of events at lower levels (downward causation).[51] This stream in the emergentist tradition has now nearly run dry (though see Sperry 1986).[52] Other prominent emergentists saw the mental as wholly dependent on the physical, and causally inert. In a famous discussion, T. H. Huxley held that consciousness was "the direct function of material changes" (1874: 141), but also that consciousness was as completely without power to affect the movements of our bodies "as the steam-whistle which accompanies the working of a locomotive engine is without influence upon its machinery" (p. 140). (See also Hodgson 1870; G. J. Romanes 1895.) On this view, mental activity is a shadow cast by neural activity, determined by it, but determining nothing in turn: conscious mental states are "nomological danglers," in Feigl's apt phrase (1958).

Until the second half of the twentieth century, emergentists believed that there were type-type correlations between the states of our central nervous systems and mental states that held as a matter of natural law. These laws were not purely physical, but bridge laws, since their statement involved irreducibly both mental and physical predicates. Epiphenomenalism is motivated by the thought that the universe would proceed just as it has physically if we were simply to subtract from it the bridge laws: we do not need in principle to refer to any non-physical events or laws to explain any physical event. Just as the locomotive would continue in its path if we were to remove its whistle, so our bodies would continue in their trajectories if we were to remove their souls.[53] The conjunction of the view that there are such type-type nomic correlations, and the view that the physical is a closed system, is nomological reductionism. Obviously, the further we move from nomic type-type correlations, the less plausible it becomes that we can find a place for the causal efficacy of mental properties. The perceived threat of epiphenomenalism has been one of the motivations for physicalism. It is an irony that some popular ways of trying to ground physicalism also raise difficulties for seeing how mental properties could be causally relevant to what they are supposed to be.[54]

1.6.3 Conceptual reduction

To reject proposition (2) is to adopt conceptual reductionism for mental properties.

We consider first, briefly, non-physicalist ways of rejecting (2). There are two possibilities: that the mental is conceptually reducible to, or supervenes on something non-physical. While the latter position is an option, it has not been occupied. However, neutral monism, the view that the mental and the physical might both be understood in terms of something more basic, enjoyed a brief run at the end of the nineteenth and in the first half of the twentieth century.[55] The view is associated with William James (1904), who argued that "pure experience" is the primal stuff of the world and minds and objects were to be conceived of as different sets of experiences, so that the same experience could be taken with one set as a thought, and with another as a component of an object thought about. Neutral monism, as advocated by James, rejects the view that there is a subject of experience, and retains only what was traditionally thought of as its object. As James put it, "those who cling to it are clinging to a mere echo, the faint rumor left behind by the disappearing 'soul' upon the air of philosophy" (pp. 3–4). Ernest Mach (1886) held a similar view, and Bertrand Russell developed a version of neutral monism, inspired by James, in which sensibilia (or "sensations" as Russell put it in *The Analysis of Mind* (1921)), introduced originally as mind-independent objects of direct awareness (1917), played the role of the neutral stuff out of which minds and physical objects were to be logically constructed (1921).

It may seem as if this view should more properly be described as a version of idealism, because the terms that James, Mach, and Russell used to describe the neutral stuff are usually associated with mental phenomena. But they held that the neutral stuff was not properly thought of as mental in character, but only when it was considered in a certain arrangement. It might then seem reasonable to describe neutral monism as a double aspect theory, at least in the sense that it treats each of the fundamental things as a thing that could participate in a series of things which constituted something mental, as well as in a series of things which constituted something physical; thus, each could be said to be viewed under a physical or a mental aspect. However, since talk of thoughts and material things is conceived of as translatable into talk neither mental nor physical, neither the mental nor the physical has a fundamental status in the ontology of neutral monism.[56] Rather, both bear the relation to the neutral stuff that ordinary objects do to phenomenal experience according to idealist theories. Just as idealist theories do not countenance genuine material substance, neutral monism does not countenance genuine mental or physical substances in its fundamental ontology, though it gives an account of *talk* of each sort.

Neutral monism has some theoretical virtues. It avoids the difficulties associated with trying to reduce either the mental to the physical or vice versa, and, if successful, provides a fundamental, unified account of things of all kinds in terms of a fundamental kind, the dream of idealists and physicalists alike. Despite this, it is not a popular view. It attracts neither those who think the mental is a basic feature of reality, nor those who dream of the desert landscape of physics. Moreover, it is difficult to develop the account in detail, and difficult to understand the nature of the neutral stuff which it relies upon.

We turn now to physicalist rejections of proposition (2).

The first twentieth-century physicalist position to gain popularity was logical behaviorism, which was spurred on in part by the verificationism of the logical positivists before the Second World War, the view that the meaning of a sentence was to be sought in the empirical conditions for confirming or disconfirming it (a view with roots in classical British empiricism).[57] Logical behaviorism has a stronger and a weaker form. The strong form I will call 'translational behaviorism', and the weaker form 'criterial behaviorism'. Translational behaviorism holds that every psychological statement can be translated into a statement about actual and potential behavior of bodies. Criterial behaviorism holds, in contrast, merely that there are behavioral analytically sufficient conditions for the application of mental predicates.

Logical behaviorism has long fallen out of fashion. This is explained in part by the fall from favor of verificationism, which provided it theoretical support, but also by the fact that not only were no satisfactory translation schemes advanced, but there are reasons to think none could be forthcoming in principle. A particularly troubling problem was that what behavioral manifestations we may expect from someone with a certain mental state depends on what other mental states he has. Consequently, there can be no piecemeal translation of psychological claims into behavioral terms. In addition, behaviorism seems incompatible with our conception of mental states as (possible) causes of behavior. For to reduce talk of mental states to talk of behavior is to treat it as merely a more compendious way of describing behavior. Behavior, though, cannot cause itself.[58]

The two principal physicalist responses to the defects of behaviorism were analytic functionalism and the psychophysical identity theory. Though the psychophysical identity theory came to prominence before analytic functionalism, it will be useful to discuss functionalism first, since it is the natural successor to logical behaviorism, and this will put us in a position to usefully clarify the psychophysical identity theory, which in some early versions suffered from a number of confusions and conflicting tendencies.

Analytic functionalism holds that mental states are conceptually reducible to functional states. Functional states are held to conceptually supervene, in the sense defined in section 1.4, on physical states.[59] The identification of mental with functional states then leads to *physicalism* without conceptual reduction of the mental to the physical per se. A functional state, in the relevant sense, is a state of an object defined in terms of its relations to input to a system, other functional states of the system, and output from the system. Some of the logical behaviorists, e.g., Gilbert Ryle in *The Concept of Mind* (1949), can be seen to have been moving toward something like this (functionalism may therefore be said to be the eclosion of behaviorism). Functionalism was inspired, at least in part, by the rise of computer technology[60] after the Second World War. Its earliest form in the twentieth century, machine table functionalism, introduced by Hilary Putnam (1967), was directly inspired by theoretical work on finite state machines, which is what a (finite state) computer is.[61] A machine table describes a system in terms of a list of exhaustive and mutually exclusive inputs, a list of possible states, a list of outputs, and, for each possible state, what state it moves to and what output is produced given that it receives a given input. The operation of any computer running a program can be described exhaustively in terms of a machine table. For programmable computers, the program determines what machine table it instantiates (relative to a division of a system into states of particular interest to us). Putnam generalized the notion of a finite state automaton (a system describable using a finite state machine table with deterministic state transitions) to a probabilistic finite state automaton, in which transitions are probabilistic. The general form of the proposal is that a system is in a certain mental state iff it has an appropriate machine table description and appropriate inputs or appropriate states. Putnam treated his proposal as an *empirical* hypothesis. This is typically called 'psychofunctionalism', following Block (1978).[62] It is nonetheless one of the principal inspirations for analytic functionalism, and is easily reconstrued as a thesis about our concepts of mental states. *Theoretical* or, sometimes, *causal role* functionalism is a variant on the theme. On this view, we start with a theory that embeds psychological terms. The concepts expressed by these terms are taken to be concepts of states that are characterized exhaustively by their relations to other states and inputs and outputs as specified abstractly in the theory.[63]

Functionalism is attractive. It accommodates a thought that motivated behaviorism, namely, that our mental states are intimately tied up with understanding of behavior, but it does so in a way that distinguishes them from, and treats them as causes of, behavior. Moreover, functionalism allows for the possibility of immaterial thinking beings, since a system's having a certain functional organization does not depend on what it is made of, but rather on its causal powers with respect to inputs and outputs. It has merely to sustain the right organization mediating inputs and outputs. Functional states are *multiply realizable*. This accommodates one of the thought experiments that motivates the assumption of the conceptual independence of the mental and the physical. It finds a place for the mental in the natural world that exhibits it as grounded in the physical, in the sense that it exhibits the mental as conceptually supervening on the physical, without insisting on a conceptual reduction to physical properties. It thereby allows that the language of psychology is distinct from that of physics, while allowing that the realization of psychological states requires nothing more than objects having physical properties governed by physical laws. The multiple realizability of functional states also (prima facie) protects functionalism from a charge leveled against the psychophysical identity theory, namely, that it would be implausible, and chauvinistic, to insist that only those physically like us can have mental states.[64]

Analytic functionalism has come in for considerable criticism, but remains popular, especially outside philosophy in fields contributing to the new discipline of cognitive science. A first objection to functionalism is that no one has come up with a successful conceptual reduction of mental concepts to functional concepts. It might be said that this could equally well be a sign of the complexity of these functional concepts. A second objection to functionalism is based on the prima facie intelligibility of systems which are functionally identical to us but which have no mental states. An example is provided by a thought experiment of Ned Block's (1978).[65] Imagine a robot body actuated by a program instantiating a machine table for some person. Imagine further that we instantiate the program by providing each member of the population of China with a two-way radio with a display that shows the current input to the robotic system and an indicator of whether the system is in his state. Each person presses a button on the radio appropriate for the input when his state is active. Signals are relayed to the body for appropriate action. Suppose that the Chinese get so good at this that our robot and accessories constitute a system functionally identical to our original. Does this system now constitute an intelligent, conscious being? Most people, first confronted with the thought experiment, deny that we have created a new person (who will die when the exercise is terminated).[66]

Another important objection is also due to Ned Block (1978). Functionalists must decide how to specify inputs and outputs to the system. This presents them with a dilemma. If we specify the inputs and outputs physically using ourselves as models, it is not difficult to describe some system that could have a mind that is incapable of causing those outputs, but causes others instead (e.g., we do not want to rule out, a priori, intelligent jellyfish, or beings whose inputs and outputs are various portions of the electromagnetic spectrum, and so on). Further, it is difficult to see how we could put a priori limits on the physical character of inputs and outputs. However, if the inputs and outputs are specified barely as distinct, then it is not unlikely that we can find minds just about everywhere, for it is plausible that most complex systems will admit of some division into states and inputs and outputs that will instantiate some machine table said to be sufficient for having a mind (e.g., the world economy).

It also has been objected that it is easy to imagine functional duplicates who differ in the qualities of their experiences. A well-known thought experiment designed to show this is that of the inverted spectrum. We imagine two individuals functionally indistinguishable, and therefore behaviorally indistinguishable, but imagine that their experiences of the colors of objects in their environments are inverted with respect to one another. Where one experiences a red object, e.g., the other experiences a green object. They both utter the same sentence in describing it, but each sees it differently. If this is conceivable, then their color experiences are not conceptually reducible to their functional organization, and, hence, functionalism is false with respect to these phenomenal qualities.[67]

Another difficulty is that it is unclear that functional states can be causally relevant to the right sorts of behavior. Functionalism accommodates mental states as *causes* of behavior by definition.[68] But this may secure the causal connection in the wrong way. For a state defined in terms of its effects in various circumstances cannot be the type in virtue of which those effects come about. Causal relations between events or states are underlain by *contingent* causal laws connecting types under which they fall.[69] One type is causally relevant to another type (in certain circumstances) iff they are connected by a causal law (in the circumstances). However, the relation between a functional state and the output (type) in terms of which it is partially defined is not contingent. Thus, the state type and output type cannot feature appropriately in a contingent causal law. Therefore, functional state types are not causally relevant to output in terms of which they are defined.[70] If this reasoning is correct, analytic functionalism entails epiphenomenalism with respect to these outputs. An advantage of functionalism over behaviorism was supposed to be that it makes mental states causes of behavior. The trouble is that it does so in a way that undercuts the possibility of those states being causally relevant to what we expect them to be.

Worse, it seems quite plausible that we do conceive of our mental states as causally relevant to the behavior that we would use to define mental states on a functional analysis. Our beliefs about the causal relevance of mental states to behavior may be false. It is contingent on what causal laws hold. But if they are not necessarily false, then functionalism cannot be true, since it precludes *the possibility of* our mental states being causally relevant to our behavior.[71]

Let us now turn to the psychophysical identity theory. This is the view that mental properties are physical properties. I start with what I believe is the most plausible form of the psychophysical identity theory, which is based on an approach advocated by David Lewis (1966, 1972). The approach makes use of functionalist *descriptions* of states extracted from a "folk theory" of psychology to identify mental states with physical states.

Analytic functionalism holds that psychological concepts and properties *are* functional concepts and properties. This should be distinguished from the view that psychological properties are *picked out by functional descriptions*. This view does not reduce mental properties to functional properties. Rather, it treats mental terms as theoretical terms. Theoretical terms are treated as picking out properties in the world (and so as expressing whatever concepts are of those properties) that actually play the role the theory accords them in the systems to which it is applied. We represent our psychological theory as a single sentence, '$T(M_1, M_2, \ldots, M_n)$', where 'M_1' and so on represent psychological terms referring to properties. Then we replace each such term with a corresponding variable, 'x_1', 'x_2', and so on, and preface the whole with a quantifier for each, 'there is a unique x_1 such that' (symbolized as '$(\exists!x_1)$'), etc., to yield, '$(\exists!x_1)(\exists!x_2) \ldots (\exists!x_n)T(x_1, x_2, \ldots, x_n)$'. The property "$M_1$" picks out can be characterized as follows, where we leave out the quantifier in front of 'T(. . .)' associated with 'x_1':

M_1 is the unique property x_1 such that $(\exists!x_2) \ldots (\exists!x_n)T(x_1, x_2, \ldots, x_n)$

In application to human beings, on the assumption that the theoretical description of this property is satisfied by a physical property of our bodies or central nervous systems, it follows that M_1 *is* that physical property. Thus, we arrive at a psychophysical identity theory.

Given how we have characterized the relation between concepts, predicates, states, and properties, if we identify a mental state or property with a physical state or property, it follows that the corresponding mental concept *is* a physical concept. Therefore, the view that mental properties are picked out by functional descriptions will lead to the conclusion that mental concepts are conceptually reducible to physical concepts, if those descriptions pick out physical states or properties.[72] This is not, however, something we could know a priori. It could only emerge after empirical investigation. For on this view, the concepts expressed by our theoretical terms are hostage to the nature of the phenomena to which we apply them. We start only with descriptions of the properties, and so, in effect, only with descriptions of the concepts of them. We can reason a priori using the concepts only after we have discovered them a posteriori.

The psychophysical identity theory has the advantage over functionalism and emergentism in securing the causal relevance of mental properties. No one doubts that our physical states are causally relevant to our movements. Identifying mental states with physical states, the psychophysical identity theory makes their causal relevance unproblematic. Some philosophers have argued that since only identifying mental with physical states will secure their causal efficacy, and mental states are causally efficacious, we are justified in identifying them (Papineau 1998).

This comes at a cost, though. On this view, prior to empirical investigation it is open that there are no mental properties at all, no properties that answer to the theoretical descriptions we have of them. This shows that this view has in common with eliminativism the assumption that we do not know directly that anything has the properties we suppose to be picked out by our psychological terms. A view like this entails eliminativism when combined with the claim that no physical (or any other) states play the required roles. To the extent to which we find it implausible, perhaps even unintelligible, that we could discover we don't have any mental states, we should find equally implausible or unintelligible the argument for the psychophysical identity theory just reviewed.[73]

The psychophysical identity theory (also called "central state materialism"), like functionalism, has antecedents that stretch back to the ancient world. In the twentieth century, it was influentially advocated after the Second World War by Ullin Place (1956), Herbert Feigl (1958), and J. J. C. Smart (1959).[74] Place and Smart held that sensations were to be theoretically identified with brain processes, in the same way that lightning was identified with a certain sort of electrical discharge (this can be generalized straightforwardly to states; see Armstrong 1968).[75] They thought of this as a contingent identity, because it was empirically discovered. The position is also sometimes called 'the topic neutral approach', because Smart in particular argued that in order that we not have irreducible mental properties, and yet make sense of the possibility of contingent identity, the descriptions by which we pick out mental processes (more generally mental states), which are to be empirically identified with physical ones, must leave it open whether they are physical or not. This position came into considerable criticism for the claim that identities could be contingent (see Kripke 1980: 98–100, 144–55). If we are speaking about strict identity of things – in the present case, properties – there is no room for contingency, since identity holds of necessity between everything and itself, and between no distinct things. The view I have presented based on Lewis's approach is a descendant of these early psychophysical identity theories. It retains the view that mental properties are physical properties (on the assumption that unique physical properties play the right roles). But it rejects the view that this is contingent (given that in fact there are physical properties playing the right roles). Seeing theoretical terms as introduced to track properties that are to play certain roles helps us to see how the discovery of identities can be empirical although the identities are necessary. It also gives precise content to the idea that the descriptions that pick out mental states are topic neutral, since they are to be given by the structure induced by our folk theory of psychology.

At this point, a note on metaphysical necessity is in order. This modality is often invoked in contemporary discussions of the mind–body problem. It is said to be distinct both from nomological and conceptual necessity, stronger than the former, and weaker than the latter. How did it come to be introduced? A paradigm of metaphysical necessity is supposed to be the sort that results from theoretical identifications involving *natural kinds*, like the identification of gold with that element with atomic number 79. It is not contingent or just a matter of natural law, but necessary that gold is the element with atomic number 79, since nothing that did not have atomic number 79 would count as gold even in a world with different natural laws. Still, it was an empirical discovery, and not something we could have known purely a priori. But since conceptual truths are knowable a priori, it must be that metaphysical necessity is distinct from conceptual necessity – or so the argument goes.

The perceived utility of metaphysical necessity is that it provides a way to argue for connections between the mental and the physical stronger than nomological connections, indeed, identities, which at the same time is immune to refutation by thought experiments that seem to show mental and physical phenomena are independent. Since metaphysical necessity is supposed not to be governed by what is conceptually possible, and such thought experiments are, they fail to bear on the claim.[76]

As I said earlier, in my view no philosopher has succeeded in expressing a concept by 'metaphysical necessity' that answers to this argument. The first thing that should make us suspicious about "metaphysical necessity" is that we do not have any account of what grounds claims supposedly about it. Barring this, it is dubious that we have any precise idea of what is supposed to be expressed here by the term 'metaphysical'. The second thing that should make us suspicious is that there is available a straightforward explanation of the facts which motivate introducing metaphysical necessity that requires no mysterious new sort of necessity.

Our reading of Lewis's account of theoretical identifications provides the key. On that account, we associate with each theoretical term a description of the property that it picks out (the property P which plays such and such a role in such and such systems). It is a matter for empirical investigation what property actually satisfies the description (as it is in determining which individual is the mayor of New York). However, the concept a term expresses is, as we have seen, what determines the property it picks out: they are a matched set. Thus, to discover what property a theoretical term picks out by discovering empirically what satisfies the associated description is likewise to discover empirically what concept the term expresses. Prior to that, we had a description of a concept, but it was not given to us directly. Thus, when we discover that 'is gold' picks out the element with atomic number 79, we discover what concept it expresses. Prior to this, we did not know what concept it expressed. Once we know, we are in a position to see that 'Gold is that element with atomic number 79' expresses a conceptual truth, which is knowable a priori. What was not knowable a priori was not that gold is that element with atomic number 79, but that 'gold' expressed the concept of the element with atomic number 79. We competently use such natural kind terms prior to discovering what concepts they express. This is explained by the fact that we treat such terms as tracking properties that *explain easily identifiable features of things* we in practice apply them to. We apply the terms in accordance with those features. The mistake in the original argument was to confuse competence in applying natural kind terms with grasp of the concept expressed: given that we do not know what property is picked out, we likewise do not know what concept is expressed. What we know is just what work the property is supposed to do, which enables us to develop an application practice with the term that is to pick it out.

Thus, the introduction of 'metaphysical necessity' is gratuitous. We have no reason to suppose anything corresponds to it, and no idea of what it would be if it did. Consequently, we cannot look to metaphysical necessity for new avenues for the solution of the mind–body problem.[77]

Before we leave the topic of reductionism, it is important to consider a hybrid view that combines functionalism and externalism about thought content. Externalist accounts of mental states emphasize the importance of our relations to things in our environments in conceptually individuating them. At the same time that difficulties were mounting for functionalism, independently some influential arguments were advanced which suggested that content properties were relational properties.[78] According to these accounts, what thoughts we have depends on what actual and potential causal relations we bear to things in our environments. (Relationally individuated states are often called 'wide states' in the literature, and non-relationally individuated states 'narrow states'.) The most important division among externalist views is that between physical and social externalism. Physical externalism holds that thought contents are individuated (in part) by relations to our physical environments. Social externalism holds that thought contents are individuated (in part) by how others in our linguistic communities use the words we intend to use as they do.[79] A reductionist externalist account of thought content will typically hold that our concepts at least of contentful mental states can be reduced to functional and causal concepts, where we include systematic causal relations to external things in fixing the contents of thoughts.

Externalist theories too have come in for considerable criticism. Two are worth mentioning because they are connected with themes already touched on.[80] The first is the objection that if externalism were true, we would not be able to know the contents of our own thoughts without empirical investigation, but since we must in order to undertake empirical investigations in the first place, externalism entails unacceptably that we can never know the contents of our own thoughts.[81] The second is connected with a difficulty already noted for functionalism. It is that treating content properties as individuated in part in terms of relational properties threatens to make them unsuitable for explaining our behavior (described physically). The problem is not that relational properties cannot be causally relevant to anything. There are prima facie counterexamples to this. That something is a planet, for example, may be cited in explaining why I come to believe that it is. But the difficulty for externalism only requires that the kind of relational properties that content properties would turn out to be could not be causally relevant to our behavior. For externalist theories exploit the possibility of behavior (described physically) remaining the same because one's non-relational physical states remain the same while one's thought contents vary. This appears to show that the relational states are "screened off" from the relevant effect types by the non-relational physical states, which are sufficient to account for the behavior and are independently necessary.[82]

The conception of our (at least conscious) mental states as of a sort which are (a) non-inferentially knowable by their possessor (our concepts of which are therefore not theoretical concepts), though by no one else, and (b) as (possibly) causally relevant to other sorts of things (other mental events and states as well as non-mental events and states) may be called the core of the Cartesian conception of the mind. The difficulties we have been reviewing for reductionist proposals about the mental are connected with these features. No physical states seem capable of possessing both. The first feature stands in the way of the plausibility of the psychophysical identity theory, and, arguably, of externalism about thought content. The second seems to preclude conceptual reduction to states characterized in terms of their causal relations to other things, or, again, in terms of their relations to things in the environment.

1.6.4 Irrealism

Finally, we turn to eliminativism. Eliminativists seek absolution through denial. According to eliminativism, nothing has mental properties. Prominent proponents of this position are Paul Churchland (1981) and Stephen Stich (1983), who argue that our mental concepts are empty.[83] They are concepts deployed in a pre-scientific or "folk" theory of behavior, which are ripe for replacement by a more sophisticated theory deploying different categories, which answer better to our explanatory interests. Folk psychology goes the way of theories of disease that appeal to demonic spirits. The psychological entities of our common-sense conceptual scheme too are creatures of darkness. We must now march forward into a brighter future, out from under the shadow cast by superstitions inculcated in the childhood of civilization, shriven of the sin of belief in the mind.

Eliminativism remains, not surprisingly, a minority position. It has some advantages – as Karl Popper has said, "the difficult body–mind problem simply disappears, which is no doubt very convenient: it saves us the trouble of solving it" (1994: 8). But it is hard to credit. It must reject the view that knowledge of our own conscious mental states is epistemically prior to knowledge of other things, which seems to be in conflict with a very natural account of how we come to know things about the world around us through perceptual experience. There are also certain difficulties involved in thinking about our position in putting forward the theory, and in accounting for how we could justify it. For surely if someone maintains that the theory is true, there is at least one person who believes something, namely, that eliminativism is true, in which case, eliminativism is false. The difficulty is that we have no vocabulary for describing the acceptance, rejection, and support of theories that does not presuppose that theoreticians have mental states. Eliminativists maintain this is merely a pragmatic difficulty, but it is not one that they have overcome.

1.7   Conclusion

This concludes our survey of the mind–body problem and the principal responses to it. A summary of the positions we have considered is given in figure 1.1.

Two basic positions mark the continental divide of the mind–body problem. All the positions we have examined are expressions of one or the other of them. One accepts the mental as a basic feature of reality, not explicable in terms of other features. Its basic characteristic is that it accepts propositions (1) and (2), realism and conceptual autonomy. The other insists that the appearance that the mental is a basic feature of reality must be an illusion, and that we and all our properties can be understood exhaustively ultimately in terms that make intelligible to us at the same time the clearly non-mental phenomena of the world. Its basic characteristic is that it accepts propositions (3) and (4), constituent explanatory sufficiency and constituent non-mentalism. The second view, constrained by the assumption that the basic constituents of things are physical (constituent physicalism), is equivalent to physicalism, with eliminativism as a degenerate case. The reason the mind–body problem does not go away, despite our being clear about the options in responding to it, is because of the constant battle between common sense, which favors the view that the mental is a basic feature of reality,

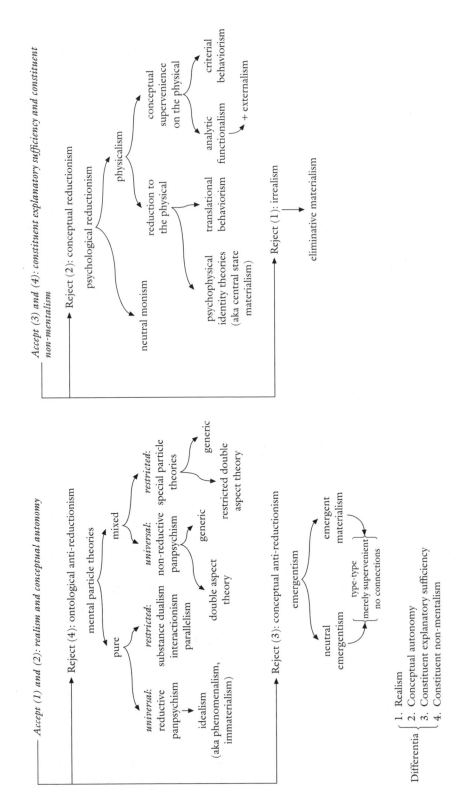

Figure 1.1 The logical space of solutions to the mind–body problem

and the pull to see it as an authoritative deliverance of science that this is not so. We find ourselves constantly pulled between these two poles, unable to see our minds as nothing over and above the physical, unwilling to see the universe as containing anything not explicable ultimately in terms of its basic, apparently non-mental, constituents.

Notes

1   The term 'the mind–body problem' is not used univocally. What guides my usage is an interest in getting at the puzzle that has generated the great variety of positions that we find in philosophical and scientific discussions of the relation of mental phenomena to physical phenomena. If I am right, there is a puzzle we can articulate clearly to which all the positions on the relation of the mental to the physical can be seen as responses. If any one problem deserves the label 'the mind–body problem' it is this.

2   In the course of discussion, a considerable amount of terminology will be introduced. This is partly to enable us to state our problem and its possible solutions with precision. More terminology is introduced than is strictly necessary for this. The excess is intended to provide a foundation for further reading in the relevant literature on the topic. I will often provide references representative of particular views or arguments. I list here some collections of papers which together give a fairly comprehensive picture of the historical and contemporary development of views on the mind–body problem: Vesey (1964), Anderson (1964), O'Connor (1969), Borst (1970), Rosenthal (1971), Block (1980), Eccles (1985), Lycan (1990), Rosenthal (1991), Beakley and Ludlow (1992), Warner and Szubka (1994), Block et al. (1997), Cooney (2000). Rosenthal (1991) is particularly comprehensive. Vesey (1964) contains historical sources not found in the others. Anderson (1964) contains early papers on the computer model of the mind. Eccles (1985) contains contributions mostly by scientists, both philosophical and scientific in character. Block et al. (1997) is devoted specifically to recent work on consciousness.

3   "By the term 'thought'," Descartes says, "I understand everything which we are aware of as happening within us, in so far as we have awareness of it" (1984, vol. I: 195 [1644: I.9]). This corresponds to the feature of consciousness I describe below as non-inferential knowledge of our modes of consciousness. Descartes held also that a state is a mental state *only if* it is conscious, but this is widely regarded as too stringent a requirement, for reasons considered below.

4   On this common-sense conception of events as changes, they are datable particulars. They may be complex as well as simple. My snapping my fingers is an event. So was the Second World War. If an object changes from being F to being non-F, the event is the changing from being F to being non-F. If we individuate events in terms of which objects, times, and properties they are changes with respect to, the question whether mental events are physical events is reduced to the question whether mental properties are physical properties.

5   It is sometimes thought that this is too strong. For one might mistakenly think, e.g., that one is in pain because one expects to be, given the occurrence of some event one had anticipated and expected to cause pain. For example, someone might think he was in pain when someone puts an ice cube on the back of his neck, if he had been

told that a piece of metal heated red hot was about to be pressed against the back of his neck. The possibility of his having a false belief in these circumstances does not show, however, that he does not know what he experienced. For he will correct his mistake. He will realize quickly that he is not, and was not, in pain. For he can recall what the experience was like. That requires knowing what character it had at the time, since one cannot remember something one did not originally know. Memory preserves but does not create knowledge.

6   For discussion of this issue, see essays 20–24 in Block et al. (1997).

7   See Nagel (1979b, 1994, 1998), and McGinn (1989, 1991, 1999). McGinn and Nagel think there must be a way of understanding how the operations of our brains give rise to consciousness, but that we currently have no conception of how that could be. McGinn is the more pessimistic, since he thinks whatever the correct explanation, it is one that we cannot in principle understand, given our cognitive make-up, while Nagel thinks we may one day develop appropriate concepts. The view that consciousness is the central difficulty is as old as discussion of the mind–body problem.

8   This terminology traces back to medieval philosophy; it is derived from the Latin verb *intendere*, for 'point at' or 'aim at'; it was used to characterize the object of a thought when it did not exist *in reality*, but had *intentional inexistence*, or *existed only intentionally in the thinking subject*.

9   Some things besides attitudes of the sorts we have been discussing can be said to represent things, and so to have intentionality; e.g., a sentence, or a portrait. However, these have representational content only because agents treat them as representations in accordance with various rules. This is derived, as opposed to original, intentionality (Searle 1983, 1984). Mental states have original intentionality. I use 'intentionality', without qualification, to mean original intentionality.

10   A *disposition* is a state of an object that consists in its settled tendency to undergo some change in certain conditions. Water solubility is a simple dispositional state possessed by salt and sugar: when placed in unsaturated water in a certain range of temperatures and pressures, they dissolve. The change undergone that characterizes a disposition is its *manifestation property*, the property that is manifested. The *manifestation condition* is that under which the manifestation property is manifested. Often both of these are encoded in the name of the disposition, as in "water solubility." Dispositional attitudes are not simple dispositions, but what Gilbert Ryle called "multi-track dispositions" (1949: 43–4). This means that they manifest themselves in various conditions in various ways. Moreover, they are interlocking dispositions: among the manifestation conditions for any given attitude will be conditions involving what other attitudes an agent has. A desire to buy a certain book will not be manifested unless I *believe* I have the opportunity to purchase it, and have no other desires whose satisfaction I rank above that for the purchase of the book, and which I think I can satisfy only to its exclusion.

11   Many recent theories of cognitive activity have appealed to in principle unconscious inferences in their explanations, thereby presupposing the two can be conceived independently. See Ludwig (1996c) for criticism of these views.

12   Some philosophers have recently argued that conscious states may be exhaustively characterized in terms of their representational content. Examples are Lycan (1996), Dretske (1997), and Tye (1997). For contrary views, see Searle (1993), Chalmers (1996), and Siewert (1998). Representational accounts of consciousness have often

been motivated by the thought that it is easier to see how intentional states could be reduced to physical states than how consciousness could be. In my view, which I do not argue for here, intentionality is ultimately to be understood as a form of consciousness, rather than the other way around, dispositional intentional states deriving their content from their manifestation in consciousness. If so, the question of the relation of consciousness to the physical is basic.

13 Importantly, I do not characterize the class of physical properties here as per se non-mental, though given the list of basic properties, they are clearly not mental per se. This leaves it open that mental properties could be analyzed as logical constructions of primary qualities, or, as conceptually supervening on them (see section 1.4).

14 See Poland (1994: esp. pp. 109–47) and Papineau (1993: 29–32).

15 More properly, a fully meaningful predicate in a language L expresses a concept and picks out a property. In different languages the same word may express different concepts, or none. I omit this relativization for brevity, but it should be understood as implicit wherever we are concerned with the relation of linguistic items to truth, concepts, and properties. I also ignore, for the most part, complications introduced by tense and other context-sensitive elements in natural languages.

16 There are other concepts of property that might be, and sometimes are, employed on which this would not be true. For example, one might individuate properties in terms of the sets of possible individuals who possessed them. Then two predicates would pick out the same property iff they were necessarily coextensive, which does not require synonymity (e.g., 'is trilateral' and 'is triangular'). But the theses about property identity that could be expressed in this way can be expressed without the dubious ontology and unhelpful innovation in terminology, which should not be encouraged.

17 More generally, we would speak of sentences as analytic relative to occasions of utterance, since what many sentences express in natural languages is relative to context of utterance.

18 There is controversy about whether there are analytic statements, conceptual truths, and truths knowable a priori, but in stating the mind–body problem it is not necessary to take a stand on this. W. V. Quine's "Two Dogmas of Empiricism" (1953) is the *locus classicus* of the case against analyticity. Grice and Strawson (1956) is an important early reply.

19 'Supervenience' in its current use is usually said to have been introduced in the context of ethical theory by R. M. Hare in the early 1950s to describe the relation of ethical properties to natural properties, and then imported into discussions in the philosophy of mind by Davidson (1980). It was in use earlier in the emergentist tradition, though perhaps not with quite as specific a meaning; see Kim (1993b: essay 8).

20 There are many changes one can ring on this formulation. For example, if we put in 'it is conceptually necessary that' before the whole right-hand side of the biconditional, we get a version of what has been called strong supervenience (Kim 1993b: essay 4). There are weaker varieties as well. I use this formulation because I wish to allow conceptual supervenience of the mental on the physical even though there could be a world of non-material objects that had mental properties. This is a possibility which functionalism, for example, leaves open. This gives content to the idea that supervenience is strictly weaker than reduction. Sometimes supervenience claims are formulated in terms of indiscernibility claims: F-properties supervene on G-properties iff necessarily

things which are alike with respect to their G-properties are alike with respect to their *F*-properties. See the essays in Kim (1993b) and Savellos and Yalçin (1995) for further discussion of the variants and their relations to one another.

21 The requirement that psychological laws (including any psychophysical laws) be entailed by physical laws is needed to avoid the problem of lucky materialism (Witmer 2000).

22 This position may appear stronger than it is. I put no constraints on physical properties other than that they be physical. Complex relational properties may figure in the supervenience base. Thus, it is equivalent to the view that a complete physical description of the world entails a complete psychological account of it.

23 It has been used in a weaker sense to denote a materialist ontology, and in a stricter sense, e.g., by the Logical Positivists, to mean that all statements are translatable into the vocabulary of physics.

24 By 'non-mental properties' here I mean properties that are classified in terms that are not mental as such, so that some members of the class, and certainly all basic (i.e., non-complex) members, are not mental. This allows that mental properties may be a subclass of the properties in question. That is to say, (2) asserts that there are no classes of properties that are not mental per se to which mental properties are conceptually reducible.

25 In the present context, by a non-relational property we mean a property that an individual has which does not require the existence of some contingently existing individual not identical with the individual possessing the property or any part of it, and does not require the non-existence of any thing or kind of thing. For example, being married and being a planet are relational properties, being round and being red are not.

26 This rules out appeal to properties that constituents have because of emergent properties of the wholes they compose.

27 This leaves open that they may have mental properties in the sense that they have relational properties which entail that something possesses mental properties, e.g., because they coexist with or are part of a thing that has irreducible mental properties but which is not itself a basic constituent of things. Also this leaves open that the basic constituents of things have properties which we might not recognize as broadly physical, but it does not allow that they be mental. Thus, constituent non-mentalism is a more liberal thesis than constituent physicalism.

28 See Bealer (1992) for a general defense of these methods for discovering what is necessary and possible; a more recent book-length defense of conceptual analysis is Jackson (1998).

29 The discovery of this paradox by Bertrand Russell, in May 1901, played an important role in foundational studies in set theory and mathematics early in the twentieth century.

30 The question of the relation of consciousness and intentionality becomes important here, for the thought experiments mentioned seem to depend on our thinking that a conscious point of view could be missing in a being physically and behaviorally like us, or be present in a being with no associated body at all. If intentional states and conscious states are independent, the support of these thought experiments for the irreducibility of the mental *tout court* is reduced.

31 With the exception, however, of the role of the notion of an observation in quantum mechanics: how seriously this is to be taken is a matter of controversy.

32 See Annas (1992) for survey of ancient philosophy of mind concentrating on the Hellenistic period.

33 This was a minority position in antiquity. Introduced by Plato, it assumed the importance it has in the later western tradition through the influence of Plato's philosophy on Catholic theology, through which it has permeated ideas about mind and body in western culture.

34 See Woolhouse (1993) for discussion of the notion of substance in early modern philosophy rationalists.

35 We must exclude here such "formal" properties as having a property.

36 The initial moves in the argument are made in the second meditation of Descartes's masterpiece *Meditations on First Philosophy* (1985 [1641]) and concluded in the sixth; see also *Principles of Philosophy* (1985 [1644]: §63).

37 This analogy was conceived by Leibniz, though his basic metaphysics rejects substance dualism.

38 Though dualism is not currently a popular view among philosophers or scientists, it is still no doubt one of the most commonly, if unreflectively, held views about the relation of mental to physical phenomena, as it is the background metaphysics of a number of the world's major religions; and it is not without contemporary proponents among philosophers and scientists, see, e.g., Foster (1996), Eccles (1953: ch. 8), Popper and Eccles (1977: ch. E7).

39 Three landmarks of the twentieth century are Carnap (1928), Lewis (1929), and Goodman (1951). A more recent proponent is Grayling (1985).

40 A detailed bibliography of sources is available at the end of the article on panpsychism in Edwards (1967).

41 Panpsychism, and other mental particle theories, as for reductive materialism, is an expression of the idea, as Popper and Eccles have put it, that there is nothing new under the sun, which is an expression of a form of the principle of sufficient reason: nothing can come from nothing (Popper and Eccles 1977: 14).

42 Nineteenth-century double aspect theorists include Shadworth Hodgson (1870: esp. ch. 3) and G. H. Lewes (1877).

43 See, e.g., the discussion of Morton Prince (1885; repr. in Vesey 1964: 187).

44 Perhaps Strawson's view that the concept of a person is more basic than that of a person's mind or body may be construed as of this sort (1958).

45 How should we classify a view such as Hume's "bundle" theory of the self? On this view, there is no thing that is the self, but rather each self is to be construed as constituted out of a set of perceptions which bear appropriate relations to one another. The perceptions are intrinsically mental in character, like mental atoms. They are not, though, apparently thought of as in space. So, while a mental particle view of a sort, it is more like substance dualism without the basic mental substances being thinking beings, but rather thoughts constitutive of thinking beings. If we take "perceptions" to be non-mental themselves, and take both the self and ordinary objects to be logical constructions out of them, we arrive at a version of the neutral monism advocated by James, Mach, and Russell (see below).

46 It is important to distinguish emergence in this sense from emergence of higher levels of organization of complex systems governed by simple rules that is often discussed in the context of "chaos" theory. The properties of the latter sort conceptually supervene on the rules governing the constituents of the system, their properties, and their

arrangement. They are emergent only in the sense of being surprising to us, and so their status as emergent, in this sense, is a function of our inability to easily predict them.

47 This requires us to disallow indefinitely long disjunctions from expressing relevant types; otherwise, by disjoining all the nomically sufficient conditions stated in physical terms for a given mental type, we could always arrive at a nomically necessary condition.

48 A token is an instance of a type. For example, in the previous sentence (inscription), there are four tokens of the letter "a." Tokens are always particulars. Every token is identical with itself. We get informative statements about token identity when we use different ways of picking out the same thing. It can be informative, e.g., to be told that Pluto is the smallest planet in the Solar System. Type-type identity, strictly speaking, is about properties. Again, every property is identical to itself and to no distinct thing. Informative type-type identity statements pick out the properties in different ways. We will see an example below of a type-type identity theory of the mental and the physical that makes this an interesting empirical discovery.

49 The conception of events articulated in note 4 is incompatible with anomalous monism, for it individuates events in terms of the objects and properties that they are changes with respect to. Thus, unless mental properties are physical properties, which on this view they are not, no mental event is token identical with any physical event. There are various weaker relations that could be articulated. For example, it might be said that every mental event occurs at the same time as and in the same object as a physical event. In any case, it is not clear that much hinges on this. The more fundamental question is about objects and properties rather than events.

50 In origin, a medical term meaning "symptom of an underlying cause" or "secondary symptom."

51 See McLaughlin (1992) for a discussion of this particular school in the broader emergentist tradition. Be aware that McLaughlin uses 'emergentism' in a narrower sense than it is used here, namely, to cover what I would call emergent materialism with downward causation. 'Emergentism' is the right term for the rejection of (3); we can distinguish epiphenomenal and non-epiphenomenal versions, the latter of which will at least include emergentism with downward causation. Alas, terminological variation in philosophy is endemic. Broad himself, who introduced the term 'emergent materialism', did not take it to imply downward causation, which he accepted tentatively as an empirical hypothesis on the basis of what he took to be the evidence of psychical research.

52 This contrast and debate between epiphenomenal emergentists and downward causation emergentists reprises a similar debate in antiquity between followers of Aristotle (Caston 1997).

53 For more recent discussions, see Armstrong (1968: 47) and Kim (1993a,b).

54 A note is in order on the term 'property dualism', which has figured prominently in recent literature on the mind–body problem. This label is often used in application to emergentism, but applies to any position that holds that there are objects that have mental properties, and there are objects that have physical properties and that both sorts are basic properties, not conceptually reducible to each other or anything more basic. (Property dualism is not coextensive with any position that holds (1) and (2) and either of (3) or (4), since, e.g., idealism embraces (1)–(3), but reduces what are ordinarily thought of as physical properties to mental properties.) *Property* dualism

is a weaker view than *substance* dualism, but is entailed by it. "Property dualism" is often used as a term of abuse by philosophers attracted by reductionism, with the idea of associating its proponents with the discredited view of substance dualism by the overlap in the spelling of their labels. The introduction of "property dualism" into the philosophical vocabulary is not an entirely happy terminological innovation, and that is one reason it does not figure prominently in my discussion. Quite apart from its association with demagoguery, the label falsely suggests that there are at most two families of properties irreducible to each other: but even setting aside the current issue, there are many mutually irreducible families of properties (color and shape properties, for example).

55 There are some possible though unoccupied positions here that we will not survey, such as the view that the mental supervenes on or is conceptually reducible to something non-mental, and the physical in turn supervenes on or is conceptually reducible to the mental.

56 In this way it is like the reduction of mathematics to logic and set theory. We can retain our old forms of speech, but our ontology includes only sets, not numbers in addition. The relation of the mental and physical to underlying reality on neutral monism is like the relation of odd and even numbers to the underlying reality on the set-theoretic reduction of mathematics. Each is distinct from the other, and has an essential property the other cannot have, but each is explained as a logical construction out of something more basic.

57 Carnap (1931) and Hempel (1935) provide early examples of logical behaviorists; both later retreated from the early position. Ryle's *The Concept of Mind* (1949) was an important and influential behaviorist manifesto (though Ryle denied the term applied to his view). Wittgenstein's *Philosophical Investigations* (1950) was an important inspiration for criterial behaviorism. See, for example, Malcolm (1958). Important psychological behaviorists were Watson (1925) and Skinner (1974), though their behaviorism was methodological rather than logical.

58 See Putnam (1968). Logical behaviorism seems to have succumbed to a danger that every reductive project faces. As C. I. Lewis put it: "Confronted with problems of analysis which there is trouble to resolve, one may sometimes circumvent them by changing the subject" (1941: 225).

59 This is held to be true as a matter of fact. Of course, if there were non-physical objects that had internal structure, they would have functional states as well.

60 Every era has its favored metaphor provided by its prestige technology. In the seventeenth and eighteenth centuries, it was the clock or the mill. In the nineteenth, it was the steam engine. In the latter half of the twentieth, it became the computer.

61 The Pythagoreans advocated the general idea of functionalism, that having a mind depends on a certain organization of the body, in antiquity. It is one of the positions that Socrates responds to in the *Phaedo* in Simmias's suggestion that the soul is to the body as the attunement of it is to a string instrument (Plato 1989: 69).

62 There are two ways of understanding psychofunctionalism's empirical character. First, it can be understood as a version of emergentism with bridge laws connecting functional with mental states (see, e.g., Chalmers 1996: ch. 6). Second, it might be maintained that the identification of mental with functional states is a theoretical identification, like the identification of lightning as an electrical discharge (this view has been advocated for intentional states in Rey 1997). If what I say below about this

is correct, this introduces an empirical element into the discovery, but not in a way that prevents this view, if correct, from collapsing into analytic functionalism. See the discussion of the identity theory below.

63 A more recent variant on the general theme is connectionism. A connectionist system consists of a set of interconnected units that can take on activation values: the interconnections determine the influence of the activation value of a given node on those connected to it. Through their connections, units may inhibit or excite other units to various degrees depending on their own activation states. Certain units may be designated input units and others output units. The activation values can be continuous, so a connectionist system is not a finite state machine. But it fits our initial very general characterization of a functional system, since different connectionist systems are wholly characterized in terms of their states' relations to input and output and other states. The difference between classical functionalism and connectionism will not be relevant at the level of our discussion here.

64 The force of this objection is unclear. Either mental properties are analyzable as functional properties or not. If not, then there is the question whether they are analyzable as physical properties. If so, that is an end to the matter, and the charge of chauvinism is bootless. If not, it is an empirical matter what physical state types, if any, mental state types are correlated with, and our hunches or prejudices about it are irrelevant. Though in the latter case, clearly difficulties will arise when we try to confirm or disconfirm claims about physical systems that are very different from ourselves.

65 See also Searle's Chinese Room thought experiment (1980), and Chalmers (1996: ch. 3) for a recent deployment of so-called zombie thought experiments to establish the irreducibility of conscious mental states.

66 Putnam was careful to exclude systems that contain parts that have organizations like the whole they constitute. This would rule out the system in Block's thought experiment as constituting a person. However, it is difficult to see what justifies the exclusion. For if our mental concepts are functional concepts, it should not matter how the system that has the appropriate functional organization is constituted.

67 See Chalmers (1996: 91–101) for a somewhat fuller discussion and some responses to objections that have appeared in the literature.

68 A functionalist need not require this. A functional system could be characterized in terms of non-causal transitions between states given input and output. But this opens the door to a great many more machine table descriptions of objects that may have minds than a functionalist will typically want to countenance.

69 The event reported in the headlines of this morning's paper caused extensive flooding in coastal areas of Florida, but it was not by virtue of being of that type that it did so, but in virtue of its being the passing of a category 3 hurricane off the coast. Causal relations hold between particulars, datable events, or states. But to explain why they hold between those particulars we must appeal to their types.

70 See Jackson and Pettit (1988), Block (1990), Fodor (1991), Dardis (1993), and Ludwig (1994a, 1998) for discussion.

71 At this point too the question whether intentional states are conceptually independent of conscious states is important, for our conviction that mental states are causally relevant to behavior seems to attach in the first instance to conscious mental states, and to dispositional states only through their manifestation conditions in consciousness.

For dispositional states too are defined in terms of manifestation conditions, and so as such are not causally relevant to those conditions.

72   The account given here departs from Lewis's own. Perhaps the departure is largely in terminology, but it is still important. Lewis has argued that despite the theoretical identification of pain with a physical property in human beings, it still makes sense to say that some being (a Martian, e.g.) could be in pain though he does not have that property which in human beings is pain (Lewis 1980). How is this possible? It is not, if we understand the relation between predicates, concepts, and properties as I have introduced them. On the account I have given, the predicate 'is in pain' expresses the concept of pain and is used to attribute the property of being in pain, and it does each of these in virtue of its meaning in English. The property is, so to speak, the shadow of the meaning of the predicate cast on the world, and the concept is the shadow it casts in our thoughts. If the property of being in pain is a physical property, so, on this view, is the concept of pain a physical concept. Lewis, however, identifies something else as the concept of pain. To put it briefly, Lewis uses 'concept of pain' to denote the concept expressed by the predicate 'is a thing that has the property P such that, for the most part, $T(P)$ for beings of kind K' where '$T(P)$' is replaced by the appropriate psychological theory with 'P' in the place of the variable representing the property of pain. That concept applies to a thing in virtue of that thing's having some property that plays a certain role mediating input and output. It might have been that a different property played that role. And in different kinds of beings, perhaps, for the most part, different properties play that role. However, Lewis does not say that the property of being in pain is the one attributed using this form of predicate. Rather, Lewis calls the property that actually plays the role the property of being in pain. This allows then that in different kinds of beings a different property can be (called) the property of being in pain. It also apparently allows that if things had been different, a different property in us would have been (called by us) the property of being in pain. Apparently, however, Lewis does want to treat the predicate 'is in pain' as if it attributed the property that plays the right role. Thus, he says "is in pain" is ambiguous when we apply it to different kinds of beings, and when we consider it in different possible worlds. For a difference in property attributed entails a difference in the meaning of the predicate. It is as if we had decided to say that the property being rich is attributed using 'has a lot more money than most people' but the concept of richness is expressed by the predicate 'is Ludwig's favorite property'. I keep the concept of pain attached to the predicate 'is in pain', and so matched with the property attributed using it. This follows the traditional alignment, and provides us a clearer view of the issues.

73   There are many arguments against the psychophysical identity theory and physicalism more generally that rest on thought experiments designed to show that nothing follows about what mental properties an object has from an exhaustive description of its physical construction. One style of argument much discussed recently has been dubbed 'the knowledge argument'. Some deployments of the argument in the latter half of the twentieth century are Meehl (1966), Nagel (1979b), Jackson (1982, 1986). Leibniz already gives a version of such an argument in *The Monadology* (1714: sec. 16): "If we imagine that there is a machine whose structure makes it think, sense, and have perceptions, we could conceive it enlarged, keeping the same proportions, so that we could enter into it, as one enters into a mill. Assuming that, when inspecting

its interior, we will only find parts that push one another, and we will never find anything to explain a perception." These arguments are certainly decisive against any version of the psychophysical identity that suggests that we can perform an armchair analysis of our mental concepts to determine that they in fact pick out neuro-physiological properties. They do not address versions of the theory that treat our ordinary terms as having their concepts fixed by description: the burden such an approach takes up, though, is scarcely less heavy, for it must allow, as we have seen, that our terms may fail to express any concepts at all.

74 The view itself was certainly not undiscussed previously in the twentieth century. Broad discusses and dismisses it (1925: 622–3). C. I. Lewis discussed and criticized a form of the identity theory, which he presents as proposing descriptive definitions of mental terms, in much the same spirit as the theory I have presented (1941: 230–1). Some of Smart's replies to objections are clearly directed at Broad's and Lewis's earlier discussions.

75 They regarded propositional attitudes as understandable behavioristically, or functionally. However, the position can easily be generalized to propositional attitudes.

76 See Bealer (1987, 1994) for arguments against this appeal to what is sometimes called scientific essentialism.

77 In any case, it should be noted that the same unclarity would attach to whatever notion of property identity would be here invoked as attaches to metaphysical necessity: if we try to explain it in accordance with the tradition, we must admit that what we discover is that, e.g., "water" and "H$_2$O" express the same concept, contrary to the supposition.

78 These began with work by Kripke (1980) on proper names and natural kind terms and Hilary Putnam (1975) on natural kind terms in the early 1970s. Initially, these arguments were directed toward showing that the meanings of various natural language terms were determined by their causal relations with things and kinds in our environments. Since we use these same terms to characterize our attitudes, however, it was soon apparent that these arguments might be used to urge also that our thought contents were individuated relative to what things and kinds were actually in our environments.

79 See Putnam (1975) and Burge (1979, 1982, 1986). Widespread uncritical acceptance of externalism is a salient feature of discussion in contemporary philosophy of mind.

80 Difficulties are discussed in Ludwig (1992a, 1992b, 1993a, 1993b, 1993c, 1994a, 1994b, 1996a, 1996b).

81 The literature on this subject is large. An earlier paper that advanced this thesis particularly in response to Putnam (1981) is Brueckner (1986). See also Boghossian (1989, 1993).

82 See Jackson (1996) for a fairly comprehensive review of discussion of mental causation.

83 Early proponents were Feyerabend (1963) and Rorty (1965, 1979). Perhaps Wittgenstein endorsed eliminativism in the *Tractatus Logico-Philosophicus* (1921), but if so on grounds more abstract than more recent eliminativists. Eliminativism may be the one modern view that is not represented in ancient philosophy. Perhaps the atomists, Leucippus and Democritus, might be thought to endorse eliminativism, since they held that reality consisted solely of atoms and the void. But they showed no inclination to deny that there were people who thought and reasoned, and

Democritus seems to have intended to explain psychological phenomena in terms of his atomistic metaphysics (see Taylor 1999). One can be a partial, as well as a wholesale eliminativist. Georges Rey argues for functionalism for intentional states, but eliminativism for qualitative states (1997).

References

Alexander, S. (1920). *Space, Time and Deity: The Gifford Lectures at Glasgow 1916–1918.* London: Macmillan.

Anderson, A. R. (ed.) (1964). *Minds and Machines.* Englewood Cliffs: Prentice Hall.

Annas, J. (1992). *Hellenistic Philosophy of Mind.* Berkeley: University of California.

Aristotle. (1984). *The Complete Works of Aristotle.* Princeton: Princeton University Press.

Armstrong, D. M. (1968). *A Materialist Theory of the Mind.* London: Routledge and Kegan Paul, Humanities Press.

Ayer, A. J. (ed.) (1959). *Logical Positivism.* New York: Free Press.

Beakley, B. and Ludlow, P. (eds.) (1992). *The Philosophy of Mind: Classical Problems/ Contemporary Issues.* Cambridge, MA: MIT Press.

Bealer, G. (1987). "The Philosophical Limits of Scientific Essentialism." *Philosophical Perspectives,* 1: 289–365.

—— (1992). "The Incoherence of Empiricism." *Proceedings of the Aristotelian Society,* 66: 99–138.

—— (1994). "Mental Properties." *The Journal of Philosophy,* 91: 185–208.

Beckermann, A., Flohr, H. et al. (1992). *Emergence or Reduction? Essays on the Prospects of Nonreductive Physicalism.* New York: W. de Gruyter.

Bedau, M. (1986). "Cartesian Interaction." *Midwest Studies in Philosophy,* 10: 483–502.

Berkeley, G. (1710). *A Treatise Concerning the Principles of Human Knowledge.* In Michael R. Ayers (ed.), *Philosophical Works.* London: The Guernsey Press, 1975: 61–128.

Block, N. (1978). "Troubles with Functionalism." In C. W. Savage (ed.), *Perception and Cognition: Issues in the Foundations of Psychology.* Minneapolis: University of Minnesota: 261–325. Reprinted in Block (1980).

—— (ed.) (1980). *Readings in the Philosophy of Psychology.* Cambridge, MA: Harvard University Press.

—— (1990). "Can the Mind Change the World?" In G. Boolos (ed.), *Meaning and Method: Essays in Honor of Hilary Putnam.* New York: Cambridge University Press: 29–59.

Block, N., Flanagan, O. et al. (eds.) (1997). *The Nature of Consciousness: Philosophical Debates.* Cambridge, MA: MIT Press.

Boghossian, P. (1989). "Content and Self-Knowledge." *Philosophical Topics,* 17: 5–26.

—— (1993). "The Transparency of Content." *Philosophical Perspectives,* 8: 33–50.

Borst, C. V. (ed.) (1970). *The Mind–Brain Identity Theory.* London: Macmillan.

Brentano, F. (1955 [1874]). *Psychologie vom Empirischen Standpunkt (Psychology from an Empirical Standpoint).* Hamburg: Felix Meiner.

Broad, C. D. (1925). *The Mind and Its Place in Nature.* New York: Harcourt, Brace and company.

Brueckner, A. (1986). "Brains in a Vat." *The Journal of Philosophy,* 83: 148–67.

Burge, T. (1979). "Individualism and the Mental." *Midwest Studies in Philosophy,* 4: 73–121.

—— (1982). "Other Bodies." In A. Woodfield (ed.), *Thought and Object: Essays on Intentionality*. Oxford: Clarendon Press: 97–120.

—— (1986). "Cartesian Error and the Objectivity of Perception." In P. Pettit (ed.), *Subject, Thought, and Context*. New York: Clarendon Press: 117–36.

Carnap, R. (1928). *The Logical Structure of the World*, trans. Rolf A. George. Berkeley: University of California Press, 1967. First published in German in 1928 under the title *Der Logische Aufbau der Welt*.

—— (1931). "Die Physikalische Sprache als Universalsprache der Wissenschaft." *Erkenntnis*, 2: 432–65. Reprinted in Ayer (1959) as "Psychology in Physical Language."

Caston, V. (1997). "Epiphenomenalisms, Ancient and Modern." *The Philosophical Review*, 106: 309–64.

Chalmers, D. (1996). *The Conscious Mind: In Search of a Fundamental Theory*. New York: Oxford University Press.

Churchland, P. (1981). "Eliminative Materialism and the Propositional Attitudes." *The Journal of Philosophy*, 78: 67–90.

Cooney, B. (ed.) (2000). *The Place of Mind*. Stamford: Wadsworth.

Dardis, A. (1993). "Sunburn: Independence Conditions on Causal Relevance." *Philosophy and Phenomenological Research*, 53: 577–98.

Davidson, D. (1980). 'Mental Events'. In *Essays on Actions and Events*. New York: Clarendon Press: 207–24.

Descartes, R. (1985 [1641]). *Meditations on First Philosophy*. In *The Philosophical Writings of Descartes*, vol. II, ed. and trans. J. Cottingham, R. Stoothoff, and D. Murdoch. Cambridge: Cambridge University Press: 1–62.

—— (1984 [1644]). *The Principles of Philosophy*. In *The Philosophical Writings of Descartes*, vol. I, ed. and trans. J. Cottingham, R. Stoothoff, and D. Murdoch. Cambridge: Cambridge University Press: 177–292.

Dretske, F. (1997). *Naturalizing the Mind*. Cambridge, MA: MIT Press.

Eccles, J. C. (1953). *The Neurophysiological Basis of Mind; The Principles of Neurophysiology*. Oxford: Clarendon Press.

—— (ed.) (1985). *Mind and Brain: The Many-Faceted Problems*. New York: Paragon House.

Edwards, P. (1967). *The Encyclopedia of Philosophy*. New York: Macmillan.

Feigl, H. (1958). "The Mental and the Physical." In H. Feigl et al., *Concepts, Theories and the Mind–Body Problem*. Minneapolis: University of Minnesota Press: 370–497.

Feyerabend, P. (1963). "Mental Events and the Brain." *The Journal of Philosophy*, 60: 295–96.

Fodor, J. A. (1991). "A Modal Argument for Narrow Content." *The Journal of Philosophy*, 88 (1): 5–26.

Foster, J. (1996). *The Immaterial Self: A Defence of the Cartesian Dualist Conception of the Mind*. London: Routledge.

Grayling, A. C. (1985). *The Refutation of Scepticism*. LaSalle, IL: Open Court.

Grice, H. P. and Strawson, P. F. (1956). "In Defense of a Dogma." *Philosophical Review*, 65: 141–58.

Goodman, N. (1951). *The Structure of Appearance*. Cambridge, MA: Harvard University Press.

Hempel, C. (1935). "The Logical Analysis of Behavior." In Block (1980: 14–23). Originally published in *Revue de Synthese*, 1935.

Hodgson, S. (1870). *The Theory of Practice*. London: Longmans, Green, Reader and Dyer.

Huxley, T. H. (1874). "On the Hypothesis that Animals are Automata, and its History." In Vesey (1964: 134–43). Originally delivered in 1874 to the British Association for the Advancement of Science, Belfast.

—— (1901). *Methods and Results: Essays*. New York: D. Appleton.

Jackson, F. (1982). "Epiphenomenal Qualia." *The Philosophical Quarterly*, 32: 127–36.

—— (1986). "What Mary Didn't Know." *The Journal of Philosophy*, 83: 291–5.

—— (1996). "Mental Causation." *Mind*, 105 (419): 377–413.

—— (1998). *From Metaphysics to Ethics: A Defense of Conceptual Analysis*. New York: Clarendon Press.

Jackson, F. and Pettit, P. (1988). "Functionalism and Broad Content." *Mind*, 97: 381–400.

James, W. (1950 [1890]). *The Principles of Psychology*. New York: Dover.

—— (1910). *Psychology*. New York: Henry Holt and Co. Page references in the text are given to Block et al. (1997), in which a portion of chapter 11 is reprinted.

—— (1904). "Does Consciousness Exist?" *The Journal of Philosophy, Psychology and Scientific Methods*, 1: 477–91. Repr. in James (1976 [1912]).

—— (1976 [1912]). *Essays in Radical Empiricism*. Cambridge, MA: Harvard University Press.

Kant, I. (1997 [1781]). *The Critique of Pure Reason*. Cambridge: Cambridge University Press. Originally published in 1781, a much revised version was published in 1787.

Kim, J. (1993a). "Mechanism, Purpose, and Explanatory Exclusion." In Kim (1993b: 237–64).

—— (1993b). *Supervenience and Mind*. New York: Cambridge University Press.

Kripke, S. (1980). *Naming and Necessity*. Cambridge, MA: Harvard University Press.

Leibniz, G. W. (1714). *Principles of Philosophy, or, The Monadology*. In *Philosophical Essays*. Indianapolis: Hackett, 1989: 213–24. Originally composed in 1714 for private correspondence as a summary of his philosophical views.

Lewes, G. H. (1877). *The Physical Basis of Mind*. London: Trubner and Co.

Lewis, C. I. (1929). *Mind and the World-order: Outline of a Theory of Knowledge*. New York: Scribner.

—— (1941). "Some Logical Considerations Concerning the Mental." *The Journal of Philosophy*, 38: 225–33.

Lewis, D. (1966). "An Argument for the Identity Theory." *The Journal of Philosophy*, 63: 17–25.

—— (1972). "Psychophysical and Theoretical Identifications." *The Australasian Journal of Philosophy*, 50: 249–58. Repr. in Lewis (1999).

—— (1980). "Mad Pain and Martian Pain." In Block (1980: 216–22).

—— (1999). *Papers in Metaphysics and Epistemology*. Cambridge: Cambridge University Press.

Ludwig, K. (1992a). "Skepticism and Interpretation." *Philosophy and Phenomenological Research*, 52 (2): 317–39.

—— (1992b). "Brains in a Vat, Subjectivity, and the Causal Theory of Reference." *Journal of Philosophical Research*, 17: 313–45.

—— (1993a). "Direct Reference in Thought and Speech." *Communication and Cognition*, 26 (1), 49–76.

—— (1993b). "Externalism, Naturalism, and Method." In E. Villanueva (ed.), *Naturalism and Normativity*. Atascadero, Ridgeview: 250–64.

Kirk Ludwig

—— (1993c). "Dretske on Explaining Behavior." *Acta Analytica*, 811: 111–24.

—— (1994a). "Causal Relevance and Thought Content." *Philosophical Quarterly*, 44: 334–53.

—— (1994b). "First Person Knowledge and Authority." In G. Preyer, F. Siebelt, and A. Ulfig (eds.), *Language, Mind, and Epistemology: On Donald Davidson's Philosophy*. Dordrecht: Kluwer: 367–98.

—— (1996a). "Singular Thought and the Cartesian Theory of Mind." *Nous*, 30 (4): 434–60.

—— (1996b). "Duplicating Thoughts." *Mind and Language*, 11 (1): 92–102.

—— (1996c). "Explaining Why Things Look the Way They Do." In K. Akins (ed.), *Perception*. Oxford: Oxford University Press: 18–60.

—— (1998). "Functionalism and Causal Relevance." *Psyche* 4 (3) (http://psyche.cs.monash. edu.an/v4/psyche-4-03-ludwig.html).

Lycan, W. G. (1996). *Consciousness and Experience*. Cambridge, MA: MIT Press.

—— (ed.) (1990). *Mind and Cognition: A Reader*. Oxford: Blackwell.

Mach, E. (1897 [1886]). *Ernst Mach: Contributions to the Analysis of Sensations*. Chicago: Open Court.

Malcolm, N. (1958). "Knowledge of Other Minds." *The Journal of Philosophy*, 55: 969–78. Reprinted in Rosenthal (1991).

McGinn, C. (1989). "Can We Solve the Mind–Body Problem?" *Mind*, 98: 349–66.

—— (1991). *The Problem of Consciousness*. Oxford: Blackwell.

—— (1999). *The Mysterious Flame: Conscious Minds in a Material World*. New York: Basic Books.

McLaughlin, B. (1992). "The Rise and Fall of British Emergentism." In Beckermann (1992).

Meehl, P. E. (1966). "The Compleat Autocerebroscopist: A Thought-Experiment on Professor Feigl's Mind–Body Identity Thesis." In P. K. Feyerabend and G. Maxwell (eds.), *Mind, Matter, and Method: Essays in Philosophy and Science in Honor of Herbert Feigl*. Minneapolis: University of Minnesota Press: 103–80.

Menzies, P. (1988). "Against Causal Reductionism." *Mind*, 97: 551–74.

Moore, G. E. (1959 [1903]). "The Refutation of Idealism." *Philosophical Studies*. Paterson, N.J.: Littlefield, Adams and Co.: 1–30. Originally published in *Mind*, 13: 433–53.

Morgan, C. L. (1923). *Emergent Evolution: The Gifford Lectures*. London: Williams and Norgate.

Nagel, T. (1979a). "Panpsychism." In *Mortal Questions*. Cambridge: Cambridge University Press: 181–95.

—— (1979b). "What Is It Like to Be a Bat?" In *Mortal Questions*. Cambridge: Cambridge University Press: 165–80.

—— (1994). "Consciousness and Objective Reality." In Richard Warner (ed.), *The Mind–Body Problem: A Guide to the Current Debate*. Oxford: Blackwell: 63–8.

—— (1998). "Conceiving the Impossible and the Mind–Body Problem." *Philosophy*, 73 (285): 337–52.

O'Connor, J. (ed.) (1969). *Modern Materialism: Readings on Mind–Body Identity*. New York: Harcourt, Brace and World.

Papineau, D. (1998). "Mind the Gap." *Philosophical Perspectives*, 12: 373–88.

—— (1993). *Philosophical Naturalism*. Oxford: Blackwell.

Place, U. T. (1956). "Is Consciousness a Brain Process?" *British Journal of Psychology*, 45: 243–55.

Plato (1989). *The Collected Dialogues of Plato*. Princeton: Princeton University Press.

Poland, J. S. (1994). *Physicalism, the Philosophical Foundations*. Oxford: Clarendon Press.

Popper, K. (1994). *Knowledge and the Body–Mind Problem: In Defence of Interaction*. London: Routledge.

Popper, K., and Eccles, J. (1977). *The Self and its Brain*. New York: Springer-Verlag.

Prince, M. (1885). *The Nature of Mind and Human Automatism*. Philadelphia: J. B. Lippincott Company.

Putnam, H. (1967). "Psychological Predicates." In W. H. Capitan and D. D. Merrill (eds.), *Art, Mind and Religion*. Pittsburgh: Pittsburgh University Press: 37–48. Reprinted under the title "The Nature of Mental States" in Rosenthal (1991).

—— (1968). "Brains and Behavior." In J. R. Butter (ed.), *Analytic Philosophy*. Oxford: Basil Blackwell: 1–19. Reprinted in Rosenthal (1991).

—— (1975). "The Meaning of 'Meaning'." In *Mind, Language and Reality: Philosophical Papers*. Cambridge: Cambridge University Press: 215–71.

—— (1981). *Reason, Truth and History*. Cambridge: Cambridge University Press.

Quine, W. V. O. (1953). "Two Dogmas of Empiricism." In *From a Logical Point of View*. Cambridge, MA: Harvard University Press: 20–46.

Rey, G. (1997). *Contemporary Philosophy of Mind: A Contentiously Classical Approach*. New York: Blackwell.

Romanes, G. J. (1895). *Mind and Motion and Monism*. New York: Longmans Green.

Rorty, R. (1965). "Mind–Body Identity, Privacy, and Categories." *The Review of Metaphysics*, 19: 24–54.

—— (1979). *Philosophy and the Mirror of Nature*. Princeton: Princeton University Press.

Rosenthal, D. (ed.) (1971). *Materialism and the Mind–Body Problem*. Englewood Cliffs: Prentice-Hall.

—— (1991). *The Nature of Mental States*. New York: Oxford University Press.

Ryle, G. (1949). *The Concept of Mind*. London: Hutchinson and Company, Ltd.

Russell, B. (1917). "On the Relation of Sense-data to Physics." In *Mysticism and Logic, and Other Essays*. London: Allen and Unwin: 108–31.

—— (1921). *The Analysis of Mind*. London: G. Allen and Unwin.

Savellos, E. and Yalçin, U. (eds.) (1995). *Supervenience: New Essays*. New York: Cambridge University Press.

Searle, J. R. (1980). "Minds, Brains, and Programs." *The Behavioral and Brain Sciences*, 3: 417–24. Reprinted in Rosenthal (1991).

—— (1983). *Intentionality: An Essay in the Philosophy of Mind*. Cambridge: Cambridge University Press.

—— (1984). "Intentionality and Its Place in Nature." *Dialectica*, 38: 87–100.

—— (1993). *The Rediscovery of the Mind*. Cambridge, MA: MIT Press.

Siewert, C. (1998). *The Significance of Consciousness*. Princeton: Princeton University Press.

Skinner, B. F. (1974). *About Behaviorism*. New York: Knopf.

Smart, J. J. C. (1959). "Sensations and Brain Processes." *The Philosophical Review*, 68: 141–56.

Sperry, R. W. (1986). "Discussion: Macro- Versus Micro-Determination." *Philosophy of Science*, 53: 265–70.

Spinoza, B. (1994). *A Spinoza Reader: The Ethics and Other Works*. Princeton: Princeton University Press.

Stich, S. (1983). *From Folk Psychology to Cognitive Science: The Case Against Belief.* Cambridge, MA: MIT Press.

Strawson, P. F. (1958). "Persons." In Herbert Feigl, Michael Scriven, and Grover Maxwell (eds.), *Minnesota Studies in the Philosophy of Science* 2. Minneapolis: University of Minnesota Press: 330–53.

Taylor, C. C. W. (1999). "The Atomists." A. A. Long (ed.), *The Cambridge Companion to Early Greek Philosophy.* Cambridge: Cambridge University Press: 181–204.

Tye, M. (1997). *Ten Problems of Consciousness: A Representational Theory of the Phenomenal Mind.* Cambridge, MA: MIT Press.

Vesey, G. N. A. (ed.) (1964). *Body and Mind: Readings in Philosophy.* London: George Allen and Unwin.

Warner, R. and Szubka, T. (eds.) (1994). *The Mind–Body Problem: A Guide to the Current Debate.* Oxford: Basil Blackwell.

Watson, J. B. (1925). *Behaviorism.* New York: W. W. Norton.

Wilson, E. O. (1998). *Consilience: The Unity of Knowledge* (1st edn). New York: Knopf.

Witmer, D. G. (2000). "Sufficiency Claims and Physicalism: A Formulation." In C. Gillett and B. Loewer (eds.), *Physicalism and Its Discontents.* New York: Cambridge University Press: 57–73.

Wittgenstein, L. (1961 [1921]). *Tractatus Logico-Philosophicus.* London: Routledge and Kegan Paul Ltd. First published in 1921 in *Annalen der Naturphilosophie.*

—— (1950). *Philosophical Investigations.* London: Macmillan.

Woolhouse, R. S. (1993). *Descartes, Spinoza, Leibniz: The Concept of Substance in Seventeenth Century Metaphysics.* London: Routledge.

Chapter 2

The Mind–Body Problem

William G. Lycan

Human beings, and perhaps other creatures, have minds as well as bodies. But what is a mind, and what is its relation to body, or to the physical in general?

2.1 Mind–Body Dualism

The first answer to the mind–body question proposed since medieval times was that of Descartes, who held that minds are wholly distinct from bodies and from physical objects of any sort. According to *Cartesian dualism*, minds are purely spiritual and radically non-spatial, having neither size nor location. On this view, a normal living human being or person is a duality, a mind and a body paired (though there can be bodies without minds, and minds can survive the destruction of their corresponding bodies). Mysteriously, despite the radical distinctness of minds from bodies, they interact causally: bodily happenings cause sensations and experiences and thoughts in one's mind; conversely, mental activity leads to action and speech, causing the physical motion of limbs or lips.

Cartesian dualism has strong intuitive appeal, since from the inside our minds do not feel physical at all; and we can easily imagine their existing disembodied or, indeed, their existing in the absence of any physical world whatever. And until the 1950s, in fact, the philosophy of mind was dominated by Descartes's "first-person" perspective, our view of ourselves from the inside. With few exceptions, philosophers had accepted the following claims: (1) that one's own mind is better known than one's body, (2) that the mind is metaphysically in the body's driver's seat, and (3) that there is at least a theoretical problem of how we human intelligences can know that "external," everyday physical objects exist at all, even if there are tenable solutions to that problem. We human subjects are immured within a movie theatre of the mind, though we may have some defensible ways of inferring what goes on outside the theatre.

Midway through the past (twentieth) century, all this suddenly changed, for two reasons. The first reason was the accumulated impact of logical positivism and the verification theory of meaning. Intersubjective verifiability or testability became the criterion both of scientific probity and of linguistic meaning itself. If the mind, in particular, was to be respected either scientifically or even as meaningfully describable in the first place, mental ascriptions would have to be pegged to publicly, physically testable verification conditions. Science takes an intersubjective, third-person perspective on everything; the traditional first-person perspective had to be abandoned for scientific purposes and, it was felt, for serious metaphysical purposes also.

The second reason was the emergence of a number of pressing philosophical objections to Cartesian dualism, such as the following:

1   Immaterial Cartesian minds and ghostly non-physical events were increasingly seen to fit ill with our otherwise physical and scientific picture of the world, uncomfortably like spooks or ectoplasm themselves. They are not needed for the explanation of any publicly observable fact, for neurophysiology promises to explain the motions of our bodies in particular and to explain them completely. Indeed, ghost-minds could not very well help in such an explanation, since nothing is known of any properties of spookstuff that would bear on public physical occurrences.
2   Since human beings evolved over aeons, by purely physical processes of mutation and natural selection, from primitive creatures such as one-celled organisms which did not have minds, it is anomalous to suppose that at some point Mother Nature (in the form of population genetics) somehow created immaterial Cartesian minds in addition to cells and physical organs. The same point can be put in terms of the development of a single human zygote into an embryo, then a fetus, a baby, and finally a child.
3   If minds really are immaterial and utterly non-spatial, how can they possibly interact causally with physical objects in space? (Descartes himself was very uncomfortable about this. At one point he suggested gravity as a model for the action of something immaterial on a physical body; but gravity is spatial in nature even though it is not tangible in the way that bodies are.)
4   In any case it does not seem that immaterial entities could cause physical motion consistently with the conservation laws of physics, such as those regarding motion and matter-energy; physical energy would have to vanish and reappear inside human brains.

2.2   Behaviorism

What alternatives are there to dualism? First, Carnap (1932–3) and Ryle (1949) noted that the obvious verification conditions or tests for mental ascriptions are behavioral. How can the rest of us tell that you are in pain, save by your wincing and groaning behavior in circumstances of presumable damage or disorder, or that you believe that parsnips are dangerous, save by your verbal avowals and your avoidance of parsnips? If the tests are behavioral, then (it was argued) the very meanings of the ascriptions, or at least the only facts genuinely described, are not ghostly or ineffable but behavioral. Thus behaviorism as a theory of mind and a paradigm for psychology.

In academic psychology, behaviorism took primarily a methodological form, and the psychologists officially made no metaphysical claims. But in philosophy, behaviorism did (naturally) take a metaphysical form: chiefly that of *analytical behaviorism*, the claim that mental ascriptions simply mean things about behavioral responses to environmental impingements. Thus, "Leo is in pain" means, not anything about Leo's putative ghostly ego, or even about any episode taking place within Leo, but that either Leo is actually behaving in a wincing and groaning way or he is disposed so to behave (in that he would so behave were something not keeping him from doing so). "Leo believes that parsnips are dangerous" means just that, if asked, Leo would assent to that proposition, and, if confronted by a parsnip, Leo would shun it, and so forth.

Any behaviorist will subscribe to what has come to be called the Turing Test. In response to the perennially popular question "Can machines think?", Alan Turing (1964) replied that a better question is that of whether a sophisticated computer could ever pass a battery of verbal tests, to the extent of fooling a limited observer (say, a human being corresponding with it by mail) into thinking it is human and sentient. If a machine did pass such tests, then the putatively further question of whether the machine really thought would be idle at best, whatever metaphysical analysis one might attach to it. Barring Turing's tendentious limitation of the machine's behavior to verbal as opposed to non-verbal responses, any behaviorist, psychological or philosophical, would agree that psychological differences cannot outrun behavioral tests; organisms (including machines) whose actual and hypothetical behavior is just the same are psychologically just alike.

Besides solving the methodological problem of intersubjective verification, philosophical behaviorism also adroitly avoided a number of the objections to Cartesian dualism, including all of (1)–(4) listed above. It dispensed with immaterial Cartesian egos and ghostly non-physical events, writing them off as metaphysical excrescences. It disposed of Descartes's admitted problem of mind–body interaction, since it posited no immaterial, non-spatial causes of behavior. It raised no scientific mysteries concerning the intervention of Cartesian substances in physics or biology, since it countenanced no such intervention. Thus it is a *materialist* view, as against Descartes's immaterialism.

Yet some theorists were uneasy; they felt that in its total repudiation of the inner, the private, and the subjective, behaviorism was leaving out something real and important. When this worry was voiced, the behaviorists often replied with mockery, assimilating the doubters to old-fashioned dualists who believed in ghosts, ectoplasm, or the Easter bunny; behaviorism was the only (even halfway sensible) game in town. Nonetheless, the doubters made several lasting points against it. First, people who are honest and not anesthetized know perfectly well that they experience, and can introspect, actual inner mental episodes or occurrences, that are neither actually accompanied by characteristic behavior nor merely static hypothetical facts of how they would behave if subjected to such-and-such a stimulation. Place (1956) spoke of an "intractable residue" of conscious mental states that bear no clear relations to behavior of any particular sort; see also Armstrong (1968: ch. 5) and Campbell (1984). Secondly, contrary to the Turing Test, it seems perfectly possible for two people to differ psychologically despite total similarity of their actual and hypothetical behavior, as in a case of "inverted spectrum" as hypothesized by John Locke: it might be that when you see a red object, you have the sort of color experience that I have when I see a green object, and vice versa. For that matter, a creature might exhibit all the appropriate stimulus-response relations and lack a mental life entirely; we can imagine building a "zombie" or stupid robot that behaves in the right ways but does not really feel or think anything at all (Block and Fodor 1972; Kirk 1974; Block 1981; Campbell 1984). Thirdly, the analytical behaviorist's behavioral analyses of mental ascriptions seem adequate only so long as one makes substantive assumptions about the rest of the subject's mentality (Chisholm 1957: ch. 11; Geach 1957: 8; Block 1981); for example, if Leo believes that parsnips are dangerous and he is offered parsnips, he would shun them only if he does not want to die. Therefore, the behaviorist analyses are either circular or radically incomplete, so far as they are supposed to exhaust the mental generally.

So matters stood in stalemate between dualists, behaviorists, and doubters, until the late 1950s, when U. T. Place (1956) and J. J. C. Smart (1959) proposed a middle way, a conciliatory compromise solution.

2.3 The Identity Theory

According to Place and Smart, contrary to the behaviorists, at least some mental states and events are genuinely inner and genuinely episodic after all. They are not to be identified with outward behavior or even with hypothetical dispositions to behave. But, contrary to the dualists, the episodic mental items are neither ghostly nor non-physical. Rather, they are neurophysiological. They are identical with states and events occurring in their owners' central nervous systems; more precisely, every mental state or event is numerically identical with some such neurophysiological state or event. To be in pain is, for example, to have one's c-fibers, or more likely a-fibers, firing in the central nervous system; to believe that broccoli will kill you is to have one's B_{bk}-fibers firing, and so on.

By making the mental entirely physical, this *identity theory* of the mind shared the behaviorist advantage of avoiding the objections to dualism. But it also brilliantly accommodated the inner and the episodic as behaviorism did not. For, according to the identity theory, mental states and events actually occur in their owners' central nervous systems. (Hence they are inner in an even more literal sense than could be granted by Descartes.) The identity theory also thoroughly vindicated the idea that organisms can differ mentally despite total outward behavioral similarity, since clearly organisms can differ neurophysiologically in mediating their outward stimulus-response regularities; that would afford the possibility of inverted spectrum. And of course the connection between a belief or a desire and the usually accompanying behavior is defeasible by other current mental states, since the connection between a B- or D-neural state and its normal behavioral effect is defeasible by other psychologically characterizable interacting neural states. The identity theory was the ideal resolution of the dualist–behaviorist impasse.

Moreover, there was a direct deductive argument for the identity theory, hit upon independently by David Lewis (1966, 1972) and D. M. Armstrong (1968). Lewis and Armstrong maintained that mental terms were defined causally, in terms of mental items' typical causes and effects. For instance, the word "pain" means a state that is typically brought about by physical damage and that typically causes withdrawal, favoring, complaint, desire for cessation, and so on. (Armstrong claimed to establish this by straightforward "conceptual analysis." More elaborately, Lewis held that mental terms are the theoretical terms of a common-sensical "folk theory," and with the positivists that all theoretical terms are implicitly defined by the theories in which they occur. That common-sense theory has since come to be called "folk psychology.") Now if, by definition, pain is whatever state occupies a certain causal niche, and if, as is overwhelmingly likely, scientific research will reveal that that particular niche is in fact occupied by such-and-such a neurophysiological state, it follows straightaway that pain is that neurophysiological state; QED. Pain retains its conceptual connection to behavior, but also undergoes an empirical identification with an inner state of its owner. (An advanced if convoluted elaboration of this already hybrid view is developed by Lewis 1980; for meticulous discussion, see Block 1978; Shoemaker 1981; Tye 1983; Owens 1986.)

Notice that although Armstrong and Lewis began their arguments with a claim about the meanings of mental terms, their "common-sense causal" version of the identity theory was itself no such claim, any more than was the original identity theory of Place and Smart. Rather, all four philosophers relied on the idea that things or properties can sometimes be identified with "other" things or properties even when there is no synonymy of terms; there is such a thing as synthetic and a posteriori identity that is nonetheless genuine identity. While the identity of triangles with trilaterals holds simply in virtue of the meanings of the two terms and can be established by reason alone, without empirical investigation, the following identities are standard examples of the synthetic a posteriori, and were discovered empirically: clouds with masses of water droplets; water with H_2O; lightning with electrical discharge; the Morning Star with Venus; Mendelian genes with segments of DNA molecules; and temperature with mean molecular kinetic energy. The identity theory was offered similarly, in a spirit of scientific speculation; one could not properly object that mental expressions do not mean anything about brains or neural firings.

So the dualists were wrong in thinking that mental items are non-physical but right in thinking them inner and episodic; the behaviorists were right in their materialism but wrong to repudiate inner mental episodes. A delightful synthesis. But alas, it was too good to be true.

2.4   Machine Functionalism

Quite soon, Hilary Putnam (1960, 1967a, 1967b) and Jerry Fodor (1968b) pointed out a presumptuous implication of the identity theory understood as a theory of "types" or kinds of mental item: that a mental state such as pain has always and everywhere the neurophysiological characterization initially assigned to it. For example, if the identity theorist identified pain itself with the firings of c-fibers, it followed that a creature of any species (earthly or science-fiction) could be in pain only if that creature had c-fibers and they were firing. But such a constraint on the biology of any being capable of feeling pain is both gratuitous and indefensible; why should we suppose that any organism must be made of the same chemical materials as we are in order to have what can be accurately recognized as pain? The identity theorist had overreacted to the behaviourists' difficulties and focused too narrowly on the specifics of biological humans' actual inner states, and in so doing they had fallen into species chauvinism.

Putnam and Fodor advocated the obvious correction: what was important was not its being c-fibers (per se) that were firing, but what the c-fiber firings were doing, what they contributed to the operation of the organism as a whole. The role of the c-fibers could have been performed by any mechanically suitable component; so long as that role was performed, the psychology of the containing organism would have been unaffected. Thus, to be in pain is not per se to have c-fibers that are firing, but merely to be in some state or other, of whatever biochemical description, that plays the same causal role as did the firings of c-fibers in the human beings we have investigated. We may continue to maintain that pain "tokens" (individual instances of pain occurring in particular subjects at particular times) are strictly identical with particular neurophysiological states of those subjects at those times – in other words, with the states that happen to be playing the appropriate roles; this is the thesis of *token identity* or "token" materialism or physicalism. But pain itself, the kind, universal, or "type," can be identified only with something more abstract: the causal or functional role that c-fiber firings share with their potential replacements or surrogates. Mental state-types are identified not with neurophysiological types but with more abstract functional roles, as specified by state-tokens' causal relations to the organism's sensory inputs, behavioral responses, and other intervening psychological states.

Functionalism, then, is the doctrine that what makes a mental state the type of state it is – a pain, a smell of violets, a belief that koalas are venomous – is its distinctive set of functional relations, its role in its subject's behavioral economy.

Putnam compared mental states to the functional or "logical" states of a computer: just as a computer program can be realized or instantiated by any of a number of physically different hardware configurations, so can a psychological "program" be realized by different organisms of various physiochemical composition, and that is why different physiological states of organisms of different species can realize one and the same mental state-type. Where an identity theorist's type-identification would take the form, "To be in mental state of type M is to be in the neurophysiological state of type N," Putnam's *machine functionalism*, as I shall call it, asserts that to be in M is to be merely in some physiological state or other that plays role R in the relevant computer program (that is, the program that at a suitable level of abstraction mediates the creature's total outputs given total inputs and so serves as the creature's global psychology). The physiological state "plays role R" in that it stands in a set of relations to physical inputs, outputs, and other inner states that matches one-to-one the abstract input–output–logical-state relations codified in the computer program.

The functionalist, then, mobilizes three distinct levels of description but applies them all to the same fundamental reality. A physical state-token in someone's brain at a particular time has a neurophysiological description, but it may also have a functional description relative to a machine program that the brain happens to be realizing, and it may further have a mental description if some mental state is correctly type-identified with the functional category it exemplifies. And so there is after all a sense in which "the mental" is distinct from "the physical." Though, presumably, there are no non-physical substances or stuffs, and every mental token is itself entirely physical, mental characterization is not physical characterization, and the property of being a pain is not simply the property of being such-and-such a neural firing. Moreover, unlike behaviorism and the identity theory, functionalism does not strictly entail that minds are physical; it might be true of non-physical minds, so long as those minds realized the relevant programs.

2.5 Homuncular Functionalism and Other Teleological Theories

Machine functionalism has been challenged on a number of points, which together motivate a specifically teleological notion of "function": we are to think of a thing's function as what the thing is for, what its job is, what it is supposed to do. Here are three reasons for thus "putting the function back into functionalism" (Sober 1985).

First, the machine functionalist still conceived psychological explanation in the logical positivists' terms of subsuming observed data under wider and wider universal laws. But Fodor (1968a), Dennett (1978), and Cummins (1983) have defended a competing picture of psychological explanation, according to which behavioral data are to be seen as manifestations of subjects' psychological capacities, and those capacities are to be explained by understanding the subjects as systems of interconnected components. Each component is a "homunculus," in that it is thought of as a little agent or bureaucrat operating within its containing subject; it is identified by reference to the function it performs. And the various homuncular components cooperate with each other in such a way as to produce overall behavioral responses to stimuli. The "homunculi" are themselves broken down into subcomponents whose functions and interactions are similarly used to explain the capacities of the subsystems they compose, and so again and again until the sub-sub-... components are seen to be neurophysiological structures. Thus biological and mechanical systems alike are hierarchically organized. (An automobile works – locomotes – by having a fuel reservoir, a fuel line, a carburetor, a combustion chamber, an ignition system, a transmission, and wheels that turn. If one wants to know how the carburetor works, one will be told what its parts are and how they work together to infuse oxygen into fuel; and so on.) But nothing in this pattern of explanation corresponds to the subsumption of data under wider and wider universal generalizations.

The second reason is that the machine functionalist treated functional "realization," the relation between an individual physical organism and the abstract program it was said to instantiate, as a simple matter of one-to-one correspondence between the organism's repertoire of physical stimuli, structural states, and behavior, on the one hand, and the program's defining input–state–output function on the other. But this criterion of realization was seen to be too liberal; since virtually anything bears a one–one correlation of some sort to virtually anything else, "realization" in the sense of mere one–one correspondence is far too easily come by (Block 1978; Lycan 1987: ch. 3); any middle-sized physical object has some set of component molecular motions that happen to correspond one–one to a given machine program. Some theorists have proposed to remedy this defect by imposing a teleological requirement on realization: a physical state of an organism will count as realizing such-and-such a functional description only if the organism has genuine organic integrity and the state plays its functional role properly for the organism, in the teleological sense of "for" and in the teleological sense of "function." The state must do what it does as a matter of, so to speak, its biological purpose. (Machine functionalism took "function" in its spare mathematical sense rather than in a genuinely functional sense. One should note that, as used here, the term "machine functionalism" is tied to the original liberal conception of "realizing;" so to impose a teleological restriction is to abandon machine functionalism.)

Thirdly, Van Gulick (1980), Millikan (1984), Dretske (1988), Fodor (1990a), and others have argued powerfully that teleology must enter into any adequate analysis of the intentionality or aboutness or referential character of mental states such as beliefs and desires, by reference to the states' psychobiological functions.

Beliefs, desires, and other propositional attitudes such as suspecting, intending, and wishing are directed upon states of affairs which may or may not actually obtain (for instance, that the Republican candidate will win), and are about individuals who may or may not exist (such as King Arthur or Sherlock Holmes). Franz Brentano (1973 [1874]) drew a distinction between psychological phenomena, which are directed upon objects and states of affairs, even non-existing ones, and physical objects, which are not so directed. If mental items are physical, however, the question arises how any purely physical entity or state could have the property of being "directed upon" or about a non-existent state of affairs or object; that is not the sort of feature that ordinary, purely physical objects (such as bricks) can have. According to the teleological theorists, a neurophysiological state should count as a belief that broccoli will kill you, and in particular as about broccoli, only if that state has the representing of broccoli as in some sense one of its psychobiological functions. If teleology is needed to explicate intentionality, and machine functionalism affords no teleology, then machine functionalism is not adequate to explicate intentionality.

All this talk of teleology and biological function seems to presuppose that biological and other "structural" states of physical systems really do have functions in the teleological sense. The latter claim is, to say the least, controversial. But, fortunately for the teleological functionalist, there is a vigorous industry whose purpose is to explicate biological teleology in naturalistic terms, typically in terms of etiology. For example, a trait may be said to have the function of doing F in virtue of its having been selected because it did F; a heart's function is to pump blood because hearts' pumping blood in the past has given them a selection advantage and so led to the survival of more animals with hearts (Wright 1973; Millikan 1984).

Functionalism inherits some of the same difficulties that earlier beset behaviorism and the identity theory. These remaining obstacles fall into two main categories: qualia problems and intentionality problems.

2.6 Problems over Qualia and Consciousness

The quale of a mental state or event (particularly a sensation) is that state or event's feel, its introspectible "phenomenal character," its nature as it presents itself to consciousness. Many philosophers have objected that neither functionalist metaphysics nor any of the allied doctrines aforementioned can "explain consciousness," or illuminate or even tolerate the notion of what it feels like to be in a mental state of such-and-such a sort. Yet, say these philosophers, the feels are quintessentially mental – it is the feels that make the mental states the mental states they are. Something, therefore, must be drastically wrong with functionalism.

"The" problem of consciousness or qualia is familiar. Indeed, it is so familiar that we tend to overlook the most important thing about it: that its name is legion, for it is many. There is no single problem of qualia; there are at least eleven quite distinct objections that have been brought against functionalism (some of them apply to materialist views generally). To mention a few:

1   Block (1978) and others have urged various "zombie"-style counterexample cases against functionalism – examples in which some entity seems to realize the right program but which lacks one of mentality's crucial qualitative aspects. (Typically the "entity" is a group of human beings, such as the entire population of China acting according to an elaborate set of instructions. It does not seem that such a group of individuals would collectively be feeling anything.) Predictably, functionalists have rejoined by arguing, for each example, either that the proposed group entity does not in fact succeed in realizing the right program (for example, because the requisite teleology is lacking) or that there is no good reason for denying that the entity does have the relevant qualitative states.

2   Nagel (1974) and Jackson (1982) have appealed to a disparity in knowledge, as a general anti-materialist argument: I can know what it is like to have such-and-such a sensation only if I have had that sensation myself; no amount of objective, third-person scientific information would suffice. In reply, functionalists have offered analyses of "perspectivalness," complete with accounts of "what it is like" to have a sensation, that make those things compatible with functionalism. Nagel and Jackson have argued, further, for the existence of a special, intrinsically perspectival kind of fact, the fact of "what it is like", which intractably and in principle cannot be captured or explained by physical science. Functionalists have responded that the arguments commit a logical fallacy (specifically, that of applying Leibniz's Law in an intensional context); some have added that in any case, to "know what it is like" is merely to have an ability, and involves no fact of any sort, while, contrariwise, some other theorists have granted that there are facts of "what it is like" but insisted that such facts can after all be explained and predicted by natural science.

3   Saul Kripke (1972) made ingenious use of modal distinctions against type or even token identity, arguing that unless mental items are necessarily identical with neurophysiological ones, which they are not, they cannot be identical with them at all. Kripke's close reasoning has attracted considerable critical attention. And even more sophisticated variants have been offered, e.g., by Jackson (1993) and Chalmers (1996).

4   Jackson (1977) and others have defended the claim that in consciousness we are presented with mental individuals that themselves bear phenomenal, qualitative properties. For instance, when a red flash bulb goes off in your face, your visual field exhibits a green blotch, an "after-image," a thing that is really green and has a fairly definite shape and exists for a few seconds before disappearing. If there are such things, they are entirely different from anything physical to be found in the brain of a (healthy) human subject. Belief in such "phenomenal individuals" as genuinely green after-images has been unpopular

among philosophers for some years, but it can be powerfully motivated (see Lycan 1987: 83–93).

This is a formidable quartet of objections, and, on the face of it, each is plausible. Materialists and particularly functionalists must respond in detail. Needless to say, materialists have responded at length; some of the most powerful rejoinders are formulated in Lycan (1987, 1996). Yet recent years have seen some reaction against the prevailing materialism, including a re-emergence of some neo-dualist views, as in Robinson (1988), Hart (1988), Strawson (1994), and Chalmers (1996).

2.7 Problems over Intentionality

The problem arising from our mention of Brentano was to explain how any purely physical entity or state could have the property of being about or "directed upon" a non-existent state of affairs. The standard functionalist reply is that propositional attitudes have Brentano's feature because the internal physical states and events that realize them represent actual or possible states of affairs. What they represent (their content) is determined at least in part by their functional roles.

There are two main difficulties. One is that of saying exactly how a physical item's supposed representational content is determined; in virtue of what does a neurophysiological state represent precisely that the Republican candidate will win? An answer to that general question is what Fodor has called a *psychosemantics*. Several attempts have been made (Dretske 1981; Millikan 1984; Fodor 1987, 1990a, 1990b, 1994), but none is very plausible. In particular, none applies to any content but that which involves actual and presently existing physical objects. Abstract entities such as numbers, future entities such as a child I hope one day to have, and Brentano's non-existent items, are just left out.

The second difficulty is that ordinary propositional attitude contents do not supervene on the states of their subjects' nervous systems, but are underdetermined by even the total state of that subject's head. Putnam's (1975) Twin Earth and indexical examples show that, surprising as it may seem, two human beings could be molecule-for-molecule alike and still differ in their beliefs and desires, depending on various factors in their spatial and historical environments. Thus we can distinguish between "narrow" properties, those that are determined by a subject's intrinsic physical composition, and "wide" properties, those that are not so determined. Representational contents are wide, yet functional roles are, ostensibly, narrow. How, then, can propositional attitudes be type-identified with functional roles, or for that matter with states of the brain under any narrow description?

Functionalists have responded in either of two ways to the second difficulty. The first is to understand "function" widely as well, specifying functional roles historically and/or by reference to features of the subject's actual environment.

The second is simply to abandon functionalism as an account of content in particular, giving some alternative psychosemantics for propositional attitudes, but preserving functionalism in regard to attitude types. (Thus what makes a state a desire that P is its functional role, even if something else makes the state a desire that P).

2.8   The Emotions

In alluding to sensory states and to mental states with intentional content, we have said nothing specifically about the emotions. Since the rejection of behaviorism, theories of mind have tended not to be applied directly to the emotions; rather, the emotions have been generally thought to be conceptually analyzable as complexes of more central or "core" mental states, typically propositional attitudes such as belief and desire (and the intentionality of emotions has accordingly been traced back to that of attitudes). Armstrong (1968: ch. 8, secn III) essentially took this line, as do Solomon (1977) and Gordon (1987). However, there is a literature on functionalism and the emotions; see Rey (1980) and some of the other papers collected in Rorty (1980). Griffiths (1997) takes a generally functionalist view, but argues that "the emotions" do not constitute a single kind.

2.9   Instrumentalism

The identity theorists and the functionalists, machine or teleological, joined common sense (and current cognitive psychology) in understanding mental states and events both as internal to human subjects and as causes. Beliefs and desires in particular are thought to be caused by perceptual or other cognitive events and as in turn conspiring from within to cause behavior. If Armstrong's or Lewis's theory of mind is correct, this idea is not only common-sensical but a conceptual truth; if functionalism is correct, it is at least a metaphysical fact.

In rallying to the inner-causal story, as we saw in section 2.3, the identity theorists and functionalists broke with the behaviorists, for behaviorists did not think of mental items as entities, as inner, or as causes in any stronger sense than the bare hypothetical. Behaviorists either dispensed with the mentalistic idiom altogether, or paraphrased mental ascriptions in terms of putative responses to hypothetical stimuli. More recently, other philosophers have followed them in rejecting the idea of beliefs and desires as inner causes and in construing them in a more purely operational or instrumental fashion. D. C. Dennett (1978, 1987) has been particularly concerned to deny that beliefs and desires are causally active inner states of people, and maintains instead that belief-ascriptions and desire-ascriptions are merely calculational devices, which happen to have predictive usefulness for a reason that he goes on to explain. Such ascriptions are often objectively true, he grants, but not in virtue of describing inner mechanisms.

Thus Dennett is an *instrumentalist* about propositional attitudes such as belief and desire. (According to a contemporary interpretation, an "instrumentalist" about Xs is a theorist who claims that although sentences about "Xs" are often true, they do not really describe entities of a special kind, but only serve to systematize more familiar phenomena. For instance, we are all instrumentalists about "the average American homeowner," who is white, male, and the father of exactly 2.2 children.) To ascribe a "belief" or a "desire" is not to describe some segment of physical reality, Dennett says, but is more like moving a group of beads in an abacus. (It should be noted that Dennett has more recently moderated his line: see 1991.)

Dennett offers basically four grounds for his rejection of the common-sensical inner-cause thesis:

1   He thinks it quite unlikely that any science will ever turn up any distinctive inner-causal mechanism that would be shared by all the possible subjects that had a particular belief.
2   He compares the belief-desire interpretation of human beings to that of lower animals, chess-playing computers, and even lightning-rods, arguing that (a) in their case we have no reason to think of belief-ascriptions and desire-ascriptions as other than mere calculational-predictive devices and (b) we have no more reason for the case of humans to think of belief-ascriptions and desire-ascriptions as other than that.
3   Dennett argues from the verification conditions of belief-ascriptions and desire-ascriptions – basically a matter of extrapolating rationally from what a subject ought to believe and want in his or her circumstances – and then he boldly just identifies the truth-makers of those ascriptions with their verification conditions, challenging inner-cause theorists to show why instrumentalism does not accommodate all the actual evidence.
4   He argues that in any case, if a purely normative assumption (the "rationality assumption," which is that people will generally believe what they ought to believe and desire what they should desire) is required for the licensing of an ascription, then the ascription cannot itself be a purely factual description of a plain state of affairs.

Stich (1981) explores and criticizes Dennett's instrumentalism at length (perhaps oddly, Stich (1983) goes on to defend a view nearly as deprecating as Dennett's, though clearly distinct from it). Dennett (1981) responds to Stich, bringing out more clearly the force of the "rationality assumption" assumption. (Other criticisms are levelled against Dennett by commentators in the *Behavioral and Brain Sciences* symposium that is headed by Dennett 1988.)

A close cousin of Dennett's view, in that it focuses on the rationality assumption, is Donald Davidson's (1970) *anomalous monism*. Unlike Dennett's instrumentalism, it endorses token physicalism and insists that individual mental tokens are causes, but it rejects on similarly epistemological grounds the possibility of any interesting materialistic type-reduction of the propositional attitudes.

2.10 Eliminativism and Neurophilosophy

Dennett's instrumentalism breaks with common sense and with philosophical tradition in denying that propositional attitudes such as belief and desire are real inner-causal states of people. But Dennett concedes – indeed, he urgently insists – that belief-ascriptions and desire-ascriptions are true, and objectively true, nonetheless. Other philosophers have taken a less conciliatory, more radically uncommon-sensical view: that mental ascriptions are not true after all, but are simply false. Common sense is just mistaken in supposing that people believe and desire things, and perhaps in supposing that people have sensations and feelings, disconcerting as that nihilistic claim may seem.

Following standard usage, let us call the nihilistic claim "eliminative materialism," or "eliminativism" for short. It is important to note a customary if unexpected alliance between the eliminativist and the token physicalist: the eliminativist, the identity theorist, and the functionalist all agree that mental items are, if anything, real inner-causal states of people. They disagree only on the empirical question of whether any real neurophysiological states of people do in fact answer to the common-sensical mental categories of "folk psychology." Eliminativists praise identity theorists and functionalists for their forthright willingness to step up and take their empirical shot. Both eliminativists and token physicalists scorn the instrumentalist's sleazy evasion. (But eliminativists agree with instrumentalists that functionalism is a pipe-dream, and functionalists agree with instrumentalists that mental ascriptions are often true and obviously so. The three views form an eternal triangle of a not uncommon sort.)

Paul Feyerabend (1963a, 1963b) was the first to argue openly that the mental categories of folk psychology simply fail to capture anything in physical reality and that everyday mental ascriptions were therefore false. (Rorty (1965) took a notoriously eliminativist line also, but, following Sellars (1963), tried to soften its nihilism; Lycan and Pappas (1972) argued that the softening served only to collapse Rorty's position into incoherence.) Feyerabend attracted no great following, presumably because of his view's outrageous flouting of common sense. But eliminativism was resurrected by Paul Churchland (1981) and others, and defended in more detail.

Churchland argues mainly from the poverty of "folk psychology;" he claims that historically, when other primitive theories such as alchemy have done as badly on scientific grounds as folk psychology has, they have been abandoned, and rightly so. P. S. Churchland (1986) and Churchland and Sejnowski (1990) emphasize the comparative scientific reality and causal efficacy of neurobiological mechanisms: given the scientific excellence of neurophysiological explanation and the contrasting diffuseness and type-irreducibility of folk psychology, why should we suppose – even for a minute, much less automatically – that the platitudes of folk psychology express truths?

Reasons for rejecting eliminativism are obvious. First, we think we know there are propositional attitudes because we introspect them in ourselves. Secondly, the attitudes are indispensable to prediction, reasoning, deliberation, and understanding, and to the capturing of important macroscopic generalizations. We could not often converse coherently without mention of them. But what of P. M. Churchland's and P. S. Churchland and Sejnowski's arguments?

One may dispute the claim that folk psychology is a failed or bad theory; Kitcher (1984) and Horgan and Woodward (1985) take this line. Or one may dispute the more basic claim that folk psychology is a theory at all. Ryle (1949) and Wittgenstein (1953) staunchly opposed that claim before it had explicitly been formulated. More recent critics include Morton (1980), Malcolm (1984), Baker (1988), McDonough (1991), and Wilkes (1993).

References

Armstrong, D. M. (1968). *A Materialist Theory of the Mind.* London: Routledge and Kegan Paul.

Baker, L. R. (1988). *Saving Belief.* Princeton, NJ: Princeton University Press.

Block, N. J. (1978). "Troubles with Functionalism." In W. Savage (ed.), *Minnesota Studies in the Philosophy of Science, Vol. IX: Perception and Cognition.* Minneapolis: University of Minnesota Press: 261–325. Excerpts reprinted in Lycan (1990, 1999).

—— (ed.) (1980). *Readings in Philosophy of Psychology,* 2 vols. Cambridge, MA: Harvard University Press.

—— (1981). "Psychologism and Behaviorism." *Philosophical Review,* 90: 5–43.

Block, N. J. and Fodor, J. A. (1972). "What Psychological States Are Not." *Philosophical Review,* 81: 159–81. Reprinted in Block (1980).

Brentano, F. (1973 [1874]). *Philosophy from an Empirical Standpoint.* London: Routledge and Kegan Paul.

Campbell, K. (1984). *Body and Mind* (2nd edn). Notre Dame, IN: University of Notre Dame Press.

Carnap, R. (1932–3). "Psychology in Physical Language." *Erkenntnis,* 3: 107–42. Excerpt reprinted in Lycan (1990).

Chalmers, D. (1996). *The Conscious Mind.* Oxford: Oxford University Press.

Chisholm, R. M. (1957). *Perceiving.* Ithaca, NY: Cornell University Press.

Churchland, P. M. (1981). "Eliminative Materialism and the Propositional Attitudes." *Journal of Philosophy,* 78: 67–90. Reprinted in Lycan (1990, 1999).

Churchland, P. S. (1986). *Neurophilosophy.* Cambridge, MA: Bradford Books/MIT Press.

Churchland, P. S. and Sejnowski, T. (1990). "Neural Representation and Neural Computation." In Lycan (1990): 224–52. Reprinted in Lycan (1999).

Cummins, R. (1983). *The Nature of Psychological Explanation.* Cambridge, MA: MIT Press/Bradford Books.

Davidson, D. (1970). "Mental Events." In L. Foster and J. W. Swanson (eds.), *Experience and Theory*. Amherst, MA: University of Massachusetts Press: 79–101. Reprinted in Block (1980) and in Lycan (1999).

Dennett, D. C. (1978). *Brainstorms*. Montgomery, VT: Bradford Books.

—— (1981). "Making Sense of Ourselves." *Philosophical Topics*, 12: 63–81. Reprinted in Lycan (1990).

—— (1987). *The Intentional Stance*. Cambridge, MA: Bradford Books/MIT Press.

—— (1988). "Précis of *The Intentional Stance*." *Behavioral and Brain Sciences*, 11: 495–505.

—— (1991). "Real Patterns." *Journal of Philosophy*, 88: 27–51.

Dretske, F. (1981). *Knowledge and the Flow of Information*. Cambridge, MA: Bradford Books/MIT Press.

—— (1988). *Explaining Behavior*. Cambridge, MA: Bradford Books/MIT Press.

Feyerabend, P. (1963a). "Materialism and the Mind–Body Problem." *Review of Metaphysics*, 17: 49–66.

—— (1963b). "Mental Events and the Brain." *Journal of Philosophy*, 60: 295–6.

Fodor, J. A. (1968a). "The Appeal to Tacit Knowledge in Psychological Explanation." *Journal of Philosophy*, 65: 627–40.

—— (1968b). *Psychological Explanation*. New York, NY: Random House.

—— (1987). *Psychosemantics*. Cambridge, MA: MIT Press.

—— (1990a). "Psychosemantics." In Lycan (1990): 312–37.

—— (1990b). *A Theory of Content*. Cambridge, MA: Bradford Books/MIT Press.

—— (1994). *The Elm and the Expert*. Cambridge, MA: Bradford Books/MIT Press.

Geach, P. (1957). *Mental Acts*. London: Routledge and Kegan Paul.

Gordon, R. M. (1987). *The Structure of Emotions*. Cambridge: Cambridge University Press.

Griffiths, P. (1997). *What Emotions Really Are*. Chicago: University of Chicago Press.

Hart, W. D. (1988). *Engines of the Soul*. Cambridge: Cambridge University Press.

Horgan, T. and Woodward, J. (1985). "Folk Psychology is Here to Stay." *Philosophical Review*, 94: 197–226. Reprinted in Lycan (1990, 1999).

Jackson, F. (1977). *Perception*. Cambridge: Cambridge University Press.

—— (1982). "Epiphenomenal Qualia." *Philosophical Quarterly*, 32: 127–36. Reprinted in Lycan (1990, 1999).

—— (1993). "Armchair Metaphysics." In J. O'Leary-Hawthorne and M. Michael (eds.), *Philosophy in Mind*. Dordrecht: Kluwer Academic Publishing.

Kirk, R. (1974). "Zombies vs. Materialists." *Aristotelian Society Supplementary Volume*, 48: 135–52.

Kitcher, P. (1984). "In Defense of Intentional Psychology." *Journal of Philosophy*, 81: 89–106.

Kripke, S. (1972). *Naming and Necessity*. Cambridge, MA: Harvard University Press.

Lewis, D. (1966). "An Argument for the Identity Theory." *Journal of Philosophy*, 63: 17–25.

—— (1972). "Psychophysical and Theoretical Identifications." *Australasian Journal of Philosophy*, 50: 249–58. Reprinted in Block (1980).

—— (1980). "Mad Pain and Martian Pain." In Block (1980).

Lycan, W. (1987). *Consciousness*. Cambridge, MA: MIT Press/Bradford Books.

—— (ed.) (1990). *Mind and Cognition: A Reader*. Oxford: Blackwell.

—— (1996). *Consciousness and Experience*. Cambridge, MA: MIT Press/Bradford Books.

—— (ed.) (1999). *Mind and Cognition: An Anthology*. Oxford: Blackwell.

Lycan, W. and Pappas, G. (1972). "What is Eliminative Materialism?" *Australasian Journal of Philosophy*, 50: 149–59.

Malcolm, N. (1984). "Consciousness and Causality." In D. Armstrong and N. Malcolm, *Consciousness and Causality: A Debate on the Nature of Mind*. Oxford: Blackwell.

McDonough, R. (1991). "A Culturalist Account of Folk Psychology." In J. Greenwood (ed.), *The Future of Folk Psychology*. Cambridge: Cambridge University Press: 263–88.

Millikan, R. G. (1984). *Language, Thought, and Other Biological Categories*. Cambridge, MA: Bradford Books/MIT Press.

Morton, A. (1980). *Frames of Mind*. Oxford: Oxford University Press.

Nagel, T. (1974). "What Is It Like to be a Bat?" *Philosophical Review*, 83: 435–50. Reprinted in Block (1980).

Owens, J. (1986). "The Failure of Lewis' Functionalism." *Philosophical Quarterly*, 36: 159–73.

Place, U. T. (1956). "Is Consciousness a Brain Process?" *British Journal of Psychology*, 47: 44–50. Reprinted in Lycan (1990, 1999).

Putnam, H. (1960). "Minds and Machines." In S. Hook (ed.), *Dimensions of Mind*. New York: Collier Books: 136–64.

—— (1967a). "The Mental Life of Some Machines." In H.-N. Castañeda (ed.), *Intentionality, Minds, and Perception*. Detroit, MI: Wayne State University Press: 177–200.

—— (1967b). "Psychological Predicates." In W. H. Capitan and D. Merrill (eds.), *Art, Mind, and Religion*, Pittsburgh, PA: University of Pittsburgh Press: 37–48. Reprinted in Block (1980) under the title "The Nature of Mental States."

—— (1975). "The Meaning of 'Meaning'." In *Philosophical Papers*. Cambridge: Cambridge University Press.

Rey, G. (1980). "Functionalism and the Emotions." In Rorty (1980): 163–95.

Robinson, W. S. (1988). *Brains and People*. Philadelphia, PA: Temple University Press.

Rorty, A. O. (ed.) (1980). *Explaining Emotions*. Berkeley and Los Angeles, CA: University of California Press.

Rorty, R. (1965). "Mind–Body Identity, Privacy, and Categories." *Review of Metaphysics*, 19: 24–54.

Ryle, G. (1949). *The Concept of Mind*. New York, NY: Barnes and Noble.

Sellars, W. (1963). *Science, Perception and Reality*. London: Routledge and Kegan Paul.

Shoemaker, S. (1981). "Some Varieties of Functionalism." *Philosophical Topics*, 12: 93–119.

Smart, J. J. C. (1959). "Sensations and Brain Processes." *Philosophical Review*, 68: 141–56.

Sober, E. (1985). "Panglossian Functionalism and the Philosophy of Mind." *Synthese*, 64: 165–93. Revised excerpt reprinted in Lycan (1990, 1999) under the title "Putting the Function Back Into Functionalism."

Solomon, R. (1977). *The Passions*. New York, NY: Doubleday.

Stich, S. (1981). "Dennett on Intentional Systems." *Philosophical Topics*, 12: 39–62. Reprinted in Lycan (1990, 1999).

—— (1983). *From Folk Psychology to Cognitive Science*. Cambridge, MA: Bradford Books/ MIT Press.

Strawson, G. (1994). *Mental Reality*. Cambridge, MA: Bradford Books/MIT Press.

Turing, A. (1964). "Computing Machinery and Intelligence." In A. R. Anderson (ed.), *Minds and Machines*. Englewood Cliffs, NJ: Prentice-Hall: 4–30.

Tye, M. (1983). "Functionalism and Type Physicalism." *Philosophical Studies*, 44: 161–74.

Van Gulick, R. (1980). "Functionalism, Information, and Content." *Nature and System*, 2: 139–62.

Wilkes, K. (1993). "The Relationship Between Scientific and Common Sense Psychology." In S. Christensen and D. Turner (eds.), *Folk Psychology and the Philosophy of Mind*. Hillsdale, NJ: Lawrence Erlbaum Associates: 144–87.

Wittgenstein, L. (1953). *Philosophical Investigations*, trans. G. E. M. Anscombe. New York, NY: Macmillan.

Wright, L. (1973). "Functions." *Philosophical Review*, 82: 139–68.

Chapter 3

Physicalism

Andrew Melnyk

Most philosophers of mind nowadays profess to be physicalists (or materialists) of one stripe or another. Generally, however, if not invariably, they regard their physicalism about the mind as a particular application to mental phenomena of a quite general thesis of physicalism to the effect that, in whatever sense of "physical" it is true to say that the mind is physical, *everything* is physical. It is with this quite general thesis of physicalism (henceforth, physicalism) that the present chapter will be concerned. One might be tempted to think that the only serious philosophical perplexities which physicalism provokes arise in the philosophy of mind; but it turns out, as we shall see, that physicalism provides much to think about even if one leaves aside the problem of giving physicalistically acceptable accounts of such traditionally recalcitrant mental phenomena as consciousness, intentionality, and rationality. In what follows, I shall first survey issues that arise in attempting even to formulate physicalism adequately; then consider attempts to justify physicalism; and finally discuss the character of objections to physicalism. Though I aspire to fair treatment of views opposed to my own, the reader is warned that my discussion will inevitably reflect substantive philosophical commitments that other writers in this area do not share.[1]

By way of background, however, let me present the philosophical problem to which physicalism can be plausibly viewed as one possible solution (though there are others). Even a casual perusal of a university course directory will reveal that there are many sciences in addition to physics: meteorology, geology, zoology, biochemistry, neurophysiology, psychology, sociology, ecology, molecular biology, and so on, not to mention honorary sciences such as folk psychology and folk physics. Each of these many sciences has its own characteristic theoretical vocabulary with which, to the extent that it gets things right, it describes a characteristic domain of objects, events, and properties. But the existence of the many sciences prompts various questions: how are the many sciences related to one another? And how is the domain of objects, events, and properties proprietary to each science related to the proprietary domains of the others? Do the many sciences somehow speak of different aspects of the same things? Or do they address themselves to distinct segments of reality? If so, do these distinct segments of reality exist quite independently of one another, save perhaps for relations of spatio-temporal contiguity, or do some segments depend in interesting ways upon others? This problem of the many sciences, as we may call it, is evidently a generalization of the mind–body problem, at least if that is understood as the problem of accounting for the relations between folk psychology, on the one hand, and scientific psychology, on the other.[2]

Physicalism provides a response to this problem. *Any* response to it, whether physicalist or not, must offer a systematic account of the relations among the many sciences, and among their many domains; it must therefore undertake the ambitious project of sketching a picture of the totality of reality as revealed to us both by science and by common sense. A physicalist response to the problem, however, is distinguished from other responses by the fact that its account of the relations among the many sciences and their domains has the effect of *privileging* physics and its domain, of assigning to physics and the physical some sort of descriptive and metaphysical primacy; we shall soon see some of the different ways in which this can be done. But non-physicalist responses are possible too. In the current climate of opinion, two are especially noteworthy. The first corresponds most closely to the intentions of traditional mind–body dualists, and claims, in effect, that physicalism is *nearly* true: what physicalism says about the relation between the non-physical sciences and physics is true of every non-physical science *except* folk psychology, which must instead be treated as describing real phenomena that are every bit as basic, and that warrant just as much privilege, as those described by fundamental physics. The second non-physicalist response claims that physicalism is entirely false, alleging instead that a kind of pluralistic egalitarianism prevails among the various sciences and honorary sciences, so that every science is on an ontological par with every other, and the world turns out not to be stratified at all. An advocate of this second sort of response will join with the traditional mind–body dualist in denying that the mental is physical, but will add that neither is the geological or the meteorological or the microbiological. Today's most influential anti-physicalists seem to favor this second response.[3]

3.1 Formulating Physicalism

A good place to begin is with the physicalist slogan, "Everything is physical." What sort of things should fall within the scope of "everything"? One important (though neglected) question here is whether the physicalist means to make a claim only about *concrete* entities (e.g., the phenomena described by the special sciences), or also about *abstract* entities (e.g., numbers or propositions as understood by a Platonist). In the absence of any literature to report on, let me make two comments. First, to the extent that there is a principled distinction between concrete and abstract entities, physicalists can perfectly well *stipulate* that the scope of their thesis be restricted to concrete entities; the thesis that results, though less controversial than an unrestricted thesis, will still be amply controversial. Secondly, the crucial question to consider in deciding whether such a restriction on the scope of physicalism would be objectionably arbitrary is this: does the rationale, whatever it might be, for holding that all *concrete* entities are physical carry over with equal force to the case of *abstract* entities? One might, for instance, consider the proposed justifications for physicalism sketched below in section 3.2 and ask, in each case, whether it can be modified to yield the conclusion that abstract entities are physical.

A second neglected question about the scope of physicalism concerns the *categories* into which the entities asserted to be physical fall. Let us assume, here and henceforth, that these entities are concrete; then the question is whether these concrete entities are objects, events, properties, facts, or what. Intuitively, it would not express the full content of physicalism to claim merely that all concrete *objects* are physical; for surely their *properties* must be physical too. But since these properties *themselves* need not be physical, so long as all their *instances* are, physicalists should perhaps claim that all concrete objects and property-instances are physical.[4] For the sake of clarity and simplicity, I shall assume that this is right. If, in addition to objects and property-instances, one's ontology also includes events or states or processes or conditions or whatever, and if these are irreducible to objects and property-instances, then (token) events, states, processes, and so on can and should be included within the scope of one's physicalism.

Let us return to the slogan, "Everything is physical." How should we understand ". . . is physical"? An attractive idea is to count an entity as physical if, and only if, it is of a kind expressed by some predicate in the consensus theories of current physics, where the nature of consensus theories of current physics can readily be discovered by consulting some up-to-date physics textbooks; examples of physical objects are therefore such things as electrons and quarks, and examples of physical properties such properties as charge and mass. Given our earlier assumptions, the resulting doctrine of physicalism will then claim that every concrete object and property-instance is of a kind expressed by some predicate in the consensus theories of current physics.

On its face, physicalism of this sort seems wildly counterintuitive, since it apparently entails the non-existence of pretty much every kind of thing described by the special sciences and by common sense. For cabbages and kings, embassies and elephants, percolators and prices – none of these things is expressed by a predicate in the consensus theories of current physics. Defenders of physicalism of this sort, when it is interpreted in this radically eliminativist way, need not deny that the world certainly *appears* to contain more than their physicalism countenances, but will aspire to explain that false appearance by appeal only to physical entities: they may deny that there are any elephants, and deny in particular that any elephant is *there*, but they will insist that *something* occupies the space where common sense locates an elephant – presumably some or other spatio-temporal arrangement of microphysical particles (see, e.g. Maxwell 1968).

In fact, however, physicalism, when understood as claiming that every concrete object and property-instance is of a kind expressed by some predicate in the consensus theories of current physics, does not *by itself* entail any eliminativist consequence whatsoever; it does so only when combined with the additional premise that the kinds of thing described by the special sciences and by common sense are not (numerically) *identical* with the kinds of thing expressed by predicates in the consensus theories of current physics. Now this additional premise is widely accepted, mainly on the grounds that the kinds of thing described by the special sciences and by common sense are *multiply realizable,* in the sense that physically very different assemblages of microphysical particles do (or merely can) nevertheless constitute individuals of the same special-scientific or common-sense kind. For suppose that an object of physical kind K and an object of incompatible physical kind J both constitute percolators; then if *being a percolator* were the very same property as *being of physical kind K*, it would follow that *every* percolator was an object of physical kind K; but since at least one percolator (the one of physical kind J) is not of physical kind K, it follows that *being a percolator* cannot be the very same property as *being of physical kind K*. However, this argument against identifying special-scientific and common-sense kinds with physical kinds may be challenged.[5] For one thing, the extent of *actual* multiple realization of certain phenomena (e.g., of phenomenal consciousness) is not clear, while the significance of the *mere conceivability* of multiple realization can be doubted by any philosopher who doubts that conceivability is a reliable guide, or even any guide at all, to genuine metaphysical possibility. For another thing, if arbitrary disjunctions of physical predicates express authentic, and authentically physical, kinds, then it looks as if the argument from multiple realizability can be evaded by simply identifying apparently non-physical kinds with the physical kinds expressed by suitable *disjunctions* of (conjunctions of) physical predicates; for example, perhaps *being a percolator* is the physical property of *being of physical kind K or of physical kind J*.

Multiple realizability arguments, however, have in fact persuaded nearly all philosophers that special-scientific and honorary-scientific kinds cannot be identified with physical kinds. Since, if this is right, the formulation of physicalism we have just been considering entails the strongly eliminativist conclusions mooted above, philosophers interested in formulating a comprehensive doctrine of physicalism have in recent decades taken a different approach. According to it, physicalism claims that every concrete object and property-instance is either physical in some *narrow* sense of "physical" or else is physical in the *broad* sense of standing in a certain relation to things that are physical in the narrow sense. Thus formulated, physicalism need not deny the existence of things of the kinds described by the special sciences and by common sense; for those things, even if they are not physical in the narrow sense, may yet stand in the right relation (whatever it turns out to be) to things that are. Nor, on this new approach, would physicalism have to claim the identity of the kinds described by the special sciences and by common sense with (narrowly) physical kinds, for (presumably) the right relation need neither be, nor entail, identity.

How, on this approach, should we understand "physical" in the narrow sense? An obvious suggestion is to recycle the account of "physical" *simpliciter* given above and therefore say that something is physical in the narrow sense (henceforth, "physical$_n$") if, and only if, it is of a kind expressed by some predicate in the consensus theories of current physics. But if "physical$_n$" is understood in this way, then the resulting formulation of physicalism can be true only if current physics itself is both true and complete, something that seems most unlikely given physics' historical track-record of error and omission; so the resulting formulation of physicalism must itself be most unlikely to be true, which certainly sounds bad for physicalism. And this difficulty, if genuine, afflicts all the formulations of physicalism discussed so far. So either physicalism cannot be formulated at all (as some anti-physicalists allege) or we should understand "physical$_n$" in some other way. But how? It will not do to suggest that something is physical$_n$ if, and only if, it is of a kind expressed by some predicate of *completed* physics. For if no constraint is placed upon what completed physics might be like, then, for all we now know, it might postulate the existence of Cartesian minds, contrary to the intentions of aspiring physicalists. Moreover, it is hard to see how any scientific findings *currently* available to us could possibly constitute evidence for a physicalism formulated by appeal to a completed physics whose content is at present entirely unknown to us. Some third way of understanding "physical$_n$" therefore seems required. Perhaps it should appeal to the idea of a *modest extension* of current physics, something similar enough to current physics for its content not to be entirely obscure to us, but flexible enough to withstand the discovery that current physics is both incomplete and (in some respects) false. But whether a third way can be found to avoid the problems besetting the two ways just considered is a question that remains unresolved and, till recently, largely unexplored.[6]

So much for "physical$_n$." How, on the approach we are presently considering, should we understand "physical" in the *broad* sense (henceforth, "physical$_b$")? Overwhelmingly, the most popular answer given over the past decade or two has been that something is physical$_b$ if, and only if, it *supervenes* upon things that are physical$_n$; and the formulation of physicalism it yields claims that every concrete object and property-instance is either itself physical$_n$ or else supervenes upon things that are physical$_n$. The concept of supervenience in philosophy (lay usage of "supervene" has little to do with its philosophical usage) can be explained intuitively like this: the mental (for example) supervenes upon the physical if, and only if, once the physical facts have been fixed, the mental facts are thereby fixed also; the way things are mentally *cannot* vary (and not merely does not vary) without variation also in the way things are physically.

Now the extensive literature on the concept of supervenience is full of proposals for how to understand claims of supervenience more precisely, and one issue which supervenience physicalists (as we may call philosophers who wish some thesis of supervenience to play an important role in the formulation of physicalism) must resolve concerns the exact kind of supervenience claim, precisely understood, that a formulation of physicalism should use. One much-discussed notion of supervenience is Jaegwon Kim's *strong supervenience*.[7] According to this, the claim that non-physical$_n$ properties supervene upon physical$_n$ properties should be understood as follows: non-physical$_n$ properties *strongly supervene* upon physical$_n$ properties if, and only if, necessarily, if a thing has a non-physical$_n$ property, then there is some physical$_n$ property that the thing has such that, necessarily, anything with that physical$_n$ property also has the original non-physical$_n$ property. According to this supervenience claim, however, all the non-physical$_n$ properties of a given object are fixed by physical$_n$ properties *of that very object* (perhaps even by physical$_n$ properties of that very object *contemporaneous* with its non-physical$_n$ properties). And this implication seems inconsistent with a number of plausible suggestions as to the constitution of various non-physical$_n$ properties; for example, the suggestion that the genuineness of a dollar bill is partially constituted by its (historical) relation to appropriate authorities, the suggestion that the possession of a function by a biological entity (e.g., a heart) is partially constituted by the selectional history of its ancestors, and the externalist suggestion widely endorsed by philosophers of mind that the representational content of propositional attitudes is partially constituted by their relations to states of affairs external to their owners' heads. For this reason, supervenience physicalists have generally preferred to employ Kim's notion of *global supervenience*. A very crude first stab at expressing the desired supervenience claim might be this: any two possible worlds exactly alike in respect of the physical$_n$ entities and property-instances they contain and the physical laws that hold there are exactly alike in respect of *all* the (concrete) entities and property-instances they contain. The literature contains sophisticated discussion of how such a claim should be refined.[8]

A second issue which aspiring supervenience physicalists must resolve concerns the character and appropriate strength of the modality their claims invoke. For modal-operator formulations (e.g., the claim of strong supervenience above), the question is what kind of necessity the necessity operators should express. Conceptual necessity? Metaphysical necessity? Nomological necessity? Something else? For possible-world formulations (e.g., the claim of global supervenience above), the question is which possible worlds the claim should quantify over. Literally all possible worlds? Merely those whose laws of nature are the same as the actual world's laws of nature? Some other set? Any adequate answer to such questions must apparently steer a middle course between two extremes. Let me illustrate with the case of claims of global supervenience. On the one hand, if such claims quantify over literally *all* possible worlds, then they seem to be false. For they entail that every world physically$_n$ indistinguishable from (say) our world is also indistinguishable mentally from our world. But surely there is a world which is indistinguishable from our world physically$_n$, but *distinguishable* mentally, since in addition to its physical$_n$ contents it contains ectoplasmic spirits which play the right functional roles to count as minds. This so-called "problem of extras" has no generally agreed solution (for critical discussion of proposed solutions, see Witmer 1999). On the other hand, claims of global supervenience cannot quantify merely over nomologically possible worlds (i.e., those in which the laws of nature are exactly the same as those in the actual world), for in that case the supervenience claims could be true while physicalism were false. Suppose, for instance, that physicalism turns out to be *false*, but only because phenomenal properties turn out to be non-physical$_b$ properties that are nevertheless linked by fundamental psychophysical laws, biconditional in form, to certain physical properties; in that case claims of global supervenience quantifying over nomologically possible worlds would still be *true*, since any nomologically possible world physically$_n$ indistinguishable from the actual world would be one in which those fundamental psychophysical laws held and therefore operated to produce exactly the same distribution of phenomenal properties as obtains in the actual world. So claims of global supervenience must quantify over some set of possible worlds distinct from both the set of all possible worlds and the set of nomologically possible worlds. There is currently no consensus on what that set is.

A third issue which aspiring supervenience physicalists must resolve concerns the exact role that a supervenience claim, however expressed, is intended to play in the overall formulation of physicalism. The intended role varies from author to author and is sometimes left rather obscure. Some authors seem to take an appropriate global supervenience claim to constitute the whole of physicalism. Others hold that at least some additional claim is required (to the effect that every object is either a physical$_n$ object or else a spatio-temporal sum of physical$_n$ objects); but it is unclear what exactly they regard as sufficient; perhaps they regard a supervenience thesis as expressing physicalism about *properties*, whereas other claims are required to express physicalism about *particulars*. At the very least there is a loose end to be tied up here.

Even when all the issues just mentioned, as well as others, have been resolved, however, the adequacy of a supervenience formulation of physicalism remains open to doubt; and enthusiasm for such formulations has declined steadily over the last decade. The content of the doubt is that although an appropriate claim of supervenience may be a logically necessary condition for physicalism, it fails as a logically sufficient condition (even for physicalism about properties). The ground of the doubt, put briefly, is this: any supervenience claim that has been pressed into service as a formulation of physicalism is merely a variation on the theme that the physical$_n$ way things are *necessitates* the non-physical$_n$ way things are. But there is no explanation, *entailed by the supervenience claim itself*, for how and why this necessitation occurs; so, for all that the supervenience claim itself says, the necessitation of the non-physical$_n$ by the physical$_n$ might constitute a brute modal fact; but if, for all that the supervenience claim itself says, the necessitation of the non-physical$_n$ by the physical$_n$ might simply be a brute modal fact, then the supervenience claim *itself* yields no intuitively satisfactory sense in which the mental is physical$_n$. No supervenience claim, therefore, suffices for physicalism about anything.[9]

No alternative to supervenience physicalism's way of understanding "physical$_b$," has as yet achieved the popularity once enjoyed by the supervenience proposal, but an alternative to it, though neglected until recently, has indeed existed for a couple of decades (Boyd 1980; Lycan 1981, 1987: ch. 4). Its leading idea is that something is physical$_b$ if, and only if, it is a *functional* kind of thing that is *realized by* the physical$_n$; and the formulation of physicalism it yields claims that every concrete object and property-instance is either itself physical$_n$ or else is functional and realized by something that is physical$_n$. *Realization physicalists* (as we may call philosophers who endorse such a formulation of physicalism) are therefore committed to holding that all (actual) non-physical$_n$ kinds are, in fact, functional kinds; but they are not committed to any conceptual or linguistic thesis whatever – no thesis, for example, alleging the functional definability of non-physical$_n$ *concepts* or *terms*. (Realization physicalism can therefore be viewed as a sort of generalization of psychofunctionalism in the philosophy of mind.) Also, realization physicalists do not *deny* appropriately expressed claims of supervenience; indeed, they may regard such claims as logically necessary conditions of the truth of physicalism. But they insist that what *explains* the supervenience of the non-physical$_n$ on the physical$_n$ (if it does so supervene) is the fact that the non-physical$_n$ is functional and realized by the physical$_n$.[10]

The companion notions of a functional kind and of realization that realization physicalists exploit are familiar, of course, from the philosophy of mind. But the very heavy load which realization physicalism requires them to bear has revealed that they are employed even in the philosophy of mind in senses that are neither uniform nor clear. So realization physicalists need to spell out how they are understanding them. One attractive approach is to treat functional kinds as higher-order kinds: a functional property, P, will then be the property of having some or other property that plays role so-and-so; a functional object-kind, O, will be the kind of object that exists if, and only if, there exists an object of some or other kind that plays such-and-such a role; and so on. The roles here referred to may be causal or nomic or computational – or of any other sort, since playing a role is really no more than meeting a certain specifiable condition, and in principle the condition could be of any sort. Realization can now be understood as role-playing. If functional property P is the property of having some or other property that plays role so-and-so, then any property Q that plays role so-and-so can be said to realize P. This approach to understanding realization, however, needs much refinement before realization physicalists have in hand a notion adequate for formulating physicalism. One issue in particular that needs attention is whether realization physicalists can give a satisfactory account of the realization of *individuals* (tokens), as opposed to *kinds* (types), and whether, in so doing, they must or should assert claims of *identity* between non-physical$_n$ individuals (objects, property-instances, and so on) and the physical$_n$ individuals that realize them.[11]

Now that we have surveyed some attempts to formulate physicalism more precisely, we are in a position briefly to consider three questions *about* the thesis of physicalism: (1) Is it contingent or necessary? (2) Is it a priori or a posteriori? (3) Is it reductionist?

On its face, physicalism seems contingent. Since (when expressed in slogan form) it is true just in case every concrete thing is physical, it is false if even one concrete thing exists that is non-physical. But it is surely contingent whether or not there exist any concrete non-physical things (e.g., ectoplasmic ghosts). So physicalism is contingent. Moreover, this conclusion still holds when physicalism is more precisely formulated as the claim that every concrete object and property-instance is of a kind expressed by some predicate in the consensus theories of current physics; for it is surely contingent whether or not any concrete object or property-instance exists that is *not* of a kind expressed by some predicate in the consensus theories of current physics. But does physicalism remain a contingent thesis when it is formulated in terms of supervenience or in terms of realization?

It does. Admittedly, any supervenience formulation of physicalism claims that the physical$_n$ way things are *necessitates* the non-physical$_n$ way things are, which certainly sounds like a non-contingent claim. On the other hand, a supervenience formulation of physicalism must apply to the *actual* world, implying at a minimum that the *actual* world is such that the physical$_n$ way things are in *it* necessitates the non-physical$_n$ way things are in it, i.e., that any world physically$_n$ just like the *actual* world is also non-physically$_n$ just like the actual world. Now one way to ensure that a supervenience formulation of physicalism succeeds in doing this is to spell it out as a global supervenience claim that quantifies over *all* possible worlds without exception; for if the claim quantifies over *all* possible worlds, asserting that *any* two worlds exactly alike physically$_n$ are exactly alike in every way, then it obviously entails that any world exactly like the *actual* world physically$_n$ is exactly like the actual world in every way. Spelled out as a quantification over literally all possible worlds, then, a supervenience formulation of physicalism does express a non-contingent claim, not dependent for its truth on what the actual world turns out to be like. However, in order to avoid the "problem of extras" discussed above, a supervenience formulation of physicalism should quantify over *fewer* than all the possible worlds; it should quantify only over all possible worlds that meet some contingent condition X (whatever that might be), thus claiming merely that any two X-*worlds* exactly alike physically$_n$ are exactly alike in every way. But in that case the claim applies to the actual world (i.e., implies that any world physically$_n$ just like the actual world is also non-physically$_n$ just like the actual world) only if the actual world meets condition X, which is a contingent matter. So, strictly speaking, a supervenience formulation of physicalism must include not only a supervenience claim which quantifies over a suitably restricted set of possible worlds, but also the contingent claim that the actual world in fact belongs to that restricted set. A plausible supervenience formulation of physicalism, therefore, is a contingent thesis, dependent for its truth on what sort of world we happen to inhabit.

Some supervenience physicalists, however, ensure that their formulations of physicalism apply to the actual world by making them explicitly refer to the actual world; according to such formulations, any world exactly like the actual world physically$_n$ is exactly like the actual world non-physically$_n$.[12] Now let "P" be a complete physical$_n$ description of the actual world, and "Q" be a complete non-physical$_n$ description of the actual world. Then, according to these formulations, if physicalism is true, the conditional "If P then Q" expresses a necessary truth. So is physicalism a non-contingent thesis, according to these formulations? No. For the conditional "If P then Q" is not logically sufficient for physicalism; it is logically sufficient only if it is conjoined with the *contingent* claim that "P" *is* a complete physical$_n$ description of the actual world, and that "Q" *is* a complete non-physical$_n$ description of the actual world. The conditional "If P then Q" simply does not entail that any world exactly like the actual world physically$_n$ is exactly like the actual world non-physically$_n$ unless it is (contingently) true that "P" expresses the physical$_n$ way the actual world is and that "Q" expresses the non-physical$_n$ way the actual world is. Think of it this way: you are given an extensive physical$_n$ world-description "S," and an extensive non-physical$_n$ world description "T," and you figure out (using a priori methods, let us suppose) that "If S then T" expresses a necessary truth; have you thereby figured out that physicalism is true? Obviously not, because you do not yet know whether "S" and "T" accurately describe the *actual* world; and whether they do is a matter of contingent fact. Strictly speaking, then, supervenience physicalism formulated so as to refer explicitly to the actual world is the thesis that (1) "P" is a complete physical$_n$ description of the actual world, (2) "Q" is a complete non-physical$_n$ description of the actual world, and (3) "If P then Q" expresses a necessary truth.

Physicalism also remains contingent when formulated with help from the notion of realization. Since, when so formulated, it claims that every concrete object and property-instance is either itself physical$_n$ or else is functional and realized by something that is physical$_n$, it is false if concrete things exist that are neither physical$_n$ nor realized by the physical$_n$. But it is surely contingent what concrete things exist; so physicalism, thus formulated, is contingent. Nor, for reasons already rehearsed, should this conclusion be rejected on the grounds that a realization formulation of physicalism entails a suitably formulated claim of supervenience.

Let us turn now to the epistemic status of physicalism. Since, on any plausible formulation, the thesis of physicalism is contingent, we can safely presume that it is a posteriori. Surely the thesis that the actual world (though maybe not others) is such that the non-physical$_n$ phenomena it contains are identical with, or supervene upon, or are realized by, the physical$_n$ phenomena it contains is a thesis whose truth or falsity could only be established by examining the actual world. Still, what about the epistemic status of the specific modal claims to which physicalists are committed, once the way things actually are has been discovered and specified? That is, what about the claim that (take the definite descriptions rigidly now) the way things actually are physically$_n$ necessitates the way things actually are non-physically$_n$? Here, opinions differ. The majority view supposes that this necessitation holds in virtue of a posteriori necessary identities between the non-physical$_n$, on the one hand, and either the physical$_n$ or the functional and physically$_n$ realized, on the other; on this view, then, even when we have learned (a posteriori) what the actual world is like physically$_n$ and non-physically$_n$, it is still a posteriori whether physicalism is true. There is a minority view, however, according to which, if physicalism is true, then someone who had a complete physical$_n$ description of the actual world *and* who possessed all the concepts used to formulate non-physical$_n$ claims could in principle deduce his way to a complete non-physical$_n$ description of the world (Chalmers 1996; Jackson 1998). If this view is correct, then, by taking a complete physical$_n$ description of the actual world and by using one's grasp of non-physical$_n$ concepts, one could deduce a complete non-physical$_n$ description *allegedly* true of the actual world and then *test* physicalism by comparing this non-physical$_n$ description with a complete non-physical$_n$ description discovered empirically.

Finally, let us ask whether physicalism is reductionist, i.e., whether it entails that the non-physical$_n$ is reducible to the physical$_n$. According to a wide consensus, of the three formulations of physicalism we have considered, the first formulation (construed as non-eliminativist) is reductionist, while the second (supervenience) and third (realization) are not; indeed, the originators of these latter formulations explicitly aimed to formulate versions of non-reductionist physicalism.[13] But this consensus must rest on the assumption of some or other account of what reducibility to the physical$_n$ *is*; and according to the account of reducibility (derived from Ernest Nagel) that seems in fact to be assumed, the non-physical$_n$ is reducible to the physical$_n$ if, and only if, all non-physical$_n$ *laws* can be deduced from physical$_n$ laws by means of additional premises (i.e., "bridge principles") asserting the *identity* of non-physical$_n$ kinds with (tractable disjunctions of) physical$_n$ kinds. Supervenience and realization formulations of physicalism do not entail the reducibility in this sense of the non-physical$_n$ to the physical$_n$, since both are consistent with the multiple realizability of non-physical$_n$ kinds by *intractably many* distinct physical$_n$ kinds. (And in fact the first formulation does not entail it either, so long as it is permissible to avoid the problem of multiple realizability by identifying non-physical$_n$ kinds with intractable, perhaps infinite, disjunctions of physical$_n$ kinds.)

But the neo-Nagelian account of reducibility is a substantive philosophical claim. What if it is incorrect? Or what if it is not *uniquely* correct (so that there is no *single* correct account of reducibility)? The core idea of reducibility seems to be this: the non-physical$_n$ is reducible to the physical$_n$ just in case the non-physical$_n$ is somehow *explainable* in terms of the physical$_n$. The neo-Nagelian account is certainly one specification of this core idea (construing explanation as a species of derivation), but it seems likely that other specifications should be possible too, and plausible that no one of them should be uniquely correct. Will physicalism in that case still emerge as non-reductionist, or as non-reductionist in important ways? Some exploration of alternative accounts of reducibility can be found in the literature (see, e.g., Waters 1990; Smith 1992; Brooks 1994; Melnyk 1995; Chalmers 1996; Bickle 1998). Also welcome would be further exploration of the different kinds of *autonomy* that a special science like psychology can – and cannot – enjoy, consistently with the truth of physicalism; it would be nice to know, for example, how far the *methodological* autonomy of psychology requires its *metaphysical* autonomy.

3.2   Justifying Physicalism

On the assumption that a thesis of physicalism can be satisfactorily formulated, and that, so formulated, it is a posteriori, the question naturally arises whether there is in fact any empirical evidence that the thesis is true. What sort of non-deductive reasoning strategies could in principle provide such evidence? And do any of those strategies yield evidence for physicalism when put into practice? For all the enthusiasm for physicalism, in philosophy of mind and elsewhere, it is surprising how little attention these issues have received. On the other hand, they have received more attention than some anti-physicalist rhetoric might suggest. Let us briefly review some suggestions as to how physicalism might be evidenced, and the issues those suggestions raise.

One proposal (modeled on David Lewis's argument for the psychophysical identity theory) is that a two-premise argument can be used to support the conclusion that some non-physical$_n$ kind N is identical with a physical$_n$ kind P (Lewis 1966; the generalization is suggested in Jackson 1998). The first premise states that N is the kind that plays so-and-so role; the second premise states that P is the kind that plays so-and-so role; and the conclusion that N = P follows by the transitivity of identity. The first premise is inferable from the allegedly a priori conceptual or linguistic claim that "N" is semantically equivalent to "the kind that plays so-and-so role"; the second premise is discoverable empirically by checking out what roles physical$_n$ kinds in fact play. But most physicalists would doubt the applicability of this argumentative strategy, on the grounds that in point of fact the proprietary concepts or terms of the special sciences are not in general, perhaps not ever, semantically equivalent to definite descriptions, as the first premise seems to require; such a doubt would form part of a general doubt about descriptivist theories of the meanings of concepts or terms. A currently open question is whether the generalized Lewisian argumentative strategy can be repaired by supposing that special scientific concepts or terms, though not semantically equivalent to definite descriptions, still have their references fixed by means of a priori knowable definite descriptions of the rigidified form "the kind that *actually* plays so-and-so role."

A second proposal is that conclusions asserting the identity of non-physical$_n$ kinds with physical$_n$ kinds can be supported by an inference to the best explanation which takes as its data the observed fact that individuals of the non-physical$_n$ kind occur when and only when, and where and only where, individuals of the physical$_n$ kind in question occur. Suppose, then, that we observe the co-instantiation, in this sense, of non-physical$_n$ kind N and physical$_n$ kind P. Surely one hypothesis which could explain this observed co-instantiation is that N = P; certainly if $N = P$, and individuals of kinds N and P are observed at all, they cannot fail to be observed together. And this identity hypothesis is plausibly regarded as a better candidate explanation than the rival which asserts the distinctness of N and P, and which accounts for their observed co-instantiation by supposing them to be connected by a fundamental law of nature. The identity hypothesis looks better than this rival because, in two separate ways, it is more *economical* than the rival: it postulates just one kind $(= N, = P)$, whereas the rival postulates two (N *and* P); and the number of laws of nature which it must treat as brute and fundamental is fewer (by one) than the number the rival must treat as brute and fundamental. Accordingly, the observed co-instantiation of N and P provides evidence that $N = P$ (for elaboration, see Hill 1991: ch. 2).

Such a pattern of reasoning might appear to be of limited usefulness, since very few contemporary physicalists wish to endorse the sort of kind-to-kind identity claims which it supports. But the reasoning suggested can be extended so that it shows how to support physicalist conclusions other than those which assert the identity of non-physical$_n$ kinds with physical$_n$ kinds. One extension is obvious: if the empirical evidence with which the reasoning begins is the observed co-instantiation of some non-physical$_n$ kind N with some *functional* (rather than physical$_n$) kind F, then the reasoning can presumably be used to support the hypothesis that $N = F$, a hypothesis which a realization physicalist would obviously find congenial. Of course, to discover that a non-physical$_n$ kind N is a functional kind is not yet to discover that N is physically realized; so, since this latter conclusion is what realization physicalism needs, a further extension of the original line of reasoning would be desirable. Suppose that the observations which serve as data are that, whenever and wherever there is an individual of physical$_n$ kind P, there is also an individual of non-physical$_n$ kind N; because of multiple realization, however, the converse is not observed. These observations are potentially explainable by adopting the hypothesis that (roughly) N is identical with some functional kind F, and is in fact realized by physical$_n$ kind P; for if N $(= F)$ is realized by P, then P is sufficient for N, and so naturally whenever and wherever there is a P, there will be an N. As before, if this hypothesis is superior to its rivals in respect of economy, then the original observations provide evidence that N is functional and physically$_n$ realized.

These proposals raise at least two important questions. One is whether it is legitimate to appeal to economy (or simplicity) in the way in which the suggested patterns of reasoning do; obviously this question turns on the resolution of large issues in epistemology. The other question is whether widely accepted scientific findings can be used to construct actual instances of these patterns of reasoning that have true premises; this question has hitherto been pretty much ignored.

A third line of empirical reasoning in support of physicalism, and the one that has received the most attention, runs as follows (see, e.g., Peacocke 1979: 134–43; Melnyk 1994). The first premise is the so-called *causal closure* (or *completeness*) of the physical$_n$. It asserts that the physical$_n$ is closed in the sense that one does not need to go outside the realm of the physical$_n$ in order to find a sufficient cause of physical$_n$ phenomena: every physical$_n$ event has a sufficient physical$_n$ cause (to the extent that it has a cause at all).[14] This premise is supported by current physics, which has investigated ever so many physical$_n$ events but which knows of none for the explanation of which it is *necessary* to invoke non-physical$_n$ causes. The second premise is that non-physical$_n$ events have physical$_n$ effects. Certainly non-physical$_n$ events have non-physical$_n$ effects (e.g., hurricanes blow down trees). But current physics assures us – and no scientific realist seriously contests this today – that non-physical$_n$ effects at least have physical$_n$ parts. Since it is hard to see how a non-physical$_n$ event could have a non-physical$_n$ effect without also having some effect of some kind on some physical$_n$ part of that non-physical$_n$ effect, non-physical$_n$ events must have some physical$_n$ effects. From these two premises, together with the assumption that the non-physical$_n$ events which have physical$_n$ effects are not physical even in some broad sense of "physical," it follows that some physical$_n$ events are *causally overdetermined*; for every physical$_n$ event which has a non-physical$_n$ (and hence, by the assumption, non-physical$_b$) cause also has an entirely distinct physical$_n$ cause. But to the extent that – and this is the third premise – it is highly implausible that physical$_n$ events are causally overdetermined, it is reasonable to *reject* the assumption that the non-physical$_n$ events which have physical$_n$ effects are not physical even in some broad sense of "physical," and hence to *accept* that, in some broad sense of "physical," they are physical. A further, enumerative-inductive step leads to the universal conclusion that *all* non-physical$_n$ events, and not merely those known to have physical$_n$ effects, are physical in some broad sense (i.e., identical with, supervenient on, or realized by, the physical$_n$).

This line of reasoning prompts many questions (for discussion, see Mills 1996; Sturgeon 1998; Witmer 2000; Papineau 2001). Is the causal overdetermination to which the rejection of physicalism allegedly leads really such a bad thing? And if so, why? Is the causal closure of the physical$_n$ something for which there is evidence that would be acceptable to someone who was not already convinced of physicalism? And are there counterexamples to it? Is it really true, in any normal sense of "cause," that non-physical$_n$ events cause physical$_n$ effects? Finally, can the argument be modified to accommodate the apparently indeterministic character of the physical$_n$ realm?

The literature contains other suggestions as to how physicalism might be evidenced (Loewer 1995; Papineau 1995; for criticism, see Witmer 1998). But in view of the surprisingly little attention that philosophers have paid to the question of justifying physicalism, it strikes me as unlikely that all the possible suggestions have yet been thought up.

3.3 Objecting to Physicalism

Since the thesis of physicalism, as we have been understanding it, has the logical form of a universal generalization, it is in principle open to counterexamples:

concrete objects or property-instances that are neither physical$_n$ nor physical$_b$. One sort of objection to physicalism, therefore, consists in grounds for thinking that such entities really do exist. Such entities might be ones (e.g., God, vital forces, astral bodies) whose sheer existence is denied by physicalists, in which case the objector must provide a posteriori or a priori grounds for thinking that they do exist. Alternatively, and more plausibly, such entities might be ones (e.g., rational decisions, episodes in embryonic development) whose sheer existence (at least on a neutral construal of what their existence entails) is undisputed by physicalists, but whose characterization as neither physical$_n$ nor physical$_b$ is disputed, in which case the objector must provide a posteriori or a priori grounds for thinking that the entities in question are indeed neither physical$_n$ nor physical$_b$. To illustrate: no physicalists deny that human beings exist (well, hardly any); but human beings are a counterexample to physicalism if it can be shown, as parapsychological researchers have tried systematically to show, that human beings have powers (e.g., psychokinetic powers) that human beings simply could not have if they were physical$_b$. Most of the objections to physicalism familiar from the philosophy of mind literature are objections of this first sort, i.e., putative counterexamples (see, e.g., Robinson 1993).

In responding to them, physicalists will naturally want to examine each case on its merits, and we obviously cannot enter into any details here. But we should pause to notice a certain philosophical outlook which is likely to underlie physicalists' particular arguments, and which may not be shared by their opponents. This outlook amounts to a deep suspicion of any allegedly a priori ground for holding *either* that some concrete entity exists *or* that (its mere existence granted) it is neither physical$_n$ nor physical$_b$. According to this outlook, grounds for holding that a concrete entity of any kind exists have to be a posteriori. Likewise, any grounds for holding that a concrete entity is neither physical$_n$ nor physical$_b$ must also be a posteriori, since they must rule out the possibility that the entity is identical a posteriori either with a physical$_n$ entity or with an entity that is functional but physically$_n$ realized. Accordingly, physicalists are unlikely to be impressed by, or perhaps even to take seriously, objections to physicalism that start with a premise about what is *conceivable* by humans.[15] The sort of objection, by contrast, which *would* really impress a physicalist with this outlook would be the identification of some non-tendentious empirical phenomenon for the best explanation of which it was required *either* to postulate anew something neither physical$_n$ nor physical$_b$, *or* to construe *as* neither physical$_n$ nor physical$_b$ something already acknowledged by everyone to exist. An example of such a phenomenon would be some type of human behavior which demonstrably *could not* be the product of the operations of a merely physical$_b$ system. The physicalist, however, denies that any such phenomena actually exist, and the plausibility of this denial, in the light of the past century of science, goes a long way to explain such popularity as physicalism enjoys.[16]

Now anti-physicalists who advance objections of this first sort are likely to adopt a positive response to the problem of the many sciences according to which physicalism is right about the physical$_b$ character of *much* of what is non-physical$_n$, though not right, of course, about it all. However, anti-physicalists who advance objections of the three remaining sorts that I shall consider are likely to adopt the pluralistic, egalitarian response to the problem of the many sciences according to which every science (or honorary science) is on an ontological par with every other, so that pretty much nothing that is non-physical$_n$ is physical$_b$.

The first such objection is that physicalism cannot be true, because it cannot even be adequately formulated; and it cannot be adequately formulated because, for reasons rehearsed in section 3.1, there is no satisfactory way to define "physical$_n$." If correct, this objection is obviously devastating to physicalism. But whether it is correct remains undecided and forms the topic of ongoing research. The second objection claims that, even if physicalism can be satisfactorily formulated, there is simply no reason whatever to think that it is true.[17] (Some philosophers, it seems, even wish to explain the popularity of physicalism by appeal to some sort of wholly irrational physics-worship.) If this is correct, then, since science certainly presents an appearance of plurality, there is no reason not to take this appearance at face value and therefore to treat all the branches of science as metaphysically equal. But it is at best premature to claim that there is no evidence for physicalism, since, as we have seen, there do exist promising lines of argument for physicalism and in any case the matter thus far has only been rather cursorily investigated by philosophers. Moreover, if physicalism *is* a mere prejudice, then it is a noticeably more prevalent one among those (I mainly mean non-philosophers) who have some idea of what condensed matter physics has to say about familiar macrophysical phenomena, what quantum mechanics has to say about chemistry, what biochemistry has to say about cell biology, and so forth. It is *possible* that the (admittedly imperfect) correlation between being a physicalist and being scientifically well informed can be explained sociologically or by appeal to some sort of systematic error in reasoning (though one would dearly like to see the hypothesis spelled out), but on the whole it seems likelier that the people in question see dimly that what they know about science *does* constitute evidence for physicalism, even if they cannot say exactly *how* it does.[18] If this conjecture is correct, then evidently there is work for philosophers to do in helping them out.

The third and final objection that I shall consider is that physicalism is implausible because it implies that no events other than physical$_n$ events are ever causes, and that no properties of events other than the physical$_n$ properties of those events are ever causally relevant in the sense of making a difference to what effects the events have (see, e.g., Lowe 1993; Moser 1996). If physicalism does imply these things, then that is bad; for surely non-physical$_n$ events (e.g., decisions, earthquakes, chemical reactions) are sometimes causes, and surely an event (e.g., a collision with a sharp knife) can sometimes have the effect it has *because* it was a collision with a sharp knife, even though the event kind, *collision with a sharp knife*, is not a physical$_n$ event kind. And physicalism does seem to imply these things. For if, for every non-physical$_n$ effect, there is an underlying physical$_n$ phenomenon sufficient for it (as physicalism requires), and if all such underlying physical$_n$ phenomena are completely caused by earlier physical$_n$ phenomena in strict accordance with physical$_n$ laws, then physical$_n$ phenomena seem to be doing all the real causal work, and the appearance of non-physical$_n$ causation is just an illusion. But physicalists will hardly allow this line of reasoning, on which the third objection clearly turns, to go unchallenged; and they may in addition try to fashion an independently plausible account of causation and causal relevance which does not entail that, if physicalism is true, only physical$_n$ events are causes and only physical$_n$ properties are causally relevant.[19]

Notes

1 The interested reader will find a full account of my views in Melnyk (2003).
2 The mind–body problem is famously cast in such terms in Churchland (1981).
3 Anti-physicalists of this sort appear to include Goodman (1978), Putnam (1987), Crane and Mellor (1990), and Dupré (1993).
4 A concrete property-instance is an instance of a concrete property (e.g., the property of having mass); an abstract property-instance is an instance of an abstract property (e.g., the property of being divisible by five).
5 One challenger is Jaegwon Kim; see Kim (1998).
6 For the difficulty here and one possible solution, see Poland (1994: ch. 3). In Melnyk (1997), I dubbed this difficulty "Hempel's dilemma," in honor of Hempel (1980), and argued that, notwithstanding the reasoning in the text, there is no good objection to defining "physical" in terms of contemporary physics. However, see Daly (1998), Montero (1999), Crook and Gillett (2001). For another approach, see Papineau (2001); for a critique, see Witmer and Gillett (2001).
7 See Kim (1984), the paper which, in the United States at least, has set the terms of the debate about supervenience. For further discussion, see Kim (1993) and the papers by McLaughlin and Post in Savellos and Yalçin (1995). An excellent survey is Horgan (1993).
8 See, for example, Hellman and Thompson (1975), Haugeland (1982), Horgan (1982, 1987), Lewis (1983), Post (1987), Jackson (1998). For a closely related (since also modal) approach, see Kirk (1996).
9 This is my way of putting the matter; see Melnyk (1998, 1999). For similar concerns, see Horgan (1993).
10 The fullest account of realization physicalism is Melnyk (2003). See also Poland (1994), which advocates a hybrid form of physicalism incorporating both supervenience and realization elements.
11 This is the only occasion on which I shall mention the thesis that every token (e.g., individual event) is identical with some or other physical$_n$ token. Though famously propounded (see, e.g., Fodor 1974; Davidson 1980), it has played a surprisingly small role in recent discussion of physicalism, perhaps because no one seems to regard it as sufficient for physicalism (unless events are treated as Kim-events, in which case it becomes equivalent to the unpopular type-identity physicalism discussed first in the text). Davidson himself, of course, advanced the thesis alongside a supervenience thesis.

12 See Chalmers (1996) and Jackson (1998). In the text, I misrepresent these authors, though harmlessly as far as the current issue goes: in order to handle the "problem of extras," they would not say "exactly like the actual world non-physically$_n$," but rather "exactly like the actual world with regard to *positive* non-physical$_n$ facts."

13 The source of this consensus may well be Fodor (1974). See also Fodor (1997).

14 Confusingly, another claim is also sometimes referred to as the "causal closure of the physical," the claim that physical$_n$ causes are the *only* causes of physical$_n$ effects. This latter claim leads swiftly to physicalism, given the further premise that non-physical$_n$ events are causes of physical$_n$ effects; but for that very reason it will be regarded as question-begging by anti-physicalists. It is not entailed by the closure claim in the text.

15 Defense of this outlook against the challenge to it presented by Chalmers (1996) may be found in my (2001).

16 The denial that any such phenomena exist is, I believe, *one* of the lines of pro-physicalist thought to be found in Smart's classic (1959).

17 Distasteful though it is to mention, I fear that it must be asked, of philosophers who claim to find no arguments for physicalism in the literature, how hard they have looked.

18 A hypothesis of this form is defended in Papineau (2001).

19 Nearly all of the philosophy of mind literature about the problems of mental causation is, of course, relevant here.

References

Bickle, John (1998). *Psychoneural Reduction: The New Wave.* Cambridge, MA: The MIT Press.

Boyd, Richard (1980). "Materialism Without Reductionism: What Physicalism Does Not Entail." In Ned Block (ed.), *Readings in the Philosophy of Psychology, Vol. 1.* London: Methuen: 268–305.

Brooks, D. H. M. (1994). "How To Perform A Reduction." *Philosophy and Phenomenological Research,* 54: 803–14.

Chalmers, David (1996). *The Conscious Mind: In Search of a Fundamental Theory.* New York: Oxford University Press.

Charles, David, and Lennon, Kathleen (1992). *Reduction, Explanation, and Realism.* New York: Oxford University Press.

Churchland, Paul (1981). "Eliminative Materialism and the Propositional Attitudes." *The Journal of Philosophy,* 78: 67–90.

Crane, Tim, and Mellor, D. H. (1990). "There Is No Question Of Physicalism." *Mind,* 90: 185–206.

Crook, Seth and Gillett, Carl (2001). "Why Physics Alone Cannot Define the 'Physical': Materialism, Metaphysics, and the Formulation of Physicalism." *Canadian Journal of Philosophy,* 31: 333–60.

Daly, Chris (1998). "What Are Physical Properties?" *Pacific Philosophical Quarterly,* 79: 196–217.

Davidson, Donald (1980). *Essays on Actions and Events.* New York: Oxford University Press.

Dupré, John (1993). *The Disorder of Things: Metaphysical Foundations of the Disunity of Science.* Cambridge, MA: Harvard University Press.

Fodor, Jerry A. (1974). "Special Sciences, or The Disunity of Science As A Working Hypothesis." *Synthèse*, 28: 97–115.

—— (1997). "Special Sciences: Still Autonomous After All These Years." In James E. Tomberlin (ed.), *Philosophical Perspectives, 11, Mind, Causation, and World*. Cambridge, MA: Blackwell: 149–63.

Gillett, Carl and Loewer, Barry (2001). *Physicalism and Its Discontents*. New York: Cambridge University Press.

Goodman, Nelson (1978). *Ways of Worldmaking*. Sussex: Harvester Press.

Haugeland, John (1982). "Weak Supervenience." *American Philosophical Quarterly*, 19: 93–103.

Hellman, Geoffrey, and Thompson, Frank (1975). "Physicalism: Ontology, Determination, and Reduction." *The Journal of Philosophy*, 72: 551–64.

Hempel, Carl G. (1980). "Comments on Goodman's *Ways of Worldmaking*." *Synthèse*, 45: 193–9.

Hill, Christopher S. (1991). *Sensations: A Defense of Type Materialism*. New York: Cambridge University Press.

Horgan, Terry (1982). "Supervenience and Microphysics." *Pacific Philosophical Quarterly*, 63: 29–43.

—— (1987). "Supervenient Qualia." *Philosophical Review*, 96: 491–520.

—— (1993). "From Supervenience To Superdupervenience: Meeting the Demands of a Material World." *Mind*, 102: 555–86.

Jackson, Frank (1998). *From Metaphysics To Ethics: A Defence of Conceptual Analysis*. New York: Oxford University Press.

Kim, Jaegwon (1984). "Concepts of Supervenience." *Philosophy and Phenomenological Research*, 45: 153–76. Reprinted in Kim (1993).

—— (1993). *Supervenience and Mind: Selected Philosophical Essays*. New York: Cambridge University Press.

—— (1998). *Mind in a Physical World: An Essay on the Mind–Body Problem and Mental Causation*. Cambridge, MA: The MIT Press.

Kirk, Robert (1996). "Strict Implication, Supervenience, and Physicalism." *Australasian Journal of Philosophy*, 74: 244–57.

Lewis, David (1966). "An Argument for the Identity Theory." *Journal of Philosophy*, 63: 17–25.

—— (1983). "New Work For A Theory Of Universals." *Australasian Journal of Philosophy*, 61: 343–77.

Loewer, Barry (1995). "An Argument for Strong Supervenience." In Savellos and Yalçin (1995): 218–25.

Lowe, E. J. (1993). "The Causal Autonomy of the Mental." *Mind*, 102: 629–44.

Lycan, William G. (1981). "Form, Function, and Feel." *Journal of Philosophy*, 78: 24–50.

—— (1987). *Consciousness*. Cambridge, MA: The MIT Press.

Maxwell, Grover (1968). "Scientific Methodology and the Causal Theory of Perception." In I. Lakatos and A. Musgrave (eds.), *Problems in the Philosophy of Science*. Holland: North Holland Publishing Company.

McLaughlin, Brian P. (1995). "Varieties of Supervenience." In Savellos and Yalçin (1995): 16–59.

Melnyk, Andrew (1994). "Being A Physicalist: How And (More Importantly) Why." *Philosophical Studies*, 74: 221–41.

—— (1995). "Two Cheers For Reductionism: Or, The Dim Prospects For Non-Reductive Materialism." *Philosophy of Science*, 62: 370–88.

—— (1997). "How To Keep The 'Physical' In Physicalism." *The Journal of Philosophy*, 94: 622–37.

—— (1998). "The Prospects for Kirk's Non-Reductive Physicalism." *Australasian Journal of Philosophy*, 76: 323–32.

—— (1999). "Supercalifragilisticexpialidocious: A Critical Study of Savellos and Yalçin's *Supervenience: New Essays*." *Nous*, 33: 144–54.

—— (2001). "Physicalism Unfalsified: Chalmers' Inconclusive Conceivability Argument." In Gillett and Loewer (2001): 329–47.

—— (2003). *A Physicalist Manifesto: Thoroughly Modern Materialism*. Cambridge: Cambridge University Press.

Mills, Eugene (1996). "Interactionism and Overdetermination." *American Philosophical Quarterly*, 33: 105–17.

Montero, Barbara (1999). "The Body Problem." *Nous*, 33: 183–200.

Moser, Paul K. (1996). "Physicalism and Mental Causes: Contra Papineau." *Analysis*, 56: 263–7.

Papineau, David (1995). "Arguments for Supervenience and Physical Realization." In Savellos and Yalçin (1995): 226–43.

—— (2001). "The Rise of Physicalism." In Gillett and Loewer (2001): 3–36.

Peacocke, Christopher (1979). *Holistic Explanation: Action, Space, Interpretation*. New York: Oxford University Press.

Poland, Jeffrey (1994). *Physicalism: The Philosophical Foundations*. New York: Oxford University Press.

Post, John F. (1987). *The Faces of Existence: An Essay in Nonreductive Metaphysics*. Ithaca, NY: Cornell University Press.

—— (1995). "'Global' Supervenient Determination: Too Permissive?" In Savellos and Yalçin (1995): 73–100.

Putnam, Hilary (1987). *The Many Faces of Realism*. Illinois: Open Court.

Robinson, Howard (1993). *Objections to Physicalism*. New York: Oxford University Press.

Savellos, Elias E. and Yalçin, Ümit D. (eds.) (1995). *Supervenience: New Essays*. New York: Cambridge University Press.

Smart, J. J. C. (1959). "Sensations and Brain Processes." *Philosophical Review*, 68: 141–56.

Smith, Peter (1992). "Modest Reductions and the Unity of Science." In Charles and Lennon (1992): 19–43.

Sturgeon, Scott (1998). "Physicalism and Overdetermination." *Mind*, 107: 411–32.

Waters, C. Kenneth (1990). "Why The Anti-Reductionist Consensus Won't Survive: The Case of Classical Mendelian Genetics." In A. Fine, M. Forbes, and L. Wessels (eds.), *PSA 1990*. East Lansing, MI: Philosophy of Science Association.

Witmer, D. Gene (1998). "What is Wrong with the Manifestability Argument for Supervenience." *Australasian Journal of Philosophy*, 76: 84–9.

—— (1999). "Supervenience Physicalism and the Problem of Extras." *The Southern Journal of Philosophy*, 37: 315–31.

—— (2000). "Locating the Overdetermination Problem." *The British Journal for the Philosophy of Science*, 51: 273–86.

Witmer, D. Gene and Gillett, Carl (2001). "A 'Physical' Need: Physicalism and the *Via Negativa*." *Analysis*, 61: 302–9.

Chapter 4

Dualism

Howard Robinson

4.1 Introduction

Dualism in the philosophy of mind is the doctrine that mind and body (or mental states and physical states) are of radically different natures. How exactly to express this difference is a matter of controversy, but it is generally taken to center on two properties possessed by the mental that are alien to the physical. One of these is the privacy or subjectivity of states of consciousness, as contrasted to the public availability of physical states. The other is the possession of intentionality or "aboutness" by mental states: physical states stand in spatio-temporal and causal relations to each other, but are not intrinsically *about* anything. The principle task for the physicalist is to give an account of these properties in physical or physical-compatible terms. A dualist is someone who thinks that this cannot be done.[1]

There are normally thought to be two forms of dualism, namely substance dualism and bundle dualism. The former is primarily associated with Descartes and the latter with Hume.[2] An important distinction must be made amongst bundle dualists, however. Some, like Hume, do not believe in either mental or physical substance, treating both as just collections of states, properties, or events (depending on how the theory is stated). For others, it is only the mind that is given this treatment: bodies are substantial entities, but minds only collections of states, properties, or events. This constitutes a relative downgrading of the mind and a move toward the *attribute* theory. According to this theory, mental states are non-physical attributes of a physical substance – the human body or brain. This theory can be regarded as the softest or least reductive form of materialism. It is materialistic because it says that the only substances are material substances. It is also a form of dualism, because it allows the irreducibility of mental states and properties.

Both substance and bundle dualisms face the same three problems. The first problem is to show why we need to be dualists at all – why a materialist account of the mind will not work. The second is to explain the nature of the unity of the immaterial mind. For the Cartesian, that means explaining how he understands the notion of immaterial substance. For the Humean, the issue is to explain the nature of the relationship between the different elements in the bundle that binds them into one thing.[3] Neither tradition has been notably successful in this latter task: indeed, Hume declared himself wholly mystified by the problem, rejecting his own initial solution (though quite why is not clear from the text).[4] The third problem is to give a satisfactory account of the relationship between the immaterial mind and the material body. Which means, for preference, to explain how they can interact, and, failing this, to render plausible either epiphenomenalism (the view that the mental is produced by the physical, but has no influence back on the physical) or parallelism (the view that mental and physical realms "march in step," but without either causally interacting with the other).

I shall use the excuse of limited space for not dealing with all these issues. Rather, I shall attempt, in Cartesian spirit, to show, first, that the thinking subject has to transcend the physical world; and, secondly, that such subjects must be essentially simple. They (that is, we) are more like the immaterial substance in which Descartes believed, than like a Humean bundle of mental events or states. So I shall be concerned with why we should be dualists, and why dualists of a Cartesian stripe. How to explain the unity of the mind – except by showing it to be essentially simple – and how to explain our relations to our bodies, are not issues I can discuss here.[5]

In order to accomplish the first of the tasks I have set myself (that is, to show that the thinking subject must transcend the physical world), I shall introduce a form of dualism not so far mentioned, and which is generally neglected in discussions of dualism, namely *predicate dualism*. That is the theory that psychological or mentalistic predicates are not reducible to physicalistic predicates. (What this means I shall discuss in the next section.) Few philosophers nowadays either believe in such reduction or think that it is necessary for physicalism. Predicate dualism is only dualism at the level of meaning, and this is generally thought to have no ontological consequences. I shall be arguing that this is a mistake, and that predicate dualism – the failure of reduction – is a threat to physicalism because the irreducibility of the special sciences in general implies that the mind is not an integral part of the physical realm with which those sciences deal.

This conclusion does not alone force us to adopt any particular form of dualism. Perhaps the mind, though it transcends the physical world about which it constructs the sciences, is no more than a bundle of mental states or properties, as Hume thought. Perhaps, that is, predicate dualism forces us to nothing more than property dualism, which may not drive one further away from physicalism than the attribute theory. I shall then attempt to show that this is not so, for property dualism is not adequate to cope with certain respects in which *personal* identity is demonstrably different from the identity conditions for physical bodies and other complex entities: these constraints on personal identity can be met only by substance dualism of a roughly Cartesian kind.

4.2 The Argument for Predicate Dualism

If physicalism is true, then it should be possible, in principle, to give what is, in some sense, a total description of the world in the vocabulary of a completed physics. To put it in the material, not the formal, mode, all the properties that there *ultimately* are should be those of the basic physical entities. But there are many ways of talking truly about the world other than that couched in the vocabulary of physics; and there are, in some obvious sense, many properties that the world possesses that are not contained in that physics. These higher-order predicates and properties are expressed in the other – or *special* – sciences, such as chemistry, biology, citology, epidemiology, geology, metereology, psychology, and the supposed social sciences; not to mention our ordinary discourse, which often expresses truths that find no place in anything we would naturally call a science. How does the fundamental level of ontology – which we are presupposing to be captured ideally in physics – sustain all these other ontologies and make true these other levels of discourse?

The logical positivists had a simple answer to this question. Any respectable level of discourse was reducible to some level below it and ultimately to physics itself. The kind of reduction of which we are talking has a *strong* form and a *very strong* form. According to the *very strong* form, all respectable statements in the special sciences and in ordinary discourse could, in principle, be translatable into statements in the language of physics. In the end, therefore, all truths could be expressed using the language of physics.[6] According to the merely *strong* form – which was the form in which reductionism was generally discussed – there had only to be scientific laws (called "bridging laws") connecting the concepts and laws in a higher-order science with those in the next lower, and ultimately to physics.[7] So the concepts and laws of psychology would be nomically connected to those of some biological science, and these, in turn, with chemistry, and chemistry would be nomically reducible to physics. So "reducible to," in this sense, meant that the entities and properties invoked in the non-basic discourse were *type identical with* certain basic structures. For example, our ordinary concept *water* is reducible to the chemical type H_2O, and this chemical molecule always consists of the same atomic arrangements. This pattern makes it easy to understand intuitively how the existence of water and the truths of sentences referring to water need involve nothing more than the existence of things in the ontology of physics.

But not all concepts in the special sciences, let alone ordinary discourse and the social sciences, can be fitted into this pattern. Not every hurricane that might be invoked in metereology, or every tectonic shift that might be mentioned in geology, will have the same chemical or physical constitution. Indeed, it is barely conceivable that any two would be similar in this way. Nor will every infectious disease, or every cancerous growth, not to mention every devaluation of the currency or every *coup d'état* share similar structures in depth. Jerry Fodor, in his important article "Special Sciences" (1974), correctly claims that the doctrine of reductionism requires that all our scientifically legitimate concepts be *natural kind* concepts and – like water – carry their similarities down to the foundations, and that this is not plausible for most of our useful explanatory concepts. It is particularly not plausible for the concepts of psychological science, understood in functionalist terms, nor for the concepts in our lay mentalistic vocabulary. All these concepts are *multiply realizable,* which means that different instances of the same kind of thing can be quite different at lower levels – in their "hard wear" – and that it is only by applying the concepts from the special science that the different cases can be seen as saliently similar at all. Whereas you could eliminate the word "water" and speak always of "H_2O" with no loss of communicative power, you could not do this for "living animal," "thought of the Eiffel Tower," "continental drift," etc.

Fodor (1974) thinks that this is no threat to physicalism, because each instance of a higher-order concept will be identical with some structure describable in terms of basic physics, and nothing more. Token reductionism is all that physicalism and the unity of the sciences require: type reduction is unnecessary. I shall now try to explain why, contrary to appearances, this is wrong.

4.3   Why Predicate Dualism leads to Dualism Proper

Fodor is quite right to think that the very same subject matter can be described in irreducibly different ways and still be just that subject matter. What, in my view, he fails to notice is that such different explanatory frameworks presuppose a perspective on that subject matter which is, prima facie, from outside of it. The outline of my position is as follows. On a realist construal, the completed physics cuts physical reality up at its ultimate joints: any special science which is nomically strictly reducible to physics also, in virtue of this reduction, it could be argued, cuts reality at its joints, but not at its minutest ones. By contrast, a science which is not nomically reducible to physics does not take its legitimation from the underlying reality in this direct way; rather, it is formed from the collaboration between, on the one hand, objective similarities in the world and, on the other, perspectives and interests of those that devise the science. If scientific realism is true, a completed physics will tell one how the world is, independently of any special interest or concern: it is just *how the world is.* Plate tectonics, however, tell you how it is from the perspective of an interest in the development of continents, and talk about hurricanes and cold fronts from the perspective of an interest in the weather. A *selection* of phenomena with a certain *teleology* in mind is required before these structures or patterns are reified. The point is that these sciences and the entities that they postulate exist from certain intellectual perspectives, and a perspective, whether perceptual or intellectual, is external to that on which it is a perspective.[8] The problem for the physicalist is to say what it is for a perspective *on* the physical world to be something *within* it. A unified naturalistic view of the world would require that the observer's perspective required by these sciences be integrated into the reality he observes. The integration of perspectives and interests into the one world requires the integration of psychological states of both perceptual and intentional kinds into the physical world. These, however, are paradigms of the kinds of state that seem to resist nomic – type – reduction to physics.

There are, of course, famous arguments that appeal to the phenomenology of consciousness for thinking that token reductions fail: but no appeal to these is involved in the current argument.[9] Even if token reductionism of the mind could meet the phenomenological problems, the fact that it is token, not type, means that it presupposes the existence of a perspective from which the physical world is seen in order to bring out these facts. The perspective that makes possible the nomically irreducible sciences, being itself irreducible, could itself exist (if it were physical) only from a perspective on physical reality. As this second perspective is essentially of the same kind as the one we are trying to explain, namely a psychological or intellectual perspective, there is no prospect of a non-vicious regress here.

We can now understand the motivation for full-blown reduction. A true basic physics represents the world as it is in itself, and if the special sciences were reducible, then the existence of their ontologies would make sense as expressions of the physical, not just as ways of seeing or interpreting it – they could be understood "from the bottom up," not from above down. The irreducibility of the special sciences creates no problem for the dualist, who sees the explanatory endeavor of the physical sciences as something carried on from a perspective conceptually outside of the physical world. Nor need it worry a physicalist, *if* he can reduce psychology, for then he could understand "from the bottom up" the acts (with their internal, intentional contents) which created the irreducible ontologies of the other sciences. But psychology is one of the least likely of sciences to be reduced.

4.4   Is the Talk of "Perspectives" Legitimate?

Someone who wished to resist this line of argument might deny the claim that the nomically irreducible sciences cannot be given a fully realist interpretation, but are a perspective on the reality. He might argue that the foundations of the special sciences are what Dennett (1991) calls "real patterns" in reality, and that these are as objective as the structures of the ultimate and reducible sciences.

This misses the point. My position is not to deny that the "real patterns" on which the special sciences are based are objective and genuine, but that, as well as this *fundamentum in re*, those sciences require an interpretative component which takes these similarities and picks them out as interesting for certain purposes.

The relation between an ideal physics and the nomically irreducible special sciences is like that between straightforward phenomena and *Gestalt* phenomena.

Entities in physics are analogous to a perfectly circular object, which needs no interpretation to be taken as a circle: those in irreducible special sciences are like a series of discontinuous dots or marks arranged roughly in a circle which one sees as circular. Two hurricanes, for example, are not perfectly similar and would present themselves as a kind only to someone with an interest in weather: plate tectonics exist only given an interest in the habitability of the earth. From a wholly detached viewpoint, both these phenomena could, perfectly correctly, be regarded simply as by-products of more fundamental processes, and not as constituting natural kinds at all. The world in itself is a continuous flow of events – which is not to say that its texture is everywhere the same. Taking some point as the start or end of some process is only non-arbitrary when seen in the light of some interest or concern.

4.5   A Surprising Ally

Support for my treatment of (most of) the special sciences can be drawn from Armstrong's account of universals (1980: vol. 2; 1989). Armstrong is a realist, but not for all properties, only for those required by basic science. Now it might be thought that this includes those in the special sciences, but I think that it does not. A real universal is one that makes a distinctive causal contribution, but non-micro entities, case by case, add nothing to the causal contribution of the micro base. Whatever reservations I may have about Armstrong's close tying of the identity of universals and properties to their causal powers, I think it is not unreasonable, in this context, to take the matter of whether a universal "does work" in its particular instances as criterial of whether a real universal is there needed. This can perhaps be reinforced by appeal to Armstrong's claim that there are no disjunctive universals (1980: 19–23; 1989: 82–4).[10] The properties of any special science not related by simple bridging laws to physics will be disjuncts – perhaps open-ended disjuncts – of more atomic universals. This reinforces the sense in which irreducible universals are not strictly necessary: the corresponding *predicates* are necessary for the schemes of explanation that constitute the special sciences, but predicates, as opposed to universals, are creatures of human thought and talk, and so presuppose the mental perspective on the subject matter.[11]

4.6   The Optionality of Non-basic Levels and the Unavoidability of Psychology

I want to take the matter further by discussing the suggestion that, if a being could understand the world in all its physical (meaning, on the level of physics) detail, but ignored the grosser levels, it would be missing out on nothing. The purpose of the discussion is to show that amongst the special sciences only psychology could not be omitted without loss, and that this shows the essential difference of the mental from the physical.

Imagine a semi-divine being who follows everything at the level of physics, but takes no notice of any of the more macroscopic patterns of events. Because of his intelligence, he can predict the position of everything with as much accuracy as is in principle possible. Are we to say that his failure to concern himself with grosser patterns is a form of substantive ignorance, or that he merely ignores certain macro patterns that are essential to us for understanding because we cannot grasp the detail: they are, for us, a necessary shorthand and for him, not necessary at all? Someone who thought such a being was substantially ignorant might start by claiming that failure to notice patterns and operative laws constitutes ignorance. But suppose that our semi-divinity were capable of noticing these things, but found them of no interest, given his ability to do everything in terms of physics. It would be necessary to argue that the non-basic levels were, in some way, *significant in their own right*, ends in themselves. The issue is closely parallel to that of the irreducibility of teleological explanation. Supposing the truth of mechanism, do teleological explanations do extra, non-heuristic work?

The situation is at its most crucial for psychology, as is brought out by Dennett's discussion in "True Believers" (in 1987: 13–42). Dennett argues that even an omnicompetent observer who was able to predict the behavior of humans by predicting the behavior of the individual atoms that make them up would need folk psychology. He would need it if he wished to understand the utterances of humans when he talked to them, and, more fundamentally, he would need it to understand what he himself was doing. So the folk psychological level of description is ineliminable, though it carries no fundamental ontological clout. The problem with Dennett's position is that there can be no explanation of why we must adopt the folk psychological perspective. If we are all just clouds of atoms, why are we obliged to see ourselves in this particular ontologically non-basic way? It is true that we cannot see ourselves as *people* or *understand* our *actions* unless we adopt this perspective, but why see ourselves in these ways? An eliminativist would argue that it is just conceptual conservatism. But if one rejects the idea that we just happen to be hooked on this way of seeing ourselves and agree that the applicability of these categories is truly fundamental, then there is the problem of explaining why this should be so. A reductionist believes that statements on this level can be true, because they are reducible. But this fact does not explain why, amongst all possible non-basic levels of discourse, this one should be unavoidable, rather than merely available if required. It is possible to argue that the question "why should we see ourselves as persons?" answers itself, because the use of "we" already presupposes the personal perspective. But this misses the point. The behavior of the physical structures that we call "people" cannot be understood in a way that seems complete or remotely adequate without the personal perspective. Physicalistically speaking, there should be no "we" that exists at some particular level. But, even if one tries to think in a physicalistic manner, one cannot avoid thinking that, at a certain level of complexity, there emerges something which is neither a matter of seeing or interpreting the organism in a certain way from outside (on pain of regress) nor is it just one of those levels of complexity which one might notice or ignore. There is present there, in a manner wholly different from other forms of emergent complexity (because others are either or both interpretative and ignorable) something of which it makes no sense to say one might ignore it. This is at least the seed of what Descartes expresses in the *cogito*.

The truth is that even if we were able to do all the predicting that physical omniscience would make possible, it would be impossible to restrict one's understanding of oneself to the physical terms. The Cartesian certainty that I *think* is absolute, not relative to adopting one possible but, like all the rest, optional level of discourse. Our existence on the personal level is a fundamental, not a pragmatic, fact. There is no way it can be thought of as a function of a certain way of thinking or conceptualizing: it is a basic fact, in the sense of being unavoidable in a more than pragmatic way, and it could not be thus basic if the physicalist ontology were correct.

4.7   Why Bundle Dualism Will Not Do

If what is said above is correct, the mind transcends the physical world and is, *ipso facto*, non-physical. But this does not indicate whether it is a substance or only a collection of states. I shall argue that bundle dualism will not suffice because this would make it into a complex entity and only by supposing it to be simple can we accommodate certain irresistible intuitions concerning personal identity.

There is a long tradition, dating at least from Reid, for arguing that the identity of persons over time is not a matter of convention or degree in the way that the identity of other (complex) substances is. Criticism of these arguments and of the intuitions on which they rest, running from Hume to Parfit, has left us with an inconclusive clash of intuitions. My argument does not concern identity through time, but the consequences for identity of certain counterfactuals concerning origin. It can, I hope, therefore, break the stalemate which faces the debate over diachronic identity. My claim will be that the broadly conventionalist ways, which are used to deal with problem cases through time for both persons and material objects, and which can also be employed in cases of counterfactuals concerning origin for bodies, cannot be used for similar counterfactuals concerning persons or minds.

It is nowadays respectable to maintain that individuals have essential properties, though it is somewhat less generally agreed that they have essences. Kripke's claim that a particular wooden table could not have been made of ice seems to be widely accepted, so there is at least one necessary condition for the existence of that individual table: but whether there are necessary and sufficient conditions –

i.e. an essence – as well as merely necessary conditions for it being the object it is, is more controversial (Kripke 1980: 39–53). Even granted that the table has some essential properties, it is doubtful whether it has an essence. We can scale sentences as follows:

1 This table might have been made of ice.
2 This table might have been made of a different sort of wood.
3 This table might have been made of 95 per cent of the wood it was made of and 5 per cent of some other wood.

There will come a point along the spectrum illustrated by (1) and (2) and towards (3) where the question of whether the hypothesized table would be the same as the one that actually exists has no obvious answer. It seems that the question of whether it "really" is the same one has no clear meaning: it is of, say, 75 per cent the same matter and of 25 per cent different matter. These are the only genuine facts in the case; the question of numerical identity can be decided in any convenient fashion, or left unresolved. There will thus be a penumbra of counterfactual cases where the question of whether two things would be the same is not a matter of fact.

Suppose that a given human individual had had origins different from those which he in fact had, such that whether that difference affected *who he was* was not obvious to intuition. What would count as such a case might be a matter of controversy, but there must be one. Perhaps it is unclear whether, if there had been a counterpart to Jones's body from the same egg but a different though genetically identical sperm from the same father, the person there embodied would have been Jones. Some philosophers might regard it as obvious that sameness of sperm is essential to the identity of a human body and to personal identity. In that case imagine a counterpart sperm in which some of the molecules in the sperm are different; would that be the same sperm? If one pursues the matter far enough there will be indeterminacy which will infect that of the resulting body. There must therefore be some difference such that neither natural language nor intuition tells us whether the difference alters the identity of the human body; a point, that is, where the question of whether we have the same body is not a matter of fact.

How one is to describe these cases is, in some respects, a matter of controversy. Some philosophers think one can talk of *vague identity* or *partial identity*, others think that such expressions are nonsensical. I do not have the space to discuss this issue. I am assuming, however, that questions of how one is allowed to use the concept of identity affect only the care with which one should characterize these cases, not any substantive matter of fact. There are cases of substantial overlap of constitution in which *that* fact is the only bedrock fact in the case: there is no further fact about whether they are "really" the same object. If there were then there would have to be a *haecceitas* or *thisness* belonging to and individuating each complex physical object, and this I am assuming to be implausible if not unintelligible. (More about the conditions under which *haecceitas* can make sense will be found below.) My claim is that no similar overlap of constitution can be applied to the counterfactual identity of minds. In Geoffrey Madell's words: "But while my present body can thus have its partial counterpart in some possible world, my present consciousness cannot. Any present state of consciousness that I can imagine either is or is not mine. There is no question of degree here" (1981: xx).[12]

Why is this so? Imagine the case where we are not sure whether it would have been Jones's body – and, hence, Jones – that would have been created by the slightly modified sperm and the same egg. Can we say, as we would for an object with no consciousness, that the story *something the same, something different* is the whole story, that overlap of constitution is all there is to it? For the Jones body as such, this approach would do as well as for any other physical object. But suppose Jones, in reflective mood, asks himself "if that had happened, would I have existed?" There are at least three answers he might give to himself: (1) "I either would or would not, but I cannot tell;" (2) "There is no fact of the matter whether I would or would not have existed: it is just a mis-posed question;" (3) "In some ways, or to some degree, I would have, and in some ways, or to some degree, I would not. The creature who would have existed would have had a kind of overlap of psychic constitution with me."

The third answer parallels the response we would give in the case of bodies. But as an account of the subjective situation, it makes no sense. Call the creature that would have emerged from the slightly modified sperm "Jones2." Is the overlap suggestion that, just as, say, 85 per cent of Jones2's original body would have been identical with Jones's, about 85 per cent of his psychic life would have been Jones's? That it would have been *like* Jones's – indeed, that Jones2 might have had a psychic life 100 per cent like Jones's – makes perfect sense, but that he might have been to that degree, the same psyche – that Jones "85 per cent existed" – makes no sense. Take the case in which Jones and Jones2 have *exactly* similar lives throughout: which 85 per cent of the 100 per cent similar mental events do they share? Nor does it make sense to suggest that Jones might have participated in the whole of Jones2's psychic life, but in a rather ghostly *only 85 per cent there* manner. Clearly, the notion of overlap of numerically identical psychic parts cannot be applied in the way that overlap of actual bodily part constitution quite unproblematically can.

This might make one try the second answer. We can apply the "overlap" answer to the Jones body, but the question of whether the minds or subjects would have been the same has no clear sense. It is difficult to see why it does not. Suppose Jones found out that he had originally been one of twins, in the sense that the zygote from which he developed had divided, but that the other half had died soon afterwards. He can entertain the thought that if it had been his half that had died, he would never have existed as a conscious being, though someone would, whose life, both inner and outer, might have been very similar to his. He might feel rather guiltily grateful that it was the other half that died. It would be strange to think that Jones is wrong to think that there is a matter of fact about this. And how is one to "manage" the transition from the case where there is a matter of fact to the case where there is not?

This only leaves us with the first option. There has to be an absolute matter of fact from the subjective point of view. But the physical examples we have considered show that when something is essentially complex, this cannot be the case. When there is constitution, degree and overlap of constitution are inevitably possible. So the mind must be simple, and this is possible only if it is something like a Cartesian substance.

4.8   Two Reflections on this Conclusion

The first reflection concerns the difference between Jones's failure to imagine his relation to the existence of Jones2, and other more traditional problems in personal identity. Unlike the other cases, Jones's is not a matter of what one might call *empathetic distance*.

Suppose that my parents had emigrated to China whilst my mother was pregnant with me, and that, shortly after my birth, both my parents had died. I was then taken in by Chinese foster parents, lived through the revolution and ended up being brought up in whatever way an alien would have been brought up in Mao's China. None of this person's post-uterine experiences would have been like mine. It seems, on the one hand, that this person would obviously have been me, and, on the other, that it is utterly unclear what kind of empathetic connection I can feel to this other "me." If I ask, like Jones, "would this have been me?," I am divided between the conviction that, as the story is told, it obviously would, and a complete inability to feel myself into the position I would then have occupied. This kind of *failure of empathy* plays an important role in many stories that are meant to throw doubt on the absoluteness of personal identity. It is important to the attempt to throw doubt on whether I am the same person as I would become in fifty years time, or whether brain damage would render me "a different person" in more than a metaphorical sense. It is also obviously something that can be a matter of degree: some differences are more empathetically imaginable than others. In all these cases our intuitions are indecisive about the effect on identity. It is an important fact that problems of empathy play no role in my argument. The twin who might have survived in my stead, or the person who would have existed if the sperm had been slightly different, could have had as exactly similar a psychic life to mine as you care to imagine. This shows the difference between the cases I have discussed and the problematic cases that involve identity through time. In those cases the idea of "similar but not quite the same" gets empirical purchase. My future self feels, in his memory, much, but not all, of what I now feel. In these cases, overlap of conscious constitution is clearly intelligible. But in the counterfactual cases, imaginative or empathetic distance plays no essential role, and the accompanying relativity of identification gets no grip.

Secondly, I think that the argument is reinforced by the light it throws on the concept of *haecceitas*. In the case of complex physical bodies it is impossible to imagine what a *haecceitas* would consist in or how it relates to the other features of the object, and so the suggestion that there is such a thing seems to be pure mystery-mongering. By contrast, in the case of minds we do have a form of *haecceitas* which, in a sense, we all understand, namely subjectivity. It is because we intuitively understand this that we feel we can give a clear sense to the suggestion that it would, or would not, have been ourselves to which something had happened, if it had happened: and that we feel we can understand very radical counterfactuals – e.g. that I might have been an ancient Greek or even a non-human – whereas such radical counterfactuals when applied to mere bodies – e.g. that this wooden table might have been the other table in the corner or even a pyramid – makes no intuitive sense. It is possible to argue that the suggestion that my mind might have been in another body ultimately makes no sense, but it makes a prima facie sense – it seems to have content – in a way that a similar suggestion for mere bodies does not. The very fact that the counterfactuals for subjects seem to make sense exhibits something not present in the other cases, which is available to function in the role of *haecceitas*. Only with consciousness understood in a Cartesian fashion can *haecceitas* be given an empirical interpretation.

4.9 An Objection

One response sometimes made to this argument is that it is correct as an account of our *concept* of the mind, but not correct about the actual nature of the mind.[13] Reality is, so to speak, deconstructive of the concept that we have. So our conceptual scheme does commit us to something like the Cartesian conception of the mind, but we have other grounds for thinking that this is a mistake. As it stands, this is more an expression of unease than a worked out objection. I shall consider two ways of filling it out.

First, one might argue as follows. If we suppose the mind to be only a collection of mental states related by a co-consciousness relation, the phenomenology would still seem to be to us as it is in fact. The argument does not, therefore, show that the bundle theory is false, for even if the bundle theory were true, it would seem to us as if we were simple substances. It could be compared to what a "hard determinist" might say about free will, namely we cannot help but feel we have it, but the feeling is mistaken.[14] There are two problems with this argument. First, it does not help Jones to answer his question. In order to avoid answer (1) – that he either would or would not be identical with Jones2 – he would have to make sense of one of the other alternatives, and this objection gives him no help with that. Is the suggestion that when Jones tries to imagine overlap of psychic constitution, our concepts prevent him from doing so, but, in reality, such a thing would be possible? If so, I do not think this very plausible. It seems to me to be a real fact that this makes no sense. My objections above to the other option – that there is no fact of the matter – seem also to be untouched. Secondly, the argument is question-begging. It is a moot point between the bundle theorist and the substantivalist whether there could be a co-consciousness relation that would produce an experientially united mind. My argument supports the view that experiential unity involves a simple substance and so supports the view that there is no such thing as a self-standing co-consciousness relation. So it is not proper simply to claim that it could be the same for us if the bundle theory were true, if that condition is in fact an impossible one. The analogy with free will, though illustrative of what the objector is driving at, does little to show that he is correct. First, the coherence of the hard determinist's position is controversial. Secondly, the determinist can give a rationale for why we *must* feel free in terms of the conceptual impossibility of replacing one's own practice of *deciding* by one of merely *predicting* one's own behavior. There seems to be no parallel explanation of why it seems all or nothing for counterfactual identity. This is especially mysterious given that it can seem be a matter of degree in cases that turn on empathetic distance.[15]

There is a completely different way of filling the objection out. It concerns my use of counterfactuals. Counterfactuals are a controversial matter and I make no attempt to discuss them. I blatantly assume the falsehood of Lewis's counterpart analysis, for if Jones's question whether he would exist only enquired whether there would be a counterpart which possessed states very like his own, then there would be no phenomenological problem. All counterparts are strictly different objects. However, I am quite happy, along with almost all other philosophers, simply to deny Lewis's theory. But it is not from this source that the challenge comes, but from someone who takes a non-realist attitude to counterfactuals. There is an empiricist tradition which denies truth values to counterfactuals and says that they express policies or attitudes. There will be no truth about what would have happened if the relevant sperm had been slightly different.

It is not possible to get deeply engaged in a discussion of counterfactuals here. I would make two points. First, most philosophers do accept a realist account of counterfactuals – the anti-realist view is not very plausible – and the argument would go through for them. Secondly, the anti-realist approach has a weaker and a stronger form. The weaker version simply denies truth value to counterfactuals: there is no fact of the matter about whether it is a or b that would have happened if C had obtained. C could have obtained and, if it had, either a or b (or something else) would have occurred: there is just no truth from the perspective of the actual world about which it would have been. This does not affect my argument at all, which only requires that the only options about what might have happened are all or nothing, not that there is a fact about which. The stronger version says that the whole notion of *might have been otherwise* is a projection of our mode of thought – of our ability to imagine things – not something that obtains in reality. This is not to say – as it might seem – that the actual world is necessary (because there is nothing else that might have been) but only that all these modal categories are mere projections. Even if we accepted this – which I do not recommend – it would not entirely deflate the argument. It would still show something interesting about the nature of mind, namely that it made no sense to treat it in the same way as bodies within the logical space of possibility that we create by projection. The fact that we create that space does not imply that what we express within it does not reflect real differences between the objects about which we are talking.

4.10   Conclusion

My arguments in this chapter have been in a Cartesian spirit. First, in sections 4.2–4.6 I argued that the thinking subject has to transcend the physical world about which (among other things) it thinks. Only if a strong reductionism were true could its thinking be part of that physical world. Then, in sections 4.7–4.9, I argued that the thinking subject has to be a simple substance, on pain of entertaining incoherent counterfactuals. These arguments complement each other, but they are logically independent and the second can establish its conclusion on its own.

Notes

1   I do not enter further into a fuller discussion of these properties here, for that belongs principally to an examination of the problems for materialism. For a fuller description of these properties and a brief outline of the strategies that modern materialists have employed to cope with them, see Robinson (1999).

2   Descartes' *Sixth Meditation* is the *locus classicus* for substance dualism. Modern defenses of the theory can be found in Popper and Eccles (1977), Swinburne (1986), and Foster (1991). Hume develops his theory in the *Treatise* (Bk I, Part iv, Section 6) and expresses his dissatisfaction with what he has said in the Appendix to the *Treatise*. There are several modern philosophers who account for the unity of the mind in terms of the relations between mental events, and so could be said to have a bundle theory, but they do not tend to be dualists. Parfit (1971; 1984) is a materialist and Dainton (2000) is neutral on ontological questions.

3   It might be thought that the attribute theory already has an account of the unity of the mind, in terms of the dependence of all the elements in a given bundle on the same brain. But, though this may be a causal explanation, it is not an analysis, of unity. Mere dependence on the same brain does not conceptually guarantee unity of consciousness. See Foster (1968) in reply to Ayer (1963).

4   For the doubts, see the Appendix to the *Treatise*.

5 I discuss embodiment – though not specifically the problem of interaction – in Robinson (1989).

6 Examples of translation reductionism are Hempel (1980) and Carnap (1934).

7 The classic source for this is Ernest Nagel (1961).

8 The withdrawal from genuine reductionism in psychology, then, began when Skinner accepted that a stimulus-response model was inadequate, and developed the notion of operant conditioning. Whereas the former required only mechanistic causal concepts, the latter is irreducibly teleological. The behavior of the rat which is learning how to get the food pellet may have a mechanical description on a lower level, but the understanding of it as operant conditioning has to be teleological, for it concerns what the rat is trying to achieve, or the point of its behavior. Furthermore, the behaviorist is prevented, by his own principled disinterest in what happens inside, from having views about the nature of the process in which the learning is realized. This brings out the ambiguity of the concept of reduction when applied to the philosophy of mind. Its central concern is to eliminate "the ghost in the machine" – that is, anything irreducibly private or subjective. This form of reduction is entirely irrelevant to any of the physical sciences. The second element is the elimination or analysis away of concepts of a kind that have no place in a purely physical science. Operant conditioning meets the first objective but not the second. It is the brunt of the argument of this part of my chapter that, contra Fodor, the second objective is as essential to the physicalist as the first.

9 These are the much discussed qualia objections to physicalism. See, for example, Jackson (1982), Robinson (1993).

10 Armstrong's acceptance of conjunctive universals also reinforces the intuition that strong reduction preserves full realism for the special sciences. Water is a conjunction of instances of the universals of hydrogen-ness and oxygen-ness in a certain spatial arrangement. These, in their turn, are conjunctions of more atomic universals.

11 It follows from this, of course, that if psychology (which includes not only the science, but our ordinary mentalistic concepts) is not reducible in a strong sense, its "properties" are only predicates and its subject matter is in part created by an act of the mind – the mind not being present until that act has been performed. Armstrong's theory becomes less different from Dennett's interpretative theory, with the attendant threat of regress, than was the intention.

12 Madell's book is an excellent treatment of the topics I discuss in this section.

13 This objection has been made to me, on different occasions, by Simon Blackburn, Derek Parfit, and Katalin Farkas. It is worth noting that this objection involves a major concession. If the argument I have presented shows that we are committed by the way we think of ourselves to a Cartesian concept of the self, this was not in virtue of some easily revisable definition. The argument was not a derivation of logical consequences from some necessary and sufficient conditions for being a subject, leaving the option of altering those conditions. It proceeded on the basis of what was conceivable for a conscious subject. The associated concept of the self must be unavoidable in a "Kantian" manner. The suggestion that it is mistaken is, therefore, a form of skeptical nihilism, which we can only live through by pretending to ignore.

14 I owe the comparison with free will to Katalin Farkas.

15 There is a more complicated version of the argument presented in sections 4.6–4.9, which would resist the objection. I believe that it can be argued that vague predicates

are never ontologically basic and can, in principle, be eliminated. Amongst these will be the notion of identity under counterfactual circumstances for physical bodies of all kinds. There is no real factual difference between an assertion that some physical body would have existed if such and such had been different, and an assertion that there would have been a "counterpart" body of a similar kind under those circumstances. This applies even if the counterfactual change does not directly involve the object in question. But this treatment is wholly unacceptable for subjects. Suppose that, contrary to fact, someone had coughed on the other side of the world just before you were conceived. On the principle that applies to bodies, there is no factual difference between the proposition that *you* would still have come into existence, and the proposition that someone with the same qualities as you would have. As the twin example shows, this difference is real and not eliminable. The full version of this argument is not in print, but for discussion of some of the relevant issues concerning vagueness, see Robinson (2001).

References

Armstrong, D. M. (1980). *Universals and Scientific Realism* (2 vols). Cambridge: Cambridge University Press.

—— (1989). *Universals: An Opinionated Introduction*. Boulder, CO: Westview Press.

Ayer, A. J. (1963). "The Concept of a Person." In *The Concept of a Person and other Essays*. London: Macmillan: 82–128.

Carnap, R. (1934). *The Unity of Science*. London: Kegan Paul.

Dainton, B. (2000). *Stream of Consciousness*. London: Routledge.

Dennett, D. (1987). *The Intentional Stance*. Cambridge, MA: MIT Press.

—— (1991). "Real Patterns." *Journal of Philosophy*, 89: 27–51.

Descartes, R. (1984–5). *The Philosophical Writings of Descartes*, trans. J. Cottingham, R. Stoothof, and D. Murdoch (2 vols). Cambridge: Cambridge University Press.

Fodor, J. (1974). "Special Sciences or the Disunity of Science as a Working Hypothesis." *Synthese*, 28: 77–115.

Foster, J. (1968). "Psychophysical Causal Relations." *American Philosophical Quarterly*, 5.

—— (1991). *The Immaterial Self*. London: Routledge.

Hempel, C. G. (1980). "The Logical Analysis of Psychology." In N. Block (ed.), *Readings in Philosophy of Psychology*, vol. 1. London: Methuen: 14–23. (Originally published in French in 1935.)

Hume, D. (1978). *A Treatise on Human Nature*, ed. P. H. Nidditch. Oxford: Clarendon Press.

Jackson, F. (1982). "Epiphenomenal Qualia." *Philosophical Quarterly*, 32: 127–36.

Kripke, S. (1980). *Naming and Necessity*. Oxford: Blackwell.

Madell, G. (1981). *The Identity of the Self*. Edinburgh: Edinburgh University Press.

Nagel, E. (1961). *The Structure of Science*. London: Routledge and Kegan Paul.

Parfit, D. (1971). "Personal Identity." *Philosophical Review*, 80: 3–27.

—— (1984). *Reasons and Persons*. Oxford: Clarendon Press.

Popper, K. R. and Eccles, J. C. (1977). *The Self and its Brain*. Berlin: Springer International.

Robinson, H. (1989). "A Dualist Account of Embodiment." In Smythies and Beloff (1989): 43–57.

—— (1993). "The Anti-materialist Strategy and the 'Knowledge Argument'." In H. Robinson (ed.), *Objections to Physicalism*. Oxford: Clarendon Press: 159–83.

—— (1999). "Materialism and the Mind–Body Problem." In E. Graig (ed.), *The Routledge Encyclopaedia of Philosophy*. London: Routledge.

—— (2001). "Vagueness, Realism, Language and Thought." In T. Horgan and M. Potric (eds.), *Essays on Vagueness*. Oxford: Oxford University Press.

Smythies, J. R. and Beloff, J. (eds.) (1989). *The Case for Dualism*. Charlottesville: University of Virginia Press.

Swinburne, R. (1986). *The Evolution of the Soul*. Oxford: Clarendon Press.

Chapter 5

Consciousness and its Place in Nature

David J. Chalmers

5.1 Introduction[1]

Consciousness fits uneasily into our conception of the natural world. On the most common conception of nature, the natural world is the physical world. But on the most common conception of consciousness, it is not easy to see how it could be part of the physical world. So it seems that to find a place for consciousness within the natural order, we must either revise our conception of consciousness, or revise our conception of nature.

In twentieth-century philosophy, this dilemma is posed most acutely in C. D. Broad's *The Mind and its Place in Nature* (1925). The phenomena of mind, for Broad, are the phenomena of consciousness. The central problem is that of locating mind with respect to the physical world. Broad's exhaustive discussion of the problem culminates in a taxonomy of seventeen different views of the mental–physical relation.[2] On Broad's taxonomy, a view might see the mental as non-existent ("delusive"), as reducible, as emergent, or as a basic property of a substance (a "differentiating" attribute). The physical might be seen in one of the same four ways. So a four-by-four matrix of views results. (The seventeenth entry arises from Broad's division of the substance/substance view according to whether one substance or two is involved.) At the end, three views are left standing: those on which mentality is an emergent characteristic of either a physical substance or a neutral substance, where in the latter case, the physical might be either emergent or delusive.

In this chapter I take my cue from Broad, approaching the problem of consciousness by a strategy of divide-and-conquer. I will not adopt Broad's categories: our understanding of the mind–body problem has advanced since the 1920s, and it would be nice to think that we have a better understanding of the crucial issues. On my view, the most important views on the metaphysics of consciousness can be divided almost exhaustively into six classes, which I will label "type

A" through "type F." Three of these (A through C) involve broadly reductive views, seeing consciousness as a physical process that involves no expansion of a physical ontology. The other three (D through F) involve broadly non-reductive views, on which consciousness involves something irreducible in nature, and requires expansion or reconception of a physical ontology.

The discussion will be cast at an abstract level, giving an overview of the metaphysical landscape. Rather than engaging the empirical science of consciousness, or detailed philosophical theories of consciousness, I will be examining some general classes into which theories of consciousness might fall. I will not pretend to be neutral in this discussion. I think that each of the reductive views is incorrect, while each of the non-reductive views holds some promise. So the first part of this chapter can be seen as an extended argument against reductive views of consciousness, while the second part can be seen as an investigation of where we go from there.

5.2   The Problem

The word "consciousness" is used in many different ways. It is sometimes used for the ability to discriminate stimuli, or to report information, or to monitor internal states, or to control behavior. We can think of these phenomena as posing the "easy problems" of consciousness. These are important phenomena, and there is much that is not understood about them, but the problems of explaining them have the character of puzzles rather than mysteries. There seems to be no deep problem in principle with the idea that a physical system could be "conscious" in these senses, and there is no obvious obstacle to an eventual explanation of these phenomena in neurobiological or computational terms.

The hard problem of consciousness is the problem of experience. Human beings have subjective experience: there is something it is like to be them. We can say that a being is conscious in this sense – or is phenomenally conscious, as it is sometimes put – when there is something it is like to be that being. A mental state is conscious when there is something it is like to be in that state. Conscious states include states of perceptual experience, bodily sensation, mental imagery, emotional experience, occurrent thought, and more. There is something it is like to see a vivid green, to feel a sharp pain, to visualize the Eiffel Tower, to feel a deep regret, and to think that one is late. Each of these states has a *phenomenal character*, with *phenomenal properties* (or qualia) characterizing what it is like to be in the state.[3]

There is no question that experience is closely associated with physical processes in systems such as brains. It seems that physical processes give rise to experience, at least in the sense that producing a physical system (such as a brain) with the right physical properties inevitably yields corresponding states of experience. But how and why do physical processes give rise to experience? Why do not these processes take place "in the dark," without any accompanying states of experience? This is the central mystery of consciousness.

What makes the easy problems easy? For these problems, the task is to explain certain behavioral or cognitive functions: that is, to explain how some causal role is played in the cognitive system, ultimately in the production of behavior. To explain the performance of such a function, one need only specify a mechanism that plays the relevant role. And there is good reason to believe that neural or computational mechanisms can play those roles.

What makes the hard problem hard? Here, the task is not to explain behavioral and cognitive functions: even once one has an explanation of all the relevant functions in the vicinity of consciousness – discrimination, integration, access, report, control – there may still remain a further question: why is the performance of these functions accompanied by experience? Because of this, the hard problem seems to be a different sort of problem, requiring a different sort of solution.

A solution to the hard problem would involve an account of the relation between physical processes and consciousness, explaining on the basis of natural principles how and why it is that physical processes are associated with states of experience. A *reductive explanation* of consciousness will explain this wholly on the basis of physical principles that do not themselves make any appeal to consciousness.[4] A *materialist* (or physicalist) solution will be a solution on which consciousness is itself seen as a physical process. A *non-materialist* (or non-physicalist) solution will be a solution on which consciousness is seen as non-physical (even if closely associated with physical processes). A *non-reductive* solution will be one on which consciousness (or principles involving consciousness) is admitted as a basic part of the explanation.

It is natural to hope that there will be a materialist solution to the hard problem and a reductive explanation of consciousness, just as there have been reductive explanations of many other phenomena in many other domains. But consciousness seems to resist materialist explanation in a way that other phenomena do not. This resistance can be encapsulated in three related arguments against materialism, summarized in what follows.

5.3 Arguments Against Materialism

5.3.1 The explanatory argument[5]

The first argument is grounded in the difference between the easy problems and the hard problem, as characterized above: the easy problems concern the explanation of behavioral and cognitive functions, but the hard problem does not. One can argue that by the character of physical explanation, physical accounts explain *only* structure and function, where the relevant structures are spatio-temporal structures, and the relevant functions are causal roles in the production of a system's behavior. And one can argue as above that explaining structures and functions does not suffice to explain consciousness. If so, no physical account can explain consciousness.

We can call this the *explanatory argument*:

(1)   Physical accounts explain at most structure and function.
(2)   Explaining structure and function does not suffice to explain consciousness.

_____

(3)   No physical account can explain consciousness.

If this is right, then while physical accounts can solve the easy problems (which involve only explaining functions), something more is needed to solve the hard problem. It would seem that no reductive explanation of consciousness could succeed. And if we add the premise that what cannot be physically explained is not itself physical (this can be considered an additional final step of the explanatory argument), then materialism about consciousness is false, and the natural world contains more than the physical world.

Of course, this sort of argument is controversial. But before examining various ways of responding, it is useful to examine two closely related arguments that also aim to establish that materialism about consciousness is false.

5.3.2   The conceivability argument[6]

According to this argument, it is conceivable that there be a system that is physically identical to a conscious being, but that lacks at least some of that being's conscious states. Such a system might be a *zombie*: a system that is physically identical to a conscious being but that lacks consciousness entirely. It might also be an *invert*, with some of the original being's experiences replaced by different experiences, or a *partial zombie*, with some experiences absent, or a combination thereof. These systems will look identical to a normal conscious being from the third-person perspective: in particular, their brain processes will be molecule-for-molecule identical with the original, and their behavior will be indistinguishable. But things will be different from the first-person point of view. What it is like to be an invert or a partial zombie will differ from what it is like to be the original being. And there is nothing it is like to be a zombie.

There is little reason to believe that zombies exist in the actual world. But many hold that they are at least conceivable: we can coherently imagine zombies, and there is no contradiction in the idea that reveals itself even on reflection. As an extension of the idea, many hold that the same goes for a *zombie world*: a universe physically identical to ours, but in which there is no consciousness. Something similar applies to inverts and other duplicates.

From the conceivability of zombies, proponents of the argument infer their *metaphysical possibility*. Zombies are probably not naturally possible: they probably cannot exist in our world, with its laws of nature. But the argument holds that zombies *could have* existed, perhaps in a very different sort of universe. For example, it is sometimes suggested that God could have created a zombie world, if he had so chosen. From here, it is inferred that consciousness must be non-physical. If there is a metaphysically possible universe that is physically identical to ours but that lacks consciousness, then consciousness must be a further, non-physical component of our universe. If God could have created a zombie world, then (as Kripke puts it) after creating the physical processes in our world, he had to do more work to ensure that it contained consciousness.

We can put the argument, in its simplest form, as follows:

(1) It is conceivable that there be zombies.
(2) If it is conceivable that there be zombies, it is metaphysically possible that there be zombies.
(3) If it is metaphysically possible that there be zombies, then consciousness is non-physical.

___

(4) Consciousness is non-physical.

A somewhat more general and precise version of the argument appeals to P, the conjunction of all microphysical truths about the universe, and Q, an arbitrary phenomenal truth about the universe. (Here "$\wedge$" represents "and" and "$\neg$" represents "not".)

(1) It is conceivable that $P \wedge \neg Q$.
(2) If it is conceivable that $P \wedge \neg Q$, it is metaphysically possible that $P \wedge \neg Q$.
(3) If it is metaphysically possible that $P \wedge \neg Q$, then materialism is false.

___

(4) Materialism is false.

5.3.3 The knowledge argument[7]

According to the knowledge argument, there are facts about consciousness that are not deducible from physical facts. Someone could know all the physical facts, be a perfect reasoner, and still be unable to know all the facts about consciousness on that basis.

Frank Jackson's canonical version of the argument provides a vivid illustration. On this version, Mary is a neuroscientist who knows everything there is to know about the physical processes relevant to color vision. But Mary has been brought up in a black-and-white room (on an alternative version, she is colorblind[8]) and has never experienced red. Despite all her knowledge, it seems that there is something very important about color vision that Mary does not know: she does not know what it is like to see red. Even complete physical knowledge and unrestricted powers of deduction do not enable her to know this. Later, if she comes to experience red for the first time, she will learn a new fact of which she was previously ignorant: she will learn what it is like to see red.

Jackson's version of the argument can be put as follows (here the premises concern Mary's knowledge when she has not yet experienced red):

(1) Mary knows all the physical facts.
(2) Mary does not know all the facts.

———

(3) The physical facts do not exhaust all the facts.

One can put the knowledge argument more generally:

(1) There are truths about consciousness that are not deducible from physical truths.
(2) If there are truths about consciousness that are not deducible from physical truths, then materialism is false.

———

(3) Materialism is false.

5.3.4 The shape of the arguments

These three sorts of argument are closely related. They all start by establishing an *epistemic gap* between the physical and phenomenal domains. Each denies a certain sort of close epistemic relation between the domains: a relation involving what we can know, or conceive, or explain. In particular, each of them denies a certain sort of *epistemic entailment* from physical truths P to the phenomenal truths Q: deducibility of Q from P, or explainability of Q in terms of P, or conceiving of Q upon reflective conceiving of P.

Perhaps the most basic sort of epistemic entailment is a priori entailment, or *implication*. On this notion, P implies Q when the material conditional P⊃Q is a priori; that is, when a subject can know that if P is the case then Q is the case, with justification independent of experience. All of the three arguments above can be seen as making a case against an a priori entailment of Q by P. If a subject who knows only P cannot deduce that Q (as the knowledge argument suggests), or if one can rationally conceive of P without Q (as the conceivability argument suggests), then it seems that P does not imply Q. The explanatory argument can be seen as turning on the claim that an implication from P to Q would require a functional analysis of consciousness, and that the concept of consciousness is not a functional concept.

After establishing an epistemic gap, these arguments proceed by inferring an ontological gap, where ontology concerns the nature of things in the world. The conceivability argument infers from conceivability to metaphysical possibility; the knowledge argument infers from failure of deducibility to difference in facts; and the explanatory argument infers from failure of physical explanation to non-physicality. One might say that these arguments infer from a failure of epistemic entailment to a failure of ontological entailment. The paradigmatic sort of onto-logical entailment is *necessitation*: P necessitates Q when the material conditional P⊃Q is metaphysically necessary, or when it is metaphysically impossible for P to hold without Q holding. It is widely agreed that materialism requires that P necessitates all truths (perhaps with minor qualifications). So if there are phenom-enal truths Q that P does not necessitate, then materialism is false.

We might call these arguments *epistemic arguments* against materialism. Epistemic arguments arguably descend from Descartes's arguments against materialism (although these have a slightly different form), and are given their first thorough airing in Broad's book, which contains elements of all three arguments above.[9] The general form of an epistemic argument against materialism is as follows:

(1) There is an epistemic gap between physical and phenomenal truths.
(2) If there is an epistemic gap between physical and phenomenal truths, then there is an ontological gap, and materialism is false.

_____

(3) Materialism is false.

Of course, this way of looking at things oversimplifies matters, and abstracts away from the differences between the arguments.[10] The same goes for the precise analysis in terms of implication and necessitation. Nevertheless, this analysis pro-vides a useful lens through which to see what the arguments have in common, and through which to analyze various responses to the arguments.

There are roughly three ways that a materialist might resist the epistemic arguments. A type-A materialist denies that there is the relevant sort of epistemic gap. A type-B materialist accepts that there is an unclosable epistemic gap, but denies that there is an ontological gap. And a type-C materialist accepts that there is a deep epistemic gap, but holds that it will eventually be closed. In what follows, I discuss all three of these strategies.

5.4 Type-A Materialism

According to type-A materialism, there is no epistemic gap between physical and phenomenal truths; or at least, any apparent epistemic gap is easily closed. Ac-cording to this view, it is not conceivable (at least on reflection) that there be duplicates of conscious beings that have absent or inverted conscious states. On this view, there are no phenomenal truths of which Mary is ignorant in principle from inside her black-and-white room (when she leaves the room, she gains at most an ability). And on this view, on reflection there is no "hard problem" of explaining consciousness that remains once one has solved the easy problems of explaining the various cognitive, behavioral, and environmental functions.[11]

Type-A materialism sometimes takes the form of eliminativism, holding that consciousness does not exist, and that there are no phenomenal truths. It sometimes takes the form of analytic functionalism or logical behaviorism, holding that consciousness exists, where the concept of "consciousness" is defined in wholly functional or behavioral terms (e.g., where to be conscious might be to have certain sorts of access to information, and/or certain sorts of dispositions to make verbal reports). For our purposes, the difference between these two views can be seen as terminological. Both agree that we are conscious in the sense of having the functional capacities of access, report, control, and the like; and they agree that we are not conscious in any further (non-functionally defined) sense. The analytic functionalist thinks that ordinary terms such as "conscious" should be used in the first sort of sense (expressing a functional concept), while the eliminativist thinks that they should be used in the second. Beyond this terminological disagreement about the use of existing terms and concepts, the substance of the views is the same.

Some philosophers and scientists who do not explicitly embrace eliminativism, analytic functionalism, and the like are nevertheless recognizably type-A materialists. The characteristic feature of the type-A materialist is the view that on reflection there is nothing in the vicinity of consciousness that needs explaining over and above explaining the various functions: to explain these things is to explain everything in the vicinity that needs to be explained. The relevant functions may be quite subtle and complex, involving fine-grained capacities for access, self-monitoring, report, control, and their interaction, for example. They may also be taken to include all sorts of environmental relations. And the explanation of these functions will probably involve much neurobiological detail. So views that are put forward as rejecting functionalism on the grounds that it neglects biology or neglects the role of the environment may still be type-A views.

One might think that there is room in logical space for a view that denies even this sort of broadly functionalist view of consciousness, but still holds that there is no epistemic gap between physical and phenomenal truths. In practice, there appears to be little room for such a view, for reasons that I will discuss under type C, and there are few examples of such views in practice.[12] So I will take it for granted that a type-A view is one that holds that explaining the functions explains everything, and will class other views that hold that there is no unclosable epistemic gap under type C.

The obvious problem with type-A materialism is that it appears to deny the manifest. It is an uncontested truth that we have the various functional capacities of access, control, report, and the like, and these phenomena pose uncontested explananda (phenomena in need of explanation) for a science of consciousness. But in addition, it seems to be a further truth that we are conscious, and this phenomenon seems to pose a further explanandum. It is this explanandum that raises the interesting problems of consciousness. To flatly deny the further truth, or to deny without argument that there is a hard problem of consciousness over and above the easy problems, would be to make a highly counterintuitive claim that begs the important questions. This is not to say that highly counterintuitive claims are always false, but they need to be supported by extremely strong arguments. So the crucial question is: are there any compelling *arguments* for the claim that, on reflection, explaining the functions explains everything?

Type-A materialists often argue by analogy. They point out that in other areas of science, we accept that explaining the various functions explains the phenomena, so we should accept the same here. In response, an opponent may well accept that in other domains the functions are all we need to explain. In explaining life, for example, the only phenomena that present themselves as needing explanation are phenomena of adaptation, growth, metabolism, reproduction, and so on, and there is nothing else that even calls out for explanation. But the opponent holds that the case of consciousness is different and possibly unique, precisely because there is something else, phenomenal experience, that calls out for explanation. The type-A materialist must either deny even the appearance of a further explanandum, which seems to deny the obvious, or accept the apparent disanalogy and give further substantial arguments for why, contrary to appearances, only the functions need to be explained.

At this point, type-A materialists often press a different sort of analogy, holding that at various points in the past, thinkers held that there was an analogous epistemic gap for other phenomena, but that these turned out to be physically explained. For example, Dennett (1996) suggests that a vitalist might have held that there was a further "hard problem" of life over and above explaining the biological function, but that this would have been misguided.

On examining the cases, however, the analogies do not support the type-A materialist. Vitalists typically *accepted*, implicitly or explicitly, that the biological functions in question were what needed explaining. Their vitalism arose because they thought that the functions (adaptation, growth, reproduction, and so on) would not be physically explained. So this is quite different from the case of consciousness. The disanalogy is very clear in the case of Broad. Broad was a vitalist about life, holding that the functions would require a non-mechanical explanation. But at the same time, he held that in the case of life, unlike the case of consciousness, the only evidence we have for the phenomenon is behavioral, and that "being alive" means exhibiting certain sorts of behavior. Other vitalists were less explicit, but very few of them held that something more than the functions needed explaining (except consciousness itself, in some cases). If a vitalist had held this, the obvious reply would have been that there is no reason to believe in such an explanandum. So there is no analogy here.[13]

So these arguments by analogy have no force for the type-A materialist. In other cases, it was always clear that structure and function exhausted the apparent explananda, apart from those tied directly to consciousness itself. So the type-A materialist needs to address the apparent further explanandum in the case of consciousness head on: either flatly denying it, or giving substantial arguments to dissolve it.

Some arguments for type-A materialists proceed indirectly, by pointing out the unsavory metaphysical or epistemological consequences of rejecting the view: e.g., that the rejection leads to dualism, or to problems involving knowledge of consciousness.[14] An opponent will either embrace the consequences or deny that they are consequences. As long as the consequences are not completely untenable, then for the type-A materialist to make progress, this sort of argument needs to be supplemented by a substantial direct argument against the further explanandum.

Such direct arguments are surprisingly hard to find. Many arguments for type-A materialism end up presupposing the conclusion at crucial points. For example, it is sometimes argued (e.g., Rey 1995) that there is no reason to postulate qualia, since they are not needed to explain behavior; but this argument presupposes that only behavior needs explaining. The opponent will hold that qualia are an explanandum in their own right. Similarly, Dennett's (1991) use of "heterophenomenology" (verbal reports) as the primary data to ground his theory of consciousness appears to rest on the assumption that these reports are what need explaining, or that the only "seemings" that need explaining are dispositions to react and report.

One way to argue for type-A materialism is to argue that there is some intermediate X such that (i) explaining functions suffices to explain X, and (ii) explaining X suffices to explain consciousness. One possible X here is *representation*: it is often held both that conscious states are representational states, representing things in the world, and that we can explain representation in functional terms. If so, it may seem to follow that we can explain consciousness in functional terms. On examination, though, this argument appeals to an ambiguity in the notion of representation. There is a notion of *functional representation*, on which P is represented roughly when a system responds to P and/or produces behavior appropriate for P. In this sense, explaining functioning may explain representation, but explaining representation does not explain consciousness. There is also a notion of *phenomenal representation*, on which P is represented roughly when a system has a conscious experience as if P. In this sense, explaining representation may explain consciousness, but explaining functioning does not explain representation. Either way, the epistemic gap between the functional and the phenomenal remains as wide as ever. Similar sorts of equivocation can be found with other X's that might be appealed to here, such as "perception" or "information."

Perhaps the most interesting arguments for type-A materialism are those that argue that we can give a physical explanation of our *beliefs* about consciousness, such as the belief that we are conscious, the belief that consciousness is a further explanandum, and the belief that consciousness is non-physical. From here it is argued that once we have explained the belief, we have done enough to explain, or to explain away, the phenomenon (e.g., Clark 2000, Dennett forthcoming). Here it is worth noting that this only works if the beliefs themselves are functionally analyzable; Chalmers (2002a) gives reason to deny this. But even if one accepts that beliefs are ultimately functional, this claim then reduces to the claim that explaining our dispositions to talk about consciousness (and the like) explains everything. An opponent will deny this claim: explaining the dispositions to report may remove the third-person warrant (based on observation of others) for accepting a further explanandum, but it does not remove the crucial first-person warrant (from one's own case). Still, this is a strategy that deserves extended discussion.

At a certain point, the debate between type-A materialists and their opponents usually comes down to intuition: most centrally, the intuition that consciousness (in a non-functionally defined sense) exists, or that there is something that needs to be explained (over and above explaining the functions). This claim does not gain its support from argument, but from a sort of observation, along with rebuttal of counterarguments. The intuition appears to be shared by the large majority of philosophers, scientists, and others; and it is so strong that to deny it, a type-A materialist needs exceptionally powerful arguments. The result is that even among materialists, type-A materialists are a distinct minority.

5.5 Type-B Materialism[15]

According to type-B materialism, there is an epistemic gap between the physical and phenomenal domains, but there is no ontological gap. According to this view, zombies and the like are conceivable, but they are not metaphysically possible. On this view, Mary is ignorant of some phenomenal truths from inside her room, but nevertheless these truths concern an underlying physical reality (when she leaves the room, she learns old facts in a new way). And on this view, while there is a hard problem distinct from the easy problems, it does not correspond to a distinct ontological domain.

The most common form of type-B materialism holds that phenomenal states can be *identified* with certain physical or functional states. This identity is held to be analogous in certain respects (although perhaps not in all respects) with the identity between water and H_2O, or between genes and DNA.[16] These identities are not derived through conceptual analysis, but are discovered empirically: the concept *water* is different from the concept H_2O, but they are found to refer to the same thing in nature. On the type-B view, something similar applies to consciousness: the concept of consciousness is distinct from any physical or functional concepts, but we may discover empirically that these refer to the same thing in nature. In this way, we can explain why there is an epistemic gap between the physical and phenomenal domains, while denying any ontological gap. This yields the attractive possibility that we can acknowledge the deep epistemic problems of consciousness while retaining a materialist worldview.

Although such a view is attractive, it faces immediate difficulties. These difficulties stem from the fact that the character of the epistemic gap with consciousness seems to differ from that of epistemic gaps in other domains. For a start, there do not seem to be analogs of the epistemic arguments above in the cases of water, genes, and so on. To explain genes, we merely have to explain why systems function a certain way in transmitting hereditary characteristics; to explain water, we have to explain why a substance has a certain objective structure and behavior. Given a complete physical description of the world, Mary would be able to deduce all the relevant truths about water and about genes, by deducing which systems have the appropriate structure and function. Finally, it seems that we cannot coherently conceive of a world physically identical to our own, in which there is no water, or in which there are no genes. So there is no epistemic gap between the *complete* physical truth about the world and the truth about water and genes that is analogous to the epistemic gap with consciousness.

(Except, perhaps, for epistemic gaps that derive from the epistemic gap for consciousness. For example, perhaps Mary could not deduce or explain the perceptual *appearance* of water from the physical truth about the world. But this would just be another instance of the problem we are concerned with, and so cannot help the type-B materialist.)

So it seems that there is something unique about the case of consciousness. We can put this by saying that while the identity between genes and DNA is empirical, it is not *epistemically primitive*: the identity is itself deducible from the complete physical truth about the world. By contrast, the type-B materialist must hold that the identification between consciousness and physical or functional states is epistemically primitive: the identity is not deducible from the complete physical truth. (If it were deducible, type-A materialism would be true instead.) So the identity between consciousness and a physical state will be a sort of primitive principle in one's theory of the world.

Here, one might suggest that something has gone wrong. Elsewhere, the only sort of place that one finds this sort of primitive principle is in the fundamental laws of physics. Indeed, it is often held that this sort of primitiveness – the inability to be deduced from more basic principles – is the mark of a fundamental law of nature. In effect, the type-B materialist recognizes a principle that has the epistemic status of a fundamental law, but gives it the ontological status of an identity. An opponent will hold that this move is more akin to theft than to honest toil: elsewhere, identifications are grounded in explanations, and primitive principles are acknowledged as fundamental laws.

It is natural to suggest that the same should apply here. If one acknowledges the epistemically primitive connection between physical states and consciousness as a fundamental law, it will follow that consciousness is distinct from any physical property, since fundamental laws always connect distinct properties. So the usual standard will lead to one of the non-reductive views discussed in the second half of this chapter. By contrast, the type-B materialist takes an observed connection between physical and phenomenal states, unexplainable in more basic terms, and suggests that it is an identity. This suggestion is made largely in order to preserve a prior commitment to materialism. Unless there is an independent case for primitive identities, the suggestion will seem at best ad hoc and mysterious, and at worst incoherent.

A type-B materialist might respond in various ways. First, some (e.g., Papineau 1993) suggest that identities do not *need* to be explained, so are always primitive. But we have seen that identities in other domains can at least be *deduced* from more basic truths, and so are not primitive in the relevant sense. Secondly, some (e.g., Block and Stalnaker 1999) suggest that even truths involving water and genes cannot be deduced from underlying physical truths. This matter is too complex to go into here (see Chalmers and Jackson 2001 for a response[17]), but one can note that the epistemic arguments outlined at the beginning suggest a very strong disanalogy between consciousness and other cases. Thirdly, some (e.g., Loar 1990/1997) acknowledge that identities involving consciousness are unlike other identities by being epistemically primitive, but seek to explain this uniqueness by appealing to unique features of the concept of consciousness. This response is perhaps the most interesting, and I will return to it.

There is another line that a type-B materialist can take. One can first note that an *identity* between consciousness and physical states is not strictly required for a materialist position. Rather, one can plausibly hold that materialism about consciousness simply requires that physical states *necessitate* phenomenal states, in that it is metaphysically impossible for the physical states to be present while the phenomenal states are absent or different. That is, materialism requires that entailments P⊃Q be necessary, where P is the complete physical truth about the world and Q is an arbitrary phenomenal truth.

At this point, a type-B materialist can naturally appeal to the work of Kripke (1980), which suggests that some truths are necessarily true without being a priori. For example, Kripke suggests that "water is H_2O" is necessary – true in all possible worlds – but not knowable a priori. Here, a type-B materialist can suggest that P⊃Q may be a Kripkean a posteriori necessity, like "water is H_2O" (though it should be noted that Kripke himself denies this claim). If so, then we would *expect* there to be an epistemic gap, since there is no a priori entailment from P to Q, but at the same time there will be no ontological gap. In this way, Kripke's work can seem to be just what the type-B materialist needs.

Here, some of the issues that arose previously arise again. One can argue that in other domains, necessities are not epistemically primitive. The necessary connection between water and H_2O may be a posteriori, but it can itself be deduced from a complete physical description of the world (one can deduce that water is identical to H_2O, from which it follows that water is necessarily H_2O). The same applies to the other necessities that Kripke discusses. By contrast, the type-B materialist must hold that the connection between physical states and consciousness is epistemically primitive, in that it cannot be deduced from the complete physical truth about the world. Again, one can suggest that this sort of primitive necessary connection is mysterious and ad hoc, and that the connection should instead be viewed as a fundamental law of nature.

I will discuss further problems with these necessities in the next section. But here, it is worth noting that there is a sense in which any type-B materialist position gives up on reductive explanation. Even if type-B materialism is true, we cannot give consciousness the same sort of explanation that we give genes and the like, in purely physical terms. Rather, our explanation will always require explanatorily primitive principles to bridge the gap from the physical to the phenomenal. The *explanatory* structure of a theory of consciousness, on such a view, will be very much unlike that of a materialist theory in other domains, and very much like the explanatory structure of the non-reductive theories described below. By labeling these principles identities or necessities rather than laws, the view may preserve the letter of materialism; but by requiring primitive bridging principles, it sacrifices much of materialism's spirit.

5.6 The Two-Dimensional Argument Against Type-B Materialism

As discussed above, the type-B materialist holds that zombie worlds and the like are conceivable (there is no contradiction in P¬Q) but are not metaphysically possible. That is, P⊃Q is held to be an a posteriori necessity, akin to such a posteriori necessities as "water is H_2O." We can analyze this position in more depth by taking a closer look at the Kripkean cases of a posteriori necessity. This material is somewhat technical (hence the separate section) and can be skipped if necessary on a first reading.

It is often said that in Kripkean cases, conceivability does not entail possibility: it is conceivable that water is not H_2O (in that it is coherent to suppose that water is not H_2O), but it is not possible that water is not H_2O. But at the same time, it seems that there is *some* possibility in the vicinity of what one conceives. When one conceives that water is not H_2O, one conceives of a world W (the XYZ-world) in which the watery liquid in the oceans is not H_2O, but XYZ, say. There is no reason to doubt that the XYZ-world is metaphysically possible. If Kripke is correct, the XYZ-world is not correctly described as one in which water is XYZ. Nevertheless, this world is relevant to the truth of "water is XYZ" in a slightly different way, which can be brought out as follows.

One can say that the XYZ-world could *turn out* to be actual, in that for all we know a priori, the actual world is just like the XYZ-world. And one can say that *if* the XYZ-world turns out to be actual, it will turn out that water is XYZ. Similarly: if we hypothesize that the XYZ-world is actual, we should rationally conclude on that basis that water is not H_2O. That is, there is a deep *epistemic* connection between the XYZ-world and "water is not H_2O." Even Kripke allows that it is *epistemically possible* that water is not H_2O (in the broad sense that this is not ruled out a priori). It seems that the epistemic possibility that the XYZ-world is actual is a specific instance of the epistemic possibility that water is not H_2O.

Here, we adopt a special attitude to a world W. We think of W as an epistemic possibility: as a way the world might actually be. When we do this, we consider W *as actual*. When we think of W as actual, it may make a given sentence S true or false. For example, when thinking of the XYZ-world as actual, it makes "water is not H_2O" true. This is brought out in the intuitive judgment that if W turns out to be actual, it will turn out that water is not H_2O, and that the epistemic possibility that W is actual is an instance of the epistemic possibility that water is H_2O.

By contrast, one can also consider a world W *as counterfactual*. When we do this, we acknowledge that the character of the actual world is already fixed, and we think of W as a counterfactual way things might have been but are not. If Kripke is right, then if the watery stuff *had been* XYZ, XYZ would nevertheless not have been water. So when we consider the XYZ-world as counterfactual, it does not make "water is not H_2O" true. Considered as counterfactual, we describe the XYZ-world in light of the actual-world fact that water is H_2O, and we conclude that XYZ is not water but merely watery stuff. These results do not conflict: they simply involve two different ways of considering and describing possible worlds. Kripke's claims consider *counterfactual* evaluation of worlds, whereas the claims in the previous paragraph concern the *epistemic* evaluation of worlds.

One can formalize this using *two-dimensional semantics*.[18] We can say that if W considered as actual makes S true, then W *verifies* S, and that if W considered as counterfactual makes S true, then W *satisfies* S. Verification involves the epistemic evaluation of worlds, whereas satisfaction involves the counterfactual evaluation of worlds. Correspondingly, we can associate S with different *intensions*, or functions from worlds to truth values. The *primary* (or epistemic) intension of S is a function that is true at a world W iff W verifies S, and the *secondary* (or subjunctive) intension is a function that is true at a world W if W satisfies S. For example, where S is "water is not H_2O," and W is the XYZ-world, we can say that W verifies S but W does not satisfy S; and we can say that the primary intension of S is true at W, but the secondary intension of S is false at W.

With this in mind, one can suggest that when a statement S is conceivable – that is, when its truth cannot be ruled out a priori – then there is some world that verifies S, or equivalently, there is some world at which S's primary intension is true. This makes intuitive sense: when S is conceivable, S represents an epistemic possibility. It is natural to suggest that corresponding to these epistemic possibilities are specific worlds W, such that when these are considered *as* epistemic possibilities, they verify S. That is, W is such that intuitively, if W turns out to be actual, it would turn out that S.

This model seems to fit all of Kripke's cases. For example, Kripke holds that it is an a posteriori necessity that heat is the motion of molecules. So it is conceivable in the relevant sense that heat is not the motion of molecules. Corresponding to this conceivable scenario is a world W in which heat sensations are caused by something other than the motion of molecules. W represents an epistemic possibility: and we can say that if W turns out to be actual, it will turn out that heat is not the motion of molecules. The same goes in many other cases. The moral is that these Kripkean phenomena involve two different ways of thinking of possible worlds, with just one underlying space of worlds.

If this principle is applied to the case of type-B materialism, trouble immediately arises. As before, let P be the complete physical truth about the world, and let Q be a phenomenal truth. Let us say that S is conceivable when the truth of S is not ruled out a priori. Then one can mount an argument as follows:[19]

(1) P∧¬Q is conceivable.
(2) If P∧¬Q is conceivable, then a world verifies P∧¬Q.
(3) If a world verifies P∧¬Q, then a world satisfies P∧¬Q or type-F monism is true.
(4) If a world satisfies P∧¬Q, materialism is false.
———
(5) Materialism is false or type-F monism is true.

The type-B materialist grants premise (1): to deny this would be to accept type-A materialism. Premise (2) is an instance of the general principle discussed above. Premise (4) can be taken as definitive of materialism. As for premise (3): in general one cannot immediately move from a world verifying S to a world satisfying S, as the case of "water is H_2O" (and the XYZ-world) suggests. But in the case of P∧¬Q, a little reflection on the nature of P and Q takes us in that direction, as follows.

First, Q. Here, it is plausible that if W verifies "there is consciousness," then W satisfies "there is consciousness," and vice versa. This corresponds to the Kripkean point that in the case of consciousness, there is no distinction analogous to that between water itself and mere watery stuff. To put it intuitively, if W verifies "there is consciousness," it contains something that at least *feels* conscious, and if something *feels* conscious, it *is* conscious. One can hold more generally that the primary and secondary intensions of our core phenomenal concepts are the same (see Chalmers 2002a). It follows that if world W verifies ¬Q, W satisfies ¬Q. (This claim is not required for the argument to go through, but it is plausible and makes things more straightforward.)

Second, P. A type-B materialist might seek to evade the argument by arguing that while W verifies P, it does not satisfy P. On reflection, the only way this might work is as follows. If a world verifies P, it must have at least the *structure* of the actual physical world. The only reason why W might not satisfy P is that it lacks the intrinsic properties underlying this structure in the actual world. (On this view, the primary intension of a physical concept picks out whatever property plays a certain role in a given world, and the secondary intension picks out the actual intrinsic property across all worlds.) If this difference in W is responsible for the absence of consciousness in W, it follows that consciousness in the actual world is not necessitated by the structural aspects of physics, but by its underlying intrinsic nature. This is precisely the position I call type-F monism, or "panprotopsychism." Type-F monism is an interesting and important position, but it is much more radical than type-B materialism as usually conceived, and I count it as a different position. I will defer discussion of the reasoning and of the resulting position until later.

It follows that premise (4) is correct. If a world verifies $P \wedge \neg Q$, then either a world satisfies $P \wedge \neg Q$, or type-F monism is true. Setting aside type-F monism for now, it follows that the physical truth about our world does not necessitate the phenomenal truth, and materialism is false.

This conclusion is in effect a consequence of (i) the claim that $P \wedge \neg Q$ is conceivable (in the relevant sense), (ii) the claim that when S is conceivable, there is a world that verifies S, and (iii) some straightforward reasoning. A materialist might respond by denying (i), but that is simply to deny the relevant epistemic gap between the physical and the phenomenal, and so to deny type-B materialism. I think there is little promise for the type-B materialist in denying the reasoning involved in (iii). So the only hope for the type-B materialist is to deny the central thesis (ii).[20]

To do this, a type-B materialist could deny the coherence of the distinction between verification and satisfaction, or accept that the distinction is coherent but deny that thesis (ii) holds even in the standard Kripkean cases, or accept that thesis (ii) holds in the standard Kripkean cases but deny that it holds in the special case of consciousness. The first two options deserve exploration, but I think they are ultimately unpromising, as the distinction and the thesis appear to fit the Kripkean phenomena very well. Ultimately, I think a type-B materialist must hold that the case of consciousness is special, and that the thesis that holds elsewhere fails here.

On this view, the a posteriori necessities connecting the physical and phenomenal domains are much stronger than those in other domains in that they are verified by all worlds. Elsewhere, I have called these unusual a posteriori necessities *strong necessities*, and have argued that there is no good reason to believe they exist. As with explanatorily primitive identities, they appear to be primitive facts postulated in an ad hoc way, largely in order to save a theory, with no support from cases elsewhere. Further, one can argue that this view leads to an underlying *modal dualism*, with independent primitive domains of logical and metaphysical possibility; and one can argue that this is unacceptable.

Perhaps the most interesting response from a type-B materialist is to acknowledge that strong necessities are unique to the case of consciousness, and to try to explain this uniqueness in terms of special features of our conceptual system. For example, Christopher Hill (1997) has argued that one can predict the epistemic gap in the case of consciousness from the fact that physical concepts and phenomenal concepts have different conceptual roles. Brian Loar (1990/1997) has appealed to the claim that phenomenal concepts are recognitional concepts that lack contingent modes of presentation. Joseph Levine (2000) has argued that phenomenal concepts have non-ascriptive modes of presentation. In response, I have argued (Chalmers 1999) that these responses do not work, and that there are systematic reasons why they cannot work.[21] But it is likely that further attempts in this direction will be forthcoming. This remains one of the key areas of debate on the metaphysics of consciousness.

Overall, my own view is that there is little reason to think that explanatorily primitive identities or strong necessities exist. There is no good *independent* reason to believe in them: the best reason to postulate them is to save material-ism, but in the context of a debate over whether materialism is true this reasoning is uncompelling, especially if there are viable alternatives. Nevertheless, further investigation into the key issues underlying this debate is likely to be philosophic-ally fruitful.

5.7 Type-C Materialism

According to type-C materialism, there is a deep epistemic gap between the physical and phenomenal domains, but it is closable in principle. On this view, zombies and the like are conceivable for us now, but they will not be conceivable in the limit. On this view, it currently seems that Mary lacks information about the phenomenal, but in the limit there would be no information that she lacks. And on this view, while we cannot see now how to solve the hard problem in physical terms, the problem is solvable in principle.

This view is initially very attractive. It appears to acknowledge the deep ex-planatory gap with which we seem to be faced, while at the same time allowing that the apparent gap may be due to our own limitations. There are different versions of the view. Nagel (1974) has suggested that just as the Presocratics could not have understood how matter could be energy, we cannot understand how consciousness could be physical, but a conceptual revolution might allow the relevant understanding. Churchland (1997) suggests that even if we cannot now imagine how consciousness could be a physical process, that is simply a psycho-logical limitation on our part that further progress in science will overcome. Van Gulick (1993) suggests that conceivability arguments are question-begging, since once we have a good explanation of consciousness, zombies and the like will no longer be conceivable. McGinn (1989) has suggested that the problem may be unsolvable by humans because of deep limitations in our cognitive abilities, but that it nevertheless has a solution in principle.

One way to put the view is as follows. Zombies and the like are prima facie conceivable (for us now, with our current cognitive processes), but they are not *ideally* conceivable (under idealized rational reflection). Or we could say: phe-nomenal truths are deducible in principle from physical truths, but the deducibility is akin to that of a complex truth of mathematics: it is accessible in principle (perhaps accessible a priori), but is not accessible to us now, perhaps because the reasoning required is currently beyond us, or perhaps because we do not cur-rently grasp all the required physical truths. If this is so, then it will appear to us that there is a gap between physical processes and consciousness, but there will be no gap in nature.

Despite its appeal, I think that the type-C view is inherently unstable. Upon examination, it turns out either to be untenable, or to collapse into one of the other views on the table. In particular, it seems that the view must collapse into a version of type-A materialism, type-B materialism, type-D dualism, or type-F monism, and so is not ultimately a distinct option.

One way to hold that the epistemic gap might be closed in the limit is to hold that in the limit, we will see that explaining the functions explains everything, and that there is no further explanandum. It is at least coherent to hold that we currently suffer from some sort of conceptual confusion or unclarity that leads us to believe that there is a further explanandum, and that this situation could be cleared up by better reasoning. I will count this position as a version of type-A materialism, not type-C materialism: it is obviously closely related to standard type-A materialism (the main difference is whether we have yet had the relevant insight), and the same issues arise. Like standard type-A materialism, this view ultimately stands or falls with the strength of (actual and potential) first-order arguments that dissolve any apparent further explanandum.

Once type-A materialism is set aside, the potential options for closing the epistemic gap are highly constrained. These constraints are grounded in the nature of physical concepts, and in the nature of the concept of consciousness. The basic problem has already been mentioned. First: physical descriptions of the world characterize the world in terms of structure and dynamics. Secondly: from truths about structure and dynamics, one can deduce only further truths about structure and dynamics. And thirdly: truths about consciousness are not truths about structure and dynamics. But we can take these steps one at a time.

First, a microphysical description of the world specifies a distribution of particles, fields, and waves in space and time. These basic systems are characterized by their spatio-temporal properties, and properties such as mass, charge, and quantum wave function state. These latter properties are ultimately defined in terms of spaces of states that have a certain abstract structure (e.g., the space of continuously varying real quantities, or of Hilbert space states), such that the states play a certain causal role with respect to other states. We can subsume spatio-temporal descriptions and descriptions in terms of properties in these formal spaces under the rubric of *structural* descriptions. The state of these systems can change over time in accord with dynamic principles defined over the relevant properties. The result is a description of the world in terms of its underlying spatio-temporal and formal structure, and dynamic evolution over this structure.

Some type-C materialists hold we do not yet have a complete physics, so we cannot know what such a physics might explain. But here we do not need to have a complete physics: we simply need the claim that physical descriptions are in terms of structure and dynamics. This point is general across physical theories. Such novel theories as relativity, quantum mechanics, and the like may introduce new structures, and new dynamics over those structures, but the general point (and the gap with consciousness) remains.

A type-C materialist might hold that there could be new physical theories that go beyond structure and dynamics. But given the character of physical explanation, it is unclear what sort of theory this could be. Novel physical properties are postulated for their potential in explaining existing physical phenomena, themselves characterized in terms of structure and dynamics, and it seems that structure and dynamics always suffice here. One possibility is that instead of postulating novel properties, physics might end up appealing to consciousness itself, in the way that some theorists hold that quantum mechanics does. This possibility cannot be excluded, but it leads to a view on which consciousness is itself irreducible, and is therefore to be classed in a non-reductive category (type D or type F).

There is one appeal to a "complete physics" that should be taken seriously. This is the idea that current physics characterizes its underlying properties (such as mass and charge) in terms of abstract structures and relations, but it leaves open their intrinsic natures. On this view, a complete physical description of the world must also characterize the intrinsic properties that ground these structures and relations; and once such intrinsic properties are invoked, physics will go beyond structure and dynamics, in such a way that truths about consciousness may be entailed. The relevant intrinsic properties are unknown to us, but they are knowable in principle. This is an important position, but it is precisely the position discussed under type F, so I defer discussion of it until then.

Secondly, what can be inferred from this sort of description in terms of structure and dynamics? A low-level microphysical description can entail all sorts of surprising and interesting macroscopic properties, as with the emergence of chemistry from physics, of biology from chemistry, or more generally of complex emergent behaviors in complex systems theory. But in all these cases, the complex properties that are entailed are nevertheless structural and dynamic: they describe complex spatio-temporal structures and complex dynamic patterns of behavior over those structures. So these cases support the general principle that, from structure and dynamics, one can infer only structure and dynamics.

A type-C materialist might suggest there are some truths that are not themselves structural-dynamical that are nevertheless implied by a structural-dynamical description. It might be argued, perhaps, that truths about *representation* or *belief* have this character. But as we saw earlier, it seems clear that any sense in which these truths are implied by a structural-dynamic description involves a tacitly functional sense of representation or of belief. This is what we would expect: if claims involving these can be seen (on conceptual grounds) to be true *in virtue* of a structural-dynamic descriptions holding, the notions involved must themselves be structural-dynamic, at some level.

One might hold that there is some intermediate notion X, such that truths about X hold in virtue of structural-dynamic descriptions, and truths about consciousness hold in virtue of X. But as in the case of type-A materialism, either X is functionally analyzable (in the broad sense), in which case the second step fails, or X is not functionally analyzable, in which case the first step fails. This is brought out clearly in the case of representation: for the notion of functional representation, the first step fails, and for the notion of phenomenal representation, the second step fails. So this sort of strategy can only work by equivocation.

Thirdly, does explaining or deducing complex structure and dynamics suffice to explain or deduce consciousness? It seems clearly not, for the usual reasons. Mary could know from her black-and-white room all about the spatio-temporal structure and dynamics of the world at all levels, but this will not tell her what it is like to see red. For any complex macroscopic structural or dynamic description of a system, one can conceive of that description being instantiated without consciousness. And explaining structure and dynamics of a human system is only to solve the easy problems, while leaving the hard problems untouched. To resist this last step, an opponent would have to hold that explaining structure and dynamics *thereby* suffices to explain consciousness. The only remotely tenable way to do this would be to embrace type-A materialism, which we have set aside.

A type-C materialist might suggest that instead of leaning on dynamics (as a type-A materialist does), one could lean on structure. Here, spatio-temporal structure seems very unpromising: to explain a system's size, shape, position, motion, and so on is clearly not to explain consciousness. A final possibility is leaning on the structure present in conscious states themselves. Conscious states have structure: there is both internal structure within a single complex conscious state, and there are patterns of similarities and differences between conscious states. But this structure is a distinctively *phenomenal* structure, quite different in kind from the spatio-temporal and formal structure present in physics. The structure of a complex phenomenal state is not spatio-temporal structure (although it may involve the representation of spatio-temporal structure), and the similarities and differences between phenomenal states are not formal similarities and differences, but differences between specific phenomenal characters. This is reflected in the fact that one can conceive of any spatio-temporal structure and formal structure without any associated phenomenal structure; one can know about the first without knowing about the second; and so on. So the epistemic gap is as wide as ever.

The basic problem with any type-C materialist strategy is that epistemic implication from A to B requires some sort of *conceptual hook* by virtue of which the condition described in A can satisfy the conceptual requirements for the truth of B. When a physical account implies truths about life, for example, it does so in virtue of implying information about the macroscopic functioning of physical systems, of the sort required for life: here, broadly functional notions provide the conceptual hook. But in the case of consciousness, no such conceptual hook is available, given the structural-dynamic character of physical concepts, and the quite different character of the concept of consciousness.

Ultimately, it seems that any type-C strategy is doomed for familiar reasons. Once we accept that the concept of consciousness is not itself a functional concept, and that physical descriptions of the world are structural-dynamic descriptions, there is simply no conceptual room for it to be implied by a physical description. So the only room left is to hold that consciousness is a broadly functional concept after all (accepting type-A materialism), to hold that there is more in physics than structure and dynamics (accepting type-D dualism or type-F monism), or to hold that the truth of materialism does not require an implication from physics to consciousness (accepting type-B materialism).[22] So in the end, there is no separate space for the type-C materialist.

5.8   Interlude

Are there any other options for the materialist? One further option is to reject the distinctions on which this taxonomy rests. For example, some philosophers, especially followers of Quine (1951), reject any distinction between conceptual truth and empirical truth, or between the a priori and the a posteriori, or between the contingent and the necessary. One who is sufficiently Quinean might therefore reject the distinction between type-A and type-B materialism, holding that talk of epistemic implication and/or modal entailment is ungrounded, but that materialism is true nevertheless. We might call such a view type-Q materialism. Still, even on this view, similar issues arise. Some Quineans hold that explaining the functions explains everything (Dennett may be an example); if so, all the problems of type-A materialism arise. Others hold that we can postulate identities between physical states and conscious states in virtue of the strong isomorphic connections between them in nature (Paul Churchland may be an example); if so, the problems of type-B materialism arise. Others may appeal to novel future sorts of explanation; if so, the problems of type-C materialism arise. So the Quinean approach cannot avoid the relevant problems.

Leaving this sort of view aside, it looks like the only remotely viable options for the materialist are type-A materialism and type-B materialism. I think that other views are either ultimately unstable, or collapse into one of these (or the three remaining options).[23] It seems to me that the costs of these views – denying the manifest explanandum in the first case, and embracing primitive identities or strong necessities in the second case – suggest very strongly that they are to be avoided unless there are no viable alternatives.

So the residual question is whether there are viable alternatives. If consciousness is not necessitated by physical truths, then it must involve something ontologically novel in the world: to use Kripke's metaphor, after fixing all the physical truths, God had to do more work to fix all the truths about consciousness. That is, there must be ontologically fundamental features of the world over and above the features characterized by physical theory. We are used to the idea that some features of the world are fundamental: in physics, features such as spacetime, mass, and charge are taken as fundamental and not further explained. If the arguments against materialism are correct, these features from physics do not exhaust the fundamental features of the world: we need to expand our catalog of the world's basic features.

There are two possibilities here. First, it could be that consciousness is itself a fundamental feature of the world, like spacetime and mass. In this case, we can say that phenomenal properties are fundamental. Secondly, it could be that consciousness is not itself fundamental, but is necessitated by some more primitive fundamental feature X that is not itself necessitated by physics. In this case, we might call X a *protophenomenal* property, and we can say that protophenomenal properties are fundamental. I will typically put things in terms of the first possibility for ease of discussion, but the discussion that follows applies equally to the second. Either way, consciousness involves something novel and fundamental in the world.

The question then arises: how do these novel fundamental properties relate to the already acknowledged fundamental properties of the world, namely those invoked in microphysics? In general, where there are fundamental properties, there are fundamental laws. So we can expect that there will be some sort of fundamental principles – psychophysical laws – connecting physical and phenomenal properties. Like the fundamental laws of relativity or quantum mechanics, these psychophysical laws will not be deducible from more basic principles, but instead will be taken as primitive.

But what is the character of these laws? An immediate worry is that the microphysical aspects of the world are often held to be causally closed, in that every microphysical state has a microphysical sufficient cause. How are fundamental phenomenal properties to be integrated with this causally closed network?

There seem to be three main options for the non-reductionist here. First, one could deny the causal closure of the microphysical, holding that there are causal gaps in microphysical dynamics that are filled by a causal role for distinct phenomenal properties: this is type-D dualism. Secondly, one could accept the causal closure of the microphysical and hold that phenomenal properties play no causal role with respect to the physical network: this is type-E dualism. Thirdly, one could accept that the microphysical network is causally closed, but hold that phenomenal properties are nevertheless integrated with it and play a causal role, by virtue of constituting the intrinsic nature of the physical: this is type-F monism.

In what follows, I will discuss each of these views. The discussion is necessarily speculative in certain respects, and I do not claim to establish that any one of the views is true or completely unproblematic. But I do aim to suggest that none of them has obvious fatal flaws, and that each deserves further investigation.

5.9 Type-D Dualism

Type-D dualism holds that microphysics is not causally closed, and that phenomenal properties play a causal role in affecting the physical world.[24] On this view, usually known as *interactionism*, physical states will cause phenomenal states, and phenomenal states cause physical states. The corresponding psychophysical laws will run in both directions. On this view, the evolution of microphysical states will not be determined by physical principles alone. Psychophysical principles specifying the effect of phenomenal states on physical states will also play an irreducible role.

The most familiar version of this sort of view is Descartes's substance dualism (hence D for Descartes), on which there are separate interacting mental and physical substances or entities. But this sort of view is also compatible with a property dualism, on which there is just one sort of substance or entity with both physical and phenomenal fundamental properties, such that the phenomenal properties play an irreducible role in affecting the physical properties. In particular, the view is compatible with an "emergentist" view such as Broad's, on which phenomenal properties are ontologically novel properties of physical systems (not deducible from microphysical properties alone), and have novel effects on microphysical properties (not deducible from microphysical principles alone). Such a view would involve basic principles of "downward" causation of the mental on the microphysical (hence also D for downward causation).

It is sometimes objected that distinct physical and mental states could not interact, since there is no causal nexus between them. But one lesson from Hume and from modern science is that the same goes for any fundamental causal interactions, including those found in physics. Newtonian science reveals no causal nexus by which gravitation works, for example; rather, the relevant laws are simply fundamental. The same goes for basic laws in other physical theories. And the same, presumably, applies to fundamental psychophysical laws: there is no need for a causal nexus distinct from the physical and mental properties themselves.

By far the most influential objection to interactionism is that it is incompatible with physics. It is widely held that science tells us that the microphysical realm is causally closed, so that there is no room for mental states to have any effects. An interactionist might respond in various ways. For example, it could be suggested that although no experimental studies have revealed these effects, none has ruled them out. It might further be suggested that physical theory allows any number of basic *forces* (four as things stand, but there is always room for more), and that an extra force associated with a mental field would be a reasonable extension of existing physical theory. These suggestions would invoke significant revisions to physical theory, so are not to be made lightly; but one could argue that nothing rules them out.

By far the strongest response to this objection, however, is to suggest that far from ruling out interactionism, contemporary physics is positively encouraging to the possibility. On the standard formulation of quantum mechanics, the state of the world is described by a wave function, according to which physical entities are often in a superposed state (e.g., in a superposition of two different positions), even though superpositions are never directly observed. On the standard dynamics, the wave function can evolve in two ways: linear evolution by the Schrödinger equation (which tends to produce superposed states), and non-linear *collapses* from superposed states into non-superposed states. Schrödinger evolution is deterministic, but collapse is non-deterministic. Schrödinger evolution is constantly ongoing, but on the standard formulation, collapses occur only occasionally, on measurement.

The collapse dynamics leaves a door wide open for an interactionist interpretation. Any physical non-determinism might be held to leave room for non-physical effects, but the principles of collapse do much more than that. Collapse is supposed to occur on measurement. There is no widely agreed definition of what a measurement is, but there is one sort of event that everyone agrees is a measurement: observation by a conscious observer. Further, it seems that no purely physical criterion for a measurement can work, since purely physical systems are governed by the linear Schrödinger dynamics. As such, it is natural to suggest that a measurement is precisely a conscious observation, and that this conscious observation causes a collapse.

The claim should not be too strong: quantum mechanics does not force this interpretation of the situation onto us, and there are alternative interpretations of quantum mechanics on which there are no collapses, or on which measurement has no special role in collapse.[25] Nevertheless, quantum mechanics appears to be perfectly *compatible* with such an interpretation. In fact, one might argue that if one were to design elegant laws of physics that allow a role for the conscious mind, one could not do much better than the bipartite dynamics of standard quantum mechanics: one principle governing deterministic evolution in normal cases, and one principle governing non-deterministic evolution in special situations that have a prima facie link to the mental.

Of course such an interpretation of quantum mechanics is controversial. Many physicists reject it precisely because it is dualistic, giving a fundamental role to consciousness. This rejection is not surprising, but it carries no force when we have independent reason to hold that consciousness may be fundamental. There is some irony in the fact that philosophers reject interactionism on largely physical grounds[26] (it is incompatible with physical theory), while physicists reject an interactionist interpretation of quantum mechanics on largely philosophical grounds (it is dualistic). Taken conjointly, these reasons carry little force, especially in light of the arguments against materialism elsewhere in this chapter.

This sort of interpretation needs to be formulated in detail to be assessed.[27] I think the most promising version of such an interpretation allows conscious states to be correlated with the total quantum state of a system, with the extra constraint that conscious states (unlike physical states) can never be superposed. In a conscious physical system such as a brain, the physical and phenomenal states of the system will be correlated in a (non-superposed) quantum state. Upon observation of a superposed system, then Schrödinger evolution at the moment of observation would cause the observed system to become correlated with the brain, yielding a resulting superposition of brain states and so (by psychophysical correlation) a superposition of conscious states. But such a superposition cannot occur, so one of the potential resulting conscious states is somehow selected (presumably by a non-deterministic dynamic principle at the phenomenal level). The result is that (by psychophysical correlation) a definite brain state and a definite state of the observed object are also selected. The same might apply to the connection between consciousness and non-conscious processes in the brain: when superposed non-conscious processes threaten to affect consciousness, there will be some sort of selection. In this way, there is a causal role for consciousness in the physical world.

(Interestingly, such a theory may be empirically testable. In quantum mechanics, collapse theories yield predictions slightly different from no-collapse theories, and different hypotheses about the location of collapse yield predictions that differ from each other, although the differences are extremely subtle and are currently impossible to measure. If the relevant experiments can one day be performed, some outcomes would give us strong reason to accept a collapse theory, and might in turn give us grounds to accept a role for consciousness. As a bonus, this could even yield an empirical criterion for the presence of consciousness.)

There are any number of further questions concerning the precise formulation of such a view, its compatibility with physical theory more generally (e.g., relativity and quantum field theory), and its philosophical tenability (e.g., does this view yield the sort of causal role that we are inclined to think consciousness must have). But at the very least, it cannot be said that physical theory immediately rules out the possibility of an interactionist theory. Those who make this claim often raise their eyebrows when a specific theory such as quantum mechanics is mentioned; but this is quite clearly an inconsistent set of attitudes. If physics is supposed to rule out interactionism, then careful attention to the detail of physical theory is required.

All this suggests that there is at least room for a viable interactionism to be explored, and that the most common objection to interactionism has little force. Of course it does not entail that interactionism is true. There is much that is attractive about the view of the physical world as causally closed, and there is little direct evidence from cognitive science of the hypothesis that behavior cannot be wholly explained in terms of physical causes. Still, if we have independent reason to think that consciousness is irreducible, and if we wish to retain the intuitive view that consciousness plays a causal role, then this is a view to be taken very seriously.

5.10 Type-E Dualism

Type-E dualism holds that phenomenal properties are ontologically distinct from physical properties, and that the phenomenal has no effect on the physical.[28] This is the view usually known as *epiphenomenalism* (hence type-E): physical states cause phenomenal states, but not vice versa. On this view, psychophysical laws run in one direction only, from physical to phenomenal. The view is naturally combined with the view that the physical realm is causally closed: this further claim is not essential to type-E dualism, but it provides much of the motivation for the view.

As with type-D dualism, type-E dualism is compatible with a substance dualism with distinct physical and mental substances or entities, and is also compatible with a property dualism with one sort of substance or entity and two sorts of property. Again, it is compatible with an emergentism such as Broad's, on which mental properties are ontologically novel emergent properties of an underlying entity, but in this case although there are emergent qualities, there is no emergent downward causation.

Type-E dualism is usually put forward as respecting both consciousness and science: it simultaneously accommodates the anti-materialist arguments about consciousness and the causal closure of the physical. At the same time, type-E dualism is frequently rejected as deeply counterintuitive. If type-E dualism is correct, then phenomenal states have no effect on our actions, physically construed. For example, a sensation of pain will play no causal role in my hand's moving away from a flame; my experience of decision will play no causal role in my moving to a new country; and a sensation of red will play no causal role in my producing the utterance "I am experiencing red now." These consequences are often held to be obviously false, or at least unacceptable.

Still, the type-E dualist can reply that there is no direct *evidence* that contradicts their view. Our evidence reveals only regular connections between phenomenal states and actions, so that certain sorts of experience are typically followed by certain sorts of action. Being exposed to this sort of constant conjunction produces a strong *belief* in a causal connection (as Hume pointed out in another context); but it is nevertheless compatible with the absence of a causal connection. Indeed, it seems that if epiphenomenalism *were* true, we would have exactly the same evidence, and be led to believe that consciousness has a causal role for much the same reasons. So if epiphenomenalism is otherwise coherent and acceptable, it seems that these considerations do not provide strong reasons to reject it.[29]

Another objection holds that if consciousness is epiphenomenal, it could not have evolved by natural selection. The type-E dualist has a straightforward reply, however. On the type-E view, there are fundamental psychophysical laws associating physical and phenomenal properties. If evolution selects appropriate physical properties (perhaps involving physical or informational configurations in the brain), then the psychophysical laws will ensure that phenomenal properties are instantiated, too. If the laws have the right form, one can even expect that, as more complex physical systems are selected, more complex states of consciousness will evolve. In this way, physical evolution will carry the evolution of consciousness along with it as a sort of by-product.

Perhaps the most interesting objections to epiphenomenalism focus on the relation between consciousness and representations of consciousness. It is certainly at least strange to suggest that consciousness plays no causal role in my utterances of "I am conscious." Some have suggested more strongly that this rules out any *knowledge* of consciousness. It is often held that if a belief about X is to qualify as knowledge, the belief must be caused in some fashion by X. But if consciousness does not affect physical states, and if beliefs are physically constituted, then consciousness cannot cause beliefs. And even if beliefs are not physically constituted, it is not clear how epiphenomenalism can accommodate a causal connection between consciousness and belief.

In response, an epiphenomenalist can deny that knowledge always requires a causal connection. One can argue on independent grounds that there is a stronger connection between consciousness and beliefs about consciousness: consciousness plays a role in *constituting* phenomenal concepts and phenomenal beliefs. A red experience plays a role in constituting a belief that one is having a red experience, for example. If so, there is no causal distance between the experience and the belief. And one can argue that this immediate connection to experience and belief allows for the belief to be justified. If this is right, then epiphenomenalism poses no obstacle to knowledge of consciousness.

A related objection holds that my zombie twin would produce the same reports (e.g., "I am conscious"), caused by the same mechanisms, and that his reports are unjustified; if so, my own reports are unjustified. In response, one can hold that the true bearers of justification are beliefs, and that my zombie twin and I have *different* beliefs, involving different concepts, because of the role that consciousness plays in constituting my concepts but not the zombie's. Further, the fact that we produce isomorphic reports implies that a third-person observer might not be any more justified in believing that I am conscious than that the zombie is conscious, but it does not imply a difference in first-person justification. The first-person justification for my belief that I am conscious is not grounded in any way in my reports but rather in my experiences themselves, experiences that the zombie lacks.

I think that there is no knock-down objection to epiphenomenalism here. Still, it must be acknowledged that the situation is at least odd and counterintuitive. The oddness of epiphenomenalism is exacerbated by the fact that the relationship between consciousness and reports about consciousness seems to be something of a lucky coincidence, on the epiphenomenalist view. After all, if psychophysical laws are independent of physical evolution, then there will be possible worlds where physical evolution is the same as ours but the psychophysical laws are very different, so that there is a radical mismatch between reports and experiences. It seems lucky that we are in a world whose psychophysical laws match them up so well. In response, an epiphenomenalist might try to make the case that these laws are somehow the most "natural" and are to be expected; but there is at least a significant burden of proof here.

Overall, I think that epiphenomenalism is a coherent view without fatal problems. At the same time, it is an inelegant view, producing a fragmented picture of nature, on which physical and phenomenal properties are only very weakly integrated in the natural world. And of course it is a counterintuitive view that many people find difficult to accept. Inelegance and counterintuitiveness are better than incoherence; so if good arguments force us to epiphenomenalism as the most coherent view, then we should take it seriously. But at the same time, we have good reason to examine other views very carefully.

5.11 Type-F Monism

Type-F monism is the view that consciousness is constituted by the intrinsic properties of fundamental physical entities: that is, by the categorical bases of fundamental physical dispositions.[30] On this view, phenomenal or protophenomenal properties are located at the fundamental level of physical reality, and, in a certain sense, underlie physical reality itself.

This view takes its cue from Bertrand Russell's discussion of physics in *The Analysis of Matter* (1927). Russell pointed out that physics characterizes physical entities and properties by their relations to one another and to us. For example, a quark is characterized by its relations to other physical entities, and a property such as mass is characterized by an associated dispositional role, such as the tendency to resist acceleration. At the same time, physics says nothing about the intrinsic nature of these entities and properties. Where we have relations and dispositions, we expect some underlying intrinsic properties that ground the dispositions, characterizing the entities that stand in these relations.[31] But physics is silent about the intrinsic nature of a quark, or about the intrinsic properties that play the role associated with mass. So this is one metaphysical problem: what are the intrinsic properties of fundamental physical systems?

At the same time, there is another metaphysical problem: how can phenomenal properties be integrated with the physical world? Phenomenal properties seem to be intrinsic properties that are hard to fit in with the structural/dynamic character of physical theory; and arguably, they are the only intrinsic properties of which we have direct knowledge. Russell's insight was that we might solve both these problems at once. Perhaps the intrinsic properties of the physical world are themselves phenomenal properties. Or perhaps the intrinsic properties of the physical world are not phenomenal properties, but nevertheless constitute phenomenal properties: that is, perhaps they are protophenomenal properties. If so, then consciousness and physical reality are deeply intertwined.

This view holds the promise of integrating phenomenal and physical properties very tightly in the natural world. Here, nature consists of entities with intrinsic (proto)phenomenal qualities standing in causal relations within a spacetime manifold. Physics as we know it emerges from the relations between these entities, whereas consciousness as we know it emerges from their intrinsic nature. As a bonus, this view is perfectly compatible with the causal closure of the microphysical, and indeed with existing physical laws. The view can retain the *structure* of physical theory as it already exists; it simply supplements this structure with an intrinsic nature. And the view acknowledges a clear causal role for consciousness in the physical world: (proto)phenomenal properties serve as the ultimate categorical basis of all physical causation.

This view has elements in common with both materialism and dualism. From one perspective, it can be seen as a sort of materialism. If one holds that physical terms refer not to dispositional properties but the underlying intrinsic properties, then the protophenomenal properties can be seen as physical properties, thus preserving a sort of materialism. From another perspective, it can be seen as a sort of dualism. The view acknowledges phenomenal or protophenomenal properties as ontologically fundamental, and it retains an underlying duality between structural-dispositional properties (those directly characterized in physical theory) and intrinsic protophenomenal properties (those responsible for consciousness).

One might suggest that while the view arguably fits the letter of materialism, it shares the spirit of anti-materialism.

In its protophenomenal form, the view can be seen as a sort of neutral monism: there are underlying neutral properties X (the protophenomenal properties), such that the X properties are simultaneously responsible for constituting the physical domain (by their relations) and the phenomenal domain (by their collective intrinsic nature). In its phenomenal form, it can be seen as a sort of idealism, such that mental properties constitute physical properties, although these need not be mental properties in the mind of an observer, and they may need to be supplemented by causal and spatio-temporal properties in addition. One could also characterize this form of the view as a sort of panpsychism, with phenomenal properties ubiquitous at the fundamental level. One could give the view in its most general form the name *panprotopsychism*, with either protophenomenal or phenomenal properties underlying all of physical reality.

A type-F monist may have one of a number of attitudes to the zombie argument against materialism. Some type-F monists may hold that a complete physical description must be expanded to include an intrinsic description, and may consequently deny that zombies are conceivable. (We only think we are conceiving of a physically identical system because we overlook intrinsic properties.) Others could maintain that existing physical concepts refer via dispositions to those intrinsic properties that ground the dispositions. If so, these concepts have different primary and secondary intensions, and a type-F monist could correspondingly accept conceivability but deny possibility: we misdescribe the conceived world as physically identical to ours, when in fact it is just structurally identical.[32] Finally, a type-F monist might hold that physical concepts refer to dispositional properties, so that zombies are both conceivable and possible, and the intrinsic properties are not physical properties. The differences between these three attitudes seem to be ultimately terminological rather than substantive.

As for the knowledge argument, a type-F monist might insist that for Mary to have complete physical knowledge, she would have to have a description of the world involving concepts that directly characterize the intrinsic properties; if she had this (as opposed to her impoverished description involving dispositional concepts), she might thereby be in a position to know what it is like to see red. Regarding the explanatory argument, a type-F monist might hold that physical accounts involving intrinsic properties can explain more than structure and function. Alternatively, a type-F monist who sticks to dispositional physical concepts will make responses analogous to one of the other two responses above.

The type-F view is admittedly speculative, and it can sound strange at first hearing. Many find it extremely counterintuitive to suppose that fundamental physical systems have phenomenal properties: e.g., that there is something it is like to be an electron. The protophenomenal version of the view rejects this claim, but retains something of its strangeness: it seems that any properties responsible for constituting consciousness must be strange and unusual properties, of a sort that we might not expect to find in microphysical reality. Still, it is not clear that this strangeness yields any strong objections. Like epiphenomenalism, the view appears to be compatible with all our evidence, and there is no direct evidence against it. One can argue that if the view were true, things would appear to us just as they in fact appear. And we have learned from modern physics that the world is a strange place: we cannot expect it to obey all the dictates of common sense.

One might also object that we do not have any conception of what proto-phenomenal properties might be like, or of how they could constitute phenomenal properties. This is true, but one could suggest that this is merely a product of our ignorance. In the case of familiar physical properties, there were principled reasons (based on the character of physical concepts) for denying a constitutive connection to phenomenal properties. Here, there are no such principled reasons. At most, there is ignorance and absence of a connection. Of course it would be very desirable to form a positive conception of protophenomenal properties. Perhaps we can do this indirectly, by some sort of theoretical inference from the character of phenomenal properties to their underlying constituents; or perhaps knowledge of the nature of protophenomenal properties will remain beyond us. Either way, this is no reason to reject the truth of the view.[33]

There is one sort of principled problem in the vicinity, pointed out by William James (1890: ch. 6). Our phenomenology has a rich and specific structure: it is unified, bounded, differentiated into many different aspects, but with an underlying homogeneity to many of the aspects, and appears to have a single subject of experience. It is not easy to see how a distribution of a large number of individual microphysical systems, each with their own protophenomenal properties, could somehow add up to this rich and specific structure. Should one not expect something more like a disunified, jagged collection of phenomenal spikes?

This is a version of the *combination problem* for panpsychism (Seagar 1995), or what Stoljar (2001) calls the *structural mismatch* problem for the Russellian view (see also Foster 1991: 119–30). To answer it, it seems that we need a much better understanding of the *compositional* principles of phenomenology: that is, the principles by which phenomenal properties can be composed or constituted from underlying phenomenal properties, or protophenomenal properties. We have a good understanding of the principles of physical composition, but no real understanding of the principles of phenomenal composition. This is an area that deserves much close attention: I think it is easily the most serious problem for the type-F monist view. At this point, it is an open question whether or not the problem can be solved.

Some type-F monists appear to hold that they can avoid the combination problem by holding that phenomenal properties are the intrinsic properties of *high-level* physical dispositions (e.g., those involved in neural states), and need not be constituted by the intrinsic properties of microphysical states (hence they may also deny panprotopsychism). But this seems to be untenable: if the low-level network is causally closed and the high-level intrinsic properties are not constituted by low-level intrinsic properties, the high-level intrinsic properties will be epiphenomenal all over again, for familiar reasons. The only way to embrace this position would seem to be in combination with a denial of microphysical causal closure, holding that there are fundamental dispositions above the microphysical level, which have phenomenal properties as their grounds. But such a view would be indistinguishable from type-D dualism.[34] So a distinctive type-F monism will have to face the combination problem directly.

Overall, type-F monism promises a deeply integrated and elegant view of nature. No one has yet developed any sort of detailed theory in this class, and it is not yet clear whether such a theory can be developed. But at the same time, there appear to be no strong reasons to reject the view. As such, type-F monism is likely to provide fertile grounds for further investigation, and it may ultimately provide the best integration of the physical and the phenomenal within the natural world.

5.12   Conclusions

Are there any other options for the non-reductionist? There are two views that may not fit straightforwardly into the categories above.

First, some non-materialists hold that phenomenal properties are ontologically wholly distinct from physical properties, that microphysics is causally closed, but that phenomenal properties play a causal role with respect to the physical nevertheless. One way this might happen is by a sort of causal overdetermination: physical states causally determine behavior, but phenomenal states cause behavior at the same time. Another is by causal mediation: it might be that in at least some instances of microphysical causation from A to B, there is actually a causal connection from A to the mind to B, so that the mind enters the causal nexus without altering the structure of the network. And there may be further strategies here. We might call this class type-O dualism (taking overdetermination as a paradigm case). These views share much of the structure of the type-E view (causally closed physical world, distinct phenomenal properties), but escapes the charge of epiphenomenalism. The special causal setups of these views may be hard to swallow, and they share some of the same problems as the type-E view (e.g., the fragmented view of nature, and the "lucky" psychophysical laws), but this class should nevertheless be put on the table as an option.[35]

Second, some non-materialists are *idealists* (in a Berkeleyan sense), holding that the physical world is itself constituted by the conscious states of an observing agent. We might call this view type-I monism. It shares with type-F monism the property that phenomenal states play a role in constituting physical reality, but on the type-I view this happens in a very different way: not by having separate "microscopic" phenomenal states underlying each physical state, but rather by having physical states constituted holistically by a "macroscopic" phenomenal mind. This view seems to be non-naturalistic in a much deeper sense than any of the views above, and in particular seems to suffer from an absence of causal or explanatory closure in nature: once the natural explanation in terms of the external world is removed, highly complex regularities among phenomenal states have to be taken as unexplained in terms of simpler principles. But again, this sort of view should at least be acknowledged.

As I see things, the best options for a non-reductionist are type-D dualism, type-E dualism, or type-F monism: that is, interactionism, epiphenomenalism, or panprotopsychism. If we acknowledge the epistemic gap between the physical and the phenomenal, and we rule out primitive identities and strong necessities, then we are led to a disjunction of these three views. Each of the views has at least some promise, and none has clear fatal flaws. For my part, I give some credence to each of them. I think that in some ways the type-F view is the most appealing, but this sense is largely grounded in aesthetic considerations whose force is unclear.

The choice between these three views may depend in large part on the development of specific theories within these frameworks. Especially for the type-D view and type-F view, further theoretical work is crucial in assessing the theories (e.g., in explicating quantum interactionism, or in understanding phenomenal composition). It may also be that the empirical science of consciousness will give some guidance. As the science progresses, we will be led to infer simple principles that underlie correlations between physical and phenomenal states. It may be that these principles turn out to point strongly toward one or the other of these views: e.g., if simple principles connecting microphysical states to phenomenal or protophenomenal states can do the explanatory work, then we may have reason to favor a type-F view, while if the principles latch onto the physical world at a higher level, then we may have reason to favor a type-D or type-E view. And if consciousness has a specific pattern of effects on the physical world, as the type-D view suggests, then empirical studies ought in principle to be able to find these effects, although perhaps only with great difficulty.

Not everyone will agree that each of these views is viable. It may be that further examination will reveal deep problems with some of these views. But this further examination needs to be performed. There has been little critical examination of type-F views to date, for example; we have seen that the standard arguments against type-D views carry very little weight; and while arguments against type-E views carry some intuitive force, they are far from making a knock-down case against the views. I suspect that even if further examination reveals deep problems for some views in this vicinity, it is very unlikely that all such views will be eliminated.

In any case, this gives us some perspective on the mind–body problem. It is often held that even though it is hard to see how materialism could be true, materialism *must* be true, since the alternatives are unacceptable. As I see it, there are at least three prima facie acceptable alternatives to materialism on the table, each of which is compatible with a broadly naturalistic (even if not materialistic) worldview, and none of which has fatal problems. So given the clear arguments against materialism, it seems to me that we should at least tentatively embrace the conclusion that one of these views is correct. Of course all of the views discussed in this chapter need to be developed in much more detail, and examined in light of all relevant scientific and philosophical developments, in order to be comprehensively assessed. But as things stand, I think that we have good reason to suppose that consciousness has a fundamental place in nature.

Notes

1   This chapter is an overview of issues concerning the metaphysics of consciousness. Much of the discussion in this chapter (especially the first part) recapitulates discussion in Chalmers (1995; 1996; 1997), although it often takes a different form, and sometimes goes beyond the discussion there. I give a more detailed treatment of many of the issues discussed here in the works cited in the bibliography.

2   The taxonomy is in the final chapter, chapter 14, of Broad's book (set out on pp. 607–11, and discussed until p. 650). The dramatization of Broad's taxonomy as a 4 × 4 matrix is illustrated on Andrew Chrucky's website devoted to Broad, at http://www.ditext.com/broad/mpn14.html#t.

3   On my usage, qualia are simply those properties that characterize conscious states according to what it is like to have them. The definition does not build in any further substantive requirements, such as the requirement that qualia are intrinsic or non-intentional. If qualia are intrinsic or non-intentional, this will be a substantive rather than a definitional point (so the claim that the properties of consciousness are non-intrinsic or that they are wholly intentional should not be taken to entail that there are no qualia). Phenomenal properties can also be taken to be properties of individuals (e.g., people) rather than of mental states, characterizing aspects of what it is like to be them at a given time; the difference will not matter much for present purposes.

4   Note that I use "reductive" in a broader sense than it is sometimes used. Reductive explanation requires only that high-level phenomena can be explained wholly in terms of low-level phenomena. This is compatible with the "multiple realizability" of high-level phenomena in low-level phenomena. For example, there may be many different ways in which digestion could be realized in a physiological system, but one can nevertheless reductively explain a system's digestion in terms of underlying physiology. Another subtlety concerns the possibility of a view on which consciousness can be explained in terms of principles which do not make appeal to consciousness but cannot themselves be physically explained. The definitions above count such a view as neither reductive nor non-reductive. It could reasonably be classified either way, but I will generally assimilate it with the non-reductive class.

5   A version of the explanatory argument as formulated here is given in Chalmers (1995). For related considerations about explanation, see Levine (1983) on the "explanatory gap" and Nagel (1974). See also the papers in Shear (1997).

6   Versions of the conceivability argument are put forward by Campbell (1970), Kirk (1974), Kripke (1980), Bealer (1994), and Chalmers (1996), among others. Important predecessors include Descartes's conceivability argument about disembodiment, and Leibniz's "mill" argument.

7 Sources for the knowledge argument include Nagel (1974), Maxwell (1968), Jackson (1982), and others. Predecessors of the argument are present in Broad's discussion of a "mathematical archangel" who cannot deduce the smell of ammonia from physical facts (1925: 70–1), and Feigl's discussion of a "Martian superscientist" who cannot know what colors look like and what musical tones sound like (1967[1958]: 64, 68, 140).

8 This version of the thought experiment has a real life exemplar in Knut Nordby, a Norwegian sensory biologist who is a rod monochromat (lacking cones in his retina for color vision), and who works on the physiology of color vision. See Nordby (1990).

9 For limited versions of the conceivability argument and the explanatory argument, see Broad (1925: 614–15). For the knowledge argument, see pp. 70–2, where Broad argues that even a "mathematical archangel" could not deduce the smell of ammonia from microscopic knowledge of atoms. Broad is arguing against "mechanism," which is roughly equivalent to contemporary materialism. Perhaps the biggest lacuna in Broad's argument, to contemporary eyes, is any consideration of the possibility that there is an epistemic but not an ontological gap.

10 For a discussion of the relationship between the conceivability argument and the knowledge argument, see Chalmers (1996 and 2002b).

11 Type-A materialists include Ryle (1949), Lewis (1988), Dennett (1991), Dretske (1995), Rey (1995), and Harman (1990).

12 Two specific views may be worth mentioning: (1) Some views (e.g., Dretske 1995) deny an epistemic gap while at the same time denying functionalism, by holding that consciousness involves not just functional role but also causal and historical relations to objects in the environment. I count these as type-A views: we can view the relevant relations as part of functional role, broadly construed, and exactly the same considerations arise. (2) Some views (e.g., Strawson 2000 and Stoljar 2001) deny an epistemic gap not by functionally analyzing consciousness but by expanding our view of the physical base to include underlying intrinsic properties. These views are discussed under type-F (sectn 5.11).

13 In another analogy, Churchland (1996) suggests that someone in Goethe's time might have mounted analogous epistemic arguments against the reductive explanation of "luminescence." But on a close look, it is not hard to see that the only further explanandum that could have caused doubts here is the *experience* of seeing light (see Chalmers 1997). This point is no help to the type-A materialist, since this explanandum remains unexplained.

14 For an argument from unsavory metaphysical consequences, see White (1986). For an argument from unsavory epistemological consequences, see Shoemaker (1975). The metaphysical consequences are addressed in the second half of this chapter. The epistemological consequences are addressed in Chalmers 2002a.

15 Type-B materialists include Levine (1983), Loar (1990/1997), Papineau (1993), Tye (1995), Lycan (1996), Hill (1997), Block and Stalnaker (1999), and Perry (2001).

16 In certain respects, where type-A materialism can be seen as deriving from the logical behaviorism of Ryle and Carnap, type-B materialism can be seen as deriving from the identity theory of Place and Smart. The matter is complicated, however, by the fact that the early identity theorists advocated "topic-neutral" (functional) analyses of phenomenal properties, suggesting an underlying type-A materialism.

17　Block and Stalnaker (1999) argue against deducibility in part by arguing that there is usually no explicit conceptual analysis of high-level terms such as "water" in microphysical terms, or in any other terms that could ground an a priori entailment from microphysical truths to truths about water. In response, Chalmers and Jackson (2001) argue that explicit conceptual analyses are not required for a priori entailments, and that there is good reason to believe that such entailments exist in these cases.

18　Two-dimensional semantic frameworks originate in the work of Stalnaker (1978), Evans (1979), and Kaplan (1989). The version used in these arguments is somewhat different: for discussion of the differences, see Chalmers (forthcoming).

19　This is a slightly more formal version of an argument in Chalmers (1996: 131–6). It is quite closely related to Kripke's modal argument against the identity theory, though different in some important respects. The central premise 2 can be seen as a way of formalizing Kripke's claim that where there is "apparent contingency," there is some misdescribed possibility in the background. The argument can also be seen as a way of formalizing a version of the "dual property" objection attributed to Max Black by Smart (1959), and developed by Jackson (1979) and White (1986). Related applications of the two-dimensional framework to questions about materialism are given by Jackson (1994) and Lewis (1994).

20　I have passed over a few subtleties here. One concerns the role of indexicals: to handle claims such as "I am here," primary intensions are defined over *centered worlds*: worlds with a marked individual and time, corresponding to indexical "locating information" about one's position in the world. This change does not help the type-B materialist, however. Even if we supplement P with indexical locating information I (e.g., telling Mary about her location in the world), there is as much of an epistemic gap with Q as ever; so $P \wedge I \wedge \neg Q$ is conceivable. And given that there is a centered world that verifies $P \wedge I \wedge \neg Q$, one can see as above that either there is a world satisfying $P \wedge \neg Q$, or type-F monism is true.

21　Hill (1997) tries to explain away our modal intuitions about consciousness in cognitive terms. Chalmers (1999) responds that any modal intuition might be explained in cognitive terms (a similar argument could "explain away" our intuition that there might be red squares), but that this has no tendency to suggest that the intuition is incorrect. If such an account tells us that modal intuitions about consciousness are unreliable, the same goes for all modal intuitions. What is really needed is not an explanation of our modal intuitions about consciousness, but an explanation of why these intuitions in particular should be unreliable.

　　Loar (1990/1997) attempts to provide such an explanation in terms of the unique features of phenomenal concepts. He suggests that (1) phenomenal concepts are recognitional concepts ("*that* sort of thing"); that (2) like other recognitional concepts, they can co-refer with physical concepts that are cognitively distinct; and that (3) unlike other recognitional concepts, they lack contingent modes of presentation (i.e., their primary and secondary intensions coincide). If (2) and (3) both hold (and if we assume that physical concepts also lack contingent modes of presentation), then a phenomenal-physical identity will be a strong necessity in the sense above. In response, Chalmers (1999) argues that (2) and (3) cannot both hold. The co-reference of other recognitional concepts with theoretical concepts is *grounded* in their contingent modes of presentation; in the absence of such modes of presentation, there is no reason to think that these concepts can co-refer. So accepting (3) undercuts any support for (2).

Chalmers (1999) also argues that by assuming that physical properties can have phenomenal modes of presentation non-contingently, Loar's account is in effect presupposing rather than explaining the relevant strong necessities.

22 Of those mentioned above as apparently sympathetic with type-C materialism, I think McGinn is ultimately a type-F monist, Nagel is either a type-B materialist or a type-F monist, and Churchland is either a type-B materialist or a type-Q materialist (below).

23 One might ask about specific reductive views, such as representationalism (which identifies consciousness with certain representational states), and higher-order thought theory (which identifies consciousness with the objects of higher-order thoughts). How these views are classified depends on how a given theorist regards the representational or higher-order states (e.g., functionally definable or not) and their connection to consciousness (e.g., conceptual or empirical). Among representationalists, I think that Harman (1990) and Dretske (1995) are type-A materialists, while Tye (1995) and Lycan (1996) are type-B materialists. Among higher-order thought theorists, Carruthers (2000) is clearly a type-B materialist, while Rosenthal (1997) is either type-A or type-B. One could also in principle hold non-materialist versions of each of these views.

24 Type-D dualists include Popper and Eccles (1977), Sellars (1981), Swinburne (1986), Foster (1991), Hodgson (1991), and Stapp (1993).

25 No-collapse interpretations include Bohm's "hidden-variable" interpretations, and Everett's "many-worlds" (or "many-minds") interpretation. A collapse interpretation that does not invoke measurement is the Ghirardi-Rimini-Weber interpretation (with random occasional collapses). Each of these interpretations requires a significant revision to the standard dynamics of quantum mechanics, and each is controversial, although each has its benefits (see Albert 1993 for discussion of these and other interpretations). It is notable that there seems to be no remotely tenable interpretation that preserves the standard claim that collapses occur upon measurement, except for the interpretation involving consciousness.

26 I have been as guilty of this as anyone, setting aside interactionism in Chalmers (1996) partly for reasons of compatibility with physics. I am still not especially inclined to endorse interactionism, but I now think that the argument from physics is much too glib. Three further reasons for rejecting the view are mentioned in Chalmers (1996). First, if consciousness is to make an interesting qualitative difference to behavior, this requires that it act non-randomly, in violation of the probabilistic requirements of quantum mechanics. I think there is something to this, but one could bite the bullet on non-randomness in response, or one could hold that even a random causal role for consciousness is good enough. Secondly, I argued that denying causal closure yields no special advantage, as a view with causal closure can achieve much the same effect via type-F monism. Again there is something to this, but the type-D view does have the significant advantage of avoiding the type-F view's "combination problem." Thirdly, it is not clear that the collapse interpretation yields the *sort* of causal role for consciousness that we expect it to have. I think that this is an important open question that requires detailed investigation.

27 Consciousness-collapse interpretations of quantum mechanics have been put forward by Wigner (1961), Hodgson (1991), and Stapp (1993). Only Stapp goes into much detail, with an interesting but somewhat idiosyncratic account that goes in a direction different from that suggested above.

28 Type-E dualists include Huxley (1874), Campbell (1970), Jackson (1982), and Robinson (1988).

29 Some accuse the epiphenomenalist of a double standard: relying on intuition in making the case against materialism, but going counter to intuition in denying a causal role for consciousness. But intuitions must be assessed against the background of reasons and evidence. To deny the relevant intuitions in the anti-materialist argument (in particular, the intuition of a further explanandum) appears to contradict the available first-person evidence; but denying a causal role for consciousness appears to be compatible on reflection with all our evidence, including first-person evidence.

30 Versions of type-F monism have been put forward by Russell (1927), Feigl (1967[1958]), Maxwell (1979), Lockwood (1989), Chalmers (1996), Griffin (1998), Strawson (2000), and Stoljar (2001).

31 There is philosophical debate over the thesis that all dispositions have a categorical basis. If the thesis is accepted, the case for type-F monism is particularly strong, since microphysical dispositional must have a categorical basis, and we have no independent characterization of that basis. But even if the thesis is rejected, type-F monism is still viable. We need only the thesis that microphysical dispositions *may* have a categorical basis to open room for intrinsic properties here.

32 Hence type-F monism is the sort of "physicalism" that emerges from the loophole mentioned in the two-dimensional argument against type-B materialism. The only way a "zombie world" W could satisfy the primary intension but not the secondary intension of P is for it to share the dispositional structure of our world but not the underlying intrinsic microphysical properties. If this difference is responsible for the lack of consciousness in W, then the intrinsic microphysical properties in our world are responsible for constituting consciousness. Maxwell (1979) exploits this sort of loophole in replying to Kripke's argument.

Note that such a W must involve either a different corpus of intrinsic properties from those in our world, or no intrinsic properties at all. A type-F monist who holds that the only coherent intrinsic properties are protophenomenal properties might end up denying the conceivability of zombies, even under a structural-functional description of their physical state – for reasons very different from those of the type-A materialist.

33 McGinn (1989) can be read as advocating a type-F view, while denying that we can know the nature of the protophenomenal properties. His arguments rests on the claim that these properties cannot be known either through perception or through introspection. But this does not rule out the possibility that they might be known through some sort of inference to the best explanation of (introspected) phenomenology, subject to the additional constraints of (perceived) physical structure.

34 In this way, we can see that type-D views and type-F views are quite closely related. We can imagine that if a type-D view is true and there are microphysical causal gaps, we could be led through physical observation alone to postulate higher-level entities to fill these gaps – "psychons," say – where these are characterized in wholly structural/dispositional terms. The type-D view adds to this the suggestion that psychons have an intrinsic phenomenal nature. The main difference between the type-D view and the type-F view is that the type-D view involves fundamental causation above the microphysical level. This will involve a more radical view of physics, but it might have the advantage of avoiding the combination problem.

35 Type-O positions are advocated by Lowe (1996), Mills (1996), and Bealer (forthcoming).

References

Albert, D. Z. (1993). *Quantum Mechanics and Experience*. Cambridge, MA: Harvard University Press.
Bealer, G. (1994). "Mental Properties." *Journal of Philosophy*, 91: 185–208.
Bealer, G. (forthcoming). "Mental Causation."
Block, N. and Stalnaker, R. (1999). "Conceptual Analysis, Dualism, and the Explanatory Gap." *Philosophical Review*, 108: 1–46.
Broad, C. D. (1925). *The Mind and its Place in Nature*. London: Routledge and Kegan Paul.
Campbell, K. K. (1970). *Body and Mind*. London: Doubleday.
Carruthers, P. (2000). *Phenomenal Consciousness: A Naturalistic Theory*. Cambridge: Cambridge University Press.
Chalmers, D. J. (1995). "Facing up to the Problem of Consciousness." *Journal of Consiousness Studies*, 2: 200–19. Reprinted in Shear (1997). http://consc.net/papers/facing.html.
—— (1996). *The Conscious Mind: In Search of a Fundamental Theory*. Oxford: Oxford University Press.
—— (1997). "Moving Forward on the Problem of Consciousness." *Journal of Consciousness Studies*, 4: 3–46. Reprinted in Shear (1997). http://consc.net/papers/moving.html.
—— (1999). "Materialism and the Metaphysics of Modality." *Philosophy and Phenomenological Research*, 59: 473–93. http://consc.net/papers/modality.html.
—— (2002a). "The Content and Epistemology of Phenomenal Belief." In Q. Smith and A. Jokic (eds.), *Consciousness: New Philosophical Essays*. Oxford: Oxford University Press. http://consc.net/papers/belief.html.
—— (2002b). "Does Conceivability Entail Possibility?" In T. Gendler and J. Hawthorne (eds.), *Conceivability and Possibility*. Oxford: Oxford University Press. http://consc.net/papers/conceivability.html.
—— (forthcoming). "The Foundations of Two-Dimensional Semantics." http://consc.net/papers/foundations.html.
Chalmers, D. J. and Jackson, F. (2001). "Conceptual Analysis and Reductive Explanation." *Philosophical Review*, 110: 315–61. http://consc.net/papers/analysis.html.
Churchland, P. M. (1996). "The Rediscovery of Light." *Journal of Philosophy*, 93: 211–28.
Churchland, P. S. (1997). "The Hornswoggle Problem." In Shear (1997).
Clark, A. (2000). "A Case Where Access Implies Qualia?" *Analysis*, 60: 30–8.
Dennett, D. C. (1991). *Consciousness Explained*. Boston, MA: Little, Brown.
—— (1996). "Facing Backward on the Problem of Consciousness." *Journal of Consciousness Studies*, 3: 4–6.
—— (forthcoming). "The Fantasy of First-Person Science." http://ase.tufts.edu/cogstud/papers/chalmersdeb3dft.htm.
Dretske, F. (1995). *Naturalizing the Mind*. Cambridge, MA: MIT Press.
Evans, G. (1979). "Reference and Contingency." *The Monist*, 62: 161–89.

Feigl, H. (1967[1958]). "The 'Mental' and the 'Physical'." *Minnesota Studies in the Philosophy of Science*, 2: 370–497. Reprinted (with a postscript) as *The "Mental" and the "Physical"*. University of Minnesota Press.

Foster, J. (1991). *The Immaterial Self: A Defence of the Cartesian Dualist Conception of the Mind*. Oxford: Oxford University Press.

Griffin, D. R. (1998). *Unsnarling the World-Knot: Consciousness, Freedom, and the Mind-Body Problem*. Berkeley: University of California Press.

Harman, G. (1990). "The Intrinsic Quality of Experience." *Philosophical Perspectives*, 4: 31–52.

Hill, C. S. (1997). "Imaginability, Conceivability, Possibility, and the Mind–Body Problem." *Philosophical Studies*, 87: 61–85.

Hodgson, D. (1991). *The Mind Matters: Consciousness and Choice in a Quantum World*. Oxford: Oxford University Press.

Huxley, T. (1874). "On the Hypothesis that Animals are Automata, and its History." *Fortnightly Review*, 95: 555–80. Reprinted in *Collected Essays*. London, 1893.

Jackson, F. (1979). "A Note on Physicalism and Heat." *Australasian Journal of Philosophy*, 58: 26–34.

—— (1982). "Epiphenomenal Qualia." *Philosophical Quarterly*, 32: 127–36.

—— (1994). "Finding the Mind in the Natural World." In R. Casati, B. Smith, and G. White (eds.), *Philosophy and the Cognitive Sciences*. Vienna: Holder-Pichler-Tempsky.

James, W. (1890). *The Principles of Psychology*. Henry Holt and Co.

Kaplan, D. (1989). "Demonstratives." In J. Almog, J. Perry, and H. Wettstein (eds.), *Themes from Kaplan*. New York: Oxford University Press.

Kirk, R. (1974). "Zombies vs Materialists." *Proceedings of the Aristotelian Society (Supplementary Volume)*, 48: 135–52.

Kripke, S. A. (1980). *Naming and Necessity*. Cambridge, MA: Harvard University Press.

Levine, J. (1983). "Materialism and Qualia: The Explanatory Gap." *Pacific Philosophical Quarterly*, 64: 354–61.

—— (2000). *Purple Haze: The Puzzle of Conscious Experience*. Cambridge, MA: MIT Press.

Lewis, D. (1988). "What Experience Teaches." *Proceedings of the Russellian Society* (University of Sydney).

—— (1994). "Reduction of Mind." In S. Guttenplan (ed.), *Companion to the Philosophy of Mind*. Oxford: Blackwell.

Loar, B. (1990/1997). "Phenomenal States." *Philosophical Perspectives*, 4: 81–108. Revised edition in N. Block, O. Flanagan, and G. Güzeldere (eds.), *The Nature of Consciousness*. Cambridge, MA: MIT Press.

Lockwood, M. (1989). *Mind, Brain, and the Quantum*. Oxford: Oxford University Press.

Lowe, E. J. (1996). *Subjects of Experience*. Cambridge: Cambridge University Press.

Lycan, W. G. (1996). *Consciousness and Experience*. Harvard, MA: MIT Press.

Maxwell, G. (1979). "Rigid Designators and Mind–Brain Identity." *Minnesota Studies in the Philosophy of Science*, 9: 365–403.

Maxwell, N. (1968). "Understanding Sensations." *Australasian Journal of Philosophy*, 46: 127–45.

McGinn, C. (1989). "Can We Solve the Mind–Body Problem?" *Mind*, 98: 349–66.

Mills, E. (1996). "Interactionism and Overdetermination." *American Philosophical Quarterly*, 33: 105–15.

Nagel, T. (1974). "What Is It Like To Be a Bat?" *Philosophical Review*, 83: 435–50.

Nordby, K. (1990). "Vision in a Complete Achromat: A Personal Account." In R. Hess, L. Sharpe, and K. Nordby (eds.), *Night Vision: Basic, Clinical, and Applied Aspects*. Cambridge: Cambridge University Press.

Papineau, D. (1993). "Physicalism, Consciousness, and the Antipathetic Fallacy." *Australasian Journal of Philosophy*, 71: 169–83.

Perry, J. (2001). *Knowledge, Possibility, and Consciousness*. Cambridge, MA: MIT Press.

Popper, K. and Eccles, J. (1977). *The Self and Its Brain: An Argument for Interactionism*. New York: Springer.

Quine, W. V. (1951). "Two Dogmas of Empiricism." *Philosophical Review*, 60: 20–43.

Rey, G. (1995). "Toward a Projectivist Account of Conscious Experience." In T. Metzinger (ed.), *Conscious Experience*. Paderborn: Ferdinand Schöningh.

Robinson, W. S. (1988). *Brains and People: An Essay on Mentality and its Causal Conditions*. Philadelphia: Temple University Press.

Rosenthal, D. M. (1997). "A Theory of Consciousness." In N. Block, O. Flanagan, and G. Güzeldere (eds.), *The Nature of Consciousness*. Cambridge, MA: MIT Press.

Russell, B. (1927). *The Analysis of Matter*. London: Kegan Paul.

Ryle, G. (1949). *The Concept of Mind*. London: Hutchinson and Co.

Seagar, W. (1995). "Consciousness, Information and Panpsychism." *Journal of Consciousness Studies*, 2.

Sellars, W. (1981). "Is Consciousness Physical?" *The Monist*, 64: 66–90.

Shear, J. (ed.) (1997). *Explaining Consciousness: The Hard Problem*. Cambridge, MA: MIT Press.

Shoemaker, S. (1975). "Functionalism and Qualia." *Philosophical Studies*, 27: 291–315.

Smart, J. J. C. (1959). "Sensations and Brain Processes." *Philosophical Review*, 68: 141–56.

Stalnaker, R. (1978). "Assertion." In P. Cole (ed.), *Syntax and Semantics: Pragmatics, Vol. 9*. New York: Academic Press.

Stapp, H. (1993). *Mind, Matter, and Quantum Mechanics*. Berlin: Springer-Verlag.

Stoljar, D. (2001). "Two Conceptions of the Physical." *Philosophy and Phenomenological Research*, 62: 253–81.

Strawson, G. (2000). "Realistic Materialist Monism." In S. Hameroff, A. Kaszniak, and D. Chalmers (eds.), *Toward a Science of Consciousness III*. Cambridge, MA: MIT Press.

Swinburne, R. (1986). *The Evolution of the Soul*. Oxford: Oxford University Press.

Tye, M. (1995). *Ten Problems of Consciousness: A Representational Theory of the Phenomenal Mind*. Cambridge, MA: MIT Press.

Van Gulick, R. (1993). "Understanding the Phenomenal Mind: Are We All Just Armadillos?" In M. Davies and G. Humphreys (eds.), *Consciousness: Philosophical and Psychological Aspects*. Oxford: Blackwell.

White, S. (1986). "Curse of the Qualia." *Synthese*, 68: 333–68.

Wigner, E. P. (1961). "Remarks on the Mind–Body Question." In I. J. Good (ed.), *The Scientist Speculates*. London: Basic Books.

Chapter 6

Thoughts and Their Contents: Naturalized Semantics

Fred Adams

6.1 Overview

Famously, Wittgenstein asked the question "What makes my thought about you a thought *about you?*" If I do have a thought about you, let's say that you are a part of the *content* of my thought. You are a part of what my thought is *about*.

We can think about all sorts of things: objects (the Eiffel Tower), properties (being a famous landmark), relations (being East of London), events (the tower's construction), and thoughts themselves (the thought that the Eiffel Tower is one of Paris's most famous landmarks). This is not intended to be exhaustive, but to help broaden the question to "what makes one's thought about *x* a thought *about x?*" We know[1] we have thoughts about things.[2] What we will be interested in here are accounts of how this happens.

We will focus on *thoughts* and their contents, but beliefs, desires, hopes, wishes, intentions, and so on are often loosely considered thoughts. And Descartes, among others, would have included sensations as kinds of thoughts, but it is customary to consider them differently, since they are not propositional attitudes and do not have truth-values (though they may be veridical or non-veridical). Sensations clearly have contents and on some accounts (Dretske 1995) there is a remarkable similarity to how they and thoughts acquire their contents.

Since the late 1970s and early 1980s there have been several attempts to naturalize semantics. While there are subtle differences between the various attempts, they share the view that minds are natural physical objects, and that the way they acquire content is also a natural (or physical) affair. At least since the mid 1970s, externalistic theories of content have urged that thought contents depend crucially upon one's environment, and do not depend solely upon what is inside the head (for most thoughts). The very same sort of physical state that is a thought of water (H_2O)

in Al's head on Earth may be a thought of twin-water (XYZ) in Twin-Al's head on Twin-Earth. The difference of thought content is not due to anything internal to Al or Twin-Al (themselves physical duplicates), but due to differences in the watery substances in their respective environments. What the naturalizers of meaning add to the picture of meaning externalism is a mechanism. We need an account of the mechanism that explains how external physical objects become correlated with the internal physical states of one's head (mind) such that the internal physical states come to mean or be about the external physical objects. Naturalistic theories of content offer naturalistic mechanisms.

Meaning mechanisms cannot rely upon meaning or content. The goal is to naturalize meaning and explain how meaningful bits of nature arise out of non-meaningful bits. So we cannot rely on the meanings of words or intentions of agents to explain how thoughts acquire contents. Of course, once contentful thoughts exist and meaningful language exists, these may explain how further meaning or content arises. But we need some unmeant meaners to get things rolling. Naturalistic accounts of thought content must appeal to mechanisms that generate thoughts and content without using thoughts or content in the explanation – at least initially. Perhaps a way to think about naturalism is to ask how the first mind could think its first[3] thought(s). What conditions would make this possible?

In this chapter, we will look at two of the more prominent theories that attempt to naturalize semantics. We will consider mechanisms that generate thought content on these theories, and then consider important objections. There are far too many theories and issues to cover all of the important ones, but what we lose in breadth we will gain in depth. Many of the issues arise for the other theories as well.

6.2   A Medium for Thought

In order for thoughts to acquire content they need not only a mechanism but also a medium. When Al thinks that the Eiffel Tower is in Paris, his thought is in part about the Tower itself, in part about Paris, and in part about the geographical relation of the one to the other. How thoughts are able to do this, to be sensitive to objects, properties, and relations, is in dispute. Other chapters in this volume will emphasize the options for the cognitive architecture of a mind: classicism, connectionism, and more. The correct view must show how different parts of thought are dedicated to different parts or features of the environment. This will involve differentiation of physical states of the mind (brain) to serve as differentially representative vehicles for thought. Something that was completely uniform[4] would not be able to represent or think that the Eiffel Tower is in Paris.

One way this might go is if there is a language of thought (LOT), a symbol system that mirrors a public, natural language in structure. A very good reason to think that LOT is not a public, natural language is that we need the resources of a language in order to learn a first natural language, viz. hypothesis formation about what words and phrases mean and confirmation procedures to test those hypotheses (Fodor 1975). Thus, we have to be able to think in order to learn our first natural language.[5] It is even argued that just about all of our adult thoughts are in a natural language – at least for conscious thoughts (Carruthers 1996). Whether or not some thoughts are actually thought in a public, natural language,[6] they seem expressible in a natural language. When Al thinks that the Eiffel Tower is in Paris, it is widely agreed that Al can express his thought in English (as an English speaker). One way this might be true is if, corresponding to each element in the expression of the thought, there is an element in the thought itself. There would be an element for the definite article "the," an element to stand for the Eiffel Tower, an element to stand for Paris, and an element to stand for the relation of being in. Essentially, if the language of thought is a symbol system with a compositional syntax and semantics that are isomorphic to the compositional logical syntax and semantics of natural language (Harman 1973), plus or minus a bit (Fodor 1981), that would explain how thoughts can be expressed in natural language. Of course, matters are never easy, and many issues about such an isomorphism remain unresolved (Fodor 1975). But surely there are dependency relations and functions from the one to the other that preserve content. That much seems clear. And it seems safe to say that thoughts are part of a symbolic system because they have representational characteristics that depend on their structure (Harman 1973: 59).

Thought's medium makes it productive in just the way that natural languages are *productive*. We can think that 1 is the positive integer that is less than 2, which is the integer that is less than 3, which is the integer that is less than 4, . . . You get the picture. We can do this type of iteration and composition for thoughts of unbounded complexity. The medium of thought also makes it *systematic* – if one can think that object a stands in relation R to object b, then one can think that object b stands in relation R to object a. What explains these features is in dispute, but at least one thing that seems just right for explaining it is a language of thought.[7]

A further reason to think there is a symbolic medium of thought also ties into the naturalistic program. Intelligent behavior seems to depend upon the contents of our thoughts (beliefs, desires, intentions, sensations, and so on). Jerry's going to the fridge to get a beer (Dretske 1988) seems to require that Jerry's reasons for going to the fridge are represented in his mind. Something gets him to the fridge. Something else gets him reaching for the beer. Folk psychology (and cognitive science, too) seems to cry out for vehicles of thought that play an explanatory role in guiding Jerry to the fridge and then in guiding his reaching for the beer. These seem to require different causal elements guiding different portions of his total trajectory.

Furthermore, consider linguistic behavior. If I say that Ken is taller than Gary because I believe this and desire to communicate it, there would seem to be distinct elements producing my saying "Ken" and "Gary," etc. The intentional realist and semantic naturalist who also embraces LOT tries to explain purposive behavior by appeal to the contents of one's propositional attitudes and other thoughts. One tries to account for the contents of one's thoughts as computational operations (taken quite literally) over internal formulae (or sequences of formulae) (Fodor

1975) in LOT. On this view, thinking that a is F is standing in the computational relation to a symbol in the language of thought that means that a is F. Therefore, the thought symbols for "a" and for "F" have to be able to cause or explain the behavior that one intelligently produces, with respect to a and to F (let a = the particular bottle of beer and F = being opened by Jerry). If we are to explain Jerry's opening the beer by appeal to his desire to open it and his belief that he can do so thusly (the manner of opening), his internal thought symbols or vehicles must be able to cause behavior (or movements) in virtue of their contents.[8]

Already we can see how interesting things can get. How does this work for vacuous thoughts where the term "a" or "F" is vacuous (planet Vulcan is small, phlogiston has negative weight)? How can behavior be explained in virtue of the contents of one's thoughts in those cases (Adams et al. 1993)? Indeed, what is the content of one's thought in those cases (Adams and Stecker 1994; Everett and Hofweber 2000)? How could one ever think truly a thought of the form "a does not exist?" And if a and F are external to the head and are the contents of the thought vehicles "a" and "F," how can the external content (what is known as "wide" or "broad" content) be causally relevant to what "a" and "F" can cause? How can broad content be relevant to the explanation of intelligent behavior (Adams et al. 1990; Adams 1991; Adams et al. 1993)?

Standard Frege puzzles can be seen from this context, as well. If I think "a is F" and $a = b$, have I thereby thought that b is F, or not? Indeed, standard Frege cases provide another excellent reason why there just about must be thought vehicles. When I think that a is F, I might behave differently than when I think that b is F, even when $a = b$. How is that possible? LOT provides the answer that the thought vehicle "a" is not identical to "b." My mind may concatenate "a" with "F," but not "b" with "F," even though $a = b$ (but I don't know that). So while I am blindfolded, Bernie Schwartz may enter the room. I may believe that he did, but not ask him about Jamie Lee or ask for his autograph. Although Bernie Schwartz = Tony Curtis (someone whom I would ask about Jamie Lee Curtis or from whom I would request an autograph), my mind does not concatenate my mental vehicle for Tony Curtis "b" with my mental vehicle for being in this room "F." I literally have an "Fa" ("Bernie Schwartz is here") in my mind but no "Fb" ("Tony Curtis is here") (Adams and Fuller 1992).

Let us now suppose that thoughts have vehicles and they take external objects, properties, and relations as contents (at least very often, if not always), and that we are working with natural causes. Now let us consider some meaning mechanisms.

6.3 Naturalization

The naturalization of semantics is really about the mechanisms[9] that connect thought vehicles (symbols) with their contents. The line of influence goes back at least to Grice (1957), and runs through Stampe (1977), Dretske (1981, 1988), and Fodor (1987, 1990a), to name only some of the key players. Naturalization is an attempt to capture the mechanisms of content and explain how objects of thought become paired with thought vehicles.

The story begins with Grice's notion of "natural meaning." This notion is closely linked with the notions of "information" and "indication." All three are about property correlations (and dependencies). If, under locally stable environmental conditions, things with property G are correlated with things with property F, in a relation of nomic dependency, then the occurrence of something's being G can be a natural sign or indicator of something's being F. Smoke (G) naturally means fire (F). Footprints in the snow indicate that someone walked through the snow. Rings in the tree carry information about the age of the tree. The thermometer's rising indicates rising temperature.

For natural meaning (indication or information) to exist, these property dependencies must be locally stable. There must not be causal overdetermination (artificial smoke, artificial footprints, or tree-boars), and there must be no other factors that would disrupt such dependencies (seasons of non-tree-growth, imperceptible cracks in the thermometer). The need to specify these dependencies led Dretske[10] away from an early formulation ("there wouldn't be smoke unless there were fire") to an information theoretic one ("the probability of fire, given smoke, must be 1 (unity)"). Subtle differences aside, natural meaning (or indication or information) has been there from the start of the naturalization project – with good reason. If something in Al's head is going to mean or be about fire, then Al needs a thought vehicle that can naturally mean fire as surely as smoke naturally means fire. Perhaps the thought vehicle itself is caused by perceptual mechanisms that are triggered by sensory detection of fire (or there are symbols in the perceptual system[11] that naturally mean fire and in turn cause symbols in the central system that come to mean fire).

This requires an identity between the environmental (or ecological) conditions necessary for knowledge and those necessary for univocal content (Dretske 1989). Suppose that in one's environment it is not possible to know that something is F by evidence that something is G. Suppose this is because, in this environment, things that are G are also nomically correlated with (and dependent upon) things that are H – suppose Gs are alternately caused by Fs or Hs. How, in such an environment, could one build a detector mechanism for Fs, out of a detector of Gs? One could not. Since Gs are dependent on Fs or Hs, such a detector would be of Fs or Hs, *not of Fs alone.* In an environment where Gs are reliably dependent upon (and correlated with) Fs or Hs, something's being G detects that something is *F or H*. Call this the *disjunction problem.* With respect to knowledge, the most such a detector could tell us is that something is F or H. This is because the most it could indicate or naturally mean is that something is F or H. With respect to thoughts, if thought content derives from natural meaning, from disjunctive natural meaning, disjunctive thought content derives. To avoid this, the naturalization project has to solve the disjunction problem and explain how a thought symbol may have univocal meaning. In the case at hand, if "G" were a thought symbol that had only disjunctive natural meaning, at best it would allow one to think a disjunctive thought about Fs or Hs (not about Fs alone). Further, to be a thought symbol *at all*, "G" would have to rise to a level above natural meaning – as we shall soon see. For natural meaning to be part of a mechanism that generates univocal thought content, it must spring from non-disjunctive natural meaning. We can also see that something's having univocal natural meaning is just the sort of thing that is required to know that something is F by its being G. This is why there is a connection between knowledge and thought content. If one's environment is not locally stable enough to know that something is F (univocally by some G), then it is not stable enough to acquire a non-disjunctive thought symbol "G" in the deployment of the thought that something is F (alone).

Putnam (1975) gives the example of jadeite (F) and nephrite (H). Suppose that I don't know that jade comes in two varieties. I've heard the term "jade" but don't know what it means. You show me some jadeite, but both jadeite and nephrite look exactly alike to me (G). Then I cannot by their look (G) know if I'm seeing jadeite (F) or nephrite (H). Nor could I form a univocal thought ("this is jade") of jadeite alone. My thought would be as much about jadeite as nephrite – though I have only the thought symbol "jade" (whatever that would be in LOT).

Natural meaning (indication or information), therefore, is an important ingredient of the mechanism that underwrites thought content. Still, thought content cannot be merely a matter of natural meaning, for indication and thought have divergent properties. When Al sees a particular beer, his perceptual symbols of the beer may naturally indicate presence of beer. And this may cause Al to think that there is a beer present. But Al may think of beer when there is none[12] present, when he wishes some were. Al's perceptual mechanisms don't work this way (barring dreaming, hallucination, or something out of the ordinary). Perceptual mechanisms are tuned in to what is happening now. Thoughts are able to focus on the here and now (via "here" and "now"), but are not bound by the present. This gives thought an element of freedom that perception and sensation (when veridical) do not have.

Unfortunately, the same cognitive ability that frees us to think frees us to think falsely. When Al's perceptual mechanisms are working properly, he will not see beer that isn't there. But when his thinking mechanisms are working properly,[13] he may well think there is a beer (in the fridge) that isn't there (he may lose count, someone he trusts may tell him there is one left). That this can happen is not a cognitive deficit. Indeed, it is a benefit that the mind can free itself from its immediate environmental contingencies. But the fact that Al can falsely think something of the form "*Fa*" tells us that *thought content is not natural meaning*. Grice called it "non-natural meaning." I prefer to call it *semantic content* – content that can be falsely tokened. If "*Fa*" has natural meaning, *a* must be *F*, but if "*Fa*" has semantic content, *a* need not be *F*. The question becomes how something goes from natural meaning to semantic thought content? For instance, smoke naturally means fire. Al, thinking he smells smoke, may mentally token "smoke." But "smoke" semantically means smoke, not fire. How is this possible? How does something "fire" go from indicating fire (thereby requiring fire's presence) to semantically meaning fire (not requiring fire's presence)?

6.4 Mechanisms of Meaning

What is required to make the jump from natural meaning to semantic thought content is that a symbol becomes dedicated to its content.[14] For "F" to have Fs as its semantic content, the symbol must become dedicated to the property of being an F. It must mean Fs whether one is currently thinking of something that is F, that it is F or of something that is not F, that it is F. Indeed, it must have the content that something is F even if it is tokened by thoughts unrelated to whether something is an F. This would secure the possibility both of *robust* and *false* tokening – two of the properties that distinguish thoughts from percepts and other items with only natural meaning.

So the problem is to articulate a mechanism of *dedication*. Dretske (1981) once suggested the possibility of a *learning period* – a time period during which a concept formed and acquired its meaning. Let us think of a concept, for our purposes here, as a thought symbol or vehicle. Dretske's suggestion was that someone might acquire the concept (an "F") of an F by being shown Fs and non-Fs under conditions appropriate for detecting Fs. If the property of being an F is the most specific piece of information the subject becomes selectively sensitive to (in digital form of representation), then the subject's "F"-tokens (or "F"s) become dedicated or locked to Fs, as we might put it. "F"s become activated by Fs and Fs only as the subject learns to discriminate Fs and non-Fs shown during the learning period. The idea of a learning period makes perfect sense, if one thinks of a thought symbol locking to its content along the lines of a baby duck's imprinting on its "mother." A window of opportunity for content acquisition opens, the symbol is receptive of a most specific piece of information, locks to it, and the window of opportunity for content acquisition (the learning period) closes. On such a view, a learning period might just work. It seems to work just fine for imprinting in baby ducks.

The problems (Fodor 1990a) with a learning period are that there is no good reason to think that concept acquisition is anything like imprinting – with a window closing after a certain time period. And even if there were such a window of opportunity for concepts to form on specific instances of objects presented to a learner, there is no guarantee that the information delivered to the learner is exhausted by the properties of items presented. Consider "jade" again. Since, as we supposed, I cannot discriminate jadeite from nephrite, if my thought symbol "jade" is tokened exclusively by showing me jadeite during the learning period, the information delivered may still be that something is jadeite or nephrite. So my symbol "jade" is locking to *jadeite or nephrite*, even though I am exclusively shown jadeite. After the learning period, if I am shown nephrite and it tokens my symbol "jade," I am not falsely believing that this is jadeite, but truly believing that it is jadeite or nephrite. Though I would not put it that way, this is the content of my thought. So, in effect, this example illustrates the problems for the learning period approach. It neither solves the disjunction problem, nor explains the possibility of falsehood.

Dretske revised his account of how misrepresentation was possible (1986), and finally settled on an even different account (1988) which not only attempts to explain how symbols lock to their contents, but also how their having content is explanatorily relevant for behavior. However, before looking at this account, let us consider Fodor's own approach to meaning mechanisms.

6.5   Fodor's Meaning Mechanisms

Fodor (1987, 1990a, 1994)[15] offers conditions sufficient for a symbol "X" to mean something X. Since he offers sufficient conditions only, his view inspires concerns that his conditions don't apply to us (or to anyone). And Fodor is perfectly happy if there are other sufficient conditions for meaning (since his aren't intended to be necessary). As much as possible, I hope to minimize these issues because it is pretty clear that Fodor would not be offering these conditions if he thought they didn't apply to us. So we will proceed as though his conditions are supposed to explain the mechanisms by which our thoughts have the contents that they do.

Let's also be clear that Fodor is offering conditions for the meanings of primitive, non-logical thought symbols. This may well be part of the explanation of why he sees his conditions as only sufficient for meaning. The logical symbols and some other thought symbols may come by their meanings differently. Symbols with non-primitive (molecular) content may derive from primitive or atomic symbols by decomposing into atomic clusters. It is an empirical question when something is a primitive term, and Fodor is the first to recognize this. Still he tries to see how far his account can extend by trying to determine whether it would apply to many terms not normally taken to be primitive ("unicorn," "doorknob").

Fodor's conditions have changed over time and are not listed by him anywhere in the exact form below, but I believe this to be the best representation of his current considered theory.[16] (This version is culled from Fodor 1987, 1990a, and 1994.) The theory says that "X" means X if:

(1)   "Xs cause 'X's" is a law,
(2)   for all Ys not = Xs, if Ys qua Ys actually cause "X"s, then Y's causing "X"s is asymmetrically dependent on Xs causing "X"s,

(3) there are some non-X-caused "X"s,
(4) the dependence in (2) is *synchronic* (not diachronic).

Condition (1) represents Fodor's version of natural meaning (information, indication). If it is a law that Xs cause "X"s, then a tokened "X" may indicate an X. Whether it does will depend on one's environment and its laws, but this condition affords[17] natural meaning a role to play in this meaning mechanism. It is clear that this condition is not sufficient to make the jump from natural meaning to semantic content. For "X" to become a symbol for Xs requires more than being tokened by Xs. "X"s must be dedicated to, faithful to, locked to Xs *for their content.*

Condition (2) is designed to capture the jump from natural meaning to semantic content and solve the disjunction problem, at the same time. It does the work of Dretske's learning period, giving us a new mechanism for locking "X"s to Xs. Rather than a window opening and closing where "X"s become dedicated to Xs, Fodor's fix is to make all non-X-tokenings of "X"s nomically dependent upon X-tokenings of "X"s from the very start. There is then no need for a learning period.[18] The condition says that not only will there be a law connecting a symbol "X" with its content X, but for any other items that are lawfully connected with the symbol "X", there is an asymmetrical dependency of laws or connections. The asymmetry is such that, while other things (Ys) are capable of causing the symbol to be tokened, the Y→"X" law depends upon the X→"X" law, but not vice versa. But for the latter, the former would not hold. Hence, the asymmetrical dependence *of laws* locks the symbol to its content.

Condition (3) establishes "robust" tokening. It acknowledges that there are non-X-caused "X"s. Some of these are due to false thought content, as when I mistake a horse on a dark night for a cow, and falsely token "cow" (believing that there is a cow present). Others are due to mere associations, as when one associates things found on a farm with cows and tokens "cow" (but not a case of false belief). These tokenings do not corrupt the meaning of "cow" because "cow" is dedicated to cows in virtue of condition (2).

Condition (4) is designed to circumvent potential problems due to kinds of asymmetrical dependence that are not meaning conferring (Fodor 1987: 109). Consider Pavlovian conditioning. Food causes salivation in the dog. Then a bell causes salivation in the dog. It is likely that the bell causes salivation only because the food causes it. Yet, salivation hardly means food. It may well naturally mean that food is present, but it is not a thought or thought content and it is not ripe for false semantic tokening. Condition (4) allows Fodor to block saying that salivation[19] itself has the semantic content that food is present, for its bell-caused dependency upon its food-caused dependency is diachronic, not synchronic. First there is the unconditioned response to the unconditioned stimulus, then, over time, there comes to be the conditioned response to the conditioning stimulus. Fodor's stipulation that the dependencies be synchronic not diachronic screens off Pavlovian conditioning and many other types of diachronic dependencies, as well.

That would be the end of the discussion of Fodor's meaning mechanisms, if it were not for a further historical instantiation condition (HIC) that has shown up (Fodor 1990a), and subsequently disappeared (Fodor 1994), in Fodor's writings. It is unquestionable that the middle versions of his theory state HIC.

HIC: Some "X"s are actually caused by Xs.

The fact that this was once a stated condition complicates matters. With HIC included as a fifth condition, (2)–(4) seem to be conditions on actual instances of causation, not just counterfactuals (Warfield 1994). This makes a rather important difference. It makes Fodor's theory historical in virtue of requiring actual empirical encounters with objects and their properties. This is a problem, given that Fodor wants to say a symbol such as "unicorn" may lock to uninstantiated properties, such as the property of being a unicorn (Fodor 1990a, and 1991). Further, condition (4) seems only to make sense if we include something like HIC. Without it, what sense would it make to say that a dependency between laws is diachronic (Adams and Aizawa 1993)? Laws are timeless. So without HIC, conditions (1)–(2), at least, seem only to be about counterfactuals, not instances of laws (Fodor 1994).

HIC makes perfectly good sense if one is worried about excluding thoughts for Davidson's (1987) Swampman or accounting for the differences of content of "water" here or on Twin-Earth. Let me explain. First consider the content of "water." In Jerry, the thought symbol "water" means water (our water, H_2O). In Twin-Jerry, the thought symbol "water" means twin-water (XYZ). How is that possible on conditions (1)–(4) alone? There is an $H_2O \rightarrow$ "water" law. But there is also an XYZ$\rightarrow$"water" law. Since Jerry and Twin-Jerry are physically type-identical, the same laws hold of each. There exists no asymmetrical dependency of laws to fix univocal content. It might help to invoke the HIC. For Jerry does not instantiate the XYZ$\rightarrow$"water" law and Twin-Jerry does not instantiate the $H_2O \rightarrow$ "water" law. Thus, it would be possible for Jerry's "water" symbol to lock to one thing, due to actual causal contact with that kind of substance, while Twin-Jerry's "water" symbol locks to another kind of substance via actual causal contact with it. By including (HIC), at least prima facie the theory would be able to explain these differences of broad content.[20] For then the dependencies of (2) would hold only for the instantiated laws.

In the same way, the theory would be able to explain why Davidson's Swampman lacks thoughts. His vehicles lack content. Although the same counterfactuals may be true of Jerry and of SwampJerry, since SwampJerry has no causal truck with the same objects and properties as Jerry, SwampJerry fails to satisfy historical condition HIC.

Useful though this condition may be, Fodor jettisons it because he now (1994) denies that Twin-Earth examples are problems that need to be addressed. He also now accepts that SwampJerry has the same thoughts as Jerry. Therefore, Fodor's considered theory drops this condition. Later we will consider whether this is wise. Next we will look at Dretske's considered view and then we will examine problems for both naturalized theories.

6.6   Dretske's Meaning Mechanisms

Dretske's recipe for content involves three interlocking pieces. (i) The content of a symbol "C" must be tied to its natural meaning F (Fs – objects that are F). (ii) Natural meaning (indication, information) must be transformed to semantic content. There must be a transformation of perceptually acquired information content into cognitive (semantic) content – encoded in a form capable of being harnessed to beliefs and desires in service of the production of behavior M. (iii) The causal explanation of the resultant behavior M must be in virtue of the contents of the cognitive states (via their possession of content). Thus, if a symbol "C" causes bodily movements M because tokenings of "C" indicate (naturally mean) Fs, then "C" is elevated from merely naturally meaning Fs to having the semantic content that something is F.

F← indicates "C" and causes →M (because it indicates F)

While Fodor flirted with an historical account of content (via HIC), Dretske's account is way beyond flirtation. His account is essentially historical. In different environments, the same physical natural signs may signify different things, and have different natural meaning. On Earth, Al's fingerprints are natural signs or indicators of Al's presence. On Twin-Earth, the same physical types of prints indicate Twin-Al's presence, not Al's. For this to be true, there must be something like an *ecological boundary*[21] that screens off what is possible in one environment from what is possible in another. On Earth, for Al's prints to indicate Al's presence, there must be a zero probability of these types of prints being left by Twin-Al (who can't get here from Twin-Earth, or would not come here, let us suppose). Indeed, there must be a zero probability that, given the occurrence of these prints, anything but Al made them. If the mob learns how to fake prints, no prints may have univocal natural meaning. So whether a natural sign has one natural meaning or another will depend upon the ecological conditions in which the sign occurs. This makes Dretske's theory historical to the max. All laws exist everywhere, but not all laws are instantiated everywhere. So which laws are relevant depends upon where you are, and your history of interaction with your environment. Physically identical thought symbols "S" in different, but qualitatively similar organisms, in different environments, may acquire different thought contents.[22] What contents the symbols acquire will depend on what natural meanings they could acquire, in their respective ecological niches.

Dretske's solution to the disjunction problem has at least two components. The first component has already been addressed. The symbol "C" must start out with the ability to naturally mean Fs (and only Fs). If it indicates Fs or Gs, then a disjunctive content is the only semantic content it could acquire. The second component is the jump to semantic content. Even if "C"s indicate Fs only, to acquire semantic content, a symbol must lose its guarantee of possessing natural meaning. It needs to become locked to Fs and permit robust, and even false, tokening, without infecting its semantic content. We've seen why an appeal to a "learning period" doesn't quite work, unembellished. And we've seen that Fodor tries to turn this trick with asymmetrical causal dependencies of laws. Where Fodor uses asymmetrical dependencies of tokenings of "C," Dretske appeals to the explanatory relevance of the natural meaning. For Dretske, it is not just what causes "C"s, but what "C"s in turn cause, and why they cause this that is important in locking "C"s to their content (F).

Let's suppose that a ground squirrel needs to detect Fs (predators) to stay alive. If Fs cause "C"s in the ground squirrel, then the tokening of "C"s indicate Fs. Dretske claims that "C"s come to have the content that something is an F, when "C"s come to have the function of indicating the presence of Fs. When will that be? For every predator is not just a predator, it is an animal (G), a physical object (H), a living being (I), and so on for many properties. Hence, tokens of "C" will indicate all of these, not just Fs. Dretske's answer is that when "C"s indication of Fs (alone) *explains* the animal's behavior, then "C"s acquire the semantic content that something is a predator (F). Hence, it is the *intensionality* of explanatory role[23] that locks "C"s to F, not to G or H or I.

For Dretske, behavior is a complex of a mental state's causing a bodily movement. So when "C" causes some bodily movement M (say, the animal's movement into its hole), the animal's movement consists of its trajectory into its hole. The animal's behavior is its causing that trajectory. The animal's behavior – running into its hole – consists of "C"s causing M ("C"→M). There is no specific behavior that is required to acquire an indicator function. Sometimes the animal slips into its hole (M1). Sometimes it freezes (M2). Sometimes it scurries away (M3). This account says that "C"s become *recruited* to cause such movements because of what "C"s indicate (naturally mean). The animal needs to keep track of Fs and it needs to behave appropriately in the presence of Fs (to avoid predation). Hence, the animal thinks there is a predator when its token "C" causes some appropriate movement M (and hence the animal behaves) because of "C"'s indication (natural meaning). Not until "C"'s natural meaning *has an explanatory role* does "C" lock to its semantic content F. So "C"'s acquired function to indicate or detect predators elevates its content to the next, semantic level.

Now "C" can be falsely or otherwise robustly tokened. The animal may run into its hole because it thinks there is a predator, even when spooked only by a sound or a shadow, as long as the presence of sounds or shadows doesn't explain why the "C"s cause relevant Ms (don't explain the animal's behavior).[24] So even when falsely or robustly tokened, the semantic content of the "C"s is not infected with disjunctive content.

Notice that this doesn't exactly require a learning period or window to open or close, but it does require a determinate function. For Dretske an indicator function becomes fixed when an explanatory role for its indication is fixed (or determinate). Could this change over time? Yes, it could.[25] Functions of any kind can change when the conditions of their sustained causing change. Cognitive systems may adapt to changes in the external environment or the internal economy of the cognitive agent.

On this view, indicator functions are like other natural functions, such as the function of the heart or kidneys or perceptual mechanisms. The account of natural functions favored by Dretske is one on which the X acquires a function to do Y when doing Y contributes some positive effect or benefit to an organism and so doing helps explain why the organism survives. Then there is a type of selection for organisms with Xs that do Y. Consequently, part of the reason Xs are still present, still doing Y, is that a type of selection for such organisms has taken place. Of course, this doesn't explain how X got there or began doing Y in the beginning.

Naturally, the selection for indicator functions has to be within an organism's lifetime, not across generations. Dretske thinks of this kind of selection as a type of biological process of "recruitment" or "learning" that conforms with standard, etiological models of natural functions (Adams 1979; Adams and Enc 1988; Enc and Adams 1998).

Now the third piece of the puzzle is to show that the content of "C" at some level is relevant to the explanation of the organism's behavior. "C" may cause M, but not because of its natural meaning. "C"'s meaning may be idle. For this purpose, Dretske distinguishes triggering and structuring causes. A triggering cause may be the thing that causes "C" to cause M right now. Whereas, a structuring cause is what explains why "C" causes M, rather than some other movement N. Or, alternatively, structuring causes may explain why it is "C" rather than some other state of the brain D that causes M. So structuring causes highlight *contrastives*: (a) why "C"s cause M, or alternatively, (b) why "C"s cause *M*. In either case, if it is because of "C"'s natural meaning, then we have a case of structuring causation, and content plays a role on this account of meaning mechanisms.

Let's illustrate this with a comparison of a non-intelligent robot cat and an intelligent cat.[26] Both may produce the identical movements, but their *behaviors* may not be the same. Suppose that both appear to be stalking a mouse. This does not mean that both are stalking, not even if the robot cat's "brain" has structures that resemble the brain of the cat. For there may be nothing in the robot cat that is in any way *about a mouse*. There will be something in the cat that is about this, given its learning history. It will also have a desire to catch the mouse and beliefs about how to do so. Though their bodily movements may be physically similar, it would be stretching things to say the robot cat was "stalking" the mouse, and teleological nonsense to try to explain why. Since unintelligent, the best we could do is explain how. It would be quite sensible to say that the cat was stalking the mouse and it would make perfect sense teleologically to explain why – it is stalking in order to catch the mouse. Inside the workings of the robot cat's "brain" there are triggering causes of its movements. But since the robot cat's internal states have no semantic content, there are no structuring causes[27] that produce movements because of what they indicate or naturally mean. Thus, there is no intelligent behavior here, unlike in the case of the cat. Hence, semantic content makes an important difference in the origin and explanation of intelligent behavior, on this view.

This completes the basic sketch of the meaning mechanisms of Fodor and Dretske. Let's consider some objections that have been raised to both accounts. This will help us see more deeply into the nature of these theories and detect their strengths and weaknesses.

6.7 Objections

Names

Neither Fodor's nor Dretske's theories are designed to handle names and their contents. For both theories are designed to explain how thought symbols become locked to properties. Since objects have a wealth of properties, unless they have individual essences, these theories do not easily account for the contents of names. Names and demonstratives are widely thought to have their referents determined by causal chains that connect their introduction into a language (or thought system). Aristotle's family named him and used "Aristotle" to refer to him. The mental symbol that corresponds to the term in natural language also gets its reference determined via this causal chain. And this chain can be passed on from person to person, generation to generation.

Perhaps the problem is easiest to see on Fodor's theory, since he states his theory in terms of laws. For "Aristotle" to mean Aristotle, when we look at condition (1) we see that it must be a law that "Aristotle causes 'Aristotle's.'" The difficulty is immediately apparent. The theory requires the individual Aristotle to feature in a law. But laws feature kinds of properties, not individuals. So the theory is not designed to handle contents of names (Adams and Aizawa 1994a).

Fodor noticed and tried to fix this problem (1994: 118) by suggesting that the relevant law in (1) would be this: "Property of being Aristotle → 'Aristotle's.'" While he gets an A for effort, this still seems to make "Aristotle" mean a *property*, not *Aristotle* (the man) (Adams and Aizawa, 1997a). Fodor may want to insist that for every individual, there is a property of being that individual. But if it were this easy for there to be properties, why would anyone ever have thought that individuals do not feature in laws? There could be as many such laws as you please. It seems much more likely that there is a difference between properties and individuals and that names like "Aristotle" name the individual and that phrases like "property of being Aristotle" name a property.

Since Fodor is giving only sufficient conditions for meaning, it would not be the end of the world if his theory didn't apply to names. He himself suggests that it doesn't apply to demonstratives or logical terms. Perhaps a causal theory of reference, such as the direct reference theory, is adequate for names and demonstratives (Adams and Stecker 1994; Adams and Fuller 1992). Names in thought may connect one directly to an individual, supplying that individual for the propositional content of a thought (consisting of that individual and a property, relation, or sequence).

Dretske's theory too has to be able explain how "C" can mean Aristotle. Something must indicate[28] Aristotle (for example, fingerprints would, DNA would). Presumably, Aristotle had features via which his family recognized him. "Aristotle" does not mean these features or properties. "Aristotle" means Aristotle, but a constellation of features in that space and time unique to Aristotle would permit a structure "C" to be selectively sensitive to Aristotle's presence in virtue of them, and thereby to naturally mean that he is present. Of course, there must be a causal chain[29] linking Aristotle to percepts of Aristotle and percepts to "C" in those who named him (Dretske 1981: 66–7, and ch. 6). Dretske can tell the rest of his story about how "C" causes some relevant M in virtue of naturally meaning Aristotle. A relevant M may have been his mother's calling him "Aristotle," for example. This would make Aristotle (the individual) the content of the thought symbol "Aristotle."

Uninstantiated properties

People can think about unicorns and fountains of youth and so on, but none of these things exists. So it is an important question how uninstantiated properties might be the semantic contents of such thoughts.[30] One way is if such contents of thought symbols are complex and decompose into meaningful primitive constituents. So, for example, the content of thoughts about unicorns may decompose into content of horses with horns. "Horse," "horn," and "possession" may be primitive symbols with primitive contents (and if not, they may further decompose). These primitive symbols may have instantiated properties as their contents.

This is a standard strategy of empiricists, and is followed by Dretske (1981). It is clear that "unicorn"s cannot naturally mean or indicate unicorns, if unicorns don't exist. Thus, meaningful symbols having complex uninstantiated properties as their contents would decompose into their meaningful parts (with simpler, instantiated properties as contents). Notice that such a view must maintain that there are no meaningful primitive terms that have uninstantiated properties as their contents.

Fodor, being a rationalist, has a harder time with uninstantiated properties as contents of thoughts. He has open to him the strategy of decomposition, but he believes that it is at least possible that "unicorn" is a primitive thought symbol. So suppose that "unicorn" is a primitive. One way to get an organism to lock to a property is to rub its nose in instantiations. This is a bit hard when there are no instantiations of the unicorns→"unicorns" law. One suspects that it is for reasons like this that Fodor dropped HIC.

Another way is to suggest that non-unicorn-caused "unicorn"s in this world asymmetrically depend on unicorn-caused "unicorn"s in close possible worlds (Fodor 1991). Of course this doesn't tell us what metric to use for closeness of worlds (Cummins 1989; Sterelny 1990; Loar 1991). Worse yet, it doesn't tell us how unicorns cause "unicorns" in the close possible worlds. Presumably it is because the property is instantiated in those close worlds. If so, then the HIC condition seems to be employed in those worlds and needs to be put back into Fodor's theory in some fashion.

When pressed, Fodor (1991) notes that he can always retreat and say that "unicorn" is a complex term, not primitive, after all.[31] But he is reluctant to do so. What is more, his reluctance baits others (Wallis 1995) into attempts to invent primitive terms for nomically uninstantiable properties. Suppose a giant ant (gant) is a nomological impossibility for biological reasons – its legs would crush under its own weight and its circulation would not allow sufficient heat transfer. Then Wallis would contend that there are no close worlds where the gant→"gant" law is instantiated. Were Fodor stubbornly to stick to his story, he would say that "gant" locks to the property of being a gant, because in the closest worlds where the laws of nature are different from ours gants cause "gants"s. Whatever causes "gant"s in us here does so only because gants cause "gant"s there (and not vice versa). How plausible this is becomes the question.

Of course, Fodor himself notes that he must use the decompositional strategy for logically impossible properties such as being a round square (Fodor 1998a). (Let "roundsquare" suggest a primitive term.) There are no worlds where a roundsquares→"roundsquare"s law holds. Of course, if Fodor really rejects HIC even when appealing to close worlds that ground asymmetrical dependencies of laws, he could maintain that it is not that roundsquares or gants or unicorns *do* cause "roundsquares" or "gants" or "unicorns," but they *would* if they were to be instantiated. However, it is highly doubtful that Fodor would say such a thing. For then the mechanisms of meaning evaporate. This would be to resort not only to the uninstantiated, but to the uninstantiable and there is no reason to believe in such a metaphysics of semantic mechanisms.

The disjunction problem – again

Critics argue that semantic naturalists still have not solved the disjunction problem. Fodor (1990a) alerted us to it originally in response to Dretske's appeal to a learning period. Dretske modified his account so that it was not dependent upon a learning period, temporally construed. However, there remains a residual learning element in Dretske's new account (1988, 1995) of indicator functions. It remains true that during a process of what Dretske calls "recruitment" some internal structure acquires its indicator function, and thereby acquires its representational content. This is not temporally determined and it is not arbitrary. However, it does require a structure "C" having its indicator function become fixed or set. As we noted above, Dretske thinks that indicator functions become fixed in ways similar to the ways any natural function becomes fixed or set. The most skeptical critics worry that all function attributions are indeterminate (Enc, manuscript). Others worry that functions are far less determinate than is required for determinate semantic content.

The above is a representative sample of the objections to Dretske's solution to the disjunction problem. There is a similar range of attacks upon Fodor's solution. The objections to Fodor's use of asymmetrical dependencies began early (Dennett 1987a, 1987b; Adams and Aizawa 1992). Aizawa and I pointed out that Twin-Earth examples should be a problem for Fodor. Since Al and his Twin are physically similar in every relevant way, if a law would apply to Al, it would apply to Twin-Al. Hence, if there is an $H_2O \rightarrow$ "water" law and an XYZ$\rightarrow$"water" law[32] there can hardly be an asymmetrical dependency of laws. Breaking either law should break the other, since, by hypothesis of Twin-Earth cases, Al and Twin-Al cannot discriminate water from twin-water.

As noted above, Fodor might try to use HIC to explain that Al instantiates the first law (about water) and Twin-Al instantiates the second law (about XYZ) and neither instantiates both. So, that is why Al's "waters" mean water and Twin-Al's mean twin-water (Warfield 1994). Ultimately, I don't think this helps (Adams and Aizawa 1994a, 1994b) and Fodor drops HIC, anyway. His theory no longer blocks saying that Al's "water" tokens symmetrically depend on both the water law and the twin-water law, thereby having disjunctive meaning.

Fodor (1994) seems no longer worried about Twin-Earth cases – metaphysical possibilities are too remote to be worrisome. He may be correct that mere possibilities are so remote that they are, as if by an ecological boundary, screened off. Twin-water is screened off from Al's environment (and vice versa for Twin-Al). These cases are not "relevant alternatives," to use a familiar term from the epistemology literature. Still, as Dennett (1987b) and a long line of others (Baker 1989; Cummins 1989; Godfrey-Smith 1989; Maloney 1990; Sterelny 1990; Boghossian 1991; Jones et al. 1991; Adams and Aizawa 1992, 1994a; Manfredi and Summerfield 1992; Wallis 1994) have pointed out, Twin-Earth may not be a relevant alternative, but other things are (or might be). We can assume that there is nothing metaphysically outre about lookalikes. What keeps "X" from meaning X or X-lookalike?

Cummins (1989) picks mice for his Xs and shrews for his X-lookalikes. It would be easy for someone to confuse these two animals by their looks. There will be a mouse$\rightarrow$"mouse" law, satisfying Fodor's condition (1), but there will also be a shrew$\rightarrow$"mouse" law. The question is whether the second law is asymmetrically dependent upon the first law. Cummins considers the various ways of explaining why this asymmetry seems unlikely. It seems clear that for Al, his thought symbol "mouse" might symmetrically depend upon mice or shrews. His thought symbol "mouse" would lock to *mouse or shrew*.[33] Of course, there are other properties than "mousey looks" that might be involved in getting Al to lock to mice. There may be properties that mice have and that shrews lack, such that if mice didn't have their properties, shrews wouldn't be able to poach upon the mouse→"mouse" law. This is what Fodor needs to explain how "mouse" locks to the property of being a mouse, for Al. But it seems at least plausible that Al's "mouse" symbol might have disjunctive semantic content, by Fodor's conditions.

Cummins's example may not be a problem for Fodor. I'll explain why. Fodor can surely accept that it is possible that one's idiolect, or its equivalent in thought, has disjunctive meaning. If Al really mistakes mice for shrews, this is to be expected. What Fodor doesn't want is that no tokens of "mouse" mean mouse, by his conditions. To avoid this, he might appeal to a division of linguistic labor. Since there is a division of labor in the introduction of terms into our natural language, as long as the experts can tell mice from shrews, the English word "mouse" may still mean mouse (alone). If Al acquires his thought symbol "mouse" from experts and English speakers, there can be *semantic borrowing*. Semantic borrowing occurs when person A acquires a term from person B and A's term thereby means what A's term means. If Al hears Frank talk about the Australian echidna, but Al has not seen these animals, Al can still think about echidnas. He can wonder what they look like, what they eat, and so on. Al's thought symbol for echidnas may be rather impoverished, but lock to echidnas nonetheless. So thought symbols can lock to their semantic content via causal chains going through other minds. We must take Cummins to be arguing that there are no experts in the mouse/shrew case. Then Al's thought symbol "mouse" will not derive univocal content from the English word. Still, Fodor could accept that "mouse" locks to mouse or shrew for Al. It even could lock to something disjunctive for everyone, if no one can tell mice from shrews. But surely this is not true. To be a problem one must show that "mouse" is univocal, but would be disjunctive on Fodor's conditions (and not because of semantic borrowing).

Baker (1989, 1991) uses cats for Xs and robot-cats for X-lookalikes to argue that Fodor's theory gives the wrong content assignment. She imagines Jerry first seeing robot-cats, later seeing cats, and discovering still later that he was wrong about cats (thinking that they were not robots). There are both of the following laws: robot-cats→"cat"s and cats→"cat"s. What is the content of Jerry's thought symbol "cat"? Baker argues strenuously that "cat" cannot mean cat, for Jerry (and I think she is right, if we exclude the possibility of semantic borrowing). Baker also argues that "cat" cannot have cats as its semantic content (here too, I agree). The asymmetrical dependency clause of Fodor's conditions (condition 2) is not satisfied for either of these contents. Baker also claims that Jerry's "cat"s cannot have the disjunctive content *cat or robot-cat* because if it did, Jerry could not later discover that he was mistaken about cats. But it seems to me, and Fodor (1991) agrees, that this *is* a case of disjunctive content. There is a cats or robot-cats→"cat"s law upon which all other tokenings of "cat"s asymmetrically depend. The rest of Fodor's conditions are easily met, consistent with this interpretation, and Baker's claim about Fodor's discovering his mistake about cats is consistent with this interpretation. It becomes a second-order mistake. Fodor's later discovery is that his former thoughts about cats were mistaken because he finds out that the content of his thoughts was disjunctive (where he thought they were non-disjunctively about robot-cats).[34] So Baker's example may not be a problem for Fodor, after all.

Manfredi and Summerfield (1992) try a different tack. They suggest that a thought symbol "cow" may remain locked to cows, even if the cow→"cow"s law is broken. They ask us to imagine that Jerry has seen lots of cows and acquired a thought symbol "cow." Suppose that all of Fodor's conditions are met and then cows change their appearance (through evolution or radiation, say). They argue that the change may break the cow→"cow" law, but not change the content of Jerry's "cow"s. Barring semantic borrowing, a plausible reply is that the cow→"cow" law has not been broken, just masked. As long as the essence of being a cow has not changed, the cow→"cow" law may manifest itself through different appearances over time. No doubt the earliest cows in history looked different from what they do now. The fact that one of those early cows might not cause a "cow" in Jerry doesn't show that the cow→"cow" law is broken. Why should it if there were a sudden change in the appearance, rather than a slow gradual change? That Jerry wouldn't recognize cows by their appearance would not be a problem for Fodor's theory (though it might present practical problems for Jerry). This, too, doesn't seem to present an insurmountable worry.

Too much meaning (semantic promiscuity)

Adams and Aizawa (1994a) have argued that Fodor's theory attributes meaning to things that it shouldn't – attributes too much meaning, if you will. Dretske's theory may have this difficulty as well. An interesting example brought to my attention by Colin Allen seems to apply to both theories. If semantic content is as easy to come by as it appears in this example, it may be ubiquitous on naturalized theories. Kudu antelope eat the bark of the acacia tree. Consequently, the tree emits tannin that the kudu don't like. Not only that, the wind carries this down wind to other trees which emit tannin too. Were a human to disturb the bark of the acacia tree, it would emit tannin too. If we let tannin molecules count as symbols, all of Fodor's conditions are satisfied. Kudu bites→tannin (condition 1). Human disturbance→tannin (condition 3). Law (3) is asymmetrically dependent upon law (1) (Condition 2). The dependencies are synchronic (condition 4).

For Dretske's theory too, some structure (C) in the acacia detected and naturally meant kudu. That structure also had the ability to turn on the tannin production (M). Hence, C became locked to kudu, when the function of indicating kudu explained the tannin production in the acacia. C's indicator function became locked to kudu (who would otherwise have decimated the acacia forests).

The easy way out, I think, is to restrict both theories to symbols in LOT (or its products).[35] There is nothing in the acacia tree that comes close to LOT.

Fodor originally (1990c) had such a requirement, but dropped it, and Dretske's theory seems to be designed for creatures that have conscious experience, beliefs, desires, and a full cognitive economy.[36] Still examples like this, if successful, yield what may be a surprising result to some: that semantic content can exist outside of minds.[37]

Proximal projections

Both Fodor and Dretske face the problem of why a thought symbol means its distal cause (cow) and not a more proximal cause (retinal projection of a cow) that serves to mediate between thought and reality (Sterelny 1990; Antony and Levine 1991). Dretske's (1981) solution was to say that constancy mechanisms may operate and result in "cow" indicating cows without thereby indicating proximal projections of cows. This is because Dretske believes there are multiple projections (P1 v P2 . . . v Pn) and the most specific piece of information that "cow" carries in digitalized form will be that a cow is present, not that P1, not that P2, . . . not that Pn.

Note that "cow" will still carry the conjunctive information that F (a cow is present) and P (some or other proximal projections – P1 v P2 . . . v Pn) are occurring. I think Dretske should say what he now (1988) says in reply to "C" 's indicating that there is a predator (F) and an animal (G) and a physical object (H) present. Namely, if "C"s indication of Fs explains why it causes relevant Ms then it semantically means Fs, even though it indicates F and G and H. Similarly, "cow" may indicate cows and P (where P is the finite disjunctive property). Still "cow" may cause relevant Ms because it indicates cows, enabling us to perceive the cow and think about the cow, not the proximal projections.

Fodor's solution to the problem of proximal projections relies on his condition (3). All of the cow-caused "cows" are also proximal projections of cow-caused "cow"s. So there is no robust causation of "cow"s by proximal projections of cows, and "cow" cannot mean *projection of cow*.

For Fodor, it seems false that there is not robust causation of "cow" even if all perceptions of cows asymmetrically depend on proximal projections of cows. For thoughts of cows cause "cow"s and plausibly this asymmetrically depends upon proximal projections causing "cow"s. If so, the content of "cow" should be *proximal projection of cows* (Adams and Aizawa 1997b). Thus, this still seems to be a problem for Fodor's account.

Swampman

Here we have a significant difference between Dretske and Fodor (minus HIC).[38] Clearly, on Dretske's view, Swampman has no thought content when he instantaneously materializes. None of his symbols has functions to indicate. No symbols have semantic contents. Of course, whether Swampman can acquire semantic contents is up for grabs, even on Dretske's account. That would depend on whether his internal neural states are capable of natural meaning and sustained causing of relevant movements M because of their natural meaning (i.e., learning). If possible, then in time there would be no reason in principle why Swampman could not acquire semantic thought content.

However, Fodor (1994) claims that Swampman has thoughts from the instant of his materialization. He believes that the same meaning mechanisms that apply to Jerry apply to SwampJerry. Fodor's justifications for maintaining this are six, none of which seems sufficient (Adams and Aizawa 1997a). First, it is simpler ("more aesthetic") to have one meaning mechanism for all. I am for unified theories, but Fodor's theory has its warts. He has to handle demonstratives and names and logical terms differently. Why not Swampman? Secondly, he notes that one may token "X"s in the absence of Xs (implying the rejection of something like HIC). But this is true whether the "X"s have semantic content or not. "Giz" can be tokened in absence of gizs, but "giz" doesn't mean anything. Thirdly, Fodor's intuitions are strong that Swampman has thoughts. Yes, and Euclid's intuitions were strong that the parallel postulate was true of all lines and points off them. Fourthly, Fodor thinks that the only explanation of why Swampman says "Wednesday" when asked the current date is that he thinks it is Wednesday. However, a syntactic but non-contentful "today is Wednesday" in what would be his belief box[39] would explain it as well.[40] A current thoughtless computer program with a speech module driven by its syntax proves this. The syntax is meaningful to us, but not to existing computers (compuJerry, if you will). Fifthly, Fodor claims that the best explanation of why it is more plausible to say that SwampJerry's "water" tokens mean H_2O and Twin-SwampJerry's mean XYZ is that they have these respective semantic contents. I would maintain that it is as good to explain that if SwampJerry's thoughts had content, they'd have the content of the most proximate population of believers (viz. Earth), while Twin-SwampJerry would have the content of his most proximate population of believers (viz. Twin-Earth). If these Swampmen had thoughts, these are the thoughts they would have, but they have none. These counters are, I believe, just as strong or stronger than Fodor's.

Mind dependence

Shope (1999) objects that Dretske's account employs the concept of explanation and explanation is a mind-dependent activity. So Dretske's account is not really a naturalized account. This is true only if the appeal to explanation is ineliminable. A naturalized account needs intensionality (with an "s"), such that "C"s cause Ms because of their indicating Fs (not Gs, though they indicate Gs). This intensionality is fully supplied by that of laws and teleological functions. So the mind-dependent activity of explaining is eliminable.

Functions don't work like that

Many critics complain that Dretske doesn't have the right theory of functions or that there is no consensus about teleological functions. Dretske (1990) would be happy to abandon the term "function" if need be. His account would be the same if a new term for "indicator function" were substituted.

Also Shope (1999) and Godfrey-Smith (1992), among others, argue that it is not necessary for an organism to have a symbol that naturally means Fs to acquire the function of indicating Fs (a semantic content F). Something less will do. Perhaps a predatory animal will recruit a "C" that is best correlated with prey. The suggestion is that "C" still will mean prey. I think the proper question is whether Shope or Godfrey-Smith (or anyone) has a way around the example above where "jade" seems semantically to mean jadeite or nephrite for precisely the reasons that it naturally indicates this disjunction. So far as I can see, Shope and Godfrey-Smith and others assert that this can happen ("F" means F without ever having naturally meant Fs), but they don't explain how it can happen. Until they do, they have not established that it happens. The examples they give are consistent with the animals' having disjunctive contents, despite their claims to the contrary.

Vacuity

The fact that Fodor gives only sufficient conditions for content invites the worry that, while ingenious, his theory is vacuous. It may apply to no actual meaningful items, or, if it does, it may yield the wrong contents (Baker 1991; Seager 1993; Adams and Aizawa 1992, 1994a). Water may be capable of causing "water"s in Janet, but so may hallucinogenic drugs, brain tumors, or high fevers. Since Fodor drops HIC, the abilities of each of these to cause "water"s in Janet must asymmetrically depend on the water→"water" law. But do they? Why would they? "Water"s are structures in the brain that are identifiable independently of content[41] (by Fodor's own conditions). So why wouldn't something in the brain be capable of causing such a structure, independently of the structure's content? I can type "Giz" whether "Giz" has a meaning or not. Why couldn't my brain do something similar with "water"? On the assumption that it can, Fodor's conditions alone do not explain how Janet's "water"s lock to water. Janet's and our thoughts have content, but not because of the conditions of Fodor's theory. Hence, his conditions are vacuous.

A natural way out of this worry is to bring back HIC. Indeed, this is what Dretske would do. He would say that it may be possible in some people that a symbol "water" is triggered by something other than water (prior[42] to "water"s acquiring its semantic content). If so, "water" does not have water as its natural meaning and it could not acquire water as its semantic content, for those individuals in those contexts. But there may very well be stable conditions that screen off these causes in persons free of drugs, tumors, fevers, XYZ, and so on. Fodor needs to explain why these other things are screened off and, minus[43] HIC, simply has no mechanism to do this (Warfield 1994; Adams and Aizawa 1994b). Fodor will have to say that worlds where water causes "water"s in Janet are closer than worlds where pathological causes do. But no world could be closer than the actual world. And people just like Janet in all other relevant physical respects seem perfectly capable of having these kinds of deviant causes of things in the brain, in this world. So Fodor's theory may not apply to them (or Janet).

Which came first: meaning or asymmetry?

Many authors have doubted whether asymmetrical dependencies generate meaning (Seager 1993; Gibson 1996; Adams and Aizawa 1994a, 1994b; Wallis 1995). Fodor's asymmetries are supposed to bring meaning into the world, not result from it. If Ys cause "X"s only because Xs do, this must not be because of any semantic facts about "X"s. What sort of mechanism would bring about such syntactic asymmetric dependencies? In fact, why wouldn't lots of things be able to cause "X"s besides Xs, quite independently of the fact that Xs do? The instantiation of "X"s in the brain is some set of neurochemical events. There should be natural causes capable of producing such events in one's brain (and under a variety of circumstances). Why on earth would steaks be able to cause "cow"s in us only because cows can (given that "cows" are uninterpreted neural events)? Is it brute?

Often, in explaining the existence of such asymmetries, Fodor relies on the "experts," on their intentions to use terms (1990c: 115). But, of course, this won't do. One cannot appeal to meanings to explain the existence of underived meanings. So where do the underived asymmetries come from? My best guess is that it goes like this: "cow" means cow, "steak" means steak, we associate steaks with cows and that is why steaks cause "cow"s only because cows cause "cow"s. We wouldn't associate steaks with "cow"s unless we associated "cow"s with cows and steaks with cows. This explanation of the asymmetrical dependency exploits meanings – it does not generate them. Unless there is a better explanation of such asymmetrical dependencies, it may well be that Fodor's theory is misguided to attempt to rest meaning upon them.

6.8 Conclusion

Warts and all, these are among the best theories of thought content that we have. They are not the only theories, but they exhibit the basic project to naturalize content. The differences between these two theories and other naturalized theories are relatively minor. And these theories are not really too bad, especially when you consider the alternatives – but that is a project for another time.[44]

Notes

1 If Dretske (manuscript) is right, it may be harder to explain *how* we know these things than we previously believed.

2 In this chapter, I will be adopting the view of an intentional realist. Intentional realists maintain that thought and other mental states have content and explain behavior (and other mental states) in virtue of having content. There are views that maintain that attributions of contents to thoughts is a matter of interpretation, but that having content is not a matter that could do explanatory work.

3 There is a dispute between content holists and content atomists. Holists would say that thoughts come in clusters – no mind could have just one. Atomists believe that thoughts and minds could be punctate – a mind could have just one thought. We may not be able to go deeply into this dispute here, but see Fodor and Lepore (1992).

4 This is a way in which meaning is different from information. I suppose a uniform signal would be able to indicate or inform that the Eiffel Tower was in Paris. Suppose we prearranged that a specific light's going on will signal that the Tower is in Paris. Then a light's going on would be able to inform one who did not know that the Tower is in Paris. But a light's going on would not be able to constitute the thought that the Tower is in Paris.

5 Another good reason – to which almost everyone appeals – is that non-verbal infants and animals think. Of course, there are dissenters (Davidson 1982; Carruthers 1996).

6 Harman (1973) and Carruthers (1996) claim that most thoughts are in natural public languages. Dissenters include Fodor (1998b).

7 Fodor and Pylyshyn (1988), Fodor, and Fodor and McLaughlin in Fodor (1998b) and Aizawa (1997) for dissent on the efficacy of some LOT arguments for systematicity.

8 At least, they must if intentional realism is true.

9 I hope it is clear that when I talk about mechanisms, I am abstracting from the material basis of thought in humans (the particular structures of neurons or chemistry of neurotransmitters), and even from the particular psychophysical mechanisms of perception. I'm talking about the informational requirements, not particular physical or psychological implementations that meet those requirements.

10 Dretske originally (1971) came up with the notion of a "conclusive reason" where the thing that was the reason R (which could be Smith's fingerprints on the gun) wouldn't be the case unless p (Smith touched the gun). R's being the case would allow one to know that p was true. Dretske later (1981) turned to information theory to find a more exact specification of the relation between properties necessary to have knowledge (necessary to know Smith touched the gun).

11 See Barsalou (1999) for the view that perceptual symbols in the perceptual system are themselves used as thought symbols or vehicles. For dissent, see Adams and Campbell (1999) and many of the other peer commentaries.

12 Fodor (1990b) makes much of this and eventually (1990a) dubs it "robustness."

13 Descartes may dissent (*Meditation IV*) about whether one is using his cognitive abilities properly when thinking falsely.

14 Fodor now, aptly, calls this "locking" to a property (or content).

15 Fodor's conditions for meaning are in flux and (subtly) change across these three works.

16 Below we will consider another incarnation of the theory that adds a condition and discuss why he may have added and then dropped that condition. For more about this see Adams and Aizawa (1994b).

17 Fodor likes to refer to his view as an "informational" semantics (1994).

18 Nor is there a need for learning (period) – consistent with Fodor's penchant for nativism.

19 One might think that it doesn't need blocking because salivation is not a vehicle in the language of thought. But Fodor does not restrict his theory to items in LOT. So, in principle, even things outside the head can have meaning.

20 Actually, there are still problems about whether there are disjunctive laws of the form "water or twin-water" → "water"s (Adams and Aizawa 1994a) or whether there is a symmetrical dependence of laws here, but I shall ignore those for now.

21 Let's think of an ecological boundary as akin to what Dretske (1981) calls a "channel condition."

22 Perhaps it goes without saying, but, because of this, Dretske is an empiricist. The same cognitive structures "water" may be in Al and Twin-Al innately, but since the Als have different histories, their thoughts (via "water") will acquire different contents.

23 We will return to this later when considering an objection by Shope.

24 Sticks and stones may break one's bones, but shadows and sounds cannot harm you. Every ground squirrel knows this. So no "C" is recruited to be an indicator of shadows or sounds. Predators – that is altogether different.

25 See Dretske (1988: 150).

26 It's okay with me if the intelligent cat is a robot too, but it has got to be able to think. For my purposes, a Davidsonian swampcat would do as well for the non-intelligent cat.

27 There may be things in the robot-cat that cause things because the engineers wired it up to cause those things. But there will not be structures that cause things because the structures indicate *to the cat* that there is a mouse present, thereby causing bodily movements in conjunction with beliefs and desires. For the robot-cat has no beliefs and desires, being unintelligent.

28 Here is where Dretske's theory may have an easier time of it. For a fingerprint to carry information about Aristotle, on Dretske's information-theoretic account (1981), the probability that Aristotle touched an object, given that his fingerprint is on it, must be one. On the face of it, this doesn't say that Aristotle enters into a law. No one knew about fingerprints in Aristotle's day, but that isn't the point. His appearance may have been as individuating as a fingerprint. So identifying properties of individuals may enable one to track information about that individual, without thereby saying the individual enters into laws.

29 This is why percepts of Aristotle may be qualitatively identical to those of Twin-Aristotle, but they naturally mean that Aristotle is present (not Twin-Aristotle) because Aristotle caused them (not Twin-Aristotle).

30 A related problem exists, of course, for vacuous names (Adams and Stecker 1994; Everett and Hofweber 2000), but there won't be time to discuss these here.

31 I think it is Fodor's hatred of semantic holism that accounts for his avoidance of this strategy (Fodor and Lepore 1992).

32 Clearly there must be both, since Earth water causes "water"s in Al and twin-water causes "water"s in Twin-Al.

33 There are moves one could make by bringing in HIC, but I will leave those to the reader.

34 Once again, barring the possibility of semantic borrowing, Dretske's theory would conclude the same thing as Fodor's on Baker's example – the content is disjunctive. It must be, if Jerry has no way to distinguish cats from robot-cats by their appearance. The natural meaning of mental states from which Jerry's "cat" symbols derive their indicator function is itself disjunctive.

35 The need for this is obvious. Symbols in natural languages exist outside the mind and have meaning, but their meaning is derived from mental content.

36 Of course, if one hoped to identify having a mind with having semantic contents, this would be a disappointing move.

37 I don't know what Fodor's reaction would be to this possibility, but Dretske (personal communication) told me that he figured all along that states of the early visual system (and possibly others) would satisfy his conditions for semantic content. Dretske joked about the acacia that "it sounds like a pretty boring mental life." But this is only a "mental life" at all, boring or not, if one attempts to identify having minds with having semantic content.

38 With HIC Fodor and Dretske would both deny that Swampman has thoughts. For Swampman, by hypothesis, has no history of instantiation of relevant laws between properties and symbols.

39 By stipulation of the Swampman thought experiment, Jerry and SwampJerry have all the same syntactic objects in their heads (where syntax supervenes on purely physical states). But the syntactic objects may not be locked to properties.

40 Note that there are still very good reasons why content is still relevant to the explanation of behavior, and why one may not retreat to a purely syntactic theory, such as Stich's (Adams et al. 1990).

41 Semantic content is a product of asymmetrical dependency, not a source of it, on this theory.

42 If this happens after semantic content is locked, it is a false (or otherwise robust) tokening.

43 There are similar problems for Fodor's theory even with HIC (Adams and Aizawa 1994a, 1994b). For example, with (HIC), if we show Janet only jadeite, she instantiates only the "jade"→jadeite law. And any thing that robustly or falsely tokens "jade" would thus asymmetrically depend upon jadeite's tokening "jade". So the theory would say "jade" locks to jadeite because she doesn't instantiate nephrite→"jade." But this seems to be a classic case where "jade" would still have the content jadeite or nephrite because there are plenty of both around and Janet cannot tell them apart. So Fodor's theory with (HIC) would still be in trouble.

44 Thanks to Ken Aizawa and Fred Dretske for conversations and advice.

References

Adams, F. (1979). "A Goal-State Theory of Function Attribution." *Canadian Journal of Philosophy*, 9: 493–518.

—— (1991). "Causal Contents." In B. McLaughlin (ed.), *Dretske and His Critics*. Oxford: Basil Blackwell.

Adams, F. and Aizawa, K. (1992). " 'X' Means X: Semantics Fodor-Style." *Minds and Machines*, 2: 175–83.

—— (1993). "Fodorian Semantics, Pathologies, and 'Block's Problem'." *Minds and Machines*, 3: 97–104.

—— (1994a). "Fodorian Semantics." In S. Stich and T. Warfield (eds.), *Mental Representations*. Oxford: Basil Blackwell.

—— (1994b). " 'X' Means X: Fodor/Warfield Semantics." *Minds and Machines*, 4: 215–31.

—— (1997a). "Rock Beats Scissors: Historicalism Fights Back." *Analysis*, 57: 273–81.

—— (1997b). "Fodor's Asymmetrical Causal Dependency and Proximal Projections." *The Southern Journal of Philosophy*, 35: 433–7.

Adams, F. and Campbell, K. (1999). "Modality and Abstract Concepts." *Behavioral and Brain Sciences*, 22 (4): 610.

Adams, F. and Enc, B. (1988). "Not Quite By Accident." *Dialogue*, 27: 287–97.

Adams, F. and Fuller, G. (1992). "Names, Contents, and Causes." *Mind & Language*, 7: 205–21.

Adams, F. and Stecker, R. (1994). "Vacuous Singular Terms." *Mind & Language*, 9: 387–401.

Adams, F., Drebushenko, D., Fuller, G., and Stecker, R. (1990). "Narrow Content: Fodor's Folly." *Mind & Language*, 5: 213–29.

Adams, F., Fuller, G., and Stecker, R. (1993). "Thoughts Without Objects." *Mind & Language*, 8: 90–104.

Aizawa, K. (1997). "Explaining Systematicity." *Mind & Language*, 12: 115–36.

Antony, L. and Levine, J. (1991). "The Nomic and the Robust." In B. Loewer and G. Rey (eds.), *Meaning in Mind: Fodor and His Crtics*. Oxford: Basil Blackwell.

Baker, L. (1989). "On a Causal Theory of Content." *Philosophical Perspectives*, 3: 165–86.

—— (1991). "Has Content Been Naturalized?" In B. Loewer and G. Rey (eds.), *Meaning in Mind: Fodor and His Critics*. Oxford: Basil Blackwell.

Barsalou, L. (1999). "Perceptual Symbol Systems." *Behavioral and Brain Sciences*, 22: 577–660.

Boghossian, P. (1991). "Naturalizing Content." In B. Loewer and G. Rey (eds.), *Meaning in Mind: Fodor and His Critics*. Oxford: Basil Blackwell.

Carruthers, P. (1996). *Language Thought and Consciousness: An Essay in Philosophical Psychology*. Cambridge: Cambridge University Press.

Cummins, R. (1989). *Meaning and Mental Representation*. Cambridge, MA: MIT/Bradford.

Davidson, D. (1982). "Rational Animals." *Dialectica*, 36: 317–27.

—— (1987). "Knowing One's Own Mind." *Proceedings and Addresses of the American Philosophical Association*, 60: 441–58.

Dennett, D. (1987a). *The Intentional Stance*. Cambridge, MA: MIT Press.

—— (1987b). "Review of J. Fodor's *Psychosemantics*." *Journal of Philosophy*, 85: 384–9.

Dretske, F. (1971). "Conclusive Reasons." *Australasian Journal of Philosophy*, 49: 1–22.

—— (1981). *Knowledge and the Flow of Information*. Cambridge, MA: MIT/Bradford Press.

—— (1986). "Misrepresentation." In R. Bogdan (ed.), *Belief*. Oxford: Oxford University Press.

—— (1988). *Explaining Behavior: Reason in a World of Causes*. Cambridge, MA: MIT/Bradford Press.

—— (1989). "The Need to Know." In M. Clay and K. Lehrer (eds.), *Knowledge and Skepticsm*. Boulder: Westview Press.

—— (1990). "Replies to Reviewers." *Philosophy and Phenomenological Research*, 50: 819–39.

—— (1995). *Naturalizing the Mind*. Cambridge, MA: MIT/Bradford Press.

—— (manuscript) "How Do You Know You Are Not A Zombie?"

Enc, B. (manuscript). "Indeterminacy of Function Attributions."

Enc, B. and Adams, F. (1998). "Functions and Goal-Directedness." In C. Allen, M. Bekoff, and G. Lauder (eds.), *Nature's Purposes*. Cambridge, MA: MIT/Bradford.

Everett, A. and Hofweber, T. (2000). *Empty Names, Fiction and the Puzzles of Non-Existence*. Stanford: CSLI Publications.

Fodor, J. (1975). *The Language of Thought*. New York: Thomas Crowell.

—— (1981). *Representations: Philosophical Essays on the Foundations of Cognitive Science*. Cambridge, MA: MIT/Bradford.

—— (1987). *Psychosemantics*. Cambridge, MA: MIT/Bradford Press.

—— (1990a). *A Theory of Content and Other Essays*. Cambridge, MA: MIT/Bradford Press.

—— (1990b). "Information and Representation." In P. Hanson (ed.), *Information, Language, and Cognition*. Vancouver: University of British Columbia Press.

—— (1990c). "Psychosemantics or: Where Do Truth Conditions come from?" In W. Lycan (ed.), *Mind and Cognition*. Oxford: Basil Blackwell.

—— (1991). "Replies." In B. Loewer and G. Rey (eds.), *Meaning in Mind: Fodor and His Critics*. Oxford: Basil Blackwell.

—— (1994). *The Elm and the Expert: Mentalese and its Semantics*. Cambridge, MA: MIT/Bradford Press.

—— (1998a). *Concepts: Where Cognitive Science Went Wrong*. Oxford: Oxford University Press.

—— (1998b). *In Critical Condition: Polemical Essays on Cognitive Science and the Philosophy of Mind*. Cambridge, MA: MIT/Bradford Press.

Fodor, J. and Lepore, E. (1992). *Holism: A Shopper's Guide*. Oxford: Blackwell.

Fodor, J. and Pylyshyn, Z. (1988). "Connectionism and Cognitive Architecture: A Critical Analysis." *Cognition*, 28: 3–71.

Gibson, M. (1996). "Asymmetric Dependencies, Ideal Conditions, and Meaning." *Philosophical Psychology*, 9: 235–59.

Godfrey-Smith, P. (1989). "Misinformation." *Canadian Journal of Philosophy*, 19: 533–50.

—— (1992). "Indication and Adaptation." *Synthese*, 92: 283–312.

Grice, H. P. (1957). "Meaning." *Philosophical Review*, 66: 377–88.

Harman, G. (1973). *Thought*. Princeton: Princeton University Press.

Jacob, Pierre (1997). *What Minds Can Do*. Cambridge: Cambridge University Press.

Jones, T., Mulaire, E., and Stich, S. (1991). "Staving Off Catastrophe: A Critical Notice of Jerry Fodor's *Psychosemantics*." *Mind & Language*, 6: 58–82.

Loar, B. (1991). "Can We Explain Intentionality?" In B. Loewer and G. Rey (eds.), *Meaning in Mind: Fodor and His Critics*. Oxford: Basil Blackwell.

Maloney, C. (1990). "Mental Representation." *Philosophy of Science*, 57: 445–8.

Manfredi, P. and Summerfield, D. (1992). "Robustness Without Asymmetry: A Flaw in Fodor's Theory of Content." *Philosophical Studies*, 66: 261–83.

Putnam, H. (1975). "The Meaning of 'Meaning.'" In *Mind, Language and Reality.* Cambridge: Cambridge University Press.

Seager, W. (1993). "Fodor's Theory of Content: Problems and Objections." *Philosophy of Science*, 60: 262–77.

Shope, R. (1999). *The Nature of Meaningfulness: Representing, Powers and Meaning.* Boston: Rowman and Littlefield.

Stampe, D. (1977). "Towards a Causal Theory of Linguistic Representation." In *Midwest Studies in Philosophy.* Vol. 2, *Contemporary Perspectives in the Philosophy of Language*, ed. P. French, T. Uehling Jr., and H. Wettstein. Minneapolis: University of Minnesota Press.

Sterelny, K. (1990). *The Representational Theory of Mind.* Oxford: Blackwell.

Wallis, C. (1994). "Representation and the Imperfect Ideal." *Philosophy of Science*, 61: 407–28.

—— (1995). "Asymmetrical Dependence, Representation, and Cognitive Science." *The Southern Journal of Philosophy*, 33: 373–401.

Warfield, T. (1994). "Fodorian Semantics: A Reply to Adams and Aizawa." *Minds and Machines*, 4: 205–14.

Chapter 7

Cognitive Architecture: The Structure of Cognitive Representations

Kenneth Aizawa

Although theories of cognitive architecture are concerned with the nature of the basic structures and processes involved in cognition, philosophical interest in this area has largely focused on the structure of hypothetical cognitive representations.[1] The classical theory of cognitive architecture, for example, maintains that

1   There exist syntactically and semantically combinatorial mental representations, i.e., there is a distinction to be made between syntactically and semantically atomic and syntactically and semantically molecular representations.
2   Each token of a molecular representation literally contains a token of each of the representations of which it is constructed.
3   The meaning of a molecular representation is a function of the meanings of its parts and the way in which those parts are put together.
4   Each of the syntactic parts of a molecular representation has the same content in whatever context it occurs.
5   There exist computational mechanisms that are sensitive to the structure of the mental representations.

One alternative to classicism is atomic representationalism (AR). AR maintains that cognitive representations are one and all syntactically and semantically atomic, hence it rejects (1)–(5). Another rival, with a considerable following in some quarters, is functional combinatorialism (FC).[2] FC maintains that, while there are combinatorial representations, they are not of the sort postulated by classicism. Somewhat more specifically, FC asserts that molecular representations are merely (computable) functions of their atoms, hence that the atoms need not be literal parts of the molecules from which they are derived.

Rather than attempt to survey the whole of the field of cognitive architecture, or even the whole of the debates over cognitive representations, this paper will focus on Jerry Fodor and Zenon Pylyshyn's systematicity arguments for classicism. In rough outline, the arguments are simple. There are certain features of thought, namely, the systematicity of inference, the systematicity of thought, and the compositionality of representations, which are best explained by classicism, hence we have some defeasible reason to believe that classicism is true. This survey of the arguments has a number of goals. In the first place, it aims to address a range of misunderstandings about what is to be explained in the arguments. Secondly, it will draw attention to a relatively underappreciated feature of the systematicity arguments, namely, that there is some principle of better explanation at work. Thirdly, it will indicate how, classicist contentions notwithstanding, the usual formulations of the systematicity arguments do not in fact support classicism. Finally, it will draw attention to another kind of systematicity argument suggested by Fodor and Pylyshyn's critique. This argument has the explanatory virtue Fodor and Pylyshyn have in mind and shows a strength of classicism lacking in AR and FC.

The plan of this chapter will be to survey the systematicity of inference, the systematicity of cognitive representations, the compositionality of representations arguments, and a new type of systematicity argument. Each argument will be introduced via an explanandum, along with possible AR and classical explanations. After the first pass through the arguments, we will return to see how the systematicity arguments bear on a specific version of FC, namely, the hypothesis that cognitive representations have the structure of Gödel numerals.

7.1 The Systematicity of Inference

Fodor and Pylyshyn suggest that cognition has the following general feature: "inferences that are of similar logical type ought, pretty generally, to elicit correspondingly similar cognitive capacities. You shouldn't, for example, find a kind of mental life in which you get inferences from P&Q&R to P but don't get inferences from P&Q to P" (1988: 47). Further:

> The hedge ["pretty generally"] is meant to exclude cases where inferences of the same logical type nevertheless differ in complexity in virtue of, for example, the length of their premises. The inference from (AvBvCvDvE) and (¬B&¬C&¬D&¬E) to A is of the same logical type as the inference from AvB and ¬B to A. But it wouldn't be very surprising, or very interesting, if there were minds that could handle the second inference but not the first. (Ibid.: fn. 28)

The question, then, arises, "Why is it that inferential capacities are systematic?" A number of features of the explanandum bear comment. In the first place, the explanandum involves inferences of the same logical type.[3] A normal cognitive agent that can perform one instance of, say, conjunction elimination can, *ceteris paribus*, perform another instance. A normal cognitive agent that can perform one instance of *modus ponens* can, *ceteris paribus*, perform another instance. For simplicity, in what follows we will consider only a limited range of systematicity of conjunction elimination. In the second place, the explanandum involves cognitive capacities, or cognitive competences, in logical inference. The explanandum here does not maintain that any normal cognitive agent that infers P from P&Q will also infer P from P&Q&R. Because the explanandum is concerned with capacities for inference, rather than actual performance in inference, the experimental literature on human performance in reasoning – the literature that has detected various content effects, frequency effects, and so forth – does not, as it stands, directly address Fodor and Pylyshyn's explanandum.[4] Thirdly, the systematicity arguments assume only a finite human cognitive competence. They do not rely on the view that human competence involves an unbounded representational capacity. Fodor and Pylyshyn write:

> [W]e propose to view the status of productivity arguments for Classical architectures as moot; we're about to present a different sort of argument for the claim that mental representations need an articulated internal structure. It is closely related to the productivity argument, but it doesn't require the idealization to unbounded competence. Its assumptions should thus be acceptable even to theorists who – like Connectionists – hold that the finitistic character of cognitive capacities is intrinsic to their architecture. (1988: 36–7)[5]

Fourthly, it is crucial to see that in foregoing recourse to the idea of an unbounded representational capacity, classicists do not thereby forgo recourse to the competence/performance distinction. Clearly, classicists believe that actual human performance in reasoning is a function of many capacities.[6] One of these is a logical inferential capacity, but one must also admit recognitional, attentional, and memory capacities. Indeed, any competent experimentalist will recognize that there are many features of an experimental situation – such as those affecting motivation, recognition, attention, and memory – that must be controlled in order to detect a capacity for logical inference. Recognizing this multiplicity of factors is the essence of recognizing the competence/performance distinction. So, even though Fodor and Pylyshyn propose to run the systematicity of inference argument without relying on the supposition that there is an unbounded capacity for inference, they do not thereby propose to do without the competence/performance distinction *in toto*.[7]

So much for the explanandum. What about the explanans? Some critics of the systematicity arguments have observed that it is possible to develop systems that display various forms of systematic relations.[8] From this, they conclude that the real issue in the systematicity debate is over exactly what sorts of systematic relations exist in human thought and the extent to which a given theory of cognition can generate those systematic relations. While data-fit is an important factor in rational scientific theory choice, it is not the only one. More importantly, it is not the one Fodor and Pylyshyn invoke in the systematicity arguments. The issue in these arguments is not one of merely accommodating the available data, but one of accounting for it in a certain important sort of way. Fodor and Pylyshyn's commentary on the systematicity of inference argument bears this point out nicely:

> A Connectionist can certainly model a mental life in which, if you can reason from P&Q&R to P, then you can also reason from P&Q to P. . . . But notice that *a Connectionist can equally model a mental life in which you get one of these inferences and not the other.* In the present case, since there is no structural relation between the P&Q&R node and the P&Q node . . . there's no reason why a mind that contains the first should also contain the second, or vice versa. Analogously, there's no reason why you shouldn't get minds that simplify the premise *John loves Mary and Bill hates Mary* but no others; or minds that simplify premises with 1, 3, or 5 conjuncts, but don't simplify premises with 2, 4, or 6 conjuncts; or, for that matter, minds that simplify premises that were acquired on Tuesdays . . . etc. In fact, the Connectionist architecture is *utterly indifferent* as among these possibilities. (1988: 47–8)

The idea that there is more at stake in the systematicity arguments than merely fitting the data is further supported by a later passage by Fodor and McLaughlin:

> No doubt it is possible for [a Connectionist] to wire a network so that it supports a vector that represents *aRb* if and only if it supports a vector that represents *bRa* . . . The trouble is that, although the architecture permits this, it equally permits [a Connectionist] to wire a network so that it supports a vector that represents *aRb* if and only if it supports a vector that represents *zSq*; or, for that matter, if and only if it supports a vector that represents *The Last of the Mohicans*. The architecture would appear to be absolutely indifferent as among these options. (1990: 202)

Clearly, more is at stake in explaining the systematic relations in thought than simply covering the data.

Many critics have responded to the foregoing passages, indicating weaknesses in the way in which Fodor et al. develop this idea.[9] While there are genuine weaknesses in the formulation, in the end, Fodor et al. appear to be on to something that is of scientific import, something that philosophers of science would do well to analyze, and something to which cognitive scientists ought to pay greater attention.[10] Given space limitations, these contentions can be supported only with an apparently analogous case from the history of science. In the *Origin of Species*, Charles Darwin notes regularities in morphology, taxonomy, embryology, and biogeography that he takes to be better explained by evolution than by a theory of divine creation.[11] The idea is that, although both evolution and creationism have accounts of these putative regularities, the evolutionary account does not rely on arbitrary hypotheses in the way the creationist account does. One instance involves the biogeography of batrachians:

> Bory St. Vincent long ago remarked that Batrachians (frogs, toads, newts) have never been found on any of the many islands with which the great oceans are

studded. I have taken pains to verify this assertion, and I have found it strictly true. I have, however, been assured that a frog exists on the mountains of the great island of New Zealand; but I suspect that this exception (if the information be correct) may be explained through glacial agency. This general absence of frogs, toads, and newts on so many oceanic islands cannot be accounted for by their physical conditions; indeed it seems that islands are peculiarly well fitted for these animals; for frogs have been introduced into Madeira, the Azores, and Mauritius, and have multiplied so as to become a nuisance. But as these animals and their spawn are known to be immediately killed by sea-water, on my view we can see that there would be great difficulty in their transportal across the sea, and therefore why, on the theory of creation, they should not have been created there, it would be very difficult to explain. (1859: 393)

According to the theory of evolution, batrachian forms first appeared on the mainland, but because seawater kills them, thereby hindering their migration across oceans, one finds that (almost without exception) there are no batrachians on oceanic islands. According to creationism, God distributed life on the planet according to some plan. The problem is that it appears that God's plan could as easily have placed batrachians on oceanic islands as not. The evidence for this latter claim is that naturalists had already observed that it is possible for humans to transport batrachians to Madeira, the Azores, and Mauritius and have them survive quite well.

Creationism and evolution have what might be identified as central hypotheses and auxiliary hypotheses. The central hypothesis in creationism is, of course, that species are the product of divine creation, where the central hypothesis in evolution is, of course, that species are the product of descent with modification. The difference in the accounts the theories offer lies in their appeals to auxiliary hypotheses. The evolutionary account relies on auxiliary hypotheses that are confirmed independently of the explanatory task at hand. The evolutionary account assumes that the mainland is older than oceanic islands, a fact that is confirmed by geological observations of erosion. The evolutionary account also assumes that saltwater constitutes a migration barrier to batrachians, a fact easily confirmed by simple experiments. By contrast, creationist hypotheses concerning God's plan for distributing life forms are not independently confirmable; the nature of God's plan in creation would seem to be inaccessible unless one had antecedently verified that God did, in fact, separately create organisms according to a plan. In this sense, the creationist relies on an arbitrary hypothesis.

With this rough characterization of the explanatory standard at work in the systematicity arguments, we can consider what AR might have to say about the systematicity of conjunction elimination. The atomic representationalist will postulate a set of syntactically atomic representations $\{\alpha, \beta, \gamma\}$, where

α means John loves Mary and Bill loves Mary and Alice loves Mary,
β means John loves Mary and Bill loves Mary, and
γ means John loves Mary.

A system for inferring that John loves Mary from the premise that John loves Mary and Bill loves Mary and Alice loves Mary and from the premise that John loves Mary and Bill loves Mary might have the Turing-machine-like program

(P1) $s_0 \, \alpha \, \gamma \, s_1$
      $s_0 \, \beta \, \gamma \, s_1$

This program is such that, if the system is in state s_0 scanning an α or β, then it will print a γ, and go into state s_1. But, such a system might just as easily have the program

(P2) $s_0 \, \alpha \, \gamma \, s_1$

(P1) allows a system to infer P from P&Q and from P&Q&R, where (P2) only allows a system to infer P from P&Q. So, recalling what Fodor and Pylyshyn had to say about this possibility, AR can certainly model a mental life in which an agent can reason from both P&Q and P&Q&R to P, but can equally model a mental life in which you get one of these inferences and not the other. One can, of course, add to the central AR hypothesis concerning the existence of atomic mental representations the auxiliary hypothesis that the AR system has a program like (P1), rather than (P2), but here we have an objectionable auxiliary. This auxiliary cannot be confirmed independently of the truth of AR just as the creationist hypothesis about the plan of God in creation could not be confirmed independently of the truth of creationism.

A classical account of the systematicity of conjunction elimination will begin with the syntactically atomic symbols, $\{\alpha, \beta, \gamma, \&, b\}$, where α means John loves Mary, β means Bill loves Mary, γ means Alice loves Mary, & means conjunction, and b is a meaningless blank symbol.[12] One Turing-machine-like program that enables a system to infer its first conjunct regardless of whether there are two or more conjunctions in the whole is

(P3) $s_0 \, \alpha \, R \, s_0$ $s_2 \, \alpha \, b \, s_3$
      $s_0 \, \beta \, R \, s_0$ $s_2 \, \beta \, b \, s_3$
      $s_0 \, \gamma \, R \, s_0$ $s_2 \, \gamma \, b \, s_3$
      $s_0 \, \& \, b \, s_1$ $s_2 \, \& \, b \, s_3$
      $s_1 \, b \, R \, s_2$ $s_3 \, b \, R \, s_2$

The instructions in the left column direct the system to scan over the first symbol on the tape and erase the first "&," while those in the second column direct it to erase the non-blank symbols from the remainder of the tape. The evident problem with this approach is that, while there are classical programs, such as (P3), that give rise to systematicity of conjunction elimination, there are other programs meeting classicist specifications that do not give rise to the systematicity of conjunction elimination. In other words, given classicism, one can as easily have a program that gives rise to the systematicity of conjunction elimination as some other program that does not. Of course, one might add some further auxiliary hypothesis to classicism, saying that the program of the mind is like (P3), rather than not, but this auxiliary would appear to be inaccessible to confirmation independent of the truth of classicism. The classicist can no better independently confirm this auxiliary than could the creationist independently confirm her auxiliary about God's plan of creation. Further, the classicist can no better independently confirm this auxiliary than could the atomic representationalist confirm her auxiliary about the nature of the computer program of the mind. The upshot, therefore, is that neither classicism nor AR has an adequate explanation of the systematicity of inference.

7.2 The Systematicity of Cognitive Representations

For this argument, Fodor and Pylyshyn claim that, in normal cognitive agents, the ability to have some thoughts is intrinsically connected to the ability to have certain other thoughts. This intrinsic connection might be spelled out in terms of two types of psychological-level dependencies among thought capacities. On the one hand, were a normal cognitive agent to lack the capacity for certain thoughts, that agent would also lack the capacity for certain other thoughts.[13] On the other hand, were a normal cognitive agent to have the capacity for certain thoughts, that agent would thereby have the capacity for certain other thoughts. It should be noted that this feature of normal cognitive agents is not logically or conceptually necessary. Minds could be entirely punctate in the sense that the ability to have certain thoughts might have no consequences at all for the possession of any other thoughts. So, what needs to be explained is why normal cognitive agents have systematic, rather than punctate, minds.

As a way of further clarifying the putative explanandum, consider where the classicist expects to find these dependencies. For a normal cognitive agent, one expects to find an intrinsic connection between the capacity for the thought that John loves Mary and the capacity for the thought that Mary loves John. Were a normal cognitive agent to lack the capacity to have the thought that John loves Mary, then that agent would also lack the capacity to have the thought that Mary loves John. This is one aspect of the idea of intrinsic connections among thoughts; here is another. Were a normal cognitive agent to be able to think that John loves Mary, then that cognitive agent would also be able to think that Mary loves John. Bear in mind that the thing to be explained in the systematicity of cognitive representations argument is the very existence of systematic relations among thoughts, not where those relations lie. Bringing out where these dependencies lie is merely an expository move that may lend some intuitive credibility to the claim that thought is systematic. Once again, we want to know why some thoughts are connected to others, rather than to none at all.

How, then, might AR attempt to explain the systematicity of thought? AR might conjecture that, because of the structure of the computer program of the mind, the loss of a representation corresponding to one thought brings with it a loss of the representation corresponding to one or more additional thoughts. Further, the program is such that the addition of representations corresponding to some thoughts brings with it the addition of representations corresponding to additional thoughts. Since representations are (part of) the underlying basis for thoughts, having the connections between the various representations would constitute (in part) the connections between the capacities for the corresponding thoughts.

The problem with the AR account of the systematicity of thought is essentially the same as that with the AR account of the systematicity of inference. Let us suppose, if only for the sake of argument, that one can in fact program a computer to give rise to dependencies among the capacities for tokening various representations. Suppose there is a class of AR computer programs that display dependencies among representations. Even if there exist such computer programs, it is clear that there also exist computer programs that meet the conditions of AR, yet do not give rise to dependencies among representations. One might say that an AR computer program can as easily be systematic, as not. One can, of course, add to AR some auxiliary hypothesis to the effect that the computer program of the mind is such as to give rise to the dependencies among thoughts, rather than not. But, once again, this hypothesis would appear to be inaccessible to independent confirmation short of confirming AR.

Although we see why AR does not explain the systematicity of thought, we must also consider whether classicism can pass muster by the same explanatory standard. Suppose that there is a set of syntactically atomic representations, Γ = {John, Jane, Mary, Lisa, loves, hates}. There are, of course, computer programs that combine the atoms in Γ so as to yield the formulas in the set $\Gamma_1^* =$

{John loves John   John loves Jane   John loves Mary   John loves Lisa
Jane loves John   Jane loves Jane   Jane loves Mary   Jane loves Lisa
Mary loves John   Mary loves Jane   Mary loves Mary   Mary loves Lisa
Lisa loves John   Lisa loves Jane   Lisa loves Mary   Lisa loves Lisa
John hates John   John hates Jane   John hates Mary   John hates Lisa
Jane hates John   Jane hates Jane   Jane hates Mary   Jane hates Lisa
Mary hates John   Mary hates Jane   Mary hates Mary   Mary hates Lisa
Lisa hates John   Lisa hates Jane   Lisa hates Mary   Lisa hates Lisa}

but there are also computer programs that combine the atoms of Γ so as to yield the formulas in the set $\Gamma_2^* =$ {John loves Mary, Jane hates Lisa}. Γ_1^* is systematic, where Γ_2^* is not; there are dependencies among the representations in Γ_1^*, but not among those in Γ_2^*. So, given that one has a classical system of representation, one can as easily have a systematic set of representations, as not. The classicist will, thus, wish to add some auxiliary hypothesis to the effect that Γ forms a set like Γ_1^*, rather than a set like Γ_2^*. The refrain, however, is that we lack independent confirmation of this auxiliary. So, again, even though AR lacks a satisfactory account of the systematicity of thought, classicism is in no better shape in this regard.

7.3   The Compositionality of Representations

The systematicity of cognitive representations is a matter of some thoughts being dependent on other thoughts. The compositionality of representations has to do with an additional property of thoughts: possible occurrent thoughts are semantically related. Roughly speaking, thoughts predicate the same properties and relations of the same objects. Thus, the previous section indicated where we should expect to find intrinsic connections among thoughts, namely, among those that are semantically related. Now, this semantic relatedness is converted into an explanandum.

Fodor and Pylyshyn (1988: 41) suggest that systematicity is closely related to compositionality and that they might best be viewed as two aspects of a single phenomenon. Be this as it may, systematicity and compositionality are logically distinct properties. So, on the one hand, it is logically possible that were one, as a matter of psychological fact, to lose the capacity to have the thought that John loves Mary, one might thereby lose the capacity to have the thought that Aristotle was a shipping magnate. It is also logically possible that, as a matter of psychological fact, were one to have the capacity to have the thoughts that John loves Mary and that Mary loves herself, one would also have the capacity to have the thought that Aristotle is a shipping magnate. The discovery of cognitive agents that were systematic, but not compositional, would be puzzling in the extreme, but such a discovery is nonetheless a possibility. On the other hand, it is also possible to have thoughts that are contentfully related without their being interdependent. One could have the capacity for the thoughts that John loves Mary, that Mary loves John, that John hates Mary, and that Mary hates John without the loss of one of these capacities precipitating the loss of any others; further, one could have the capacity for the thoughts that John loves Mary, that Mary loves John, and that John hates Mary, without having the capacity for the thought that Mary hates John. Dependence among thoughts does not logically imply contentful relations among the thoughts, and contentful relations among thoughts does not logically imply dependence among thoughts.

How then might AR explain the putative fact that the set of possible occurrent thoughts for a normal cognitive agent are contentfully related? AR will say that the thought that John loves Mary involves a syntactic atom α that means that John loves Mary, and that the thought that Mary loves John involves a syntactic atom β that means that Mary loves John. Now while there may well be computer programs meeting this description, there are also clearly computer programs that do not meet this description. Computers can be as easily programmed to be like this as not, hence AR alone does not lead to the compositionality of thought. Moreover, should AR add an auxiliary hypothesis to the effect that the computer program of the mind is such that were the agent not to be able to handle α it would not be able to handle β, the situation is not improved. This auxiliary is of exactly the sort that admits of no confirmation independent of the truth of AR.

The classical account of the compositionality of representations invokes the hypothesis that thoughts involve a set of syntactic atoms and some way of composing them into syntactic molecules. Yet, there are ways of building molecules and there are ways of building molecules. A set of syntactic atoms $\Sigma = \{$John, Jane, loves, hates$\}$ can be combined to form the set of strings $\Sigma_1^* =$

{John loves John   John loves Jane   Jane loves John   Jane loves Jane
John hates John   John hates Jane   Jane hates John   Jane hates Jane}

or it can be combined to form the set of strings $\Sigma_2^* = \{$John loves John, Jane hates Jane$\}$. The set of classicist hypotheses we have enumerated does not lead to there being content relations among thoughts. Classicism must, therefore, invoke an auxiliary hypothesis to the effect that Σ is combined to form syntactic items in a set like Σ_1^*, rather than those in a set like Σ_2^*. But such an auxiliary is not independently confirmed, leaving classicism without a bona fide explanation of the compositionality of representations. Again, we find that neither AR nor classicism has an explanation of the compositionality of thought.

7.4   Another Systematicity Argument

Thus far we have had three illustrations of the basic weakness in current attempts to use systematicity arguments to justify hypothesizing a classical system of cognitive representations. All current attempts rely on auxiliary hypotheses that are in some sense arbitrary. This might suggest that the explanatory standard being invoked in the systematicity arguments is unrealistically high.[14] The argument of this section will show that the standard is not too high. It will maintain the explanatory standard implicit in Fodor and Pylyshyn's work, but invoke another explanandum in another systematicity argument. This approach will not, of course, show us how to explain the systematic relations that Fodor and Pylyshyn have introduced, but it will provide us with some defeasible reason to believe that there exists a combinatorial language of thought.

In the last section, we noted the logical separability of the systematicity and compositionality of representations. We can have one as a psychological fact without the other. Here, however, is another psychological fact. If a normal cognitive agent has a systematic mind, then it also has a compositional mind. Why is this? Why is it that the interdependent thoughts are, in addition, contentfully related? We have noted that neither AR nor classicism has an appropriate account of these independent regularities, but what about one following upon the other?

Classicism appears to have the right sort of account of the co-occurrence. Given the apparatus classicism needs to account for systematicity, one has, without further assumption, the apparatus necessary to account for compositionality. Thus, a classical account of systematicity relies on the hypothesis that there exist syntactically atomic representations that combine to form syntactically molecular representations and that these atomic representations satisfy the principle of semantic compositionality. The reason that some thoughts are dependent on others is that they have common atomic or molecular representations. Thus, the reason the thought that John loves Mary is dependent on the thought that Mary loves John is that they share (a) an atomic representation "John" (which means John in both the context of "– loves Mary" and "Mary loves –," (b) an atomic representation "Mary" (which means Mary in both the context of "John loves –" and "– loves John," (c) an atomic representation "loves" (which means loving in both the context of "John – Mary" and "Mary – John," and (d) a common grammatical structure. Given this sort of account of the interdependence of the John loves Mary thought and the Mary loves John thought, the fact that thoughts will be content-related follows without additional assumption. The set of classical assumptions that are needed in order to account for systematicity entail compositionality.

By contrast, AR has no satisfactory method for connecting the systematicity of thought with the compositionality of thought. This arises because the content of one syntactically atomic representation is completely independent of the content of any other syntactically atomic representation. Given what AR needs in order to account for the interdependence of thoughts, there is no reason why those interdependent thoughts should at the same time be contentfully related. Even if the AR theorist can make good on the hypothesis that the program of the mind is such that two syntactic items α and β, with their respective contents, are dependent on each other, it would require an auxiliary hypothesis regarding the specific semantic content of α and β to have it work out that α and β are also contentfully related. Such an additional hypothesis, however, would be just the sort of hypothesis that could not be confirmed independent of the hypothesis of an AR system of mental representation.

The strength of this sort of explanatory argument is borne out in an example. Ancient astronomers had observed that, as a very gross approximation, the superior planets Mars, Jupiter, and Saturn move through the fixed stars from west to east. This very general tendency, however, is periodically interrupted by a period of retrograde motion which involves the superior planets slowing in their normal eastward motion, stopping, moving for a time in a westward retrograde manner, before again slowing, stopping, and finally resuming a normal eastward motion. Ptolemaic astronomers were aware of these irregularities and were able to provide a qualitatively correct model of them. The basic idea is to have a superior planet, such as Mars, orbiting on an epicycle. This epicycle then orbits at the end of a deferent. By careful adjustment of the relative sizes and relative rates of rotation of the epicycle and deferent, it is possible to generate, to a first approximation, the observed motions of the superior planets. The Copernican account of retrograde motions is fundamentally different. According to Copernicans, retrograde motions are merely apparent motions that arise from the Earth's overtaking a superior planet as both orbit the Sun. Where the Copernican account proves to be far superior to the Ptolemaic account is in its ability to account for a particular feature of retrograde motions: they always occur when the superior planet stands in opposition to the sun. Whenever a planet is in the very middle of its westward retrograde motion, it is found to be separated from the Sun by 180°. By clever manipulation of features of the epicycle on the deferent system, Ptolemaic astronomy could provide an account of this feature of retrograde motion, but the Copernican system generated the further fact without any additional hypothesis. Simply given the proposed nature of retrograde motions on the Copernican system, it follows of necessity that retrograde motions will occur at opposition. The necessary elements of the Copernican account of retrograde motions suffice to account for retrograde motions occurring at opposition. The Ptolemaic account doesn't have this strength.

7.5 Can Functional Combinatorialism Explain the Systematic Relations in Thought?

To this point, we have considered how a range of systematicity arguments bears on classicism and AR. One response to these arguments, however, has been to claim that cognition involves a third form of representationalism, a non-classical FC. According to FC, molecular representations are merely (computable) functions of their atoms; the atoms need not be literal spatio-temporal parts of the molecules from which they are derived. One way this idea is fleshed out is through Paul Smolensky's (1995) Tensor Product Theory. Another way is through Gödel numerals. In fact, Gödel numerals are frequently cited to show the impeccable scientific stature of functionally combinatorial representations.[15] Fodor and McLaughlin (1990) and Fodor (1996) have raised a number of technical and conceptual problems with Smolensky's theory, ultimately carrying the discussion in directions we do not have time to explore here. This, however, gives us an opening to explore a more conservative line of criticism. We can press the explanatory standard implicit in Fodor and Pylyshyn (1988) to show that the kind of functionally combinatorial representations embodied in Gödel numerals cannot explain the systematic relations in thought.

Suppose we try to use Gödel numerals to explain how a cognitive agent can infer John loves Mary from John loves Mary and John loves Jane and from John loves Mary and John loves Jane and John loves Alice. The Gödel numerals story might begin with the following atomic representations

"1" means John loves Mary
"2" means John loves Jane
"3" means John loves Alice
"4" means and.

The n atomic representations that will constitute a molecular representation give us a sequence of n numerals. Thus, to represent the proposition that John loves Mary and John loves Jane we will use the sequence <1, 4, 2>, while to represent the proposition that John loves Mary and John loves Jane and John loves Alice we will use the sequence <1, 4, 2, 4, 3>. This sequence of n numerals gives us exponents for the first n prime numbers, which are then multiplied in order to complete our Gödel representations. So, we have it that

"1" means John loves Mary.
"144" ($= 1 \times 2^4 \times 3^2$) means John loves Mary and John loves Jane.
"30870000" ($= 1 \times 2^4 \times 3^2 \times 5^4 \times 7^3$) means John loves Mary and John loves Jane and John loves Alice.

Here the system of representation is non-classical, since a token of a given syntactic molecule, such as "30870000," need not literally contain a token of each of the syntactic atoms of which it is constructed, i.e., tokens of "1," "2," "3," or "4."[16] To get the systematicity of conjunction elimination in these cases, we simply hypothesize that there exists a computer program that produces a "1" in response to both "144" and "30870000."

The problem here is what we have come to expect. Speaking loosely, it is just as easy to produce a computer program that writes "1" in response to both "144" and "30870000" as it is to produce a computer program that writes "1" in response to "144" but not to "30870000." Adding some hypothesis to the effect that the program does produce "144" and "30870000" will, however, be unproductive, since such an hypothesis cannot be confirmed short of confirming the hypothesis that the system uses Gödel numerals as cognitive representations.

What about the systematicity of thought? Suppose we have the set of propositions

John loves John   John loves Mary   John loves Jane
Mary loves John   Mary loves Mary   Mary loves Jane
Jane loves John   Jane loves Mary   Jane loves Jane.

We begin setting up a Gödel numeral representation of these propositions using numerals from the familiar base ten Arabic system and giving them the following semantic interpretations:

"1" means John,
"2" means Mary,

"3" means Jane, and
"4" means loving.

Here we have our Gödel numeral system's atomic representations. We next associate with each proposition a sequence of numerals. Thus, the proposition John
loves Mary is associated with the sequence <1, 4, 2> and the proposition that
John loves Jane is associated with the sequence <1, 4, 3>. We take the n numbers
represented by the n numerals in the sequence and use them as the powers of n
prime numbers. The product of these n prime numbers yields another number
whose Arabic decimal representation we can then take to be the representation of
our proposition. Thus, we take the three-member sequence <1, 4, 2> (which is
associated with John loves Mary) and apply it to three prime numbers to give us
the number two thousand and twenty five (= $2 \times 3^4 \times 5^2$) which is written in
Arabic notation as "2025." Similarly, we take the three-member sequence <1, 4,
3> (which is associated with the proposition John loves Jane) and use this in
conjunction with three prime numbers, so that John loves Jane is associated with
the numeral "20250" (= $2 \times 3^4 \times 5^3$). Following this arrangement, we represent
our set of propositions with the following numerals:

810 (= $2 \times 3^4 \times 5$) represents John loves John
2025 (= $2 \times 3^4 \times 5^2$) represents John loves Mary
20250 (= $2 \times 3^4 \times 5^3$) represents John loves Jane
1620 (= $2^2 \times 3^4 \times 5$) represents Mary loves John
8100 (= $2^2 \times 3^4 \times 5^2$) represents Mary loves Mary
40500 (= $2^2 \times 3^4 \times 5^3$) represents Mary loves Jane
3240 (= $2^3 \times 3^4 \times 5$) represents Jane loves John
16200 (= $2^3 \times 3^4 \times 5^2$) represents Jane loves Mary
81000 (= $2^3 \times 3^4 \times 5^3$) represents Jane loves Jane.

Inspecting the representations generated in this way, we see that the mutual
dependence of representations on one another gives rise to systematic relations
among thoughts. That is, given that, say, the representation of John loving Jane
and the representation of Jane loving John both depend on the capacity for
having a "0" in the ones place, we can see that there will be a dependency
between the capacity for thinking that John loves Jane and the capacity for Jane
loves John.

From the previous discussion, however, we should have learned that the foregoing only shows that Gödel numerals can exhibit a dependence among thoughts.
It does not show that Gödel numerals can explain the interdependence of thoughts.
We have to consider whether or not there is some arbitrary auxiliary hypothesis in
the account. Moreover, as we may have come to expect, there is. One assumption
underlying the system above is that the Gödel numerals (i.e., the products of the
exponeniated primes) are expressed in the familiar base ten notation. In virtue of
this assumption and the choice of numerals for the atomic representations, it

turns out that some of the Gödel numerals for the propositions have common elements, hence that there are dependencies among the molecular representations. The assumption that the mind uses a base ten representational system for the products of the primes is, however, arbitrary. To put matters as Fodor and Pylyshyn would, one can as easily use a base ten representational system as not all the while remaining within the framework of a Gödel numeral system. Alternatively, we may say that the hypothesis that a Gödel numeral system of representation is a base ten system is not confirmed independently of the present explanatory challenge. An alternative assumption is that the Gödel numerals occur in, say, a base 100,000 system in which none of the 100,000 atomic symbols will have anything syntactic in common. So, the set of atomic numerals in the system might be something like {0, 1, 2, 3, 4, 5, 6, 7, 8, 9, a, A, b, B, . . . , z, Z, . . . , ♥, ♦, ♣, ♠}. In such a system, none of the numerals for our propositions would have common elements, hence there would be no interdependencies among any of the numerals representing the propositions in our set, hence no interdependence among the corresponding thoughts. So, Gödel numerals cannot explain the interdependencies among thoughts.[17]

Next, what is wrong with the Gödel numeral account of the content relations among possible thoughts? Essentially, the same thing that was wrong with the classical account: a "Gödel numerals grammar" can as easily generate a contentfully related set of molecular representations as not. Take, again, the set of atomic representations, {1, 2, 3, 4}, where

"1" means John,
"2" means Mary,
"3" means Jane,
"4" means loving, and
"5" means hating

This set of atomic representations can generate the representations with the contents

John loves John	John loves Jane	John loves Mary	John loves Lisa
Jane loves John	Jane loves Jane	Jane loves Mary	Jane loves Lisa
Mary loves John	Mary loves Jane	Mary loves Mary	Mary loves Lisa
Lisa loves John	Lisa loves Jane	Lisa loves Mary	Lisa loves Lisa
John hates John	John hates Jane	John hates Mary	John hates Lisa
Jane hates John	Jane hates Jane	Jane hates Mary	Jane hates Lisa
Mary hates John	Mary hates Jane	Mary hates Mary	Mary hates Lisa
Lisa hates John	Lisa hates Jane	Lisa hates Mary	Lisa hates Lisa,

as easily as it can generate representations with the contents

John loves Mary   Jane hates Lisa.

Bear in mind, Gödel numerals must allow some way of generating different sets of molecular representations on a given set of atomic representations. For purposes of cognitive theory, there must be some principle or hypothesis that makes it the case that a "Gödel numeral grammar" does not generate representations with such "contents" as John John John, John John loves, and John loves loves. Whatever hypothesis a theory of Gödel numerals has to do, this will be the problematic hypothesis that is the undoing of its account of the content relations in thought. This hypothesis will be one for which there will be no independent confirmation. So, like classicism, Gödel numerals cannot explain the systematicity of thought.

This brings us to the less familiar feature of systematicity examined above, the co-occurrence of systematicity and semantic relatedness. How do Gödel numerals fare here? It should be clear that, while it is possible to generate dependencies between representations that are semantically related, it is also possible to generate dependencies between representations that are not semantically related. The representation "20250" (which in our example above represented John loves Jane) is intrinsically connected to the representation "3240" (which in our example above represented Jane loves John), but this connection is independent of the contents of "20250" and "3240." What a theory of Gödel numerals hypothesizes in order to account for the intrinsic connection among thoughts does not imply that there must be semantic relations among thoughts, hence does not explain the correlation.

7.6   Conclusion

Aside from the relatively minor task of clarifying the arguments, this chapter has had other more important objectives. First, it draws greater attention to the fact that the systematicity arguments involve some principle concerning choice among competing explanations. There is much that needs to be said about the principle, but at heart it appears to have something to do with explanations having to avoid ad hoc auxiliary hypotheses. Secondly, while defending the classicist contention that theories such as atomic representationalism and functional combinatorialism do not explain the systematicity relations in thought, this chapter urges that even classicism fails to explain the systematic relations in thought. Thirdly, the chapter points out another kind of systematicity argument suggested by Fodor and Pylyshyn's critique. This argument has the explanatory virtue Fodor and Pylyshyn have in mind and shows a strength of classicism lacking in AR and FC.

Notes

1   Alas, a tradition of semantic eliminativism that would warm a behaviorist's heart lives on in the representational eliminativism of Brooks (1997), and van Gelder (1997).

Another substantial area of investigation that has concerned philosophers is the "modularity of mind" (cf. Fodor 1983; Karmiloff-Smith 1992). Any adequate discussion of the modularity of mind would, however, have to be the subject of another chapter.

2   Cf., e.g., Smolensky (1995), Cummins (1996), and Horgan and Tienson (1996).

3   See Cummins (1996: 612), where this point appears to be missed.

4   Both van Gelder and Niklasson (1994) and Cummins (1996) overestimate the significance of the human reasoning literature for the systematicity of inference argument.

5   See, as well, ibid.: 37, 38, 40, where the limitation imposed on the systematicity argument is to an hypothesis of a bounded cognitive capacity.

6   That, after all, was part of the point of the note 5.

7   Both Niklasson and van Gelder (1994) and Cummins (1996) seem to miss this point.

8   Cf. Niklasson and van Gelder (1994), Cummins (1996), Hadley and Hayward (1996).

9   See, for example, the discussions of necessitating the explanandum and principled explanations in Smolensky (1995), Cummins (1996), and Hadley (1997).

10 These claims, undefended here, are defended in Aizawa (in preparation).

11 Aizawa (1997a, 1997b) examine additional illustrations.

12 Here α, β, and γ abbreviate sentences, rather than formulae in first-order logic. This is still a classical account, since combinatorial representations, structure sensitivity, the principle of compositionality, and so forth are still in play. Having α, β, and γ represent sentences merely simplifies the discussion.

13 The force of this counterfactual is not that, were one to perform a brain lesion that removes one thought, at least one other thought would thereby be lesioned. Such an explanandum would presumably be an implementational fact, hence not the sort of fact to be explained by a purely psychological-level theory. The dependence Fodor et al. are aiming for must be understood as a purely psychological-level dependence.

14 Hadley (1997) offers this response to the way in which we have formulated the systematicity arguments.

15 Cf., e.g., van Gelder (1990).

16 Of course, "30870000" does contain a token of "3," which is one of the atoms from which it is derived, but this is accidental.

17 A point of clarification is in order here. Recall that, for the systematicity arguments, we suppose that only a finite stock of thoughts is involved. Note that, for any finite stock of thoughts, there will be some base for the expressing the Gödel numerals such that the base will not lead to dependencies among the thoughts. Given this, the Gödel numerals proposal cannot explain the interdependencies among thoughts.

References

Aizawa, K. (1997a). "Exhibiting versus Explaining Systematicity: A Reply to Hadley and Hayward." *Minds and Machines*, 7: 39–55.

—— (1997b). "Explaining Systematicity." *Mind and Language*, 12: 115–36.

—— (in preparation). *The Systematicity Arguments*.

Brooks, R. (1997). "Intelligence without Representation." In J. Haugeland (ed.), *Mind Design II*. Cambridge, MA: MIT Press: 395–420.

Cummins, R. (1996). "Systematicity." *Journal of Philosophy*, 93: 591–614.

Darwin, C. (1859). *The Origin of Species*. London: John Murray.

Fodor, J. (1983). *The Modularity of Mind*. Cambridge, MA: MIT Press.

—— (1996). "Connectionism and the Problem of Systematicity (continued): Why Smolensky's Solution *Still* Doesn't Work." *Cognition*, 62: 109–19.

Fodor, J. and McLaughlin, B. (1990). "Connectionism and the Problem of Systematicity: Why Smolensky's Solution Doesn't Work." *Cognition*, 35: 183–204.

Fodor, J. and Pylyshyn, Z. (1988). "Connectionism and Cognitive Architecture: A Critical Analysis." *Cognition*, 28: 3–71.

Hadley, R. (1997). "Explaining Systematicity: A Reply to Kenneth Aizawa." *Minds and Machines*, 7: 571–9.

Hadley, R. and Hayward, M. (1996). "Strong Semantic Systematicity from Hebbian Connectionist Learning." *Minds and Machines*, 7: 1–37.

Horgan, T. and Tienson, J. (1996). *Connectionism and the Philosophy of Psychology*. Cambridge, MA: MIT Press.

Karmiloff-Smith, A. (1992). *Beyond Modularity: A Developmental Perspective on Cognitive Science*. Cambridge, MA: MIT Press.

Niklasson, L. and van Gelder, T. (1994). "On Being Systematically Connectionist." *Mind and Language*, 9: 288–302.

Smolensky, P. (1995). "Reply: Constituent Structure and Explanation in an Integrated Connectionist/Symbolic Cognitive Architecture." In C. MacDonald and G. MacDonald (eds.), *Connectionism: Debates on Psychological Explanation*: 223–90.

van Gelder, T. (1990). "Compositionality: A Connectionist Variation on a Classical Theme." *Cognitive Science*, 14: 355–84.

van Gelder, T. (1997). "Dynamics and Cognition." In J. Haugeland (ed.), *Mind Design II*. Cambridge, MA: MIT Press: 421–50.

van Gelder, T. and Niklasson, L. F. (1994). "Classicism and Cognitive Architecture." *Proceedings of the Sixteenth Annual Conference of the Cognitive Science Society*. Atlanta, GA: 905–9.

Chapter 8

Concepts

Eric Margolis and Stephen Laurence

The human mind has a prodigious capacity for representation. We aren't limited to thinking about the here and now, just as we aren't limited to thinking about the objects and properties that are relevant to our most immediate needs. Instead, we can think about things that are far away in space or time (e.g., Abraham Lincoln, Alpha Centauri) and things that involve considerable abstraction from immediate sensory experience (e.g., democracy, the number pi). We can even think about things that never have or never will exist in the actual world (e.g., Santa Claus, unicorns, and phlogiston). One of the central questions in the history of philosophy has been how we are able to do this. How is it that we are able to represent the world to ourselves in thought? In answering this question, philosophers and psychologists often take our capacity for thought to be grounded in our conceptual abilities. Thoughts are seen as having constituents or parts, namely, concepts.[1] As a result, all of science, literature, and the arts – as well as everyday thought – can be seen to stem from the astounding expressive power of the human conceptual system.

Given the foundational role that concepts have for understanding the nature of cognition, it's not possible to provide a theory of concepts without taking sides on a number of fundamental questions about the mind. In fact, the theory of concepts has become a focal point for demarcating vastly different approaches to the mind and even different worldviews. For example, it interacts with such questions as whether there really are thoughts at all and whether semantic properties are relevant to the study of human action.[2] Similarly, it is at the root of the disagreement about whether philosophy is an a priori enterprise. Needless to say, we will not discuss all of these sorts of issues here. In order to keep the discussion focused and manageable it will be necessary to make certain assumptions about matters that remain controversial both within the philosophy of mind in general and within the theory of concepts in particular.[3]

The theory of concepts has been one of the most active areas of research in both philosophy and psychology in the past 50 years, with many important and lasting results. In what follows, we will survey a number of the most influential theories with an eye toward the key issue that divides them – the issue of conceptual structure.[4] We will argue that none of the various types of conceptual structure currently on offer is entirely satisfactory. This has led us to rethink the nature of conceptual structure itself and to distinguish several categorically different types of structure.

8.1   Definitional Structure

Theorizing about the nature of concepts has been dominated since antiquity by an account known as the *Classical Theory* of concepts. So dominant has this account been that it was not until the 1970s that serious alternatives first began to be developed. Moreover, though these alternative theories are in some respects radically different from the Classical account, they are all deeply indebted to it. In fact, it would hardly be an exaggeration to say that all existing theories of concepts are, in effect, reactions to the Classical Theory and its failings. So appreciating the motivations for the Classical Theory and its pitfalls is essential to understanding work on the nature of concepts.

According to the Classical Theory, concepts are complex mental representations whose structure generally[5] encodes a specification of necessary and sufficient conditions for their own application.[6] Consider, for example, the concept BACHELOR. The idea is that BACHELOR is actually a complex mental representation whose constituents are UNMARRIED and MAN. Something falls under, or is in the extension of, BACHELOR just in case it satisfies each of these constituent concepts. Or, to take another example, the concept KNOWLEDGE might be analyzed as JUSTIFIED TRUE BELIEF. In that case, something falls under the concept KNOWLEDGE just in case it is an instance of a true belief that's justified.[7]

This simple and intuitively appealing theory has much to recommend it. A good deal of the power and elegance of the theory derives from the fact that it is able to provide accounts of a variety of key psychological phenomena, accounts that seamlessly mesh with the treatment of reference determination just sketched. Categorization, for example, is one of the most fundamental of all processes involving concepts. Most of our higher cognitive abilities – not to mention our own survival – depend upon our ability to quickly and reliably determine which categories different objects in our environment belong to. The Classical Theory's account of this capacity is natural and compelling. What happens in categorizing something as a bird, for example, is that one accesses and decomposes the concept BIRD and checks whether its constituents apply to the object in question. If each does, then the object is deemed a bird; if at least one doesn't, then the object is not. The Classical Theory offers an equally powerful account of concept learning. The process of concept learning works in much the same way as categorization, but the process runs backwards. That is, to acquire a concept one starts out with its constituents and assembles them in light of one's experience. Learning, on this view, is a constructive operation. One has certain concepts to begin with and brings these together to form novel, complex concepts. In short, the Classical Theory offers an elegantly unified account of reference determination, categorization, and learning.[8]

As attractive as it may be, the Classical Theory has few adherents today. This is because it faces a number of extremely challenging objections. In the remainder of this section we briefly review some of these objections to bring out certain motivations behind competing theories and to highlight a number of themes that will be relevant later on.

Perhaps the most pressing objection to the Classical Theory is the sheer lack of uncontroversial examples of definitions. This wouldn't be such a problem if the Classical Theory were part of a new research program. But the truth is that in spite of more than two thousand years of intensive sustained philosophical analysis, there are few, if any, viable cases where a concept can be said to have been defined. In fact, the failures of this research program are notorious.

To take one well-known example, consider the definition that we cited a moment ago for the concept KNOWLEDGE. The proposal was that KNOWLEDGE can be analyzed as JUSTIFIED TRUE BELIEF. As plausible as this definition sounds at first, it is subject to a family of powerful counterexamples, first noticed by Edmund Gettier. The following example is adapted from Dancy (1985). Henry is following the Wimbledon men's singles tournament. He turns on the television to watch the final match and sees McEnroe triumph over Connors. As a result, Henry comes to believe that McEnroe won the match and he has every reason to infer that McEnroe is this year's champion. But what Henry doesn't know is that, due to a problem with the network's cameras, the game can't be shown as it takes place and, instead, a recording of last year's game is being shown. Still, at this year's tournament, McEnroe repeats last year's performance, beating Connors in the final match. So Henry's belief that McEnroe is this year's champion is true and justified as well, but few people would want to say that he *knows* that McEnroe is champion this year.

It's not just philosophically interesting concepts that have problems like this. As Wittgenstein famously argued in his *Philosophical Investigations*, ordinary concepts don't seem to be any more definable than philosophical ones. One of Wittgenstein's main examples is the concept GAME, for which he considers a number of initially plausible definitions, each of which ends up being subject to a devastating counterexample. Even philosophy's stock example, BACHELOR, isn't unproblematic. Is the Pope a bachelor? How about a self-declared gay man who lives with his lover in a monogomous long-term relationship? Both are cases of unmarried men, yet neither seems to be a bachelor.

Defenders of the Classical Theory could respond that while definitions are indeed hard to come by, this doesn't necessarily mean that there aren't any. Perhaps definitions are tacit and so not easily accessible to introspection (see, e.g., Rey 1993; Peacocke 1998). The general feeling, however, is that the most likely reason why definitions are so hard to find is simply that there aren't any.

Another problem for the Classical Theory is that, because of its commitment to definitions, it is also committed to a form of the analytic/synthetic distinction – a distinction which, in the wake of Quine's famous critique, is thought by many philosophers to be deeply problematic. One strand of Quine's criticism centers around his view that confirmation is holistic. Confirmation involves global properties such as simplicity, conservatism, overall coherence, and the like. Moreover, since confirmation relies upon auxiliary hypotheses, when a theoretical claim is confronted by recalcitrant data, one can't say in advance whether it's this claim rather than some auxiliary hypothesis that needs to be abandoned. All of this seems to show that we don't have a priori access to truths that are within the realm of scientific investigation. Moreover, we don't know in advance just how far the reach of science is. What may look like a conceptual necessity (and therefore look analytic and immune to revision) may turn out to be a case where people are being misled by their own lack of theoretical imagination.

Notice, however, that if a concept has a definition, this definition will strongly constrain theoretical developments in science and place a priori limits on what we are capable of discovering about the world. For example, if the proper analysis of STRAIGHT LINE were SHORTEST DISTANCE BETWEEN TWO POINTS, then, it would seem, one couldn't discover that a straight line isn't always the shortest distance between two points. And if the proper analysis of CAT were (SUCH AND SUCH TYPE OF) ANIMAL, then one couldn't discover that cats aren't animals. These sorts of definitions would seem to be about as plausible and unassailable as they come. Yet, as Hilary Putnam (1962) has pointed out, the situation isn't so simple. With the discovery that space is non-Euclidian, we can now see that the first definition is actually wrong. And with the help of a little science fiction, we can see that it at least seems possible to discover that the second is wrong too. (Perhaps cats are actually Martian-controlled robots, and not animals at all.) But if STRAIGHT LINE and CAT had the definitions that the Classical Theory suggests, then these discoveries would be entirely prohibited; they wouldn't be possible at all. Examples like these threaten the very foundations of the Classical Theory. A definition may appear to capture the structure of a concept, but the appearance may only be an illusion which later discoveries help us to see beyond.[9]

Related to cases such as these, one finds other considerations that argue against definitions – in particular, Saul Kripke's and Hilary Putnam's influential work on the semantics of names and natural kind terms (see esp. Kripke 1972/1980; Putnam 1970, 1975). Kripke's and Putnam's target was the description theory of reference, according to which someone is able to use a name or kind term by virtue of knowing a description that picks out its reference. Notice, however, that the Classical Theory just is a form of the description theory, only it holds at the level of concept not words. For this reason, all of Kripke's and Putnam's arguments are pertinent to its evaluation. One of their arguments is an elaboration of the Quinean point that we can make discoveries about a kind that reveal that we were wrong about its nature – the problem of error. Closely related is the problem of ignorance: if people are sometimes wrong about certain properties of a kind, they are also often ignorant of the features that really are essential to it.[10] What turns out to be crucial to the identity of gold is its atomic number, and not, for example, its color, or weight. Similarly, the crucial feature of the bubonic plague is its bacterial source, and not the chills, fever, or nausea that it is associated with, and certainly not a connection with sinful deeds (in spite of the widespread belief that the plague was a form of divine retribution). What bears emphasizing here is that such ignorance doesn't prevent people from possessing the concept GOLD or PLAGUE. If it did, people wouldn't be able genuinely to disagree with one another about the cause of the plague; they'd always end up talking at cross purposes.

The philosophical considerations weighing against the Classical Theory are impressive. But its worries don't end there. The Classical Theory also faces a number of daunting problems based on psychological considerations.

Perhaps the most glaring of these is that definitions have failed to show up in experimental situations that are explicitly designed to test for the psychological complexity of concepts (see, e.g., Kintsch 1974; J. D. Fodor et al. 1975; J. A. Fodor et al. 1980). If, for example, CONVINCE is analyzed as CAUSE TO BELIEVE (following standard Classical treatments), one would expect that CONVINCE would impose a greater processing burden than BELIEVE; after all, CONVINCE is supposed to have BELIEVE as a constituent. Yet this sort of effect has never been demonstrated in the laboratory. Not only do definitions fail to reveal themselves in processing studies, there is also no evidence of them in lexical acquisition either (Carey 1982). Of course it is always possible that these experiments aren't subtle enough or that there is some other explanation of why definitions fail to have detectable psychological effects. But it certainly doesn't help the Classical Theory's case that definitions refuse to reveal themselves experimentally.

The most powerful psychological arguments against the Classical Theory, however, are based upon so-called *typicality effects*. Typicality effects are a variety of psychological phenomena connected to the fact that people willingly rate subcategories for how typical or representative they are for a given category. For example, subjects tend to say that robins are better examples of the category *bird* than chickens are; i.e., they say robins are more "typical" of *bird*. In and of itself, this result may not be terribly interesting. What makes typicality judgments important is the fact that they track a variety of other significant psychological variables (for reviews, see Rosch 1978; Smith and Medin 1981; for a more critical review, see Barsalou 1987).

Eleanor Rosch and Carolyn Mervis (1975) found that when subjects are asked to list properties that are associated with a given category and its subordinates, the distribution of properties on these lists is predicted by independent typicality rankings. The more typical a subordinate is judged to be, the more properties it will share with other exemplars of the same category. For instance, robins are taken to have many of the same properties as other birds, and, correspondingly, robins are judged to be highly typical birds; in contrast, chickens are taken to have fewer properties in common with other birds, and chickens are judged to be less typical birds. Another finding is that typicality has a direct reflection in categorization. In cases where subjects are asked to judge whether an X is a Y, independent measures of typicality predict the speed of correct affirmatives. Subjects are quicker in their correct response to "Is a robin a bird?" than to "Is a chicken a bird?" Error rates, as well, are predicted by typicality. The more typical the probe (X) relative to the target category (Y), the fewer the errors. Typicality also correlates with lexical acquisition and a variety of other phenomena, such as the order in which subjects will provide exemplars for a given category – more typical items are cited first. In sum, typicality effects seem to permeate every aspect of a concept's life, significantly determining its acquisition, use, and even misuse. It's no wonder that psychologists have required that a theory of concepts do justice to these data.

It's in this context that most psychologists have given up on the Classical Theory. The problem is that the Classical Theory simply has nothing to say about any of these phenomena. The classical models of categorization and concept acquisition that we sketched above don't predict any of the effects, and classical attempts to accommodate them appear ad hoc and quickly run into further problems. Moreover, as we'll see in the next section, there are alternative theories of concepts that provide natural and highly explanatory accounts of the full range of typicality effects.

The Classical Theory faces a battery of powerful philosophical and psychological objections. Definitions are very hard to come by, they don't have any psychological effects, they can't explain any of the most significant psychological facts that are known about concepts, they fly in the face of Quine's critique of the analytic–synthetic distinction, and they aren't equipped to explain how the reference of a concept is determined. As a result, it's hard to resist the thought that, in spite of its considerable attractions, the Classical Theory isn't worth saving.

8.2 Probabilistic Structure

The 1970s saw the development of a new theory of concepts, one that gained considerable support as an alternative to the Classical Theory. This new theory – the *Prototype Theory* – gave up on the idea that a concept's internal structure provides a definition of the concept.[11] Instead, the Prototype Theory adopted a probabilistic treatment of conceptual structure. According to the Prototype Theory, most lexical concepts are complex mental representations whose structure encodes not defining necessary and sufficient conditions, but, rather, conditions that items in their extension *tend to have*. So in contrast with the Classical Theory, for an object to be in the extension of a concept, it needn't satisfy each and every property encoded in the concept's structure as long as it satisfies a sufficient number of them.

Notice, right off, that one of the advantages of the Prototype Theory is that it doesn't require that concepts have definitions. It's no problem for the Prototype

Theory that people have had so much difficulty formulating them. According to the Prototype Theory, concepts, by and large, lack definitional structure; they have prototype structure instead. For this reason, it also shouldn't be a surprise that definitions never show up in studies of psychological processing. In fact, it's when we turn to the empirical psychological data that Prototype Theory becomes especially appealing. The way the theory is generally understood, it takes categorization to be a feature-matching process where an exemplar or individual is compared to a target category for how similar they are. So long as enough features match, they are deemed sufficiently similar and one comes to judge that the item falls under the category. This reliance on similarity provides the resources for an extremely natural explanation of the typicality phenomena (see, e.g., Smith 1995). One need only assume that typicality judgments are also formed by the very same process. In other words, the reason why robins are judged to be more typical birds than chickens is because ROBIN shares more features with BIRD; it ranks higher in the similarity-comparison process.

Consider also the finding by Rosch and Mervis, that typicality judgments track the number of features that a concept shares with other exemplars for a superordinate category. Again, the Prototype Theory has a natural explanation of why this happens. The reason is because the properties that subjects list that are common among the subordinate categories correspond to the features of the superordinate concept; that is, they characterize the structure of the superordinate concept. As a result, concepts that share many features with their fellow subordinates will automatically share many features with the superordinate. Sticking to the example of the concept BIRD, the idea is that the properties that are commonly cited across categories such as *robin, sparrow, ostrich, hawk,* and so on, are the very properties that are encoded by the structure of BIRD. Since ROBIN has many of the same structural elements, and CHICKEN has few, robins will be judged to be more typical birds than chickens are.

In short, the Prototype Theory has tremendous psychological advantages. It's no wonder that the psychological community embraced the theory as an alternative to the Classical Theory. But the Prototype Theory isn't without its difficulties either, and a full appreciation of some of these difficulties is essential to arriving at a satisfactory theory of concepts. To keep things brief, we'll mention only three.

The first problem is that the Prototype Theory is subject to the problems of ignorance and error, just like the Classical Theory. Once again, the problem is that people can possess a concept and yet have erroneous information about the items in its extension or lack a sufficient amount of correct information to pick them out uniquely. Moreover, prototypes are notoriously bad in dealing with the question of reference determination. Take, for example, the concept GRANDMOTHER. Prototypical grandmothers are women with gray hair, they have wrinkled skin, they wear glasses, and so on. Yet we all know that there are people who fail to exhibit these characteristics who are grandmothers, and that there are people who do exhibit these characteristics who are not. Mrs. Doubtfire (the Robin Williams character) may look like a grandmother, but Tina Turner really is a grandmother.

The second problem is that many concepts simply lack prototypes. This is especially clear in the case of certain complex concepts. As Jerry Fodor puts it: "[T]here may be prototypical *grandmothers* (Mary Worth) and there may be prototypical *properties of grandmothers* (*good, old* Mary Worth). But there are surely no prototypical properties of, say *Chaucer's grandmothers*, and there are no prototypical properties of *grandmothers most of whose grandchildren are married to dentists*" (1981: 297; see also Fodor 1998).

The third problem is that prototypes don't appear to compose in accordance with the principles of a compositional semantics (see Fodor 1998; Fodor and Lepore 1996). The difficulty is that, on the standard account of how the conceptual system is productive (i.e., of how we are capable of entertaining an unbounded number of concepts), concepts must have a compositional semantics. Fodor illustrates the argument with the concept PET FISH. The PET prototype encodes properties that are associated with dogs and cats, and the FISH prototype encodes properties that are associated with things like trout, yet the PET FISH prototype encodes properties that are associated with goldfish and other small colorful fish. So it's hard to see how the prototype for PET FISH could be computed from the prototypes for PET and FISH.

Together, these three criticisms pose a serious threat to the Prototype Theory. However, prototype theorists do still have some room to maneuver. What all three objections presuppose is that prototype theorists must hold that a concept's structure is *exhausted* by its prototype. But prototype theorists could simply abandon this constraint. They could maintain, instead, that a concept's prototype is a crucial part of its structure, but that there is more to a concept than its prototype.

In fact, a number of prototype theorists have suggested theories along just these lines in order to deal with the first of our three criticisms, viz., the problem that prototypes aren't suited to determining reference. According to this *Dual Theory*, a concept has two types of structure, one type constitutes the concept's "core" and the second its "identification procedure" (Osherson and Smith 1981; Smith et al. 1984; Landau 1982). Prototypes are supposed to be confined to identification procedures. They account for quick categorization processes as well as all of the typicality effects. On the other hand, cores are supposed to have some other type of structure that accounts for reference determination and is responsible for our most considered categorization judgments – the default view being that cores exhibit classical structure.[12]

The Dual Theory handles the first objection by its commitment to conceptual cores. The idea is that it's perfectly fine if prototypes can't determine reference, since by hypothesis cores fulfil that role. It handles the second objection by adding that some concepts lack prototypes but that this doesn't prohibit anyone from possessing the concepts; they need only grasp the cores of these concepts. Finally, it handles the third objection by maintaining that the productivity of the conceptual system is established so long as conceptual cores combine in accordance with a compositional semantics, and that examples such as PET FISH don't tell against this possibility.

Though none of these responses is without merit, notice that they work by insulating prototype structure from many of the theoretical roles for which conceptual structure is introduced in the first place. As a result, the Dual Theory places a great deal of weight on the conceptual structure associated with a concept's core. To the extent that this other structure is supposed to be *classical* structure, the Dual Theory inherits most of the problems that were associated with the Classical Theory. For example, the Dual Theory faces the problem of ignorance and error, it has to overcome Quinean objections to the analytic–synthetic distinction, it has to confront the difficulty that there are few examples of true definitions, and so on. In short, the Dual Theory may expand the logical space somewhat, but, without an adequate account of conceptual cores, it isn't much of an improvement on either the Classical Theory or the Prototype Theory.

8.3   Theory Structure

The Dual Theory continues to enjoy widespread support in spite of these difficulties. We suspect that this is because of the feeling that psychology has found a way to abandon its residual ties to the Classical Theory. The idea is that conceptual cores should be understood in terms of the *Theory Theory* (see, e.g., Keil 1994). This is the view that concepts are embedded in mental structures that are in important ways like scientific theories and that they apply to the things that satisfy the descriptive content given by the roles that they have within their respective mental theories (see, e.g., Carey 1985; Murphy and Medin 1985; Gopnik and Meltzoff 1997).[13] For a mental structure to be theory-like, it must embody an explanatory schema, that is, a set of principles or rules that a thinker uses in trying to make sense of an event in the course of categorizing it. Examples of such theories include so-called common-sense psychology, common-sense physics, and common-sense biology – the sets of principles that ordinary people use in explaining psychological, physical, and biological events.[14]

One of the main advantages of the Theory Theory is the model of categorization that it encourages. Many psychologists have expressed dissatisfaction with earlier theories of concepts on the grounds that they fail to incorporate people's tendency toward essentialist thinking – a view that Medin and Ortony (1989) have dubbed *psychological essentialism*. According to psychological essentialism, people are apt to view category membership for some kinds as being less a matter of an instance's exhibiting certain observable properties than the item's having an appropriate internal structure or some other "hidden" property (including, perhaps, relational and historical properties). The Theory Theory readily accommodates psychological essentialism since the Theory Theory takes people to appeal to a mentally represented theory in making certain category decisions. Rather than passing quickly over a check-list of properties, people ask whether the item has the right hidden property. This isn't to say that the Theory Theory requires that people have a detailed understanding of genetics and chemistry. They needn't even have clearly developed views about the specific nature of the property. As Medin and Ortony put it, people may have little more than an "essence placeholder" (1989: 184). This suggests that different people represent different sorts of information in thinking of a kind as having an essence. In some cases they may have detailed views about the essence. In most, they will have a schematic view, for instance, the belief that genetic makeup is what matters, even if they don't represent particular genetic properties and know very little about genetics in general.

The Theory Theory is best suited to explaining our considered acts of categorization. What matters in such cases is not so much an object's gross perceptual properties, but, rather, the properties that are taken to be essential to its nature. At the same time, the Theory Theory is not terribly well suited to explaining our more rapid categorization judgments where concepts are deployed under pressures of time and resources. And in general, the Theory Theory makes little contact with typicality effects; like the Classical Theory, it has nothing to say about why some exemplars seem more typical than others and why typicality correlates with so many other variables. On the other hand, if the Theory Theory were combined with Prototype Theory, the resulting version of the Dual Theory would seem to have considerable promise. Cores with theory structure would seem to be a vast improvement on cores with classical structure.

Unfortunately, this revised Dual Theory still faces a number of serious difficulties. We will mention two that are specifically associated with the Theory Theory as an account of conceptual cores. The first problem is one that has already cropped up, so it shouldn't be much of a surprise (the problem of reference determination); the other problem is new (the problem of stability).

The problem of reference determination affects the Theory Theory in several ways. For one thing, we've seen that theory theorists typically allow that people can have rather sketchy theories, where the essence placeholder for a concept includes relatively little information. Notice, however, that to the extent that this is true, concepts will most likely encode inadequate information to pick out a correct and determinate extension. If people don't represent an essence for cats or dogs apart from some thin ideas about genetic endowment, then the concepts CAT and DOG will be embedded in theories that look about the same. Depending on how anemic the theories are, there may then be nothing to pull apart their concepts CAT and DOG.

On the other hand, people may have detailed enough theories to differentiate any number of concepts, yet this comes with the danger that they may have incorporated incorrect information into their theories. To return to our earlier example, someone might hold that the plague is caused by divine retribution, or that the illness itself involves the possession of evil spirits. But, again, someone who believes such things should still be capable of entertaining the very same concept as we do – the PLAGUE. Indeed, it is necessary for them to have the very same concept in order to make sense of the idea that we can disagree with them about the nature and cause of the disease. Ignorance and error are as problematic for the Theory Theory as they were for the Classical Theory.

Still, whether two people are employing the same concept or not[15] is a difficult question. We suppose that many theorists would claim that it's simply inappropriate to insist that the *very same concept* may occur despite a difference in surrounding beliefs. The alternative suggestion is that people need only have *similar concepts*. The idea is that differences in belief do yield distinct concepts, but this is not problematic because two concepts might still be similar enough in content that they would be subsumed by the same psychological generalizations – and perhaps that's all that really matters.

As tempting as this position may be, it is actually fraught with difficulty. The problem is that when the notion of content similarity is unpacked it generally presupposes a prior notion of content identity (Fodor and Lepore 1992). For example, a common strategy for measuring content similarity is in terms of the number of constituents that two concepts share. If they overlap in many of their constituents, then they are said to have similar contents (see, e.g., Smith et al. 1984). But notice that this proposal works only on the assumption that the shared, overlapping constituents are the same. So the notion of content similarity is illicitly building on the very notion it is supposed to replace.

Since the scope of this problem hasn't been absorbed in either philosophical or psychological circles, it pays to explore some other proposed solutions. Consider, for example, a suggestion by Eric Lormand (1996). Lormand claims that even a completely holistic theory of content needn't have any difficulties with stability; in other words, stability isn't supposed to be a problem even for a theory that claims that any change in the total belief system changes the content of every single belief. The trick to establishing stability, Lormand claims, is the idea that a given symbol has *multiple meanings*. Each of its meanings is given in terms of a subset of its causal/inferential links. Lormand calls these subsets *units* and asks us to think of a unit "as a separable rough test for the acceptable use of that representation" (1996: 57). The proposal, then, is that a holistic system of representation can allow for stability of content, since, as the system exhibits changes, some of a concept's meanings change, but some don't. To the extent that it keeps some of its units intact, it preserves those meanings.

Unfortunately, this suggestion doesn't work. Since Lormand's units are themselves representations, they are part of the holistic network that determines the content of every concept in the system. As a result, every concept embedded in any unit will change its meaning as the other meanings in the inferential network change. And if they change their meaning, they can't be the basis of the stability for other concepts (Margolis and Laurence 1998).

Paul Churchland (1998) has proposed a different solution. For some time, Churchland has been developing an approach to mental content known as *state-space semantics*. State-space semantics is a theory of content for neural networks where content is supposed to be holistic. To a first approximation, the content of an activation vector – i.e., a pattern of activation across an assembly of nodes in such a network – is supposed to be determined by its position within the larger structure of the network. Since this position will be relative to the positions of many other nodes in the network, state-space semantics should have considerable difficulties in achieving content stability. As a result, Churchland is quick to reject content identity in favor of content similarity.

In earlier work, Churchland adopted a model much like the one in Smith et al. (1984). Imagine a connectionist network with a series of input nodes, output nodes, and an intermediary set of so-called hidden nodes. Taking the hidden nodes as specifying contentful dimensions, we can construct a semantic space of as many dimensions as there are hidden nodes, where points within the space correspond to patterns of activation across the hidden nodes. Supposing for simplicity that there are only three hidden nodes, the resulting semantic space would be a cube, each of whose axes corresponds to a particular hidden node and its level of activation. On Churchland's early treatments, content similarity was understood as relative closeness in a space of this sort. But this approach runs into much the same problem as the Smith et al. account. It only explains similarity of content by presupposing a prior notion of identity of content, one that applies to the constituting dimensions of the space.

In light of this difficulty, Churchland has recently put forward a new account of similarity of content. In the new model, Churchland suggests:

> A point in activation space acquires a specific semantic content not as a function of its position relative to the constituting axes of that space, but rather as a function of (1) its spatial position relative to all of the *other contentful points within that space*; and (2) its causal relations to stable and objective *macrofeatures of the external environment*. (1998: 8)

This new position, Churchland tells us, "constitute[s] a decisive answer to Fodor and Lepore's challenge" (ibid: 5) to provide a workable holistic account of content similarity.

Yet far from being a decisive answer to the challenge, Churchland's new account is really no improvement at all. His first determinant of content – spatial position relative to other contentful points in the space – immediately confronts a serious difficulty. Supposing that two networks do have nodes with the same overall relative positions, this alone doesn't suffice to fix their contents; one might well wonder why any given node in either network has the particular content it has (and not some other content). For example, Churchland describes one type of network as representing distinct families as it extracts four prototypical faces given photographs as input. But what makes it the case that the network's nodes represent families and faces as opposed to any of a wide variety of potential objects? In response to this problem, Churchland can only appeal to the resources of his second determinant of content – causal relations to features of the environment. The problem with this answer, however, is that this isn't a version of the Theory Theory at all. Rather, it relies on an atomistic theory of content of the sort we discuss in the next section. The relation of the node to its surrounding nodes turns out to have nothing to do with its content; what matters for content is just the existence of a reliable causal link to features of the environment.[16] Of course, these reliable links provide stability, but that's because they underwrite a theory of content identity: Two nodes have identical contents just in case they are linked to the same environmental feature. So it's no surprise that Churchland can have a notion of similar content, since he helps himself to an independent account of sameness of content, despite his rhetoric to the contrary.[17]

Stability, it turns out, is a robust constraint on a theory of concepts. What this means for the Theory Theory is that mental theories make for bad cores. They have as much trouble as the Prototype Theory when it comes to reference, and they are especially bad in securing stability. If a version of the Dual Theory of concepts is to succeed, it looks like it's not going to be one whose cores have either classical structure or theory structure.

8.4 Concepts Without Structure

We've seen that the main views of conceptual structure are all problematic. In light of these difficulties, a number of theorists have proposed to explore the possibility that lexical concepts don't have any structure – a view known as *Conceptual Atomism* (see, e.g., Fodor 1998; Leslie 2000; Millikan 1998, 2000). Central to Conceptual Atomism is the thesis that a concept's content isn't determined by its relation to any other particular concepts. Instead, it's determined by a mind–world relation, that is, a causal or historical relation between the symbol and what it represents. Not surprisingly, Atomism finds its inspiration in Kripke's and Putnam's treatment of natural kind terms, only it's intended to cover a broader range of semantic items and is directed, in the first instance, to the nature of the conceptual system, not to language.

The most difficult task for an atomist is to provide a sufficiently detailed account of the mind–world relation that's supposed to determine conceptual content. One general strategy is to explain content in terms of the notion of co-variation (the same notion that we saw was illicitly at play in Churchland's treatment of stability). The idea is that a concept represents what it causally co-varies with. For example, if the concept D were tokened as a reliable causal consequence of the presence of dogs, then, on the present account, the symbol would express the property *dog* and be the concept DOG. Notice, however, that this simple account won't do. The reason is because all sorts of other things will reliably cause tokenings of the symbol D. This might happen, for example, as a result of perceptual error. On a dark night you might catch a fox out of the corner of your eye and mistake it for a dog running past your car.

Atomists have a number of resources for ruling out the non-dogs. One is to add the further condition that a concept represents what it would co-vary with under *ideal conditions* (allowing for the possibility that non-dogs cause DOGS when the conditions aren't ideal; see, e.g., Stampe 1977; Fodor 1981/90). Another option is to say that a concept represents what it has the *function* of co-varying with (allowing for the possibility that the concept, or the system that produces it, isn't functioning properly in the non-dog cases; see, e.g., Dretske 1995; Millikan 1984, 1993). Yet another possibility is to say that the dog/DOG dependence is, in a sense, more basic than the non-dog-yet-dog-like/DOG dependence. For instance, the former dependence may hold whether or not the latter does, but not the other way around (Fodor 1990).

Though each of these strategies has its own difficulties, we want to focus on more general problems with Atomism, ones that aren't tied to the details of any particular atomistic theory. We'll mention three.

The first objection concerns the explanatory role of concepts. Most theories tie a concept's explanatory potential to its structure. This is evident in the other theories we've reviewed. For instance, the Prototype Theory explains a wide variety of psychological phenomena by reference to conceptual structure – categorization, typicality judgments, efficiency of use, and so on. The problem with Conceptual Atomism, however, is that it says that concepts have no structure. So it would seem that they can't really explain anything. Then what good are they?

The second objection is the worry that Conceptual Atomism is committed to an extremely implausible degree of innateness. In fact, Jerry Fodor, the most vocal defender of Atomism, has made this connection explicitly, defending the claim that virtually all lexical concepts are innate, including such unlikely candidates as CARBURETOR and QUARK. As Fodor sees it, the only way that a concept could be learned is via a process of construction, where it is assembled from its constituents. Since Atomism maintains that lexical concepts have no constituents, they must all be innate (Fodor 1981). But if CARBURETOR is innate, something has definitely gone wrong; maybe that something is Atomism itself.

The third objection is that atomistic theories individuate concepts too coarsely. Since they reduce content to a causal or historical relation between a representation and what it represents, concepts would seem to be no more finely individuated than the worldly items they pick out. Yet surely that isn't fine enough. The concept WATER isn't the same thing as the concept H_2O – someone could have the one without the other – but presumably they pick out the very same property. Or to take a more extreme case, the concept UNICORN isn't the same thing as the concept CENTAUR, yet because they are empty concepts, they would seem to pick out the very same thing, viz., nothing. So it's hard to see how an atomistic theory could tease such concepts apart.

Let's take these objections in reverse order. No doubt, the problem of achieving a fine-grained individuation is a serious concern for Atomism, but atomists do have a few resources they can call upon. For instance, in the case of empty concepts, they can maintain that the content determining co-variation relation is a nomic relation between properties. This helps because it's plausible there can be nomic relations between properties even if they are uninstantiated (Fodor 1990).

With other examples, atomists can distinguish co-referential concepts by insisting that one of the concepts is really complex and that its complexity isn't in dispute. Presumably, this is how they would handle the WATER/H$_2$O case – by maintaining that the concept H$_2$O incorporates, among other things, the concept HYDROGEN (Fodor 1990). Of course, there are other challenging cases for which neither of these strategies will work. Here we have in mind pairs of primitive concepts that express nomologically co-extensive properties (e.g., BUYING/SELLING, CHASING/FLEEING, EXTENDED/SHAPED). These prove to be the most difficult cases, since the natural solution for distinguishing them is to say they are associated with different content-determining inferences. Whether atomists have an alternative solution is very hard to say.

But let's turn to the other objections to Atomism, which, on the face of it, leave the atomist with even less room to maneuver. If Atomism says that lexical concepts have no structure, must they all be innate? And if lexical concepts have no structure, why aren't they explanatorily inert?

Fodor's argument for radical concept nativism has caused quite a stir in philosophy of mind, with theorists of different sorts dropping any doctrine thought to be tied up with the thesis.[18] As a result, the argument has not received the sort of careful critical scrutiny that it deserves. We believe that Atomism has been unfairly burdened with Fodor's strong nativist thesis, and that in fact it is possible to provide a satisfying account of how new primitive concepts can be acquired in a way that is compatible with Conceptual Atomism. The key here is the notion of a *sustaining mechanism*. Sustaining mechanisms are mechanisms that underwrite the mind–world relation that determines a concept's content. These will typically be inferential mechanisms of one sort or another, since people clearly lack transducers for most of the properties they can represent. Importantly, however, these inferential mechanisms needn't give rise to any analyticities or to a concept's having any semantic structure, since no particular inference is required for concept possession. Thus, such inferential mechanisms are fully compatible with Conceptual Atomism.

We are now in a position to see why Atomism is not committed to radical concept nativism. What the atomist ought to say is that the general question of how to acquire a concept should be framed in terms of the more refined question of how, given the correct theory of content, someone comes to be in a state of mind that satisfies the theory (Margolis 1998; Laurence and Margolis 2002). On an atomistic treatment of content this is to be understood in terms of the possession of a suitable sustaining mechanism. So the question of acquisition just is the question of how sustaining mechanisms are assembled. And here there are many things that an atomist can say, all consistent with the claim that concepts have no structure. For example, one type of sustaining mechanism that we've explored in detail supports the possession of natural kind concepts (see Margolis 1998; Laurence and Margolis, forthcoming). The model is based on what we call a *syndrome-based sustaining mechanism*, one that incorporates highly indicative perceptual information about a kind together with a disposition to treat something as a member of the same kind so long as it shares the same constitutive hidden properties (and not necessarily the same perceptual properties) as the category's paradigmatic instances. The suggestion is that people have a general tendency to assemble syndrome-based sustaining mechanisms in accordance with their experience. Such a mechanism then establishes the mind–world relation that atomists say is constitutive of content, and together with environmental input is capable of delivering a wide range of unstructured concepts. Since the mechanism respects the character of one's experience – acquisition proceeds by the collection, storage, and manipulation of information to produce a representation that tracks things in the concept's extension – we think it is fair to say that this is a learning model.

Turning finally to the charge that Atomism leaves concepts explanatorily inert, the best strategy for the atomist is to say that the explanatory roles that are often accounted for by a concept's structure needn't actually be explained directly in terms of the concept's nature. The idea is that the atomist can appeal to information that happens to be associated with the concept; that is, the atomist can make use of the relations that a concept c bears to other concepts, even though these others aren't constitutive of c. This may seem a drastic step, but virtually any theory of concepts will do the same in order to explain at least some inferences in which concepts participate. Perhaps as a child you were frightened by a dog and as a result you've come to believe that dogs are dangerous. This belief may well explain quite a lot of your behavior toward dogs. Nonetheless, a classical theorist would not likely suppose that it was part of the definition of DOG that dogs are dangerous. All theories of concepts say that some of a concept's relations to other concepts are constitutive of its identity and some are not. And having made that distinction, it's sometimes going to be the case that how a concept is deployed will reflect its non-constitutive relations. The atomist simply takes this position to the limit and says that this is always the case. A concept's role in thought can't help but reflect its non-constitutive relations, since what's constitutive of a concept isn't its relation to any other particular concepts but just how it is causally (or historically) related to things in the world. One wonders, however, whether the atomist has gone too far. Could it really be that *none* of the ways in which a concept is deployed is explained by its nature?

8.5   Rethinking Conceptual structure

There's something unsettling about the claim that the explanatory functions of concepts are handled by their incidental relations. Consider once again typicality effects. Typicality effects are so pervasive and so rich in their psychological import that they constitute one of the central explananda of any theory of concepts. Indeed, it is largely because of the Classical Theory's failure to account for these effects that psychologists abandoned the Classical Theory in droves. Notice, however, that Conceptual Atomism is no different than the Classical Theory in its capacity to deal with typicality effects. By maintaining that concepts have no structure, atomists are committed to the view that a concept's nature has no bearing whatsoever on its role in typicality effects. Of course, this doesn't mean that atomists have to deny the existence of typicality effects. Yet it is puzzling that some of the most important psychological data involving concepts end up having nothing at all to do with their nature.

At the same time, there are compelling pressures mitigating in favor of Atomism's central claim that concepts don't have any structure. In particular, all attempts to explain reference determination in terms of a concept's structure run into formidable difficulties. The Classical Theory, the Prototype Theory, and the Theory Theory all fall prey to the problems of ignorance and error, and each theory has its own peculiar difficulties as well.

The way out of this impasse lies in two related insights about conceptual structure that are implicit in the Dual Theory. The first of these is simply that concepts can have multiple structures. Thus in the original Dual Theory concepts were taken to have cores and identification procedures. The second insight is less obvious but it's really the crucial one. This is that concepts can have categorically different types of structure answering to very different explanatory functions.[19] The Dual Theory implicitly recognizes this possibility in the distinct motivations that it associates with cores and identification procedures. But once the point is made explicit, and once it is made in perfectly general terms, a whole new range of theoretical possibilities emerges.

The most immediate effect is the Dual Theory's recognition that the function of explaining reference may have to be teased apart from certain other functions of concepts. This would free the other types of structure that a concept has from a heavy burden and, crucially, would imply that not all conceptual structure is reference-determining structure. Having taken this step, one can then inquire about what other types of conceptual structure there are and about the specific functions they answer to.

We suggest that there are at least four central types of structure:

Compositional reference-determining structure This is structure that contributes to the content and reference of a concept via a compositional semantics. This type of structure is familiar from the Classical Theory. Whether any lexical concepts have this type of structure will depend on whether the problems of analyticity and ignorance and error can be met and whether definitions can actually be found. However, it is more or less uncontroversial that phrasal concepts such as BROWN DOG have this kind of structure. BROWN DOG is composed of BROWN and DOG and its reference is compositionally determined by the referential properties of its constituents: Something falls under BROWN DOG just in case it's brown and a dog.

Non-semantic structure This is structure that doesn't contribute to the content of a concept but does contribute significantly to some other theoretically important explanatory function of concepts. Though the Dual Theory is not explicit about this, it seems plausible to think of Dual Theory's commitment to prototypes as a commitment to non-semantic structure.

Non-referential semantic structure This is structure that contributes to the content of a concept but is isolated from referential consequences. Though our discussion of the meaning or content of concepts has focused on their referential properties, these may well not exhaust the semantic properties that concepts possess. This type of structure would apply to, among other things, so-called narrow content.[20]

Sustaining mechanism structure This is structure that contributes to the content of a concept indirectly by figuring in a theoretically significant sustaining mechanism. Sustaining mechanism structure determines the referential properties of a concept, but not via a compositional semantics. Rather, this type of structure supports the mind–world relation that (directly) determines a concept's content.

These four different types of structure point to a range of new theoretical options that bear exploring. By way of illustration, we will briefly sketch a resolution to the impasse between Conceptual Atomism and the pressure to appeal to a concept's structure in explaining its most salient behavior.

If we look back at the Dual Theory, the main problems it faces center around its treatment of conceptual cores. We've seen that both definitional structure and theory structure are equally problematic in this regard. Neither is especially suited to reference determination; and, in any case, definitions have proven to be quite elusive, while theory structure has its difficulties with stability. Notice, however, that there is now an alternative account of cores available. Given the distinctions we have just drawn among the four types of conceptual structure, Conceptual Atomism is best construed not in terms of the global claim that lexical concepts have no structure at all, but rather as claiming that they have no *compositional reference-determining structure*. This opens the possibility that the cores of concepts might be atomic.

Indeed, atoms seem to be almost perfectly suited to fill the explanatory roles associated with conceptual cores. If cores are atomic, then one doesn't have to worry about the fact that concepts aren't definable. Atomism implies that they aren't. Similarly, if cores are atomic, then one doesn't have to worry about stability. Atomism implies that a concept's relations to other concepts can change as much as you like so long as the mind–world relation that determines reference remains in place. Atomic cores also explain the productivity of concepts: complex concepts are generated through the classical compositionality of atomic cores. The only explanatory role associated with cores that atoms seem to have trouble with is accounting for our most considered judgments about category membership. However, it's hardly clear that this is a legitimate desideratum for a theory of conceptual cores in the first place. If Quine's work on analyticity shows anything, it's that people's most considered judgments of this sort are holistic, so it's not plausible to suppose that all of this information could be isolated for each concept taken individually. Dropping this last desideratum, then, there is a good case to be made for thinking that cores should be atomic.

At the same time, a model of this sort avoids the objection that Atomism is psychologically unexplanatory. We can agree with atomists that lexical concepts generally lack compositional reference-determining structure, but this doesn't mean we have to say that concepts are entirely unstructured. For example, proto- types and sustaining mechanisms may very well be part of a concept's structure. It's just that this structure doesn't directly determine its reference; reference is fixed by the mind–world relation that implicates cores, leaving prototypes (and other types of structure) to explain other things. And prototypes, for one, do explain many other things. Given their tremendous psychological significance, prototypes should be taken to be partly constitutive of concepts if anything is.

Concepts are psychological kinds. As we see it, the best theory of concepts is one that takes their psychological character seriously. The way to do this is to adopt a theory that admits different types of conceptual structure while tying them together by maintaining that concepts have atomic cores. In any event, it pays to focus on the nature of conceptual structure itself. Articulating the differ- ent explanatory roles for postulating conceptual structure and teasing these apart opens up a range of unexplored and potentially very promising theoretical options in the study of concepts.

Notes

This paper was fully collaborative; the order of the authors' names is arbitrary.

1 This view of the nature of thought is not entirely uncontroversial. Yet it's difficult to see how finite creatures without access to a structured system of representation could be capable of entertaining the vast number of thoughts that humans have available to them. Even if we stick to relatively simple thoughts, the number of these is truly astronomical. For example, there are 10^{18} simple statements of sums involving num- bers less than a million. This is more than the number of seconds since the beginning of the Universe and more than a million times the number of neurons in the human brain. How could a theory of thought accommodate these facts without postulating a structured representational system in which the same elements – concepts – can occur in different positions within a structured assembly? In any event, if a theory really says that thoughts don't have constituents, perhaps the best thing to say is that, according to that theory, there aren't any such things as concepts.

2 We will assume that thoughts and concepts have semantic properties and that chief among these are their truth-theoretic properties. We take it to be an important constraint on a theory of concepts that, e.g., the concept DOG refers to dogs.

3 Still, it is worth noting that the theories we discuss can be adapted with slight modifica- tion to alternative frameworks that take different stands on these foundational questions.

4   For more detailed surveys and development of the views here, see Laurence and Margolis (1999; in prep.). See also Smith and Medin (1981).

5   The main reason for the qualification is that, according to the Classical Theory, some concepts have to have no structure; these are the primitive concepts out of which all others are composed. Classical theorists have had little to say about how the reference of a primitive concept is fixed. But the most venerable account, owing to the British empiricists, is that primitive concepts express sensory properties and that they refer to these simply because they are causally linked to such properties via sensory transducers.

6   Work on the theory of concepts has become increasingly interdisciplinary, and many of the theories we will discuss bear the marks of ideas and motivations which have been transferred across disciplinary boundaries, particularly between psychology and philosophy. In line with much of this research, we take concepts to be mental representations (and thus mental particulars), since this perspective makes the most sense of the various psychological explananda that have rightly exerted considerable pressure on theorizing about concepts – even in philosophical circles. The reader should note that this is not a universally shared perspective and that many philosophers insist on construing concepts as abstract entities of one sort or another. Nonetheless, theorists who take concepts to be abstracta also take a deep interest in questions about conceptual structure. It's just that the structure in question is supposed to be the structure of abstract entities. See, e.g., Peacocke (1992) and Bealer (1982).

7   As the examples here indicate, the Classical Theory (and indeed all the theories we will be discussing) is, in the first instance, a theory about the nature of concepts that correspond to words in natural language – what are called *lexical concepts*. This is because theorists interested in concepts assume that the representations corresponding to natural language phrases or sentences are structured.

8   The motivation for the Classical Theory is by no means limited to these virtues. For example, another influential point in favor of this theory is its ability to explain our intuitions that certain statements or arguments are valid even though, on the face of it, they fail to express logical truths, e.g., "John is a bachelor, so John is unmarried" (see, e.g., Katz 1972).

9   Classical theorists have had little to say in defense of the notion of analyticity. E.g., Christopher Peacocke's seminal book on concepts (1992) falls squarely in the classical tradition, especially in its commitment to definitions, yet Peacocke takes little notice of the problems associated with analyticity, simply stating in a footnote that he is committed to some version of the analytic/synthetic distinction (see p. 244, fn 7). See Katz (1997), however, for a rare classical defense of analyticity, especially in the face of the present considerations.

10   In the most extreme cases, people know hardly any information at all. For instance, Putnam remarks that he can't distinguish elms from beeches, that for him they are both just trees. Yet arguably, he still has two distinct concepts that refer separately to elms and beeches. That wouldn't be possible if the mechanism of reference had to be an internalized definition.

11   What we are calling "the Prototype Theory" is an idealized version of a broad class of theories, one that abstracts from many differences of detail. This is true of each of the theories we present, though the diversity is perhaps more pronounced in the case of the Prototype Theory. For discussion of some of the different varieties, see Smith and Medin (1981).

12   The Dual Theory should not be confused with so-called *Two Factor* theories in philosophy. Though there are similarities, the Dual Theory and Two Factor theories address different issues. Two Factor theories are primarily concerned with distinguishing two different types, or aspects, of content. One factor accounts for all aspects of content that supervene on a person's body or that would be shared by molecule for molecule duplicates ("narrow content"). The other factor accounts for aspects of content that go beyond this, involving the person's relation to her environment ("wide content"). As a result, the two types of structure in the Dual Theory cross-classify the two aspects of content in Two Factor theories (see note 20 below).

13   According to the Theory Theory, the structure of a concept is constituted by its relations to the other concepts that are implicated in an embedding theory. Notice that on this account the structure of a concept can't be understood in terms of part/whole relations. For this reason, we have distinguished two models of conceptual structure (see Laurence and Margolis 1999). The first, the Containment Model, says that one concept, C_1, is included in the structure of another, C_2, just in case C_1 is literally contained in (i.e., is a proper part of) C_2. The second, the Inferential Model, says that C_1 is included in the structure of C_2 just in case C_1 stands in a privileged inferential relation to C_2. As should be evident from this characterization, the Theory Theory has to be construed in terms of the Inferential Model, but the Classical Theory and the Prototype Theory could be construed in terms of either model, depending on the exact motivations that support the postulation of classical and prototype structure.

14   These particular domains have been the subject of intense interdisciplinary investigation in recent years. For common-sense psychology, see Davies and Stone (1995a, 1995b), Carruthers (1996); for common-sense physics, see Spelke (1990), Baillargeon (1993), Xu and Carey (1996); for common-sense biology, see Medin and Atran (1999).

15   Or, for that matter, whether the same person is employing the same concept over time.

16   At best, Churchland's model shows how psychological *processes* could be holistic. They are holistic because they involve activation patterns across massively connected nodes in a network. But this doesn't mean that the *semantics* of the network are holistic.

17   It should be noted that Churchland is something of a moving target on these issues, though he often neglects to acknowledge changes in his view. For instance, in addition to the positions mentioned in the text, Churchland also tries maintaining that content similarity is a matter of similarity of "downstream processing" (see esp. 1996: 276),

> It is this downstream aspect of the vector's computational role that is so vitally important for reckoning sameness of cognitive content across individuals, or across cultures. A person or culture that discriminated kittens reliably enough from the environment, but treated them in absolutely every respect as a variant form of wharf-rat, must be ascribed some conception of "kitten" importantly different from our own. On the other hand, an alien person or species whose expectations of and behavior towards kittens precisely mirror our own must be ascribed the same concept "kitten," even though they might discriminate kittens principally by means of alien olfaction and high-frequency sonars beamed from their foreheads.

Apart from making his "state space semantics" have nothing whatsoever to do with the state space, this position falls prey to exactly the same sorts of problems as Churchland's first position, namely, it presupposes a notion of content identity for the "downstream" states that fix the content of the *kitten* vector.

18 See, e.g., Churchland (1986) and Putnam (1988).

19 These two points go hand in hand, since it's to be expected that if a concept has multiple structures that these would be of categorically different types.

20 The nature of narrow content is controversial but the main idea is that narrow content is shared by molecule-for-molecule duplicates even if they inhabit different environments. On some Two Factor theories (see note 12), a concept's narrow content is determined by its inferential role – a view that closely resembles the Theory Theory's account of conceptual structure. The difference is that, on a Two Factor theory, the inferential role of a concept isn't supposed to determine its reference.

References

Baillargeon, R. (1993). "The Object Concept Revisited: New Directions in the Investigation of Infants' Physical Knowledge." In C. Granrund (ed.), *Visual Perception and Cognition in Infancy*. Hillsdale, NJ: Lawrence Erlbaum Associates.

Bealer, G. (1982). *Quality and Concept*. Oxford: Clarendon Press.

Barsalou, L. (1987). "The Instability of Graded Structure: Implications for the Nature of Concepts." In U. Neisser (ed.), *Concepts and Conceptual Development: Ecological and Intellectual Factors in Categorization*. New York: Cambridge University Press.

Carey, S. (1982). "Semantic Development: The State of the Art." In E. Wanner and L. Gleitman (eds.), *Language Acquisition: The State of the Art*. New York: Cambridge University Press.

—— (1985). *Conceptual Change in Childhood*. Cambridge, MA: MIT Press.

Carruthers, P. (ed.) (1996). *Theories of Theories of Mind*. Cambridge: Cambridge University Press.

Churchland, P. M. (1996). "Fodor and Lepore: State-Space Semantics and Meaning Holism." In R. McCauley (ed.), *The Churchlands and Their Critics*. Cambridge, MA: Blackwell.

—— (1998). "Conceptual Similarity across Sensory and Neural Diversity: The Fodor/Lepore Challenge Answered." *Journal of Philosophy*, XCV (1): 5–32.

Churchland, P. S. (1986). *Neurophilosophy: Toward a Unified Science of the Mind/Brain*. Cambridge, MA: The MIT Press.

Dancy, J. (1985). *Introduction to Contemporary Epistemology*. Cambridge, MA: Blackwell.

Davies, M. and Stone, T. (eds.) (1995a). *Folk Psychology*. Oxford: Blackwell.

—— (eds.) (1995b). *Mental Simulation*. Oxford: Blackwell.

Dretske, F. (1995). *Naturalizing the Mind*. Cambridge, MA: MIT Press.

Fodor, J. D., Fodor, J. A., and Garrett, M. (1975). "The Psychological Unreality of Semantic Representations." *Linguistic Inquiry*, 6: 515–32.

Fodor, J. A. (1981). "The Present Status of the Innateness Controversy." In *Representations: Philosophical Essays on the Foundations of Cognitive Science*. Cambridge, MA: MIT Press.

—— (1981/90). "Psychosemantics; or, Where Do Truth Conditions Come From?" In N. G. Lycan (ed.), *Mind and Cognition*. Oxford: Blackwell.

—— (1990). "A Theory of Content, II: The Theory." In *A Theory of Content and Other Essays*. Cambridge, MA: MIT Press.

—— (1998). *Concepts: Where Cognitive Science Went Wrong*. New York: Oxford University Press.

Fodor, J. A., Garrett, M., Walker, E., and Parkes, C. (1980). "Against Definitions." *Cognition*, 8: 263–367.

Fodor, J. A. and Lepore, E. (1992). *Holism: A Shopper's Guide*. Cambridge, MA: Basil Blackwell.

—— (1996). "The Red Herring and the Pet Fish: Why Concepts Still Can't Be Prototypes." *Cognition*, 58: 253–70.

Gettier, E. (1963). "Is Justified True Belief Knowledge?" *Analysis*, 23: 121–3.

Gopnik, A. and Meltzoff, A. (1997). *Words, Thoughts, and Theories*. Cambridge, MA: MIT Press.

Katz, J. (1972). *Semantic Theory*. New York: Harper and Row.

—— (1997). "Analyticity, Necessity, and the Epistemology of Semantics." *Philosophy and Phenomenological Research*, LVII: 1–28.

Keil, F. (1994). "Explanation, Association, and the Acquisition of Word Meaning." In L. Gleitman and B. Landau (eds.), *The Acquisition of the Lexicon*, Cambridge, MA: MIT Press.

Kintsch, W. (1974). *The Representation of Meaning in Memory*. Hillsdale, NJ: Lawrence Erlbaum Associates.

Kripke, S. (1972/1980). *Naming and Necessity*. Cambridge, MA: Harvard University Press.

Landau, B. (1982). "Will the Real Grandmother Please Stand Up? The Psychological Reality of Dual Meaning Representations." *Journal of Psycholinguistic Research*, 11 (1): 47–62.

Laurence, S. and Margolis, E. (1999). "Concepts and Cognitive Science." In E. Margolis and S. Laurence (eds.), *Concepts: Core Readings*. Cambridge, MA: MIT Press.

—— (2002). "Radical Concept Nativism." *Cognition*, 86 (1): 22–55.

—— (in preparation). *The Building Blocks of Thought*.

Leslie, A. (2002). "How to Acquire a 'Representational Theory of Mind'." In D. Sperber and S. Davis (eds.), *Metarepresentations*. Vancouver Studies in Cognitive Science, vol. 10. Oxford: Oxford University Press.

Lormand, E. (1996). "How to Be a Meaning Holist." *Journal of Philosophy*, XCIII: 51–73.

Margolis, E. (1998). "How to Acquire a Concept." *Mind and Language*, 13 (3): 347–69.

Margolis, E., and Laurence, S. (1998). "Multiple Meanings and the Stability of Content." *Journal of Philosophy*, XCV (5): 255–63.

Medin, D. and Atran, S. (1999). *Folkbiology*. Cambridge, Mass: MIT Press.

Medin, D. and Ortony, A. (1989). "Psychological Essentialism." In S. Vosniadou and A. Ortony (eds.), *Similarity and Analogical Reasoning*. New York: Cambridge University Press.

Millikan, R. (1984). *Language, Thought, and Other Biological Categories: New Foundations for Realism*. Cambridge, MA: MIT Press.

—— (1993). *White Queen Psychology and Other Essays for Alice*. Cambridge, MA: MIT Press.

—— (1998). "A Common Structure for Concepts of Individuals, Stuffs, and Real Kinds: More Mama, More Milk, and More Mouse." *Behavioral and Brain Sciences*, 21: 55–65.

—— (2000). *On Clear and Confused Ideas: An Essay about Substance Concepts*. New York: Cambridge University Press.

Murphy, G. and Medin, D. (1985). "The Role of Theories in Conceptual Coherence." *Psychological Review*, 92 (3): 289–316.

Osherson, D. and Smith, E. (1981). "On the Adequacy of Prototype Theory as a Theory of Concepts." *Cognition*, 9: 35–58.

Peacocke, C. (1992). *A Study of Concepts*. Cambridge, MA: MIT Press.

—— (1998). "Implicit Conceptions, Understanding and Rationality." In E. Villanueva (ed.), *Philosophical Issues, 9: Concepts*. Atascadero, CA: Ridgeview Publishing Company.

Putnam, H. (1962). "The Analytic and the Synthetic." In H. Feigl and G. Maxwell (eds.), *Minnesota Studies in the Philosophy of Science, Volume III*. Minneapolis: University of Minnesota Press.

—— (1970). "Is Semantics Possible?" In H. Kiefer and M. Munitz (eds.), *Languages, Belief and Metaphysics*. New York: State University of New York Press: 50–63.

—— (1975). "The Meaning of 'Meaning'." In K. Gunderson (ed.), *Language, Mind and Knowledge*. Minneapolis: University of Minnesota Press.

—— (1988). *Representation and Reality*. Cambridge, Mass.: MIT Press.

Quine, W. (1951/1980). "Two Dogmas of Empiricism." In *From a Logical Point of View: Nine Logico-Philosophical Essays*. Cambridge, MA: Harvard University Press: 20–46.

Rey, G. (1993). "The Unavailability of What We Mean: A Reply to Quine, Fodor and Lepore." In J. A. Fodor and E. Lepore (eds.), *Holism: A Consumer Update*. Atlanta: Rodopi BV: 61–101.

Rosch, E. (1978). "Principles of Categorization." In E. Rosch and B. Lloyd (eds.), *Cognition and Categorization*. Hillsdale, NJ: Lawrence Erlbaum Associates.

Rosch, E. and Mervis, C. (1975). "Family Resemblances: Studies in the Internal Structure of Categories." *Cognitive Psychology*, 7: 573–605.

Smith, E. (1995). "Concepts and Categorization." In E. Smith and D. Osherson (eds.), *Thinking: An Invitation to Cognitive Science, Vol. 3*. Second Edition. Cambridge, MA: MIT Press.

Smith, E. and Medin, D. (1981). *Categories and Concepts*. Cambridge, MA: Harvard University Press.

Smith, E., Medin, D., and Rips, L. (1984). "A Psychological Approach to Concepts: Comments on Rey's 'Concepts and Stereotypes'." *Cognition*, 17: 265–74.

Spelke, E. (1990). "Principles of Object Perception." *Cognitive Science*, 14: 29–56.

Stampe, D. (1977). "Towards a Causal Theory of Linguistic Representation." *Midwest Studies in Philosophy*. Minneapolis: University of Minnesota Press.

Wittgenstein, L. (1953/1958). *Philosophical Investigations*, trans. E. Anscombe. 3rd edition. Oxford: Blackwell.

Xu, F. and Carey, S. (1996). "Infants' Metaphysics: The Case of Numerical Identity." *Cognitive Psychology*, 30: 111–53.

Chapter 9

Mental Causation

John Heil

9.1 The Cartesian Background

Descartes set the tone for the modern discussion of the relation of minds to bodies. According to Descartes, minds and bodies are distinct kinds of *substance*. (In this context, a substance should be thought of, not as a kind of stuff, something that might stain your shirt or stick to the bottom of your shoe, for instance, but as a particular object or entity: the tree outside your window, a pebble, the Moon, your right ear.) Bodies, Descartes thought, are spatially extended substances, incapable of feeling or thought; minds, in contrast, are unextended, thinking, feeling substances.

You might be led to such a view by considering mental and physical characteristics. These seem vastly different on the face of it. States of mind exhibit qualities that appear to fall outside the physical realm: a feeling you have when you bump your elbow, the smell of peat, the sound of a mosquito circling your head seem to differ qualitatively from anything belonging to the physical world. The *causes* of these experiences are perfectly unexceptional physical occurrences. The mental effects of these causes, however – their *appearances* – seem to include qualities not locatable in the physical world. For their part, physical bodies exhibit characteristics that appear decisively non-mental. A stone has a particular size, shape, mass, and definite spatial location. Sensations and thoughts, in contrast, apparently lack these characteristics. A pain can be intense, but not three inches long; your thoughts of an impending holiday lack mass.

To be sure, we say that thoughts occur *in* the head and that a pain in the toe is *in* the toe. This suggests that states of mind are at least spatially locatable. The sense in which a pain or a thought has a spatial location apparently differs from the sense in which a physical object has a spatial location, however. Descartes was well aware of the phenomenon of *phantom pain*: the apparent occurrence of pains in amputated limbs. This suggests that, in describing a pain as occurring in your toe, what you are really describing is a sensation of a particular kind: a sensation *as of a pain in your toe*; a pain-in-the-toe kind of sensation. Such a sensation might occur – and indeed such sensations *do* occur – in agents whose toes have been amputated.

Mental and physical items appear to differ in another respect as well. Your thoughts and feelings are *private*. Others can guess or infer what you are thinking and feeling, but only you have "direct" access to your thoughts and feelings. You and I standing side by side can observe the same tree or the same person. I can observe your having a thought or experiencing a pain. But I cannot, as you evidently can, encounter your thought or pain. My experience is not of your pain but of its effects on you and your behavior.

Considerations like these encourage us to follow Descartes and place sensation and thought outside the physical world. For Descartes, this meant that mental qualities must be qualities of mental substances, entities distinct from physical substances, themselves entities possessing distinctive characteristics. What we should regard as mental properties are, Descartes contended, modes of thought: ways of being a thinking substance. In contrast, physical properties are modes of extension: ways of being extended in or occupying space. Once we embrace this picture, the question arises: how *could* mental and physical substances interact causally? In a letter to Descartes, Princess Elizabeth of Bohemia observes that "it would be easier for me to attribute matter and extension to the soul, than to attribute to an immaterial body the capacity to move and be moved by a body" (Kenny 1970: 140).

One way to see the difficulty facing Descartes is to note that causal interaction of mental and physical substances apparently obliges us to abandon the idea that the physical world is *causally autonomous*. Physics treats the physical world as a closed system. Occurrences in this system reflect only occurrences elsewhere in the system (perhaps together with "boundary conditions"). Suppose these occurrences are ultimately motions of elementary particles. These motions are affected only by the motions of other particles. If we imagine a non-physical entity interacting causally with a physical system, we should have to countenance motions of particles not produced by motions of other particles.[1]

This appeal to the causal autonomy of the physical realm is not intended as an a priori argument against the possibility of causal links between the mental and the physical. Rather, it is a reminder that the prospect of causal interaction between a non-physical mind and a purely physical world would oblige us to rethink the character of the fundamental natural laws and broaden our notion of what constitutes the world as a whole. We should expect to discover particles behaving in ways that could not be accounted for solely by reference to laws governing inter-particle relations. This need not imply the possibility of non-material causes *violating* natural law. Natural laws, unlike legal statutes, are inviolable. A leaf fluttering slowly to the ground does not *violate* laws of gravity. Rather, an explanation of the leaf's behavior requires appeal to complex features of a system that includes the falling leaf, the Earth, and the swirling gaseous atmosphere through which the leaf is falling. The introduction of non-physical causes would complicate the causal picture, not by countenancing violations of physical law, but by introducing heretofore unanticipated causal factors.

The worry expressed by Princess Elizabeth reflects a worry common among Descartes's contemporaries. If minds are spatially unextended entities, how *could* they affect a spatially extended world? How could a non-spatial thing, as it were, get a grip on a spatial thing? What is the nature of the *causal mechanism*? To see the force of these worries, think of a simple case of mechanical causation: a rotating gear engages a second gear causing the second gear to rotate. In this case we have a distinctive causal mechanism: we can see how the second gear's turning is brought about by the rotation of the first gear. Now imagine the first gear's being replaced by a non-spatial entity. How could such an entity engage the second gear?

Of course, rotating gears afford merely one example of an easily visualizable causal nexus. Think of the action of a magnet on iron filings or the effects of the Moon on the tides. In neither case can we observe anything like a mechanical connection between cause and effect, yet we do not regard cases of this kind as worrisome. This is due, in part, to the fact that such phenomena are so familiar, and in part to our having accepted the idea that objects can affect one another at a distance when the objects are contained within a *field*. A magnet creates a magnetic field. Iron filings are affected by characteristics of this field. The Earth and Moon alter the contours of a gravitational field that includes them both, and by way of this field affect objects in it. Perhaps minds act on bodies, not by pushing those bodies around, but by creating or affecting the contours of fields which in turn affect the behavior of bodies in them.

You might still worry that a field has a definite location, but a Cartesian mind is utterly non-spatial. How could something that is not here – indeed not anywhere – bear responsibility for the character of a field present in a definite spatial region? This, however, is to misunderstand the idea that minds are non-extended. A point is non-extended, yet possesses a definite spatial location. It would seem possible, then, for a non-material substance, utterly lacking in extension, to exist at a spatial location or move from place to place and to affect contiguous spatial regions.

If all this were so, however, we should have to include mental substances among the fundamental entities making up our world. This would require, at the very least, supplementing laws we now take to govern the elementary constituents. A link of this kind between the mental and the physical might suggest that we are losing the distinction between the mental and the physical and in effect subsuming the mental under the physical.

At this point, we should do well to remind ourselves of the vast gulf between mental and physical qualities. It is hard to find a place for the qualities of conscious experience alongside the qualities of ordinary objects. The hardness, sphericity, and mass of a billiard ball seem to be nothing at all like the quality of your experience of a headache or the taste of a mango. It is not just that mental and physical phenomena differ qualitatively: there are endless qualitative differences among physical phenomena. Rather, the qualities of states of mind seem not to overlap in any way at all with physical qualities.

It may be possible to understand how the qualities of a billiard ball, for instance, could be grounded in features of the billiard ball's constituent particles. But it is another matter altogether to understand how mental qualities might be grounded in features of the particles that make us up (or for that matter make up our brains). In this case we seem to be faced with what Joseph Levine (1983) has called an "explanatory gap." Even if we accept the familiar idea that minds are somehow dependent on brains, we have no clear idea of the nature of this dependence. The mental–physical relation appears utterly mysterious.

9.2 Intentionality

Difficulties concerning the causal role of mental qualities make up one component of the problem of mental causation. A second difficulty is harder to motivate, and is best tackled in stages. The difficulty in question stems from the fact that many states of mind exhibit representational content. (Philosophers call such states of mind *intentional states*.) When you stub your toe, you experience a qualitatively distinctive kind of experience. You may also come to form a thought you might express in English by saying "I've stubbed my toe!" This thought, unlike your feeling of pain, is representational.[2]

Let us bracket for the moment incipient worries about mental qualities, and consider an influential attempt by Donald Davidson to come to terms with intentional states of mind (see Davidson 1970, 1974). Davidson's account of the relation that mental events bear to physical events is standardly characterized as a token identity theory. Davidson argues that although mental properties or types are not reducible to (that is, analyzable in terms of or identifiable with) physical types, every mental *token* is identical with some physical token.[3] Your being in pain at midnight is (let us imagine) identical with some physical (presumably neurological) event occurring in your body at midnight, although there is no prospect of translating talk of pain into neurological talk. Davidson does not appeal to familiar arguments for the "multiple realizability" of mental types, although these arguments might be taken to support his position. (I shall discuss multiple realizability presently.) Physically indiscernible agents must be mentally indiscernible, according to Davidson (the mental "supervenes" on the physical), but this does not imply that agents in the same state of mind must be physically indiscernible. You and an octopus may both be in pain, but your physical condition is very different from that of the octopus.

Davidson hoped to solve the problem of mental causation by appealing to token identity. If every (particular, token) mental event is identical with some (particular, token) physical event, and if physical events are unproblematically causes and effects, then mental events can be causes and effects as well. How can mental events be identical with physical events if mental properties or types are not reducible to physical properties or types? Davidson's idea is that an event counts as a mental event if it falls under a mental description. Similarly, an event is a physical event just in case it falls under a physical description. One and the same event (an occurrence in your brain, for instance) could fall under a mental description ("being a pain") and satisfy a physical description ("being a neurological occurrence of kind N"). The principles we use to ascribe states of mind to agents differ importantly from those we use to ascribe neurological states, however. This means that although every (true) ascription of a state of mind to an agent holds in virtue of that agent's being in a particular physical state, there is no way to reconstitute talk of states of mind in neurological terms. Indeed, in applying mental terms to agents, we need have no idea what complex physical features of those agents answer to those terms. This is so quite generally. When I correctly ascribe a headache to you, I do so on the basis of your behavior: what you say and do. But what makes my ascription correct is not your behavior, but some complex state of your brain about which I may be utterly ignorant.

Davidson's contention that mental terms cannot be reduced to physical terms can be illustrated by means of an analogy. Whenever a batter hits into a double play, the double play is constituted by a sequence of physical events. It does not follow, however, that we could redefine "double play" in terms of precise sequences of physical motions. This is so despite the fact that, if a particular physical sequence constitutes a double play, any physically indiscernible sequence would constitute a double play as well. (So being a double play "supervenes" on physical sequences.)

Davidson's proposed solution to the problem of mental causation, although influential, has been widely attacked. In general, the attacks have had the following form. Suppose we concede token identity: every mental event is identical with some physical event or other. Suppose we concede, as well, that every such physical event is causally unproblematic. Suppose your having a headache tonight at midnight is identical with your then being in neurological state N, and suppose your being in neurological state N causes a particular bodily motion (you reach for a bottle of aspirin). We can, it seems, still ask: did you reach for the aspirin in virtue of being in pain or in virtue of being in state N? (The question is sometimes put like this: did the event that caused a certain bodily motion do so qua being a pain or qua being neurological state N?)

Consider a parallel case. The ball hit by Mark McGwire for his 65th home run of the season strikes Gus in the head, causing a concussion. The ball's striking Gus *is* Gus's being struck by McGwire's 65th home run ball, but the ball's being McGwire's 65th home run ball is irrelevant to its having this physical effect. (One way to see this is to note that any object with the ball's mass and velocity would have had precisely the same effect.) The worry is that mental states could be like this. Mental events might figure in causal transactions but not in virtue of being mental (not qua mental), only in virtue of their physical characteristics – characteristics picked out by purely physical descriptions.

9.2.1 "Broad" states of mind

You might be suspicious of this example. After all, a baseball's being one hit by Mark McGwire is not an intrinsic ("built in") property of the ball, but a feature of the ball it possesses only by virtue of standing in a particular relation to something else (for starters, it was hit by Mark McGwire). And it is hard to see how any relational feature of an object could affect that object's causal capacities. The aspirin tablet you take for a headache could be the millionth tablet produced in May by the Bayer Company, but this feature of the tablet plays no role in the operation of the aspirin in your bloodstream. In general, it would seem that only an object's intrinsic – built-in – features could affect its causal capacities. You could concede that an object's relational properties are causally irrelevant to what it does or could do, but wonder what this has to do with mental causation. The answer, according to many philosophers: everything!

A tradition in twentieth-century philosophy of mind extending from Wittgenstein through Putnam and Burge rejects the Cartesian picture of the mind as a self-contained entity that undergoes sensations, entertains thoughts, and manipulates the body. Sensations, perhaps, can be understood as states and processes intrinsic to agents. Intentional states of mind, however, beliefs, desires, intentions, and the like, are held to incorporate an ineliminable relational component.

The thesis might be illustrated by imagining two intrinsically indiscernible agents situated in distinct environments. One of these, Wayne, lives on Earth. When Wayne entertains thoughts he would express by uttering sentences such as "The glass is full of water," his thoughts concern water. Wayne's twin, Dwayne, exactly resembles Wayne intrinsically (Wayne and Dwayne are "molecular duplicates"). Dwayne inhabits a planet physically resembling Earth down to the last detail, with one important exception. On Dwayne's planet (which Dwayne calls "Earth," but we shall call "Twin Earth"), the stuff in rivers, bathtubs, and ice trays, although *called* "water" is not water at all, but XYZ, a very different chemical substance that superficially resembles water: XYZ looks, feels, tastes, and behaves as ordinary water does on Earth. When Dwayne entertains a thought he would express by uttering "The glass is full of water," his thoughts do not concern *water* (water after all is H_2O) but XYZ, *twin*-water (a clear colorless liquid with a distinctive chemical make-up).

The guiding idea here is that the *contents* of thoughts depend not merely on agents' intrinsic features, but also, and crucially, on their context. If it is essential to a belief, desire, or intention that it have a particular content (if belief B_1 and belief B_2 differ in content, then $B_1 \neq B_2$), then beliefs, desires, intentions – intentional states generally – depend on agents' contexts.

Suppose this is so. Returning to Davidson, imagine a case in which an agent, A, is in a given neurological state, N, and that N is identical with a belief, B (that is, by virtue of being in neurological state N, A can be said to have B). Imagine, as well, that N causes some bodily motion, M. A's belief, B, *is* N, but, given that

N is B partly in virtue of A's context, it is hard to see how N's being a belief (as opposed to being a certain kind of neurological state) has any bearing on the occurrence of M. N *is* A's belief, but this is so only because, *in this context*, A can be said to have belief B. Why should this purely extrinsic fact about N have any bearing at all on what N causes?

A particular physical object *is* a dollar bill. Its being a dollar bill depends on a host of broadly contextual factors: the bill has a certain kind of causal history: it was printed by the US Treasury Department. These contextual factors, although essential to the bill's being a dollar bill, play no role whatever in the operation of a vending machine into which the bill is inserted. An event involving a particular object causes the machine to dispense a candy bar, and the object in question *is* a dollar bill. But the object's being a dollar bill is irrelevant to the operation of the machine.

The conclusion appears inescapable. Even if Davidson is right, and every mental event is identical with some physical (causally unproblematic) event, it seems not to follow that events have physical effects in virtue of being mental (qua mental). At least, this seems so for events involving intentionality if we grant that intentional character is contextual.

Where does this leave us? We have uncovered two kinds of worry concerning mental causation. One worry concerns mental qualities. Such qualities seem not to engage with physical goings on. A second, less obvious, worry focuses on intentional states of mind – beliefs, desires, intentions, and the like. Such states of mind appear to have irreducibly contextual or relational components that disqualify them as candidate causes of physical effects (bodily motions of agents, for instance). In either case, the action of mind on the physical world is hard to understand.

Perhaps this is too hasty, however. We have yet to look at the most influential account of the mind today: functionalism. Functionalism purports to offer a way through the thicket of problems associated with mental–physical causal interaction.

9.3   Functionalism

Functionalism has many sources, but as an explicit conception of mind it can be traced to Hilary Putnam's 1967 paper, "Psychological Predicates."[4] Functionalists hold that states of mind are functional states of creatures to whom they are ascribed. The idea of a functional state is most easily understood by reference to the notion of a functional characterization. What is an egg-beater? An egg-beater is a device the function of which is to beat eggs. Egg-beaters can take many forms. An egg-beater might be a wire whisk, a hand-cranked device made of metal or plastic, or a gleaming solid state Cuisinart. Think of each of these devices as being an egg-beater differently embodied or "realized." Each counts as an egg-beater because each performs a particular function: each takes unbeaten eggs as inputs and yields as outputs beaten eggs.

How could states of mind be functional states? Think of pain. Your being in pain is a matter of your being in a state with a particular kind of causal role. Pains are caused by tissue damage or malfunction, for instance, pains give rise to various bodily responses, and pains have assorted mental effects as well. When you stub your toe you go into a state produced by a collision between your toe and some bulky object, you react by rubbing your toe, and you form the belief that your toe hurts and a desire to take appropriate medicinal action.

Looked at this way, your being in pain is a matter of your being in a state of a kind with characteristic kinds of cause and effect. This state is "realized" in you by a particular physiological state. What is important to that state's realizing your pain is not its intrinsic make-up, but the fact that the state occupies the right sort of causal role. Other kinds of creature – octopodes, for instance, or reptiles – might have utterly different kinds of physical constitution, yet be capable of going into states with similar causal profiles: they are brought about by tissue damage, and they result in aversive responses. These states are said to realize pain in creatures of those kinds. Suppose we encountered a being from a remote galaxy with a silicon-based "biology." Could such a creature feel pain? We should be inclined to say so, functionalists argue, insofar as we have evidence that the alien creatures have a capacity for going into states that resemble our pain states in their characteristic causes and effects. If, when the aliens suffer bodily injury, they cry out, withdraw, and seek relief, functionalists sensibly contend, it would be churlish to deny that the aliens suffer pain solely on the grounds that their bodily make-up differs from that of terrestrial species.

We are thus led to the view that pains (and states of mind generally) are functional states, states characterizable not by their intrinsic make-up, but by their occupying an appropriate causal role. A view of this sort appears to solve the problem of mental causation in a stroke. If states of mind are functional states, states that owe their nature to patterns of physical causes and effects, it would seem that there can be no mental–physical "gap." States of mind, after all, *are* states of mind by virtue of what causes them and what they cause.

9.3.1   Multiple realizability

Matters are not so clear, however. Functionalists do not identify states of mind with physical states of their possessors. On the contrary, functionalists regard such states as the *realizers* of mental states. Pain is realized in you by one kind of physical state; but it is realized in other creatures (and other possible creatures) by states of very different sorts. States of mind are in this way multiply realizable. You are in mental state S by virtue of being in physical state P_1; an octopus is in state S by virtue of being in a very different kind of physical state, P_2; and an Alpha Centaurian is in state S by virtue of being in state P_3. P_1, P_2, and P_3 are very different kinds of physical realizer of S. Pain cannot be identified with any one of these kinds of state without thereby excluding the rest. What makes a pain a pain,

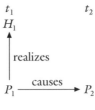

Figure 9.1

functionalists hold, is not the physical character of the state that realizes the pain, but the fact that the state has the right kind of causal profile.

This is not the place to discuss the pros and cons of functionalism (see chapter 1). We can, however, see how the problem of mental causation arises for a functionalist. A functional state is not identifiable with the physical states that realize it. Functionalists put this by describing functional states as "higher-level" states: states creatures are in by virtue of being in particular lower-level realizing states.[5] Now, however, it is hard to see how a higher-level state could have a lower-level effect. In the case of your being in pain (which, we are supposing, is realized in you by your being in some physical state P_1), it looks as though the physical *realizer* of your pain – P_1 – is responsible for any physical responses associated with the pain. The pain itself appears merely to float above its physical realizer, and so to do nothing. The situation is illustrated in figure 9.1. (H_1 is a higher-level state – your being in pain, for instance – P_1 is that state's lower-level realizer, P_2 is some physical effect – your taking aspirin, for instance – and t_1 and t_2 reflect the passage of time.)

This difficulty attaches not merely to functionalism but to any account of mentality that regards states of mind as "higher-level" states, states realized by, but distinct from, lower-level physical states. Davidson is not a functionalist, but many have found it natural to read him as endorsing the idea that states of mind are higher-level states "supervenient" on, but not reducible to, lower-level physical states. Indeed, philosophers of many different persuasions have been attracted to the idea that mental properties, although in some way dependent on physical properties, are not thereby reducible to physical properties. The argument for multiple realizability seems to establish that while states of mind are realized by physical states, mental states are not reducible to physical states. If the mental is not reducible to the physical, however, we must either assume that mental states are something "over and above" their physical realizers or – more radically – to suppose that there are no mental states at all, only physical states and goings-on.

The latter position, *eliminativism* (see chapter 2), strikes most people as a non-starter. Surely, it might be argued, our having mental states is a datum to be explained, not a candidate for elimination. Eliminativists cite cases in which entities (caloric, phlogiston, the ether are three commonly cited examples) postulated by scientific theories were subsequently abandoned. With the abandonment of the theories came abandonment of the entities. Such cases do not fit well our own direct experience of mentality. States of mind and their properties are not theoretical posits like caloric, phlogiston, or the ether, but objects of direct experience (or better: *experiences*). What sense could there be in the thought that there are no pains, no feelings of grief or happiness, no thoughts, only neurological goings-on?

Eliminativism as to states of mind appears unpromising, a desperate move that attempts to answer the question of how states of mind are related to the physical world by subtracting states of mind and leaving only the physical world. The alternatives – the idea that minds are higher-level entities and reductionism – appear to have serious problems of their own, however. We have noted already that reductionism is at odds with the evident possibility of multiple realizability. That worry aside, many theorists consider reductionism to be a covert form of eliminativism, a conception of mind that stems from the benighted thought that science is the measure of all things. We should admit (such theorists argue) that mental states are a species of irreducible higher-level phenomena that deserve treatment on their own terms. If we have difficulty reconciling the role of such phenomena in the causal structure of the physical world, we should not doubt the phenomena, but abandon the "scientistic" idea that all genuine causal relations are reducible to basic physical processes (see, for instance, Post 1991, Dupré 1993, and Poland 1994).

9.4 Levels of Reality

The sense that we are faced with three unpalatable options is due perhaps less to the nature of things and more to the network of concepts that dictates these options. We shall (as management texts advise) need to "think outside the box" if we are to make progress in our understanding of the mind's place in nature.

Consider, first, what it is to be a realist about states of mind. In general, you are a realist about a phenomenon or a domain of phenomena to the extent that you believe that phenomena of the sort in question exist independently of your thoughts about them. Most of us are realists about tables, chairs, mountains, and galaxies, but not about ghosts, witches, or phlogiston. Some philosophers endorse realism about value, regarding objects as valuable or not quite independently of our valuing them. Others are value anti-realists, preferring to think of an object's value as depending in some way on attitudes valuers take up toward it. What is required for realism about states of mind? As will become evident, the way this somewhat obscure question is answered can dramatically affect the conceptual framework within which questions about mental causation are posed and answered.

Philosophers are trained to think about realism in a particular way. You are a realist about ghosts, or quarks, or the ether if you think that ghosts, or quarks, or the ether exist independently of your thoughts about such things. Philosophers, seeking precision, prefer to characterize realism in terms of attitudes we evince toward terms or predicates:

(P) You are a realist about F's if you think the term, "F," designates a property shared by every object to which it (truly) applies.[6]

You are a realist about colors, for instance, if you think that "is red" designates a property possessed by some objects and shared by every object to which "is red" correctly applies.

Note, first, that (P) goes beyond the innocuous claim that when "is red" applies to an object, it does so in virtue of some property possessed by that object. This claim is innocuous because it does not imply, as (P) does, that every object to which "is red" applies possesses one and the same property – presumably the property of being red. To see the difference, think of two red balls. One ball is crimson, one is scarlet. Both balls (in virtue of their respective colors) answer to the predicate "is red." But it is easy to doubt that there is some one property, that of being red, possessed by each ball *in addition to* that ball's being some particular shade of red. Is it false, then, that both balls are red? Only a philosopher would say this; only a philosopher who accepted (P).[7] It seems more natural to say that "is red" applies – truly and literally – to objects by virtue of those objects possessing any of a (possibly open-ended) range of colors, those we classify as shades of red.

My suggestion is that a similar point holds for the kinds of mental term thought to range over multiply realizable properties and states. "Is in pain," for instance, might be taken to hold of diverse creatures in virtue of those creatures being in distinct kinds of state.[8] Although the states differ, they are pertinently similar. If the functionalists are right, then they are similar with respect to the kinds of event that evoke them and the kinds of event they themselves evoke. If the functionalists are wrong, if there is more to being in pain than being in a particular kind of functional state, then a creature answers to "is in pain" in virtue of being in a state that is relevantly similar – perhaps similar qualitatively – to states of other creatures to whom "is in pain" applies. The operative word here is "similar." When you and an octopus are in pain, you are in similar but not perfectly similar states. There is no need to postulate, as the functionalists do, some further higher-level state that both you and the octopus are in, a state with respect to which you and the octopus are perfectly similar, a state answering directly to the pain predicate but differently realized in you and the octopus.

If this is right, we can at least see our way around one prominent puzzle about mental causation: how could higher-level states or properties have lower-level effects? My suggestion is that the higher-level states and properties are philosophical artifacts, traceable to a covert acceptance of something like principle (P). We can turn our backs on higher-level states and properties without giving up realism about putatively higher-level items. "Is in pain" might apply truly and literally to you, to an octopus, and to an Alpha Centaurian. The pain predicate applies to you, the octopus, and the Alpha Centaurian, not because you share a single higher-level property, but because you, the octopus, and the Alpha Centaurian possess similar, although not precisely similar, properties.

The view I am advancing is ontologically reductive but not reductionist in the sense that many anti-reductionists find objectionable. I do not imagine for a moment that we could translate talk of states of mind into talk of biological states, much less into talk of states involving elementary particles. Nor is the position advanced here a form of eliminativism. Particular mental terms can apply truly and literally to creatures in virtue of those creatures' being in any of a very large number of relevantly similar physical states. In each individual case, a definite physical state answers to the term. On such a view, all that is eliminated is an alleged higher-level state or property, a purely philosophical posit.

The abandonment of the levels picture resolves one component of the problem of mental causation. It does not provide an exhaustive solution, however. We are left with at least two residual issues: the problem of "broad" contextually determined states of mind, and the qualia problem.

9.5 Causation and Broad States of Mind

Recall the idea that intentional states – beliefs, desires, intentions, and the like – vary with context.[9] One result of such a conception of intentionality is that, differently situated, intrinsically indiscernible agents ("molecular duplicates") might be entertaining utterly different thoughts. This, coupled with the idea that an object's causal powers are wholly a function of its intrinsic make-up, leads to the idea that differences in the contents of states of mind make no causal difference. To the extent that the content of your mental states depends on factors external to you (broadly speaking, on your context), the contents of those states – what they concern – could make no difference to your behavior. But surely what you believe, or desire or intend, does make a difference to what you do.

Again, we are faced with various options. One option is to bite the bullet. Your intrinsic properties determine what you do (how you respond to incoming stimuli, for instance). The fact that, in virtue of your intrinsic state together with your context, it is true of you that you have particular beliefs and desires is beside the point causally. A view of this kind is simply an extension of the eliminativist impulse to a new domain. In either case it is hard to see eliminativism as much more than an admission of defeat.

A second option parallels functionalist appeals to levels of reality. Suppose we replace talk of *causation* with talk of *explanation*. We routinely describe and explain one another's behavior (and, significantly, the behavior of non-human creatures) by appealing to intentional states of mind. Why did you visit the pantry? Because you wanted some cheese and believed there was cheese in the pantry. You subsequently formed an intention to visit the pantry and, on the basis of this intention, visited the pantry. We seem willing to accept such explanations as fundamental. Our conception of causation, it could be argued, is founded on our grasp of this kind of explanation. If that is so, it is no good trying to undercut a successful explanatory practice by appeals to metaphysical qualms about the nature of causation. Causes are what we appeal to in successful explanations of the behavior of objects. It is a conceptual mistake to imagine that we could discover that, in general, successful explanations lacked a causal grounding.[10]

If you regard the problem of mental causation as a significant metaphysical problem, then you will not be attracted to purported solutions that seek to replace talk of causation with talk of explanation. To do so would be to put the cart before the horse. This might appear to beg the question against the idea that causal explanation is conceptually prior to causation. We are faced with a stand-off between two positions, each of which relies on premises that entail the denial of the other. How might we break the deadlock?

We arrived at worries about mental causation via deeply held metaphysical convictions about causation. Few theorists would dispute the practice of explaining agents' intelligent behavior by reference to agents' states of mind. One question is how we might accommodate such a practice to other practices that seem no less fundamental – including the practice of explaining the behavior of physical bodies exclusively by reference to the intrinsic physical properties of those bodies. Few philosophers would be tempted to dismiss fine-grained physical accounts of a cake's falling on the grounds that we already have a perfectly acceptable everyday explanation of this event: the cake fell because Lilian slammed the oven door. The same holds, I believe, for mental causation. True, there would be something fishy about any view that entailed the utter falsehood of everyday explanations of intelligent behavior. This does not imply that such explanations constitute bedrock, however. By persevering, we can hope to find an account of mental causation that accommodates such explanations. In so doing, we may find it convenient to modify the way we think of intelligent behavior and the intentional states that seem to drive it.

What might we say, then, about "broad" (contextually determined) states of mind and their causal efficacy? First, we should not be quick to abandon the idea that the causal powers of an object (hence what it does or could do) depend wholly on its intrinsic make-up.[11] Second, we should look more carefully at the contextual model of intentionality. Perhaps the projective character of states of mind can, after all, be accounted for by reference to agents' intrinsic make-up. A view of this sort could allow that what our thoughts concern – in the sense of what they include reference to – depends on the way the world is independent of agents. But this relational matter, although it can enter into descriptions of states of mind, need not oblige us to imagine that those states of mind are themselves constituted by relations between agents and external factors.[12]

9.6 Qualia

Many readers will by now have grown impatient. The deep worry about mental causation – indeed the deep problem for accounts of minds generally (what David

Chalmers (1996) calls "the hard problem") – is the worry about how to fit the qualities of conscious experiences, the so-called qualia, into a causally self-contained physical world. Let me focus on just two difficulties posed by qualia for any account of mental causation.

Imagine that you are gazing at cherry trees in bloom around the Jefferson Memorial. You have a vivid visual experience you would find difficult to put into words. Imagine now that a scientist who believes that experiences are goings-on in the brain carefully inspects your brain while you are undergoing this experience. The scientist observes a dull gray mass. On closer inspection (and with the aid of expensive instruments), the scientist observes fine-grained neural activity: cells firing, chemical reactions along axons, and the like. These activities might correspond to your experience. Your experience has a definite qualitative character, but the scientist's observation reveals nothing of this, only boring neurological qualities. Where are these qualities of your experience, if not in your brain? Perhaps they lie outside the physical world.

This line of reasoning betrays a confusion over qualities of experience.[13] Your experience is of pink blossoms, white marble, and shimmering water. Pinkness, whiteness, and the shimmering character you perceive are qualities of the objects you perceive, not qualities of your experience. When you perceive a ball, the ball, but not your experience, is spherical. If you were to think, then, that on looking into your brain and observing your experiences a scientist ought to observe pink, white, shimmering, or spherical items, you would be in error. If neurological goings-on in your brain *are* your experiences, those goings-on need not have qualities ascribable to the objects you are experiencing. The scientist looking into your brain experiences occurrences of your experiences, let us suppose. But the scientist's experiences need not resemble yours; your experiences are of cherry trees, the scientist's experiences are of something quite different: your *experiences* of cherry trees.

This is not to say that experiences lack qualities (does *anything* lack qualities?), only that we must take care to distinguish qualities of experiences from qualities of objects experienced. When we do this, is it so clear that the qualities of experiences differ radically from the qualities of brains? In considering this question, we tend to forget that, in describing brains as gray, mushy, and the like, we are describing the way brains look to us: *brains as we experience them*. There is no reason to think that the qualities of our experiences of brains ought to resemble qualities of experiences of objects other than brains (cherry blossoms, for instance). Considered in this light, there is no obvious problem with the thought that your experience of cherry blossoms and the Jefferson Memorial is an occurrence in your brain and that its qualities are qualities of that neurological occurrence. This means that, if there is no special problem with the idea that the qualitative changes in your brain affect your behavior, then conscious qualities pose no special problem of mental causation.

Many philosophers will disagree. Qualities, they will suppose, are causally inert. When a baseball causes a concussion, it is the causal powers (dispositionalities) of the baseball, not its qualities, that matter. A view of this kind is founded on the practice of distinguishing dispositional properties (properties regarded as bestowing causal powers on their possessors) and categorical properties (purely qualitative non-causal properties).[14] One seldom noticed problem with such a view is that it apparently flies in the face of ordinary experience. You enjoy viewing cherry blossoms because of their visually perceived qualities; you take pleasure in eating ice cream because of its gustatory qualities. An artist selects a particular medium in which to work in part because of the qualities of that medium. In each of these cases, it looks for all the world as though agents are responding to qualities of the objects in question. How might we reconcile these deliverances of common sense with a view of properties according to which properties must be either causal or qualitative?

Perhaps we should reject the division of properties into exhaustive and mutually exclusive classes: dispositional and categorical. Philosophers who have done so have typically attempted to reduce one class to the other – arguing, for instance, that properties are exclusively dispositional (Shoemaker 1980). A more attractive possibility is that every property (and here I have in mind natural properties of concrete objects, not abstracta) is simultaneously dispositional and qualitative. This is sometimes put by saying that properties have dispositional and qualitative *aspects*. Talk of aspects, however, brings to mind properties and leads to the thought that every property might be (or might be made up of) two properties, one qualitative one dispositional. I prefer to follow C. B. Martin and see qualities and dispositions as strictly identical (see Martin 1997; Martin and Heil 1999; Heil 1998: ch. 6). Consider the sphericity of a particular ball. The ball's sphericity is a particular quality possessed by the ball and it is in virtue of this quality that the ball is disposed to roll. The quality and disposition do not merely co-vary, they are one and the same property differently considered and described.

Pretend that something like this is right. It would follow that there is no particular mystery as to how the qualities of experience bear on causal transactions in the physical realm – providing we are willing to countenance the possibility that conscious experiences are, at bottom, physical events. This, of course, is a weighty proviso, one many theorists would not concede without a fight. Rather than attempt a defense of these ideas here, I propose to apply them to a particular puzzle case and note how they stack up.

9.7 Zombies

Be forewarned: the philosophical notion of a zombie differs dramatically from the popular conception.[15] The philosopher's zombie is not a member of the "undead," requiring human blood in order to remain, if not exactly alive, at least undead. A philosopher's zombie is a being indistinguishable from ordinary people in every respect, save one: zombies lack conscious experiences. You might have a zombie counterpart. This counterpart would behave exactly as you do, would exhibit all your preferences and prejudices. Indeed, no observer could distinguish you from your zombie twin. When interrogated, your zombie twin will deny being a zombie (and indeed, if you believe you are conscious, your twin will believe the same). From time to time your twin complains of headaches and reports a fondness for chocolate. Differences between you and zombie-you are literally invisible to any observer, even a neuroscientist armed with brain-scanning instruments.

Zombies have figured in thought experiments attacking functionalism. The idea is straightforward. You and your zombie twin are functionally indiscernible. You, however, enjoy conscious experiences, while your twin, despite protestations to the contrary, does not: "all is dark inside." If such cases are conceivable (they need not be *really* possible, "possible in the actual world," only *logically* possible in the way your leaping tall buildings with a single bound is logically possible), it would seem that functionalism falls short of providing a complete account of the nature of mind. Functionalism leaves out a central feature of minds: consciousness.

Some functionalists deny the possibility of zombies on the grounds that any being with the right sort of functional architecture *thereby* has a mind. This amounts to the claim that there is nothing more to having a mind than having the right kind of functional architecture, however; this is the very point at issue.

In a recent, much discussed book, David Chalmers (1996) takes a different tack. Chalmers defends functionalism in the face of the possibility of zombies. He argues that, while zombies are logically possible, they are naturally impossible. Laws of nature, he thinks, tie consciousness to particular sorts of functional state. In the actual world, a creature with a functional architecture identical to yours would be conscious. Consciousness "emerges" from functional architecture by virtue of the holding of certain irreducible laws of nature. Zombies are possible, but only in a world lacking these basic laws.[16]

Chalmers's view is intended to work consciousness into the physical world while at the same time showing why consciousness does not find a place in ordinary accounts of physical processes. Conscious experiences are salient to conscious agents, but because the qualities of such experience are merely emergent by-products of functional systems, they have no direct effects on physical processes. (Hence the possibility of zombies.)

A position of this kind mandates fundamental laws of nature relating properties of conscious experiences – conscious qualities, qualia – to functional properties of creatures to whom the experiences belong. Chalmers accepts the functionalist contention that functional properties are higher-level properties, properties possessed by agents by virtue of those agent's possession of some lower-level property (see section 9.3 above). You, for instance, possess a particular functional property, F, by virtue of possessing a neurological property, P_1. An octopus possesses F by virtue of possessing a very different neurological property, P_2; and an Alpha Centaurian possesses F by virtue of possessing an altogether different physical property, P_3. It is important for functionalism that the class of physical realizers of F ($P_1, P_2, P_3, \ldots$) is open-ended. Functional properties are not in any sense reducible to physical properties. (To imagine that functional properties are

– possibly infinite – disjunctions of physical properties is to make hash of the notion of a property.) This leads to a remarkable picture of the basic laws of nature. The emergence of conscious properties from functional properties requires basic laws of nature that tie simple properties of consciousness to open-ended disjunctions of physical properties (the realizers of the functional properties from which the latter emerge). Such laws would be very odd indeed, unlike anything thus far encountered in basic physics.

Worries of this kind aside, let us look at the implications of the conception of mentality sketched earlier for the possibility of zombies. I have argued against the functionalist thesis that states of mind are higher-level states, and its corollary the thesis that mental properties are higher-level properties – properties possessed by agents by virtue of their possession of lower-level realizing properties. The functionalist idea that mental properties are multiply realized is better captured by the idea that mental predicates ("is in pain," for instance) hold of diverse agents, not in virtue of those agents' sharing a single multiply realized higher-level property, but by virtue of those agents' possessing any property from among a sprawling, somewhat unruly family of *similar* properties. Mental predicates are "projectable" (they figure in explanations of agents' behavior, for instance) because they hold of agents in virtue of those agents' possessing causally similar properties.

In addition to bestowing "causal powers" on their possessors, however, these same properties contribute to the agent's qualitative nature. There are not two kinds of property, qualitative and dispositional, only properties themselves differently considered. If this "identity theory" of properties is right, then it is flatly impossible to vary dispositions and qualities independently. If a zombie is a precise duplicate of you dispositionally (hence a functional replica), the zombie must be a qualitative duplicate as well. This result, coupled with the idea that your states of mind are physical states (states of your nervous system, for instance), yields the further result that zombies are impossible – not just impossible given laws of nature in our world, but flatly impossible. There might be creatures functionally similar to us in some respects that differ in their conscious experiences (or even lack them altogether). But there could not be creatures with *all* our physical properties who differed from us in this regard.

You may be unimpressed by this result. It depends, after all, on certain substantive, hence controversial, philosophical theses. But at the very least it should serve to undermine the air of inevitability that often accompanies discussion of the "hard problem" of consciousness. There are still problems, to be sure, puzzles remaining to be answered. But philosophy can ill afford to make hard problems harder.

9.8 Conclusion

Cartesian worries about mental causation stem from the thought that minds are non-physical substances. The problem then arises: how can something non-physical have physical effects (for that matter, how could something physical have non-physical effects)? This is the venerable mind–body problem, nowadays referred to as the problem of mental causation.

Philosophers have largely given up Cartesian dualism. Property dualism – the thesis that there are two distinctive kinds of property, mental and physical – is widely accepted, however. The result is a collection of problems every bit as resistant to solution as those issuing from Cartesianism. If accounts of sensation and thought require the postulation of mental properties, what is the bearing of these properties on physical processes, in particular on those physical processes that underlie intelligent action? I have suggested that the frame of mind required to regard mental properties as special kinds of non-physical property is induced by certain philosophical theses we need not accept. These theses are ripe for replacement. In so doing, we can see our way past many of the worries that dog the mind–body debate. Difficulties undoubtedly remain. In philosophy we must rest content with the kind of progress that results when we can see our way around self-imposed barriers. So it is in the case of mental causation.

Notes

I am indebted to Davidson College for funding a research leave during 2000–1 and to the Department of Philosophy, Monash University for its hospitality and for supporting an invigorating philosophical environment. My greatest debt is to C. B. Martin, the most ontologically serious of the ontologically serious.

1   Descartes (1596–1650), who died before Newton (1642–1727) produced his monumental work on physics, held that the mind might affect the particles, not by imparting motion to them, but by altering their direction. In this way *motion* in the physical system was conserved. Newton's laws required conservation of *momentum*, however, and this is violated if changes in the direction in which particles move has a non-material source.

2   Some philosophers, hoping to assimilate qualities of experiences to representations, regard sensory experiences as purely representational (see, e.g., Harman 1990; Dretske 1995; Tye 1995; Lycan 1996). Although I have doubts about any such view, nothing I say here requires that it be accepted or rejected. If you do accept it, then worries about the place of mental qualities in a physical world are replaced by worries about the causal significance of representational states.

3   Consider the box: Saginaw Saginaw . How many words does this box contain? Well, you might say the box contains two occurrences or instances of one word. Philosophers say that the box includes two *tokens* of a single *type*.

4   Aristotle embraced a species of functionalism, and functional explanation has had a long history in the biological and social sciences (see Winch 1958). In light of what follows, it is perhaps worth noting that Putnam subsequently (and, as I shall suggest, inappropriately!) retitled the paper "The Nature of Mental States."

5   See Block (1980) for a discussion of two species of functionalism: the functional identity theory (what I have been calling functionalism), and the functional specifier

theory (a view associated with Lewis 1966; Armstrong 1968; and Smart 1959). On the latter view, your being in pain *is* your being in a particular physical state. On the former view, your physical state is thought merely to be the *realizer* of pain in you (for reasons mentioned earlier). This is sometimes put by saying that a state of mind is a functional role, not the occupant of the role. Today, most functionalists embrace the functional identity conception of functionalism, so I shall omit discussion of the functional specifier version here. Functional specifiers avoid problems stemming from the identification of functional states with higher-level states, but at the cost of sacrificing the core functionalist thesis that functional states are multiply realizable – or so functional identity theorists insist.

6   See, for instance, Boghossian (1990: 161). This formulation holds for "characterizing predicates" (roughly, terms, such as "is red" or "is wise," used to ascribe properties). A slightly different formulation is required for "substantial predicates" (those, such as "is a horse" or "is gold" used to classify objects as *kinds*). Whether or not the distinction is a deep one is a matter of controversy. I shall ignore it here in order to keep the discussion simple.

7   Some philosophers are anti-realists about colors quite generally. I use color here merely as a stalking horse, however. If you doubt the colors, substitute some other property – being triangular, for instance, or having mass.

8   This suggestion calls to mind the functional specifier version of functionalism (see note 5).

9   If such a conception of intentional states of mind still seems odd, think of a component in a painting – a smiling face. Imagine this face transferred from one pictorial context to another. In one painting, the face appears in the midst of a joyous wedding scene. In another painting, the face belongs to a soldier in a concentration camp. Context affects the significance of the expression on the face, despite there being no intrinsic differences in the faces themselves.

10   This is my reading of Baker (1993) and, perhaps, Burge (1993).

11   Some philosophers (e.g. Teller 1986) have argued that certain kinds of quantum state violate this principle. Even if correct, it is hard to see how this could help resolve the puzzle posed by "broad" states of mind.

12   This is a huge issue, not one to be addressed in a few paragraphs. The interested reader is referred to Martin and Heil (1998) and Heil (1998: 115–19, 148–58) for a more detailed discussion. It is worth noting here that causes are routinely described by reference to their extrinsic features: if my flipping the light switch results in the room's being illuminated, my action – flipping the switch – can be described as my illuminating the room, and we can say that this action frightened a burglar.

13   The confusion is discussed by Smart (1959) and by Place (1956), who dubs it "the phenomenological fallacy." (For further discussion, see Heil 1998: 78–81, 206–9.)

14   Some theorists argue that dispositional properties are grounded in categorical properties, others that all properties are dispositional. For a discussion of the possibilities, see Mumford (1998); see also Heil (1998: ch. 6).

15   Zombies were first used as a philosophical example by Robert Kirk (1974). More recently, they have been discussed at length by David Chalmers (1996).

16   One consequence of this view is that the laws underlying consciousness must be basic in the strong sense that they are not derivable from laws governing the basic particles and forces.

References

Armstrong, D. M. (1968). *A Materialist Theory of the Mind*. London: Routledge and Kegan Paul.

Baker, Lynne Rudder (1993). "Metaphysics and Mental Causation." In Heil and Mele (1993): 75–95.

Block, Ned (1980). "What is Functionalism?" In *Readings in Philosophy of Psychology*, vol. I. Cambridge, MA: Harvard University Press: 171–84.

Boghossian, Paul (1990). "The Status of Content." *Philosophical Review*, 99: 157–84.

Burge, Tyler (1993). "Mind–Body Causation and Explanatory Practice." In Heil and Mele (1993): 97–120.

Capitan, W. H. and Merrill, D. D. (eds.) (1967). *Art, Mind, and Religion*. Pittsburgh: University of Pittsburgh Press.

Chalmers, David (1996). *The Conscious Mind: In Search of a Fundamental Theory*. New York: Oxford University Press.

Davidson, D. (1970). "Mental Events." In L. Foster and J. W. Swanson (eds.), *Experience and Theory*. Amherst, MA: University of Massachusetts Press: 79–101. Reprinted in Davidson (1980).

—— (1974). "Psychology as Philosophy." In S. C. Brown (ed.), *Philosophy of Psychology*. New York: Barnes and Noble Books: 41–52. Reprinted in Davidson (1980): 231–9.

—— (1980). *Essays on Actions and Events*. Oxford: Clarendon Press.

Dretske, Fred (1995). *Naturalizing the Mind*. Cambridge, MA: MIT Press.

Dupré, John (1993). *The Disorder of Things: Metaphysical Foundations of the Disunity of Science*. Cambridge, MA: Harvard University Press.

Harman, Gilbert (1990). "The Intrinsic Quality of Experience." *Philosophical Perspectives*, 4: 31–52.

Heil, John (1998). *Philosophy of Mind: A Contemporary Introduction*. London: Routledge.

Heil, John and Mele, Alfred (eds.) (1993). *Mental Causation*. Oxford: Clarendon Press.

Kenny, A., trans. and ed. (1970). *Descartes: Philosophical Letters*. Oxford: Clarendon Press.

Kirk, Robert (1974). "Zombies vs. Materialists." *Proceedings of the Aristotelian Society*, Supplementary vol. 48: 135–52.

Levine, Joseph (1983). "Materialism and Qualia: The Explanatory Gap." *Pacific Philosophical Quarterly*, 64: 354–61.

Lewis, David (1966). "An Argument for the Identity Theory." *Journal of Philosophy*, 63: 17–25. Reprinted in *Philosophical Papers*, vol. 1. New York: Oxford University Press (1983): 99–107.

Lycan, W. G. (1996). *Consciousness and Experience*. Cambridge, MA: MIT Press.

Martin, C. B. (1997). "On the Need for Properties: The Road to Pythagoreanism and Back." *Synthese*, 112: 193–231.

Martin, C. B. and Heil, John (1998). "Rules and Powers." *Philosophical Perspectives*, 12: 283–312.

—— (1999). "The Ontological Turn." *Midwest Studies in Philosophy*, 23: 34–60.

Mumford, Stephen (1998). *Dispositions*. Oxford: Clarendon Press.

Place, U. T. (1956). "Is Consciousness A Brain Process?" *The British Journal of Psychology*, 47: 44–50.

Poland, Jeffrey (1994). *Physicalism: The Philosophical Foundations.* Oxford: Clarendon Press.

Post, John F. (1991). *Metaphysics: A Contemporary Introduction.* New York: Paragon House.

Putnam, Hilary (1967). "Psychological Predicates." In W. H. Capitan and D. D. Merrill (eds.), *Art, Mind, and Religion.* Pittsburgh: University of Pittsburgh Press: 37–48. Reprinted as "The Nature of Mental States," in Putnam's *Mind, Language, and Reality: Philosophical Papers*, vol. 2. Cambridge: Cambridge University Press (1975): 429–40; and in Ned Block (ed.), *Readings in Philosophy of Psychology*, vol. I. Cambridge, MA: Harvard University Press (1980): 223–31.

Shoemaker, Sydney (1980). "Causality and Properties." In Peter van Inwagen (ed.), *Time and Cause.* Dordrecht: Reidel Publishing Co.: 109–35. Reprinted in *Identity, Cause, and Mind: Philosophical Essays.* Cambridge: Cambridge University Press (1984): 206–33.

Smart, J. J. C. (1959). "Sensations and Brain Processes." *Philosophical Review*, 68: 141–56.

Teller, Paul (1986). "Relational Holism and Quantum Mechanics." *British Journal for Philosophy of Science*, 37: 71–81.

Tye, M. (1995). *Ten Problems of Consciousness: A Representational Theory of the Phenomenal Mind.* Cambridge: MIT Press.

Winch, Peter (1958). *The Idea of a Social Science and its Relation to Philosophy.* London: Routledge and Kegan Paul.

Chapter 10

Folk Psychology

Stephen P. Stich and Shaun Nichols

Discussions and debates about common-sense psychology (or "folk psychology," as it is often called) have been center stage in contemporary philosophy of mind. There have been heated disagreements both about what folk psychology is and about how it is related to the scientific understanding of the mind/brain that is emerging in psychology and the neurosciences. In this chapter we will begin by explaining why folk psychology plays such an important role in the philosophy of mind. Doing that will require a quick look at a bit of the history of philosophical discussions about the mind. We will then turn our attention to the lively contemporary discussions aimed at clarifying the philosophical role that folk psychology is expected to play and at using findings in the cognitive sciences to get a clearer understanding of the exact nature of folk psychology.

10.1 Why Does Folk Psychology Play an Important Role in the Philosophy of Mind?

To appreciate philosophers' fascination with folk psychology, it will be useful to begin with a brief reminder about the two most important questions in the philosophy of mind, and the problems engendered by what was for centuries the most influential answer to one of those questions. The questions are the mind–body problem, which asks how mental phenomena are related to physical phenomena, and the problem of other minds, which asks how we can know about the mental states of other people. On Descartes's proposed solution to the mind–body problem, there are two quite different sorts of substance in the universe: physical substance, which is located in space and time, and mental substance, which is located in time but not in space. Mental phenomena, according to Descartes, are events or states occurring in a mental substance, while physical phenomena are events or states occurring in a physical substance. Descartes insisted that there is two-way causal interaction between the mental and the physical, though many philosophers find it puzzling how the two could interact if one is in space and the other isn't. Another problem with the Cartesian view is that it seems to make the other minds problem quite intractable. If, as Descartes believed, I am the only person who can experience my mental states, then there seems to be no way for you to rule out the hypothesis that I am a mindless zombie – a physical body that merely behaves as though it was causally linked to a mind.

In the middle of the twentieth century the verificationist account of meaning had a major impact on philosophical thought. According to the verificationists, the meaning of an empirical claim is closely linked to the observations that would verify the claim. Influenced by verificationism, philosophical behaviorists argued that the Cartesian account of the mind as the "ghost in the machine" (to use Ryle's (1949) memorable image) was profoundly mistaken. If ordinary mental state terms such as "belief," "desire," and "pain" are to be meaningful, they argued, they can't refer to unobservable events taking place inside a person (or, worse still, not located in space at all). Rather, the meaning of sentences invoking these terms must be analyzed in terms of conditional sentences specifying how someone would behave under various circumstances. So, for example, a philosophical behaviorist might suggest that the meaning of

(1)   John believes that snow is white

could be captured by something like the following:

(2)   If you ask John, "Is snow white?" he will respond affirmatively.

Perhaps the most serious difficulty for philosophical behaviorists was that their meaning analyses typically turned out to be either obviously mistaken or circular – invoking one mental term in the analysis of another. So, for example, contrary to (2), even though John believes that snow is white, he may not respond affirmatively unless he is paying *attention, wants* to let you know what he thinks, *believes* that this can be done by responding affirmatively, etc.

While philosophical behaviorists were gradually becoming convinced that there is no way around this circularity problem, a very similar problem was confronting philosophers seeking verificationist accounts of the meaning of scientific terms. Verificationism requires that the meaning of a theoretical term must be specifiable in terms of observables. But when philosophers actually tried to provide such definitions, they always seemed to require additional theoretical terms (Hempel 1964). The reaction to this problem in the philosophy of science was to explore a quite different account of how theoretical terms get their meaning. Rather than being defined exclusively in terms of observables, this new account proposed, a cluster of theoretical terms might get their meaning collectively by being embedded within an empirical theory. The meaning of any given theoretical term lies in its theory-specified interconnections with other terms, *both observational and theoretical.* Perhaps the most influential statement of this view is to be found in the work of David Lewis (1970, 1972). According to Lewis, the meaning of theoretical terms is given by what he calls a "functional definition." Theoretical entities are "defined as the occupants of the causal roles *specified by the theory* . . . ; as *the* entities, whatever those may be, that bear certain causal relations *to one another* and to the referents of the O[bservational]-terms" (1972: 211; first and last emphases added).

Building on an idea first suggested by Wilfrid Sellars (1956), Lewis went on to propose that ordinary terms for mental or psychological states could get their meaning in an entirely analogous way. If we "think of commonsense psychology as a term-introducing scientific theory, though one invented before there was any such institution as professional science," then the "functional definition" account of the meaning of theoretical terms in science can be applied straightforwardly to the mental state terms used in common-sense psychology (Lewis 1972: 212). And this, Lewis proposed, is the right way to think about common-sense psychology:

> Imagine our ancestors first speaking only of external things, stimuli, and responses . . . until some genius invented the theory of mental states, with its newly introduced T[heoretical] terms, to explain the regularities among stimuli and responses. But that did not happen. Our commonsense psychology was never a newly invented term-introducing scientific theory – not even of prehistoric folk-science. The story that mental terms were introduced as theoretical terms is a myth.
>
> It is, in fact, Sellars' myth. . . . And though it is a myth, it may be a good myth or a bad one. It is a good myth if our names of mental states do in fact mean just what they would mean if the myth were true. I adopt the working hypothesis that it is a good myth. (Ibid.: 212–13)

In the three decades since Lewis and others[1] developed this account, it has become the most widely accepted view about the meaning of mental state terms. Since the account maintains that the meanings of mental state terms are given by functional definitions, the view is often known as *functionalism.*[2] We can now see one reason why philosophers of mind have been concerned to understand the exact nature of common-sense (or folk) psychology. According to functionalism, *folk psychology is the theory that gives ordinary mental state terms their meaning.*

A second reason for philosophers' preoccupation with folk psychology can be explained more quickly. The crucial point is that, according to accounts such as Lewis's, folk psychology is an *empirical* theory which is supposed to explain "the regularity between stimuli and responses" to be found in human (and perhaps animal) behavior. And, of course, if common-sense psychology is an empirical theory, it is possible that, like any empirical theory, it might turn out to be *mistaken.* We might discover that the states and processes intervening between stimuli and responses are not well described by the folk theory that fixes the meaning of mental state terms. The possibility that common-sense psychology *might* turn out to be mistaken is granted by just about everyone who takes functionalism seriously. However, for the last several decades a number of prominent philosophers of mind have been arguing that this is more than a *mere* possibility. Rather, they maintain, a growing body of theory and empirical findings in the cognitive and neurosciences strongly suggest that common-sense psychology *is* mistaken, and not just on small points. As Paul Churchland, an enthusiastic supporter of this view, puts it:

> FP [folk psychology] suffers explanatory failures on an epic scale . . . it has been stagnant for at least twenty-five centuries, and . . . its categories appear (so far) to be incommensurable with or orthogonal to the categories of the background physical sciences whose long term claim to explain human behavior seems undeniable. Any theory that meets this description must be allowed a serious candidate for outright elimination. (1981: 212)

Churchland does not stop at discarding (or "eliminating") folk psychological theory. He and other "eliminativists" have also suggested that because folk psychology is such a seriously defective theory, we should also conclude that the theoretical terms embedded in folk psychology don't really refer to anything. Beliefs, desires, and other posits of folk psychology, they argue, are entirely comparable to phlogiston, the ether, and other posits of empirical theories that turned out to be seriously mistaken; like phlogiston, the ether, and the rest, *they do not exist*. Obviously, these are enormously provocative claims. Debating their plausibility has been high on the agenda of philosophers of mind ever since they were first suggested.[3] Since the eliminativists' central thesis is that folk psychology is a massively mistaken theory, philosophers of mind concerned to evaluate that thesis will obviously need a clear and accurate account of what folk psychology is and what it claims.

10.2 What is Folk Psychology? Two Possible Answers

Functionalists, as we have seen, maintain that the meaning of ordinary mental state terms is determined by the role they play in a common-sense psychological theory. But what, exactly, is this theory? In the philosophical and cognitive science literature there are two quite different approaches to this question.[4] For Lewis, and for many of those who have followed his lead, common-sense or folk psychology is closely tied to the claims about mental states that almost everyone would agree with and take to be obvious.

> Collect all the platitudes you can think of regarding the causal relations of mental states, sensory stimuli, and motor responses. . . . Add also the platitudes to the effect that one mental state falls under another – "toothache is a kind of pain" and the

like. Perhaps there are platitudes of other forms as well. Include only platitudes that are common knowledge among us – everyone knows them, everyone knows that everyone else knows them, and so on. For the meanings of our words are common knowledge, and I am going to claim that *names of mental states derive their meaning from these platitudes.* (1972: 212; emphasis added)

So, on this approach, folk psychology is just a collection of platitudes, or perhaps, since that set of platitudes is bound to be large and ungainly, we might think of folk psychology as a set of generalizations that systematizes the platitudes in a perspicuous way. A systematization of that sort might also make it more natural to describe folk psychology as a theory. We'll call this the *platitude account* of folk psychology.

The second approach to answering the question focuses on a cluster of skills that have been of considerable interest to both philosophers and psychologists. In many cases people are remarkably good at *predicting* the behavior of other people. Asked to predict what a motorist will do as she approaches the red light, almost everyone says that she will stop, and fortunately our predictions are usually correct. We are also often remarkably good at *attributing* mental states to other people[5] – at saying what they perceive, think, believe, want, fear, and so on, and at *predicting* future mental states and *explaining* behavior in terms of past mental states.[6] In recent discussions, the whimsical label *mindreading* has often been used for this cluster of skills, and since the mid-1980s developmental and cognitive psychologists have generated a large literature aimed at exploring the emergence of mindreading and explaining the cognitive mechanisms that underlie it.

The most widely accepted view about the cognitive mechanisms underlying mindreading (and until the mid-1980s the *only* view) is that people have a rich body of mentally represented information about the mind, and that this information plays a central role in guiding the mental mechanisms that generate our attributions, predictions, and explanations. Some of the psychologists who defend this view maintain that the information exploited in mindreading has much the same structure as a scientific theory, and that it is acquired, stored, and used in much the same way that other common-sense and scientific theories are. These psychologists often refer to their view as *the theory theory* (Gopnik and Wellman 1994; Gopnik and Meltzoff 1997). Others argue that much of the information utilized in mindreading is innate and is stored in mental "modules" where it can only interact in very limited ways with the information stored in other components of the mind (Scholl and Leslie 1999). Since modularity theorists and theory theorists agree that mindreading depends on a rich body of information about how the mind works, we'll use the term *information-rich theories* as a label for both of them. These theories suggest another way to specify the theory that (if functionalists are right) fixes the meaning of mental state terms – it is the theory (or body of information) that underlies mindreading. We'll call this the *mindreading account* of folk psychology.

Let's ask, now, how the platitude account of folk psychology and the mindreading account are related. How is the mentally represented information about the mind posited by information-rich theories of mindreading related to the collection of platitudes which, according to Lewis, determines the meaning of mental state terms? One possibility is that the platitudes (or some systematization of them) is near enough *identical* with the information that guides mindreading – that mindreading invokes little or no information about the mind beyond the common-sense information that everyone can readily agree to. If this were true, then the platitude account of folk psychology and the mindreading account would converge. But, along with most cognitive scientists who have studied mindreading, we believe that this convergence is *very* unlikely. One reason for our skepticism is the comparison with other complex skills that cognitive scientists have explored. In just about every case, from face recognition (Young 1998) to decision-making (Gigerenzer et al. 1999) to common-sense physics (McCloskey 1983; Hayes 1985), it has been found that the mind uses information and principles that are simply not accessible to introspection. In these areas our minds use a great deal of information that people cannot recognize or assent to in the way that one is supposed to recognize and assent to Lewisian platitudes. A second reason for our skepticism is that in many mindreading tasks people appear to attribute mental states on the basis of cues that they are not aware they are using. For example, Ekman has shown that there is a wide range of "deception cues" that lead us to believe that a target does not believe what he is saying. These include "a change in the expression on the face, a movement of the body, an inflection to the voice, a swallowing in the throat, a very deep or shallow breath, long pauses between words, a slip of the tongue, a micro facial expression, a gestural slip" (1985: 43). In most cases, people are quite unaware of the fact that they are using these cues. So, while there is still much to be learned about mental mechanisms underlying mindreading, we think it is very likely that the information about the mind that those mechanisms exploit is substantially richer than the information contained in Lewisian platitudes.

If we are right about this, then those who think that the functionalist account of the meaning of ordinary mental state terms is on the right track will have to confront a quite crucial question: which account of folk psychology picks out the theory that actually determines the meaning of mental state terms? Is the meaning of these terms fixed by the theory we can articulate by collecting and systematizing platitudes, or is it fixed by the much richer theory that we can discover only by studying the sort of information exploited by the mechanisms underlying mindreading?

We don't think there is any really definitive answer to this question. It would, of course, be enormously useful if there were a well-motivated and widely accepted general theory of meaning to which we might appeal. But, notoriously, there is no such theory. Meaning is a topic on which disagreements abound even about the most fundamental questions, and there are many philosophers who think that the entire functionalist approach to specifying the meaning of mental state terms is utterly wrongheaded.[7] Having said all this, however, we are inclined to think that those who are sympathetic to the functionalist approach should prefer the mindreading account of folk psychology over the platitude account. For on the mindreading account, folk psychology is the theory that people actually use in recognizing and attributing mental states, in drawing inferences about mental states, and in generating predictions and explanations on the basis of mental state attributions. It is hard to see why someone who thinks, as functionalists do, that mental state terms get their meaning by being embedded in a theory would want to focus on the platitude-based theory whose principles people can easily acknowledge, rather than the richer theory that is actually guiding people when they think and talk about the mind.

10.3   The Challenge from Simulation Theory

Let's take a moment to take stock of where we are. In section 10.1 we explained why folk psychology has played such an important role in recent philosophy of mind: functionalists maintain that folk psychology is the theory that implicitly defines ordinary mental state terms, and eliminativists (who typically agree with functionalists about the meaning of mental state terms) argue that folk psychology is a seriously mistaken theory, and that both the theory and the mental states that it posits should be rejected. In section 10.2 we distinguished two different accounts of folk psychology, and we argued, albeit tentatively, that functionalists should prefer the mindreading account on which folk psychology is the rich body of information or theory that underlies people's skill in attributing mental states and in predicting and explaining behavior. In this section, we turn our attention to an important new challenge that has emerged to all of this. Since the mid-1980s a number of philosophers and psychologists have been arguing that it is a mistake to think that mindreading invokes a rich body of information about the mind. Rather, they maintain, mindreading can be explained as a kind of *mental simulation* that requires little or no information about how the mind works (Gordon 1986; Heal 1986; Goldman 1989; Harris 1992) If these simulation theorists are right, and if we accept the mindreading account of folk psychology, then *there is no such thing as folk psychology.* That would be bad news for functionalists. It would also be bad news for eliminativists, since if there is no such thing as folk psychology, then their core argument – which claims that folk psychology is a seriously mistaken theory – has gone seriously amiss.

How could it be that the mental mechanisms underlying mindreading do not require a rich body of information? Simulation theorists often begin their answer by using an analogy. Suppose you want to predict how a particular airplane will behave in certain wind conditions. One way to proceed would be to derive a prediction from aeronautical theory along with a detailed description of the plane. Another, quite different, strategy would be to build a model of the plane, put it in a wind tunnel that reproduces those wind conditions, and then simply observe how the model behaves. The second strategy, unlike the first, does not require a rich body of theory. Simulation theorists maintain that something like this second strategy can be used to explain people's mindreading skills. For if you are trying to predict what another person's mind will do, and if that person's mind is similar to yours, then you might be able to use components of your own mind as models of the similar components in the mind of the other person (whom we'll call the "target").

Here is a quick sketch of how the process might work. Suppose that you want to predict what the target will decide to do about some important matter. The target's mind, we'll assume, will make the decision by utilizing a decision-making or "practical reasoning" system which takes his relevant beliefs and desires as input and (somehow or other) comes up with a decision about what to do. The lighter lines in figure 10.1 are a sketch of the sort of cognitive architecture that might underlie the normal process of decision-making. Now suppose that your mind can momentarily take your decision making system "off-line" so that you do not actually act on the decisions that it produces. Suppose further that in this off-line mode your mind can provide your decision-making system with some hypothetical or "pretend" beliefs and desires – beliefs and desires that you may not actually have but that the target does. Your mind could then simply sit back and let your decision-making system generate a decision. If your decision-making system is similar to the target's, and if the hypothetical beliefs and desires that you've fed into the off-line system are close to the ones that the target has, then the decision that your decision-making system generates will be similar or identical to the one that the target's decision-making system will produce. If that off-line decision is now sent on to the part of your mind that generates predictions about what other people will do, you will predict that that is the decision the target will make, and there is a good chance that your prediction will be correct. All of this happens, according to simulation theorists, with little or no conscious awareness on your part. Moreover, and this of course is the crucial point, the process does not utilize any theory or rich body of information about how the decision-making system works. Rather, you have simply used your own decision-making system to *simulate* the decision that the target will actually make. The dark lines in figure 10.1 sketch the sort of cognitive architecture that might underlie this kind of simulation-based prediction.

The process we have just described takes the decision-making system off-line and uses simulation to predict decisions. But much the same sort of process might be used to take the inference mechanism or other components of the mind off-line, and thus to make predictions about other sorts of mental processes. Some of the more enthusiastic defenders of simulation theory have suggested that *all* mindreading skills could be accomplished by something like this process of simulation, and thus that we need not suppose that folk psychological theory plays *any* important role in mindreading. If this is right, then both functionalism and eliminativism are in trouble.[8]

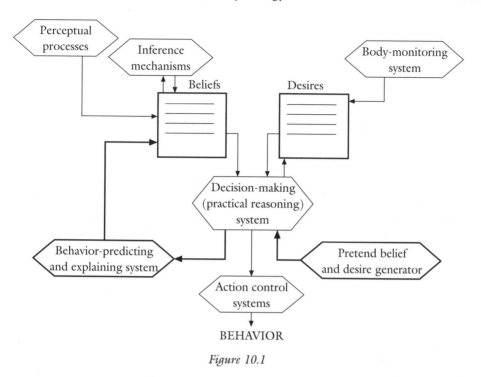

Figure 10.1

10.4 Three Accounts of Mindreading: Information-rich, Simulation-based and Hybrid

Simulation theorists and advocates of information-rich accounts of mindreading offer competing empirical theories about the mental processes underlying mindreading,[9] and much of the literature on the topic has been cast as a winner-takes-all debate between these two groups.[10] In recent years, however, there has been a growing awareness that mindreading is a complex, multifaceted phenomenon and that some aspects of mindreading might be subserved by information-poor simulation-like processes, while others are subserved by information-rich processes. This hybrid approach is one that we have advocated for a number of years (Stich and Nichols 1995; Nichols et al. 1996; Nichols and Stich, forthcoming), and in this section we will give a brief sketch of the case in favor of the hybrid approach.[11] We will begin by focusing on one important aspect of mindreading for which information-rich explanations are particularly implausible and a simulation-style account is very likely to be true. We will then take up two other aspects of mindreading where, we think, information-rich explanations are clearly to be preferred to simulation-based explanations.

10.4.1 *Inference prediction: a mindreading skill subserved by simulation*

One striking fact about the mindreading skills of normal adults is that we are remarkably good at predicting the inferences of targets, even their obviously *non-demonstrative* inferences. Suppose, for example, that Fred comes to believe that the President of the United States has resigned, after hearing a brief report on the radio. Who does Fred think will become President? We quickly generate the prediction that Fred thinks the Vice-President will become President. We know perfectly well, and so, we presume, does Fred, that there are lots of ways in which his inference could be mistaken. The Vice-President could be assassinated; the Vice-President might resign before being sworn in as President; a scandal might lead to the removal of the Vice-President; there might be a coup. It is easy to generate stories on which the Vice-President would not become the new President. Yet we predict Fred's non-demonstrative inference without hesitation. And in most cases like this, our predictions are correct. Any adequate theory of mindreading needs to accommodate these facts.

Advocates of information-rich approaches to mindreading have been notably silent about inference prediction. Indeed, so far as we have been able to determine, no leading advocate of that approach has even *tried* to offer an explanation of the fact that we are strikingly good at predicting the inferences that other people make. And we are inclined to think that the reason for this omission is pretty clear. For a thorough-going advocate of the information-rich approach, the only available explanation of our inference prediction skills is *more information*. If we are good at predicting how other people will reason, that must be because we have somehow acquired a remarkably good theory about how people reason. But that account seems rather profligate. To see why, consider the analogy between predicting inferences and predicting the grammatical intuitions of someone who speaks the same language that we do. To explain our success at this latter task, an advocate of the information-rich approach would have to say that we have a *theory* about the processes subserving grammatical intuition production in other people. But, as Harris (1992) pointed out, that seems rather far-fetched. A much simpler hypothesis is that we rely on *our own* mechanisms for generating linguistic intuitions, and having determined our own intuitions about a particular sentence, we attribute them to the target.

Harris's *argument from simplicity*, as we shall call it, played an important role in convincing us that a comprehensive theory of mindreading would have to invoke many different sorts of process, and that simulation processes would be among them. However, we don't think that the argument from simplicity is the only reason to prefer a simulation-based account of inference prediction over an information-rich account. Indeed, if the argument from simplicity were the only one available, a resolute defender of the information-rich approach might simply dig in her heels and note that the systems produced by Mother Nature are often far from simple. There are lots of examples of redundancy and apparently unnecessary complexity in biological systems. So, the information-rich theorist might argue, the mere fact that a theory-based account of inference prediction would be less simple than a simulation-style account is hardly a knock-down argument against it. There is, however, another sort of argument that can be mounted against an information-rich approach to inference prediction. We think it is a particularly important argument since it can be generalized to a number of other mindreading skills, and thus it can serve as a valuable heuristic in helping us to decide which aspects of mindreading are plausibly treated as simulation-based.

This second argument, which we will call the *argument from accuracy*, begins with the observation that inference prediction is remarkably accurate over a wide range of cases, including cases that are quite different from anything that most mindreaders are likely to have encountered before. There is, for example, a rich literature in the "heuristics and biases" tradition in cognitive social psychology chronicling the ways in which people make what appear to be very bad inferences on a wide range of problems requiring deductive and inductive reasoning.[12] In all of this literature, however, there is no suggestion that people are bad at *predicting* other people's inferences, whether those inferences are good or bad. This contrasts sharply with the literature on desire-attribution that we discuss below, where it is often remarked how surprising and *un*predictable people's desires and decisions are. Although it hasn't been studied systematically, we think it is quite likely that people typically predict others will make just those bad inferences that they would make themselves, even on problems that are quite different from any they have encountered before. If that is indeed the case, it poses a problem for information-rich accounts: How do ordinary mindreaders manage to end up with such an *accurate* theory about how people draw inferences – a theory which supports correct predictions even about quite unfamiliar sorts of inferences? The problem is made more acute by the fact that there are other sorts of mindreading tasks on which people do very badly. Why do people acquire the right theory about inference and the *wrong* theory about other mental processes? A simulation-based account of inference prediction, by contrast, has a ready explanation of our accuracy. On the simulation account, we are using the same inference mechanism for both *making* and *predicting* inferences, so it is to be expected that we would predict that other people make the same inferences we do.

Obviously, the argument from accuracy is a two-edged sword. In those domains where we are particularly good at predicting or attributing mental states in unfamiliar cases, the argument suggests that the mindreading process is unlikely to be subserved by an information-rich process. But in those cases where we are *bad* at predicting or attributing mental states, the argument suggests that the process is unlikely to be subserved by a *simulation* process. We recognize that there are various moves that might be made in response to the argument from accuracy, and thus we do not treat the argument as definitive. We do, however, think that the argument justifies a strong initial presumption that accurate mindreading processes are subserved by simulation-like processes and that inaccurate ones are not. And if this is right, then there is a strong presumption in favor of the hypothesis that inference prediction is simulation based.

10.4.2 Desire-attribution: a mindreading skill that cannot be explained by simulation

Another quite central aspect of mindreading is the capacity to attribute desires to other people. Without that capacity we would not know what other people want, and we would be severely impaired in trying to predict or explain their actions. There are a number of processes that can give rise to beliefs about a target's desires. In some cases we use information about the target's verbal and non-verbal behavior (including their facial expressions) to determine what they want. In other cases we attribute desires on the basis of what other people say about the target. And in all likelihood a variety of other cues and sources of data are also used in the desire-attribution process. It is our contention that these desire-attribution skills do not depend on simulation, but rather are subserved by information-rich processes. We have two quite different reasons for this claim.

First, desire-attribution exhibits a pattern of systematic inaccuracy and that supports at least an initial presumption that the process is not simulation-based. One very striking example comes from what is perhaps the most famous series of experiments in all of social psychology. Milgram (1963) had a "teacher" subject flip switches that were supposed to deliver shocks to another subject, the "learner" (who was actually an accomplice). For each mistake the learner made, the teacher was instructed to deliver progressively stronger shocks, including one labeled "Danger: Severe Shock" and culminating in a switch labeled "450-volt, XXX." If the teacher subject expressed reservations to the experimental assistant, he was calmly told to continue the experiment. The result of the experiment was astonishing. A clear majority of the subjects administered *all* the shocks. People often find these results hard to believe. Indeed, the Milgram findings are so counterintuitive that in a verbal re-enactment of the experiment, people still didn't predict the results (Bierbrauer 1973, discussed in Nisbett and Ross 1980: 121). One plausible interpretation of these findings is that in the Milgram experiment the instructions from the experimenter generated a desire to comply, which, in most cases, overwhelmed the subject's desire not to harm the person they believed to be on the receiving end of the electric shock apparatus. The fact that people find the results surprising and that Bierbrauer's subjects did not predict them indicates an important limitation in our capacity to determine the desires of others.

There is a large literature in cognitive social psychology detailing many other cases in which desires and preferences are affected in remarkable and unexpected ways by the circumstances subjects encounter and the environment in which they are embedded. The important point, for present purposes, is that people typically find these results surprising and occasionally quite unsettling, and the fact that they are surprised (even after seeing or getting a detailed description of the experimental situation) indicates that the mental mechanisms they are using to predict the subjects' desires and preferences are systematically inaccurate. Though this is not the place for an extended survey of the many examples in the literature, we cannot resist mentioning one of our favorites.[13]

Loewenstein and Adler (1995) looked at the ability of subjects to predict *their own* preferences when those preferences are influenced by a surprising and little-known effect. The effect that Loewenstein and Adler exploit is the *endowment effect*, a robust and rapidly appearing tendency for people to set a significantly higher value for an object if they actually own it than they would if they did not own it (Thaler 1980). Here is how Loewenstein and Adler describe the phenomenon:

> In the typical demonstration of the endowment effect . . . one group of subjects (sellers) are endowed with an object and are given the option of trading it for various amounts of cash; another group (choosers) are not given the object but are given a series of choices between getting the object or getting various amounts of cash. Although the objective wealth position of the two groups is identical, as are the choices they face, endowed subjects hold out for significantly more money than those who are not endowed. (1995: 929–30).

In an experiment designed to test whether "unendowed" subjects could predict the value they would set if they were actually to own the object in question, the experimenter first allowed subjects (who were members of a university class) to examine a mug engraved with the school logo. A form was then distributed to approximately half of the subjects, chosen at random, on which they were asked "to imagine that they possessed the mug on display and to predict whether they would be willing to exchange the mug for various amounts of money" (ibid.: 931). When the subjects who received the form had finished filling it out, *all* the subjects were presented with a mug and given a second form with instructions analogous to those on the prediction form. But on the second form it was made clear that they actually could exchange the mug for cash, and that the choices they made on this second form would determine how much money they might get. "Subjects were told that they would receive the option that they had circled on one of the lines – which line had been determined in advance by the experimenter" (ibid.). The results showed that subjects who had completed the first form substantially underpredicted the amount of money for which they would be willing to exchange the mug. In one group of subjects, the mean predicted exchange price was $3.73, while the mean actual exchange price for subjects (the *same* subjects who made the prediction) was $5.40. Moreover, there seemed to be an "anchoring effect" in this experiment which depressed the actual exchange price, since the mean actual exchange price for subjects who did not make a prediction about their own selling price was even higher, at $6.46. Here again we find that people are systematically inaccurate at predicting the effect of the situation on desires, and in this case the desires they fail to predict are their own. If these desire predictions were subserved by a simulation process, it would be something of a mystery why the predictions are systematically inaccurate. But if, as we believe, they are subserved by an information-rich process, the inaccuracy can be readily explained. The theory or body of information that guides the prediction simply does not have accurate information about the rather surprising mental processes that give rise to these desires.

Our second reason for thinking that the mental mechanisms subserving desire-attribution use information-rich processes rather than simulation is that it is hard to see how the work done by these mechanisms *could* be accomplished by simulation. Indeed, so far as we know, simulation theorists have made only one proposal about how some of these desire detection tasks might be carried out, and it is singularly implausible. The proposal, endorsed by both Gordon (1986) and Goldman (1989), begins with the fact that simulation processes like the one sketched in figure 10.1 can be used to make behavior predictions, and goes on to suggest that they might also be used to generate beliefs about the desires and beliefs that give rise to observed behavior by exploiting something akin to the strategy of analysis-by-synthesis (originally developed by Halle and Stevens (1962) for phoneme recognition). In using the process in figure 10.1 to predict behavior, hypothetical or "pretend" beliefs and desires are fed into the mindreader's decision-making system (being used "off-line" of course), and the mindreader predicts that the target would do what the mindreader would decide to do, given those beliefs and desires. In an analysis-by-synthesis account of the generation of beliefs about desires and beliefs, the process is, in effect, run backwards. It starts with a behavioral episode that has already occurred and proceeds by trying to find hypothetical beliefs and desires which, when fed into the mindreader's decision mechanism, will produce a decision to perform the behavior we want to explain.

An obvious problem with this strategy is that it will generate too many candidates, since typically there are endlessly many possible sets of beliefs and desires that might lead the mindreader to decide to perform the behavior in question. Gordon is well aware of the problem, and he seems to think he has a solution:

> No matter how long I go on testing hypotheses, I will not have tried out all candidate explanations of the [target's] behavior. Perhaps some of the unexamined candidates would have done at least as well as the one I settle for, if I settle: perhaps indefinitely many of them would have. But these would be "far fetched," I say intuitively. Therein I exhibit my inertial bias. The less "fetching" (or "stretching," as actors say) I have to do to track the other's behavior, the better. I tend to feign only when necessary, only when something in the other's behavior doesn't fit. . . . This inertial bias may be thought of as a "least effort" principle: the "principle of least pretending." It explains why, other things being equal, I will prefer the less radical departure from the "real" world – i.e. from what I myself take to be the world. (Gordon 1986: 164)

Unfortunately, it is not at all clear what Gordon has in mind by an inertial bias against "fetching." The most obvious interpretation is that attributions are more "far-fetched" the further they are, on some intuitive scale, from one's own mental states. But if that's what Gordon intends, it seems clear that the suggestion won't work. For in many cases we explain behavior by appealing to desires or beliefs (or both) that are *very* far from our own. I might, for example, explain the cat chasing the mouse by appealing to the cat's desire to eat the mouse. But there are indefinitely many desires that would lead me to chase a mouse that are intuitively much closer to my actual desires than the desire to eat a mouse. Simulation theorists have offered no other proposal for narrowing down the endless set of candidate beliefs and desires that the analysis-by-synthesis strategy would generate, and without some plausible solution to this problem the strategy looks quite hopeless. So it is not surprising that accounts of this sort have largely disappeared from the simulation theory literature over the last decade. And that, perhaps, reflects at least a tacit acknowledgement, on the part of simulation theorists, that desire-attribution can only be explained by appealing to information-rich processes.

10.4.3 Discrepant belief-attribution: another mindreading skill that cannot be explained by simulation

Yet another important aspect of mindreading is the capacity to attribute beliefs that we ourselves do not hold – *discrepant beliefs*, as they are sometimes called. There are a number of processes subserving discrepant belief-attribution, some relying on beliefs about the target's perceptual states, others exploiting information about the target's verbal behavior, and still others relying on information about the target's non-verbal behavior. All of these, we suspect, are subserved by information-rich mechanisms, rather than by a mechanism that uses simulation. Our reasons are largely parallel to the ones we offered for desire-attribution. First, there is abundant evidence that the discrepant belief-attribution system exhibits systematic inaccuracies of the sort we would expect from an information-rich system that is not quite rich enough and does not contain information about the process generating certain categories of discrepant beliefs. Second, there is no plausible way in which prototypical simulation mechanisms could do what the discrepant belief-attribution system does.

One disquieting example of a systematic failure in discrepant belief-attribution comes from the study of belief-perseverance. In the psychology laboratory, and in everyday life, it sometimes happens that people are presented with fairly persuasive evidence (e.g. test results) indicating that they have some hitherto unexpected trait. In light of that evidence people typically form the belief that they do have the trait. What will happen to that belief if, shortly after this, people are presented with a convincing case discrediting the first body of evidence? Suppose, for example, they are convinced that the test results they relied on were actually someone else's, or that no real test was conducted at all. Most people expect that the undermined belief will simply be discarded. And that view was shared by a generation of social psychologists who duped subjects into believing all sorts of things about themselves, often by administering rigged psychological tests, observed their reactions, and then "debriefed" the subjects by explaining the ruse. The assumption was that no enduring harm could be done because once the ruse was explained the induced belief would be discarded. But in a widely discussed series of experiments, Ross and his co-workers have demonstrated that this is simply not the case. Once a subject has been convinced that she has a trait, showing her that the evidence that convinced her was completely phony does not succeed in eliminating the belief (Nisbett and Ross 1980: 175–9). If the trait in question is being inclined to suicide, or being "latently homosexual," belief perseverance can lead to serious problems. The part of the discrepant belief-attribution system that led both psychologists and everyone else to expect that these discrepant beliefs would be discarded after debriefing apparently has inaccurate information about the process of belief-perseverance and thus it leads to systematically mistaken belief-attributions.

Another example, with important implications for public policy, is provided by the work of Loftus (1979) and others on the effect of "post-event interventions" on what people believe about events they have witnessed. In one experiment subjects were shown a film of an auto accident. A short time later they were asked a series of questions about the accident. For some subjects, one of the questions was: "How fast was the white sports car traveling when it passed the barn while traveling along the country road?" Other subjects were asked: "How fast was the white sports car traveling while traveling along the country road?" One week later all the subjects were asked whether they had seen a barn. Though there was no barn in the film that the subjects had seen, subjects who were asked the question that mentioned the barn were five times more likely to believe that they had seen one. In another experiment, conducted in train stations and other naturalistic settings, Loftus and her students staged a "robbery" in which a male confederate pulled an object from a bag that two female students had temporarily left unattended and stuffed it under his coat. A moment later, one of the women noticed that her bag had been tampered with and shouted, "Oh my God, my tape recorder is missing." She went on to lament that her boss had loaned it to her and that it was very expensive. Bystanders, most of whom were quite cooperative, were asked for their phone numbers in case an account of the incident was needed for insurance purposes. A week later, an "insurance agent" called the eyewitnesses and asked about details of the theft. Among the questions asked was "Did you see the tape recorder?" More than half of the eyewitnesses remembered having seen it, and nearly all of these could describe it in detail – this despite the fact that *there was no tape recorder*. On the basis of this and other experiments, Loftus concludes that even casual mention of objects that were not present or of events that did not take place (for example, in the course of police questioning) can significantly increase the likelihood that the objects or events will be incorporated into people's beliefs about what they observed. A central theme in Loftus's work is that the legal system should be much more cautious about relying on eyewitness testimony. And a major reason why the legal system is *not* as cautious as it should be is that our information-driven discrepant belief-attribution system lacks information about the post-event processes of belief-formation that Loftus has demonstrated.

As in the case of desire-attribution, we see no plausible way in which the work done by the mental mechanisms subserving discrepant belief-attribution *could* be accomplished by simulation. Here again, the only proposal that simulation theorists have offered is the analysis-by-synthesis account, and that strategy won't work any better for belief-attribution than it does for desire-attribution.

10.5 Conclusion

In the previous section we sketched some of the reasons for accepting a hybrid account of mindreading in which some aspects of that skill are explained by appeal to information-rich processes, while other aspects are explained by simulation. Though we only looked at a handful of mindreading skills, we have argued elsewhere (Nichols and Stich, forthcoming) that much the same pattern can be found more generally. Mindreading is a complex and multifaceted phenomenon, many facets of which are best explained by an information-rich approach, while many other facets are best explained by simulation. If this is correct, it presents both functionalists and eliminativists with some rather awkward choices. Functionalists, as we have seen, hold that the meaning of ordinary mental state terms is determined by folk psychology, and eliminativists typically agree. In section 10.2 we argued that functionalism is most plausible if folk psychology is taken to be the information-rich theory that subserves mindreading. But now it appears that only *parts* of mindreading rely on an information-rich theory. Should functionalists insist that the theory underlying these aspects of mindreading fixes the meaning of mental state terms, or should they retreat to the platitude account of folk psychology? We are inclined to think that whichever option functionalists adopt, their theory will be less attractive than it was before it became clear that the platitude approach and the mindreading approach would diverge, and that only part of mindreading relies on folk psychology.

Notes

1   Though we will focus on Lewis's influential exposition, many other philosophers developed similar views, including Putnam (1960), Fodor and Chihara (1965), and Armstrong (1968).
2   Though beware. In the philosophy of mind, the term "functionalism" has been used for a variety of views. Some of them bear a clear family resemblance to the one we've just sketched, while others do not. For good overviews, see Lycan (1994) and Block (1994).

3 For an overview of these debates, see Stich (1996: ch. 1), and chapter 2 in this volume.

4 The distinction was first noted in Stich and Ravenscroft (1994).

5 Though not always, as we'll see in section 10.4.

6 Eliminativists, of course, would not agree that we do a good job at attributing and predicting mental states or at explaining behavior in terms of past mental states, since they maintain that the mental states we are attributing do not exist. But they would not deny that there is an impressive degree of *agreement* in what people say about other people's mental states, and that that agreement needs to be explained.

7 See, for example, Fodor and LePore (1992). For a useful overview of many of the disputes about the theory of meaning, see Devitt (1996).

8 Robert Gordon is the most avid defender of the view that all mindreading skills can be explained by simulation. Here is a characteristic passage:

> It is . . . uncanny that folk psychology hasn't changed very much over the millennia. . . . Churchland thinks this a sign that folk psychology is a bad theory; but it could be a sign that it is no theory at all, not, at least, in the accepted sense of (roughly) a system of laws implicitly defining a set of terms. Instead, it might be just the capacity for practical reasoning, supplemented by a special use of a childish and primitive capacity for pretend play. (1986: 71)

Of course, an eliminativist might object that the simulation theorist begs the question since the simulation account of decision prediction presupposes the existence of beliefs, desires and other posits of folk psychology, while eliminativists hold that these common-sense mental states do not exist. Constructing a plausible reply to this objection is left as an exercise for the reader.

9 Though Heal (1998) has argued that there is one interpretation of simulation theory on which it is true a priori. For a critique, see Nichols and Stich (1998).

10 Many of the important papers in this literature are collected in Davies and Stone (1995a, 1995b).

11 We have also argued that some important aspects of mindreading are subserved by processes that can't be comfortably categorized as either information-rich or simulation-like. But since space is limited, we will not try to make a case for that here. See Nichols and Stich (forthcoming).

12 Among the best-known experiments of this kind are those illustrating the so-called *conjunction fallacy*. In one quite famous experiment, Kahneman and Tversky (1982) presented subjects with the following task.

> Linda is 31 years old, single, outspoken, and very bright. She majored in philosophy. As a student, she was deeply concerned with issues of discrimination and social justice, and also participated in anti-nuclear demonstrations.
>
> Please rank the following statements by their probability, using 1 for the most probable and 8 for the least probable.
>
> (a) Linda is a teacher in elementary school.
> (b) Linda works in a bookstore and takes Yoga classes.
> (c) Linda is active in the feminist movement.

(d) Linda is a psychiatric social worker.

(e) Linda is a member of the League of Women Voters.

(f) Linda is a bank teller.

(g) Linda is an insurance sales person.

(h) Linda is a bank teller and is active in the feminist movement.

In a group of naive subjects with no background in probability and statistics, 89 per cent judged that statement (h) was more probable than statement (f) despite the obvious fact that one cannot be a *feminist* bank teller unless one is a *bank teller*. When the same question was presented to statistically sophisticated subjects – graduate students in the decision science program of the Stanford Business School – 85 per cent gave the same answer! Results of this sort, in which subjects judge that a compound event or state of affairs is more probable than one of the components of the compound, have been found repeatedly since Kahneman and Tversky's pioneering studies, and they are remarkably robust. For useful reviews of research in the heuristics and biases tradition, see Kahneman et al. (1982), Nisbett and Ross (1980), Baron (2001), and Samuels et al. (2003).

13   For an excellent review of the literature, see Ross and Nisbett (1991).

References

Armstrong, D. (1968). *A Materialist Theory of the Mind.* New York: Humanities Press.

Baron, J. (2001). *Thinking and Deciding*, 3rd edn. Cambridge: Cambridge University Press.

Bierbrauer, G. (1973). *Effect of Set, Perspective, and Temporal Factors in Attribution*, unpublished doctoral dissertation, Stanford University.

Block, N. (1994). "Functionalism." In S. Guttenplan (ed.), *A Companion to the Philosophy of Mind.* Oxford: Blackwell: 323–32.

Churchland, P. (1981). "Eliminative Materialism and Propositional Attitudes." *Journal of Philosophy*, 78: 67–90. Reprinted in W. Lycan (ed.), *Mind and Cognition.* Oxford: Blackwell (1990): 206–23. Page reference is to the Lycan volume.

Davies, M. and Stone, T. (1995a). *Folk Psychology.* Oxford: Blackwell.

—— (1995b). *Mental Simulation.* Oxford: Blackwell.

Devitt, M. (1996). *Coming to Our Senses: A Naturalistic Program for Semantic Localism.* Cambridge: Cambridge University Press.

Ekman, P. (1985). *Telling Lies: Clues to Deceit in the Marketplace, Politics, and Marriage.* New York: W. W. Norton and Co.

Fodor, J. and C. Chihara (1965). "Operationalism and Ordinary Language." *American Philosophical Quarterly*, 2 (4). Reprinted in J. Fodor, *Representations.* Cambridge, MA: MIT Press (1981): 35–62.

Fodor, J. and LePore, E. (1992). *Holism: A Shopper's Guide.* Oxford: Blackwell.

Gigerenzer, G., Todd, P. and the ABC Research Group (1999). *Simple Heuristics that Make Us Smart.* Oxford: Oxford University Press.

Goldman, A. (1989). "Interpretation Psychologized." *Mind and Language*, 4: 161–85.

Gopnik, A. and Meltzoff, A. (1997). *Words, Thoughts and Theories.* Cambridge, MA: MIT Press.

Gopnik, A. and Wellman, H. (1994). "The Theory-Theory." In L. Hirschfeld and S. Gelman (eds.), *Mapping the Mind: Domain Specificity in Cognition and Culture*. New York: Cambridge University Press: 257–93.

Gordon, R. (1986). "Folk Psychology as Simulation." *Mind and Language*, 1: 158–70. Reprinted in Davies and Stone (1995a). Page reference is to the Davies and Stone volume.

Halle, M. and Stevens, K. (1962). "Speech Recognition: A Model and a Program for Research." In J. Fodor and J. Katz (eds.), *The Structure of Language: Readings in the Philosophy of Language*. Englewood Cliffs, NJ: Prentice-Hall.

Harris, P. (1992). "From Simulation to Folk Psychology: The Case for Development." *Mind and Language*, 7: 120–44.

Hayes, P. (1985). "The Second Naive Physics Manifesto." In J. Hobbs and R. Moore (eds.), *Formal Theories of the Commonsense World*. Norwood, NJ: Ablex: 1–36.

Heal, J. (1986). "Replication and Functionalism." In J. Butterfield (ed.), *Language, Mind and Logic*. Cambridge: Cambridge University Press: 135–50.

—— (1998). "Co-cognition and Off-line Simulation: Two Ways of Understanding the Simulation Approach." *Mind and Language*, 13: 477–98.

Hempel, C. (1964). "The Theoretician's Dilemma: A Study in the Logic of Theory Construction." In C. Hempel, *Aspects of Scientific Explanation*. New York: The Free Press: 173–226.

Kahneman, D. and Tversky, A. (1982). "The Psychology of Preferences." *Scientific American*, 246 (1): 160–73.

Kahneman, D., Slovic, P., and Tversky, A. (eds.) (1982). *Judgment Under Uncertainty: Heuristics and Biases*. Cambridge: Cambridge University Press.

Lewis, D. (1970). "How to Define Theoretical Terms." *Journal of Philosophy*, 67: 17–25.

—— (1972). "Psychophysical and Theoretical Identifications." *Australasian Journal of Philosophy*, 50: 249–58. Reprinted in N. Block (ed.), *Readings in the Philosophy of Psychology*, vol. I. Cambridge, MA: Harvard University Press: 207–15. Page references are to the Block volume.

Loewenstein, G. and Adler, D. (1995). "A Bias in the Prediction of Tastes." *The Economic Journal: The Quarterly Journal of the Royal Economic Society*, 105: 929–37.

Loftus, E. (1979). *Eyewitness Testimony*. Cambridge, MA: Harvard University Press.

Lycan, W. (1994). "Functionalism." In S. Guttenplan (ed.), *A Companion to the Philosophy of Mind*. Oxford: Blackwell: 317–23.

McCloskey, M. (1983). "Intuitive Physics." *Scientific American*, 248 (4): 122–9.

Milgram, S. (1963). "Behavioral Study of Obedience." *Journal of Abnormal and Social Psychology*, 67: 371–8.

Nichols, S. and Stich, S. (1998). "Rethinking Co-cognition: A Reply to Heal." *Mind and Language*, 13: 499–512.

—— (forthcoming). *Mindreading*. Oxford: Oxford University Press.

Nichols, S., Stich, S., Leslie, A., and Klein, D. (1996). "Varieties of Off-line Simulation." In P. Carruthers and P. Smith (eds.), *Theories of Theories of Mind*. Cambridge: Cambridge University Press: 39–74.

Nisbett, R. and Ross, L. (1980). *Human Inference*. Englewood Cliffs, NJ: Prentice-Hall.

Putnam, H. (1960). "Minds and Machines." In S. Hook (ed.), *Dimensions of Mind*. New York: New York University Press: 138–64.

Ross, L. and Nisbett, R. (1991). *The Person and the Situation: Perspectives of Social Psychology*. Philadelphia: Temple University Press.

Ryle, G. (1949). *The Concept of Mind*. London: Hutchinson.

Samuels, R., Stich, S., and Faucher, L. (2003). "Reasoning and Rationality." In I. Niiniluoto, M. Sintonen, and J. Wolenski (eds.), *Handbook of Epistemology*. Dordrecht: Kluwer: 1–50.

Scholl, B. and Leslie, A. (1999). "Modularity, Development, and 'Theory of Mind' ". *Mind and Language*, 14: 131–53.

Sellars, W. (1956). "Empiricism and the Philosophy of Mind." In H. Feigl and M. Scriven (eds.), *The Foundations of Science and the Concepts of Psychology and Psychoanalysis: Minnesota Studies in the Philosophy of Science*, vol. 1. Minneapolis: University of Minnesota Press: 253–329.

Stich, S. (1996). *Deconstructing the Mind*. Oxford: Oxford University Press.

Stich, S. and Nichols, S. (1995). "Second Thoughts on Simulation." In Davies and Stone (1995b): 86–108.

Stich, S. and Ravenscroft, I. (1994). "What *is* Folk Psychology?" *Cognition*, 50: 447–68. Reprinted in Stich (1996).

Thaler, R. (1980). "Toward a Positive Theory of Consumer Choice." *Journal of Economic Behavior and Organization*, 1: 39–60.

Young, A. (1998). *Face and Mind*. Oxford University Press.

Chapter 11

Individualism

Robert A. Wilson

11.1   Introduction

Much discussion has been generated in the philosophy of mind over the last 25 years or so on the general issue of the relationship between the nature of the mind of the individual and the character of the world in which that individual, and hence her mind, exists. The basic issue here is sometimes glossed in terms of whether psychological or mental states are "in the head," but to the uninitiated that is likely to sound like a puzzling issue to debate: of course mental states are in the head! (but see Rowlands 1999; Wilson 2000a, 2001). So one of our first tasks is to articulate a version of the issue that makes more perspicuous why it has been a topic of some contention for so long, and that begins to convey something of its importance for a range of diverse issues, such as the methodology of cognitive science, the possibility of self-knowledge, and the nature of intentional representation.

Consider the question of whether the character of an agent's environment plays some crucial role in determining or fixing the nature of that agent's mind. A natural thought, one shared by those who disagree about the answer to the question above, would be that agents causally interact with their world, gathering information about it through their senses, and so the nature of their minds, in particular what their thoughts are about, *are* in part determined by the character of their world. Thus, the world is a *causal* determinant of one's thoughts, and thus one's mind. That is, the world is a contributing cause to the *content* of one's mind, to what one perceives and thinks about. This is just to say that the content of one's mind is not causally isolated from one's environment. Separating individualists and anti-individualists in the philosophy of mind is the question of whether there is some *deeper* sense in which the nature of the mind is determined by the character of the individual's world.

We can approach this issue by extending the brief discussion above of the idea that the content of the mind is in part causally determined by the agent's environment to explore the conditions under which a difference in the world implies a difference in the mind. Individualists hold that this is so just in case that difference in the world makes some corresponding change to what occurs inside the boundary of the individual; anti-individualists deny this, thus allowing for the possibility that individuals who are identical with respect to all of their *intrinsic* features could nonetheless have psychological or mental states with different contents. And, assuming that mental states with different contents are *ipso facto* different types or kinds of state, this implies that an individual's intrinsic properties do not determine or fix that individual's mental states.

This provides us with another way, a more precise way, of specifying the difference between individualism (or *internalism*) and its denial, anti-individualism (or *externalism*), about the mind. Individualists claim, and externalists deny, that what occurs inside the boundary of an individual *metaphysically* determines the nature of that individual's mental states. The individualistic determination thesis, unlike the causal determination thesis, expresses a view about the nature or essence of mental states, and points to a way in which, despite their causal determination by states of the world, mental states are autonomous or independent of the character of the world beyond the individual. What individualism implies is that two individuals who are identical in all their intrinsic respects *must have* the same psychological states. This implication, and indeed the debate over individualism, is often made more vivid through the fantasy of *doppelgangers*, molecule-for-molecule identical individuals, and the corresponding fantasy of Twin Earth. I turn to these dual fantasies via a sketch of the history of the debate over individualism.

11.2 Getting to Twin Earth: What's in the Head?

Hilary Putnam's "The Meaning of 'Meaning'" (1975) introduced both fantasies in the context of a discussion of the meaning of natural language terms. Putnam was concerned to show that "meaning" does not and cannot jointly satisfy two theses that it was often taken to satisfy by then prevalent views of natural language reference: the claim that the meaning of a term is what determines its reference, and the claim that meanings are "in the head," where this phrase should be understood as making a claim of the type identified above about the metaphysical determination of meanings. These theses typified *descriptive* theories of reference, prominent since Frege and Russell first formulated them, according to which the reference of a term is fixed or metaphysically determined by the descriptions that a speaker attaches to that term. To take a classic example, suppose that I think of Aristotle as a great, dead philosopher who wrote a number of important philosophical works, such as the *Nicomachean Ethics*, and who was a student of Plato and teacher of Alexander the Great. Then, on a descriptivist view of reference, the reference of my term "Aristotle" is just the thing in the world that satisfies the various descriptions that I attach to that term: it is the thing in the world that is a great philosopher, is dead, wrote a number of important philosophical works (e.g., *Nicomachean Ethics*), was a student of Plato, and was a teacher of Alexander the Great.

Such descriptivist views of the reference of *proper names* were the critical focus of Saul Kripke's influential *Naming and Necessity* (1980), while in his attack on this cluster of views and their presuppositions, Putnam focused on *natural kind terms*, such as "water" and "tiger." Both Kripke and Putnam intended their critiques and the subsequent alternative theory of natural language reference, the causal theory of reference, to be quite general and to provide an alternative way to think about the relationship between language and the world. But let us stay close to Putnam's argument and draw out its connection to individualism.

Consider an ordinary individual, Oscar, who lives on Earth and interacts with water in the ways that most of us do: he drinks it, washes with it, and sees it falling from the sky as rain. Oscar, who has no special chemical knowledge about the nature of water, will associate a range of descriptions with his term "water": it is a liquid that one can drink, that is used to wash, and that falls from the sky as rain. On a descriptive view of reference, these descriptions determine the reference of Oscar's term "water." That is, Oscar's term "water" refers to whatever it is in the world that satisfies the set of descriptions he attaches to the term. And since those descriptions are "in the head," natural language reference on this view is individualistic.

But now, to continue Putnam's argument, imagine a molecule-for-molecule doppelganger of Oscar, Oscar*, who lives on a planet just like Earth in all respects but one: the substance that people drink, wash with, and see falling from the sky is *not* water (i.e., H_2O), but a substance with a different chemical structure, XYZ. Call this planet "Twin Earth." This substance, whose chemical composition we might denote with "XYZ," is called "water" on Twin Earth, and Oscar*, as a doppelganger or twin of Oscar, has the same beliefs about it as Oscar has about water on Earth. (Recall that Oscar, and thus Oscar* as his twin, have no special knowledge of the chemical structure of water.) Twin Earth has what we might call "*twin-water*" or "*twater*" on it, not water, and it is twater that Oscar* interacts with, not water – after all, there is no water on Twin Earth. Given that Oscar's term "water" refers to or is about water, then Oscar*'s term "water" refers to or is about *twater*. That is, they have natural language terms that *differ* in their meaning, assuming that reference is at least one aspect of meaning. But, by hypothesis, Oscar and Oscar* are doppelgangers, and so are identical in all their intrinsic properties, and so are identical with respect to what's "in the head." Thus, Putnam argues, the meaning of the natural language terms that Oscar uses are not metaphysically determined by what is in Oscar's head.

Putnam's target was a tradition of thinking about language which was, in terms that Putnam appropriated from Rudolph Carnap's *The Logical Construction of the World* (1928), *methodologically solipsistic*: it treated the meanings of natural language terms and language more generally in ways that did not suppose that the world beyond the individual language user exists. Since Putnam's chief point was one about natural language terms and the relationship of their semantics to what's inside the head, one needs at least to extend his reasoning from language to thought to arrive at a position that denies individualism about the mind itself. But given the tradition to which he was opposed, such an extension might be thought to be relatively trivial, since in effect those in the tradition of methodological solipsism – from Brentano, to Russell, to Husserl, to Carnap – conceived of natural languages and their use in psychological terms.

The introduction of the term "individualism" itself can be found in Tyler Burge's "Individualism and the Mental" (1979), where Burge developed a series of thought experiments in many ways parallel to Putnam's Twin Earth thought experiment. Burge identified individualism as an overall conception of the mind prevalent in modern philosophical thinking, at least since Descartes in the mid-seventeenth century, and argued that our common-sense psychological framework for explaining behavior, our *folk psychology*, was not individualistic. Importantly, Burge was explicit in making a case against individualism that did not turn on perhaps controversial claims about the semantics of natural kind terms – he developed his case against individualism using agents with thoughts about arthritis, sofas, and contracts – and so his argument did not presuppose any type of scientific essentialism about natural kinds. Like Putnam's argument, however, Burge's argument does presuppose some views about natural language understanding.

The most central of these is that we can and do have *incomplete* understanding of many of the things that we have thoughts about and for which we have natural language terms. Given that, it is possible for an individual to have thoughts that turn on this incomplete understanding, such as the thought that one has arthritis in one's thigh muscle. Arthritis is a disease only of the joints, or as we might put it, "arthritis" in our speech community applies only to a disease of the joints. Consider an individual, Bert, with the belief that he would express by saying "I have arthritis in my thigh." In the actual world, this is a belief about arthritis; it is just that Bert has an incomplete or partially mistaken view of the nature of arthritis, and so expresses a false belief with the corresponding sentence.

But now imagine Bert as living in a different speech community, one in which the term "arthritis" *does* apply to a disease of both the joints and of other parts of the body, including the thigh. In *that* speech community, Bert's thought would not involve the sort of incomplete understanding that it involves in the actual world; in fact, his thought in such a world would be *true*. Given the differences in the two speech communities, it seems that an individual with thoughts about what he calls "arthritis" will have different thoughts in the two communities: in the actual world, Bert has thoughts about arthritis, while in the counterfactual world he has thoughts about *some other disease* – what *we* might refer to as "tharthritis," to distinguish it from the disease that we have in the actual world. In principle, we could suppose that Bert himself is identical across the two contexts – that is, he is identical in all intrinsic respects. Yet we attribute thoughts with different contents to Bert, and seem to do so *solely* because of the differences in the language community in which he is located. Thus, the content of one's thoughts is not metaphysically determined by the intrinsic properties of the individual. And again taking a difference in the content of two thoughts to imply a difference between the thoughts themselves, this implies that thoughts are not individuated individualistically.

One contrast that is sometimes (e.g., Segal 2000: chs. 2–3) drawn between the anti-individualistic views of Putnam and Burge is to characterize Putnam's view as a form of *physical* externalism and Burge's view as a form of *social* externalism: according to Putnam, it is the character of the physical world (e.g., the nature of water itself) that, in part, metaphysically determines the content of one's mind, while according to Burge it is the character of the social world (e.g., the nature of one's linguistic community) that does so. While this difference may serve as a useful reminder of one way in which these two views differ, we should also keep in mind the "social" aspect to Putnam's view of natural language as well: his linguistic division of labor. Important to both views is the idea that language users and psychological beings depend and rely on one another in ways that are reflected in our everyday, common-sense ways of thinking about language and thought. Thus there is a social aspect to the nature of meaning and thought on both views, and this is in part what justifies the appropriateness of the label anti-*individualism* for each of them.

11.3   The Cognitive Science Gesture

Philosophers who see themselves as contributing to cognitive science have occupied the most active arena in which the debate between individualists and externalists has been played out. At around the time that individualism was coming under attack from Putnam and Burge, it was also being defended as a view of the mind particularly apt for a genuinely scientific approach to understanding the mind, especially of the type being articulated within the nascent interdisciplinary field of cognitive science. For those offering this defense, there was something suspiciously unnaturalistic about the Putnam–Burge arguments, as well as something about their conclusions that seemed anti-scientific, and part of the defense of individualism and the corresponding attack on externalism turned on what I will call the *cognitive science gesture*: the claim that, as contemporary empirical work on cognition indicated, any truly scientific understanding of the mind would need to be individualistic.

Picking up on Putnam's use of "methodological solipsism", Jerry Fodor defended methodological solipsism as the doctrine that psychology ought to concern itself only with *narrow* psychological states, where these are states that do not presuppose "the existence of any individual other than the subject to whom that state is ascribed" (Fodor 1980: 244). Fodor saw methodological solipsism as the preferred way to think of psychological states, given especially the Chomskyan revolution in linguistics and the accompanying computational revolution in psychology. If mental states were transitions governed by computational rules, then the task of the cognitive sciences would be to specify those rules; insofar as mental states were computational, broader considerations about the physical or social worlds in which an individual is located seem irrelevant to that individual's psychological nature.

Stephen Stich's (1978) principle of autonomy provides an alternative way to articulate an individualistic view of cognitive science, variations on which have become the standard ways to formulate individualism. The principle says that "the states and processes that ought to be of concern to the psychologist are those that supervene on the current, internal, physical state of the organism" (Stich 1983: 164–5). The notion of *supervenience* provides a more precise way to specify the type of metaphysical determination that we introduced earlier. A set of properties, S (the supervening properties), supervenes on some other set of properties, B (the base properties), just if anything that is identical with respect to the B properties must also be identical with respect to the S properties. In part because of the prominence of supervenience in formulating versions of physicalism, together with the perceived link between physicalism and individualism (more of which in a moment), but also in part because of the emphasis on doppelgangers in the Putnam and Burge arguments, it has become most typical to express individualism and its denial in terms of one or another supervenience formulation.

Common to both Fodor and Stich's views of cognitive science is the idea that an individual's psychological states should be *bracketed off* from the mere, beyond-the-head environments that individuals find themselves in. Unlike Putnam and Burge in the papers discussed above, Fodor and Stich have focused on the relevance of individualism for explanatory practice in psychology, using their respective principles to argue for substantive conclusions about the scope and methodology of psychology and the cognitive sciences. Fodor contrasted a solipsistic psychology with what he called a naturalistic psychology, arguing that since the latter (amongst which he included J. J. Gibson's approach to perception, learning theory, and the naturalism of William James) was unlikely to prove a reliable research strategy in psychology, methodological solipsism provided the only fruitful research strategy for understanding cognition (see also Fodor 1987). Stich argued for a syntactic or computational theory of mind which made no essential use of the notion of intentionality or mental content at all, and so used the principle of autonomy in defense of an *eliminativist* view about content (see also Stich 1983).

Although I think that the cognitive science gesture *is* a gesture (rather than a solid argument that appeals to empirical practice), it is not an *empty* gesture. While Fodor's and Stich's arguments have not won widespread acceptance in either the philosophical or cognitive science communities, they have struck a chord with those working in cognitive science, perhaps not surprisingly since the dominant research traditions in cognitive science have been at least implicitly individualistic. Relatively explicit statements of a commitment to an individualistic view of aspects of cognitive science include Chomsky's (1986, 1995, 2000) deployment of the distinction between two conceptions of language (the "I"-language and the "E"-language, for "internal" and "external", respectively), Jackendoff's (1991) related, general distinction between "psychological" and "philosophical" conceptions of the mind, and Cosmides and Tooby's (1994) emphasis on the constructive nature of our internal, evolutionary-specialized cognitive modules.

Part of the attraction of individualism for practicing cognitive scientists is its perceived connection to the representational theory of mind, which holds that we interact with the world perceptually and behaviorally through internal mental representations of how the world is (as the effects of perceiving) or how the world should be (as instructions to act). Jackendoff expresses such a view when he says:

> Whatever the nature of real reality, the way reality can look to us is determined and constrained by the nature of our internal mental representations. . . . Physical stimuli (photons, sound waves, pressure on the skin, chemicals in the air, etc.) act mechanically on sensory neurons. The sensory neurons, acting as transducers in Pylyshyn's (1984) sense, set up peripheral levels of representation such as retinal arrays and whatever acoustic analysis the ear derives. In turn, the peripheral representations stimulate the construction of more central levels of representation, leading eventually to the construction of representations in central formats such as the 3D level model. (1991: 159–61)

Provided that the appropriate, internal, representational states of the organism remain fixed, the organism's more peripheral causal involvement with its environment is irrelevant to cognition, since the only way in which such causal involvement can matter to cognition is by altering the internal mental states that represent that environment.

11.4 Functionalism, Physicalism, and Individualism

For many philosophers interested in the cognitive sciences, individualism has been attractive because of a perceived connection between that view and both physicalism and functionalism in the philosophy of mind, both of which have been widely accepted since the 1980s. Physicalism (or materialism) is a view that has been expressed in various ways, perhaps the most common of which is in terms of the notion of supervenience: all facts, properties, processes, events, and things supervene on the physical facts, properties, processes, events, and things, as they are posited in elementary physics. This ontological formulation of physicalism (concerned with what *exists*) is often accompanied by an *explanatory* thesis, which states that physical explanations are, in some sense, the ultimate explanations for any phenomenon whatsoever.

Individualism has been thought to be linked to physicalism, since it implies, via the supervenience formulation, that there is no psychological difference without a corresponding difference in the intrinsic, physical states of the individual. Those rejecting individualism have sometimes been charged (e.g., by Block 1986 and Fodor 1987: ch. 2) with endorsing some form of dualism about the mind, or making a mystery of mental causation by ignoring or misconstruing the role of causal powers in psychological taxonomy. Connecting this up with the methodological formulations that have had influence in cognitive science itself, individualism has been claimed to be a minimal constraint on arriving at psychological explanations that locate the mind suitably in the physical world, a psychology that taxonomizes its entities by their causal powers. (We have seen, however, that individualists themselves disagree about what this implies about psychology.)

Functionalism is the view that psychological states and processes should be individuated by their causal or functional roles – that is, by their place within the overall causal economy of the organism – and it has been common to suppose that these functional or causal roles are individualistic. Certainly, these causal roles can be understood in different ways, but the two (complementary) ways most prevalent in cognitive science – in terms of the notion of computation (e.g., Fodor 1980; Pylyshyn 1984), and in terms of the idea of analytical decomposition (e.g., Dennett 1978; Cummins 1983) – lend themselves to an individualistic reading. Computational processes, operating solely on the *syntactic* properties of mental states, have been plausibly thought to be individualistic; and it is natural to think of analytical decomposition as beginning with a psychological capacity (e.g., memory, depth perception, reasoning) and seeking the intrinsic properties of the organism in virtue of which it instantiates that capacity.

Despite their prima facie plausibility, however, neither of these connections – between physicalism and individualism, and between functionalism and individualism – is unproblematic, and in fact I think that upon closer examination neither purported inference holds. These claims can be explored more fully by examining explicit arguments for individualism that specify these connections more precisely.

11.5   The Appeal to Causal Powers

An argument for individualism that has been widely discussed derives from chapter 2 of Fodor's *Psychosemantics* (1987). Although a series of related criticisms (van Gulick 1989; Egan 1991; Wilson 1992, 1995: ch. 2) seem to me decisive in showing the argument to be fatally flawed, the argument itself taps into an intuition, or perhaps a cluster of intuitions, running deep in the philosophical community. The argument itself is easy to state. Taxonomy or individuation in the sciences in general satisfies a generalized version of individualism: sciences taxonomize the entities they posit and discover by their causal powers. Psychology and the cognitive sciences should be no exception here. But the causal powers of anything supervene on that thing's intrinsic, physical properties. Thus, scientific taxonomy, and so psychological taxonomy, must be individualistic.

One way to elicit the problem with this argument is to ask what it is that makes the first premise (about scientific taxonomy in general) true. Given the naturalistic turn supposedly embraced by those working in contemporary philosophical psychology, one would think that the support here comes from an examination of actual taxonomic practice across the sciences. However, once one does turn to look at these practices, it is easy to find a variety of sciences that *don't* taxonomize "by causal powers;" rather, they individuate their kinds *relationally*, where often enough it is the *actual* relations that determine kind membership. Examples often cited here include species in evolutionary biology, which are individuated phylogenetically (and so historically), and continents in geology, whose causal powers are pretty much irrelevant to their identity as continents (see Burge 1986a). The problem is particularly acute in the context of this argument for individualism, since a further premise in the argument states that a thing's causal powers supervene on that thing's intrinsic properties, and so one cannot simply stipulate that individuation in these sciences is "by causal powers" in some extended sense of "causal powers." (If one does that, then "causal powers" no longer so supervene.)

The intuition that persists despite an acknowledgment that the argument itself is flawed in something like the way identified above is that individualism *does* articulate a constraint for the explanation of cognition that sciences more generally satisfy, one that would make for a physicalistically respectable psychology (e.g., see Walsh 1999). My view is that this intuition itself seriously underestimates the diversity in taxonomic and explanatory practice across the sciences (see Wilson 2000b), and it simply needs to be given up. Attempts to revitalize this sort of argument for individualism proceed by making the sorts of a priori assumptions about the nature of scientific taxonomies and explanations that are reminiscent of the generalized, rational reconstructions of scientific practice that governed logical positivist views of science, and this should sound alarm bells for any self-professed contemporary naturalistic philosopher of mind.

11.6 Externalism and Metaphysics

What, then, of the more general, putative connection between physicalism and individualism? If the denial of individualism could be shown to entail the denial of a plausibly general version of physicalism, then I think that externalism would itself be in real trouble. But like the individualist's appeal to causal powers and scientific taxonomy, I suspect that the move from the general intuitions that motivate such an argument to the argument itself will itself prove problematic. For example, externalists can respect the physicalist slogan "no psychological difference without a physical difference" because the relevant physical differences lie beyond the boundary of the individual; attempts to refine this slogan (e.g., no psychological difference without a here-and-now physical difference) are likely either to beg the question against the externalist or invoke a construal of physicalism that is at least as controversial as individualism itself.

What is true is that externalists themselves have not been as attentive to the metaphysical notions at the core of contemporary materialism as they could have been, and when they have so attended they have sometimes sounded opposed to physicalism. The most prominent case here is Burge's (1979) original discussion of the implications of individualism for related views about the mind, where he claimed that the rejection of individualism implied the rejection of both type-type and token-token identity theories of the mind, these being two of the major forms of materialism.

To my mind, the most under-discussed of these notions is that of *realization*. Although it has been common to express materialism as entailing that all mental states are realized as physical states, and to take the relevant physical states to be states of the brain, there has been little general discussion of the properties of this relation of realization, or of the properties of realizer states (see Shoemaker 2000, Gillett 2002, though). This creates a problem for externalists, since the standard view of realization smuggles in an individualistic bias. On this standard view, realizers are held to be both *metaphysically sufficient* for the states they realize and *physically constitutive* of the individuals with the realized properties. Denying the second of these conjuncts, as I think an externalist should, creates space for the idea that mental states have a *wide realization*, an option that I have attempted elsewhere to defend in the context of a more general discussion of realization (Wilson 2001).

11.7 The Debate Over Marr's Theory of Vision

I have already said that individualism receives prima facie support from the computational and representational theories of mind, and thus from the cognitive science community in which those theories have been influential. But I have also indicated that I think that the claim that a truly explanatory cognitive science will be individualistic has an epistemic basis more like a gesture than a proof. One way to substantiate this second view in light of the first is to turn to examine the continuing philosophical debate over whether David Marr's celebrated theory of early vision is individualistic. Apart from the intrinsic interest of the debate itself, our examination here will also help to elicit some of the broader issues about the mind to which the individualism issue is central, including the nature of computation and representation.

In the final section of "Individualism and the Mental," Burge had suggested that his thought experiment and the conclusion derived from it – that mental content and thus mental states with content were not individualistic – had implications for computational explanations of cognition. These implications were twofold. First, purely computational accounts of the mind, construed individual-istically, were inadequate; and second, insofar as such explanations did appeal to a notion of mental content, they would fail to be individualistic. It is the latter of these ideas that Burge pursued in "Individualism and Psychology" (1986a), in which he argued, strikingly, that Marr's theory of vision was *not* individualistic. This was the first attempt to explore a widely respected view within cognitive science vis-à-vis the individualism issue, and it was a crucial turning point in moving beyond the cognitive science gesture toward a style of argument that really does utilize empirical practice in cognitive science itself.

As has often been pointed out, what is called "Marr's theory of vision" is an account of a range of processes in early or "low-level" vision that was developed by Marr and colleagues, such as Ellen Hildreth and Tomas Poggio, at the Massa-chussetts Institute of Technology from the mid-1970s. These processes include stereopsis, the perception of motion, and shape and surface perception, and the approach is explicitly computational. Marr's *Vision: A Computational Investiga-tion into the Human Representation and Processing of Visual Information* (1982), published posthumously after Marr's tragic early death in 1980, became the paradigm expression of the approach, particularly for philosophers, something facilitated by Marr's comfortable blend of computational detail with broad-brushed, programmatic statements of the perspective and implications of his approach to understanding vision. Since the publication of Marr's book, work on his theory of vision has continued, being extended to cover the processes constituting low-level vision more extensively (e.g., see Hildreth and Ullman 1989). Interestingly, by and large, the philosophical literature on individualism that appeals to Marr's theory has been content to rely almost exclusively on his *Vision* in interpreting the theory.

Critical to the computational theory that Marr advocates is a recognition of the different levels at which one can – indeed, for Marr, must – study vision. According to Marr, there are three levels of analysis to pursue in studying an information-processing device. First, there is the level of the computational theory (hereafter, the *computational level*), which specifies the goal of the computa-tion, and at which the device itself is characterized in abstract, formal terms as "mapping from one kind of information to another" (1982: 24). Second is the level of representation and algorithm (hereafter, the *algorithmic level*), which selects a "representation for the input and output and the algorithm to be used to transform one into the other" (ibid.: 24–5). And third is the level of hardware implementation (hereafter, the *implementational level*), which tells us how the representation and algorithm are realized physically in the actual device.

Philosophical discussions, like Marr's own discussions, have been focused on the computational and algorithmic levels for vision, what Marr himself (ibid.: 23) characterizes, respectively, as the "what and why" and "how" questions about vision. As we will see, there is particular controversy over what the computational level involves. In addition to the often-invoked trichotomy of levels at which an informational-processing analysis proceeds, there are two further interesting dimensions to Marr's approach to vision that have been somewhat neglected in the philosophical literature. These add some complexity not only to Marr's theory, but also to the issue of how "computation" and "representation" are to be understood in it.

The first is the idea that visual computations are performed sequentially in *stages of computational inference*. Marr states that the overall goal of the theory of vision is "to understand how descriptions of the world may efficiently and reliably be obtained from images of it" (ibid.: 99). Marr views the inferences from intensity changes in the retinal image to full-blown three-dimensional descriptions as proceeding via the construction of a series of preliminary representations: the raw primal sketch, the full primal sketch, and the $2^1/_2$-D sketch. Call this the *temporal dimension* to visual computation. The second is that visual processing is subject to modular design, and so particular aspects of the construction of 3-D images – stereopsis, depth, motion, etc. – can be investigated in principle independently. Call this the *modular dimension* to visual computation.

A recognition of the temporal and modular dimensions to visual computation complicates any discussion of what "the" computational and algorithmic levels for "the" process of vision are. Minimally, in identifying each of Marr's three levels, we need first to fix at least the modular dimension to vision in order to analyze a given visual *process*, and to fix at least the temporal dimension in order to analyze a given visual *computation*.

Burge's argument that Marr's theory is not individualistic is explicitly and fully presented in the following passage:

> (1) The theory is intentional. (2) The intentional primitives of the theory and the information they carry are individuated by reference to contingently existing physical items or conditions by which they are normally caused and to which they normally apply. (3) So if these physical conditions and, possibly, attendant physical laws were regularly different, the information conveyed to the subject and the intentional content of his or her visual representations would be different. (4) It is not incoherent to conceive of relevantly different (say, optical) laws regularly causing the same non-intentionally, individualistically individuated physical regularities in the subject's eyes and nervous system. . . . (5) In such a case (by (3)) the individual's visual representations would carry different information and have different representational content, though the person's whole non-intentional physical history . . . might remain the same. (6) Assuming that some perceptual states are identified in the theory in terms of their informational or intentional content, it follows that individualism is not true for the theory of vision. (1986a: 34)

The second and third premise make specific claims about Marr's theory of vision, while the first premise, together with (4) and (5), indicate the affinity between this argument and the Twin Earth-styled argument of Burge's that we discussed earlier.

Burge himself concentrates on defending (2)–(4), largely by an appeal to the ways in which Marr appears to rely on "the structure of the real world" in articulating both the computational and algorithmic levels for vision. Marr certainly does make a number of appeals to this structure throughout *Vision*. For example, he says

The purpose of these representations is to provide useful descriptions of aspects of the real world. The structure of the real world therefore plays an important role in determining both the nature of the representations that are used and the nature of the processes that derive and maintain them. An important part of the theoretical analysis is to make explicit the physical constraints and assumptions that have been used in the design of the representations and processes. (1982: 43; cf. also pp. 68, 103–5, 265–6)

And Marr does claim that the representational primitives in early vision – such as "blobs, lines, edges, groups, and so forth" – that he posits "correspond to real physical changes on the viewed surface" (ibid.: 44). Together, these sorts of comment have been taken to support (2) and (3) in particular.

Much of the controversy over how to interpret Marr's theory turns on whether this is the correct way to understand his appeals to the "structure of the real world." There are at least two general alternatives to viewing such comments as claiming the importance of the beyond-the-head world for the computational taxonomy of visual states.

The first is to see them as giving the real world a role to play *only* in constructing what Marr calls the computational theory. Since vision is a process for extracting information from the world in order to allow the organism to act effectively in that world, clearly we need to know something of the structure of the world in our account of what vision is *for*, what it is that vision *does*, what function vision is *designed to perform*. If this is correct, then it seems possible to argue that one does *not* need to look beyond the head in constructing the theory of the representation and algorithm. As it is at this level that visual states are taxonomized qua the objects of computational mechanisms, Marr's references to the "real world" do not commit him to an externalist view of the taxonomy of visual states and processes.

The second is to take these comments to suggest merely a *heuristic* role for the structure of the real world, not only in developing a computational taxonomy but in the computational theory of vision more generally. That is, turning to the beyond-the-head world is merely a useful short-cut for understanding how vision works and the nature of visual states and computations, either by providing important *background* information that allows us to understand the representational primitives and thus the earliest stages of the visual computation, or by serving as interpretative lenses that allow us to construct a *model* of computational processes in terms that are meaningful. Again, as with the previous option, the beyond-the-head world plays only a peripheral role within computational vision, even if Marr at times refers to it prominently in outlining his theory.

Individualists have objected to Burge's argument in two principal ways. First, Segal (1989) and Matthews (1988) have both in effect denied (2), with Segal arguing that these intentional primitives (such as edges and generalized cones) are better interpreted within the context of Marr's theory as individuated by their *narrow content*. Second, Egan (1991, 1992, 1995, 1999) has more strikingly denied (1), arguing that, qua computational theory, Marr's theory is not intentional at all. Both objections are worth exploring in detail, particularly insofar as they highlight issues that remain contentious in contemporary discussions. In fact, the discussion of Marr's theory raises more foundational questions than it solves about the nature of the mind and how we should investigate it.

Segal points out that there are two general interpretations available when one seeks to ascribe intentional contents to the visual states of two individuals. First, one could follow Burge and interpret the content of a given visual state in terms of what normally causes it. Thus, if it is a crack in a surface that plays this role, then the content of the corresponding visual state is "crack;" if it is a shadow in the environment that does so, then the content of the visual state is "shadow." This could be so even in the case of doppelgangers, and so the visual states so individuated are not individualistic. But second and alternatively, one could offer a more liberal interpretation of the content of the visual states in the two cases, one that was neutral as to the cause of the state, and to which we might give the name "crackdow" to indicate this neutrality. This content would be shared by doppelgangers, and so *would* be individualistic.

The crucial part of Segal's argument is his case for preferring the second of these interpretations, and it is here that one would expect to find an appeal to the specifics of Marr's theory of vision. While some of Segal's arguments here do so appeal, he also introduces a number of quite general considerations that have little to do with Marr's theory in particular. For example, he points to the second interpretation as having "economy on its side" (1989: 206), thus appealing to considerations of simplicity, and says:

> The best theoretical description will *always* be one in which the representations fail to specify their extensions at a level that distinguishes the two sorts of distal cause. It will *always* be better to suppose that the extension includes both sorts of thing. (ibid.: 207; my emphasis)

Why "always"? Segal talks generally of the "basic canons of good explanation" (ibid.) in support of his case against externalism, but as with the appeals to the nature of scientific explanation that turned on the idea that scientific taxonomy and thus explanation individuates by "causal powers," here we should be suspicious of the level of generality (and corresponding lack of substantive detail) at which scientific practice is depicted. Like Burge's own appeal to the objectivity of perceptual representation in formulating a general argument for externalism (1986a: section 3; 1986b), these sorts of a priori appeals seem to me to represent gestural lapses entwined with the more interesting, substantive, empirical arguments over individualism in psychology.

When Segal does draw more explicitly on features of Marr's theory, he extracts three general points that are relevant for his argument that the theory is individualistic: each attribution of a representation requires a "bottom-up account" (1989: 194), a "top-down motivation" (ibid.: 195) and is "checked against behavioral evidence" (ibid.: 197). Together, these three points imply that positing represen-tations in Marr's theory does not come cheaply, and indeed is tightly constrained by overall task demands and methods. The first suggests that any higher-level representations posited by the theory must be derived from lower-level input representations; the second that all posited representations derive their motiva-tion from their role in the overall perceptual process; and the third that "inten-tional contents are inferred from discriminative behavior" (ibid.: 197).

Segal uses the first assumption to argue that since the content of the earliest representations – "up to and including zero-crossings" (ibid.: 199) – in doppelgangers are the same, there is a prima facie case that downstream, higher-level representations must be the same, unless a top-down motivation can be given for positing a difference. But since we are considering doppelgangers, there is no behavioral evidence that could be used to diagnose a representational differ-ence between the two (Segal's third point), and so no top-down motivation available. As he says, "[t]here would just be no theoretical point in invoking the two contents [of the twins], where one would do. For there would be no the-oretical purpose served by distinguishing between the contents" (ibid.: 206).

How might an externalist resist this challenging argument? Three different tacks suggest themselves, each of which grants less to Segal than that which precedes it.

First, one could grant the three points that Segal extracts from his reading of Marr, together with his claim that the lowest levels of representation are individu-alistic, but question the significance of this. Here one could agree that the gray arrays with which Marr's theory begins do, in a sense, represent light intensity values, and that zero-crossings do, in that same sense, represent a sudden change in the light intensity. But these are both merely representations of some state of the retina, not of the world, and it should be no surprise that such intra-organismic representations have narrow content. Moreover, the depth of the intentionality or "aboutness" of such representations might be called into question precisely be-cause they don't involve any causal relation that extends beyond the head; they might be thought to be representational in much the way that my growling stomach represents my current state of hunger. However, once we move to downstream processes, processes that are later on in the temporal dimension to visual processing, *genuinely* robust representational primitives come into play, primitives such as "edge" and "generalized cone." And the contents of states deploying *these* primitives, one might claim, as representations of a state of the world, metaphysically depend on what they correspond to in the world, and so are not individualistic. The plausibility of this response to Segal turns on both the strength of the distinction between a weaker and a stronger sense of "representa-tion" in Marr's theory, and the claim that we need the stronger sense to have states that are representational in some philosophically interesting sense.

Secondly, and more radically, one could allow that all of the representational primitives posited in the theory represent in the same sense, but challenge the claim that the content of *any* of the corresponding states is narrow: it is wide content all the way out, if you like. The idea that the representational content of states deploying gray arrays and zero-crossings is in fact wide might itself take its cue from Segal's second point – that representations require a top-down motivation – for it is by reflecting on the point of the overall process of constructing reliable, three-dimensional images of a three-dimensional visual world that we can see that even early retinal representations must be representations of states and conditions in the world. This view would of necessity go beyond Marr's theory itself, which is explicitly concerned only with the computational problem of how we infer three-dimensional images from impoverished retinal information, but would be, I think, very much in the spirit of what we can think of as a Gibsonian aspect to Marr's theory (cf. Shapiro 1993).

Thirdly, and least compromisingly, one could reject one or more of Segal's three points about Marr's theory or, rather, the significance that Segal attaches to these points. Temporally later representations *are* derived from earlier representations, but this itself doesn't tell us anything about how to individuate the contents of *either*. Likewise, that Marr himself begins with low-level representations of the retinal image tells us little about whether such representations are narrow or wide. Top-down motivations *are* needed to justify the postulation of representations, but since there is a range of motivations within Marr's theory concerning the overall point of the process of three-dimensional vision, this also gives us little guidance about whether the content of such representations is narrow or wide. Behavioral evidence does play a role in diagnosing the content of particular representations, but since Marr is not a behaviorist, behavioral discrimination does not provide a litmus test for representational difference (Shapiro 1993: 498–503).

This third response seems the most plausible to develop in detail, but it also seems to me the one that implies that there is likely to be no definitive answer to the question of whether Marr's theory employs either a narrow or a wide notion of content, or both or neither. Although Marr was not concerned at all himself with the issue of the intentional nature of the primitives of this theory, the depth of his methodological comments and asides has left us with an embarrassment of riches when it comes to possible interpretations of his theory. This is not simply an indeterminacy about what Marr meant or intended, but one within the computational approach to vision itself, and, I think, within computational psychology more generally. With that in mind, I shall turn now to Egan's claim that the theory is *not intentional at all*, a minority view of Marr's theory that has not, I believe, received its due (cf. critiques of Egan by Butler 1996 and 1998 and Shapiro 1997; see also Chomsky 1995: 55, fn. 25).

At the heart of Egan's view of Marr is a particular view of the nature of Marr's *computational* level of description. Commentators on Marr have almost universally taken this to correspond to what others have called the "knowledge level" (Newell 1980) or the "semantic level" (Pylyshyn 1984) of description, i.e., as offering an *intentional* characterization of the computational mechanisms governing vision and other cognitive processes. Rather than ignoring Marr's computational level, as some (e.g., Shapiro 1997) have claimed she does (supposedly in order to focus exclusively on Marr's algorithmic level of description), Egan rejects this dominant understanding of the computational level, arguing instead that what makes it a computational level is that it specifies the function to be computed by a given algorithm in precise, mathematical terms. That is, while this level of description is functional, what makes it the first stage in constructing a *computational* theory is that it offers a function-theoretic characterization of the computation, and thus abstracts away from all other functional characterizations. Thus, while vision might have all sorts of functions that can be specified in language relatively close to that of common sense (e.g., it's for extracting information from the world, for perceiving an objective world, for guiding behavior), none of these, in Egan's view, forms a part of Marr's computational level of description. Given this view, the case for Marr's theory being individualistic because computational follows readily:

> A computational theory prescinds from the actual environment because it aims to provide an abstract, and hence completely general, description of a mechanism that affords a basis for predicting and explaining its behavior in any environment, even in environments where what the device is doing cannot comfortably be described as *cognition*. When the computational characterization is accompanied by an appropriate intentional interpretation, we can see how a mechanism that computes a particular mathematical function can, in a particular context, subserve a cognitive function such as vision. (1995: 191).

According to Egan, while an intentional interpretation links the computational theory to our common-sense-based understanding of cognitive functions, it forms no part of the computational theory itself. Egan's view naturally raises questions not only about what Marr meant by the computational level of description but, more generally, about the nature of *computational* approaches to cognition.

There are certainly places in which Marr does talk of the computational level as simply being a high-level functional characterization of what vision is for, and thus primarily as orienting the researcher to pose certain general questions. For example, one of his tables offers the following summary questions that the theory answers at the computational level: "What is the goal of the computation, why is it appropriate, and what is the logic of the strategy by which it can be carried out?" (1982: 25, fig. 1–4). Those defending the claim that Marr's theory is externalist have typically rested with this broad and somewhat loose understanding of the computational level of the theory (see, e.g., Burge 1986a: 28; Shapiro 1993: 499–500; 1997: 134).

The problem with this broad understanding of the computational level, and thus of computational approaches to cognition, is that while it builds a bridge between computational psychology and more folksy ways of thinking about cognition, it creates a gap within the computational approach between the computational and algorithmic levels. For example, if we suppose that the computational level specifies simply that some visual states have the function of representing edges, others the function of representing shapes, etc., there is nothing about such descriptions that guides us in constructing *algorithms* that generate the state-to-state transitions at the heart of computational approaches to vision. More informal elaborations of what vision is for, or of what it evolved to do, do little by themselves to bridge this gap.

The point here is that computational specifications themselves are a very special kind of functional characterization, at least when they are to be completed or implemented in automatic, algorithmic processes. Minimally, proponents of the broad interpretation of computational approaches to cognition need either to construe the computational level as encompassing but going beyond the function-theoretic characterizations of cognitive capacities that Egan identifies, or they must allocate those characterizations to the algorithmic level. The latter option simply exacerbates the "gap" problem identified above. But the former option seems to me to lump together a variety of quite different things under the heading of "the computational level," and subsequently fails to recognize the constraints that computational assumptions bring in their wake. The temporal and modularity dimensions to Marr's theory exacerbate the problem here.

There is a large issue lurking here concerning how functionalism should be understood within computational approaches to cognition, and correspondingly how encompassing such approaches really are. Functionalism has usually been understood as offering a way to reconcile our folk psychology, our manifest image (Sellars 1962) of the mind, with the developing sciences of the mind, even if that reconciliation involves revising folk psychology along individualistic lines (e.g., factoring it into a *narrow* folk psychology via the notion of narrow content). And computationalism has been taken to be one way of specifying what the relevant functional roles are: they are "computational roles." But if Egan is right about Marr's understanding of the notion of computation as a function-theoretic notion, and we accept the view that this understanding is shared in computational approaches to cognition more generally, then the corresponding version of functionalism about the mind must be correspondingly function-theoretic: it must not only "prescind from the actual environment," as she claims the computational level must do, but also from the sort of *internal* causal role that functionalists have often appealed to. Cognitive mechanisms, on this view, take mathematically characterizable inputs to deliver mathematically characterizable outputs, and qua computational devices, that is all. Any prospects for the consilience of our "two images" must lie elsewhere.

In arguing for the non-intentional character of Marr's theory of vision, Egan presents an austere picture of the heart of computational psychology, one that accords with the individualistic orientation of computational cognitive science as it has traditionally been developed (cf. Chomsky 1995), even if computational psychologists have sometimes (e.g., Pylyshyn 1984) attempted to place their theories within more encompassing contexts. One problem with such a view of computation, as Shapiro (1997: 149) points out, is that a computational theory of X tells us very little about the nature of X, including information sufficient to individuate X as (say) a *visual* process at all. While Egan (1999) seems willing to accept this conclusion, placing this sort of concern outside of computational theory proper, this response highlights a gap between computational theory, austerely construed, and the myriad of theories – representational, functional, or ecological in nature – with which such a theory must be integrated for it to constitute a complete, mechanistic account of any given cognitive process. The more austere the account of computation, the larger this gap becomes, and the less a computational theory contributes to our understanding of cognition. One might well think that Egan's view of computational theory in psychology errs on the side of being *too* austere in this respect.

11.8   Exploitative Representation and Wide Computationalism

As a beginning on an alternative way of thinking about computation and representation, consider an interesting difference between individualistic and externalist interpretations of Marr's theory that concerns what it is that Marrian computational systems have built into them. Individualists about computation, such as Egan and Segal, hold that they incorporate various *innate assumptions* about what the world is like. This is because the process of vision involves recovering 3-D information from a 2-D retinal image, a process that without further input would be underdetermined. The only way to solve this underdetermination problem is to make innate assumptions about the world. The best known of these is Ullman's *rigidity assumption*, which says that "any set of elements undergoing a two-dimensional transformation has a unique interpretation as a rigid body moving in space and hence should be interpreted as such a body in motion" (1979: 146). The claim that individualists make is that assumptions like this are part of the computational systems that drive cognitive processing. This is the standard way to understand Marr's approach to vision.

Externalists like Shapiro have construed this matter differently. Although certain assumptions must be true of the world in order for our computational mechanisms to solve the underdetermination problem, these are simply assumptions that are *exploited* (Shapiro 1997: 135, 143; cf. Rowlands 1999) by our computational mechanisms, rather than innate in our cognitive architecture. That is, the assumptions concern the relationships between features of the external world, or between properties of the internal, visual array and properties of the external world, but those assumptions are not themselves encoded in the organism. To bring out the contrast between these two views, consider a few simple examples.

An odometer keeps track of how many miles a car has traveled, and it does so by counting the number of wheel rotations and being built so as to display a number proportional to this number. One way in which it could do this would be for the assumption that 1 rotation = x meters to be part of its calculational machinery; another way of achieving the end would be for it to be built so as simply to record x meters for every rotation, thus exploiting the fact that 1 rotation = x meters. In the first case it encodes a representational assumption, and uses this to compute its output; in the second, it contains no such encoding but instead *uses* an existing relationship between its structure and the structure of the world. In either case, if it finds itself in an environment in which the relationship between rotations to distance traveled is adjusted (e.g., larger wheels, or being driven on a treadmill), it will not function as it is supposed to, and will misrepresent the distance traveled.

Consider two different strategies for learning how to hit a baseball that is falling vertically to the ground. Since the ball accelerates at 9.8 ms^{-2}, there is a time lag between swinging and hitting. One could either assume that the ball is falling (say, at a specific rate of acceleration), and then use this assumption to calculate when one should swing; alternatively, one could simply aim a certain distance below where one perceives the ball at the time of swinging (say, two feet). In this latter case one would be exploiting the relationship between acceleration, time, and distance without having to encode that relationship in the assumptions one brings to bear on the task.

The fact that there are these two different strategies for accomplishing the same end should, minimally, make us wary of accepting the claim that innate assumptions are the *only* way that a computational system could solve the underdetermination problem. But I also want to develop the idea that our perceptual system in particular and our cognitive systems more generally typically exploit rather than encode information about the world and our relationship to it, as well as say something about where Marr himself seems to stand on this issue (see also Wilson, forthcoming).

An assumption that Egan makes and that is widely shared in the philosophical literatures both on individualism and computation is that at least the *algorithmic* level of description within computational psychology is individualistic. The idea here has, I think, seemed so obvious that it has seldom been spelled out: algorithms operate on the syntactic or formal properties of symbols, and these are intrinsic to the organisms instantiating the symbols. We might challenge this neither by disputing how much is built into Marr's computational level, nor by squabbling over the line between Marr's computational and algorithmic levels, but, rather, by arguing that computations themselves can extend beyond the head of the organism and involve the relations between individuals and their environments. This position, which holds that at least some of the computational systems that drive cognition, especially human cognition, reach beyond the limits of the organismic boundary, I have elsewhere (1994; 1995: ch. 3) called *wide computationalism*, and its application to Marr's theory of vision marks a departure from the parameters governing the standard individualist-externalist debate over that theory. Wide computationalism constitutes one way of thinking about the way in which cognition, even considered computationally, is "embedded" or "situated" in its nature (cf. also Hutchins 1995; McClamrock 1995), and it provides a framework within which an exploitative conception of representation can be pursued.

The basic idea of wide computationalism is simple. Traditionally, the sorts of computation that govern cognition have been thought to begin and end at the skull. But why think that the skull constitutes a magic boundary beyond which true computation ends and mere causation begins? Given that we are creatures embedded in informationally rich and complex environments, the computations that occur inside the head are an important part but are not exhaustive of the corresponding computational systems. This perspective opens up the possibility of exploring computational units that include the brain as well as aspects of the brain's beyond-the-head environment. Wide computational systems thus involve minds that literally extend beyond the confines of the skull into the world.

One way to bring out the nature of the departure made by wide computationalism within the individualism debate draws on a distinction between a *locational* and a *taxonomic* conception of psychological states (see also Wilson 2000a; cf. Rowlands 1999: chs. 2–3). Individualists and externalists are usually presented as disagreeing over how to taxonomize or individuate psychological states, but both typically (though not always) presume that the relevant states are what we might call *locationally individualistic*: they are located within the organismic envelope. What individualists and externalists typically disagree about is whether in addition to being locationally individualistic, psychological states must also be taxonomically individualistic. Wide computationalism, however, rejects this assumption of locational individualism by claiming that some of the "relevant states" – some of those that constitute the relevant computational system – are located not in the individual's head but in her environment.

The intuitive idea behind wide computationalism is easy enough to grasp, but there are two controversial claims central to defending wide computationalism as a viable model for thinking about and studying cognitive processing. The first is that it is sometimes appropriate to offer a formal or computational characterization of an organism's environment, and to view parts of the brain of the organism, computationally characterized, together with this environment so characterized, as constituting a unified computational system. Without this being true, it is difficult to see wide computationalism as a coherent view. The second is that this resulting mind–world computational system itself, and not just the part of it inside the head, is genuinely cognitive. Without this second claim, wide computationalism would at best present a zany way of carving up the computational world, one without obvious implications for how we should think about real cognition in real heads. Rather than attempting to respond to each of these problems in the space available, I shall turn to the issue of how this general perspective on representation and computation sits with Marr's theory of vision.

As we have seen, Marr himself construes the task of a theory of vision to be to show how we extract visual information from "arrays of image intensity values as detected by the photoreceptors in the retina" (1982: 31). Thus, as we have already noted, the problem of vision *begins* with retinal images, not with properties of the world beyond those images, and "the true heart of visual perception is the inference *from* the structure of an image about the structure of the real world outside" (ibid.: 68; my emphasis). Marr goes on to characterize a range of physical constraints that hold true of the world that "make this inference possible" (ibid.), but he makes it clear that "the constraints are used by turning them into an assumption that may or may not be internally verifiable" (ibid.: 104). For all of Marr's talk of the importance of facts about the beyond-the-head world for constructing the computational level in a theory of vision, this is representative of how he conceives of that relevance (e.g., ibid.: 43, 68, 99, 103–5, 265–6). It seems to me clear that, in terms that I introduced earlier in this section, Marr himself adopts an encoding view of computation and representation, rather than an exploitative view of the two. The visual system is, according to Marr, a locationally individualistic system.

Whatever Marr's own views here, the obvious way to defend a wide computational interpretation of his theory is to resist his inference from "x is a physical constraint holding in the world" to "x is an assumption that is encoded in the brain." This is, in essence, what I have previously proposed one should do in the case of the multiple spatial channels theory of form perception pioneered by Campbell and Robson (1968). Like Marr's theory of vision, which in part builds on this work (see esp. Marr 1982: 61–4), this theory has usually been understood as postulating a locationally individualistic computational system, one that begins with channels early in the visual pathway that are differentially sensitive to four parameters: orientation, spatial frequency, contrast, and spatial phase. My suggestion (Wilson 1994; 1995: ch. 3) was to take seriously the claim that any visual scene (in the world) can be decomposed into these four properties, and so see the computational system itself as extending into the world, with the causal relationship between stimulus and visual channels itself modeled by transition rules. Rather than simply having these properties encoded in distinct visual channels in the nervous system, view the in-the-head part of the form perception system as exploiting formal properties in the world beyond the head. With respect to Marr's theory, there is a respect in which this wide computational interpretation is *easy* to defend, and another in which it is *difficult* to defend.

The first of these is that Marr's "assumptions," such as the spatial coincidence assumption (1982: 70) and the "fundamental assumption of stereopsis" (ibid.: 114), typically begin as physical constraints that reflect the structure of the world; in the above examples, they begin as the constraint of spatial localization (ibid.: 68–9) and three matching constraints (ibid.: 112–14). Thus, the strategy is to argue that the constraints *themselves*, rather than their derivative encoding, play a role in defining the computational system, rather than simply filling a heuristic role in allowing us to offer a computational characterization of a locationally individualistic cognitive system.

The corresponding respect in which a wide computational interpretation of Marr's theory is difficult to defend is that these constraints themselves do not specify what the computational primitives are. One possibility would simply be to attribute the primitives that Marr ascribes to the *image* to features of the scenes perceived themselves, but this would be too quick. For example, Marr considers zero-crossings to be steps in a computation that represent sharp changes in intensity in the image, and while we could take them to represent intensity changes in the stimuli in the world, zero-crossings themselves are located somewhere early in the in-the-head part of the visual system, probably close to the retina. A better strategy, I think, would be to deflate the interpretation of the retinal image and look "upstream" from it to identify richer external structures in the world, structures which satisfy the physical constraints that Marr postulates. That is, one should extend the temporal dimension to Marr's theory so that the earliest stages in basic visual processes *begin in the world*, not in the head. Since the study of vision has been largely conducted within an overarching individualistic framework, this strategy would require recasting the theory of vision itself so that it ranges over a process that causally extends beyond the retinal image (see also Rowlands 1999: ch. 5).

11.9 Narrow Content and Marr's Theory

Consider the very first move in Segal's argument for the conclusion that Marr's theory of vision is individualistic, the claim that there are two general interpretations available when one seeks to ascribe intentional contents to the visual states of two individuals: one "restrictive" (Burge's) and one "liberal" (Segal's). Something like these two general alternatives was implicit in the basic Twin Earth cases with which we – and the debate over individualism – began; the idea that twins must share some intentional state about watery substances (or about arthritis-like diseases, in Burge's standard case) is the basis for attempts to articulate a notion of *narrow* content, i.e., intentional content that does supervene on the intrinsic, physical properties of the individual. I have elsewhere (Wilson 1995: ch. 9) expressed my skepticism about such attempts, and here I want to tie this skepticism to the innocuous-looking first step in Segal's interpretation.

   This first step in Segal's interpretation, the presupposition of a liberal interpretation for Marr's theory, and a corresponding view of the original Twin Earth cases in general, are themselves questionable. Note first that the representations that we might, in order to make their disjunctive content perspicuous, label "crackdow" or "water or twater," *do* represent their reliable, environmental causes: "crackdow" is reliably caused by cracks or shadows, and has the content crack or shadow; similarly for "water or twater." But then this disjunctive content is a species of wide, not narrow content, as Egan (1995: 195) has pointed out. In short, although being shared by twins is necessary, it is not sufficient for mental content to be narrow.

   To press further, if the content of one's visual state is to be individualistic, it must be shared by doppelgangers *no matter how different their environments.* Thus, the case of "twins" is merely a heuristic for thinking about a potentially infinite number of individuals. But then the focus on a content shared by two individuals, and thus on a content that is neutral between two environmental causes, represents a misleading simplification insofar as the content needed won't simply be "crackdow," but something more wildly disjunctive, since there is a potentially infinite number of environments that might produce the same intrinsic, physical state of the individual's visual system as (say) cracks do in the actual world (see also Egan 1991: 200, fn. 35). It is not that we can't simply make up a name for the content of such a state (we can: call it "X"), but that it is difficult to view a state so individuated as being *about anything*. And if being about something is at the heart of being intentional, then this calls into question the status of such narrowly individuated states as intentional states.

Segal (1991: 490) has claimed that the narrow content of "crackdow," or by implication "water or twater," need not be disjunctive, just simply more encompassing than, respectively, crack or water (see also Segal 2000). But casting the above points in terms of disjunctive content simply makes vivid the general problems that (1) the individuation of states in terms of their content still proceeds via reference to what does or would cause them to be tokened; and (2) once one prescinds from a conception of the cognitive system as embedded in and interacting with the actual world in thinking about how to taxonomize its states, it becomes difficult to delineate clearly those states as intentional states with some definite content. As it is sometimes put, narrow content becomes *inexpressible*. Two responses might be made to this second objection.

First, one might concede that, strictly speaking, narrow content *is* inexpressible, but then point out ways of "sneaking up on it" (Fodor 1987: 52). One might do so by talking of how one can "anchor" narrow content to wide content (ibid.: 50–3); or of how to specify the *realization conditions* for a proposition (Loar 1988). But these suggestions, despite their currency, seem to me little more than whistling in the dark, and the concession on which they rest, fatal. All of the ways of "sneaking up on" narrow content involve using wide contents in some way. Yet if wide content is such a problematic notion (because it is not individualistic), then surely the problem spreads to any notion, such as snuck-up-on narrow content, for whose intelligibility the notion of wide content is crucial.

Moreover, if narrow content really is inexpressible, then the idea that it is this notion that is central to psychological explanation as it is actually practiced, and this notion that does or will feature in the natural kinds and laws of the cognitive sciences, cannot reasonably be sustained. Except in Douglas Adamsesque spoofs of science, there are no sciences whose central explanatory constructs are inexpressible. Moreover, this view would make the claim that one arrives at the notion of narrow content via an examination of actual explanatory practice in the cognitive sciences extremely implausible, since if narrow content is inexpressible, then one won't be able to find it expressed in any existing psychological theory. In short, and in terms that I introduced earlier, the idea that snuck-up-on narrow content is what cognitive science needs or uses represents a reversion to the cognitive science gesture.

Secondly, it might be claimed that although it is true that it *is* difficult for common-sense folk to come up with labels for intentional contents, those in the relevant cognitive sciences can and do all the time, and we should defer to them. For example, one might claim that many if not all of the representational primitives in Marr's theory, such as blob, edge, and line, have narrow contents. These concepts, like many scientific terms, are technical and, as such, may bear no obvious relationship to the concepts and terms of common sense, but they still allow us to see how narrow content can be expressed. One might think that this response has the same question-begging feel to it as does the claim that our folk psychological states are themselves narrow. However, the underdetermination of philosophical views by the data of the scientific theories, such as Marr's, that they interpret remains a problem for both individualists and externalists alike here. As my discussion of exploitative representation and wide computation perhaps suggests, my own view is that we need to reinvigorate the ways in which the computational and representational theories of mind have usually been construed within cognitive science. If this can be done in more than a gestural manner, then the issue of the (in)expressibility of narrow content will be largely moot.

11.10   Individualism and the Problem of Self-knowledge

Thus far, I have concentrated on discussions of individualism and externalism in contemporary philosophy of mind with a primary affinity to cognitive science. It is testimony to the centrality of individualism and externalism for philosophy more generally – quite apart from their relevance to empirical cognitive science – that there is a variety of discussions that explore the relationship between these positions and traditional issues in the philosophy of mind and philosophy more generally. The most interesting of these seem to me to cluster around three related epistemological issues: self-knowledge, a priori knowledge, and skepticism.

Basic to self-knowledge is knowledge of one's own mind, and traditionally this knowledge has been thought to involve some form of privileged access to one's own mental states. This first-person privileged access has often been understood in terms of one or more distinctive properties that the resulting second-order mental states have. These states, such as my belief that I believe that the Earth goes around the sun, have been claimed to be *infallible* (i.e., incapable of being false or mistaken), which would imply that simply having the second-order belief guarantees that one has the first-order belief that is its object; or *incorrigible* (i.e., even if mistaken, incapable of being corrected by anyone other than the person who has them), which would at least imply that they have a form of epistemic security that other types of mental state lack. In either case, there is an asymmetry between knowledge of one's own mind and knowledge of the minds of others, as well as knowledge of other things in the world. Indicative of the depth of these asymmetries in modern philosophy is the fact that an introduction to epistemology, particularly one with a historical slant, that reflects on skepticism, will likely introduce the *problem of other minds* and the *problem of our knowledge of the external world*, but not the corresponding *problem of self-knowledge*. Skepticism about one's own mind has seemed to be precluded by the very nature of self-knowledge.

Although the contrast between first- and third-person knowledge of mental states has softened in recent philosophy of mind, it remains part of our common-sense conception of the mind that the ways in which I know about my own mental life are distinctive from the ways in which I know about that of others (cf. Siewert 1998). Thus, not unreasonably, the idea of first-person epistemic privilege survives. Knowledge about one's *self*, about the condition or state of one's mind or body, often enough seems to be simply a matter of introspection, of inward-directed reflection or attention, rather than requiring the collection of evidence through observation or experiment. I simply *feel* my skin itching, or upon attending notice that my toes are squashed up in my shoes; to find out whether *your* skin is itching or whether your toes are squashed up in your shoes, I observe your body and its behavior (including what you *say*), and then draw an inference from that observation to a conclusion about your bodily state. Self-knowledge is *direct*, while knowledge of others is inferential or mediated in some way, based on observation and other forms of evidence. Since one's own mental states are typically the object of first-person thoughts, we are acquainted with our own minds in a way that we are not acquainted with the minds of others.

Individualistic conceptions of the mind have seemed well-suited to making sense of first-person privileged access and the subsequent asymmetry between self-knowledge and knowledge of the mental states of others. If mental states are individuated in abstraction from the beyond-the-individual environment, then there seems to be no problem in understanding how the process of introspection, turning our mind's eye inwards (to use a common metaphor), reveals the content of those states. To invoke the Cartesian fantasy in a way that brings out the asymmetry between self-knowledge and other forms of knowledge, even if there were an evil demon who deceived me about the existence of an external world – including the existence of other people with mental states like mine – the one thing that I could be sure about would be that I am having experiences with a certain content. As it is sometimes put, even if I could be deceived about whether there is really a tree in front of me and thus about whether I am actually seeing a tree, I cannot be deceived about whether *it seems to me that I am seeing a tree*. Thus individualism seems to facilitate a sort of epistemic security for first-person knowledge of one's own mental states that the corresponding third-person knowledge lacks.

Externalism, by contrast, poses a prima facie problem for even the more modest forms of first-person privileged access, and has even been thought to call into question the possibility of any form of self-knowledge. For externalism claims that what mental states *are* is metaphysically determined, in part, by the nature of the world beyond the boundary of the subject of those states. Thus it would seem that in order to know *what* one is thinking, i.e., to know the content of one's mental states, one would have to know something about the world beyond one's self. But this would be to assimilate our first-person knowledge of our own minds to our knowledge of other things, and so deny any *privileged* access that self-knowledge might be thought to have. It implies that in order to know my own mind I need to know about perhaps difficult-to-discern facts about the nature of the physical or social world in which I live, and so it also suggests that in a range of ordinary cases where we might unreflectively attribute self-knowledge, I don't actually have self-knowledge at all.

We can express the problem here in another way that abstracts from the differences between both specific accounts of privileged access and specific versions of externalism. Whether it be infallible, incorrigible, self-intimating, introspective, or a priori, knowledge of one's own mental states has a special character. Knowing one's own mental states involves, *inter alia*, knowing their contents. Now, according to externalism, the contents of a subject's mental states are metaphysically determined, in part, by facts about her physical or social environment. Knowledge of these facts, however, does not have this special character. But then how is the special character of self-knowledge compatible with the non-special character of worldly knowledge, given the dependence of the former on the latter (see also Ludlow and Martin 1998: 1)? Others have stated the problem more dramatically. For example, Davidson presents it as "a transposed image of Cartesian skepticism" (1987: 94), according to which "[o]ur beliefs about the external view are . . . directed onto the world, but we don't know what we believe" (ibid.), claiming thus that externalism seems to imply that we don't have self-knowledge at all; Heil points out that "if externalism were true, one could not discover a state's intentional properties merely by inspecting that state" (1988: 137), going on to connect this up with Davidson's focus on a "nastier skeptic, one who questions the presumption that we think what we think we think" (ibid.).

The problem can be schematized as a supposedly inconsistent triad of propositions (cf. also McKinsey 1991, whose triad differs; see below). Let P = the contents of our mental states, E = facts about the environment, and let "by introspection" stand in for the distinctive character of self-knowledge:

1   We know P by introspection. (Self-knowledge)
2   P are metaphysically determined in part by E. (Externalism)
3   E are not known by introspection. (Common Sense)

The claim is that one of these three propositions must be given up. If we reject Self-knowledge, then we give up on the idea that we have privileged access to our own minds; if we reject Externalism, then we give up on an independently plausible view of the mind; and if we reject Common Sense, then we make a strange and implausible claim about our knowledge of the physical or social world.

When it is stated so starkly, I think that the right response to the "problem of self-knowledge" is to argue that all three propositions are true, and so consistent, and thus that there is no problem of self-knowledge for an externalist to solve. Their consistency turns on the fact that (1) and (3), which make epistemological claims, are connected only by (2), which makes a metaphysical claim. As a counterexample to the charge of formal inconsistency, consider an instance of the argument where P = the state of being in pain, and E = a particular, complicated state of the central nervous system. There is no inconsistency in these instances of (1)–(3): we do know that we are in pain by introspection; that state is metaphysically determined by some particular state of our central nervous system; but we don't know about *that* state by introspection. (Or, to put it more carefully: we don't about it qua state of our central nervous system by introspection.) The same is true of our original triad, as well as of variations on those propositions which substitute some other distinctive feature of self-knowledge for "by introspection."

If this is the correct way to represent the supposed problem for externalists, and the basis for an adequate response to that problem, then two features of the problem are worth noting.

The first is that at the heart of the problem is not an externalist view of the mind itself but, rather, any thesis of metaphysical determination, where the determining state is not something that is known in the special way that mental states are known. Since not all of an organism's internal, individualistically individuated states are so known, there is a variation on the problem of self-knowledge that individualists must face, if it is a real problem. Thus, even if one rejects the way of dissolving the problem posed above, a version of the problem of self-knowledge remains for both externalists and individualists to solve. This implies that externalists do *not*, despite initial appearances, face a *special* problem concerning self-knowledge.

The second is that the problem and response so characterized have affinities with a family of problem–response pairs, including on the "problem" side Moore's open question argument and the paradox of analysis, and whose closest relative perhaps is a standard objection to the mind–brain identity theory. Pain, it was claimed, couldn't be identical to C-fiber firing, since one can know that one is in pain but not know that one's C-fibers were firing. And the now-standard response is that such an objection, in attempting to derive an ontological conclusion from epistemological premises, commits a fallacy. Now, as a purportedly inconsistent triad, rather than an argument that draws such a conclusion, the problem of self-knowledge itself does not suffer from this specific problem, although the rejection of externalism as a response to the problem *would* be subject to just this objection. However, the broad affinity here is worth keeping in mind. How adequate one finds the proposed dissolution of the problem of self-knowledge is likely to correlate with how adequate one finds this type of response to this type of objection more generally.

Proponents of the problem of self-knowledge should object to the claim that (1)–(3) adequately expresses the dilemma. In particular, they should (and in fact do) reject (2) as a member of the triad. Rather, the problem of self-knowledge is constituted by the following triad (cf. McKinsey 1991):

A   We have a priori knowledge of P. (Self-Knowledge*)
B   We have a priori knowledge that P entails E. (Knowledge of Externalism)
C   We cannot know E a priori. (Common Sense*)

(A)–(C) *are* inconsistent. But in contrast to (1)–(3), this construal of the problem of self-knowledge can be challenged at *every* point.

First, is an externalist committed to (B)? For an affirmative answer, two prior questions need to be answered affirmatively: according to externalism, (i) do we know that P entails E? and (ii) does P entail E? Take (ii): does externalism claim that, for example, having a mental state with the content "arthritis occurs in the thigh" entail that arthritis does actually occur in the thigh? One reason to think not is that, as we have seen, externalism incorporates the idea that there is a social division of labor in both thought and language, which allows for intentionality even in "vacuous cases": we can think P not because P, but because others think P.

Given, however, that externalism claims that there is a deep, individuative relation between the nature of an individual's mental states and how the world beyond the individual is, some such entailment between P and E seems plausible. This suggests that E needs to be construed in a more nuanced way, encompassing perhaps various disjuncts which together must be true if the externalist's view of the mind is correct. For example, it might be claimed that having the thought that arthritis occurs in the thigh entails either that arthritis does occur in the thigh or that one lives in a linguistic community of a certain character; perhaps more (or more complicated) disjuncts need to be added here (cf. Brown 1995). But then it seems less plausible that "we," i.e., each of us ordinary folk, know (2) so construed, let alone know this a priori. After all, few of us have reflected systematically on what the contents of our thoughts imply about the world; indeed, many of those who have thus reflected – individualists – have concluded that they tell us *nothing* about the character of the world.

This in turn invites the response that to form an inconsistent triad with (A) and (C), (B) need only claim that we *can* have such knowledge, and if externalism is true, and at least some people believe it and what it entails, then that is sufficient to generate the inconsistency.

This seems to me to be a strange way to develop the problem of self-knowledge, since it now sounds like a problem that arises chiefly for the self-knowledge of those versed in the externalism literature, rather than self-knowledge per se. But the real problem here, and the second problem with this construal of the triad, is that the triad now includes a questionable reading of (C). For now (C), even if it *is* a dictate of common sense (and modalized, as (3) is not, this seems doubtful), seems false, since although it is usual for ordinary folk to know about what is mentioned in E through empirical means, and so they don't usually know E a priori, in light of this reading of (B), it seems at least possible that someone could know about E in this fashion. Combined with the reminder that this is not usually how we come to know facts about the empirical world, this concession seems fairly innocuous, and preserves the intuition that self-knowledge is epistemically privileged.

We can see how this construal of the triad undermines its status as a problem for externalism by turning to (A): do we know the contents of our thoughts a priori? McKinsey conceives of a priori knowledge as knowledge "obtained independently of empirical investigation" (1991: 175), and relies on introspection and reasoning as paradigm processes through which we gain such knowledge. Externalists should be wary of this claim if it is taken to imply that self-knowledge can be gained *completely independently* of empirical investigation of the world; what they can allow, and perhaps all that is needed for (A), is that we know the contents of our mental states on particular occasions without empirically investigating the world on those occasions.

On this reading, (A) is made true by the existence of introspection, while (B)'s truth turns on our ability to follow the arguments for the externalist nature of content and so intentional mental states. While (C) may seem true if we think only of introspection or reasoning alone as means of securing a priori knowledge (in the sense above), it becomes more dubious once we consider introspection and reasoning *together*. Since it is unusual for us to both introspect our own mental states and engage in sophisticated philosophical reasoning using the results of such introspection as premises, the circumstances under which (C) will be falsified are themselves unusual; but (C) nonetheless is, strictly speaking, false.

Note

I should like to thank Gabriel Segal, Frances Egan, and Lawrence Shapiro for reading an earlier version of this review.

References

Block, N. (1986). "Advertisement for a Semantics for Psychology." In P. French, T. Uehling Jr., and H. Wettstein (eds.), *Midwest Studies in Philosophy*, vol. 10 (Philosophy of Mind). Minneapolis: University of Minnesota Press.

Brown, J. (1995). "The Incompatibility of Anti-Individualism and Privileged Access." *Analysis*, 55: 149–56. Reprinted in Ludlow and Martin (1998).

Burge, T. (1979). "Individualism and the Mental." In P. French, T. Uehling Jr., and H. Wettstein (eds.), *Midwest Studies in Philosophy*, vol. 4 (Metaphysics). Minneapolis: University of Minnesota Press.

—— (1986a). "Individualism and Psychology." *Philosophical Review*, 95: 3–45.

—— (1986b). "Cartesian Error and the Objectivity of Perception." In P. Pettit and J. McDowell (eds.), *Subject, Thought, and Context*. Oxford: Oxford University Press. Also in Grimm and Merrill (eds.), *Contents of Thought*. Tucson, AZ: University of Arizona Press (1988).

Butler, K. (1996). "Individualism and Marr's Computational Theory of Vision." *Mind and Language*, 11: 313–37.

—— (1998). "Content, Computation, and Individuation." *Synthese*, 114: 277–92.

Campbell, F. W. and Robson, J. G. (1968). "Application of Fourier Analysis to the Visibility of Gratings." *Journal of Physiology*, 197: 151–66.

Carnap, R. (1928). *The Logical Construction of the World*, trans. by R. George, 1967. Berkeley, CA: University of California Press.

Chomsky, N. (1986). *Knowledge of Language*. New York: Praeger.

—— (1995). "Language and Nature." *Mind*, 104: 1–61.

—— (2000). *New Horizons in the Study of Language and Mind*. New York: Cambridge University Press.

Cosmides, L. and Tooby, J. (1994). "Foreword" to S. Baron-Cohen, *Mindblindness*. Cambridge, MA: MIT Press.

Cummins, R. C. (1983). *The Nature of Psychological Explanation*. Cambridge, MA: MIT Press.

Davidson, D. (1987). "Knowing One's Own Mind." *Proceedings of the American Philosophical Association*. Reprinted in Ludlow and Martin (1998).

Dennett, D. C. (1978). "Artificial Intelligence as Philosophy and as Psychology." In M. Ringle (ed.), *Philosophical Perspectives on Artificial Intelligence*. New York: Humanities Press and Harvester Press. Reprinted in D. C. Dennett, *Brainstorms*. Cambridge, MA: MIT Press.

Egan, F. (1991). "Must Psychology be Individualistic?" *Philosophical Review*, 100: 179–203.

—— (1992). "Individualism, Computation, and Perceptual Content." *Mind*, 101: 443–59.

—— (1995). "Computation and Content." *Philosophical Review*, 104: 181–203.

—— (1999). "In Defense of Narrow Mindedness." *Mind and Language*, 14: 177–94.

Fodor, J. A. (1980). "Methodological Solipsism Considered as a Research Strategy in Cognitive Psychology." *Behavioral and Brain Sciences*, 3: 63–73. Reprinted in J. A. Fodor, *Representations*. Sussex: Harvester Press (1981).

—— (1987). *Psychosemantics*. Cambridge, MA: MIT Press.

Gillett, C. (2002). "The Dimensions of Realization: A Critique of the Standard View." *Analysis* (October).

Heil, J. (1988). "Privileged Access." *Mind*, 97: 238–51. Reprinted in Ludlow and Martin (1998).

Hildreth, E. and Ullman, S. (1989). "The Computational Study of Vision." In M. Posner (ed.), *Foundations of Cognitive Science*. Cambridge, MA: MIT Press.

Hutchins, E. (1995). *Cognition in the Wild*. Cambridge, MA: MIT Press.

Jackendoff, R. (1991). "The Problem of Reality." Reprinted in his *Languages of the Mind*. Cambridge, MA: MIT Press (1992).

Kripke, S. (1980). *Naming and Necessity*. Cambridge, MA: Harvard University Press.

Loar, B. (1988). "Social Content and Psychological Content." In R. Grimm and D. Merrill (eds.), *Contents of Thought*. Tucson, AZ: University of Arizona Press.

Ludlow, P. and Martin, N. (eds.) (1998). *Externalism and Self-Knowledge*. Palo Alto, CA: CSLI Publications.

Marr, D. (1982). *Vision: A Computational Investigation into the Human Representation and Processing of Visual Information*. San Francisco, CA: W. H. Freeman.

Matthews, R. (1988). "Comments on Burge." In R. Grimm and D. Merrill (eds.), *Contents of Thought*. Tuscon, AZ: University of Arizona Press.

McClamrock, R. (1995). *Existential Cognition: Computational Minds in the World*. Chicago: University of Chicago Press.

McKinsey, M. (1991). "Anti-Individualism and Privileged Access." *Analysis*, 51: 9–16.

Newell, A. (1980). "Physical Symbol System." *Cognitive Science*, 4: 135–83.

Putnam, H. (1975). "The Meaning of 'Meaning'." In K. Gunderson (ed.), *Language, Mind and Knowledge*. Minneapolis, MN: University of Minnesota Press. Reprinted in H. Putnam, *Mind, Language, and Reality*. New York: Cambridge University Press (1975).

Pylyshyn, Z. (1984). *Computation and Cognition*. Cambridge, MA: MIT Press.

Rowlands, M. (1999). *The Body in Mind*. New York: Cambridge University Press.

Segal, G. (1989). "Seeing What is Not There." *Philosophical Review*, 98: 189–214.

—— (1991). "Defence of a Reasonable Individualism." *Mind*, 100: 485–94.

—— (2000). *A Slim Book About Narrow Content*. Cambridge, MA: MIT Press.

Sellars, W. (1962). "Philosophy and the Scientific Image of Man." In R. Colodny (ed.), *Frontiers of Science and Philosophy*. Pittsburgh: University of Pittsburgh Press. Reprinted in W. Sellars, *Science, Perception, and Reality*. Atascadero, CA: Ridgeview Publishing Company (1963).

Shapiro, L. (1993). "Content, Kinds, and Individualism in Marr's Theory of Vision." *Philosophical Review*, 102: 489–513.

—— (1997). "A Clearer Vision." *Philosophy of Science*, 64: 131–53.

Shoemaker, S. (2000). "Realization and Mental Causation." Reprinted in C. Gillett and B. Loewer (eds.), *Physicalism and it Discontents*. New York: Cambridge University Press.

Siewert, C. (1998). *The Significance of Consciousness*. Princeton, NJ: Princeton University Press.

Stich, S. (1978). "Autonomous Psychology and the Belief-Desire Thesis." *Monist*, 61: 573–91.

—— (1983). *From Folk Psychology to Cognitive Science*. Cambridge, MA: MIT Press.

Ullman, S. (1979). *The Interpretation of Visual Motion*. Cambridge, MA: MIT Press.

Van Gulick, R. (1989). "Metaphysical Arguments for Internalism and Why They Don't Work." In S. Silvers (ed.), *Rerepresentation*. Dordrecht, The Netherlands: Kluwer.

Walsh, D. M. (1999). "Alternative Individualism." *Philosophy of Science*, 66: 628–48.

Wilson, R. A. (1992). "Individualism, Causal Powers, and Explanation." *Philosophical Studies*, 68: 103–39.

—— (1994). "Wide Computationalism." *Mind*, 103: 351–72.

—— (1995). *Cartesian Psychology and Physical Minds: Individualism and the Sciences of the Mind*. New York: Cambridge University Press.

—— (2000a). "The Mind Beyond Itself." In D. Sperber (ed.), *Metarepresentation*. New York: Oxford University Press.

—— (2000b). "Some Problems for 'Alternative Individualism'." *Philosophy of Science*, 67: 671–9.

—— (2001). "Two Views of Realization." *Philosophical Studies*, 104: 1–31.

—— (forthcoming). *The Individual in the Fragile Sciences I: Cognition*.

Chapter 12

Emotions

Paul E. Griffiths

12.1 Brute Feelings or Rational Judgments?

12.1.1 The feeling theory of emotions

Until the early twentieth century it was taken for granted that emotions are feelings: subjective states of experience. Darwin carried out extensive empirical investigations of the physiological and behavioral components of emotion but never regarded these as anything other than "expressions" of the feelings experienced by people and animals. Following Herbert Spencer, Darwin defined emotions as sensations caused by states of affairs outside the body, intending by this to differentiate them from sensations such as hunger and pain. Feeling is also central to William James's theory of emotion. Although James made the radical suggestion that emotion feelings are caused by the physiological changes associated with emotion, rather than causing those physiological changes, he still identifies the emotion with the feeling, not the physiological changes or the earlier neural processes that cause them. Naturally enough, the behaviorists were the first to question the feeling theory. John B. Watson argued that adult emotional behaviors were conditioned responses based on three unconditioned reactions in infants that he termed fear, rage, and pleasure. Later, under the influence of behaviorism and the verification theory of meaning, philosophical behaviorists such as Gilbert Ryle claimed that a correct analysis of the meanings of emotion words involves no reference to subjective states of experience.

In the 1960s philosophers enthusiastically embraced the "cognitive revolution" in psychology, linguistics, and the new field of artificial intelligence. The rejection of behaviorism was thus not accompanied by a revival of the feeling theory. Instead, a consensus emerged in the philosophy of emotion in the early 1960s that emotions are defined by the cognitions they involve. This consensus has persisted to the present day. Some philosophers have allowed feelings a role in emotion, but never one that determines the identity of the emotion. Emotion feelings merely add the "heat" to "hot cognition." Patricia Greenspan (1988), for example, argues that emotions are feelings of comfort or discomfort directed toward an evaluative thought about an external (or imaginary) stimulus. It is the evaluative thought that defines the emotion. Different negative emotions, such as anger and fear, are differentiated only by the different evaluative thoughts they involve. Philosophers have generally held it to be a conceptual truth that emotions derive their identities from the thoughts associated with them, but psychological research on the "cognitive labeling" of states of arousal has been cited as evidence that empirical findings converge on the same conclusion as conceptual analysis. The most frequently cited study showed that subjects could be induced to describe the sensations produced by adrenaline injections as either euphoria or anger under the influence of contextual cues provided by the experimenters (Schachter and Singer 1962).

12.1.2   Propositional attitude theories

Since the early 1960s the cognitivist or propositional attitude school has dominated the philosophy of emotion (Griffiths 1989; Deigh 1994). The basic commitments of this school are twofold. First, emotions are differentiated from one another by the cognitive states that they involve. Secondly, the cognitive states involved in emotion can be understood in terms of a propositional attitude theory of mental content. Mental states are attitudes, such as belief, desire, hope, and intention, to propositions. The simplest propositional attitude theory identifies emotions with evaluative judgments (Solomon 1976). A person is angry if they have the attitude of belief to the proposition that they have been wronged. Other prominent varieties of propositional attitude theory are belief/desire theories, hybrid feeling theories, and "seeing as" theories. Belief/desire theories analyze emotions as combinations of beliefs and desires (Marks 1982). Hope, for example, is analyzed as the belief that some state of affairs is possible and the desire that it be actual. Hybrid feeling theories, such as that of Greenspan discussed above, analyze emotions as combinations of propositional attitudes and feelings. The feeling component is used to differentiate cold cognition from hot (emotional) cognition and in some theories to distinguish positive from negative emotions. The specific identity of the emotion is given by the propositional attitude component. Finally, the increasingly popular "seeing as" approach argues that a subject's beliefs and desires about an object are not sufficient to constitute an emotion unless the subject "sees" the object in the right way. A typical anecdote involves a mountain climber who is said to retain the same beliefs and desires as she fluctuates between seeing a climb as terrifying and seeing it as exhilarating. Earlier versions of this approach were inclined to treat "seeing as" as a primitive concept, following some aspects of the later work of Wittgenstein (Lyons 1980). Contemporary versions analyze "seeing as" in terms of attentional phenomena in cognition. Emotions are biases in cognition that direct attention at some sources of information rather than others or lead to a higher weighting for one consideration than for another and thus lead to actions that would not have eventuated in the absence of the emotion (Calhoun 1984; De Sousa 1987).

The main concern of the propositional attitude school in the philosophy of emotion has been with whether emotions are "rational," meaning that an emotional response can be judged right or wrong in relation to the stimulus that elicits it. The feeling theory of emotion is condemned for placing emotions outside the realm of rational evaluation. This is seen as part of a wider and invidious tendency to separate the realm of the moral from the realm of the rational. The simplest judgmentalist theory brings emotions back into the domain of reason by identifying them with beliefs. An emotion is rational if the evaluative beliefs composing it are justified by the evidence available to the subject. More complex propositional attitude theories give more complex accounts of the rationality of emotions. Belief/desire theories face the difficulty that formal accounts of rationality, such as decision theory, are confined to evaluating the suitability of means to ends and take the ends (desires) as given. So these theories must provide an account of what it is rational to desire. Hybrid feeling theories can evaluate the rationality of having one emotion rather than another in the same ways as the theories just mentioned, since the identity of an emotion is determined solely by its propositional attitude component. Whether the state is an emotion in the first place, however, relies on the feeling component and so hybrid feeling theories must give some account of when it is rational to take one's cognition hot rather than cold. "Seeing as" theories face their own difficulties, such as giving a non-circular account of what it is to perceive in an angry or loving manner, but they have some promising resources to bring to bear on the rationality question. The cognitive biases that constitute emotions on this theory can be evaluated for their heuristic value in generating true belief, successful action, and so forth, and judged rational if they are successful in these respects.

12.2 Evolutionary Theories of Emotion

12.2.1 Darwin and the emotions

Facial expressions have been the subject of careful investigation in anatomy for centuries, generally with the aim of assisting painting and sculpture. This tradition provided a wealth of anatomical data for Charles Darwin's *The Expression of the Emotions in Man and Animals* (1872). Darwin had been collecting data on the emotions since the M and N notebooks of the late 1830s, and he originally intended to include this material in *The Descent of Man* (1871). The two books are therefore intimately related. In *Descent* . . . Darwin aimed to show evolutionary continuity between animal social behavior and human morality and between the aesthetic sense of animals and of humans. In *Expression* . . . he aimed to show evolutionary continuity in the facial expressions of humans and animals and thus, by implication, evolutionary continuity in the emotions underlying those expressions. The fundamental aim of both books was to show that in every respect humans differ from animals only in degree and thus that humans might have evolved from simpler precursors. In the Preface to *Expression* . . . Darwin explicitly targeted Sir Charles Bell's claim that the muscles of the human face were created by God to express human emotions. With this in mind, he argued that many movements that now express emotion were vestiges of previous ways of life: "With mankind some expressions, such as the bristling of the hair under the influence of extreme terror, or the uncovering of the teeth under that of furious rage, can hardly be understood, except in the belief that man once existed in a much lower and animal-like condition" (1872: 12).

Darwin argued that expressions of emotion could be understood through three complementary evolutionary principles. The most important of these was the "principle of serviceable associated habits," which is a straightforward application of Darwin's theory of instincts to the case of emotion. Darwin believed that instinctive behaviors derive from habits acquired by psychological reinforcement. The consistent acquisition of the same habit for many generations causes it to become a hereditary, or instinctive, behavior by the inheritance of acquired characteristics, in which Darwin was a firm believer. Most of the distinctive behaviors associated with particular emotions, such as the erection of the hair in fear, reflect long-since vanished lifestyles in which those behaviors were rewarded and reinforced in each generation until they were finally incorporated into the hereditary material as instincts. Darwin supplements this principle with two others, the "principle of antithesis" and the "principle of direct action." His antithesis principle postulates an intrinsic tendency for opposite states of feeling to produce opposite behaviors. Darwin remarks of a submissive dog that:

> Not one of the movements, so clearly expressive of affection, are of the least direct service to the animal. They are explicable, as far as I can see, solely from their being in complete opposition or antithesis to the attitude expressive of anger. (1872: 51).

Darwin explains the behaviors left over after the application of these two principles as the results of the "direct action" of the nervous system. Excess nerve energy built up in an emotional episode is released in behaviors such as sweating and trembling for no other reason than that it must go somewhere and that these channels are physiologically available for its release.

12.2.2   The emotions in classical ethology

The concept of instinctive behavior had little currency in the 1920s and 1930s when behaviorism was the dominant school in comparative psychology. It was revived by the founders of classical ethology, who saw themselves as the direct heirs of Darwin's work on mental evolution (Lorenz 1965). Their account of the evolution of emotional expression retains Darwin's principles, but reinterprets them to fit the theory of evolution as it emerged during the 1930s in the "modern synthesis" of Darwinism and Mendelian genetics. The principle of serviceable associated habits is transformed into the ethological concepts of "ritualization" and "derived activity" (Tinbergen 1952). Derived activities are behaviors that originally evolved for one purpose but were later selected for another purpose. Ritualized behaviors are derived activities that originally evolved to fulfill some practical function but which were later selected to function as signals. Thus, although piloerection in fear and rage does not make a human being appear larger to an opponent, it does communicate their emotional state. Derived activities require a special pattern of evolutionary explanation. They cannot be understood purely in terms of the function they currently perform and the selection pressures that currently maintain them in the population. This is particularly obvious in the case of signals. Having one's hairs stand on end is not intrinsically better as a signal of fear than smiling or laughing. This particular behavior was selected as a signal only because it was already associated with certain emotional states in the distant past. It was associated with those states not because it was a signal, but because it made the animal appear larger. The concept of ritualization allowed ethology to reconstruct Darwin's principle of serviceable associated habits whilst avoiding his commitment to the inheritance of acquired characteristics. Most of Darwin's descriptions of the pay-offs to the organism that cause certain emotional behaviors to become habitual are equally plausible as descriptions of the *selective advantage* that led to the evolution of those behaviors by natural selection. Darwin's other two principles are equally open to reinterpretation. The principle of antithesis is explained by the selective value of unambiguous signals. It is as important for a dog to signal that it wants to avoid conflict as it is for it to signal aggression. Hence there can be selection of behaviors merely because they look different from the behaviors that signal aggression. The principle of direct action was transformed into the ethological concept of a displacement activity. The early ethologists shared Darwin's view that instinctive motivations cause a build-up of mental energy that must be released in some behavior or other. An example commonly given is that of an angry cat that is unwilling to attack and begins to wash itself. Niko Tinbergen remarks: "I think it is probable that displacements do serve a function as outlets, through a safety valve, of dangerous surplus impulses" (1952: 23). This wholesale reinterpretation of Darwin's three principles works so smoothly and allows the retention of so much of the detail of his work that the early ethologists seem almost unaware of the differences between Darwin's theory and their own.

As well as modernizing Darwin's account of emotional expressions, classical ethology offered an account of the emotions themselves, an account encapsulated in Oskar Heinroth's epigram, "I regard animals as very emotional people with very little intelligence" (in Lorenz 1966: 180). Lorenz and his early followers believed that animal behavior is organized around a definite number of innate behavior sequences that are performed as a unit in the presence of a suitable releasing stimulus. In contrast to earlier instinct theorists, Lorenz denied that animals are motivated to seek the actual evolutionary goals of animal behavior – nutrition, shelter, procreation, and so forth. Instead, animals are motivated to perform specific innate behaviors, such as gathering nest materials or weaving a nest, behaviors that unbeknownst to them will lead to their obtaining shelter and other fitness-enhancing goals (Lorenz 1957 [1937]). Emotions are the psychological accompaniments to the performance of these innate behavior patterns. Thus, for example, the bird inserting a twig into the nest with a stereotyped, species-specific movement of the neck experiences a satisfying emotion (ibid.: 138). The earlier behaviors that have placed it in a position to perform this satisfying movement will be reinforced by this and performed more frequently in future. Conversely, a wild turkey's performance of its aerial predator response is accompanied by a negative emotion that will cause it to avoid in future the circumstances associated with performance of that behavior pattern. One of the most distinctive tenets of Lorenz's theory of emotion is that animals have many more kinds of emotion than humans (ibid.: 163). According to Lorenz, performance of a pleasurable innate behavior, such as catching prey or producing a territorial display, is frequently preceded by "appetitive behavior" in which the animal actively seeks out the "releaser" that will discharge the innate behavior pattern. In human beings, innate behavior sequences become increasingly vestigial and appetitive behaviors become elaborated into intelligent, goal-directed behaviors. Whereas a bird builds a nest because in a certain hormonal state it finds it rewarding to gather twigs and, quite separately, rewarding to stamp twigs that have been gathered into place, a human builds a shelter as a goal-directed behavior so that it can obtain the single, rewarding feeling of being "at home." The loss of so many highly specific innate behaviors in humans means the loss of many highly specific emotions. Instead of an emotional response to aerial threats of predation and a separate emotional response to terrestrial threats of predation, there is a single emotion of fear (ibid.). Similarly, whilst another primate might have separate emotions to accompany dominant threat and defensive, subordinate threat, humans have a single emotion of anger.

The emotion theory of Lorenz and his early followers did not survive the rejection in the 1960s of the whole classical ethological theory of motivation – the so-called "hydraulic model." However, the idea that emotion feelings play a critical role in some kind of internal conditioning process is an important part of many contemporary theories, such as that of Antonio Damasio discussed below. Another idea that has remained popular almost without interruption since Lorenz's work is that emotions are a phylogenetically ancient form of behavior control some parts of which have been retained in humans despite the later evolution of intelligent behavior. Finally, some of the arguments used against Lorenz's theory by the ethologist Robert Hinde have suggested a radically new way to look at emotion, as discussed below.

12.2.3 Ekman and "basic emotions"

Until the 1970s there was a fairly solid consensus in psychology and anthropology that human emotions vary widely across cultures. In stark contrast to the views of their contemporaries in the animal behavior community, many scientists in these fields believed that culturally specific emotional states were signaled in a culturally specific code of facial expressions and gestures acquired by the individual during their upbringing. This culturalist tradition was displaced in the late 1960s by a powerful revival in the Darwinian approach within psychology itself. Today, the work of Paul Ekman (1972) and his collaborators has produced an equally solid consensus that certain "basic emotions" are found in all human cultures. One famous experiment used subjects from the Fore language group in New Guinea with a minimum of prior contact with westerners and their cultural products. These subjects were given three photographs, each showing a face, and told a story which was designed to involve only one emotion. They were asked to pick the photograph showing the person in the story. This design has the advantage that no translation of the names of emotions is needed. The subjects were very successful in picking the photograph of the appropriate emotional expression. The New Guinean subjects were also asked to act out the facial behavior of the people described in the stories. Videotapes of their responses were shown to US college students. The students were generally accurate in their judgments of the emotion intended by the New Guineans. At around the same time, human ethologists demonstrated the early emergence of some of these expressions in human infants (Eibl-Eibesfeldt 1973) and primatologists reasserted the homology between human facial expressions and those of non-human primates (Chevalier-Skolnikoff 1973). The widely accepted "basic emotions" are fear, anger, surprise, sadness, joy, and disgust, where each term in this list refers to a brief, involuntary response with a distinctive facial expression.

Ekman (1984) sees facial expressions as components of *affect programs*. Each basic emotion corresponds to an affect program stored somewhere in the brain. When activated, this program coordinates a complex of actions that include facial expression, autonomic nervous system changes, expressive vocal changes, and muscular-skeletal responses such as flinching or orienting. The concept of an affect program inherits many of the features of the earlier ethological concept of an innate behavior sequence. Both concepts suggest that certain apparently complex behaviors are really atomic units of behavior that unfold in the same, stereotyped sequence whenever they are triggered by a suitable releasing stimulus. Ekman calls the mechanism that releases affect programs the "automatic appraisal mechanism." This is a specialized neural system that applies its own distinctive rules for stimulus evaluation to a limited set of data derived from the earliest stages of the processing of perceptual information. Considered together, the appraisal mechanisms and affect programs form a cognitive module in the sense favored by more recent evolutionary psychologists (Barkow et al. 1992).

The affect program theory was accompanied by a theory of the evolution of the emotion system. The system was interpreted as an ancient form of cognition that had originally operated on its own and had later been supplemented by higher cognitive functions. This view was supported by the neuroscientist Paul D. MacLean's (1952) theory of the "triune brain," according to which the emotions are located in the "paleomammalian" portions of the brain while higher cognitive functions are realized in more recently evolved, "neomammalian" structures. The survival of these ancient forms of behavior control in primates was explained by their value as fail-safe responses ensuring that vital behaviors are performed whenever necessary even if that means they are performed too often. This view of the emotion system as a collection of primitive but reliable fail-safe mechanisms remains influential in contemporary neuroscience (Panksepp 1998).

Ekman's account of basic emotions was a radical departure not only because of the earlier emphasis on cultural variation in emotion, but also because it reintroduced a typological account of the emotions themselves. Underlying emotional behavior, there are a determinate number of discrete emotions. In this respect Ekman's work shows the influence of Silvan S. Tomkins, whose arguments for reintroducing emotions as the "primary motivators" helped to rehabilitate emotion as a topic in mainstream psychology (Tomkins 1962). One of the most persistent lines of criticism of basic emotions theory has been from theorists who believe that emotional states do not fall into discrete types but are distributed more or less continuously along a number of axes such as pleasure and arousal (Russell and Fehr 1987; Russell 1997).

12.2.4 Sociobiology and the emotions

Sociobiology brought a new perspective to bear on the evolution of emotion in the 1970s and 1980s. It moved the focus of investigation from the basic emotions to the moral and quasi-moral emotions involved in human social interaction. Emotions such as trust, loyalty, guilt, and shame play an obvious role in mediating the competitive social interactions that were the focus of most research in human sociobiology. Numerous sociobiologists made brief comments to the effect that the moral emotions must have evolved as psychological mechanisms to implement evolutionary stable strategies of social interaction (Weinrich 1980). Robert A. Frank (1988) suggested that the moral emotions evolved as solutions to "commitment problems." A commitment problem arises when the winning strategy in an evolutionary interaction involves making a binding but conditional commitment to do something that would be against one's own interests if the condition were ever met. If such a commitment is to be credible, some special mechanism is needed which would cause the organism to act against its own interests. Frank suggests that emotions such as rage and vengefulness evolved to allow organisms to engage in credible deterrence, threatening self-destructive aggression to deter a more powerful aggressor. Conversely, emotions such as love and guilt evolved to allow organisms to engage in reciprocal altruism in situations where no retaliation is possible if one partner fails to reciprocate. Game-theoretic accounts of emotion such as Frank's have had a considerable influence on recent moral psychology (Gibbard 1990).

12.2.5 *Narrow evolutionary psychology and the emotions*

The term "evolutionary psychology" is frequently used in a narrow sense to refer to the specific approach championed by John Tooby and Leda Cosmides (Barkow et al. 1992). The mind is a collection of highly specialized, domain-specific cognitive devices, or modules, each adapted to a specific ecological problem in our evolutionary past. Like the emotion system, these modules operate on specific kinds of data using algorithms that differ from those used by other modules. Hence, evolutionary psychology endorses the affect program theory of basic emotions, but wants to go further, both by adding to the complexity of the known affect programs and by finding modular mechanisms underlying other emotional behaviors (Tooby and Cosmides 1990; Cosmides and Tooby 2000). David Buss has argued for the existence of a module for sexual jealousy – one of the additional modules predicted by Tooby and Cosmides. Buss argues that sexual jealousy has simple perceptual elicitors such as unusual scents, changed sexual behavior, excessive eye contact, and violation of rules governing personal space (2000: 45). The jealousy module uses special-purpose algorithms and, like the basic emotions, it functions as a fail-safe mechanism "designed to sound the alarm not just when an infidelity has been discovered, but also when the circumstances make it slightly more likely" (ibid.: 224). The module produces various forms of violence against female sexual partners, including, under conditions in which this behavior would have been adaptive in ancestral environments, murder. A noticeable contrast between these recent theories and more traditional accounts of the evolution of emotion is the absence of the idea that emotions represent a more primitive form of behavioral control that can be contrasted to rational, planned action. The emotions are seen as just another cognitive module reflecting details of the environment of evolutionary adaptedness. The idea that there are a few basic emotions and that these are components of more complex emotional responses has been criticized by some evolutionary psychologists, since, they argue, every emotion is a specific module designed to solve a unique evolutionary problem, and so all emotions are equally basic. Even Paul Ekman has allegedly fallen victim to the "standard social science model" and failed to appreciate that all aspects of our emotional lives are equally open to evolutionary explanation (Gaulin and McBurney 2001: 265–7).

12.2.6 The transactional theory of emotion

Evolutionary theory has also been used to defend the transactional view of emotion, according to which emotions are "moves" made in social interactions between organisms. The very idea that emotional behavior is the expression of discrete, underlying emotions is called into question by transactional theorists on evolutionary grounds and on the basis of animal models of emotion. The transactional view can be traced back to the work of Robert A. Hinde, an important figure in the development of the ethological tradition in animal behavior research. From the mid-1950s Hinde (1956) argued that Lorenz's and Tinbergen's classical model of animal motivation in terms of action-specific drives had outlived its usefulness. By the late 1960s analyses of animal behavior in terms of postulated underlying mechanisms had been replaced by adaptive models of the role of the behaviors themselves in interactions between animals and between animals and their environments. Behaviors that had previously been treated as the expression of instinctive drives were now treated as signals of the animal's likely future behavior or of its motivational state. But the application of evolutionary game theory to emotional behavior predicts that it will be designed to manipulate the expectations of other organisms rather than to transparently "express" the true motivational state of the organism. Rather than expressing the animal's underlying motivation, an emotional behavior sends a signal about the animal's motivation that is credible and the acceptance of which by other organisms would be advantageous: "[threat] signals make sense only if the threatening individual is attempting to bluff, deceive or manipulate the rival . . . or else is uncertain about what to do next because what he should do depends in part on the behavior of the other" (Hinde 1985b: 989). These ideas about animal communication were commonplace by the 1980s, but Hinde used them to question whether the folk psychology of human emotion is a good starting point for studying the animal behavior that appears homologous to emotional behavior in humans. Folk psychology leads us to expect that an animal engaged in an aggressive territorial display is "feeling angry." It also suggests that it is the basic stimulus situation – an intrusion into the territory – that produces anger and that not displaying anger involves a mental effort to control or suppress it, something that is difficult and may only partially succeed. Finally, folk psychology suggests that it is the same state – the anger – that motivates an attack performed by the animal on the intruder immediately after the display. Hinde suggested that while some emotional behavior in animals meets these expectations, much does not. Territorial displays were, he argued, a sign of ambivalent motivation – not so much an expression of aggression as part of the process that determines whether the animal becomes aggressive. Most importantly, the social context and the likely effect of the behavior do not merely determine whether the animal will express or suppress its "true feelings" but actually determine what emotion the animal has.

Although Hinde (1985a, 1985b) conducted his discussion mainly in terms of non-human animals, he clearly thought that these ideas were applicable to human emotion, and that the study of animal behavior could be used to loosen the grip of a model of emotion built into folk-psychological discourse and to allow the consideration of alternatives. Hinde's ideas have attracted the attention of psychologists interested in the role of social cognition in the production and modulation of emotion. The best known of these is probably Alan Fridlund (1994, 1997), who has developed his ideas as a critique of Ekman's model of basic emotions. Fridlund argues that facial expressions of emotion are unlikely to be obligate responses to simple stimuli situations in the way Ekman suggests, because such obligate communication of information would often not be in the interests of the organism. If human beings are able to determine one another's motivation from facial information, Fridlund argues, this must be the result of an "arms race" in which signaling organisms struggle to hide their motivation whilst recipients struggle to discover it. Fridlund's argument is certainly in line with the fundamental orientation of the game-theoretic literature on animal communication. However, evolutionary theory is notorious for its inability to predict the course of evolutionary change and it would be a mistake to give this theoretical argument much weight in comparison to empirical studies of the reliability, or lack thereof, with which people recognize one another's emotions. Transactional theorists have tried to meet this challenge with empirical studies of the importance of context in the interpretation of facial expression (Russell and Fernández-Dols 1997). They argue that observers read emotional significance into faces in the light of their understanding of the social interaction in which the face occurs. While it is clear that context is important and that people are often unaware of its role, it also seems undeniable that people, like other primates, do derive some information about the motivation and action tendencies of other organisms from facial behavior itself. This may be the result of an "arms race" in which signal recipients have outcompeted signal senders, but is probably in large part due to the fact that, as Hinde recognized, communicative interactions are not purely competitive. Evolutionary "games" range from zero-sum games to games of almost pure coordination, and the evolutionary games that have shaped facial expressions lie at various points on that continuum.

Fridlund's own empirical work has concentrated on the role of social context in the production of emotional behavior. He and other transactional theorists have documented audience effects on the production of the basic emotions and have argued that this is inconsistent with the affect program theory. For example, smiling is more strongly predicted by the kind of social interaction taking place at some point in time than by the degree of subjective satisfaction felt by the smiling person. In a series of ingenious experiments Fridlund has also tried to show that solitary displays of facial behavior are predicted by the presence of an "audience in the head" – potential social interactants who are the focus of the solitary person's thoughts (Fridlund et al. 1990). Fridlund frames these results as a refutation of basic emotion theory, but it is not clear that the results support this interpretation. It is true that Ekman has argued that the "display rules" that modulate emotional behaviors according to social context are acquired, culturally specific, and do not interfere with the actual internal working of the automatic appraisal mechanism and the affect programs (see below). But there is nothing to prevent an affect program theorist from building audience effects into the evolved "emotion module" itself. Emotional behavior exhibits audience effects in many organisms in which it seems much more likely that they are part of the evolved emotion system itself than that they are acquired behaviors – organisms such as domestic chickens (Marler 1997).

In his definitive review of the animal communication literature, Mark Hauser has also argued that Fridlund and Ekman's views are consistent. He has suggested that Fridlund's arguments bear on questions about the biological function of emotional behavior, whilst Ekman's affect program model is concerned with the mechanisms that produce that behavior (Hauser 1996: 495–6). This undoubtedly explains some part of their disagreement. In some places, however, Fridlund does seem to be discussing the nature of the underlying emotional processes and not merely their biological function. The broader, transactional perspective on emotion certainly involves a challenge to standard ideas about the psychological processes underlying emotional behavior. An angry person has perceived that a wrong has been done to them and is motivated to right that wrong or to obtain redress for it. To behave angrily *because* of the social effects of that behavior is to be angry insincerely. This, however, is precisely what transactional theories of emotion propose: emotions are "nonverbal strategies of identity realignment and relationship reconfiguration" (Parkinson 1995: 295). While this sounds superficially like the better-known idea that emotions are "social constructions" (learnt social roles), the evolutionary rationale for the emotions view, and the existence of audience effects in non-human animals, warn against any facile identification of the view that emotions are social transactions with the view that they are learnt or highly variable across cultures. Indeed, the transactional view may seem less paradoxical to many people once the idea that emotions are strategic, social behaviors is separated from the idea that they are learnt behaviors or that they are intentional actions.

12.3 The Universality of Emotion

12.3.1 Why it matters

Emotions are widely believed to be a critical element of moral agency and of aesthetic response. The claim that all healthy people display, recognize, and respond to the same emotions has been used to support the view that moral and aesthetic judgments can have universal validity. Conversely, if human emotions are as diverse as the concepts of emotion embodied in different languages and if humans can only understand the expressive repertoire of their own cultural group, this would seem to support cultural relativism about ethics and aesthetics.

12.3.2   Ekman's "neurocultural theory"

Ekman and his collaborators have handled cultural differences in the expression of basic emotions with the concept of a *display rule*, a concept exemplified in another of their well-known experiments (Ekman 1971, 1972). Neutral and stress-inducing films were shown to 25 American and 25 Japanese college students whilst they were alone in a room. The repertoire of facial behaviors shown during the stress phase by the two sets of subject was very similar. However, when an experimenter was introduced into the room and allowed to ask questions about the subject's emotions as the stress film was shown again, the facial behavior of the Japanese diverged radically from that of the Americans. Videotapes showed the momentary occurrence of negative emotional expressions and their replacement with polite smiles. This exemplifies an important feature of the display rule conceptualization of cultural differences: the evolved expressions remain intact but interact with culturally specific behaviors to determine the observable pattern of facial action. Attempts to disguise emotions are subject to "leakage" from the operation of the involuntary emotional response. Such attempts to suppress emotional behavior can only operate by simultaneously using the muscles involved in the expression for some other purpose. They cannot interfere with the actual operation of the emotion system. I have discussed above the possibility that social context might play a role in the actual operation of this system. This is, of course, entirely consistent with the further operation of display rules of the kind exemplified in the experiment just outlined.

12.3.3   Social constructionism about emotions

Cultural relativism about emotions was revived in the 1980s as part of a broader interest in the social construction of mental phenomena. This led to the first real involvement by analytic philosophers in the debate over universality, since the new arguments for social constructionism were as much conceptual as empirical (Solomon 1984; Harré 1986). One influential argument starts from the widely accepted idea that an emotion involves a cognitive evaluation of the stimulus. In that case, it is argued, cultural differences in how stimuli are represented will lead to cultural differences in emotion. If two cultures think differently about danger, then, since fear involves an evaluation of a stimulus as dangerous, fear in these two cultures will be a different emotion. Adherents of Ekman's basic emotions theory are unimpressed by this argument since they define emotions by their behavioral and physiological characteristics and allow that there is a great deal of variation in what triggers the same emotion in different cultures. Social constructionists also define the domain of emotion in a way that makes basic emotions research less relevant. The six or seven basic emotions seem to require minimal cognitive evaluation of the stimulus. Social constructionists often refuse to regard these physiological responses as emotions in themselves, reserving that term for the broader cognitive state of a person involved in a social situation in which they might be described as, for example, angry or jealous. It is thus unclear whether the debate between the constructionists and their universalist opponents is more than merely semantic. One side has a preference for tractable, reductive explanations, even if these are of limited scope, and the other is concerned that science may neglect the social and cultural aspects of human emotion.

12.3.4 Conceptual confusions in the debates over universality

Ekman's work and subsequent discussion have helped to clarify some of the issues about the universality of emotion. The affect programs have the same output across cultures, but they do not have the same input. There are some universal elicitors of affect programs in childhood, such as unexpected loud noises, which elicit fear. There are also systematic biases in the conditioning of affect program responses that could lead to a convergence in the eliciting conditions for adult responses (Öhman 1993). The general picture, however, is that affect programs come to be associated with whatever stimuli locally fulfill a broad functional role, so that the fear affect program comes to be associated with whatever locally constitutes a threat, the disgust response with whatever locally appears noxious or unclean, and so forth. The universality of basic emotions does not, therefore, imply that there are no cultural differences in what leads to emotion. Further clarification results from distinguishing the question of whether emotions are pan-cultural (found in all cultures) from the question of whether emotions are monomorphic (found in all healthy individuals). The types of evidence normally gathered by universalists are designed to show that emotions are pan-cultural and have little bearing on the question of monomorphicity. Emotions might be pan-cultural but still be like blood type or eye color, with several different types of individual in each population. Models of the evolution of social emotions typically predict that competing types will be maintained in the same population through competition. It is surprising that the issue of whether emotions have evolved is still so strongly linked to the issue of whether there is a single, universal, human emotional nature.

The debate over universality could also be clarified by abandoning the last vestiges of the traditional dichotomy between learnt and innate behaviors. Some critics of the affect program theory have argued that a biological perspective on emotion is inappropriate merely because the emergence and maintenance of emotional responses depends upon environmental factors (Ratner 1989). Conversely, evidence that emotions are pan-cultural and thus likely to be the products of evolution is still thought to imply that these emotions are genetically determined and resistant to modification by environmental changes. These inferences ignore the facts that the environment plays a rich and constructive role in the development of even the most stereotypically biological traits, such as bodily morphology or sexual behavior. Evolved emotions, like the rest of evolved psychology, will likely make use of many reliable features of the environment of the developing child in order to construct and maintain themselves. They will be open to cultural and individual variation as a result of changes in these features, as well as through genetic variation. Narrow evolutionary psychologists have embraced this idea and suggested that psychological differences between cultures may represent different options available within a flexible program for development designed by evolution. This idea, however, does not allow that environmental changes may produce emotional phenotypes that have no specific evolutionary history and so do not form part of the evolved program for development. To get around this difficulty, I have suggested that questions of universality can often be usefully reframed in terms of the Darwinian concept of *homology* (Griffiths 1997: 135). Two emotional responses are homologous if they are modified forms of a response in a common ancestor of those individuals or cultures. Using the concept of homology avoids sterile disputes about how similar two responses must be to count as "the same" response. If two responses are homologous, they share an evolutionary history, and no matter how far they have diverged since then, that shared history can be brought to bear in explaining the common features that they have retained.

12.4 The Emotions in Cognitive Science

12.4.1 *The resurgence of the feeling theory*

Recent work in cognitive neuroscience has shed new light on the relationship between emotion and cognition and led to a revival of the feeling theory of emotion. Antonio Damasio has argued that practical reasoning is dependent on the capacity to experience emotion. Patients with bilateral lesions to the prefrontal cortex show both reduced emotionality and a diminished ability to allocate cognitive resources in such a way as to solve real world problems. They do not, however, have deficits in abstract reasoning ability. Damasio (1994) interprets these findings as showing that emotion plays an essential role in labeling both data and goals for their relevance to the task in hand. These suggestions have aroused interest in cognitive scientists who have seen in "affective computing" a possible solution to the "frame problem": the problem of choosing all and only the relevant data without assessing all the available data for possible relevance (Picard 1997). Damasio's theory bears a resemblance to some of the philosophical "seeing as" theories that identify emotions with heuristic biases in cognition. In contrast to those theories, however, Damasio sees emotions themselves as feelings. This is important, since if emotions functioned cognitively, then his proposal would be that cognitive priorities are assigned by calculating what is most relevant and important. This would not be a solution to the frame problem, but an instance of that problem. Damasio avoids this trap by using emotion feelings to prioritize cognition. He describes a class of "primary emotions" that bear a strong affinity to Ekman's basic emotions. Damasio envisages emotional development as a process in which the feelings associated with the basic emotions become attached to particular cognitive states giving rise to cognition/feeling composites that he labels "secondary emotions." Damasio has so far given only a suggestive outline of his theory and it remains to be seen whether this sketch can be developed into a workable model of cognitive processes. Attempts to expand on Damasio's ideas to date resemble traditional behavior conditioning with thoughts taking the place of behaviors and emotion feelings acting as reinforcers. The limitations of conditioning models as explanations of complex cognitive performances are well known.

12.4.2 *Neurological support for twin-pathway models of emotion*

One of the most heated controversies in emotion theory in the 1980s concerned Robert Zajonc's "affective primacy thesis" (1980). Zajonc showed that subjects could acquire preferences for subliminal stimuli while showing no ability to recognize those stimuli when they were presented for longer periods. He argued that, in the normal case, two separate pathways led to emotional responses and paradigmatic cognitive responses such as conscious awareness and recall. Zajonc's claims were controversial because of the widespread view that an emotion essentially involves an "evaluation" of the stimulus, something that was taken to be a paradigmatically cognitive process (Lazarus 1982; Lazarus et al. 1984; Zajonc 1984). Zajonc's concept of twin pathways to cognition and emotion has obvious similarities to Ekman's proposal that an "automatic appraisal mechanism" is associated with the basic emotions and operates independently of the formation of conscious or reportable judgments about the stimulus situation. In more recent years, Joseph LeDoux's (1996) detailed mapping of the neural pathways involved in fear conditioning has confirmed something like Zajonc's twin-pathway model for fear. Information about the stimulus activates many aspects of emotional response via a fast, "low road" through sub-cortical structures, amongst which the amlygdala is particularly important. A slower, "high road" activates cortical structures and is essential for longer-term, planned, and often conscious responses to the same stimulus. Le Doux's findings suggest that at least for certain basic emotions the idea that an emotion involves a cognitive evaluation of the stimulus needs to be replaced with the idea that it involves two evaluations, which can conflict and which have complimentary but independent cognitive functions. Twin-pathway models also provide some support for the many evolutionary accounts that see the basic emotions as "quick and dirty" solutions to common survival problems.

12.5 Is Emotion a Natural Kind?

Damasio has defined an emotion as "a specifically caused transition of the organism state" (1999: 282). Confronted by similar definitions, Fridlund has remarked: "Here, the logical question is what *isn't* emotion. Emotion has, in fact, replaced Bergson's *élan vital* and Freud's *libido* as the energetic basis of all human life" (1994: 185). For many theorists, emotion has indeed become synonymous with motivation as a whole. Damasio is well aware of this situation and is self-consciously using a familiar term for his own purposes in order to facilitate communication in what he sees as a period of conceptual upheaval (Damasio 1999: 341). Given the extreme difficulty of, for example, distinguishing between mood and emotion or deciding whether (some?) desires are emotions except in the light of an actual theory of the emotions, adopting Damasio's broad definition as a starting point for inquiry has something to recommend it. I have argued elsewhere, however, that the scientific investigation of the domain of affective phenomena has been hindered by a continued belief that "the emotions" are a unitary kind of psychological state (Griffiths 1997). Science aims to group phenomena into "natural kinds": categories about which there are many, reliable generalizations to be discovered. The folk-psychological domain of emotion is so diverse that it is unlikely that all the psychological states in that domain form a natural kind. Hence there will be few if any reliable generalizations about emotion or, in other words, no theory of emotion in general. Scientific progress would be served by dividing up the domain and investigating groups of phenomena that are likely to form natural kinds, as has occurred in research into memory. New, more specific concepts will be required to replace the emotion concept and a central role for philosophers of emotion is to facilitate this kind of conceptual revision.

Most philosophers of emotion see no serious problem with the category of emotion, although they admit that it is vague and covers a diverse range of phenomena. Their concern is with the word "emotion" in everyday language and the concept that lies behind it. Philosophical analyses of the emotion concept are in reasonable agreement with those produced by psychologists studying the use of the term "emotion" in western cultures (Fehr and Russell 1984). There are clear paradigms of emotion, such as love, happiness, anger, fear, and sadness, and most philosophers define emotion so as to include these. Their definitions disagree over the same cases that produce disagreement between subjects in empirical studies, cases such as pride, hope, lust, pain, and hunger. Philosophical definitions include features that psychologists have argued are part of the prototype of the emotion concept. Emotions are directed onto external states of affairs, are relatively short-lived, and have an evaluative aspect to them, such that their objects are judged to be either attractive or aversive. Most definitions also provide a role for emotion feelings. Hence philosophers, like ordinary speakers, can achieve a reasonable level of agreement about what counts as an emotion, as opposed to a mood, a desire, or an intention. Whether the psychological states grouped together in this way form a single, productive object of scientific investigation and whether other cultures conceptualize emotion in the same way remains to be seen.

12.6 Conclusion

The philosophical psychology of emotion is a thriving field, with a large number of books and articles appearing each year. There is a trend toward closer integration with the sciences of the mind, an integration of the kind familiar from the philosophical psychology of cognition, perception, and action. The evolutionary psychology of emotion has received philosophical attention in recent years (Griffiths 1997; Horst 1998; Evans 2001), as has the potential of emotion to challenge views in cognitive science derived from the study of cognition (Delancey 2001; Evans, in press). The emotion theories proposed by neuroscientists on the basis of recent advances in affective neuroscience have also been exposed to philosophical scrutiny (Prinz, forthcoming). More traditional philosophical work, oriented towards issues in ethics and aesthetics, has also begun to draw on the claims of affective neuroscience, perhaps because Damasio's claim that emotion and rationality are inseparable resonates so strongly with older philosophical views (Blackburn 1998; Nussbaum 2001).

References

Barkow, J. H., Cosmides, L., and Tooby, J. (eds.) (1992). *The Adapted Mind: Evolutionary Psychology and the Generation of Culture*. Oxford: Oxford University Press.

Blackburn, S. (1998). *Ruling Passions: A Theory of Practical Reasoning*. Oxford and New York: Oxford University Press.

Buss, D. M. (2000). *The Dangerous Passion: Why Jealousy is as Essential as Love and Sex*. New York: Simon and Schuster.

Calhoun, C. (1984). "Cognitive Emotions?" In C. Calhoun and R. C. Solomon (eds.), *What is an Emotion: Classic Readings in Philosophical Psychology*. New York: Oxford University Press.

Chevalier-Skolnikoff, S. (1973). "Facial Expression of Emotion in Non-human Primates." In P. Ekman (ed.), *Darwin and Facial Expression: A Century of Research in Review*. New York and London: Academic Press: 11–89.

Cosmides, L. and Tooby, J. (2000). "Evolutionary Psychology and the Emotions." In M. Lewis and J. M. Haviland-Jones (eds.), *Handbook of the Emotions*, 2nd edn. New York and London: Guildford Press: 91–115.

Damasio, A. R. (1994). *Descartes Error: Emotion, Reason and the Human Brain*. New York: Grosset/Putnam.

—— (1999). *The Feeling of What Happens: Body and Emotion in the Making of Consciousness*. New York: Harcourt Brace.

Darwin, C. (1872). *The Expressions of Emotions in Man and Animals*, 1st edn. New York: Philosophical Library.

—— (1981/1871). *The Descent of Man and Selection in Relation to Sex*, Facsimile of the 1st edn. Princeton: Princeton University Press.

De Sousa, R. (1987). *The Rationality of Emotions*. Cambridge, MA: MIT Press.

Deigh, J. (1994). "Cognitivism in the Theory of Emotions." *Ethics*, 104: 824–54.

Delancey, C. (2001). *Passionate Engines: What Emotions Reveal About Mind and Artificial Intelligence*. New York and Oxford: Oxford University Press.

Eibl-Eibesfeldt, I. (1973). "Expressive Behaviour of the Deaf and Blind Born." In M. von Cranach and I. Vine (eds.), *Social Communication and Movement*. London and New York: Academic Press: 163–94.

Ekman, P. (1971). "Universals and Cultural Differences in Facial Expressions of Emotion." In J. K. Cole (ed.), *Nebraska Symposium on Motivation 4*. Lincoln, Nebraska: University of Nebraska Press: 207–83.

—— (1972). *Emotions in the Human Face*. New York: Pergamon Press.

—— (1984). "Expressions and the Nature of Emotions." In K. Scherer and P. Ekman (eds.), *Approaches to Emotions*. Hillsdale, NJ: Erlbaum.

Evans, D. (2001). *Emotion: The Science of Sentiment*. Oxford: Oxford University Press.

—— (In Press). *Rethinking Emotion: A Study in the Foundations of Mind*. Cambridge, MA: MIT Press.

Fehr, B., and Russell, J. A. (1984). "Concept of Emotion Viewed from a Prototype Perspective." *Journal of Experimental Psychology: General*, 113; 464–86.

Frank, R. H. (1988). *Passions Within Reason: The Strategic Role of the Emotions*. New York: Norton.

Fridlund, A. (1994). *Human Facial Expression: An Evolutionary View*. San Diego: Academic Press.

—— (1997). "The New Ethology of Human Facial Expressions." In J. A. Russell and J. M. Fernández-Dols (eds.), *The Psychology of Facial Expressions*. Cambridge: Cambridge University Press: 103–29.

Fridlund, A. J., Schaut, J. A., Sabini, J. P., Shenker, J. I., Hedlund, L. E., and Knauer, M. J. (1990). "Audience Effects on Solitary Faces During Imagery: Displaying to the People in Your Head." *Journal of Nonverbal Behaviour*, 14(2): 113–37.

Gaulin, S. J. C. and McBurney, D. H. (2001). *Psychology: An Evolutionary Approach*. Upper Saddle River, NJ: Prentice Hall.

Gibbard, A. (1990). *Wise Choices, Apt Feelings: A Theory of Normative Judgment*. Cambridge, MA: Harvard University Press.

Greenspan, P. (1988). *Emotions and Reasons: An Inquiry into Emotional Justification*. New York: Routledge.

Griffiths, P. E. (1989). "The Degeneration of the Cognitive Theory of Emotion." *Philosophical Psychology*, 2 (3): 297–313.

—— (1997). *What Emotions Really Are: The Problem of Psychological Categories*. Chicago: University of Chicago Press.

Harré, R. (1986). "An Outline of the Social Constructionist Viewpoint." In Harré (ed.), *The Social Construction of Emotion*. Oxford: Oxford University Press: 2–14.

Hauser, M. D. (1996). *The Evolution of Communication*. Cambridge, MA: MIT Press.

Hinde, R. A. (1956). "Ethological Models and the Concept of 'Drive'." *British Journal for the Philosophy of Science*, 6: 321–31.

—— (1985a). "Expression and Negotiation." In G. Zivin (ed.), *The Development of Expressive Behavior*. New York: Academic Press: 103–16.

—— (1985b). "Was 'The Expression of Emotions' a Misleading Phrase?" *Animal Behaviour*, 33: 985–92.

Horst, S. (1998). "Our Animal Bodies." In P. A. French and H. K. Wettstein (eds.), *The Philosophy of Emotion*. Notre Dame, IN: University of Notre Dame Press.

Lazarus, R. S. (1982). "Thoughts on the Relations Between Emotion and Cognition." *American Psychologist*, 37: 1019–24.

Lazarus, R. S., Coyne, J. C., and Folkman, S. (1984). "Cognition, Emotion and Motivation: Doctoring Humpty Dumpty." In K. Scherer and P. Ekman (eds.), *Approaches to Emotions*. Hillsdale, NJ: Erlbaum: 221–37.

LeDoux, J. (1996). *The Emotional Brain: The Mysterious Underpinnings of Emotional Life*. New York: Simon and Schuster.

Lorenz, K. (1957 [1937]). "The Nature of Instinct." In C. H. Schiller (ed.), *Instinctive Behavior: The Development of a Modern Concept*. New York: International Universities Press: 129–75.

—— (1965). *Preface to "The Expression of the Emotions in Man and Animals" by Charles Darwin*. Chicago: University of Chicago.

—— (1966). *On Aggression*, trans. by M. K. Wilson. New York: Harcourt, Brace and World.

Lyons, W. (1980). *Emotion*. Cambridge: Cambridge University Press.

MacLean, P. D. (1952). "Some Psychiatric Implications of Physiological Studies on Frontotemporal Portions of the Limbic System (Visceral Brain)." *Electroencephlography and Clinical Neurophysiology*, 4: 407–18.

Marks, J. (1982). "A Theory of Emotions." *Philosophical Studies*, 42: 227–42.

Marler, P. (1997). "Animal Sounds and Human Faces: Do they have Anything in Common?" In J. A. Russell and J. M. Férnandez-Dols (eds.), *The Psychology of Facial Expression*. Cambridge: Cambridge University Press: 133–226.

Nussbaum, M. C. (2001). *Upheavals of Thought: The Intelligence of Emotions*. Cambridge and New York: Cambridge University Press.

Öhman, A. (1993). "Stimulus Prepotency and Fear: Data and Theory." In N. Birbaumer and A. Öhman (eds.), *The Organization of Emotion: Cognitive, Clinical and Psychological Perspectives*. Toronto: Hogrefe.

Panksepp, J. (1998). *Affective Neuroscience: The Foundations of Human and Animal Emotions*. Oxford and New York: Oxford University Press.

Parkinson, B. (1995). *Ideas and Realities of Emotion*. London and New York: Routledge.

Picard, R. (1997). *Affective Computing*. Cambridge, MA: MIT Press.

Prinz, J. (forthcoming). *Emotional Perception*. Oxford: Oxford University Press.

Ratner, C. (1989). "A Social Constructionist Critique of the Naturalistic Theory of Emotion." *Journal of Mind and Behaviour*, 10 (3): 211–30.

Russell, J. A. (1997). "Reading Emotion from and into Faces: Resurrecting a Dimensional-Contextual Perspective." In J. A. Russell and J. M. Fernández-Dols (eds.), *The Psychology of Facial Expression*. Cambridge: Cambridge University Press: 295–320.

Russell, J. A. and Fehr, B. (1987). "Relativity in the Perception of Emotion in Facial Expressions." *Journal of Experimental Psychology (General)*, 116: 223–37.

Russell, J. A. and Fernández-Dols, J. M. (1997). *The Psychology of Facial Expression*. Cambridge: Cambridge University Press.

Schachter, S. and Singer, J. E. (1962). "Cognitive, Social and Physiological Determinants of Emotional State." *Psychological Review*, 69: 379–99.

Solomon, R. (1976). *The Passions*. New York: Doubleday.

——(1984). "Getting Angry: The Jamesian Theory of Emotion in Anthropology." In R. A. Schweder and R. A. LeVine (eds.), *Culture Theory: Essays on Mind, Self and Emotion*. Cambridge: Cambridge University Press: 238–54.

Tinbergen, N. (1952). "Derived Activities: Their Causation, Biological Significance, Origin and Emancipation During Evolution." *Quarterly Review of Biology*, 27 (1): 1–32.

Tomkins, S. S. (1962). *Affect, Imagery and Consciousness*. New York: Springer.

Tooby, J. and Cosmides, L. (1990). "The Past Explains the Present: Emotional Adaptations and the Structure of Ancestral Environments." *Ethology and Sociobiology*, 11: 375–424.

Weinrich, J. D. (1980). "Towards a Sociobiological Theory of Emotions." In R. Plutchik and H. Kellerman (eds.), *Emotion: Theory, Research and Experience, vol. 1: Theories of Emotion*. New York: Academic Press: 113–40.

Zajonc, R. B. (1980). "Feeling and Thinking: Preferences Need no Inference." *American Psychologist*, 35: 151–75.

——(1984). "On the Primacy of Affect." In K. Scherer and P. Ekman (eds.), *Approaches to Emotion*. Hillsdale, NJ: Lawrence Erlbaum Associates: 259–70.

Chapter 13

Artificial Intelligence and the Many Faces of Reason

Andy Clark

13.1 Pulling a Thread

I shall focus this discussion on one small thread in the increasingly complex weave of artificial intelligence (AI) and philosophy of mind: the attempt to explain how rational thought is mechanically possible. This is, historically, the crucial place where AI meets philosophy of mind. But it is, I shall argue, a place in flux. For our conceptions of what rational thought and reason *are*, and of what kinds of mechanism might explain them, are in a state of transition. To get a sense of this sea change, I shall compare several visions and approaches, starting with what might be termed the Turing–Fodor conception of mechanical reason, proceeding through connectionism with its skill-based model of reason, then moving to issues arising from robotics, neuroscientific studies of emotion and reason, and work on "ecological rationality." As we shall see, there is probably both more, and less, to human rationality than originally met the eye.

First, though, the basic (and I do mean basic) story.

13.2 The Core Idea, Classically Morphed

One core idea, common to *all* the approaches I'll consider in this chapter, is that sometimes form can do duty for meaning. This is surely the central insight upon which all attempts to give a mechanical account of reason are based. Broadly understood, it is this same trick that is at work in logic, in the Turing Machine, in symbolic AI, in connectionist AI, and even in "anti-representationalist" robotics. The trick is to organize and orchestrate some set of non-semantically specifiable properties or features so that a device thus built, in a suitable environment, can end up displaying "semantic good behavior." The term "semantic good behavior" covers, intentionally, a wide variety of things. It covers the capacity to carry out deductive inferences, to make good guesses, to behave appropriately upon receipt of an input or stimulus, and so on. Anything that (crudely put) *looks like it knows what it is doing* is exhibiting semantic good behavior: cases include the logician who infers −A from (−A v B, −B), the person who chooses to take out an umbrella because they believe it will rain and desire to stay dry, the dog who chooses the food rather than the toxin, the robot that recovers its balance and keeps on walking after one leg is damaged. There's a *lot* of semantic good behavior around, and we understand some of it a whole lot better than the rest. Where, though, does *reason* come into the picture?

Reason-governed behavior is, arguably at least, a special subset of what I am calling semantic good behavior. It is Jerry Fodor's view, for example, that it was not until the work of Turing that we began to have a sense of how *rationality* (which I'll assume to mean reason-governed behavior) could be mechanically possible (for a nice capsule statement, see Fodor 1998: 204–5). Formal logic showed us that truth preservation could be insured simply by attending to form, not meaning. B follows from A and B *regardless* of what A means and what B means, and if your keep to rules defined over the shapes of symbols and connectives you will never infer a falsehood from true premises, even if you have no idea what either the premises or the conclusions are about. Turing, as Fodor notes, showed that for all such formally ("by shape") specifiable routines, a well-programmed machine could replace the human.

It is at about this point that what was initially just an assertion of physicalist faith (that somehow or other, semantic good behavior has always and everywhere an explanatorily sufficient material base) morphs into a genuine research program targeting reason-governed behavior. The idea, rapidly enshrined in the research program of classical, symbolic AI, was that reason could be mechanically explained as the operation of appropriate computational processes on symbols, where symbols are non-semantically indivisible items (items typed by form, shape, voltage, whatever) and computational processes are mechanical, automatic processes that recognize, write, and amend symbols in accordance with rules (which themselves, up to a certain point, can be expressed as symbols). In such systems, as Haugeland famously remarks, "if you take care of the syntax [the non-semantic features and properties] the semantics will take care of itself" (1981: 23). The core idea, as viewed through the lens of both Turing's remarkable achievements and then further developments in classical AI, thus began to look both more concrete, and less general. It became the idea, in Fodor's words, that "some, at least, of what makes minds rational is their ability to perform computations on thoughts; when thoughts . . . are assumed to be syntactically structured, and where 'computation' means formal operations in the manner of Turing" (1998: 205).

The general idea of using form (broadly construed) to do duty for meaning thus gently morphed into the Turing Machine-dominated vision of reading, writing, and transposing symbols: a vision which found full expression in early work in AI. Here we encounter Newell and Simon's (1976) depiction of intelligence as grounded in the operations of so-called *physical symbol systems*: systems in which non-semantically identifiable entities act as the vehicles of specific contents (thus becoming "symbols") and are subject to a variety of familiar operations (typically copying, combining, creating, and destroying the symbols, according to instructions). For example, the story-understanding program of Schank (1975) used a special event-description language to encode the kind of background knowledge needed to respond sensibly to questions about simple stories, thus developing a symbolic database to help it "fill in" the missing details.

Considered as stories about how rational, reason-guided thought is mechanically possible, the classical approach thus displays a satisfying directness. It explains semantically sensible thought transitions ("they enjoyed the meal, so they probably left a tip;" "it's raining, I hate the rain, so I'll take an umbrella") by imagining that each participating thought has an inner symbolic echo, and that these inner echoes share relevant aspects of the structure of the thought. As a result, syntax-sensitive processes can regulate processes of inference (thought-to-thought transitions) in ways that respect semantic relations between the thoughts.

13.3   The Core Idea, Non-classically Morphed

The idea that reason-guided thought transitions are grounded in syntactically driven operations on inner symbol strings has a famous competitor. The competing idea, favored by (many) researchers working with artificial neural networks, is that reason-guided thought transitions are grounded in the vector-to-vector transformations supported by a parallel web of simple processing elements. A proper expression of the full details of this contrast is beyond the scope of this chapter (see Clark 1989, 1993 for my best attempts). But we can at least note one especially relevant point of (I think) genuine contrast. It concerns what I'll call the "best targets" of the two approaches. For classical (Turing Machine-like) AI, the best targets are rational inferences that can be displayed and modeled in *sentential space*. By "sentential space" I mean an abstract space populated by meaning-carrying structures (interpreted syntactic items) that share the logical form of sentences: sequential strings of meaningful elements, in which different kinds of syntactic item reliably stand for different things, and in which the overall meaning is a function of the items (tokens) and their sequential order, including the modifying effects of other tokens (e.g. the "not" in "it is not raining"). Rational inferences that can be satisfyingly reconstructed in sentential space include all of Fodor's favorite examples (about choosing to take the umbrella, etc.), all cases of deductive inference defined over sentential expressions, and all cases of abductive inference (basically, good guessing) in which the link between premises and conclusions can be made by the creative retrieval or deployment of additional sentences (as in Schank's story-understanding program mentioned earlier).

The best targets for the artificial neural network approach, by contrast, are various species of reasonable "inference" in which the inputs are broadly speaking perceptual and the outputs are (often) broadly speaking motoric. Reasonable inferences of this kind are implicit in, for example, the cat's rapid assessment of the load-bearing capacity of a branch, leading to a swift and elegant leap to a more secure resting point, or the handwriting expert's rapid intuitive conviction that the signature is a forgery, a conviction typically achieved in advance of the conscious isolation of specific tell-tale signs.

This is not to say, however, that the connectionist approach is limited to the perceptuo-motor domain. Rather, the point is that its take on rational inference (and, more broadly, on rational choice) is structurally continuous with its take on perceptuo-motor skill. Reasoning and inference are reconstructed, *on all levels*, as (roughly speaking) processes of pattern-completion and pattern-evolution carried out by cascades of vector-to-vector transformations between populations of simple processing units. For example, a network exposed to an input depicting the visual features of a red-spotted young human face may learn to produce as output a pattern of activity corresponding to a diagnosis of measles. This diagnosis may lead, via a similar mechanism, to a prescription of penicillin. The vector-to-vector transformations involved are perfectly continuous (on this model) with those by which we perform more basic acts of recognition and control, as when we recognize a familiar face or coordinate visual proprioceptive inputs in walking. Such pattern-completing processes, carried out in networks of simple processing units connected by numerically weighted links, are prima facie quite unlike the sentential AI models in which a medical judgment (for example) might depend on the consultation of a stored set of rules and principles. One important source of the difference lies in the way the connectionist system typically *acquires* the connection weights that act both as knowledge-store and processing-engine. Such weightings are acquired by exposing the system to a wide range of exemplars (training instances): a regime which leads, courtesy of the special learning rules deployed, to the development of a *prototype-dominated knowledge base* (see Churchland 1989). What this means in practice is that the system learns to "think about" a domain in terms of the most salient features of a body of exemplar cases, and that its responses, judgments, and actions are guided by the perceived similarity of the current case to the patterns of features and responses most characteristic of the exemplars. And what this means, in turn, is that what such a system knows is seldom, if ever, neatly expressible as a set of sentences, rules, or propositions about the domain. Making the expert medical judgment, on this model, has more in common with knowing how to ride a bicycle than with consulting a set of rules in a symbolic database. A well-tuned connectionist network may thus issue judgments that are rationally appropriate but that nonetheless resist quasi-deductive sentential reconstruction as the conclusion of an argument that takes symbolic expressions as its premises. Such appropriate responses and judgments are, on this view, the fundament of reason, and of rationality. Lingua-form argument and inference is depicted as just a special case of this general prototype-based reasoning capacity, different only in that the target and training domain here involve the symbol strings of public speech and text.

Connectionism and classicism thus differ (at least in the characteristic incarnations I am considering) in their visions of reason itself. The latter depicts reason as, at root, symbol-guided state transitions in quasi-linguistic space. The former depicts reason as, at root, the development of prototype-style knowledge guiding vector-to-vector transformations in the same kinds of (typically) non-sentential space that also underlie perceptuo-motor response. Beneath this contrast, however, lies a significant agreement. Both camps agree that rational thoughts and actions involve the use of inner resources to represent salient states of affairs, and the use of transformative operations (keyed to non-semantic features of those internal representations) designed to yield further representations (in a cascade of vector-to-vector transformations in the connectionist case) and, ultimately, action.

13.4 Robotics: Beyond the Core?

Is it perhaps possible to explain reasoned action without appeal to inner, form-based vehicles of meaning at all? Might internal representations be tools we can live without?

Consider the humble house-fly. Marr (1982: 32–3, reported by McClamrock 1995: 85) notes that the fly gets by without in any sense encoding the knowledge that the action of flying requires the command to flap your wings. Instead, the fly's feet, when not in contact with ground, automatically activate the wings. The decision to jump thus automatically results (via abolition of foot contact) in the flapping of wings.

Now imagine such circuitry multiplied. Suppose the "decision to jump" is *itself* by-passed by e.g. directly wiring a "looming shadow" detector to the neural command for jumping. And imagine that the looming shadow detector is itself nothing but a dumb routine that uses the raw outputs of visual cells to compute some simple, perceptual invariant. Finally, imagine if you will a whole simple creature, made up of a fairly large number of such basic, automatic routines, but with the routines themselves orchestrated – by exactly the same kind of tricks – so that they turn each other on and off at (generally speaking) ecologically appropriate moments. For example, a "consume food" routine may be overridden by the "something looming-so-jump" routine, which in turn causes the "flap wings" routine, and so on. What you have imagined is, coarsely but not inaccurately, the kind of "subsumption architecture" favored by robotists such as Rodney Brooks (1991), and responsible for such provocative titles of articles as "Intelligence Without Representation" and slogans (now co-opted as movie titles!) such as "Fast, Cheap, and Out of Control."

It is not *at all* obvious, however, that such a story could (even in principle) be simply scaled-up so as to give us "rationality without representation." For one thing, it is not obvious when we should say of some complex inner state that it constitutes at least *some kind* of representation of events, or states of affairs. The house-fly wing-flapping routine looks like a simple reflex, yet even here there is room for someone to suggest that, given the evolutionary history of the reflex circuit, certain states of that circuit (the ones activated by the breaking of foot-surface contact) represent the fact that the feet have left the surface. What Brooks and others are really suggesting, it often seems, is rather the absence of a certain *type* of internal representation, viz. the broadly linguaform representations favored by classical AI.

A more fundamental difficulty, however, (which goes well beyond the vagueness of the term "internal representation") concerns the *kinds* of behavior that can plausibly be explained by any complex of reflex-like mechanisms. The problematic cases here are obviously deliberative reason and abstract thought. The kinds of behavior that might be involved include planning next year's family vacation, thinking about US gun control issues (e.g. "should gun manufacturers be held responsible for producing more guns than the known *legal* market requires?"), using mental images to count the number of windows in your Spanish apartment while relaxing on the River Thames, and so on. These cases are by no means all of a piece. But they share at least one common characteristic: they are all "representation hungry" (to use a term from Clark and Toribio 1994) in quite a strong sense. All these cases, on the face of it, require the brain to use internal *stand-ins* for external states of affairs, where a "stand-in," in this strong sense (see Clark and Grush 1999) is an item designed not just to carry information about some state of affairs (in the way that, e.g., the inner circuit might carry information about the breaking of foot-surface contact in the fly) but to allow the system to key its behavior to features of specific states of affairs *even in the absence of direct physical connection.* A system which must coordinate its activity with the distal (the windows in my Spanish apartment) and the non-existent (the monster in the tool-shed) is thus a good candidate for the use of (strong) internal representations: inner states that are meant to act as full-blooded stand-ins, not just as ambient information-carriers. (For some excellent discussion of the topics of connection and disconnection, see Smith 1996.) By contrast, nearly all (but see Stein 1994 and Beer 2000) the cases typically invoked to show representation-free adaptive response are cases in which the relevant behavior is continuously driven by, and modified by, ambient input from the state of affairs to which the behavior is keyed.

Rational behavior is, in some sense, behavior that is guided by, or sensitive to, reasons. Intuitively, this seems to involve some capacity to step back and assess the options; to foresee the consequences, and to act accordingly. But *this* vision of rationality ("deliberative rationality") places rational action squarely in the "representation-hungry" box. For future consequences, clearly, cannot directly guide current action (in the way that, say, an ambient light source may directly guide a photo-sensitive robot). Such consequences will be effective only to the extent that the system uses something else to stand-in for those consequences during the process of reasoning. And that, at least on the face of it, requires the use of internal representations in some fairly robust sense.

13.5 Emotions and Reason

A mechanical explanation of our capacities to display reason-guided behavior cannot, it seems, afford to dispense with the most basic notion of inner stand-ins capable of directing behavior and inference in the absence of the events and states of affairs concerned. Work in connectionism and real-world robotics is best viewed (I believe) as expanding our conceptions of the possible *nature* of such stand-ins, and as highlighting the many ways in which bodily and environmental structures, motion, and active intervention may all serve to transform the *problems* that the brain needs to solve. The use of pen and paper, for example, may greatly alter the problems that the brain needs to solve when confronting complex arithmetical tasks, when planning a long-term strategy, and even when reasoning about gun control. But such transformations do not by-pass the need for internal structure-sensitive operations defined over inner content-bearing vehicles: rather, they reshape the problems that such an inner economy needs to solve.

The stress on reason-sensitive thought and inference can, however, blind us to the crucial importance of a further dimension of human cognition. For human reason is tightly, perhaps inextricably, interwoven with human emotion. Doing justice to this significant interaction is one of the two major challenges for the next generation of AI models.

Emotions were long regarded (at least in a broadly Kantian tradition) as the enemy of reason. And we certainly do speak of (for example) judgments being clouded by envy, acts as being driven by short-lived bursts of fury and passion rather than by reasoned reflection, and so on. It is becoming increasingly clear, however, that the normal contributions of emotion to rational response are far from detrimental. They are, in fact, best seen as part of the mechanism of reason itself. Consider, to take a famous example, the case of Phineas Gage. Gage was a nineteenth-century railway worker whose brain was damaged when an iron rod was driven through his skull in an explosion. Despite extensive damage to prefrontal cortex, the injury left Gage's language, motor skills, and basic reasoning abilities intact. It seemed as if he had escaped all cognitive compromise. Over subsequent years, however, this proved sadly incorrect. Gage's personal and professional life took noticeable turns for the worse. He lost jobs, got into fights, failed to plan for the future and to abide by normal conventions of social conduct, became a different and markedly less successful person. The explanation, according to Damasio et al. (1994) was that the damage to prefrontal cortex had interfered with a system of (what they termed) "somatic markers" – brain states that tie the image/trace of an event to a kind of gut reaction (aversion or attraction, according to the outcome). This marker system operates automatically (in normal subjects) influencing both on-the-spot response and the array of options that we initially generate for further consideration and reflection. It is active also – and crucially – when we imagine an event or possible action, yielding a positive or negative affective signal that manifests itself in (among other things) galvanic skin response. Gage, it is hypothesized, would have lacked such responses, and would not have had his reasoning and deliberations constrained by the automatic option-pruning and choice-influencing operations of the somatic marker system gradually acquired during his lifetime's experience of social and professional action. Contemporary studies seem to confirm and clarify this broad picture. E. V. R. (a patient displaying similar ventromedial frontal damage) shares Gage's profile. Though scoring well on standard IQ and reasoning tests, E. V. R. likewise lost control of his professional and social life. In an interesting series of experiments (Bechera et al. 1997) normal controls and prefrontally lesioned patients played a card game involving (unbeknownst to the subjects) two winning decks and two losing decks. Subjects could choose which deck (A, B, C, or D) to select cards from. After a little play, the normal controls fix on the better decks (smaller immediate rewards, but fewer secure penalties and more reliable in the long term) and rapidly show a heightened galvanic skin response when reaching for the "bad" decks. This skin response, interestingly, appears before the subjects could articulate any reasons for preferring the better decks. E. V. R., by contrast, shows no such skin response. And this absence of somatic cues seems to interfere with his capacity to choose the better decks *even once his conscious mind has figured it all out* – he will know that A and B are losing decks, yet continue to favor them during play.

There is obviously much to discuss here. Are these cases best understood, as Churchland suggests, as arising from "the inability of emotions to affect [the patient's] reason and decision-making" (1998: 241)? Or is it a case of *inappropriate* emotional involvement – the triumph of short-term reward over deferred (but greater) gratification? Perhaps these are not really incompatible: either way it is the lack of the on-the-spot unconscious negative responses (evidenced by the flat galvanic skin responses) that opens the door to cognitive error.

Human reason, it seems fair to conclude, is not best conceived as the operation of an emotionless logic engine occasionally locked into combat with emotional outbursts. Instead, truly rational behavior (in humans) is the result of a complex and iterated series of interactions in which deliberative reason and subtle (often quite unconscious) affect-laden responses conspire to guide action and choice. Emotional elements (at least as suggested by the somatic marker hypothesis) function, in fact, to help rational choice operate across temporal disconnections. Somatic markers thus play a role deeply analogous to internal representations (broadly construed); they allow us to reason projectively, on the basis of past experience. What could be more appropriately deemed part of the mechanism of reason itself than something that allows us to imaginatively probe the future, using the hard-won knowledge of a lifetime's choices and experiences all neatly distilled into a network of automatic affective reverberations?

13.6   Global Reasoning

A further source of complication concerns what Fodor (1983: 111) calls "global properties of belief systems." AI, according to Fodor, confronts a special problem hereabouts. For the Turing Machine model of rational inference (recall section 13.2 above) is said to be irredeemably *local*. It is great at explaining how the thought (syntactically tokened) that it is raining gives way to the thought that an umbrella is indicated. It is great, too, at explaining (given a few classical assumptions – see Fodor and Pylyshyn 1988) why the space of possible thoughts (for an individual) exhibits a certain kind of closure under recombination – the property of "systematicity," wherein those who can think aRb typically also think bRa, and so on. But where current AI-based models crash and burn, Fodor insists, is when confronting various forms of more globally sensitive inference. For example, cases of abductive inference in which the best explanation for some event might be hidden anywhere in the entire knowledge base of the system: a knowledge base deemed too large by far to succumb to any process of exhaustive search. Fodor rejects classical attempts to get around this problem by the use of heuristics and simplifying assumptions (such as the use of "frames" – see Minsky 1975; Fodor 1983: 116) arguing that this simply relocates the problem as a problem of "executive control" – viz. how to find the *right* frames (or whatever) at the right time. Since even the decision to take the umbrella against the rain is potentially sensitive to countervailing information coming from anywhere in the knowledge base, Fodor is actually left with a model of mechanical rationality which (as far as I can see) can have nothing to say about any genuine but non-deductive case of reasoning whatsoever. The Fodor–Turing model of rational mechanism works best, as Fodor frequently seems to admit, only in the domain of "informationally encapsulated systems" – typically, perceptual systems that process a restricted range of input signals in a way allegedly insensitive to all forms of top-down knowledge-driven inference. Hardly the seat of reason, one cannot help but feel.

Give this pessimistic scenario – enshrined in Fodor's "first law of the non-existence of cognitive science: the more global . . . a cognitive process is, the less anybody understands it. Very global processes . . . aren't understood at all" (1983: 107) – it is not surprising to find some theorists (Churchland 1989: 178; Clark 1993: 111) arguing for connectionist approaches as one solution to this problem of "globally sensitive reason." Such approaches are independently rejected by Fodor for failing to account for systematicity and local syntax-sensitive inference. But it now seems to me (though this is a long story – see Clark, 2002) that the problem of global abductive inference really does affect connectionist approaches too. Very roughly, it emerges therein as a problem of routing and searching: a question of how to use information, which could be drawn from anywhere in the knowledge base, to sculpt and redirect the flow of processing itself, ensuring that the right input probes are processed by the right neural sub-populations at the right times.

Churchland (1989) and Clark (1993) depict this problem as solved (in the connectionist setting) because "relevant aspects of the creature's total information are automatically accessed by the coded stimuli themselves" (Churchland 1989: 187). And certainly, input probes will (recall section 13.3 above) automatically activate the prototypes that best fit the probe, along whatever stimulus dimensions are represented. But this is at best a first step in the process of rational responsiveness. For having found these best syntactic fits (for this is still, ultimately, a form-driven process), it is necessary to see if crucially important information is stored elsewhere, unaccessed because of a lack of surface matching the probe. And it is this step which, I think, does most of the work in the types of case with which Fodor is (properly) concerned.

The good news, which I make much of in Clark (2002) but cannot pursue here, is that this second step now looks potentially computationally tractable, thanks to an odd combination of neuro-connectionist research and an innovative "second-order" search procedure developed for use on the world wide web (Kleinberg 1997). The idea is to combine a first pass (dumb, pattern-matching, syntax-based) search with a follow-up search based on the patterns of connections into and away from the elements identified on the first pass. But the point, for present purposes, is simply to acknowledge the special problems that truly globally sensitive processing currently presents to all existing models of the neural computations underlying human reason.

13.7 Fast and Frugal Heuristics

It might reasonably be objected, however, that this whole vision of human rationality is wildly inflated. Very often, we *don't* manage to access the relevant items of knowledge; very often, we *don't* choose that which makes us happiest, or most successful; we even (go on, admit it) make errors in simple logic. What is nonetheless surprising is that we very often do as well as we do. The explanation, according to recent theories of "ecological rationality," is our (brain's) use of simple, short-cut strategies designed to yield good results given the specific constraints and opportunities that characterize the typical contexts of human learning and human evolution. A quick example is the so-called "recognition heuristic." If you ask me which city has the larger population, San Diego or San Antonio, I may well assume San Diego, simply because I have *heard of* San Diego. Should I recognize both names, I might deploy a different fast and frugal heuristic, checking for other cues. Maybe I think a good cue is "have I heard of their symphony?" and so on. The point is that I don't try any *harder* than that. There may be multiple small cues and indicators, which I could try to "factor in." But doing so, according to an impressive body of research (see e.g. Chase et al. 1998) is likely to be both time-consuming and (here's the cruncher) unproductive. I'll probably choose *worse* by trying to replace the fast and frugal heuristic with something slower and (apparently) wiser.

It is not yet clear how (exactly) this important body of research should impact our vision of just *what* you need to explain in order to explain how rationality is mechanically possible. A likely alliance might see fans of robotics and artificial life-based approaches (section 13.4) using relatively simple neural network controllers (section 13.3) to learn fast and frugal heuristics that maximally exploit local opportunities and structures. The somatic marker mechanism (section 13.5) might be conceived as, in a sense, implementing just another kind of fast and frugal heuristic enabling current decision-making to profit cheaply from past experience. Under such an onslaught, it is possible that much of the worry about global abductive inference (section 13.6) simply dissolves. My own view, as stated above, is that something of the puzzle remains. But the solution I favor (see Clark, 2002) can *itself* be seen as a special instance of a fast and frugal heuristic: a cheap procedure that replaces global content-based search with something else (the second pass, connectivity pattern-based search, mentioned earlier).

13.8   Conclusions: Moving Targets and Multiple Technologies

Rationality, we have now seen, involves a whole lot more, and a whole lot less, than originally met the eye. It involves a whole lot more than local, syntax-based inference defined over tractable sets of quasi-sentential encodings. Even Fodor admits this – or at least, he admits that it is not yet obvious how to explain global abductive inference using such resources. It also involves a whole lot more than (as it were) the dispassionate deployment of information in the service of goals. For human reason seems to depend on a delicate interplay in which emotional responses (often unconscious ones) help sift our options and bias our choices in ways that *enhance* our capacities of fluent, reasoned, rational response. These emotional systems, I have argued, are usefully seen as a kind of wonderfully distilled store of hard-won knowledge concerning a lifetime's experiences of choosing and acting.

But rationality may also involve significantly *less* than we tend to think. Perhaps human rationality (and I am taking that as our constant target) is essentially a quick-and-dirty compromise forged in the heat of our ecological surround. Fast and frugal heuristics, geared to making the most of the cheapest cues that allow us to get by, may be as close as nature usually gets to the space of reasons. Work in robotics and connectionism further contributes to this vision of less as more, as features of body and world are exploited to press maximal benefit from basic capacities of on-board, prototype-based reasoning. Even the bugbear of global abductive reason, it was hinted, just might succumb to some wily combination of fast and frugal heuristics and simple syntactic search.

Where then does this leave the reputedly fundamental question "how is rationality mechanically possible?" It leaves it, I think, at an important crossroads, uncertainly poised between the old and the new. If (as I believe) the research programs described in sections 13.4–13.8 are each tackling important aspects of the problem, then the problem of rationality becomes, precisely, the problem of explaining the production, in social, environmental, and emotional context, of broadly appropriate adaptive response. Rationality (or as much of it as we humans typically enjoy) is what you get when this whole medley of factors are tuned and interanimated in a certain way. Figuring out this complex ecological balancing act just *is* figuring out how rationality is mechanically possible.

References

Bechera, A., Damasio, H., Tranel, D., and Damasio, A. R. (1997). "Deciding Advantageously Before Knowing the Advantageous Strategy." *Science*, 275: 1293–5.

Beer, R. D. (2000). "Dynamical Approaches to Cognitive Science." *Trends in Cognitive Sciences*, 4 (3): 91–9.

Brooks, R. (1991). "Intelligence Without Representation." *Artificial Intelligence*, 47: 139–59.

Chase, V., Hertwig, R., and Gigerenzer, G. (1998). "Visions of Rationality." *Trends in Cognitive Sciences*, 2 (6): 206–14.

Churchland, P. M. (1989). *The Neurocomputational Perspective*. Cambridge: MIT/Bradford Books.

Churchland, P. S. (1998). "Feeling Reasons." In P. M. Churchland and P. S. Churchland (eds.), *On The Contrary*. Cambridge, MA: MIT Press: 231–54.

Clark, A. (1989). *Microcognition: Philosophy, Cognitive Science and Parallel Distributed Processing*. Cambridge, MA: MIT Press.

—— (1993). *Associative Engines: Connectionism, Concepts and Representational Change*. Cambridge, MA: MIT Press.

—— (1996). "Connectionism, Moral Cognition and Collaborative Problem Solving." In L. May, M. Friedman, and A. Clark (eds.), *Minds and Morals*. Cambridge, MA: MIT Press: 109–28.

—— (2002). "Local Associations and Global Reason: Fodor's Frame Problem and Second-Order Search." *Cognitive Science Quarterly*.

Clark, A. and Grush, R. (1999). "Towards a Cognitive Robotics." *Adaptive Behavior*, 7 (1): 5–16.

Clark, A. and Toribio, J. (1994). "Doing Without Representing?" *Synthese*, 101: 401–31.

Clark, A. and Thornton, C. (1997). "Trading Spaces: Connectionism and the Limits of Uninformed Learning." *Behavioral and Brain Sciences*, 20 (1): 57–67.

Damasio, H., Grabowski, T., Frank, R., Galaburda, A. M., and Damasio, A. R. (1994). "The Return of Phineas Gage: Clues about the Brain from the Skull of a Famous Patient." *Science*, 264: 1102–5.

Fodor, J. (1983). *The Modularity of Mind*. Cambridge, MA: MIT Press.

—— (1998). *In Critical Condition: Polemical Essays on Cognitive Science and the Philosophy of Mind*. Cambridge, MA: MIT Press.

Fodor, J. and Lepore, E. (1993). "Reply to Churchland." *Philosophy and Phenomenological Research*, 53: 679–82.

Fodor, J. and Pylyshyn, Z. (1988). "Connectionism and Cognitive Architecture: A Critical Analysis." *Cognition*, 28: 3–71.

Haugeland, J. (1981). "Semantic Engines: An Introduction to Mind Design." In J. Haugeland (ed.), *Mind Design: Philosophy, Psychology, Artificial Intelligence.* Cambridge, MA: MIT Press: 1–34.

Kleinberg, J. (1997). "Authoritative Sources in a Hyperlinked Environment." IBM Research Report (RJ 10076). A version also appears in H. Karloff (ed.), *Proceedings of the 9th ACM-SIAM Symposium on Discreet Algorithms* (1998), and an extended version in *Journal of the ACM* 46 (1999).

Marr, D. (1982). *Vision.* San Francisco, CA: W. H. Freeman.

McClamrock, R. (1995). *Existential Cognition.* Chicago, IL: Chicago University Press.

Minsky, M. (1975). "A Framework For Representing Knowledge." In P. Winston (ed.), *The Psychology of Computer Vision.* New York: McGraw-Hill.

Newell, A. and Simon, H. (1976). "Computer Science as Empirical Inquiry: Symbols and Search." *Communications of the Association for Computing Machinery*, 19: 113–26.

Schank, R. (1975). "Using Knowledge to Understand." *TINLAP*: 75.

Smith, B. C. (1996). *On the Origin of Objects.* Cambridge, MA: MIT Press.

Stein, L. A. (1994). "Imagination and Situated Cognition." *Journal of Experimental and Theoretical Artificial Intelligence*, 6: 393–407.

Chapter 14

Philosophy of Mind and the Neurosciences

John Bickle

Nearly two decades have passed since Patricia Churchland exclaimed, with her characteristic verve, that "nothing is more obvious than that philosophers of mind could profit from knowing at least something of what there is to know about how the brain works" (1986: 4). Neuroscience has since developed exponentially. We are now on the other side of "the Decade of the Brain." We know much about the neural machinery that generates cognition, perception, and action. Our knowledge spans every level, from the biophysics of membrane channels to the large-scale dynamics of massively parallel neuronal networks. One might have thought that "philosophy of neuroscience" would now dominate philosophy of mind. One might have thought that philosophers would feel ashamed to argue about, e.g., consciousness, cognitive representation, the epistemology of perception, and even some normative issues, when ignorant of relevant and available information from neural science. One would be wrong. For the most part, mainstream philosophy of mind remains indifferent. (How much neuroscience do you find in this collection?)

Why would otherwise rational, intelligent thinkers ignore the "obvious"? Part of the answer isn't complicated. Historically, and especially in its present form, neuroscience is a *reductive* enterprise. And "reductionism" isn't popular in contemporary philosophy. In the same book, Churchland asserted that "often as not opposing sides in a debate on reductionism go right by each other because they have not agreed upon what they disagree about" (1986: 278). This assessment still holds. Reduction remains deeply misunderstood by philosophers, including its methodological implications for the "special," potentially reduced sciences. One principal goal of this chapter is to clarify the sense and methodological import of the kind of "reductionism" that inspires contemporary neuroscience.

Other factors make "reductionist" enterprises unattractive to contemporary philosophers. Job security, for instance. Only philosophers with Village Atheist temperaments take pleasure in seeing "mind" usurped by science. This concept has been so central to philosophy for so long. And if "mind" gets wrested away by a *reductive* science, joining the ranks of "divine purpose," "natural world," and "living being," what will be left for philosophers to ruminate about?

Obviously, these remarks don't address *arguments* that motivate the dim view about reductionism, which have grown increasingly sophisticated of late. Nor do they provide anti-reductionists with any empirical reasons for pause. These are my tasks in what follows. Over the next four sections I will defend the following claims.

- the "put up or shut up challenge" to psychoneural reductionism has already been met, and residual worries about examples from recent science reveal widespread misconceptions about reduction that still pervade philosophy (and cognitive psychology);
- recent work at the level of single-cell neurophysiology is yielding results directly relevant to philosophical concerns, even about consciousness;
- philosophers are not the only theorists seeking to address the "qualitative" and "subjective" aspects of consciousness; increasingly, hard-core neuroscientists are raising questions about these features and addressing them in ingenious yet straightforwardly empirical ways. Qualia and subjectivity: they're not just for philosophers anymore.

I will close on a somewhat tangential issue by arguing that the much-ballyhooed "interdisciplinarity" between philosophers, psychologists, and neuroscientists remains mostly a myth in practice. Everybody remains convinced that everybody else is ignorant of the important contributions from one's own area. And consensus is right about this, though with proper training philosophers could make a unique contribution toward changing this.

14.1 Real Reduction in Real Neuroscience

Assessing existing theories of scientific reduction and developing an alternative is a huge task in the philosophy of science, far beyond the scope of this chapter.[1] But two features require explicit mention to fend off the verbal disputes that Churchland warned about. First, scientific reduction is *inter-theoretic reduction*. It is a relation between scientific *theories*, not entities, properties, or events. Scientific reductions might yield cross-theoretic ontological *consequences*, but these consequences are *secondary to and dependent upon* the primary inter-*theoretic* relation. Secondly, the concept of *inter-theoretic unification* lies at the heart of scientific reduction. When reductions obtain, the reducing theory fully explains the reduced theory's data, which are usually still expressed in the latter's terminology and framework. (That this condition holds in principle and not always in practice should go without saying, but often can't.)

That contemporary neuroscience aspires to reduce psychology is nicely expressed in a pair of quotes from prominent textbooks. Gordon Shepherd writes:

> Many cognitive psychologists . . . believe that *theories* about learning and memory
> should be self-consistent and self-sufficient, without recourse to neural mechanisms. . . .
> For most neurobiologists, this view is outdated, and *one of the goals of modern
> research is to join the two levels into a coherent framework.* (1994: 619; my emphases).

The emphasized phrases reflect the two features of scientific reduction stressed
above, its primarily inter-theoretic character and unificationist goal. Kandel et al.
carry the reductionist banner down one more level:

> The goal of neural science is to understand the mind, how we perceive, move, think,
> and remember. In the previous editions of this book we stressed that important
> aspects of behavior could be examined at the level of individual nerve cells. . . .
> [T]he approach . . . was for the most part framed in cell-biological terms. Now it is
> also possible to address these questions *directly on the molecular level.* (1991: xii; my
> emphasis)

They urged this reorientation in the early 1990s, when the "molecular revolution" was just beginning to sweep through neuroscience. Five minutes perusal of
Society for Neuroscience Abstracts from the early 1990s up through the present
reveals how *more* prevalent molecular theories and experimental methodologies have become. Reductionism is alive and thriving in current mainstream
neuroscience.

However, research goals are one thing, while accomplished results are another.
Is current neurobiology actually developing theories to which *genuinely cognitive*
psychological theories reduce? I've termed this question "the put up or shut up
challenge" for psychoneural reduction, and have argued for an affirmative answer
(Bickle 1995; 1998: ch. 5). My argument involves two planks:

1   Current psychological theories of associative learning appeal to resources (rep-
    resentations and computations over their contents) that meet the standard,
    widely accepted "mark of the genuinely cognitive."
2   These psychological theories reduce to neurobiological theories about the
    neuronal circuitries in the appropriate brain regions and the cellular and
    molecular mechanisms of some forms of synaptic plasticity (the mechanisms
    by which the efficiency of electrochemical transmission between neurons
    increases or decreases over time).

The neurobiological reduction of genuinely cognitive psychological theories is
already an accomplished fact.

The case for the first plank is interesting and widely unknown among both
philosophers and cognitive psychologists (Rescorla 1988); but I've told it twice in
print (cited in the previous paragraph) and won't repeat the details here. Suffice
it to say that owing to advances in experimental technology, ingenious experimental design, and a quantitative model yielding counterintuitive predictions that
were verified empirically, associative learning theory, since the 1970s,

emphasizes the *information* that one stimulus gives about another. . . . These theories emphasize the importance of a discrepancy between the actual state of the world and the organism's *representation* of that state. They see learning as a *process by which these two are brought into line*. . . . A useful shorthand is that organisms adjust their Pavlovian associations only when they are "surprised." (Rescorla 1988: 152–3)

This approach is completely general. Learning theorists applied it to exotic associative phenomena such as the blocking effect and behaviorally silent learning, but also to classical conditioning. In the paper where they first articulated one such theory in precise, quantified fashion, Rescorla and Wagner state it in "explicitly cognitivist terms":

Organisms only learn when events violate their expectations. Certain expectations are built up about the events following a stimulus complex: expectations initiated by that complex and its component stimuli are then only modified when consequent events disagree with the composite expectation. (1972: 75)

Further development and empirical testing of their model quickly followed, and by the late 1970s it dominated the field (Dickinson 1980).

What about the case for my second plank? Going back to Ramon y Cajal, and first developed explicitly by Hebb (1949), neuroscientists have maintained that learning and memory involve changes in central nervous system (CNS) circuits. Since the mid-twentieth century, the site that has attracted the most attention is the synapse, the tiny cleft between neurons where the transmission of electrochemical activity takes place. In the CNS this transmission primarily is by way of chemical neurotransmitters released by the presynaptic neuron into the synaptic cleft, which then bind with membrane-bound proteins (receptors) on the postsynaptic neuron. This binding initiates a chain of biochemical events that open ion-selective membrane channels, resulting in either depolarization (excitatory postsynaptic potentials, or EPSPs) or hyperpolarization (inhibitory postsynaptic potentials, or IPSPs) at that patch of postsynaptic membrane. A large number of presynaptic, postsynaptic, and intra-cleft biochemical factors affect the efficacy of synaptic transmission. These factors are *plastic*: changeable at the behest of a huge variety of endogenous and external biochemical events.[2]

Abundant and widely varied experimental evidence supports synaptic plasticity as a principal mechanism of learning and memory.[3] Drawing on a variety of experimental methodologies, animal preparations (both vertebrate and invertebrate), anatomical regions, and behavioral tasks, a general model of the synaptic basis of learning and long-term memory has emerged (Shepherd 1994: 648–9). The basic cell-biological concept is *long-term potentiation* (LTP) (see figure 14.1). An action potential, spreading down the presynaptic axon membrane to its terminal bulb, opens voltage-gated calcium ion (Ca^{2+}) channels. Ca^{2+} flows into the presynaptic terminal (along its concentration and electric gradient). This influx produces a biochemical cascade that results in the increased binding of vesicles

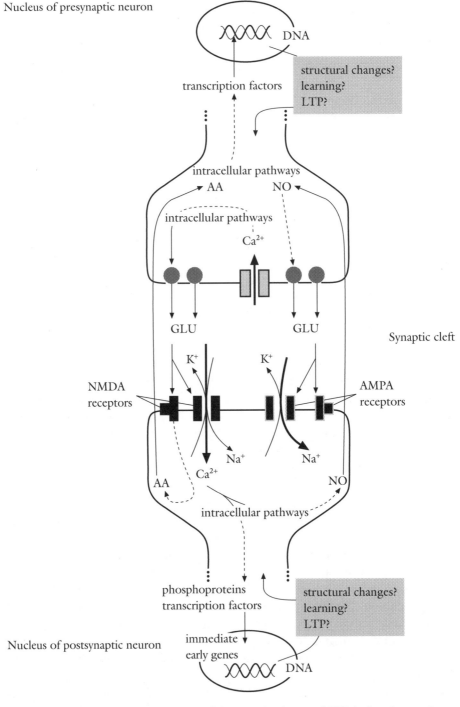

Figure 14.1 Simplified illustration of the current theory of LTP-induced synaptic plasticity. See text for explanation and abbreviations. (Adapted from Shepherd 1994: 648, figure 29.18.)

containing the neurotransmitter glutamate (GLU) to active zones on the pre-synaptic membrane, and subsequent glutamate release into the synaptic cleft.[4] The glutamate binds to two types of postsynaptic receptor. One type is ionotrophic AMPA (α-amino-3-hydroxy-5-methyl-4-isoxazole proprionic acid) receptors, which open direct sodium ion (Na^+) channels, resulting in the influx of Na^+ (along both its concentration and electric gradients) and subsequent EPSPs. The other type is NMDA (N-methyl-D-aspartate) receptors. At or near resting membrane potential, glutamate binding yields no ionic influx because NMDA receptors are blocked by magnesium. However, when the membrane is sufficiently depolarized (i.e., by glutamate binding at nearby AMPA receptors), the magnesium block pops off and glutamate binding to NMDA receptors opens postsynaptic Ca^{2+} channels.

Postsynaptically, Ca^{2+} acts as a second messenger. It activates:

- a cascade of Ca^{2+} binding proteins and protein kinases that break down and then reconstruct the cytoskeleton of the postsynaptic neuron into a different configuration, yielding changes in receptor numbers and locations;
- phosphoproteins and (probably) other transcription factors that in turn activate immediate early genes in the nucleus of the postsynaptic neuron, producing long-term changes in receptor and other protein synthesis;
- nitric oxide synthesis, which serves as a retrograde transmitter back on the presynaptic neuron to enhance subsequent glutamate release.

In addition, postsynaptic activation of NMDA receptors generates production of arachidonic acid (AA), which also appears to act as a retrograde transmitter. Presynaptically, AA initiates a cascade of protein kinases which interact ultimately with genetic transcription factors, yielding long-term changes in protein production, cell structure, and function.[5]

How does the theory of LTP-induced synaptic plasticity figure into reductions of cognitivist learning theories (such as modern associative learning theory)? The key is what Hawkins and Kandel (1984) called the "cell-biological alphabet of learning" and I called "combinatorial reduction" (Bickle 1995; 1998; ch. 5). The cell-biological and molecular mechanisms provide the "letters," and their *sequences and combinations* (the "words") made available by increasingly complex neural anatomies and physiologies explain all the behavioral data addressed by the cognitive psychological theory. For example, behavioral changes resulting from classical conditioning are explained by stimulus-paired increases in presynaptic neurotransmitter release. (This is one of Hawkins and Kandel's "letters.") Initially, the neutral conditioned stimulus (CS) elicits weak neurotransmitter release (above baseline rates) in central pathways leading from the stimulated sensory receptors. The behaviorally significant unconditioned stimulus (US) elicits strong release. Activity in the US pathway activates interneurons that synapse on the presynaptic terminal bulbs in the CS pathway. These interneurons release the neurotransmitter serotonin, which binds to receptors on the presynaptic CS pathway terminals. This initiates a biochemical cascade in these terminals that inhibits potassium ion

(K^+) efflux, broadening the action potentials initiated by the CS and eliciting increased Ca^{2+} influx. The additional Ca^{2+} facilitates increased binding of vesicles to terminal membrane, neurotransmitter release, and postsynaptic response. In this way, the CS–US pairings enable the weaker CS to access the same second messenger system elicited by the salient US.[6] CS-induced activity then replaces the US in activating the unconditioned response motor pathways. The ultimate result is activity in motor neurons that produce the appropriate muscle contractions against the skeletal frame that generate the behavioral dynamics over time.

Appealing only to presynaptic mechanisms, Hawkins and Kandel (1984) explain some higher-order cognitive features of associative learning by *sequences and combinations* of the cell-biological "letters." All of their circuitry assumptions were based on known anatomy and physiology. They demonstrate how the behavioral dynamics of the blocking effect, stimulus specificity and generalization, extinction and spontaneous recovery, second-order (S-S) conditioning, and US pre-exposure can be explained directly by biologically plausible sequences and combinations of the cell-biological "letters." The ultimate outcome of these sequences and combinations over time is changes in motor neuron activity driving behavioral response. These behavioral data were the ones that prompted "cognitivist" models of associative learning (Dickinson 1980). The additional molecular resources provided by more recent discoveries about LTP-induced synaptic plasticity increase the scope of neurobiological "combinatorial reductions" to numerous types of learning and memory (Bickle 1998: ch. 5). More recently, cognitive psychological treatments of "declarative long-term memory" and the "consolidation switch" from short-term to long-term memory have been added to this group (Squire and Kandel 1999: ch. 7).

The resulting cell and molecular biological explanations do more than just capture the behavioral data qualitatively. For example, Hawkins (1989) developed a quantitative model of the presynaptic features used in his and Kandel's earlier reductions. This model enabled him to mimic these cell-biological "letters" in an anatomically plausible computer simulation. Hawkins showed that the action potential rate curves over time in simulated motor neurons matched exactly the learning curves, behavioral dynamics, and changing patterns of reinforcement predicted by the Rescorla–Wagner equations. His quantitative measure, the firing rates over time in the simulated motor neurons, was computed by parameters and changeable synaptic weight values across simulated sensory, facilitator, and motor neurons. All values were chosen to mimic known biological features. Hence even when the neurophysiological "letters" are limited to the presynaptic cell-biological mechanisms of Hawkins's and Kandel's early account, simulated motor neuron activity generated by their sequences and combinations in increasingly complex neural anatomies capture exactly the behavioral dynamics and predictions of the cognitive-psychological account.[7]

This case is just one example of a reduction of a genuinely cognitive psychological to a cell-biological/molecular neuroscientific theory. There are other examples that draw upon newer details of the current theory of LTP-induced synaptic plasticity.[8] The second plank of my argument has thus been accomplished for a variety of genuinely cognitive psychological theories. Psychoneural reduction of the genuinely cognitive is already an accomplished scientific fact.

14.2   Neurofunctions?

Psychologists Maurice Schouten and H. Looren de Jong (1999) have challenged my argument for the second plank. Their criticisms deserve discussion here for at least two reasons. First, they express popular *and scientifically motivated* anti-reductionist themes. Secondly, they address directly my empirical case study. Their arguments thus serve as good templates for responsible counters to an empirical argument for psychoneural reduction. However, their arguments also contain important flaws, and pointing these out helps to clarify general themes of the reductionism implicit in current mainstream neuroscience.

Throughout their criticisms Schouten and de Jong (1999) stress two points:

- the need to specify functions in comprehensive scientific explanations;
- the inaccessibility of functions from theories of physical mechanisms alone.

Applied specifically to *psychoneural* inter-theoretic relations, they claim that brain functions cannot be discovered by "purely bottom-up" theorizing, even by an approach that specifies complex sequences and combinations of cell-biological and molecular processes. Their first argument contains two premises. First, higher-level dispositions are *multiply supervenient* on physical substrates and mechanisms. In other words, numerous higher-level dispositions supervene on one and the same physical substrate. Many readers will recognize multiple supervenience as the reverse of the more familiar notion of *multiple realizability*. Multiple supervenience has appeared increasingly in anti-reductionist arguments (Kincaid 1988; Endicott 1994). Secondly, given multiple supervenience, a higher-level theory typically is required in a given case to distinguish the *causally relevant* lower-level traits from the *causally irrelevant* ones. Only some lower-level traits are causally relevant for a given event (out of the myriad that occur at the time). Eschewing higher-level theories will produce a loss of objective information about the particular dispositional traits of the physical substratum that are relevant for a given explanation. So the "purely bottom-up" methodology that Schouten and de Jong assume to be characteristic of combinatorial reduction and the cell-biological/molecular "alphabet" approach "won't work."[9]

There is a variety of problems with this argument. The first is a simple misunderstanding of reductionism's methodological commitments. The methodology practiced in current neuroscience (and analyzed separately by Hawkins and Kandel and by me) does not "eschew" higher-level theories. Most reductionists now explicitly embrace *coevolutionary research ideology* (first espoused by Hooker 1981).

Some even recognize higher-level theorizing as *methodologically indispensable*, both prior to and after an accomplished reduction (Bickle 1996; 1998: ch. 4). Coevolution itself is a methodological recommendation, not a constraint or imposition on theory choice. It is designed not to rule out certain higher-level theories (i.e., those lacking reductive potential), but rather to keep afloat nascent theoretical suggestions, to give them a chance to display their explanatory power and empirical veracity. Historically, and even now, it is physiological theories that face the strongest resistance in mainstream psychology, social science, and philosophy.[10] Furthermore, since an adequate psychoneural reductionism must cohere with cross-level theory relations and methodology across the board in science, psychoneural reductionists must acknowledge that higher-level generalizations can have "strong epistemic warrant" (Horgan 1993) before and after inter-theoretic reductions obtain. The history of science offers many cases of successful theories that developed for a long time with only cursory acknowledgment of theories above and below. Even the very logic of the inter-theoretic reduction relation speaks to the need to acknowledge higher-level theories. Reduction is a two-place relation between (developed) theories and so requires developed, epistemically warranted higher-level instances. The special sciences must continue to provide theories even as their reducers develop, if *inter*-theoretic reductions are to obtain. Finally, notice that the role ascribed to higher-level theories in Schouten's and de Jong's first argument, that of distinguishing causally relevant from causally irrelevant lower-level dispositional traits for particular explananda, is consistent with ascribing to them an essential but nevertheless *purely methodological role*. They can be ineliminable for guiding lower-level theory development without committing us to an anti-reductionist conclusion.

Schouten and de Jong also criticize my appeal to the learning and memory–LTP link as an *accomplished* psychoneural reduction. Their mistakes are common enough to warrant discussion here. They first point out how higher-level neuropsychological research prompted initial physiological investigations of the mammalian hippocampus, where LTP was first discovered. Their history is correct. But this only shows that higher-level theorizing is methodologically important for neuroscience and we just scouted reasons why reductionists should not deny that. The historical details don't justify anything more than a methodological role for higher-level theorizing. Schouten and de Jong also claim that since the mid-1980s, "the empirical support for the 'LTP as memory substrate' hypothesis *has come mainly from* the use of pharmacological agents . . . that appear to antagonize NMDA [receptor] activity and to impair spatial learning," and that "[i]n this type of research, spatial learning is operationally defined as *performance in a water maze*" (1999: 247; my emphasis). Even in a paper targeted for philosophers and cognitive psychologists, this "statement of fact" about neuroscientific research is naive. It wasn't even true in the early 1990s. Searching for title words or key words of abstracts of presentations at the 2000 Society for Neuroscience Annual Meeting using either "LTP" or "synaptic plasticity" yielded more than 200 presentations (www.sfn.org). Only four of these also contained "water maze" in the title or as a key word. The complete 200+ abstracts indicate the vast number and variety of molecular manipulations and behavioral paradigms now employed to study LTP, and of the naivity of Schouten's and de Jong's assertion.

This problem is far more than just one factual error about neuroscience made by non-neuroscientists. Schouten and de Jong in turn raise some methodological and interpretive problems specific to NMDA receptor antagonists and water maze tasks, implying that these problems constitute a general challenge for the claimed learning and memory–LTP reduction. Their problems provide no such thing because of the wide variety of molecular manipulations, behavioral tasks, and recent genetic knockout and transgenic manipulations (in mammals) that provide evidence for the reduction (Squire and Kandel 1999: ch. 7). In fact, the most convincing recent experimental work demonstrating that LTP is a cellular/ molecular mechanism for learning and memory involves neither pharmacological manipulations nor the Morris water maze. Instead, it comes from transgenic adult mice manipulated to overexpress a gene whose protein product blocks the cata- lytic subunit of protein kinase A in the hippocampus. It employs a dual fear- conditioning behavioral test involving environmental cues, a neutral CS, and a foot shock US (see Squire and Kandel 1999: 149–53). There is a general lesson for psychoneural anti-reductionists in Schouten's and de Jong's error: hooray for considering empirical work, but first master the scope and variety of scientific investigations being pursued on that topic.

Schouten and de Jong also raise a more general interpretive worry about the neuroscientific evidence for the learning and memory–LTP induction link. They point out that it is important to separate influences on learning and memory from those on other systems that might be contributing to the behavior. Many systems are susceptible to NMDA receptor antagonists, including sensory, motor, motiva- tional, and attentional. All of these systems are involved in the water maze task. Perhaps LTP is a mechanism primarily for plasticity in one of these other systems? Perhaps it is. But that is not news to neuroscientists. In fact, it's the reason why neuroscientists are so careful in their experimental design. (Incidentally, *specific* methodological worries about *specific* pharmacological agents have prompted neuroscientists studying the cellular and molecular mechanisms of learning and memory to shift their experimental protocols to genetic knockout and transgenic preparations; see, e.g., Squire and Kandel 1999: 119–24, 151–3.) Philosophers and cognitive psychologists should not skip over the "Methods" section of neuroscience papers. This is where neuroscientists reveal their *controls* for the experimental variable at issue – learning, vision, attention, movement, whatever – to avoid confounding factors that can wreck an interpretation. Obviously, neuroscientists will listen to anybody's fruitful criticisms of the *specific* controls they employ. But philosophers and psychologists really aren't required to inform them about a need to control for possible confounding influences as obvious as the ones Schouten and de Jong point out. It might surprise philosophers to see how subtle the controls are that neuroscientists routinely employ.[11]

Finally, Schouten and de Jong argue that functional theories *are* more than just methodologically essential or important. For only with such theories can we answer "'why' and 'what for' questions," questions about "what [the mechanism] is supposed to do," about "the requisite normative dimension" (1999: 255–6). They insist that these questions require "a more ontological interpretation of functions" (ibid.: 256). This emphasis ties in with their plumb for *teleofunctions*. A system's teleofunctions depend upon its selective (evolutionary) history. A teleofunctional theory specifies kinds that unify distinct physical systems by reference to the goals they hold in common via their selective histories. Only an appropriate functional theory can account for these "objective properties of reality" (ibid.: 256).

Teleofunctions are at present a popular notion in the philosophy of biology, psychology, mind, and language (Millikan 1984; Post 1991). They are central to the strongest scientifically inspired anti-reductionist argument around. What I am about to say should not be taken to be my "definitive response" (no such beast yet exists). But there is a lot that is problematic about this notion and argument. Why do we need a "unifying specification" of these distinct physical systems once we understand how each works individually – that is, once such a functional account has performed its essential (but exclusively) methodological role? What does this unification add to our *ontology*? Why think that answers to "why" and "what for" questions are ontologically committing, beyond the variety of physical mechanisms at work? Notice also that for most of the purposes assigned to physical mechanisms in pro-teleofunctional discussions, the "higher-level theorizing" is trivial and obvious. Consider the favorite example: the heart's teleofunction is to pump blood. Does it really take much "high-level theorizing" to reach this insight? The example is illustrative: the "teleofunction" of most systems is usually obvious, especially when we understand their physical mechanisms. (Please note that this is *not* to say that the task of unveiling their selective histories is usually trivial or obvious – it isn't, as the difficulty of *real* evolutionary biology and ecology attest.)

There is also another science besides mainstream evolutionary biology concerned with explaining *why* a trait exists in a given system. That science is *molecular genetics*, and its aspirations are ruthlessly reductive. Some molecular geneticists even think of evolutionary theory as serving an essential but exclusively methodological role. For example, molecular biologist James Shapiro has stated recently:

> Most of the basic concepts in conventional evolutionary theory predate 1953 when virtually nothing was known about DNA. In the first half of the 20th century, mathematical treatments of the evolutionary process were elaborated using terms such as genes, alleles, dominance, penetrance, mutation, epistasis, fitness, and selection. . . . Although molecular geneticists still use much of the old language . . . they actually operate in a distinct conceptual universe. The conceptual universe of molecular genetics is as different from classical genetics *and evolutionary theory* as quantum physics is from classical mechanics. (1999: 23; my emphasis)

Building on the initial insights of Nobel laureate Barbara McClintock, Shapiro's picture is of genetic variation resulting from a host of cellular biochemical events. "Most evolutionists try (unrealistically) to model the action of these cellular functions to resemble the random mutational events of conventional evolutionary theory" (ibid.: 28). Instead, internal (to the genome) "signal transduction networks" regulate the timing and location of genetic changes, including simultaneous changes at multiple loci. The "why" and "what for" questions are addressable at the level of DNA biochemistry regulation by the variety of signal transduction networks, themselves understood increasingly in molecular terms. The "environment" does nothing more than (occasionally) kick-start these internal networks. In this light *"evolution* must be viewed afresh at the end of the 20th century" (ibid.: 23; my emphasis). Molecular genetics is ignored by the philosophers of biology who have been most active in developing the teleofunction concept. They draw inspiration from a scientific theory which, according to some molecular geneticists, must now be rethought completely. Perhaps this ignorance of the new dawning of molecular genetics is the great mistake that the teleofunction concept rests upon.

Finally, in the context of both philosophy of biology and mind, an "ontological interpretation" of (teleo-) functions must be seen for what it is. The resulting account is a *dualism* of the classical property or event variety. This interpretation implies that there are properties or events not explainable by physical mechanisms. Nothing (at present) is objectionable in and of itself about such a view. Our best biology and psychology might commit us in the end to non-physical properties or events. But those who seek to defend a *physicalism* in any meaningful sense can't help themselves so cavalierly to (teleo-) functions interpreted ontologically. It also seems extremely cavalier to ignore the reductionist sympathies of contemporary neuroscience and molecular biology.[12] If any areas constitute the "crowning glory" of current mainstream biology, it is these two. That's subject to change, of course, but indifference to them by current philosophers of biology and mind is perverse.

14.3 Consciousness and Cellular Neuroscience

Consciousness is one psychological phenomenon that many think to be far removed from reductionistic neuroscience. Ignored for nearly the entire twentieth century by mainstream sciences of mind, it has roared back recently in both science and philosophy. Following in its wake have been explicit revivals of dualism (Jackson 1982; Nagel 1989), "new mysterian" worries about our (human) capacity to solve the consciousness-brain problem (McGinn 1989), and calls to "revolutionize" physics (Chalmers 1996; Penrose 1994). Even physicalists sympathetic to neuroscience assume that explaining consciousness requires "exotic," "whole-brain" resources: sophisticated brain-imaging techniques, massively parallel neural

networks, and mathematical analysis of their global activity. The shared idea has
been that the techniques of traditional neurophysiology are not up to the task,
even if neuroscience ultimately is.

One notable exception is perceptual neurophysiologist William Newsome. In
an exchange about the "single unit approach" of mainstream neuroscience, he
exclaims that "we have not yet begun to exhaust its usefulness. . . . [E]xciting to
me . . . is the recent trend toward applying the single unit approach in behaving
animals trained to perform simple cognitive tasks" (in Gazzaniga 1997: 57).
Newsome mentions tasks involving perception, attention, learning, memory, and
motor planning. Results from his own lab can be interpreted in a way that makes
them relevant to a recent *philosophical* controversy about consciousness.

Phenomenal externalism holds that the environment external to an individual's
receptor surfaces determines ("individuates") the qualitative contents ("qualia")
of his sensory experiences (Dretske 1996; Lycan 1996). Part of its motivation is
the recent stampede toward "representational" theories of qualia coupled with
the dominance of representational-content externalism in philosophy generally.
Arguments for the latter appeal to a philosopher's popular fantasy: Twin Earth.
It is common to use these thought experiments to defend externalism about linguistic meaning and cognitive content. Fred Dretske insists that nothing prevents
one who accepts them for content externalism from accepting the same arguments
for phenomenal externalism: "Just as we distinguish and identify beliefs by what
they are beliefs about, and what they are beliefs about in terms of what they stand
in the appropriate relation to, so we must distinguish and identify experiences in
terms of what they are experiences of" (1996: 145).[13] The radical nature of this
view is apparent in Dretske's sloganesque phrase: "The experiences themselves are
in the head . . . but nothing in the head . . . need have the qualities that distinguish these experiences" (ibid.: 144–5). Although they are physical duplicates,
and thereby neurophysiological duplicates, Fred's and Twin Fred's conscious
sensory experiences might have different qualia owing to differences in their
external environments.

However, an interpretation of Newsome's "single-unit" results utilizing
microstimulation of visual area MT in rhesus monkeys (see figure 14.2) demon-
strates the empirical implausibility of externalist intuitions about qualitative content. Area MT (middle temporal cortex) is the gateway to the "dorsal" ("parietal,"
"where") visual processing stream (see figure 14.3). Both lesion studies and
electrophysiological recordings have revealed its role in visual judgments of
motion direction. Most MT neurons are direction selective, firing optimally to a
visual stimulus with motion in a single direction. Like other cortical areas, MT
has a columnar organization, with neurons in a given column sharing similar
receptive fields and preferred motion selectivity. These features vary from column
to column, so MT as a whole represents all motion directions at each point in the
visual field (Albright et al. 1984).

Newsome and his colleagues developed a technique for quantifying the strength
of a motion stimulus (Salzman et al. 1992; see figure 14.4). Sequences of dots are

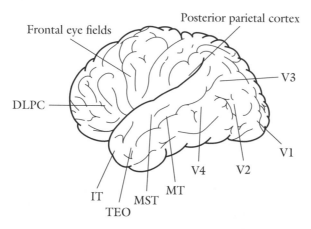

Figure 14.2 Anatomical organization of primate (macaque) visual system. Abbreviations: MT (middle temporal cortex); MST (middle superior temporal); IT (inferior temporal cortex); DLPC (dorsal lateral prefrontal cortex).

plotted on a computer screen. The strength of a motion stimulus, expressed in terms of a percentage correlation, reflects the probability that a given dot will be replotted at a fixed spatial and temporal interval. For example, in a "50 per cent correlation vertical stimulus," half the dots are replotted at a fixed upward interval (providing the illusion of vertical motion), while the other half are replotted randomly. Newsome's group also developed a behavioral paradigm for determining judgments of motion direction. Their controls are elaborate but the basic idea is straightforward. The monkey fixates on an illuminated central point, and maintains fixation while presented with a visual motion stimulus of a particular strength (see figure 14.5). Both the fixation point and the motion stimulus are extinguished, and target lights (LEDs) appear in the periphery. One LED is located in the direction of the motion stimulus. The other is located in the opposite periphery. The monkey indicates its judgment of motion direction by saccading (moving its eyes rapidly) to the appropriate LED. Monkeys are only rewarded when they saccade correctly (i.e., to the LED in the direction of the motion stimulus). By first locating an MT cell's receptive field (the portion of the visual field in which stimuli elicit a response) and preferred motion selectivity, experimenters can present the motion stimulus to only that region of the visual field. They can then compare the monkey's report about the motion direction across stimulus strengths when electrical microstimulation is applied to that cell during stimulus presentation and when it is not. The target LED in the cell's preferred motion direction is dubbed the Pref LED, and the target in the opposite direction is dubbed the Null LED. The monkey's saccade constitutes a report of apparent (perceived) motion direction.

This measure of motion strength and the behavioral paradigm enable Newsome's group to plot the proportion of the monkeys' reports of apparent motion in an MT neuron's preferred direction as a function of motion stimulus strength (see

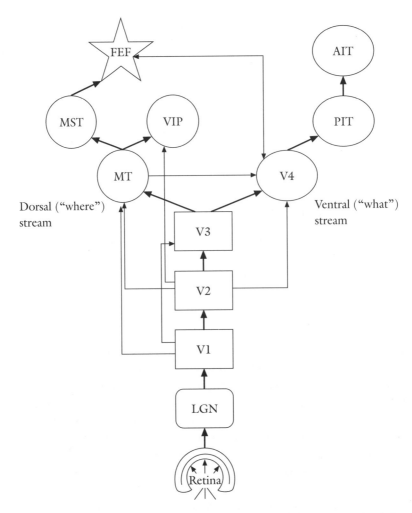

Figure 14.3 Flowchart of the major structures, cortical analyzer areas, circuitries, and processing streams in the mammalian visual system. Abbreviations: as in figure 14.2, except LGN (lateral geniculate nucleus of the dorsal thalamus); PIT (posterior inferior temporal cortex); AIT (anterior inferior temporal cortex); VIP (ventral intraparietal area); FEF (frontal eye fields).

figure 14.6). If microstimulation to direction-selective MT neurons adds "signal" to the neuronal processes underlying visual judgment of motion direction, then it will bias the monkeys' reports toward that neuron's preferred direction. Graphically, this will result in a leftward shift of the psychometric function (see again figure 14.6). These are exactly the results Newsome and his colleagues observed, under a variety of stimulus strengths and microstimulation frequencies (Salzman et al. 1992; Murasugi et al. 1993). At nearly every percentage correlation, microstimulation of a direction-selective MT cell biased significantly the monkeys' saccades to the Pref LED. This bias occurred even in the presence of strong

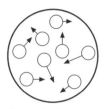 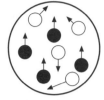 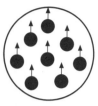

No vertical motion   50% vertical motion   100% vertical motion
    correlation   correlation   correlation

Figure 14.4 Quantitative measure of strength of motion direction stimulus.
Actual displays contained many more dots than are illustrated here. (Adapted from
Salzman et al. 1992: 2333, figure 1.)

motion stimuli in the opposite direction (e.g., > −50 per cent correlation). Recall
also that monkeys are only rewarded when they report the stimulus's motion
direction correctly. They never receive a reward for these continually incorrect
choices. Increasing microstimulation frequency increased the proportion of apparent motion reports in the neuron's preferred direction, even under conditions
of stronger motion stimuli (percent correlation) in the opposite direction.

These results lead naturally to the question: what does the monkey *see* in
microstimulation trials? Is the monkey *consciously aware* of motion in the neuron's preferred direction, even when the motion stimulus is in the opposite
direction? Newsome and his colleagues admit that their results can't answer such
questions conclusively. But they also don't shrink from offering some suggestions:

> [A] plausible hypothesis is that microstimulation *evokes a subjective sensation of
> motion* like that experienced during the motion aftereffect, or waterfall illusion. . . .
> Motion therefore appears to be *a quality that can be computed independently within
> the brain and "assigned" to patterned objects in the environment.* (Salzman et al.
> 1992: 2352; my emphases).

They are claiming that motion qualia are generated internally by neural activity
and "attached" to representations of external objects. Happily, our "internal
assignments" tend to match up well with external events. Natural selection was
crueler to creatures whose "assignments" were more haphazard. But under the
right conditions, our internally generated qualia and the external events can be
dissociated. That is what happens in Newsome's microstimulation studies.

The general idea at work here is what neuroscientist Rodolfo Llinás and
neurophilosopher Patricia Churchland call *endogenesis*. As they put it, "[t]he crux
here is that sensory experience is not created by incoming signals from the world
but by intrinsic, continuing processes of the brain" (Llinás and Churchland 1996: x).
Incoming signals from receptors keyed to external parameters function to "trellis,
shape, and otherwise sculpt the intrinsic activity to yield a survival-facilitating, me-
in-the-world representational scheme" (ibid.). Natural selection – adequacy for
exploiting an environmental niche, not truth – determines a scheme's "success."[14]

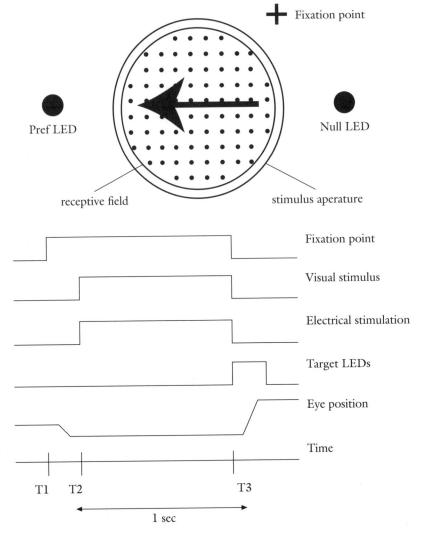

Figure 14.5 Newsome's experimental paradigm involving electrical microstimulation of individual neurons in area MT. (Adapted from Salzman et al. 1992: 2334, figure 2.)

Newsome's experimental evidence and interpretation, along with the general concept of endogenesis, count strongly against phenomenal externalism. Notice first that a monkey in a "microstimulation + (strong) null direction stimulus" trial, compared to a "no microstimulation + (strong) preferred direction stimulus" trial, is an empirical analogue of a Twin Earth case. The two brain states are (close to) identical in the two cases, at least from MT and further up the dorsal stream (the sites that matter for visual motion detection and judgment). Yet the environmental stimuli are different. In the first case, motion in the null direction correlates with that brain state (because of the microstimulation). In the second case, motion in the (opposite) preferred direction correlates with it. If

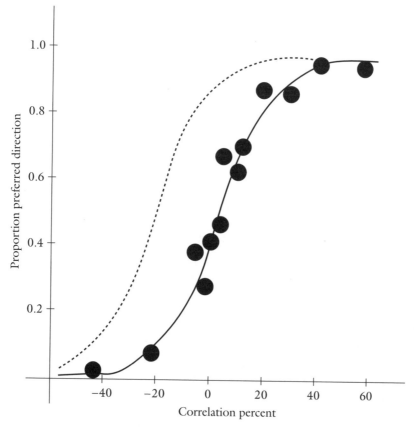

Figure 14.6 A schematic psychometric function plotting proportions of decisions in a motion-selective MT neuron's preferred direction as a function of motion signal strength (dots and solid line). The leftward shift of the function is predicted following microstimulation if microstimulation adds signal to the neuronal processes underlying visual judgment of motion direction (dotted line). (Adapted from Salzman et al. 1992: 2335, figure 3.)

phenomenal externalism is true, the motion qualia should differ. And yet the monkeys report the same direction of apparent motion in the two cases (by way of their trained saccades to the Pref LED). In accordance with Newsome and his colleagues' interpretation quoted above, this suggests that the motion qualia are similar in the two cases, not different. There is also evidence that this effect is not specific to rhesus monkeys. As Newsome and his colleagues remark, "it has recently been reported that crude motion percepts can be elicited with electrical stimulation of human parietal-occipital cortex" (Salzman et al. 1992: 2352). Nor is it specific to motion. The measure of stimulus strength, the behavioral paradigm, and the microstimulation technique generalize to other types of visual stimuli, including orientation, color, and stereoscopic disparity. More recently, Newsome and his colleagues have reported similar microstimulation results for stereoscopic depth (DeAngelis et al. 1998). With regard to the qualitative

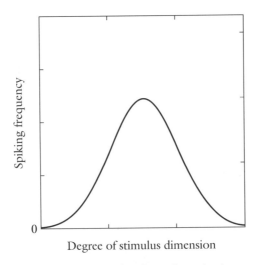

Figure 14.7 Tuning curve for a stimulus dimension-selective neuron (e.g., color, orientation) displaying a standard Gaussian response. Dimension degree on the x-axis underneath the highest point of the curve reflects the neuron's preferred stimulus dimension.

content of conscious visual experiences, what matters is what goes on "in the head" (the brain). The intuitions driving *phenomenal* externalism appear to be empirically implausible. And it is good old single-unit neurophysiology that provides the empirical evidence for this philosophical conclusion about conscious qualitative content.

Consider a second example of "single-neuron" neurophysiology yielding results that are applicable to philosophical concerns about consciousness. McAdams and Maunsell (1999) studied the effects of explicit conscious attention on activity of single neurons in macaque (visual) areas V4 and V1 (see again figure 14.2 above). V1 (primary visual cortex) receives retinotopic inputs via the lateral geniculate nucleus of the dorsal thalamus. V4, further up in extrastriate cortex, is the gateway to the "ventral" ("temporal," "what") visual processing stream (see again figure 14.3 above). V4 contains both orientation- and color-selective neurons. Most have a preferred orientation or color that elicits maximal activity. Similar stimuli elicit less activity, and dissimilar ones elicit none (over baseline response rate) (see figure 14.7).

Psychologists have known for a long time that explicit conscious attention yields improved sensory performance. Measures include improved detection thresholds and quicker discrimination. At the level of individual sensory neurons, explicit conscious attention could alter neuronal response to account for these behavioral improvements in one of two ways.[15] First, it could increase the amplitude of neurons' activity (see figure 14.8A). The neurons' stimulus selectivity remains the same, as reflected in the similar widths of the two tuning curves. Frequency of action potentials generated to stimuli increases, as reflected in the height of the tuning curve at virtually all stimulus dimensions. (This effect is

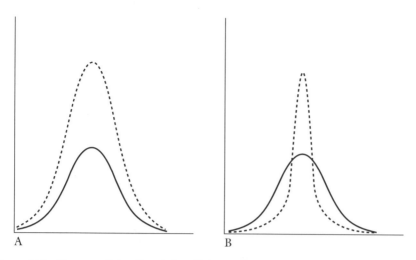

Figure 14.8 Two possible effects of explicit conscious attention to location of a visual neuron's receptive field on its activity profile. **A**: Multiplicative scaling of neuron's response (relatively constant increase in activity rate to a variety of stimulus dimension degrees) without increased stimulus selectivity. **B**: Increased stimulus selectivity, reflected by a sharpening of the neuron's tuning curve.

referred to as "multiplicative scaling.") Stronger neuronal responses typically have a better signal-to-noise ratio, which could explain improved behavioral detection thresholds and speed. However, this role for explicit conscious attention would be deflationary for consciophiles, who insist that consciousness is "special" or "unique" at least in its mode of neural realization. This result would render the effects of explicit conscious attention similar to, e.g., simply increasing the salience of the visual stimulus. Conscious attention would serve as an internal, endogenous mechanism for just "turning up the gain" on individual neurons. On the other hand, conscious attention might have a more robust and unique effect. Perhaps it alters the stimulus selectivity of individual neurons, causing activity in these neurons to signal more precisely the attributes of the attended stimulus. A sharpening of neuronal tuning curves under conditions of explicit conscious attention would reflect this effect (see figure 14.8B). A sharper tuning curve would provide a more fine-grained representation of the stimulus dimension, which could improve detection threshold and speed. Consciophiles could be heartened by this result, since increasing neurons' stimulus selectivity is not a common neurophysiological dynamic.

To test these competing explanations, McAdams and Maunsell (1999) developed a delayed matching-to-sample task conjoined with single-cell recordings in V4 and V1 (see figure 14.9). They first determined receptive fields and stimulus selectivity of V4 and V1 neurons to be recorded from during sessions. The dashed oval in all frames of figure 14.9 represents the location of the recorded neuron's receptive field. Prior to a test trial, the monkey had been cued as to which location to attend: the one within the neuron's receptive field or the one

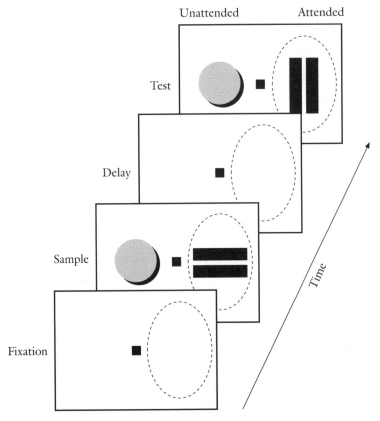

Unattended   Attended

Test

Delay

Sample

Fixation

Time

Figure 14.9 Schematic illustration of McAdams and Maunsell's delayed match-to-sample task. See text for explanation. (Adapted from their 1999: 433, figure 1.)

located diametrically opposite it. A trial began when the monkey fixated a central dot and depressed a button. Sample stimuli – orientation bars or a color patch – appeared on a screen 500 milliseconds later. One stimulus occupied the neuron's entire receptive field, the other the opposite location. The samples occupied the screen for 500 milliseconds, and then disappeared. The delay period lasted 500 milliseconds, after which test stimuli appeared. The monkey had to indicate whether the test stimulus at the cued location matched the sample by either releasing the button within 500 milliseconds if the stimuli matched, or by continuing to depress the button for at least 750 milliseconds if they did not. In the case illustrated in figure 14.9, for example, the monkey must continue to depress the button if cued to attend to the orientation location, since the sample and test orientation bars do not match. But the monkey must release the button if it had been cued to attend to the color location, since the sample and test color patches match (though this is not apparent in the black-and-white figure). Monkeys were rewarded only if they reported correctly match or non-match in the cued location. Matches and non-matches at the two locations were uncorrelated, so the monkey could gain no advantage by attending to the wrong location.

Monkeys maintained fixation on the central point throughout all phases of a trial. This insured that visual input to the cell remained constant. When presenting the same visual stimulus to the cued location in sample and test phases, any differences in recorded neuron activity could be attributed to differences in the monkey's attentional state. Since all V4 recordings were made from orientation-selective neurons, the "Attended" mode occurred when the animal performed an orientation-matching task (see figure 14.9). The recorded neuron was then responding to the stimulus relevant for the matching task. The "Unattended" mode occurred when the animal performed the color-matching task, since the recorded neuron was still responding to the orientation stimulus, but that stimulus was irrelevant to the matching task at hand. Any changes to the neuron's firing rate in Attended compared to Unattended mode reflect the neuronal effects of explicit conscious attention to the location of the neuron's receptive field.

Experimental results with more than 200 orientation-selective V4 neurons and 124 V1 neurons clearly supported the multiplicative scaling hypothesis (figure 14.8A above). (See McAdams and Maunsell 1999: figs 2, 4, 5, 6, 7, and 10.) For both individual cells and averages within populations, amplitude of Attended responses (frequency of action potentials) compared to Unattended responses to the same orientation stimulus was (statistically) significantly greater. Explicit conscious attention to the location of a sensory neuron's receptive field enhances its action potential frequency to its favored degree of the relevant stimulus dimension and to others similar to it. However, the standard deviation to the entire range of stimulus dimension degrees remained constant across Attended and Unattended modes. This means that the two tuning curves have nearly identical widths. Hence explicit conscious attention does not affect a neuron's stimulus selectivity. Finally, the Attended and Unattended tuning curves had nearly identical asymptote values. This means that explicit conscious attention has no effect on a neuron's response to "unpreferred" degrees of a stimulus dimension. Combining these results yields a clear conclusion. Directing explicit conscious attention to the location of a sensory neuron's receptive field simply increases the neuron's response to preferred and similar stimuli. It only "turns up the gain" without sharpening the neuron's stimulus selectivity.

McAdams and Maunsell point out that explicit conscious attention therefore has the same effect on single neuron activity as do procedures as mundane as manipulating stimulus saliency and contrast:

> The phenomenological similarity between the effects of attention and the effects of stimulus manipulations raises the possibility that attention involves neural mechanisms that are similar to those used in processing ascending signals from the retinas, and that cortical neurons treat retinal and attentional inputs equivalently. (1999: 439)

Their results support the "deflationary" view of consciousness mentioned above. Concerning its effects on single neurons, explicit conscious attention is just another "gain increaser."

It might sound mysterious to attribute causal effects to explicit conscious attention at the level of single neuron activity. Single neurons are biochemically complicated ion channels and pumps. Does explicit conscious attention alter channel proteins' shapes and electric membrane gradients? Is cellular neuroscience revitalizing dualism? Of course not. Extensive excitatory projections from higher neural regions in the visual streams and cross-columnar projections within a cortical region provide a straightforward physical explanation of endogenously generated single-neuron dynamics (Gilbert et al. 2000). Despite this, even physicalist consciophiles should be troubled by McAdams's and Maunsell's results. Although they have grown comfortable with the eventual physical explanation of consciousness, they still hold out for the special, unique nature of its neural realization and effects. Somehow, consciousness must do something more in the brain than just what increasing stimulus saliency and contrast accomplish. McAdams's and Maunsell's results deny consciophiles even this. This consequence by itself is *philosophically* interesting. That it was garnished by "single-cell" neurophysiology shows further the potential of reductionistic neuroscience, even for *philosophical* concerns about consciousness.

14.4   Reductionist Neuroscience and "Hard Problems"

There are neuroscientists who think of the brain as "just another organ." However, many pursue neuroscience to "know thyself" and are unashamed to express this attitude. For example, in the Introduction to his influential textbook, neurobiologist Gordon Shepherd describes some reasons for studying neurobiology. Two are especially revealing:

> As we grow older, we experience the full richness of human behavior – the ability to think and feel, to remember and create – and we wonder, if we have any wonder at all, how the brain makes this possible. (1994: 3)

> What is the neurobiological basis of racism – the fear and hatred of people who are different? Do terrorism and crime get built into our brain circuits? Why do human beings seem bent on self-destruction through environmental pollution and the development of weapons of annihilation? Why do we have this in our brains, and how can we control it? In all of science and medicine, neurobiology is the only field that can ultimately address these critical issues. (ibid.)

These aren't the rantings of some left-field crank; they are from the editor of the *Journal of Neuroscience*. Nor are they idiosyncratic to Shepherd. Similar citations could be expanded many-fold. Most neuroscientists aren't philosophical philistines.

This still won't satisfy some philosophers. Many remain jealous guardians of the "qualitative" and "subjective" aspects of mind. They seem to think that only they (along with perhaps a handful of psychologists) grapple seriously with "what it is like" to be a conscious, mindful human being. They imply that these features of mind are beyond neuroscientists' professional interest and reach. But they are wrong even about this. Consider the following quote from William Newsome. The task he refers to is the motion direction task discussed in the previous section.

> I believe *the nature of internal experience matters* for our understanding of nervous system function.... Even if I could explain a monkey's *behavior* on our task in its entirety (in neural terms), *I would not be satisfied* unless I knew whether microstimulation in MT *actually causes the monkey to see motion*. If we close up shop before answering this question and understanding its implications, we have mined silver and left the gold lying in the tailings. (in Gazzaniga 1997: 65–6; my emphases)

Yet Newsome asks for no special discipline or methodology to address "hard problems" about consciousness. There are no shortcuts around a broadly empirical, reductionist path: "For the time being . . . I suspect we must feel our way towards these ambitious goals from the bottom up, letting the new light obtained at each level of inquiry hint at the questions to be asked at the next level" (ibid.: 67).[16]

The zealous guardians of "hard problems" in the philosophy of mind should lighten up. They aren't the only ones respectful or in pursuit of the full glory of mind. If the neuroscientists themselves are to be trusted, these problems are not beyond the professional interests or reach of neuroscience. Newsome, for example, concludes: "Though I am sensitive to the issue of 'hard' limits to our understanding, the overall endeavor of cognitive neuroscience is grand. It is worth the dedication of a scientific career, and it certainly beats cloning another gene!" (in Gazzaniga 1997: 68). It also beats concocting yet another variant on worn philosophers' fantasies, like the Twins and Mary the utopian neuroscientist (to name just two).

14.5 Toward Genuinely Interdisciplinary Philosophy and Neuroscience

One of the celebrated themes of late twentieth-century "analytic" philosophy is the continuity between the sciences and philosophy. Witness Quine:

> Ontological questions are on a par with questions of natural science . . . this differ-ence is only one of degree . . . that . . . turns upon our vaguely pragmatic inclination to adjust one strand of the fabric of science rather than another in accommodating some particular recalcitrant experience. (1949: 45)

Or Wilfrid Sellars: "It is the 'eye on the whole' which distinguishes the philo-sophical enterprise. Otherwise, there is little to distinguish the philosopher from the persistently reflective specialist" (1962: 39). Or Hans Reichenbach: "To put it briefly: this book is written with the intention of showing that philosophy has proceeded from speculation to science" (1957: vii). The next generation of philosophers of mind took these claims to heart. Hilary Putnam (1960) found inspiration for his early functionalism in computability theory. Jerry Fodor (1975) found evidence for his in cognitive psychology and Chomskian linguistics. Daniel Dennett (1978) found the "intentional stance" lurking in artificial intelligence. Paul and Patricia Churchland (1985; 1986) found an alternative account of the structure and kinematics of cognition emerging from the neurosciences.

This interdisciplinary turn in philosophy was the vanguard of an entire intellectual trend. Interdisciplinary programs began springing up throughout the sciences. It is no accident that philosophy of mind saw so much of this impact. Cognitive science, especially "cognitive neuroscience" of late, is the most visible (and well-funded) example of self-proclaimed "interdisciplinarity." Psychologist Stephen Kosslyn's characterization is typical:

> [C]ognitive neuroscience is an interdisciplinary melding of studies of the brain, of behavior and cognition, and of computational systems that have properties of the brain and that can produce behavior and cognition. I don't think of cognitive neuroscience as the intersection of these areas, of the points of overlap, but rather as their union: It is not just that each approach constrains the others, but rather that each approach provides insights into different aspects of the same phenomena. (in Gazzaniga 1997: 158–9)

Yet one discovers a different attitude among cognitive neuroscientists when the kid gloves are off and decorum permits gripes to be aired. Few reject the interdisciplinary ideal in principle. But in practice, almost everybody is convinced that those in other disciplines remain ignorant of the contributions of one's own.

Finding published evidence of this attitude is not easy. Scientific writing tends to keep such attitudes subterranean, and the philosophers involved want so much to be taken seriously by the scientists that they express it only rarely. However, a book edited by neuroscientist Michael Gazzaniga (1997) provides the necessary format, and many readers will be surprised to see how deeply this attitude runs. The book contains "interviews" with ten prominent cognitive neuroscientists from the variety of disciplines making up the endeavor. Published originally in the *Journal of Cognitive Neurosciences*, the interviews were email correspondences, and were edited only minimally. The idea was to mimic the after-hours conversations that excite, invigorate, and sometimes even motivate. (The quote from Kosslyn just above comes from his interview.) One theme that emerges is that "interdisciplinarity," while commendable in principle, is still a myth in practice.

Radiologist Marcus Raichle, whose work was so instrumental in developing positron emission tomography (PET) and functional magnetic resonance imaging (fMRI) technologies and analysis, labels the "simplistic behavioral methods" and "indiscriminate use of software packages to analyze data" as the "Achilles heel" of many functional imaging experiments (in Gazzaniga 1997: 33). Psychologist

Randy Gallistel claims that neurobiological approaches to the cellular mechanisms of memory are hampered by outdated ideas about the scope of and crucial parameters for even associative learning: "[C]urrent research on [the neural basis of] memory is based on a fundamentally erroneous conception of what the elements of memory formation are" (in ibid.: 75). Computationally complex and realistic models of memory are being developed in human cognitive psychology and ethology, but these are being ignored by neuroscientists. Psychologist Endel Tulving carries this gripe a step further. Neuroscientists studying the mechanisms of memory have ignored one-half of the phenomenon entirely: retrieval. Cognitive psychologists "discovered retrieval and figured out how to separate it analytically and experimentally from storage in the 1960s." These discoveries revolutionized memory research in cognitive psychology in the 1970s, but "that revolution has not yet reached brain scientists" (in ibid.: 95–6). Linguist Steven Pinker insists that neither the importance of an evolutionary perspective on language nor even a familiarity with "mainstream evolutionary biology" has reached Chomskian psycholinguists. More generally, "the vast majority of cognitive scientists and neuroscientists have not really thought about the evolution of the brain" (in ibid.: 113–14). Neuropsychologist Alfonso Caramazza claims that outdated views from general philosophy of science about predictability have impeded acceptance of the new "cognitive neuro-psychological" approach to language, despite the variety of new deficits the approach continues to reveal (in ibid.: 142–3).

Granted, these are the attitudes of only a handful of researchers. But they are from prominent ones. One leaves Gazzaniga's interviews with the feeling that investigators at the lower levels remain wedded to behavioral methodologies and cognitive theories and concepts that have been out of date for three decades in the disciplines from which they are drawn. Similar judgments about higher-level practitioners' knowledge of cellular and molecular mechanisms from lower-level investigators are also common. Recall, for example, the quote from Shepherd near the beginning of section 14.1 above.[17] These are hardly the attitudes one would expect in an endeavor that considers itself the cutting edge of interdisciplinary science.

The problem is that each discipline comprising cognitive neuroscience is difficult. The endeavor calls for a *community* willing to teach *and learn* the relevant portions of voluminous detail gathered in individual disciplines. Researchers willing to confer with those working at other levels are a necessary first component, but eventually cognitive neuroscience needs researchers trained in the methods and factual details of a variety of levels. It needs *trans* disciplinary researchers. This is a daunting job description. But it does offer hope for philosophers wanting to contribute to real neuroscience, rather than just reflecting on the discipline. Thinkers with graduate training in both philosophy's "synoptic vision" and neuroscience's factual and experimental details would be equipped ideally for this task. The philosophy profession has been slow to recognize this potential niche, but there is some hope that a few graduate programs, publishing companies, and funding agencies are taking steps to fill it.[18]

Notes

Special thanks to Marica Bernstein, who created or adapted the figures and commented on earlier drafts of this paper, and Robert Richardson, whose comments on the penultimate draft led to numerous clarifications.

1   In Bickle (1998: chs 2 and 3), I provide such an assessment and alternative. In later chapters I extend this general account to special features of psychoneural reductions. For an assessment of the general theory, see Richardson (1999). For a critical response to my attempt to distinguish "new wave" from "classical" reductionism, see Endicott (1998). For some empirical and conceptual arguments against my extension of the general theory to psychoneural cases, see Schouten and de Jong (1999) and my discussion in section 14.2 below.

2   Good overviews of synaptic transmission are available in any passable neurobiology or physiological psychology text. Shepherd (1994: chs 6, 7, and 8) is particularly good. For those who learned their elementary neuroscience twenty years ago and haven't kept up, however, be forewarned: the story has changed! The importance of metabotrophic receptors, second messengers, retrograde transmission, and the biochemical effects on gene expression in both pre- and postsynaptic neurons yield a very different picture of synaptic transmission and plasticity. I'll introduce some of this complexity in the subsequent discussion.

3   See, e.g., tables 29.1 and 29.3 in Shepherd (1994) for a list of historical experimental support. These lists only include results prior to the mid-1970s. Both lists have grown considerably since then.

4   I will leave a *great deal* of the known biochemistry out of my discussion. See, e.g., Shepherd (1994: ch. 6) for a good introduction to that.

5   Recently, our understanding of the molecular genetics and biochemistry of LTP induction has increased dramatically. See, e.g., Squire and Kandel (1999: chs 6 and 7) for a good introduction to some of these new details. (Incidentally, this includes work for which Eric Kandel shared the 2000 Nobel Prize for Medicine.)

6   See Kandel et al. (1991: ch. 65) for the full molecular details of this cell-biological "letter." Squire and Kandel (1999: ch. 3) include more recent discoveries.

7   In Bickle (1998: ch. 5, sec. 2), I show how features of this case meet all the conditions on my general account of inter-theoretic reduction developed earlier in that book (in ch. 3).

8   In Bickle (1998: ch. 5, sec. 2), I sketch another: the reduction of a cognitive theory of hierarchically structured memory storage to the mechanisms of LTP in mammalian sensory cortex. The key neuroscientific evidence is electrophysiological and computer simulation results by neurobiologist Gary Lynch, computer scientist Richard Granger, and their colleagues (Lynch et al. 1988; Granger et al. 1989).

9   For example, Schouten and de Jong claim that "Bickle's idea was that the reductive approach *must be conducted* in a purely bottom-up fashion in the sense that it *shuns reference to higher-level functions*" (1999: 253; my emphases).

10 If a higher-level theory postulates entities or processes that are in tension or are flat-out inconsistent with those of available lower-level theories, that is sufficient reason to reject the former. But this "constraint" is part of general scientific methodology. We

don't need a special "coevolution" principle to rule out higher-level theories of this sort (see Bickle 1996; 1998: ch. 4).

11   An autobiographical note is in order here. I remember as a philosophy graduate student being frustrated in neuroscience graduate and lab seminars by the topics that dominated discussion. We had read papers from the then-current neuroscientific literature, filled with rich theoretical ideas and implications – and spent the seminar meeting talking about, e.g., the film speed in the camera and the diameter of the electrode tips. What I didn't realize then was how much graduate training in a science is in the art of experimental design. A talent for "abstract critical reasoning" is no substitute for apprenticeship with a good experimenter.

12   These two sciences are themselves becoming unified under developmental biology. In light of the shared molecular mechanisms of synaptic plasticity and neuron development, Eric Kandel invited us to "conceive of learning as . . . a late . . . stage of neuronal differentiation" (1979: 76). That was a quarter of a century ago, and since then our knowledge of the shared molecular basis of learning and neural development has increased (see, e.g., Shepherd 1994: ch. 9). *Learning* as a late stage of neuron differentiation, espoused by a leading mainstream neuroscientist: could a discipline be any more "mad dog" reductionist?

13   The modality in the final clause of this quotation is deceptive. In the essay, Dretske is careful to point out that he is urging the *availability*, not the truth, of phenomenal externalism. Lycan (1996) is a bit bolder.

14   See the essays in Llinás and Churchland (1996), especially the essay by Llinás and Paré (ch. 1), for neurobiological evidence for endogenesis.

15   For those worried that this talk of causal effects of explicit conscious attention on single neuron activity borders on the mysterious, be comforted. A neural explanation of these effects is under active development. See my brief discussion five paragraphs below.

16   Note that Newsome's "bottom-up" methodology also does not "eschew higher-level theories" in the fashion criticized by Schouten and de Jong (1999). (See section 14.2 above.)

17   See also the Preface and Introduction to Kandel et al. (1991). While the authors don't single out higher-level theorists for being ignorant of advances in cellular and molecular neuroscience, it is clear from content that they are a principal target.

18   Examples include Washington University's "Philosophy–Neuroscience–Psychology" program, Oxford University's "Philosophy, Psychology, Physiology" program, Patricia Churchland's MacArthur Foundation "Genius" grant, the McDonnell Project in Philosophy and the Neurosciences awarded recently to Kathleen Akins, and Kluwer Academic Publisher's new journal, *Brain and Mind: A Transdisciplinary Journal of Neuroscience and Neurophilosophy*.

References

Albright, T. D., Desimone, R., and Gtoss, C. G. (1984). "Columnar Organization of Directionally Selective Cells in Visual Area MT of Macaques." *Journal of Neurophysiology*, 51: 15–31.

Bickle, J. (1995). "Psychoneural Reduction for the Genuinely Cognitive: Some Accomplished Results." *Philosophical Psychology*, 8 (3): 265–85.

—— (1996). "New Wave Psychoneural Reduction and the Methodological Caveats." *Philosophy and Phenomenological Research*, 56 (1): 57–78.

—— (1998). *Psychoneural Reduction: The New Wave*. Cambridge, MA: MIT Press.

Chalmers, D. (1996). *The Conscious Mind*. Oxford: Oxford University Press.

Churchland, P. M. (1985). "Some Reductive Strategies in Cognitive Neurobiology." Reprinted in *Neurocomputational Perspective*. Cambridge, MA: MIT Press (1989): 77–110.

Churchland, P. S. (1986). *Neurophilosophy*. Cambridge, MA: MIT Press.

DeAngelis, G. C., Cumming, B. G., and Newsome, W. T. (1998). "Cortical Area MT and the Perception of Stereoscopic Depth." *Nature*, 394: 677–80.

Dennett, D. (1978). *Brainstorms*. Montgomery, VT: Bradford Books.

Dickinson, A. (1980). *Contemporary Animal Learning Theory*. Cambridge: Cambridge University Press.

Dretske, F. (1996). "Phenomenal Externalism." In E. Villaneuva (ed.), *Perception*. Atascadero, CA: Ridgeview: 143–57.

Endicott, R. (1994). "Constructive Plasticity." *Philosophical Studies*, 74 (1): 51–75.

—— (1998). "Collapse of the New Wave." *Journal of Philosophy*, 95 (2): 53–72.

Fodor, J. A. (1975). *The Language of Thought*. New York: Thomas Crowell.

Gazzaniga, M. (ed.) (1997). *Conversations in the Cognitive Neurosciences*. Cambridge, MA: MIT Press.

Gilbert, C., Ito, M., Kupadia, M., and Westheimer, G. (2000). "Interactions Between Attention, Context and Learning in Primary Visual Cortex." *Vision Research*, 40 (10–20): 1217–26.

Granger, R., Ambros-Ingerson, J., and Lynch, G. (1989). "Derivation of Encoding Characteristics of Layer II Cerebral Cortex." *Journal of Cognitive Neurosciences*, 1: 61–87.

Hawkins, R. D. (1989). "A Simple Circuit Model for Higher-order Features of Classical Conditioning." In J. H. Byrne and W. O. Berry (eds.), *Neural Models of Plasticity: Experimental and Theoretical Approaches*. San Diego: Academic Press: 74–93.

Hawkins, R. D. and Kandel, E. R. (1984). "Is There a Cell-biological Alphabet for Simple Forms of Learning?" *Psychological Review*, 91: 375–91.

Hebb, D. O. (1949). *The Organization of Behavior*. New York: Wiley.

Hooker, C. A. (1981). "Toward a General Theory of Reduction." Part I: "Historical and Scientific Setting." Part II: "Identity in Reduction." Part III: "Cross-categorial Reduction." *Dialogue*, 21: 38–59, 201–36, 496–529.

Horgan, T. (1993). "Nonreductive Materialism and the Explanatory Autonomy of Psychology." In S. Wagner and R. Werner (eds.), *Naturalism: A Critical Appraisal*. Notre Dame: University of Notre Dame Press.

Jackson, F. (1982). "Epiphenomenal Qualia." *Philosophical Quarterly*, 32: 127–36.

Kandel, E. R. (1979). "Cellular Insights into Behavior and Learning." *Harvey Lectures*, 73: 19–92.

Kandel, E. R., Schwartz, J. H., and Jessell, T. M. (eds.) (1991). *Principles of Neural Science*, 3rd edn. New York: Elsevier.

Kincaid, H. (1988). "Supervenience and Explanation." *Synthese*, 77: 251–81.

Llinás, R. and Churchland, P. S. (eds.) (1996). *The Mind–Brain Continuum*. Cambridge, MA: MIT Press.

Lycan, W. (1996). *Consciousness and Experience.* Cambridge, MA: MIT Press.

Lynch, G., Granger, R., Larson, J., and Baudry, M. (1988). "Cortical Encoding of Memory: Hypotheses Derived from Analysis and Simulation of Physiological Learning Rules in Anatomical Structures." In L. Nadel, L. Cooper, P. Culicover, and R. M. Harnish (eds.), *Neural Connections, Mental Computations.* Cambridge, MA: MIT Press: 180–224.

McAdams, C. J. and Maunsell, J. H. R. (1999). "Effects of Attention on Orientation-tuning Functions of Single Neurons in Macaque Cortical Area V4." *Journal of Neuroscience,* 19 (1): 431–41.

McGinn, C. (1989). "Can We Solve the Mind–Body Problem?" *Mind,* 98: 349–66.

Millikan, R. (1984). *Language, Thought, and Other Biological Categories.* Cambridge, MA: MIT Press.

Murasugi, C. M., Salzman, C. D., and Newsome, W. T. (1993). "Microstimulation in Visual Area MT: Effects Ovarying Pulse Amplitude and Frequency." *Journal of Neuroscience,* 13 (4): 1719–29.

Nagel, T. (1989). *The View from Nowhere.* Oxford: Oxford University Press.

Penrose, R. (1994). *Shadows of the Mind.* Oxford: Oxford University Press.

Post, J. F. (1991). *Metaphysics: A Contemporary Introduction.* New York: Paragon House.

Putnam, H. (1960). "Minds and Machines." In S. Hook (ed.), *Dimensions of Mind.* New York: Collier.

Quine, W. V. O. (1949). "Two Dogmas of Empiricism." Reprinted in *From a Logical Point of View.* Cambridge, MA: Harvard University Press.

Reichenbach, H. (1957). *The Rise of Scientific Philosophy.* Berkeley, CA: University of California Press.

Rescorla, R. A. (1988). "Pavlovian Conditioning: It's Not What You Think It Is." *American Psychologist,* 43: 151–60.

Rescorla, R. A. and Wagner, A. R. (1972). "A Theory of Pavlovian Conditioning: Variations in the Effectiveness of Reinforcement and Nonreinforcement." In A. H. Black and W. F. Prokasy (eds.), *Classical Conditioning II: Current Research and Theory.* New York: Appleton-Century-Crofts: 64–99.

Richardson, R. C. (1999). "Cognitive Science and Neuroscience: New Wave Reductionism." *Philosophical Psychology,* 12 (3): 297–308.

Salzman, C. D., Murasugi, C. M., Britten, K. R., and Newsome, W. T. (1992). "Microstimulation in Visual Area MT: Effects on Direction Discrimination Performance." *Journal of Neuroscience,* 12 (6): 2331–55.

Schouten, M. and de Jong, H. L. (1999). "Reduction, Elimination, and Levels: The Case of the LTP-learning Link." *Philosophical Psychology,* 12 (3): 237–62.

Sellars, W. (1962). "Philosophy and the Scientific Image of Man." Reprinted in *Science, Perception, and Reality.* London: Routledge and Kegan Paul.

Shapiro, J. A. (1999). "Genome System Architecture and Natural Genetic Engineering in Evolution." In L. H. Caporale (ed.), *Molecular Strategies in Biological Evolution.* New York: New York Academy of Sciences: 23–35.

Shepherd, G. (1994). *Neurobiology,* 3rd edn. Oxford: Oxford University Press.

Squire, L. and Kandel, E. (1999). *Memory: From Mind to Molecules.* New York: Scientific American Library.

Chapter 15

Personal Identity

Eric T. Olson

15.1 The Problems of Personal Identity

It is hard to say what personal identity is. Discussions that go under that heading are most often about some of the following questions.

Who am *I*? To most people, the phrase "personal identity" suggests what we might call one's individual identity. Your identity in this sense consists roughly of those attributes that make you unique as an individual and different from others. Or it is the way you see or define yourself, which may be different from the way you really are.

Persistence. When psychologists talk about personal identity, they usually mean it in the "Who am I?" sense. Philosophers generally mean something quite different. Most often they mean what it takes for a person to persist from one time to another – for the same person to exist at different times. They are asking for our persistence conditions. What sorts of adventure could you possibly survive? What sort of thing would necessarily bring your existence to an end? What determines which future being, or which past one, is you? You point to a girl in an old photograph and say that she is you. What makes you that one – rather than, say, one of the others? What is it about the way she relates to you as you are now that makes her you? Historically, this question often arises out of the hope that we might continue to exist after we die. Whether this is in any sense possible depends on whether biological death is the sort of thing that one *could* survive. Imagine that after your death there really will be someone, in the next world or in this one, related to you in certain ways. What, if anything, would make that person you – rather than me, say, or a new person who didn't exist before? How would he have to relate to you as you are now in order to be you?

Evidence. How do we find out who is who? What evidence do we appeal to in deciding whether the person here now is the one who was here yesterday? What ought we to do when different kinds of evidence support opposing verdicts? One source of evidence is memory: if you can remember doing something, or at least seem to remember it, it was probably you who did it. Another source is physical continuity: if the person who did it looks just like you, or, even better, if she is in some sense physically or spatio-temporally continuous with you, that is reason to think she is you. In the 1950s and '60s philosophers debated about which of these criteria is more fundamental: whether memory can be taken as evidence of identity all by itself, for instance, or whether it counts as evidence only insofar as it can be checked against third-person, "bodily" evidence. This is not the same as the Persistence Question, though the two are sometimes confused. What it takes for you to persist through time is one thing; how we find out whether you have is another. If the criminal had fingerprints just like yours, the courts may conclude that he is you. But even if it is conclusive evidence, having your fingerprints is not what it is for some past or future being to be you.

Population. If we think of the Persistence Question as having to do with which of the characters introduced at the beginning of a story have survived to become the characters at the end of it, we can also ask how many characters are on the stage at any one time. What determines how many of us there are now, or where one person leaves off and the next one begins? You may think that the number of people (or persons – I take these terms to be synonymous) is simply the number of human animals – members of the primate species *Homo sapiens*, perhaps discounting those in a defective state that don't count as people. But this is disputed. Surgeons sometimes cut the nerve bands connecting one's cerebral hemispheres (commissurotomy), resulting in such peculiar behavior as simultaneously pulling one's trousers up with one hand and down with the other. Does this give us two people – two thinking, conscious beings? (See e.g. Nagel 1971. Puccetti 1973 argues that there are two people within the skin of every normal human being.) Could a human being with split personality literally be the home of two, or three, or seven different thinking beings (Wilkes 1988: 127f.; Olson 2003)?

This is sometimes called the problem of "synchronic identity," as opposed to the "diachronic identity" of the Persistence Question (and the "counterfactual identity" of the "How could I have been?" Question below). I avoid these phrases because they suggest that identity comes in two kinds, synchronic and diachronic, and invite the absurd question of whether this and that might be synchronically identical but diachronically distinct or vice versa. There is only one relation of numerical identity. There are simply two kinds of situation where questions about the identity and diversity of people and other concrete things arise: synchronic situations involving just one time and diachronic ones involving several times.

Personhood. What is it to be a person? What features make something a person, as opposed to a non-person? At what point in your development from a fertilized egg did there come to be a person? What would it take for a chimpanzee or a Martian or an electronic computer to be a person, if they could ever be?

Some philosophers seem to think that all questions about personal identity reduce to this one. When we ask what it takes for a person to persist through time, or what determines whether we have one person or two at any one time, they say that we are inquiring into our concept of a person (e.g. Perry 1975: 7ff.; Wilkes 1988: viif.). I think this is a mistake. The usual definitions of "person" tell us nothing, for instance, about whether I should go along with my brain if that organ were transplanted. Suppose, as Locke thought, that a person is "a thinking intelligent being, that has reason and reflection, and can consider itself as itself, the same thinking thing, in different times and places" (1975: 335). I am a person on this account, and so is the being that would get my transplanted brain. But that doesn't tell us whether he and I would be two people or one.

What are we? What sort of things, metaphysically speaking, are you and I and other human people? Are we material or immaterial? Are we substances, attributes, events, or something different still? Are we made of matter, or of thoughts and experiences, or of nothing at all? Here are some possible answers to this admittedly rather vague question. We are human animals. Surprisingly, most philosophers, both past and present, reject this answer. I will say more about it later. Historically, the most common answer is that we are partless, immaterial souls (or, alternatively, compound things made up of an immaterial soul and a material body: see Swinburne 1984). Hume said that each of us appears to be "a bundle or collection of different perceptions, which succeed each other with an inconceivable rapidity, and are in a perpetual flux and movement" (1888: 252; see also Quinton 1962; Rovane 1998: 212). A modern descendant of this view says that you are a sort of computer program, a wholly abstract thing that could in principle be stored on magnetic tape (a common idea in science fiction). Perhaps the most popular view nowadays is that we are material objects "constituted by" human animals: you are made of the same matter as a certain animal, but you and the animal are different things because what it takes for you to persist is different (Wiggins 1967: 48; Shoemaker 1984: 112–14; Baker 2000). There is even the paradoxical view that we don't really exist at all. The existence of human people is a metaphysical illusion. Parmenides, Spinoza, Hume, and Hegel (as I read them), and more recently Russell (1985: 50) and Unger (1979), all denied their own existence. And we find the view in Indian Buddhism.

What matters? What is the practical importance of facts about our identity and persistence? Imagine that surgeons are going to put your brain into my head. Will the resulting person (who will think he is you) be responsible for my actions, or for yours? Or both? Or neither? To whose bank account will he be entitled? Suppose he will be in terrible pain after the operation unless one of us pays a large sum in advance. If we were both entirely selfish, which of us ought to pay?

You might think that the answer to these questions turns entirely on whether the resulting person will *be* you or I. Only *you* can be responsible for your actions. The only one whose future welfare you can't ignore is yourself. You have a special, selfish interest in your own future, and no one else's. But many philosophers deny this. They say that someone else could be responsible for your actions. You could have a selfish reason to care about someone else's well-being. I care, or ought rationally to care, about what happens to Olson tomorrow not because he is me, but because he is "psychologically continuous" with me, or relates to me in some other way that doesn't imply numerical identity. If someone else were psychologically continuous with me tomorrow, I ought to transfer my selfish concern to him. (See Shoemaker 1970: 284; Parfit 1971, 1984: 215; Martin 1998.)

How could I have been? How different could I have been from the way I actually am? Which of my properties do I have essentially, and which only accidentally or contingently? For instance, could I have had different parents? That is, could someone born of different parents have been me, or would it have to have been someone else? Could I – this very philosopher – have ceased to exist in the womb before I acquired any mental features? Are there possible worlds just like the actual one except for who is who – where people have "changed places" so that what is in fact your career is my career and vice versa? Whether these are best described as questions about personal identity is debatable. (They certainly aren't about whether beings in other worlds are identical with people in the actual world: see van Inwagen 1985.) But they are often discussed in connection with the others.

That completes our survey. These questions are all different, and should be kept apart. I wish I could say what common feature makes these questions, and them alone, problems of personal identity. But as far as I can see there is none, apart from the name. There is no one problem of personal identity, but only a number of loosely related problems.

I will focus in this chapter on the Persistence Question – not because it is the most important (if any, that is the "What are we?" Question), but because it has dominated the philosophical debate on personal identity since Locke. But I will touch on several of the others.

15.2 Understanding the Persistence Question

Identity and change are notoriously hard topics, and even experts often get the Persistence Question wrong. We have already mentioned the tendency to conflate it with the Evidence Question. Here are two further caveats.

First, it is about numerical identity. To say that this and that are numerically identical is to say that they are *one* thing, rather than two. If we point to you now, and then point to or describe someone or something that exists at another time – a certain aged man, say – the question is whether we are pointing to one thing twice, or pointing once to each of two things. You are numerically identical with a certain future being in that a picture of him taken then and a picture of you taken now would be two pictures of one thing.

Numerical identity isn't the same as qualitative identity. Things are qualitatively identical when they are exactly similar. A past or future person needn't be exactly like you are now in order to be you – that is, to be numerically identical with you. You don't remain qualitatively the same throughout your life: you change in size, appearance, and in many other ways. Nor does someone's being exactly like you are now guarantee that she is you. Somewhere in the universe someone else may be just like you are now, down to the last atom and quirk of personality. Nonetheless, you and she wouldn't be one and the same. (You wouldn't be in two places at once.) *Two* people, or two cats or two toasters, could be qualitatively identical.

Nothing can *change* its numerical identity. We sometimes say things like "If I lost all my memories, I wouldn't be me any longer," or "I wouldn't be the same person," or even "I would be someone else." If these claims were about numerical identity, they would be self-contradictory. Nothing can literally be one thing at one time and another, numerically different thing later on. If I say that after a certain adventure I shall be a different person, or that I am not the person I once was, I must mean that that future or past person is numerically identical with me but qualitatively different in some important way. Otherwise it wouldn't be I but someone else who was that way then. People who say these things are usually talking about someone's individual identity, in the "Who am I?" sense. Perhaps I could continue to exist without being the same person as I am now by casting off my current identity and acquiring another – that is, by changing my character or the way I see myself. I should be like a senator who, on being elected president, is no longer the same elected official as she once was, having exchanged her first elected office for another. In both cases we have numerically the same being throughout.

It is unfortunate that the words "identity" and "same" are used to mean so many different things: numerical identity, qualitative identity, individual psychological identity, and more. To make matters worse, some philosophers speak of "surviving," and "surviving as" or "becoming" someone, in a way that doesn't imply numerical identity, so that I could "survive" a certain adventure even though I won't exist afterwards. Confusion is inevitable. When *I* ask whether you would survive something, I mean whether you would exist both before and after it.

Here is a different misunderstanding. The Persistence Question is almost always stated like this:

(1)   Under what possible circumstances is a person existing at one time identical with (or the same person as) a person existing at another time?

We have a person existing at one time, and a person existing at another time, and the question is what is necessary and sufficient for "them" to be one person rather than two.

This is the wrong question to ask. We may want to know whether you were ever an embryo or a fetus, or whether you could survive the complete destruction of your mental features as a human vegetable. These are clearly questions about what it takes for us to persist, and any account of our identity through time ought to answer them. (Their answers may have important ethical implications.) However, most answers to the Personhood Question – Locke's answer quoted earlier, for instance – agree that you can't be a person without having certain mental features. And the experts say that early-term fetuses and human beings in a persistent vegetative state have no mental features. If so, they aren't strictly people. Thus, if the Persistence Question were what it takes for a past or future *person* to be you, someone who asked whether we were ever fetuses or could come to be vegetables wouldn't be asking about our identity through time. But obviously she would be.

A typical answer to question (1) illustrates the trouble: "Necessarily, a person who exists at one time is identical with a person who exists at another time if and only if the former person can, at the former time, remember an experience the latter person had at the latter time, or vice versa." We might call this the *Lockean View*, though it probably isn't quite what Locke believed. It says that a past or future person is you just in case you can now remember an experience she had then, or she can then remember an experience you are having now. It isn't very plausible, but never mind. The point is this. The Lockean View might seem to rule out your becoming a vegetable, since a vegetable can't remember anything. That is, it might seem to imply that if you were to lapse into a persistent vegetative state, the resulting vegetable wouldn't be you. You would have either ceased to exist or passed on to the next world. But in fact the Lockean View implies no such thing. That is because we don't have here a person existing at one time and a person existing at another time (assuming that a human vegetable isn't a person). The Lockean View tells us which past or future *person* you are, but not which past or future thing. It tells us what it takes for one to persist as a person, but not what it takes for one to persist without qualification. So it simply doesn't apply here. For the same reason it says nothing about whether you were ever an embryo (Olson 1997: 22–6; Mackie 1999: 224–8).

So question (1) is too narrow. Instead we ought to ask:

(2)   Under what possible circumstances is a person who exists at one time identical with *something* that exists at another time (whether or not it is a person then)?

Why, then, do so many philosophers ask (1) rather than (2)? Because they assume that every person is a person essentially: nothing that is in fact a person could possibly exist without being a person. (By contrast, something that is in fact a student could exist without being a student: no student is essentially a student.) If that is true, then whatever is a person at one time must be a person at every other time when she exists. This assumption makes questions (1) and (2) equivalent. Whether it is true, though, is a serious issue (an instance of the "How could I have been?" Question). If you are a person essentially, you couldn't possibly have been an embryo, or come to be a vegetable (if such things aren't people). The embryo that gave rise to you isn't numerically identical with you. You came into existence only when it developed certain mental capacities. The assumption also rules out our being animals, for no animal is essentially a person: every human animal started out as an unthinking embryo, and may end up as an unthinking vegetable.

Whether we are animals or were once embryos are questions that an account of personal identity ought to answer, and not matters we can settle in advance by the way we frame the issues. So we had better not assume at the outset that we are people essentially. Asking question (1) prejudges the issue by favoring some accounts of what we are and what it takes for us to persist over others. (In particular, asking (1) effectively rules out the Somatic Approach described in the next section.) It is like asking which man committed the crime before ruling out the possibility that it might have been a woman.

15.3 Accounts of Our Identity Through Time

There are three main sorts of answer to the Persistence Question. The first says that some psychological relation is either necessary or sufficient (or both) for one to persist. You are that future being that in some sense inherits its mental features – personality, beliefs, memories, and so on – from you. You are that past being whose mental features you have inherited. I will call this the *Psychological Approach*. Most philosophers writing on personal identity since Locke have endorsed some version of it. The Lockean View is a typical example.

Another answer is that our identity through time consists in some brute physical relation. You are that past or future being that has your body, or that is the same animal as you are, or the like. Whether you survive or perish has nothing to do with psychological facts. I will call this the *Somatic Approach*. It is comparatively unpopular, though I will later defend it.

You may think that the truth lies somewhere between the two: we need both mental and physical continuity to survive; or perhaps either would suffice without the other. Views of this sort are usually versions of the Psychological Approach. Here is a test case: your cerebrum – the upper brain thought to be chiefly responsible for your mental features – is transplanted into my head. (This is physically possible, though it would be a delicate business in practice.) Two beings result: the person who ends up with your cerebrum and your mental features, and the empty-headed being left behind, which may still be alive but will have no mental features. If psychological facts are at all relevant to our persistence, you will be the one who gets your cerebrum. If you would be the empty-headed vegetable, your identity consists in something non-psychological.

Both the Psychological and Somatic Approaches agree that there *is* something that it takes for us to persist – that our identity through time consists in or necessarily follows from something other than itself. A third view denies this. Mental and physical continuity are evidence for identity, but don't guarantee it, and aren't required. No sort of continuity is absolutely necessary or absolutely sufficient for you to survive. The only correct answer to the Persistence Question is that a person here now is identical with a past or future being if and only if they are identical. There are no informative, non-trivial persistence conditions for people. This is sometimes called the *Simple View* (Chisholm 1976: 108ff.; Swinburne 1984; Lowe 1996: 41ff.; Merricks 1998). It is often combined with the view that we are immaterial or have no parts, though it needn't be. (Hybrid views are also possible: mental or physical continuity may be necessary or sufficient for survival, even if nothing is both necessary and sufficient.)

The Simple View is poorly understood, and deserves more attention than it has received. However, I must pass over it. Another view I will mention and then ignore is that we don't persist at all. No past or future being could ever be numerically identical with you. Strictly speaking, you aren't the person who began reading this sentence a moment ago (Hume 1888: 253; Sider 1996). This is presumably because nothing, or at least no changing thing, can exist at two different times.

15.4   The Psychological Approach

The Psychological Approach may appear to follow trivially from the very idea of a person – from the answer to the Personhood Question (Baker 2000: 124). Nearly everyone would agree that to be a person is at least in part to have certain mental features. People are by definition psychological beings. Mustn't they therefore have psychological persistence conditions? At the very least, can't we rule out a person's surviving the complete loss of *all* her mental features? Mustn't a person who loses all her mental features not merely cease to be a person, but cease to be altogether? That would make some psychological relation necessary for a person to persist.

But matters aren't so simple. Consider a parallel argument. To be a teenager is by definition to have a certain age. Mustn't teenagers therefore have age-related persistence conditions? At the very least, can't we rule out a teenager's surviving the loss of her teen-age? Clearly not. I offer myself as living proof that one can survive one's 20th birthday. The parallel argument relies on the mistaken assumption that every teenager is essentially a teenager, or at least that once you're a teenager you can't cease to be one without perishing. The original argument relies on the analogous assumption that every person is essentially a person, or at least that ceasing to be a person means ceasing to be. As we saw earlier, that assumption is far from obvious.

So the Psychological Approach isn't obviously true, and must be argued for. The most common arguments are based on the idea that you would go along with your brain or cerebrum if it were transplanted into a different head, and that this is so because that organ carries with it your memories and other mental features. But it is notoriously difficult to get from this intuitive belief to a specific answer to the Persistence Question that has any plausibility.

We must first say what mental relation our identity through time is to consist in. The Lockean View of section 15.2 appeals to memory: a past or future being is you just in case you can now remember an experience she had then or vice versa. This faces two well-known problems, discovered in the eighteenth century by Reid and Butler (see the excerpts in Perry 1975).

First, suppose a young student is fined for overdue library books. As a middle-aged lawyer, she remembers paying the fine. Still later, in her dotage, she remembers her law career, but has entirely forgotten paying the fine, and everything else she did in her youth. The Lockean View implies that the young student is the middle-aged lawyer, that the lawyer is the old woman, but that the old woman isn't the young student: an impossible result. If *x* and *y* are one and *y* and *z* are one, *x* and *z* can't be *two*. Identity, as the logicians say, is transitive, and Lockean memory continuity isn't.

Secondly, it seems to belong to the very idea of remembering an experience that you can remember only your own experiences. To remember paying a fine (or, if you like, the experience of paying) is to remember *yourself* paying. That makes the claim that you are the person whose experiences you can remember trivial and uninformative (though it doesn't affect the claim that memory connections are necessary for identity). You can't know whether someone genuinely remembers a past experience without already knowing whether he is the one who had it. We should have to know who was who before applying the theory that is supposed to tell us who is who.

One response to the first problem is to switch from direct to indirect memory connections: the old woman is the young student because she can recall experiences the lawyer had at a time when she (the lawyer) remembered the student's life. The second problem is traditionally met by inventing a new concept, "retrocognition" or "quasi-memory," which is just like memory but without the identity requirement (Penelhum 1970: 85ff.; Shoemaker 1970). This invention has been criticized, though not, I think, in a way that matters here (McDowell 1997). But neither solution gets us very far, for the Lockean View faces the obvious problem that there are many times in my past that I can't remember at all, even indirectly. I can't now recall anything that happened to me while I was asleep last night. But if we know anything, we know that we don't stop existing when we fall asleep.

The best way forward is to explain mental continuity in terms of causal dependence (Shoemaker 1984: 89ff.). A being at a later time is *psychologically connected* with someone who exists at an earlier time just in case the later being has the psychological features she has at the later time in large part *because* the earlier being had the psychological features she had at the earlier time. I inherited my current love of philosophy from a young man called Olson who came to love it many years ago: a typical psychological connection. And you are psychologically continuous with some past or future being if your current mental features relate to those she has then by a chain of psychological connections. Then we can say that a person who exists at one time is identical with something existing at another time just in case the former is, at the former time, psychologically continuous with the latter as she is at the latter time.

This still leaves important questions unanswered. Suppose, for instance, that we could electronically copy the mental contents of your brain onto mine, thereby erasing the previous contents of both brains. The resulting being would be mentally very much like you were a moment before. Whether this would be a case of mental continuity depends on what sort of causal dependence is relevant. The resulting person would have inherited your mental properties in a way, but not in the usual way. Is it the right way, so that you could literally move from one human animal to another via "brain-state transfer"? Advocates of the Psychological Approach disagree (Unger 1990: 67–71; Shoemaker 1997).

15.5   The Fission Problem

Whatever mental continuity comes down to in the end, a far more serious worry for the Psychological Approach is that you could apparently be mentally continuous with *two* past or future people. If your cerebrum were transplanted, the resulting being would be mentally continuous with you, and so, on the Psychological Approach, would be you. Now the cerebrum has two hemispheres, and if one of them is destroyed the resulting being is also mentally continuous with the original person. Here the Psychological Approach agrees with real-life judgments: hemispherectomy (even the removal of the left hemisphere, which controls speech) is considered a drastic but acceptable treatment for otherwise-inoperable brain tumors, and not a form of murder (Rigterink 1980). No one who has actually confronted such a case doubts whether the resulting being is the original person. So the Psychological Approach implies that if we destroyed one of your cerebral hemispheres and transplanted the other, you would be the one who got the transplanted hemisphere.

But now let the surgeons transplant both hemispheres, each into a different empty head. Call the resulting people Lefty and Righty. Both will be mentally continuous with you. If you are identical with *any* future being who is mentally continuous with you, it follows that you are Lefty *and* you are Righty. That implies that Lefty is Righty: two things can't be numerically identical with one thing. But Lefty and Righty are clearly two. So you can't be identical with both. We can make the same point in another way. Suppose Lefty is hungry at a time when Righty isn't. If you are Lefty, you are hungry. If you are Righty, you aren't. If you are Lefty and you are Righty, you are both hungry and not hungry at once, which is impossible.

Short of giving up the Psychological Approach altogether, there would seem to be just two ways of avoiding this contradiction. One is to say that, despite appearances, "you" were really two people all along – a position whimsically called the double-occupancy view (Lewis 1976; Noonan 1989: 122–48; Perry 1972 offers a more complicated variant). There are two different but exactly similar people in the same place and made of the same matter at once, doing the same things and thinking the same thoughts. The surgeons merely separate them. This is implausible for a number of reasons, not least because it means that we can't know how many people there are now until we know what happens later. (The view is usually combined with "four-dimensionalism," the controversial metaphysical thesis that all persisting objects are extended in time and made up of temporal parts.)

The other way out is to give up the claim that mental continuity by itself is sufficient for you to persist. You are identical with a past or future being who is mentally continuous with you as you are now only if *no one else* is then mentally continuous with you: the "non-branching view" (Wiggins 1967: 55; Shoemaker 1984: 85; Unger 1990: 265; Garrett 1998). Neither Lefty nor Righty is you. If both your cerebral hemispheres are transplanted, that is the end of you – though you would survive if only one were transplanted and the other destroyed. This too is hard to believe. If you could survive with half your brain, how could preserving the other half mean that you *don't* survive? (See Noonan 1989: 14–18, 149–68.) For that matter, you would perish if one of your hemispheres were transplanted and the other left in place (though Nozick's 1981 variant would avoid this). And if "brain-state transfer" gives us mental continuity, you would cease to exist if your total brain state were copied onto another brain without erasing yours.

Here is another consideration. Faced with the prospect of having one of your hemispheres transplanted, there would seem to be no reason to prefer that the other be destroyed. On the contrary: wouldn't you rather have both preserved, even if they go into different heads? Yet on the non-branching view, that is to prefer death over continued existence. This is what leads Parfit and others to say that you don't really want to continue existing. Insofar as you are rational, anyway, you only want there to be someone mentally continuous with you in the future, whether or not he is strictly you. More generally, facts about who is identical with whom have no practical importance. But then we have to wonder whether we had any reason to accept the Psychological Approach in the first place. Suppose you would care about the welfare of your two fission offshoots in just the way that you ordinarily care about your own welfare, even though neither of them would be you. Then the fact that you would care about what happened to the person who got your whole brain in the original transplant case doesn't suggest that he would be you.

It is sometimes said that fission isn't a problem for the Psychological Approach per se, but afflicts all answers to the Persistence Question apart from the Simple View. I am not persuaded that it arises for the version of the Somatic Approach that says that we are animals (see section 15.7). I doubt whether anything that could happen to a human animal would produce two human animals, either of which we should be happy to identify with the original were it not for the existence of the other. But I can't argue for that claim here.

15.6 The Problem of the Thinking Animal

The Psychological Approach faces a second problem that has nothing to do with fission. It arises because that view implies that we aren't human animals. No sort of mental continuity is either necessary or sufficient for a human animal to persist. (Carter 1989; Ayers 1990: 278–92; Snowdon 1990; Olson 1997: 80f., 100–9. McDowell 1997: 237 and Wiggins 1980: 160, 180 apparently disagree.) Not necessary: every human animal starts out as an embryo, and may end up in a persistent vegetative state. Neither an embryo nor a human vegetable has any mental features at all, and so neither is mentally continuous with anything. So a human animal can persist without any sort of mental continuity. If *you* need mental continuity to persist, you aren't a human animal. Not sufficient: if your cerebrum were transplanted into another head, then the one who got that organ, and no one else, would be mentally continuous with you as you were before the operation. But the surgeons wouldn't thereby move any human animal from one head to another. They would simply move an organ from one animal to another. (The empty-headed thing left behind would still be an animal, while a detached cerebrum is no more an animal than a freshly severed arm is an animal.) No mental continuity of any sort suffices for a human animal to persist. If it suffices for you to persist, then again you aren't a human animal.

No advocate of the Psychological Approach denies that you relate in an intimate way to a certain human animal – the one you see when you look in a mirror. And human animals can think and have experiences. The immature and the brain-damaged may be exceptions, but certainly those with mature nervous systems in good working order can think. So there is a thinking human animal now located where you are. But surely *you* are the thinking thing located where you are. It follows that you are that animal. And since the animal has non-psychological persistence conditions, that contradicts the Psychological Approach. Call this the problem of the thinking animal.

The problem wouldn't arise if the human animal associated with you were unable to think. But that is implausible. It has a healthy human brain in good working order. It even has the same surroundings and evolutionary history as you have. What could prevent it from thinking? If "your" animal can't think, that must be because no animal of any sort could ever think. Strictly speaking, animals must be no more intelligent than trees. That suggests that thinking things must be immaterial: if any material thing could think, it would be an animal. But few friends of the Psychological Approach say that we are immaterial. Anyone who denies that animals can think, yet insists that we (who can think) are material, had better have an explanation for this astonishing claim. Shoemaker proposes that animals can't think because they have the wrong persistence conditions (1984: 92–7; 1997; 1999). The nature of mental properties entails that mental continuity must suffice for their bearers to persist through time. Material things with the right persistence conditions, however, can think. But he has found few followers (*Noûs* 2002).

On the other hand, if human animals *can* think, but you and I aren't animals, then there are at least two thinking things wherever we thought there was just one. This chapter was co-written by an animal and a non-animal philosopher. I ought to wonder which one I am. I may think I'm the non-animal. But the animal has the same reasons for thinking that *it* is the non-animal as I have for thinking that I am, yet is mistaken. So how do I know that I'm not the one making the mistake? If I were the animal, I'd still think I was the non-animal. So even if I am something other than an animal, it is hard to see how I could ever know it.

For that matter, if "my" animal can think, it presumably has the same mental features as I have. (Otherwise we should expect an explanation for the difference.) That ought to make it a person. People would then come in two kinds: animal people and non-animal ones. Animal people would have non-psychological persistence conditions. But the Psychological Approach claimed that all people persist by virtue of mental continuity. Alternatively, if human animals aren't people, then at most half of the rational, intelligent, self-conscious, morally responsible beings walking the earth are people. Being a person, per se, would have no practical significance. And we could never know whether we are people. That conflicts with most accounts of what it is to be a person.

Noonan proposes a linguistic hypothesis to solve some of these problems (1989: 75f.; 1998: 316). First, not just any rational, self-conscious being is a person, but only one with psychological persistence conditions. So human animals don't count as people. Secondly, personal pronouns such as "I" (and names such as "Socrates") always refer to people. Thus, when the animal associated with you says "I," it doesn't refer to itself. Rather, it refers to you, "its" person. When it says "I am a person," it isn't saying falsely that *it* is a person, but truly that you are. So the animal isn't mistaken about which thing it is, and neither are you. You can infer that you are a person from the linguistic facts that you are whatever you refer to when you say "I," and that "I" always refers to a person. You can know that you aren't an animal because people by definition have persistence conditions different from those of animals. This proposal faces difficulties that I can't go into here. In any case, it still leaves us with an uncomfortable surplus of thinking beings, and makes personhood a trivial property.

Of course, another way round the problem of the thinking animal is to accept that we are animals, and give up the Psychological Approach.

15.7 The Somatic Approach

The Psychological Approach is attractive because when we imagine cases where mental and physical continuity come apart, it is easy to think that we go along with the former. But an equally attractive idea is that we are animals. That is certainly what we appear to be. When you see yourself or another person, you see a human animal. And as we have seen, the apparent fact that human animals can think provides a strong argument for our being animals. If we are animals, though, then we have the persistence conditions of animals. And animals appear to persist through time by virtue of some sort of brute physical continuity. Thus, the most natural account of what we are leads to the Somatic Approach.

A few philosophers endorse the Somatic Approach without saying that we are animals. They say that we are our bodies (Thomson 1997), or that our identity through time consists in the identity of our bodies (Ayer 1936: 194). These are versions of the so-called Bodily Criterion of personal identity. It is unclear how they relate to the view that we are animals. It is often said that someone could have a partly or wholly inorganic body. But no animal could be partly or wholly inorganic. If you cut off an animal's limb and replace it with an inorganic prosthesis, the animal only gets smaller and has an inorganic prosthesis attached to it (Olson 1997: 135). If this is right, then you could be identical with your body without being an animal. Some philosophers say that an animal's body is always a different thing from the animal itself: an animal ceases to exist when it dies, but unless its death is particularly violent its body continues to exist as a corpse; or an animal can have different bodies at different times (Campbell 1994: 166). If so, then no one could be both an animal and identical with his body. But I won't enter into these controversies. I find the Bodily Criterion hard to understand because it is unclear to me what it is for something to be someone's body (van Inwagen 1980; Olson 1997: 142–53). I believe that the phrase "human body" or "one's body" is responsible for much philosophical confusion, and is better avoided. In any case, the view that we are animals is the clearest and most plausible version of the Somatic Approach, and I will devote the rest of this chapter to it.

Our being animals doesn't imply that all people are animals. It is consistent with the existence of wholly inorganic people: gods, angels, or robots. The claim is that we *human* people are animals. (A human person is someone who relates to a human animal as you and I do: if you insist, someone with a human body.) Nor does it imply that all animals or even all human animals are people. Human embryos and human beings in a persistent vegetative state are human organisms, but we may not want to call them people. In fact the view implies nothing about what it is to be a person.

Thus, the Somatic Approach gives persistence conditions for some people but not for others: for us but not for gods or angels, if such there be. And it assigns to some non-people the same persistence conditions it assigns to some people: human animals share their persistence conditions with dogs. This leads some to object that it isn't a view of personal identity at all (Baker 2000: 124; see also Lowe 1989: 115). There is some truth in this complaint. The Somatic Approach doesn't purport to give the persistence conditions of all and only people, or of people as such. It even implies that we are only temporarily and contingently people (on the usual definitions of that term). But why is that an objection? If some people are animals, then there *are* no persistence conditions that necessarily apply to all and only people, any more than there are persistence conditions that necessarily apply to all and only students or teenagers. That doesn't mean that being a person is no more important a property than being a student. It means only that a thing's being a person has nothing more to do with its identity through time than its being a student has. And the Somatic Approach is an account of personal identity in the sense of saying what it takes for some people to persist, namely ourselves, and in the sense of being in competition with other views, such as the Psychological Approach, which give accounts of personal identity strictly so called.

Others object to the idea that we are *merely* animals. Surely we're more than just animals? But why should our being animals imply that we are "merely" animals? Descartes was a philosopher, but not merely a philosopher: he was also a mathematician and a Frenchman. Why couldn't something be a person, a grandmother, a socialist, and many other things, as well as an animal? Although "animal" can be a term of abuse (it isn't nice to call someone an animal), our being animals in the most literal zoological sense needn't imply that we are brutish, or that we are no different from other animals, or that we have only "animal" properties. We are very special animals. But we are animals all the same.

It seems clear that our being animals is inconsistent with the Psychological Approach: animals don't persist by virtue of mental continuity. What it does take for an animal to persist is less clear. A living organism is something with a *life*: a complex biological event that maintains an organism's structure despite wholesale material turnover. This leads Locke and others to say that an organism persists just as long as its life continues (Locke 1975: 330f.; van Inwagen 1990: 142–58; Olson 1997: 131–40; Wilson 1999: 89–99). This has the surprising consequence that an organism ceases to exist when it dies and cannot be revived. Strictly speaking, there is no such thing as a dead animal; at any rate nothing can be first a living animal and then a dead and decaying one. Others argue that a living animal can continue to exist as a corpse after it dies (Feldman 1992: 89–105; Carter 1999; Mackie 1999).

As I see it, living organisms and corpses are profoundly different. A living thing, like a fountain, exists by constantly assimilating new matter, imposing its characteristic form on it, and expelling the remains (Miller 1978: 140f.). A corpse, like a marble statue, maintains its form merely by virtue of the inherent stability of its materials. The changes that take place when an organism dies are far more dramatic than anything that happens subsequently to its lifeless remains. I have never seen a plausible account of what it takes for an animal to persist that allowed for a living animal to continue to exist as a decaying corpse. But these are difficult matters.

15.8 Conclusion

I believe that the Psychological Approach owes much of its popularity to the fact that philosophers typically begin their inquiries into personal identity by asking what it takes for us to persist through time. (As we saw in section 15.2, another factor is the way this question is often put.) But an equally important question is what we are: whether we are animals, what we might be if we aren't animals, and how we relate to those animals that some call our bodies, for instance. This question is often ignored, or addressed only as an afterthought. That is why philosophers have failed to appreciate the problem of the thinking animal. Perhaps they ought instead to begin by asking what we are, and only then turn to our identity through time and other matters. Many would end up thinking differently.

References

Introductory discussions are marked with an asterisk.

Ayer, A. J. (1936). *Language, Truth, and Logic.* London: Gollancz.
Ayers, M. (1990). *Locke*, vol. 2. London: Routledge.
Baker, L. R. (2000). *Persons and Bodies.* Cambridge: Cambridge University Press.
Campbell, J. (1994). *Past, Space, and Self.* Cambridge, MA: MIT Press.
Carter, W. R. (1989). "How to Change Your Mind." *Canadian Journal of Philosophy*, 19: 1–14.
—— (1999). "Will I Be a Dead Person?" *Philosophy and Phenomenological Research*, 59: 167–72.
Chisholm, R. (1976). *Person and Object.* La Salle, IL: Open Court.
Feldman, F. (1992). *Confrontations with the Reaper.* New York: Oxford University Press.
*Garrett, B. (1998). "Personal Identity." In E. Craig (ed.), *The Routledge Encyclopedia of Philosophy.* London: Routledge.
Hume, D. (1888). *Treatise on Human Nature*, ed. L. A. Selby-Bigge. Oxford: Clarendon Press. Original work 1739. Partly reprinted in Perry (1975).
Lewis, D. (1976). "Survival and Identity." In A. Rorty (ed.), *The Identities of Persons.* Berkeley: California. Reprinted in his *Philosophical Papers*, vol. I. New York: Oxford University Press (1983).
Locke, J. (1975). *An Essay Concerning Human Understanding*, ed. P. Nidditch. Oxford: Clarendon Press. Original work, 2nd edn., first published 1694. Partly reprinted in Perry (1975).
Lowe, E. J. (1989). *Kinds of Being.* Oxford: Blackwell.
—— (1996). *Subjects of Experience.* Cambridge: Cambridge University Press.
Mackie, D. (1999). "Personal Identity and Dead People." *Philosophical Studies*, 95: 219–42.
Martin, R. (1998). *Self Concern.* Cambridge: Cambridge University Press.
McDowell, J. (1997). "Reductionism and the First Person." In J. Dancy (ed.), *Reading Parfit.* Oxford: Blackwell.
Merricks, T. (1998). "There Are No Criteria of Identity Over Time." *Noûs*, 32: 106–24.
Miller, J. (1978). *The Body in Question.* New York: Random House.
Nagel, T. (1971). "Brain Bisection and the Unity of Consciousness." *Synthèse*, 22: 396–413. Reprinted in Perry (1975) and in Nagel, *Mortal Questions.* Cambridge: Cambridge University Press (1979).
* Noonan, H. (1989). *Personal Identity.* London: Routledge.
—— (1998). "Animalism Versus Lockeanism: A Current Controversy." *Philosophical Quarterly*, 48: 302–18.
Nozick, R. (1981). *Philosophical Explanations.* Cambridge, MA: Harvard University Press.
Olson, E. (1997). *The Human Animal.* New York: Oxford University Press.
—— (2002). "What Does Functionalism Tell Us About Personal Identity?" *Noûs*, 36: 682–98.

—— (2003). "Was Jekyll Hyde?" *Philosophy and Phenomenological Research*.

—— (forthcoming). "There Is No Bodily Criterion of Personal Identity." In F. MacBride and C. Wright (eds), *Identity and Modality*. Oxford: Oxford University Press.

Parfit, D. (1971). "Personal Identity." *Philosophical Review*, 80: 3–27. Reprinted in Perry (1975).

—— (1984). *Reasons and Persons*. Oxford: Oxford University Press.

Penelhum, T. (1970). *Survival and Disembodied Existence*. London: Routledge.

Perry, J. (1972). "Can the Self Divide?" *Journal of Philosophy*, 69: 463–88.

—— (ed.) (1975). *Personal Identity*. Berkeley: University of California Press.

Puccetti, R. (1973). "Brain Bisection and Personal Identity." *British Journal for the Philosophy of Science*, 24: 339–55.

Quinton, A. (1962). "The Soul." *Journal of Philosophy*, 59: 393–403. Reprinted in Perry (1975).

Rigterink, R. (1980). "Puccetti and Brain Bisection: An Attempt at Mental Division." *Canadian Journal of Philosophy*, 10: 429–52.

Rovane, C. (1998). *The Bounds of Agency*. Princeton: Princeton University Press.

Russell, B. (1918). "The Philosophy of Logical Atomism." *Monist*, 28: 495–527; *Monist*, 29: 32–63, 190–222. Reprinted in R. Marsh (ed.), *Logic and Knowledge*. London: Allen and Unwin (1956), and in D. Pears (ed.), *The Philosophy of Logical Atomism*. La Salle, IL: Open Court (1985); page numbers from the latter.

Shoemaker, S. (1970). "Persons and Their Pasts." *American Philosophical Quarterly*, 7: 269–85.

*—— (1984). "Personal Identity: A Materialist's Account." In S. Shoemaker and R. Swinburne, *Personal Identity*. Oxford: Blackwell.

—— (1997). "Self and Substance." *Philosophical Perspectives*, 11: 283–319.

—— (1999). "Self, Body, and Coincidence." *Proceedings of the Aristotelian Society*, Supplementary volume 73: 287–306.

Sider, T. (1996). "All the World's a Stage." *Australasian Journal of Philosophy*: 433–53.

Snowdon, P. (1990). "Persons, Animals, and Ourselves." In Christopher Gill (ed.), *The Person and the Human Mind*. Oxford: Clarendon Press.

* Swinburne, R. (1984). "Personal Identity: The Dualist Theory." In S. Shoemaker and R. Swinburne, *Personal Identity*. Oxford: Blackwell.

Thomson, J. J. (1997). "People and Their Bodies." In J. Dancy (ed.), *Reading Parfit*. Oxford: Blackwell.

Unger, P. (1979). "I do not Exist." In G. F. MacDonald (ed.), *Perception and Identity*. London: Macmillan. (Reprinted in M. Rea (ed.), *Material Constitution*, Lanham, MD: Rowman and Littlefield.)

—— (1990). *Identity, Consciousness, and Value*. New York: Oxford University Press.

Van Inwagen, P. (1980). "Philosophers and the Words 'Human Body'." In van Inwagen (ed.), *Time and Cause*. Dordrecht: Reidel.

—— (1985). "Plantinga on Trans-World Identity." In J. Tomberlin and P. van Inwagen (eds.), *Alvin Plantinga*. Dordrecht: Reidel.

—— (1990). *Material Beings*. Ithaca: Cornell University Press.

Wiggins, D. (1967). *Identity and Spatio-Temporal Continuity*. Oxford: Blackwell.

—— (1980). *Sameness and Substance*. Oxford: Blackwell.

Wilkes, K. (1988). *Real People*. Oxford: Clarendon Press.

Wilson, J. (1999). *Biological Individuality*. Cambridge: Cambridge University Press.

Chapter 16

Freedom of the Will

Randolph Clarke

We commonly think that we are free in making decisions and acting,[1] and for several reasons it is important to us that we have this freedom. Deciding or acting freely is having a valuable variety of control over what one does, the possession of which, we think, is partly constitutive of human dignity. It is widely thought that only when an agent has such control over what she does are her decisions and other actions attributable to her in such a way that she may be morally responsible for what she does, deserving of praise or blame, reward or punishment, depending on the moral qualities of her decisions and other actions. Moreover, we want it to be the case that by free exercises of control, we are making a difference to what happens in the world, including what kinds of person we become. And when we deliberate, it generally seems to us that more than one option is open to us and we are free to pursue each of the alternatives we are considering; if this impression is systematically mistaken, we are routinely subject to an undesirable illusion.

Do we in fact have the freedom that we value in these respects? Some have thought that we do not because, they hold, our world is deterministic.[2] (The world is deterministic if the laws of nature are such that how the world is at any given point in time fully necessitates how it is at any later point; we shall look more closely at determinism below.) The view that there can be no free will in a deterministic world is known as incompatibilism. While some incompatibilists affirm determinism, others, called libertarians, deny determinism and affirm free will. And it is worth noting that an incompatibilist might hold that the world is not deterministic and still we do not have free will.

Many philosophers reject incompatibilism in favor of compatibilism, the view that free will can exist even in a deterministic world. Although some compatibilists believe that our world is deterministic, others hold that it is not or remain uncommitted on whether it is.

16.1   The Compatibility Question

Is free will compatible with determinism? Before addressing this question, we need to see what determinism is. We may understand it to be a feature that the world might have or lack, or as the thesis that our world actually has that feature. Understood either way, what is the feature in question?[3]

16.1.1   Determinism

Sometimes determinism is said to consist in the fact that every event has a cause. But this is not right. As we shall see below, there may be non-deterministic causation; it may be that some events are caused but not determined. In that case, it may be that every event has a cause and yet the world is not deterministic.[4]

Determinism can be well characterized in terms of how it is possible for worlds to be if they have the same laws of nature and are alike at some point in time. In such terms, our world is deterministic (in both temporal directions) just in case any possible world that has exactly the same laws of nature as ours and that is exactly like ours at any one point in time is exactly like our world at every point in time. A slightly more limited, future-directed determinism holds in our world just in case any possible world that has exactly the same laws of nature as ours and that is exactly like ours at any given point in time is exactly like our world at every *later* point in time.

If how the world is at any given point in time can be completely described by a proposition, and if, likewise, the laws of nature can be completely stated, then we may offer equivalent characterizations of determinism in terms of propositions and (broadly) logical necessity (truth in every possible world). The future-directed variety of determinism holds in our world just in case, for any proposition p that completely describes how the world is at any point in time, any true proposition q about (even part of) how the world is at some later point in time, and any proposition l that completely states the laws of nature, it is logically necessary that if (p and l) then q. In the symbolism of modal logic, we write this statement as: $\Box[(p\&l)\supset q]$.

16.1.2   The Consequence Argument

In recent years, the most widely discussed arguments in support of the view that free will is incompatible with determinism have been versions of what is called the Consequence Argument. In the context of this argument, we shall take it that an agent acts with free will just in case she has a choice about whether she performs that action, or just in case it is up to her what she does, or just in case she is able to do otherwise than perform that action. Informally, the argument may be stated as follows:

> If determinism is true, then our acts are the consequences of the laws of nature and events in the remote past. But it is not up to us what went on before we were born, and neither is it up to us what the laws of nature are. Therefore, the consequences of these things (including our present acts) are not up to us.[5]

There are various ways of making this informal argument more precise. We shall focus here on one that has received a great deal of attention.[6]

This version of the argument employs a modal operator "N" which, when attached to any sentence p, gives us a sentence that says that p and no human agent has or ever had any choice about whether p. (As it is sometimes put, "Np" says that it is power necessary for all human agents at all times that p.) For example, where "P" abbreviates a sentence expressing the proposition that the Earth revolves around the Sun, "NP" says that the Earth revolves around the Sun, and no human agent has or ever had any choice about whether the Earth revolves around the Sun.

The argument relies on the following two inference rules involving power necessity:

(α) $\Box p \vdash Np$
(β) $N(p \supset q), Np \vdash Nq$.

Rule (α) says that the premise that it is (broadly) logically necessary that p entails that it is power necessary that p; if it is logically necessary that p, it follows that p and no human agent has or ever had any choice about whether p. Rule (β) says that the two premises that it is power necessary that $p \supset q$ and that it is power necessary that p entail that it is power necessary that q; if $p \supset q$ and no human agent has or ever had any choice about whether $p \supset q$, and if p and no human agent has or ever had any choice about whether p, then it follows that q and no human agent has or ever had any choice about whether q.

Now let "H" abbreviate a sentence expressing a proposition that completely describes how the world was at some point in time prior to the existence of any human agents. Let "L" abbreviate a sentence expressing a proposition that completely states the laws of nature. And let "A" stand in for any sentence expressing a true proposition about how the world is at some point in time later than that covered by "H" (e.g., "A" may say that Clarke agrees to write this essay). Now suppose that determinism (of either variety) obtains in our world. Given our earlier characterizations of determinism, it follows from this supposition that

(1) $\Box[(H\&L) \supset A]$.

(1) is logically equivalent to

(2) $\Box[H\supset(L\supset A)]$.

By an application of rule (α) to line (2), we get

(3) $N[H\supset(L\supset A)]$.

Now the argument asserts as a premise

(4) NH.

Then, by an application of rule (β) to lines (3) and (4), we get

(5) $N(L\supset A)$.

Now the argument asserts as a second premise

(6) NL.

Then, by an application of rule (β) to lines (5) and (6), we get the conclusion

(7) NA.

The argument, if sound, shows that if the world is deterministic, then, given that in fact Clarke agrees to write this chapter, Clarke so agrees and no human agent has or ever had any choice about whether Clarke so agrees. (This would be news to me, since I think *I* had a choice in the matter!) And since "A" may be replaced with any sentence expressing a truth about how the world is at any time later than that covered by "H," the same will go for any action performed by any human agent; if the argument is sound, then it shows that if the world is deterministic, no human agent has or ever had any choice about whether any such action is performed by any such agent. Determinism, the argument purports to show, altogether precludes free will, our having a choice about what we do.

16.1.3 Assessing the argument

The argument relies on two premises. The first, line (4), says, roughly, that we have no choice about what happened in the distant past (before any of us existed). The second, line (6), says, again roughly, that we have no choice about what the laws of nature are. Both premises strike many as evidently true.[7] But, depending on how "having a choice" about something is construed, the denial of one or another of these premises may be less incredible than it first appears.

Given our characterizations of determinism, if the world is deterministic, then if any human agent had done something that she did not in fact do, either the world would have been different at every earlier point in time (and hence "H" would have been false) or the laws of nature would have been different (and hence "L" would have been false). "Multiple-Pasts Compatibilists" opt for the first disjunct, and they claim that, if the world is deterministic, then we are able to do things such that, were we to do them, the past (at every point in time) would have been different.[8] In this sense, they accept, we may be said to have a choice about the distant past. But they distinguish this claim from a stronger one to which they are *not* committed, viz., that we are able to do things that would *causally* affect the past. Once we distinguish these two claims and see clearly the one to which they are committed, they suggest, the air of incredibility about their position should dissipate.

"Local-Miracle Compatibilists" opt for the second of the disjuncts identified above, and they claim that, if the world is deterministic, then we are able to do things such that, were we to do them, the laws of nature would be different.[9] (If an agent had done something that she did not in fact do, they say, the alternative action would have been preceded by some law-breaking event (some miracle) allowing for its occurrence. The miraculous event would have been a violation of some actual law of nature, but not of any law of its world. That world includes the miraculous event, but otherwise its past resembles ours, and hence its laws differ from the actual laws.) In this sense, these compatibilists accept, we may be said to have a choice about what the laws of nature are. But they distinguish this claim from a stronger one to which they are *not* committed, viz., that we are able to perform actions that either would *be* or would *cause* law-breaking events. While the stronger claim may be incredible, the weaker claim to which they are committed is said to be merely controversial.

Many find even the claims to which these compatibilists *are* committed incredible.[10] In any case, the premises of the argument remain points of contention. There has been considerable disagreement as well about the inference rule (β) on which the argument depends.[11]

Whether (β) is a valid inference rule depends on how the operator "N" is interpreted, which depends in turn on how "having a choice" is construed. Suppose that we understand "having a choice" along the lines suggested by multiple-pasts and local-miracle compatibilists. We will say, then, that an agent has a choice about whether p just in case she is able to perform some action such that, were she to perform that action, it would not be the case that p. "Np," then, says that p and no human agent is able at any time to perform any action such that, were she to perform that action, it would not be the case that p. As it happens, there are examples showing that (β), with "N" so interpreted, is invalid.

Here is one such example.[12] Suppose that there exists just one human agent, Sam. Sam has a bit of radium, a substance that sometimes emits subatomic particles; whether or not a given bit of it emits a particle at a particular time is undetermined. Sam destroys this bit of radium before time t, thereby ensuring that the radium does not emit a particle at t, and this is the only way that Sam can ensure this. Sam has a choice about whether he destroys the radium at t; he is able to refrain from doing so. Let "R" say that the radium does not emit a particle at t; let "S" say that Sam destroys the radium before t. Then we have the following instance of (β):

(1) N(R⊃S),
(2) NR, therefore
(3) NS.

The conditional "R⊃S" is true if both the antecedent and the consequent are true, and given the example both are true. There is something that Sam can do such that, were he to do it, this conditional would be false just in case there is something he can do such that, were he to do it, R&~S. But there is nothing that Sam can do that would ensure that R&~S. (He can refrain from destroying the radium, but if he does so, the radium might emit a particle at t.) Hence, the first line of this instance of (β) is true.

The second line as well is true. The radium does not emit a particle at t. And since its emission of particles is undetermined, Sam cannot do anything that would ensure that the radium emits a particle at t. (He can refrain from destroying the radium, but if he does so, it still might not emit a particle at t.)

However, as we supposed, Sam is able to refrain from destroying the radium before t. Hence the conclusion, line (3), is false. Thus, on the current interpretation of "N," we have a counterexample to rule (β), an instance of it in which the premises are true but the conclusion is false. Rule (β), with "N" so interpreted, is thus invalid.

Defenders of the argument for incompatibilism might respond by offering a different inference rule to replace (β),[13] or by proposing a different interpretation of "N" in (β). Along the latter lines, it is easy to see that a small modification of our earlier construal of "N" will suffice to leave (β) immune from the present counterexample. Let us say that an agent has a choice about whether p just in case she is able to perform some action such that, were she to perform that action, it *might* not be the case that p. "Np" will now say that p and no human agent is able at any time to perform any action such that, were she to perform that action, it might not be the case that p.[14] With "N" so interpreted, both premises of the instance of (β) will be false in the radium example. (Sam is able to refrain from destroying the radium before t; were he to do so, it might be the case that R&~S, and were he to do so, it might be the case that ~R.) Hence the radium example is no counterexample to (β) with "N" so interpreted, nor does it appear that there can be any others. With this construal of "N," (β) appears to be a valid inference rule.[15]

The argument for incompatibilism that we have considered is quite strong. With the interpretation of "N" suggested in the previous paragraph, the inference rule (β) on which the argument relies appears valid. The premises of the argument are quite plausible as well, though, as we have seen, there remains some room to doubt that one or another of them is true.

16.2   Compatibilist Accounts

Although some compatibilists maintain that, even if the world is deterministic, it is generally the case when we act that we could have done otherwise, other compatibilists allow that determinism may preclude such an ability. Recall that in valuing free will, we are interested in a type of control that we believe to be connected to several things: human dignity, moral responsibility, making a difference, and the openness of alternatives. Some compatibilists hold that we may have a variety of control that suffices for some of these things but not for others. In particular, some hold the view that if the world is deterministic, we may always lack the ability to do otherwise, but we nevertheless generally act with the type of control that suffices for moral responsibility (and that is thus partly constitutive of human dignity). The name given to this view by some of its proponents is "semicompatibilism."[16]

16.2.1   Frankfurt cases

Semicompatibilists reject a view concerning responsibility that has long been widely held, a view that we may express in the following "principle of alternate possibilities":

(PAP)   An agent is morally responsible for what she has done only if she could have done otherwise.

Some examples presented by Harry G. Frankfurt (1969) have been most responsible for leading many, compatibilists and incompatibilists alike, to reject PAP.

Frankfurt noted that an agent might act in circumstances that constitute sufficient conditions for her performing a certain action, and that thus make it impossible for her to act otherwise, but that do not actually produce her action. When an agent acts in such circumstances, he argued, the fact that she could not have done otherwise does not excuse her from responsibility. Here is one of the cases that Frankfurt offered to illustrate these claims:

> Suppose someone – Black, let us say – wants Jones to perform a certain action. Black is prepared to go to considerable lengths to get his way, but he prefers to avoid showing his hand unnecessarily. So he waits until Jones is about to make up his mind what to do, and he does nothing unless it is clear to him (Black is an excellent judge of such things) that Jones is going to decide to do something *other* than what he wants him to do. If it does become clear that Jones is going to decide to do something else, Black takes effective steps to ensure that Jones decides to do, and that he does do, what he wants him to do. Whatever Jones' initial preferences and inclinations, then, Black will have his way. . . .

Now suppose that Black never has to show his hand because Jones, for reasons of his own, decides to perform and does perform the very action Black wants him to perform. (1969: 835–6)

Here, Frankfurt claimed, we have a case in which conditions obtain – Black's presence and his readiness to intervene – that render it impossible for Jones to do anything other than what he actually does. But Jones is unaware of these conditions, and they never influence in the least his decision or action; Jones decides and acts just as he would have if Black had been absent. We would not, and should not, excuse Jones from responsibility for what he does in this instance on the grounds that he could not have acted otherwise. Hence PAP is false.

Discussion of the case against PAP has been extensive.[17] Here, given limitations of space, let us simply note a couple of points concerning the significance of Frankfurt's argument. First, it would not follow, just from the falsehood of PAP, that responsibility is compatible with determinism. For determinism might preclude responsibility even if it does not do so by precluding the ability to do otherwise.[18] But secondly, if PAP is false, then in evaluating compatibilist accounts, we need to be alert to what they purport to be accounts of. In fact, most recently advanced compatibilist accounts of freedom of action are put forward as accounts of what, with respect to control, is required for moral responsibility. If Frankfurt is right, then these accounts cannot be shown to be mistaken just by showing (if it can be shown) that determinism precludes the ability to do otherwise.

16.2.2 A hierarchical account

Let us turn to some of the most prominent recent compatibilist accounts. Frankfurt himself has advanced a view employing the idea of a hierarchy of attitudes, a notion that has been utilized by several other compatibilists as well.[19] Persons, Frankfurt points out, are capable not only of desiring to perform (or not to perform) certain actions – of having what he calls first-order desires – but also of reflecting upon and critically evaluating our own first-order desires. Given such reflective self-evaluation, we are capable of forming second- or even higher-order desires, such as desires to have (or not to have) certain lower-order desires. Of special interest among these higher-order attitudes are what Frankfurt calls second-order volitions, desires that certain first-order desires be (or not be) the ones that move one to act. When an agent with conflicting first-order desires forms a second-order volition that a certain one of them be the one that moves her to act, she may thereby "identify herself" with that desire. A first-order desire that effectively moves an agent to action Frankfurt calls the agent's will.

Frankfurt distinguishes between having a free will and acting freely. A person's will is free, on his view, only if, with regard to any of his first-order desires, he is free either to make that desire his will or to make some other first-order desire his will instead. Whatever his will, then, the will of the person whose will is free could have been otherwise; he could have done otherwise than to constitute his will as he did. (1971: 18–19)

In contrast, Frankfurt initially maintained, it suffices for acting freely that an agent "has done what he wanted to do, that he did it because he wanted to do it, and that the will by which he was moved when he did it was his will because it was the will he wanted" (ibid.: 19). An agent may act freely, on this view, even when she is unable to do otherwise, even when she lacks free will. And it is acting freely, rather than having a free will, that is required for moral responsibility, according to Frankfurt.

A number of difficulties have been raised for this early version of Frankfurt's account of free action. First, as Frankfurt himself noted (ibid.: 21), just as there may be conflicts among an agent's first-order desires, so there may be conflicts at any higher level in the hierarchy. What are we to say about freedom of action in cases of such higher-order conflict? Secondly, and more fundamentally, higher-order desires are, after all, just desires, and it is not clear how they can have any more authority than first-order desires have with respect to an agent's identity or freedom.[20] A third problem is that Frankfurt placed no requirements on how higher-order desires are formed.[21] It appears that their formation in some case could be due to freedom-undermining compulsion, or that it could be externally controlled in a way that would undermine the agent's freedom; and thus the conditions said by Frankfurt to be sufficient for free action may not in fact suffice.[22] And finally, an agent may, on a certain occasion, desire not to act on a certain desire but nevertheless, through perversity, weakness of will, or resignation, freely act on it, and one may in some instance of free action fail to exercise one's reflective capacities. Hence, the conditions initially advanced by Frankfurt appear not to be necessary for freedom.

Frankfurt has made several revisions to his initial account in order to address some of these difficulties. An early proposal (1976) was that by *deciding* that she wants to be moved by a certain first-order desire, an agent may identify with that desire. Such a decision, he suggested, unlike a higher-order desire, is not capable itself of being something with which the agent is *not* identified; the idea here seems to be that a decision of this sort cannot lack authority in identifying one with a certain first-order desire, and that by means of making such a decision an agent can resolve any conflict among her higher-order desires.[23] In a later work (1987), Frankfurt proposed that a decision favoring a certain first-order desire effectively identifies the agent with that desire only when it leaves the agent "wholehearted." Most recently (1992), it is this notion of wholeheartedness that Frankfurt has emphasized and further articulated.[24] It requires that, if there is any conflict among the agent's higher-order attitudes, the agent is unambivalent, fully resolved concerning where she stands with respect to this conflict. Moreover, a wholehearted agent, Frankfurt says, has no interest in making changes to her commitments, and her lack of such an interest is not unreflective but derives from her understanding and evaluation of her psychic state.

A requirement of wholeheartedness addresses the first of the problems noted above, for it rules out certain types of higher-order conflict. But the requirement, although perhaps appropriate for an account of identification, is too strong for an account of acting with the type of control that is required for moral responsibility; ambivalence is not typically an excusing condition. This requirement may be thought, as well, to solve the problem of the authority of higher-order desires. But this claim seems doubtful, particularly in light of the third problem, that concerning the source of an agent's higher-order attitudes. An agent's wholeheartedly endorsing the desires on which she acts would not seem to render her action free if her endorsement, as well as her wholeheartedness, are the result of compulsion or manipulation. Frankfurt firmly denies the relevance to freedom of any facts about the causal history of higher-order volitions; what matters, he insists, is just the structure of the agent's attitudes.[25] We may grant that in wholeheartedly endorsing a certain first-order desire, an agent "takes responsibility" (1975: 121) for that desire and for acting on it. But an agent may take responsibility, in this sense, without really *being* responsible for what she does, and hence without genuinely *deserving* praise or blame for the ensuing action.[26]

16.2.3 Capacity accounts

The last of the difficulties identified for Frankfurt's account was that, it seems, we may sometimes act freely even when we do not exercise our capacity to act in accord with and on the basis of a higher-order endorsement. The problem here stems from the fact that Frankfurt requires a mesh between one's effective first-order desire and a certain higher-order attitude. What we may call capacity accounts evade this difficulty. On such views, free agency requires that one have a general ability or capacity to appreciate practical reasons and to govern one's behavior by practical reasoning (and on several versions, it requires as well a capacity to reflect rationally on one's reasons and to influence one's reason-states – such as one's desires – and hence one's behavior by means of such reflection); but it is held that one may act freely on some occasion even if one does not on that occasion exercise this capacity.[27]

There is a great variety of such views; we shall consider here a problem that faces all of them. Acting freely is acting with a certain type of control. It requires, it seems, not just that one act with a capacity for (reflective) rational self-governance, but also that one control whether and how, on a given occasion, that capacity is exercised. And a compatibilist version of a capacity account will have to explain how, if the world is deterministic, an agent may control whether and how her capacity for rational self-governance is exercised.

16.2.4   A responsiveness view

The reasons-responsiveness view advanced by John Martin Fischer and Mark Ravizza (1998) is closely related to capacity accounts, and it offers a response to the problem just identified. According to Fischer and Ravizza, the variety of control that suffices for responsibility is what they call guidance control.[28] Guidance control of a given action is characterized not in terms of the *agent* or her capacities, but in terms of the *mechanism* (or process) by which the action is produced: that mechanism must be sufficiently reasons-responsive,[29] and it must be the agent's own mechanism. Let us take these requirements in turn.

Fischer and Ravizza (1998: 69) recognize two aspects of reasons-responsiveness: receptivity and reactivity. The first is a matter of appreciating or recognizing reasons, the second a matter of producing certain decisions and other actions on the basis of one's recognition of reasons. Since responsiveness is a dispositional or modal feature, both of these aspects are characterized in terms of how the mechanism that produces an agent's action on a given occasion would function in various hypothetical (or non-actual) situations.

The receptivity that is required is an understandable pattern of recognition of reasons, minimally grounded in reality. That is, the agent must "not be substantially deluded about the nature of reality" (ibid.: 73), and there must be a variety of scenarios in which, with the mechanism in question operating, the agent would exhibit a pattern of reasons-recognition indicating that she "recognizes how reasons fit together, sees why one reason is stronger than another, and understands how the acceptance of one reason as sufficient implies that a stronger reason must also be sufficient" (ibid.: 71). (For example, if Beth has told a lie, in order for the mechanism that produced her act of lying to have been sufficiently receptive to reasons, there must be various hypothetical scenarios in which Beth has various reasons not to lie, the same type of mechanism operates, and in a suitable variety of these scenarios, she recognizes these reasons not to lie.) Further, the mechanism in question must be receptive to *moral* reasons, among others; and as with receptivity to reasons in general, the receptivity to moral reasons must exhibit an understandable pattern.

The reactivity requirement is weaker; it is satisfied if there is at least one scenario in which the agent has sufficient reason to act otherwise, the mechanism in question operates, and the agent acts otherwise because of that reason to do so. Moral responsibility, according to Fischer and Ravizza, does not require that there be any situation in which, with the mechanism in question operating, the agent would act on moral reasons. An agent who recognizes but steadfastly refuses to be moved by moral reasons may be blameworthy for her misdeeds (ibid.: 79–80).[30]

Turning to the second main requirement, a mechanism is the agent's own, according to Fischer and Ravizza, just in case the agent has "taken responsibility" for actions that stem from it. Taking responsibility (for actions stemming from mechanisms of certain types), they hold, is a process in which the agent comes to see herself as an agent – as someone whose choices and actions are efficacious in the world; she accepts that she is an appropriate target of reactive attitudes (such as gratitude and indignation) and of certain practices (such as the issuing of rewards and punishments) insofar as her actions are produced by mechanisms of those types; and these views of herself are appropriately based on the evidence.[31]

When an agent's behavior is produced by her own, sufficiently reasons-responsive mechanism, she acts with guidance control. And, it may then be held, she acts with a capacity for rational self-governance and exercises control over whether and how, on this occasion, that capacity is exercised.

However, since Fischer and Ravizza characterize ownership in terms of the agent's attitudes about herself, their account may be vulnerable to objections of the following sort.[32] Suppose that, from the beginning of his life, the mechanisms that have produced the actions of a certain agent, Allen, have on every occasion been influenced by a certain neuroscientist, Nina. Without directly altering *what* Allen desires, and without rendering him less rational than an average one of us, Nina routinely alters the relative motivational strengths of Allen's desires so that he is causally determined to choose and perform the actions that Nina selects; and were it not for Nina's interventions, Allen's decisions and other actions would have been quite different. Moreover, Nina is fond of reasons-responsiveness; in various hypothetical situations, she would influence Allen in such a way that he would display an understandable pattern of reasons-recognition (including the recognition of moral reasons) and would at least sometimes, when there is sufficient reason to act otherwise, act otherwise for that reason. And suppose that, unaware of Nina's interventions, Allen has come to hold the views of himself that Fischer and Ravizza require, and that these views are appropriately based on the evidence of which he is aware.[33] He has unwittingly "taken responsibility" for actions stemming from a type of mechanism controlled by someone else. Allen seems to meet the requirements of acting on his own, sufficiently reasons-responsive mechanism, but it does not seem that he acts freely or is morally responsible for what he does.[34]

Fischer and Ravizza claim that in a case of this sort, where an agent has been subject to repeated intervention, the agent "cannot ever have developed into a coherent self. That is, under the envisaged circumstances, there is no self or genuine individual at all" (1998: 234–5, note 28). There is no responsible agent here, they imply, because there is no genuine self or individual. This reply seems to impose a new, third requirement for free action, a requirement of genuine selfhood; and we need to be told what this requirement entails. To underscore this need, we may note that it is not at all clear why, in the present case, Allen could not be said to have developed into a coherent or genuine self. After all, Nina may like coherence as much as she likes reasons-responsiveness.[35]

16.2.5 The remaining dispute

We have thought through several cases (here and in the notes) that may be accepted by compatibilists and incompatibilists alike as showing that a certain compatibilist account fails to draw in the right place the line between influences that do and influences that don't undermine responsibility. This type of activity can yield a negative verdict about particular compatibilist accounts, but it is unlikely to settle definitively the general question whether the control that is required for responsibility is compatible with determinism. However successful we are at this activity, compatibilists may reasonably continue to search for a compatibilist account against which they, at least, find no counterexamples. And should they produce such a theory, incompatibilists might still, again without unreasonableness, maintain that *all* cases in which it is supposed that determinism holds are counterexamples to the view in question.

The general question might be more fruitfully addressed by seeking some basic principles concerning responsibility,[36] or a theory of what it is to be responsible.[37] Work in these directions might, if not settle the dispute, at least clarify the points of disagreement. But since proposed principles or a proposed theory of responsibility will themselves be controversial, a definitive resolution of the question before us does not appear imminent.

16.3 Libertarian Accounts

If deciding and acting freely are incompatible with determinism, then either such freedom is impossible or indeterminism would somehow make it possible. How might the latter be so? Recent incompatibilist (or libertarian) accounts of free action and free will offer three different answers to this question. Some hold that free decisions and other free actions must (or at least can) have no cause at all; others hold that they must be non-deterministically caused by certain prior events; and a third type holds that a free decision or other free action must be caused by the agent, a substance.[38]

Before examining representatives of each of these types of view, let us briefly consider the relation between libertarian freedom and the nature of the mental. Historically, many libertarians have been mind–body dualists, holding either that minds are immaterial substances or that mental properties and events are immaterial. But if free will and action are incompatible with determinism, dualism appears to be of no help to those who wish to find a place in the world for freedom. For one thing, recall that the characterizations of determinism offered above are not restricted to physical events; if the world is deterministic, then (assuming dualism is true) immaterial mental events are as fully determined by prior events as are any other events. Secondly, even if physical events alone were fully determined, all movements of our bodies would be fully determined, and then, if freedom is incompatible with determinism, at most we might be able to make free decisions that could make no difference to what bodily behavior we engage in. Finally, and most importantly, if freedom and determinism are incompatible, then a dualist still has the problem of explaining how indeterminism in the realm of the immaterial can make freedom possible. And if we can explain how an undetermined immaterial decision is free, then it appears that we can just as well explain how an undetermined decision that happens to be a physical event is free. Hence it is not clear that dualism confers any advantage to libertarians; and conversely, if materialism is the better view of the mind, that appears to be no problem for libertarians.[39]

16.3.1 Non-causal views

Some libertarian accounts require that a free action have no cause at all; some require that it either have no cause or be only non-deterministically caused. Since both such views hold that there are no positive causal requirements that must be satisfied in order for an action to be free, we may call them "non-causal views."

Carl Ginet (1990) has advanced one of the most sophisticated non-causal libertarian accounts.[40] On his view, every action is or begins with a causally simple mental event, i.e., a mental event with no internal causal structure. (Decisions and volitions are said to be examples of such basic actions; a volition is held to be an agent's willing or trying to make a certain exertion of her body.) And what makes some mental event a basic action, rather than a change that the agent passively undergoes, is not how that event is caused but rather its having a certain intrinsic feature, an "actish phenomenal quality" (1990: 13). This quality is best described, Ginet suggests, as its seeming to the agent as if she directly produces or determines the mental event in question. (Non-basic actions are then held to consist in an action's generating – e.g. causing – some further event, or in an aggregate of actions.[41])

Given that a certain event is an action, what more is needed in order for it to be a free action? There are no further positive conditions that must be satisfied, on Ginet's view; the additional requirements are wholly negative. The action must not be causally determined, and in performing the action, the agent must not be subject to irresistible compulsion (such as an irresistible craving induced by addiction to a drug).

Two problems arise for this view, and they confront all non-causal accounts. First, acting with free will is exercising a certain variety of control over one's behavior, and non-causal accounts appear to lack an adequate account of in what that control consists. An obvious candidate is that it consists in the action's being caused, in an appropriate way, by the agent, or by certain events involving the agent (such as her having certain reasons and a certain intention).[42] Although Ginet holds that every basic action seems to the agent as if she is directly producing it, he maintains that it is strictly false that agents cause their actions.[43] As for this actish phenomenal quality itself, it seems doubtful that how a mental event seems to the individual undergoing it can *constitute* that individual's exercise of control over that event, rather than be a (more or less reliable) sign of such control. The doubt is reinforced by the fact that, on Ginet's view (1990: 9), a mental event with an actish feel could be brought about by external brain stimulation, in the absence of any relevant desire or intention on the part of the "agent." An event so produced hardly seems to be an exercise of active control, even if it seems to the individual that it is.

Secondly, acting freely is acting with a capacity for rational self-governance and determining, oneself, whether and how one exercises that capacity on a given occasion. Hence it must be possible for a free action to be an action performed for a certain reason, an action for which there is a rational explanation. Obvious candidates for accounts of these phenomena require causal connections between reason-states (such as desires) and actions: an agent acts for a certain reason only if the corresponding reason-state (or the agent's possessing that state) causes, in an appropriate way, the agent's behavior; and citing a reason-state contributes to a rational explanation of an action only if that reason-state (or the agent's possessing it) caused, in an appropriate way, the action.[44] Non-causal views reject such proposals, but it is doubtful that the alternatives they offer are adequate.

Ginet (ibid.: 143) offers the following account of rational explanation that cites a desire. Suppose, for example, that Cate wants to cheer up Dave and believes that if she tells a joke, that will cheer him up; she then tells a joke. On Ginet's view, citing the desire to cheer him up explains her telling the joke just in case: (a) prior to her telling the joke, Cate had a desire to cheer up Dave, and (b) concurrently with telling the joke, Cate remembered that desire and intended of her act of telling the joke that it satisfy (or contribute to satisfying) that desire.[45] Note, first, that the concurrent intention required here is a second-order attitude: an attitude about (among other things) another of one's own attitudes (a certain desire). But it seems plain that one can act for a certain reason, and citing a desire can rationally explain one's action, even if one does not have when one acts any such second-order intention. Cate, for example, might act on her desire to cheer up Dave (and citing that desire might rationally explain her action) even if her only intention is an intention to cheer him up by telling the joke. Further, it is doubtful that Ginet's account provides sufficient conditions for rational explanation. For suppose that Cate also had other reasons for telling the joke, reasons that causally contributed to her doing so and of which she was quite aware when she told the joke. Then, if her desire to cheer up Dave played no role at all in bringing about (causing) her behavior, it is questionable (at best) whether she really acted on that desire and hence whether citing it truly explains what she did.[46]

16.3.2   Non-deterministic event-causal views

Both of the objections raised against non-causal accounts suggest that on an adequate libertarian view, free actions will be held to be caused. Some libertarians maintain that what is needed is an appeal to non-deterministic event causation. When one event brings about another, that instance of causation may be (on some views of causation, it must be) governed by a causal law. But causal laws may be either deterministic or non-deterministic. Statements of the former imply that events of one type always cause events of a second type. Statements of non-deterministic laws imply that events of one type might cause events of a second type. Such laws may be probabilistic, their statements implying that events of the first type probabilify (to a certain degree) events of the second type, or that when there occurs an event of the first type, there is a certain probability that it will cause an event of the second type. When one event non-deterministically causes another, the first produces the second, though there was a chance that it would not bring about that second event.[47]

The simplest event-causal libertarian view takes the requirements of a good compatibilist account and adds that certain events (such as the agent's having certain reasons) that cause the decision or other action must non-deterministically cause it. An agent may, for example, have certain reasons favoring one alternative that she is considering and other reasons favoring another. On the type of account in question, the agent may freely decide in favor of the first action if that decision is non-deterministically caused by her having the first set of reasons, while there remained a chance that she would instead decide in favor of the second alternative, where her so deciding would have been caused by her having the second set of reasons. When these conditions are satisfied, the action is performed for reasons, it is (a proponent will say) performed with a certain variety of control, and it was open to the agent to do otherwise.[48]

A common objection against such a view is that the indeterminism that it requires is destructive, that it would diminish the control with which agents act. The objection is often presented in terms of an alleged problem of luck. Suppose, for example, that a certain agent, Isabelle, has been deliberating about whether to keep a promise or not. She judges that she (morally) ought to keep it, though she recognizes (and is tempted to act on) reasons of self-interest not to. She decides to keep the promise, and her decision is non-deterministically caused by her prior deliberations, including her moral judgment. But until she made her decision, there was a chance that her deliberative process would terminate in a decision not to keep the promise, a decision non-deterministically caused by Isabelle's reasons of self-interest; everything prior to the decision, including everything about Isabelle, might have been exactly the same and yet she might have made the alternative decision. Hence, according to the objection, it is a matter of luck that Isabelle has decided to do what she judged to be morally right. (Isabelle, it might be said, has counterparts in other possible worlds who are exactly like her up to the moment of decision but who decide not to keep the promise; there, but for good luck, goes she.) To the extent that some occurrence is a matter of luck, the objection states, it is not under anyone's control. The required indeterminism is thus said to diminish Isabelle's control over the making of her decision.[49]

Motivated partly by a desire to respond to this objection, some proponents of event-causal libertarian accounts have modified the simple version of such a view that we considered two paragraphs back.[50] The most detailed modified view is that advanced by Robert Kane (1996), which differs from the simple version in two main respects.[51] First, if a decision such as Isabelle's is free, then, on Kane's view, the decision is immediately preceded by an effort of will, an effort on the agent's part to get her ends or purposes sorted out.[52] In such a case of moral conflict, the agent makes an effort to resist temptation and to decide to do what she has judged she morally ought to do. And, Kane requires, such an effort is "indeterminate" in a way analogous to the way in which, according to the laws of quantum mechanics, the position or momentum of a subatomic particle may be indeterminate. Indeed, it is due to such indeterminacy of the effort, Kane holds, that it will be undetermined which decision the agent makes.

Secondly, on Kane's view, when such a decision is free, the agent will, by making that decision, make the reasons for which she decides the reasons she wants more to act on than she wants to act on any others. In Isabelle's case, she will make her moral reasons the ones she wants most to act on by deciding for those reasons.

The first of these modifications, that requiring efforts of will, is held to address the problem of luck in two ways. The problem was raised above by noting that Isabelle has counterparts exactly like her up to the moment of decision who decide not to keep the promise. Kane claims that where there is indeterminacy – as there is on his view with the indeterminate effort of will – there can be no exact sameness from one world to another. Hence, on his view, there would be no counterpart of Isabelle who makes exactly the same effort of will and so is exactly like her up to the moment of decision but decides otherwise. And thus, he suggests, the argument from luck is defused.

But the problem is not so easily dismissed. It is not clear why there cannot be exact sameness of one world to another if there is indeterminacy. In physics, the indeterminate position of a particle may be characterized by a wave function (one specifying the probabilities of the particle's being found, upon observation, in various determinate positions), and a particle and its counterpart may both be correctly characterized by exactly the same wave function. Further, even if there is no such exact sameness, the problem remains. For it is still the case that Isabelle's decision results from the working out of a chancy process, a process that might instead have produced a decision not to keep the promise. And the objection may still be raised that then her decision is a matter of luck and hence less under her control than it would have been had her deliberations causally determined it.

The second way in which, Kane holds, the required efforts of will help to address the problem of luck concerns the fact that they are active attempts by the agent to do something in particular. On his view, when an agent such as Isabelle decides to do what she has judged she morally ought to do, it is as a result of her effort to make that very decision that she makes it. She succeeds, despite the indeterminism, in doing something that she was trying to do. And Kane points out that typically, when this is so, the indeterminism that is involved does not undermine responsibility (and hence it does not so diminish control that there is not enough for responsibility). He draws an analogy with a case (1999b: 227) in which a man hits a glass table top attempting to shatter it. Even if it is undetermined whether his effort will succeed, Kane notes, if the man does succeed, he may well be responsible for breaking the table top.

Kane (1999a, 1999b, and 2000) has recently extended this strategy to cover decisions to do what one is tempted to do as well as decisions to do what one believes one ought to do.[53] In a case such as Isabelle's, he proposes, the decision is preceded by two, simultaneous efforts of will, both of which are indeterminate. The agent tries to make the moral decision, and at the same time she tries to make the self-interested decision.[54] Whichever decision she makes, then, she succeeds, despite the indeterminism, at doing something that she was trying to do. Hence, Kane holds, whichever decision she makes, she may be, like the man who breaks the table top, responsible for what she does.

Note, however, that the man in Kane's example acts with the control that suffices for responsibility only if his attempt to break the table top is itself free. An effort's bringing about a decision can contribute in the same way to the decision's being free, then, only if the effort itself is free. Hence what is needed is an account of the agent's freedom in making these efforts.[55] And Kane faces the following dilemma in providing such an account. If the account of the freedom of an effort of will that precedes a decision such as Isabelle's requires that this effort itself result from a prior free effort, then a vicious regress looms. On the other hand, if the account of the freedom of an effort of will need not appeal to any prior free efforts of will, then it would seem that the account of a free decision itself could likewise dispense with such an appeal. In sum, it does not appear that anything is gained by the requirement that a free decision such as Isabelle's be preceded by an indeterminate effort of will.

Neither does it seem that the second modification favored by Kane helps to address the problem of luck. The problem concerns the agent's control over what she does, and control, it seems, is a causal phenomenon, a matter of what causes decisions and other actions. But an agent's wanting more to act on certain reasons is, on Kane's view, something that is brought about by making a decision, not something that brings about the decision. Hence it does not seem to contribute in any way to the agent's control over her making that decision.

These modifications to the simple, event-causal account do not seem to help with the problem of luck. But how bad is the problem for that simpler view?

First, it is clear that Isabelle's decision is not *entirely* a matter of luck. For it is caused (in an appropriate way, we may suppose) by her appreciation of her reasons, including her judgment that she ought to keep the promise. And its being caused in this way, compatibilists should agree, constitutes the agent's making the decision with a certain degree of control.[56]

Secondly, it may be questioned whether Isabelle's decision is at all a matter of luck, in an ordinary sense. The term "luck," in ordinary usage, carries connotations of something's being out of an agent's control, but it is not so obvious that the indeterminism required by an event-causal libertarian view yields control-diminishing luck. To see this, we may distinguish two importantly different kinds of case: a case in which there is indeterminism between a basic action and an intended result that is not itself an action, and a case – for example, Isabelle's – in which the indeterminism is in the causation of a basic action itself. For the first sort of case, suppose that you throw a ball attempting to hit a target, which you succeed in doing. The ball's striking the target is not itself an action, and you exercise control over this event only by way of your prior action of throwing the ball. Now suppose that, due to certain properties of the ball and the wind, the process between your releasing the ball and its striking the target is indeterministic. Indeterminism located here inhibits your succeeding at bringing about a non-active result that you were (freely, we may suppose) trying to bring about, and for this reason it clearly does diminish the control that you have over the result.[57] But the indeterminism in Isabelle's case – and the indeterminism required by the simple event-causal libertarian view – is located differently. It is located not between an action and some intended result that is not itself an action, but rather in the direct causation of the decision, which *is* itself an action. Isabelle exercises control over that decision *not* only (she need not at all) by way of her performance of some prior action. Hence indeterminism located here is not an inhibiting factor in the way that it is in the first sort of case. If the indeterminism in Isabelle's case nevertheless diminishes control, then the explanation of why it does so will have to be different from that available in the first sort of case. But it is unclear what this alternative explanation would be, and hence it is not clear that the indeterminism in Isabelle's case does in fact yield control-diminishing luck.

The luck objection against event-causal libertarian accounts appears inconclusive. But a second objection remains to be considered. Even if the required indeterminism does not diminish control, it is sometimes objected, it adds nothing of value, it is superfluous.

In order to assess this claim, let us return to the reasons why freedom is important to us. We value a freedom that grounds dignity and responsibility, in the exercise of which we make a difference to the way the world goes, and one that accords with the appearance of openness that we find in deliberating. We can distinguish two aspects of this freedom: a kind of leeway or openness of alternatives, and a type of control that is exercised in action. As we noticed when considering (in section 16.2.1) Frankfurt's attack on the principle of alternate possibilities, the freedom in which we are interested for some of the above things may involve one but not the other of these aspects. In a similar fashion, it may be that what is gained with the indeterminism that an event-causal libertarian view requires has to do with one of these aspects but not the other.

An agent's exercise of control in acting is her exercise of a positive power to determine what she does. We have seen reason to think that this is a matter of the action's being caused (in an appropriate way) by the agent, or by certain events involving the agent – such as her having certain reasons and a certain intention. An event-causal libertarian view adds no new causes to those that can be required by compatibilist accounts, and hence the former appears to add nothing to the agent's positive power to determine what she does. As far as this aspect of freedom is concerned, the requirement of indeterminism does indeed appear (at best) superfluous.

But not so with regard to the other aspect, the openness of more than one course of action. If the Consequence Argument (considered in sections 16.1.2 and 16.1.3) is correct, there is never any such openness in a deterministic world. The indeterminism required by an event-causal libertarian account suffices to secure this leeway or openness, and this may be important to us for several reasons. Some individuals, at least, may find that when they deliberate, they cannot help but presume that more than one course of action is genuinely open to them. If the world is in fact deterministic, these individuals are subject to an unavoidable illusion (since we cannot avoid deliberating). And they may reasonably judge that it would be for this reason better if things are as presented in the event-causal libertarian view. Similarly, some individuals may reasonably judge that if things are as presented in this view, that is better with regard to our making a difference, in performing our actions, to how the world goes. Even if the world is deterministic, there is a way in which, in acting, we generally make a difference: had we not done what we did, things would have gone differently. If things are as presented in an event-causal libertarian account, we still generally make a difference in this way. But we may make a difference in a second way as well: in acting we may initiate, by the exercise of active control, branchings in a probabilistic unfolding of history. There may have been a real chance of things' not going a certain way, and our actions may be the events that set things going that way. One may reasonably judge that it is better to be making a difference in this second as well as in the first way with one's actions. Since we cannot be making a difference in this second way if the world is deterministic, some individuals may have reason to find that the indeterminism required by an event-causal libertarian view is not superfluous but adds something of value.

Is there anything to be gained with respect to responsibility? That is not clear. If responsibility is not compatible with determinism, then what more is required for it than what is offered by a good compatibilist account? The leeway secured by the event-causal libertarian view doesn't seem to be the required addition; if Frankfurt is right, it isn't required at all. The actual causal process that produces a decision or other action on this view is indeterministic, but it is not clear that that makes the crucial difference. It is still, as it is on a compatibilist account, a process in which all of the causes of the decision or other action are events, which may be brought about by other events, leading back to the Big Bang. As was suggested above, it is not clear that on this view the agent exercises any greater positive powers of control. And that is what would seem to be needed if there is to be a different verdict regarding responsibility. If responsibility is not compatible with determinism, it may not be secured by an event-causal libertarian view, either.

16.3.3   Agent-causal accounts

If, on an event-causal libertarian view, agents do not exercise any greater positive powers of control than they do on compatibilist accounts, what type of libertarian view would secure greater control? A number of libertarians have maintained that such a view must hold that a free decision or other free action, while not causally determined by events, is caused by the agent,[58] and that causation by an agent is distinct from and does not consist in causation by events (such as the agent's having certain reasons).[59] An agent, it is said, is a continuant or substance, and hence not the kind of thing that can itself be an effect (though various events in its life can be). On these agent-causal accounts, then, an agent is in a strict and literal sense an originator of her free actions, an uncaused cause of her behavior. This combination of indeterminism and origination is thought to capture best the kind of freedom we desire with respect to dignity, responsibility, difference-making, and the appearance of openness.

Two main problems confront defenders of agent-causal accounts, one concerning the notion of agent causation and the other concerning the rational explicability of free decisions or other free actions on such views.

All theorists who accept a causal construal of agents' control over what they do – and this includes most compatibilists as well as many libertarians – hold that, in a sense, agents cause their free actions. However, most hold that causation by an agent is just causation by certain events involving the agent, such as the agent's having certain reasons and a certain intention. But, as we have seen, the agent causation posited by agent-causal accounts is held not to be this at all. It is said by most agent-causal theorists to be fundamentally different from event causation. And this raises the question whether any intelligible account of it can be given. Even some proponents of agent-causal views seem doubtful about this, declaring agent causation to be strange or even mysterious.[60]

Moreover, even if the notion of agent causation can be made intelligible, the question remains whether the thing itself – causation by a substance or continuant – is possible. An often repeated argument suggests that it is not. Each event, including each action, it is said, occurs at a certain time. And if an action is caused, the argument continues, then some part of that action's total cause must be an event, something that itself occurs at a certain time. Otherwise there would be no way to account for the action's occurring when it did. Hence, if an agent causes an action, there must be something the agent does, or some change the agent undergoes, that causes that action. Since either something the agent does or some change the agent undergoes would be an event, it is concluded, it cannot be the case, as most agent-causal accounts maintain, that free actions are caused by agents and not by any events.[61]

The second main problem for agent-causal views is that free actions can be performed for reasons and can be rationally explicable, but if, as most agent-causalists hold, free actions have no event causes, it does not appear that such rational free action would be possible. Earlier we saw that plausible accounts of acting for certain reasons and of rational explanation appeal to an action's being caused by the agent's having certain reasons, and it appeared that non-causal accounts of these phenomena were not adequate. In denying, then, as most agent-causalists do, that free actions have any event causes, these theorists appear to rule out rational free action.

In response to this second problem, I have proposed (Clarke 1993, 1996) an agent-causal account on which a free action is caused by the agent *and* non-deterministically caused by certain agent-involving events, such as the agent's having certain reasons. Given this appeal to reasons-causation, the view can provide the same accounts of acting for reasons and of rational explanation as can event-causal views. And since the event causation that is posited is required to be non-deterministic, the view secures the openness of alternatives, even on the assumption that this is incompatible with determinism. Finally, the agent causation itself is still held to be distinct from and not to consist in causation by any events, and so this view secures the origination of free actions that seemed an appealing feature of more traditional agent-causal accounts.[62]

This modification of traditional agent-causal views also addresses the objection described earlier to the possibility of agent causation. That objection concludes that it cannot be the case that free actions are caused by agents and not by any events; if an agent causes an action, it is said, then some event involving that agent must cause the action and account for the action's occurring when it does. On the proposed view, some events involving the agent do cause each free action and account for the action's occurring when it does.

Still, questions remain concerning the intelligibility and possibility of agent causation. Timothy O'Connor (1995a, 1996, 2000) and I (1993, 1996), though we differ on details, have both suggested that agent causation might be characterized along the same lines as event causation if the latter is given a non-reductive account. Familiar reductive accounts characterize event causation in terms of constant conjunction or counterfactual dependence or probability increase, and if event causation is so characterizable, then certainly agent causation would have to be fundamentally different. But if causation is a basic, irreducible feature of the world, then we might with equal intelligibility be able to think of substances as well as events as causes.

Even if we can understand the idea of agent causation, and even if the argument for its impossibility considered earlier is not effective, there remain reasons to doubt that it is possible for a substance to cause something. To give just one example: even if causation cannot be reduced to probability increase, it seems plausible that any cause must be the kind of thing that can affect the probability of its effect prior to the occurrence of that effect, even when the cause directly brings about that effect. Events are the sort of thing that can so affect probabilities, and this is due, it seems, to the fact that they occur at times. Substances do not occur (events involving them do), and they do not appear to be the sort of thing that can affect probabilities in the indicated way. This consideration, although not decisive, seems to count against the possibility of causation by a substance.

16.3.4   The existence question

Even if one or another of these libertarian views characterizes well the freedom that we value, and even if what that account characterizes is something that is possible, the question remains whether there is good evidence that what is posited by that account actually exists. And the answer seems to be negative.

Libertarian accounts require, first, that determinism be false. But more than this, they require that there be indeterminism of a certain sort (e.g., with some events entirely uncaused, or non-deterministically caused, or caused by agents and not deterministically caused by events) and that this indeterminism be located in specific places (generally, in the occurrence of decisions and other actions). What is our evidence with regard to these requirements' being satisfied?

It is sometimes claimed that our experience when we make decisions and act constitutes evidence that there is indeterminism of the required sort in the required place.[63] We can distinguish two parts of this claim: one, that in deciding and acting, things appear to us to be the way that one or another libertarian account says they are, and two, that this appearance is evidence that things are in fact that way. Some compatibilists deny the first part.[64] But even if this first part is correct, the second part seems dubious. If things are to be the way they are said to be by some libertarian account, then the laws of nature – laws of physics, chemistry, and biology – must be a certain way.[65] And it is incredible that how things seem to us in making decisions and acting gives us insight into the laws of nature. Our evidence for the required indeterminism, then, will have to come from the study of nature, from natural science.

The scientific evidence for quantum mechanics is sometimes said to show that determinism is false. Quantum theory is indeed very well confirmed. However, there is nothing approaching a consensus on how to interpret it, on what it shows us with respect to how things are in the world. Indeterministic as well as deterministic interpretations have been developed, but it is far from clear whether any of the existing interpretations is correct.[66] Perhaps the best that can be said here is that, given the demise of classical mechanics and electromagnetic theory, there is no good evidence that determinism is true.

The evidence is even less decisive with respect to whether there is the kind of indeterminism located in exactly the places required by one or another libertarian account. Unless there is a complete independence of mental events from physical events, then even for free decisions there has to be indeterminism of a specific sort at specific junctures in certain brain processes. There are some interesting speculations in the works of some libertarians about how this might be so;[67] but our current understanding of the brain gives us no evidence one way or the other about whether it is in fact so. At best, it seems we must remain, for the time being, agnostic about this matter.

If libertarian freedom requires agent causation, and if such a thing is possible, that is another requirement about which we lack evidence. Indeed, it is not clear that there could be any empirical evidence for or against this aspect of agent-causal views.[68]

16.4 Conclusion

The issues of whether free will is compatible with determinism and whether we have free will have usually been taken to be all-or-nothing matters: for each question, it has been assumed, the answer will be yes or no. But our interest in freedom stems from our concern for a variety of things. The control that is required for some of these things, or for some interesting version of some of them, may be compatible with determinism (and with event-causal indeterminism), while what is required for others may not be; we may have some of these things, or some interesting version of some of them, but not others. We are not controlled by neuroscientists such as Nina, and most of us are quite free from compulsions and addictions. Our recognition of reasons fits into quite comprehensible patterns, and we are not radically out of touch with reality. Who can deny that we therefore have certain valuable varieties of control, giving us a certain degree of dignity.

Even if the ability to do otherwise is not compatible with determinism, we have seen reason to think that such an ability is not required for responsibility. And even if certain aspects of responsibility are still undermined by determinism (or by event-causal indeterminism), other aspects of it may not be. Actions can be attributed to agents even if determinism is true, and it may still be appropriate to adopt certain sorts of reactive attitude (such as resentment) toward and to protect ourselves from offenders even if no one ever deserves onerous treatment in return for wrongdoing. Further, even if determinism is true, in acting we generally make a difference, in one way, to how the world goes, even if we do not make a difference in another way. In deliberating and making decisions, too, we make a difference, in one way at least, even if we are, unfortunately, subject to an illusion whenever we deliberate.

If in fact we have some but not all of the things for the sake of which we value free will, then the way of wisdom is to recognize this fact and accept it. To do so is to escape an excessive pessimism. But it is to reject both the view that some deflated variety of freedom is all that we ever wanted in the first place as well as the obstinate conviction, in the absence of evidence, that we have the most robust freedom that we can imagine.[69]

Notes

I am grateful to Charles Cross, John Martin Fischer, Robert Kane, Alfred Mele, and Bruce Waller for helpful comments on earlier drafts of this chapter.

1   Making a decision *is* acting; it is performing a mental action. I distinguish it here for emphasis. Among our actions, decisions seem to be especially important as deliberate exercises of our active control.

2   It has also been argued that divine foreknowledge would preclude our having free will, and some of the arguments offered for this view are structurally similar to some that are offered for the view that determinism is incompatible with free will. See Fischer (1994: chs. 1–6) for a discussion that highlights these parallels. Given space constraints, we shall focus here on the alleged threat of determinism.

3   A thorough discussion of determinism can be found in Earman (1986). Though parts of the book are somewhat technical, chapter 2 provides an excellent and accessible introduction to the issue. Another careful discussion may be found in van Inwagen (1983: 2–8, 58–65).

4   For further discussion of the distinction between determinism and universal causation, see van Inwagen (1983: 2–5) and Earman (1986: 5–6).

5   Van Inwagen (1983: 16).

6   Here I follow the argument set out in van Inwagen (1983: 93–105). Other arguments for incompatibilism, all of which may fairly be viewed as versions of the Consequence Argument, are advanced in Wiggins (1973), Lamb (1977), van Inwagen (1983: 68–93), and Ginet (1990: ch. 5). For general discussion of these arguments, see Fischer (1983, 1988, and 1994: chs. 1–5), Flint (1987), Vihvelin (1988), Kapitan (1991), Hill (1992), and O'Connor (2000: ch. 1). Discussions of specific aspects of the arguments are referenced in the following notes.

7   Consider what van Inwagen says. Using "P_0" for our "H," he writes:

> The proposition that P_0 is a proposition about the remote past. We could, if we like, stipulate that it is a proposition about the distribution and momenta of atoms and other particles in the inchoate, presiderial nebulae. Therefore, surely, no one has any choice about whether P_0. The proposition that L is a proposition that "records" the laws of nature. If it is a law of nature that angular momentum is conserved, then no one has any choice about whether angular momentum is conserved, and, more generally, since it is a law of nature that L, no one has any choice about whether L. (1983: 96)

8   Gallois (1977) and Narveson (1977) are representatives of this position; their papers are followed, in the same volume, by responses from van Inwagen. The discussion there concerns a somewhat different version of the Consequence Argument; I have adapted certain claims so that they apply to the version under consideration here. I borrow the name "Multiple-Pasts Compatibilists" (as well as "Local-Miracle Compatibilists" – see the text below) from Fischer (1994: ch. 4).

9 Lewis (1981) is a proponent of this position. Again, his discussion is directed at a different version of the Consequence Argument, and I have made the necessary adaptations in some of his claims. Lewis's views are discussed in Horgan (1985), Fischer (1988 and 1994: ch. 4), and Ginet (1990: 111–17).

10 The plausibility of denying (6) – NL – may depend in part on what laws of nature are, in particular, on whether they involve any irreducible necessitation. For defense of compatibilism by appeal to a non-necessitarian view of laws, see Swartz (1985: ch. 10) and Berofsky (1987: esp. chs. 8 and 9).

11 There has been extensive discussion of the validity of (β). See, for example, Slote (1982), Fischer (1983, 1986b, and 1994: ch. 2), Widerker (1987), Vihvelin (1988), O'Connor (1993), Kapitan (1996), McKay and Johnson (1996), Carlson (2000), and Crisp and Warfield (2000).

12 The example is adapted from Widerker (1987: 38–9).

13 For two such proposals, see Widerker (1987) and O'Connor (1993).

14 An inference rule with the operator understood in this way is recommended by McKay and Johnson (1996).

15 For an argument that a rule of this sort is valid, see Carlson (2000: 286–7).

16 See Fischer (1994) and Fischer and Ravizza (1998).

17 See, for example, Blumenfeld (1971), Naylor (1984), Stump (1990, 1996, 1999a, and 1999b), Rowe (1991: 82–6), Widerker (1991, 1995a, 1995b, and 2000), Haji (1993 and 1998: ch. 2), Lamb (1993), Zimmerman (1993), Fischer (1994: ch. 7, 1995, and 1999: 109–25), Fischer and Hoffman (1994), Ginet (1996), Hunt (1996 and 2000), Kane (1996: 40–3 and 142–3), Widerker and Katzoff (1996), Copp (1997), McKenna (1997), Wyma (1997), Della Rocca (1998), Mele and Robb (1998), Otsuka (1998), Goetz (1999), O'Connor (2000: 18–22 and 81–4), Vihvelin (2000), and Pereboom (2001: ch. 1).

18 For arguments that determinism precludes responsibility that do not rely on PAP, see van Inwagen (1983: 161–88 and 1999). For discussion, see Fischer (1982), Heinaman (1986), Warfield (1996), Fischer and Ravizza (1998: ch. 6), Stump (2000), and Stump and Fischer (2000).

19 Lehrer (1997: ch. 4) presents another recent hierarchical account. For a thorough discussion of such views, see Shatz (1986).

20 This point was first raised by Watson (1975: 218). Frankfurt acknowledges it when he writes:

> The mere fact that one desire occupies a higher level than another in the hierarchy seems plainly insufficient to endow it with greater authority or with any constitutive legitimacy. In other words, the assignment of desires to different hierarchical levels does not by itself provide an explanation of what it is for someone to be *identified* with one of his own desires rather than with another. (1987: 166)

21 He writes:

> [A] person may be capricious and irresponsible in forming his second-order volitions and give no serious consideration to what is at stake. Second-order volitions express evaluations only in the sense that they are preferences. There is

no essential restriction on the kind of basis, if any, upon which they are formed. (1971: note 6)

And further, "the questions of how [an agent's] actions and his identifications with their springs are caused are irrelevant to the questions of whether he performs the actions freely or is morally responsible for performing them" (1975: 122).

Frankfurt does maintain that "it is only in virtue of his rational capacities that a person is capable of becoming critically aware of his own will and of forming volitions of the second order" (1971: 17). We shall consider below compatibilist accounts that emphasize the requirement of a capacity for practical reasoning and rational action.

22 For discussion of this problem faced by Frankfurt's account (and by other similar views), see Fischer and Ravizza (1998: ch. 7). Mele (1995: ch. 9) argues that an adequate compatibilist account must place some requirements on the history of an agent's attitudes.

23 Note that freedom in performing certain actions has now been accounted for in terms of the making of certain decisions. Though Frankfurt suggests that no decision can be "external" to the agent, plainly decisions can be unfree. Hence, some account is needed of the freedom of the decisions that are now appealed to. However, since Frankfurt later drops the appeal to decisions, we need not pursue this point.

24 The ambivalence that is opposed to wholeheartedness, he notes, "cannot be over-come voluntaristically. A person cannot make himself volitionally determinate, and thereby create a truth where there was none before, merely by an 'act of will.' In other words, he cannot make himself wholehearted just by a psychic movement that is fully under his immediate voluntary control" (1992: 10). Any role for decisions in an agent's constituting her identity, then, is severely downplayed.

Bratman (1996) faults Frankfurt for denying that decision has a crucial role to play in identification, and he develops a view that combines decision and wholeheartedness (or, as he calls it, satisfaction). His view is not advanced as an account of free action, but if it were to be adapted for that purpose, then, as noted above, something would have to be said about the freedom of the required decisions.

25 See, for example, Frankfurt (1987: note 13).

26 Waller (1993) develops this objection.

27 Wallace (1994) and Wolf (1990) advance capacity accounts. Mele (1995) offers a compatibilist view that appeals to the agent's current rational capacities and to the history of her mental attitudes.

28 Guidance control is held to suffice for the "freedom-relevant" component of moral responsibility. Fischer and Ravizza (1998: 26) recognize that there may be other types of requirement (such as an epistemic or knowledge requirement) for respons-ibility.

29 Fischer and Ravizza call the required type of responsiveness "moderate reasons-responsiveness," distinguishing it (ibid.: chs. 2 and 3) from a weaker and a stronger variety that they describe.

30 This reactivity requirement may be too weak. Consider an agent, Karla, who routinely has a compulsive desire to do a certain type of thing (e.g., a compulsive desire to steal). Karla may be appropriately receptive to reasons; she may be disposed to recog-nize an understandable pattern of reasons for not stealing, including moral reasons to refrain. And it may be that Karla, like many a kleptomaniac, would refrain for *some*

good reason, for example, if there were a police officer watching her; hence she may satisfy the reactiveness requirement, even if there is no other type of situation in which she would be moved by reasons not to steal. But when, with no police officer in the vicinity, she steals, she is behaving compulsively, moved by a compulsive desire, and she is not in control of what she does in the manner that is required for moral responsibility. The reactivity to reasons that is required for responsibility, then, appears to be greater than that required on this account. (An objection of this type is raised in Mele (2000).)

Fischer and Ravizza might object that in the situation in which Karla responds to the presence of the police officer, the mechanism that operates is not the same as the one that operates when her compulsive desire to steal moves her to steal, and hence that the mechanism that produces her thefts does not count as sufficiently reasons-responsive on their view. (See their discussion (1998: 74) of a case in which a certain type of reason gives an agent more "energy or focus.") But if they so respond, then we need to know more about how to distinguish mechanisms. Otherwise, the move here appears ad hoc.

It might also be objected that in Karla's case, the second requirement for guidance control – that the mechanism be the agent's own – is not met. (This requirement is discussed in the text below.) Here it can be said briefly, in response, that such ownership is said to be a matter of the agent's having certain attitudes about herself, and there appears to be no reason why Karla could not have the required attitudes.

31   On Fischer and Ravizza's view, then, an agent must have certain beliefs about herself if she is to act with the freedom requisite for moral responsibility. Galen Strawson (1986) agrees, holding that believing that one is a free agent is a necessary condition of being a free agent.

32   The case presented in the text suggests that an agent may satisfy all the requirements of Fischer and Ravizza's view but not be morally responsible. A different kind of case (described by Alfred Mele in conversation) suggests that an agent may be morally responsible but fail to satisfy the requirements of this view. Suppose that Sam occasionally acts akratically: sometimes he judges one course of action best but, because his desire to do something different is strongest (has the greatest motivational strength), he does something different. Seeing that Sam has this problem, a well-meaning group of neuroscientists surreptitiously implants in his brain a computer chip that functions in the following way: whenever Sam judges a certain course of action best, the chip ensures that his desire to pursue that course of action is strongest. All that the chip does, then, is to help Sam overcome his weakness of will and act as he judges best. Such assistance, even if Sam is unaware of it, need not eliminate Sam's responsibility for his behavior. But it appears that it would on Fischer and Ravizza's view. At least in the period immediately following the implantation, the mechanism that operates when the chip contributes to the production of Sam's behavior would be a different type of mechanism from any for actions produced by which Sam has taken responsibility, and so it would appear not to be his own mechanism.

33   It may be thought that Allen's unawareness of Nina's influence renders his taking responsibility for his actions not appropriately based on the evidence. However, as Fischer and Ravizza recognize, to require full knowledge of the mechanisms by which our actions are produced would be to require too much, for there are numerous causal influences on our behavior of which we are routinely unaware. The evidential

requirement may be satisfied, then, by an agent (such as Allen) who is unaware of certain features of the mechanism by which his action is produced. As Fischer and Ravizza put it: "when one takes responsibility for acting from a kind of mechanism, it is as if one takes responsibility for the entire iceberg in virtue of seeing the tip of the iceberg" (1998: 216–17).

34 Note that the influences of which Allen is unaware are the deliberate interventions of another intelligent agent, whereas influences of which we are typically unaware come from unthinking causes. But it is doubtful that this difference can account for Allen's unfreedom. Indeed, we may imagine a variation of his case in which some inanimate object plays a role parallel, in relevant respects, to that of Nina. Suppose, for example, that throughout Allen's life, whenever he acts, M rays emitted by a meteorite in Mongolia happen (by coincidence) to have just the effect on him and his behavior that it was previously supposed Nina's interventions have. Again, it is not clear that any requirements of Fischer's and Ravizza's view are violated, but it seems doubtful that here we have an agent acting freely and one who is responsible for what he does.

35 As Fischer and Ravizza say (in response to a similar defense raised by Frankfurt against a similar objection): "Continuous manipulation is compatible with continuity and intelligibility. Whether an agent's history is continuous or episodic in its content is quite a different matter from whether it is internally or externally generated" (1998: 198–9).

36 The discussions cited in note 18 above pursue this strategy.

37 Two compatibilists who take this approach are Wallace (1994) and Scanlon (1998: ch. 6).

38 As will be explained below, views of this third type hold that causation by an agent does not consist in causation by events.

39 For a dissenting view, see Cover and O'Leary-Hawthorne (1996). They argue that a certain type of libertarian view – an agent-causal view – fits more comfortably with dualist views of persons and the mental.

40 Non-causal accounts are also advanced by McCall (1994: ch. 9), Goetz (1997), and McCann (1998).

41 Ginet's account of non-basic actions and particularly of generation is rather complicated. Interested readers should examine his (1990: ch. 1).

42 The expression "in an appropriate way" is included here to rule out what is called "deviant" or "wayward" causation. Proponents of causal theories of action hold that actions are distinguished by the fact that they are caused by agent-involving events of certain types. But it is recognized that a bodily movement may be caused by events of the right sorts and yet fail to be an action if the causal pathway is deviant or wayward. For discussion of this problem and proposed solutions, see Davidson (1973: 153–4), Brand (1984: 17–30), Bishop (1989: chs. 4 and 5), and Mele and Moser (1994).

43 Velleman (1992: 466, note 14) consequently objects that, on Ginet's view, the actish phenomenal quality that every basic action is said to possess is misleading, illusory. However, Ginet takes his description of the experience one has in acting to be metaphorical; the experience, he holds, does not literally represent to the agent that she is bringing about the event in question.

44 See Audi (1986) for a sophisticated causal account of acting for a certain reason.

45 Ginet claims (1990: 143) that conditions of this sort are sufficient for the truth of an explanation that cites a desire. But he seems to regard them (or at least having the

relevant concurrent intention) as necessary as well. For he maintains (ibid.: 145) that a desire that the agent has that is a reason for performing a certain action and of which the agent is aware when she acts will fail to be a reason for which the agent acts if she does not have the relevant concurrent intention.

46 This objection is developed in Mele (1992: 250–5).

47 For accounts of non-deterministic causation, see, for example, Lewis (1973 [1986]: postscript B), Tooley (1987: 289–96), and Eells (1991).

48 Relatively simple event-causal libertarian views of this sort are sketched by Wiggins (1973), Sorabji (1980: ch. 2), and van Inwagen (1983: 137–50). A similar view, though with the additional requirement that at least some free decisions be "self-subsuming" (self-explaining), is advanced by Nozick (1981: 294–316).

49 Arguments from luck are advanced by Haji (1999) and Mele (1999a and 1999b).

50 Dennett (1978), Mele (1995: ch. 12), and Ekstrom (2000: ch. 4) offer event-causal libertarian views on which indeterminism is required only at earlier stages of the deliberative process. On their views, it is allowed that some undetermined events in the deliberative process causally determine a free decision. For critical discussion of such views, see Clarke (2000).

51 For this discussion of Kane's view, I draw from Clarke (1999).

52 I assume here that Isabelle's decision is what Kane calls a "self-forming action," an action that is not causally determined by any prior events, and hence one the freedom of which does not derive from the freedom of earlier free actions that causally determine it. It may nevertheless be the case, on Kane's view, that the freedom of a self-forming action derives from the freedom of an effort of will that non-deterministically causes it. This point will be discussed later in this section.

53 This recent proposal comes in response to an objection raised by Mele (1999a: 98–9 and 1999b: 279).

54 This doubling of efforts of will introduces a troubling irrationality into the account of free decision. There is already present, in a case of moral struggle, an incoherence in the agent's motives; but this type of conflict is familiar and no apparent threat to freedom. However, to have the agent actively trying, at one time, to do two obviously incompatible things – things such that it is obviously impossible that she do both – raises serious questions about the agent's rationality. This additional incoherence may thus be more of a threat than an aid to freedom.

55 The task of providing such an account might be delayed by holding that these efforts are indirectly free, deriving their freedom from that of earlier free actions. But this maneuver would not evade the problem raised here. The question would remain why the account of the freedom of those earlier actions could not be applied directly to the decision that results from the effort of will.

56 In fact, many contemporary compatibilists (see, for example, Fischer (1999: 129–30)) hold that the control that suffices for responsibility is compatible with non-deterministic as well as deterministic causation of decisions and other actions. If the indeterminism required by the event-causal libertarian account diminishes control, these compatibilists accept, it does not do so to the extent that it undermines responsibility.

It is worth noting as well that non-deterministic causation does not constitute what has been called deviant or wayward causation. For the latter concerns the route or pathway of a causal process, and non-deterministic causation may follow the same pathway as deterministic causation.

57 Although, as Kane points out (with the example of the man who breaks the glass table top), even here indeterminism need not diminish control to the extent that the agent is not responsible for producing the result.

58 Some agent-causal theorists hold not that a free action is caused by an agent but that an agent's causing a certain event is a free action. This difference will not bear on our considerations here.

59 In recent years, agent-causal accounts have been advanced by Chisholm (1966, 1971, 1976a, 1976b, and 1978), Taylor (1966 and 1992), Thorp (1980), Zimmerman (1984), Donagan (1987), Rowe (1991), Clarke (1993 and 1996), and O'Connor (1995a, 1996, and 2000).

60 See, for example, Thorp (1980: 106) and Taylor (1992: 53).

61 This objection stems from Broad (1952: 215). It is raised as well by Ginet (1990: 13–14).

62 Even though, on this type of agent-causal view, a free action is non-deterministically caused by events involving the agent, since the agent makes a further causal contribution to what she does in addition to the contribution made by those events, it would seem that she exercises greater positive powers of control than what could be exercised if all causes were events. (For discussion of this point, see Clarke (1996: 27–30).) Hence this type of view may have a stronger defense against the problem of luck than have non-deterministic event-causal accounts. More would have to be said, however, to establish that this defense is thoroughly adequate.

63 Campbell (1957: 168–70) and O'Connor (1995a: 196–7) appeal to this experience as evidence for libertarian free will.

64 See, for example, Mele (1995: 135–7).

65 This is so for overt, bodily actions regardless of the relation between mind and body, and it is so for decisions and other mental actions barring a complete independence of mental events from physical, chemical, and biological events.

66 For a brief and accessible discussion of these issues as they bear on theories of free will, see Loewer (1996). In addition to surveying some of the more prominent interpretations of quantum mechanics, Loewer argues that libertarianism requires that some events lack objective probabilities. Many libertarians would reject that claim.

67 See, for example, Kane (1996: 128–30 and 137–42) and the sources cited there.

68 For a dissenting opinion, see Pereboom (2001: ch. 3), who argues that we now have evidence against the existence of agent causation.

69 For careful discussion of the implications of our lacking free will (or some valuable variety of freedom), see Honderich (1988: part 3), Smilansky (2000), and Pereboom (2001).

References

Audi, Robert (1986). "Acting for Reasons." *The Philosophical Review*, 95: 511–46.

Berofsky, Bernard (1987). *Freedom from Necessity: The Metaphysical Basis of Responsibility.* New York: Routledge and Kegan Paul.

Bishop, John (1989). *Natural Agency: An Essay on the Causal Theory of Action.* Cambridge: Cambridge University Press.

Blumenfeld, David (1971). "The Principle of Alternate Possibilities." *Journal of Philosophy*, 67: 339–44.

Brand, Myles (1984). *Intending and Acting: Toward a Naturalized Action Theory*. Cambridge, MA: Bradford Books.

Bratman, Michael (1996). "Identification, Decision, and Treating as a Reason." *Philosophical Topics*, 24 (2): 1–18.

Broad, C. D. (1952). *Ethics and the History of Philosophy*. London: Routledge and Kegan Paul.

Campbell, C. A. (1957). *On Selfhood and Godhood*. London: George Allen and Unwin.

Carlson, Erik (2000). "Incompatibilism and the Transfer of Power Necessity." *Noûs*, 34: 277–90.

Chisholm, Roderick M. (1966). "Freedom and Action." In Keith Lehrer (ed.), *Freedom and Determinism*. New York: Random House: 11–44.

—— (1971). "Reflections on Human Agency." *Idealistic Studies*, 1: 33–46.

—— (1976a). "The Agent as Cause." In Myles Brand and Douglas Walton (eds.), *Action Theory*. Dordrecht: D. Reidel: 199–211.

—— (1976b). *Person and Object: A Metaphysical Study*. La Salle, IL: Open Court.

—— (1978). "Comments and Replies." *Philosophia*, 7: 597–636.

Clarke, Randolph (1993). "Toward a Credible Agent-Causal Account of Free Will." *Noûs*, 27: 191–203. Reprinted in O'Connor (ed.) (1995b): 201–15.

—— (1996). "Agent Causation and Event Causation in the Production of Free Action." *Philosophical Topics*, 24 (2): 19–48. Reprinted in abbreviated form in Pereboom (ed.) (1997): 273–300.

—— (1999). "Free Choice, Effort, and Wanting More." *Philosophical Explorations*, 2: 20–41.

—— (2000). "Modest Libertarianism." *Philosophical Perspectives*, 14: 21–46.

Copp, David (1997). "Defending the Principle of Alternate Possibilities: Blameworthiness and Moral Responsibility." *Noûs*, 31: 441–56.

Cover, J. A. and O'Leary-Hawthorne, John (1996). "Free Agency and Materialism." In Jordan and Howard-Snyder (eds.) (1996): 47–71.

Crisp, Thomas M. and Warfield, Ted A. (2000). "The Irrelevance of Indeterministic Counterexamples to Principle Beta." *Philosophy and Phenomenological Research*, 61: 173–84.

Davidson, Donald (1973). "Freedom to Act." In Honderich (ed.) (1973): 139–56. Reprinted in Davidson, *Essays on Actions and Events*. Oxford: Clarendon Press (1980): 63–81.

Della Rocca, Michael (1998). "Frankfurt, Fischer and Flickers." *Noûs*, 32: 99–105.

Dennett, Daniel C. (1978). "On Giving Libertarians What They Say They Want." In Dennett, *Brainstorms: Philosophical Essays on Mind and Psychology*. Montgomery, VT: Bradford Books: 286–99.

Donagan, Alan (1987). *Choice: The Essential Element in Human Action*. London: Routledge and Kegan Paul.

Earman, John (1986). *A Primer on Determinism*. Dordrecht: D. Reidel.

Eells, Ellery (1991). *Probabilistic Causality*. Cambridge: Cambridge University Press.

Ekstrom, Laura Waddell (2000). *Free Will: A Philosophical Study*. Boulder, CO: Westview Press.

Fischer, John Martin (1982). "Responsibility and Control." *Journal of Philosophy*, 79: 24–40. Reprinted in Fischer (ed.) (1986a): 174–90.

—— (1983). "Incompatibilism." *Philosophical Studies*, 43: 127–37.

—— (ed.) (1986a). *Moral Responsibility*. Ithaca: Cornell University Press.

—— (1986b). "Power Necessity." *Philosophical Topics*, 14 (2): 77–91.

—— (1988). "Freedom and Miracles." *Noûs*, 22: 235–52.

—— (1994). *The Metaphysics of Free Will: An Essay on Control*. Oxford: Blackwell.

—— (1995). "Libertarianism and Avoidability: A Reply to Widerker." *Faith and Philosophy*, 12: 119–25.

—— (1999). "Recent Work on Moral Responsibility." *Ethics*, 110: 93–139.

Fischer, John Martin and Hoffman, Paul (1994). "Alternative Possibilities: A Reply to Lamb." *Journal of Philosophy*, 91: 321–6.

Fischer, John Martin and Ravizza, Mark (eds.) (1993). *Perspectives on Moral Responsibility*. Ithaca: Cornell University Press.

—— (1998). *Responsibility and Control: A Theory of Moral Responsibility*. Cambridge: Cambridge University Press.

Flint, Thomas P. (1987). "Compatibilism and the Argument from Unavoidability." *Journal of Philosophy*, 84: 423–40.

Frankfurt, Harry G. (1969). "Alternate Possibilities and Moral Responsibility." *Journal of Philosophy*, 66: 828–39. Reprinted in Fischer (ed.) (1986a): 143–52; in Frankfurt (1988): 1–10; and in Pereboom (ed.) (1997): 156–66.

—— (1971). "Freedom of the Will and the Concept of a Person." *Journal of Philosophy*, 68: 5–20. Reprinted in Fischer (ed.) (1986a): 65–80; in Frankfurt (1988): 11–25; in Pereboom (ed.) (1997): 167–83; and in Watson (ed.) (1982): 81–95.

—— (1975). "Three Concepts of Free Action." *Proceedings of the Aristotelian Society*, Supplementary vol. 49: 113–25. Reprinted in Fischer (ed.) (1986a): 113–23; and in Frankfurt (1988): 47–57.

—— (1976). "Identification and Externality." In Amélie O. Rorty (ed.), *The Identities of Persons*. Berkeley: University of California Press: 239–51. Reprinted in Frankfurt (1988): 58–68.

—— (1987). "Identification and Wholeheartedness." In Ferdinand Schoeman (ed.), *Responsibility, Character, and the Emotions: New Essays in Moral Psychology*. Cambridge: Cambridge University Press: 27–45. Reprinted in Fischer and Ravizza (eds.) (1993): 170–87; and in Frankfurt (1988): 159–76.

—— (1988). *The Importance of What We Care About*. Cambridge: Cambridge University Press.

—— (1992). "The Faintest Passion." *Proceedings and Addresses of the American Philosophical Association*, 66: 5–16.

Gallois, André (1977). "Van Inwagen on Free Will and Determinism." *Philosophical Studies*, 32: 99–105.

Ginet, Carl (1990). *On Action*. Cambridge: Cambridge University Press.

—— (1996). "In Defense of the Principle of Alternative Possibilities: Why I Don't Find Frankfurt's Argument Convincing." *Philosophical Perspectives*, 10: 403–17.

Goetz, Stewart (1997). "Libertarian Choice." *Faith and Philosophy*, 14: 195–211.

—— (1999). "Stumping for Widerker." *Faith and Philosophy*, 16: 83–9.

Haji, Ishtiyaque (1993). "Alternative Possibilities, Moral Obligation, and Moral Responsibility." *Philosophical Papers*, 22: 41–50.

—— (1998). *Moral Appraisability: Puzzles, Proposals, and Perplexities*. New York: Oxford University Press.

—— (1999). "Indeterminism and Frankfurt-type Examples." *Philosophical Explorations*, 2: 42–58.

Heinaman, Robert (1986). "Incompatibilism without the Principle of Alternative Possibilities." *Australasian Journal of Philosophy*, 64: 266–76. Reprinted in Fischer and Ravizza (eds.) (1993): 296–309.

Hill, Christopher S. (1992). "Van Inwagen on the Consequence Argument." *Analysis*, 52: 49–55.

Honderich, Ted (ed.) (1973). *Essays on Freedom of Action*. London: Routledge and Kegan Paul.

—— (1988). *A Theory of Determinism: The Mind, Neuroscience, and Life-Hopes*. Oxford: Clarendon Press.

Horgan, Terence (1985). "Compatibilism and the Consequence Argument." *Philosophical Studies*, 47: 339–56.

Hunt, David (1996). "Frankfurt Counterexamples: Some Comments on the Widerker–Fischer Debate." *Faith and Philosophy*, 13: 395–401.

—— (2000). "Moral Responsibility and Unavoidable Action." *Philosophical Studies*, 97: 195–227.

Jordan, Jeff and Howard-Snyder, Daniel (eds.) (1996). *Faith, Freedom, and Rationality: Philosophy of Religion Today*. Lanham: Rowman and Littlefield.

Kane, Robert (1996). *The Significance of Free Will*. New York: Oxford University Press.

—— (1999a). "On Free Will, Responsibility and Indeterminism." *Philosophical Explorations*, 2: 105–21.

—— (1999b). "Responsibility, Luck, and Chance: Reflections on Free Will and Indeterminism." *Journal of Philosophy*, 96: 217–40.

—— (2000). "Responses to Bernard Berofsky, John Martin Fischer and Galen Strawson." *Philosophy and Phenomenological Research*, 60: 157–67.

Kapitan, Tomis (1991). "How Powerful Are We?" *American Philosophical Quarterly*, 28: 331–8.

—— (1996). "Incompatibilism and Ambiguity in the Practical Modalities." *Analysis*, 56: 102–10.

Lamb, James W. (1977). "On a Proof of Incompatibilism." *The Philosophical Review*, 86: 20–35.

—— (1993). "Evaluative Compatibilism and the Principle of Alternate Possibilities." *Journal of Philosophy*, 90: 517–27.

Lehrer, Keith (1997). *Self Trust: A Study of Reason, Knowledge and Autonomy*. Oxford: Clarendon Press.

Lewis, David (1973). "Causation." *Journal of Philosophy*, 70: 556–67. Reprinted with postscripts in Lewis (1986): 159–213.

—— (1981). "Are We Free to Break the Laws?" *Theoria*, 47: 113–21. Reprinted in Lewis (1986): 291–8.

—— (1986). *Philosophical Papers*, vol. II. New York: Oxford University Press.

Loewer, Barry (1996). "Freedom from Physics: Quantum Mechanics and Free Will." *Philosophical Topics*, 24 (2): 91–112.

McCall, Storrs (1994). *A Model of the Universe*. Oxford: Clarendon Press.

McCann, Hugh J. (1998). *The Works of Agency: On Human Action, Will, and Freedom*. Ithaca: Cornell University Press.

McKay, Thomas J. and Johnson, David (1996). "A Reconsideration of an Argument against Compatibilism." *Philosophical Topics*, 24 (2): 113–22.

McKenna, Michael (1997). "Alternative Possibilities and the Failure of the Counterexample Strategy." *Journal of Social Philosophy*, 28: 71–85.

Mele, Alfred R. (1992). *Springs of Action: Understanding Intentional Behavior*. New York: Oxford University Press.

—— (1995). *Autonomous Agents: From Self-Control to Autonomy*. New York: Oxford University Press.

—— (1999a). "Kane, Luck, and the Significance of Free Will." *Philosophical Explorations*, 2: 96–104.

—— (1999b). "Ultimate Responsibility and Dumb Luck." *Social Philosophy and Policy*, 16: 274–93.

—— (2000). "Reactive Attitudes, Reactivity, and Omissions." *Philosophy and Phenomenological Research*, 61: 447–52.

Mele, Alfred R. and Moser, Paul (1994). "Intentional Action." *Noûs*, 28: 39–68.

Mele, Alfred R. and Robb, David (1998). "Rescuing Frankfurt-Style Cases." *The Philosophical Review*, 107: 97–112.

Narveson, Jan (1977). "Compatibilism Defended." *Philosophical Studies*, 32: 83–7.

Naylor, Margery Bedford (1984). "Frankfurt on the Principle of Alternate Possibilities." *Philosophical Studies*, 46: 249–58.

Nozick, Robert (1981). *Philosophical Explanations*. Cambridge, MA: Belknap Press.

O'Connor, Timothy (1993). "On the Transfer of Necessity." *Noûs*, 27: 204–18.

—— (1995a). "Agent Causation." In O'Connor (ed.) (1995b): 173–200.

—— (ed.) (1995b). *Agents, Causes, and Events: Essays on Indeterminism and Free Will*. New York: Oxford University Press.

—— (1996). "Why Agent Causation?" *Philosophical Topics*, 24 (2): 143–58.

—— (2000). *Persons and Causes: The Metaphysics of Free Will*. New York: Oxford University Press.

Otsuka, Michael (1998). "Incompatibilism and the Avoidability of Blame." *Ethics*, 108: 685–701.

Pereboom, Derk (ed.) (1997). *Free Will*. Indianapolis: Hackett.

—— (2001). *Living Without Free Will*. Cambridge: Cambridge University Press.

Rowe, William L. (1991). *Thomas Reid on Freedom and Morality*. Ithaca: Cornell University Press.

Scanlon, T. M. (1998). *What We Owe to Each Other*. Cambridge, MA: Belknap Press.

Shatz, David (1986). "Free Will and the Structure of Motivation." *Midwest Studies in Philosophy*, 10: 451–82.

Slote, Michael (1982). "Selective Necessity and the Free-Will Problem." *Journal of Philosophy*, 79: 5–24.

Smilansky, Saul (2000). *Free Will and Illusion*. Oxford: Clarendon Press.

Sorabji, Richard (1980). *Necessity, Cause, and Blame: Perspectives on Aristotle's Theory*. Ithaca: Cornell University Press.

Strawson, Galen (1986). *Freedom and Belief*. Oxford: Clarendon Press.

Stump, Eleonore (1990). "Intellect, Will, and the Principle of Alternate Possibilities." In Michael D. Beaty (ed.), *Christian Theism and the Problems of Philosophy*. Notre Dame: University of Notre Dame Press: 254–85. Reprinted in Fischer and Ravizza (eds.) (1993): 237–62.

—— (1996). "Libertarian Freedom and the Principle of Alternative Possibilities." In Jordan and Howard-Snyder (eds.) (1996): 73–88.

—— (1999a). "Alternative Possibilities and Moral Responsibility: The Flicker of Freedom." *The Journal of Ethics*, 3: 299–324.

—— (1999b). "Dust, Determinism, and Frankfurt: A Reply to Goetz." *Faith and Philosophy*, 16: 413–22.

—— (2000). "The Direct Argument for Incompatibilism." *Philosophy and Phenomenological Research*, 61: 459–66.

Stump, Eleonore and Fischer, John Martin (2000). "Transfer Principles and Moral Responsibility." *Philosophical Perspectives*, 14: 47–56.

Swartz, Norman (1985). *The Concept of Physical Law*. Cambridge: Cambridge University Press.

Taylor, Richard (1966). *Action and Purpose*. Englewood Cliffs: Prentice-Hall.

—— (1992). *Metaphysics*, 4th edn. Englewood Cliffs: Prentice-Hall.

Thorp, John (1980). *Free Will: A Defence Against Neurophysiological Determinism*. London: Routledge and Kegan Paul.

Tooley, Michael (1987). *Causation: A Realist Approach*. Oxford: Clarendon Press.

Van Inwagen, Peter (1983). *An Essay on Free Will*. Oxford: Clarendon Press.

—— (1999). "Moral Responsibility, Determinism, and the Ability to Do Otherwise." *The Journal of Ethics*, 3: 341–50.

Velleman, J. David (1992). "What Happens When Someone Acts?" *Mind*, 101: 461–81.

Vihvelin, Kadri (1988). "The Modal Argument for Incompatibilism." *Philosophical Studies*, 53: 227–44.

—— (2000). "Freedom, Foreknowledge, and the Principle of Alternate Possibilities." *Canadian Journal of Philosophy*, 30: 1–23.

Wallace, R. Jay (1994). *Responsibility and the Moral Sentiments*. Cambridge, MA: Harvard University Press.

Waller, Bruce N. (1993). "Responsibility and the Self-made Self." *Analysis*, 53: 45–51.

Warfield, Ted A. (1996). "Determinism and Moral Responsibility are Incompatible." *Philosophical Topics*, 24 (2): 215–26.

Watson, Gary (1975). "Free Agency." *Journal of Philosophy*, 72: 205–20. Reprinted in Fischer (ed.) (1986a): 81–96; and in Watson (ed.) (1982): 96–110.

—— ed. (1982). *Free Will*. Oxford: Oxford University Press.

Widerker, David (1987). "On an Argument for Incompatibilism." *Analysis*, 47: 37–41.

—— (1991). "Frankfurt on 'Ought Implies Can' and Alternative Possibilities." *Analysis*, 51: 222–4.

—— (1995a). "Libertarian Freedom and the Avoidability of Decisions." *Faith and Philosophy*, 12: 113–18.

—— (1995b). "Libertarianism and Frankfurt's Attack on the Principle of Alternative Possibilities." *The Philosophical Review*, 104: 247–61.

—— (2000). "Frankfurt's Attack on the Principle of Alternative Possibilities: A Further Look." *Philosophical Perspectives*, 14: 181–202.

Widerker, David and Katzoff, Charlotte (1996). "Avoidability and Libertarianism: A Response to Fischer." *Faith and Philosophy*, 13: 415–21.

Wiggins, David (1973). "Towards a Reasonable Libertarianism." In Honderich (ed.) (1973): 31–61.

Wolf, Susan (1990). *Freedom within Reason*. New York: Oxford University Press.

Wyma, Keith (1997). "Moral Responsibility and Leeway for Action." *American Philosophical Quarterly*, 34: 57–70.

Zimmerman, Michael J. (1984). *An Essay on Human Action*. New York: Peter Lang.

—— (1993). "Obligation, Responsibility and Alternate Possibilities." *Analysis*, 53: 51–3.

Index

vacuity of theory 164–5
Van Gulick, R. 54, 119
van Inwagen, Peter 393n6, 393n7
verification 48, 49, 118, 236–7
vision: individualism 267–8; information
   processing 266–7; Marr 265, 266,
   267–74, 278
vitalism 110

Wagner, A. R. 325
water: microphysics 137n17; natural kind
   terms 87–8, 114, 258; Twin Earth
   144, 152–3, 219, 258, 278

Watson, Gary 394n20
Watson, John B. 288
Whitman, Walt 1
wholeheartedness 377–8, 395n24
Wilson, E. O. 12
Wilson, Robert A. 265
Witmer, D. Gene 71
Wittgenstein, L. 40–1n83, 143, 192, 289
Woodward, J. 61

Zajonc, Robert 303
zero-crossings 270, 278
zombies 56, 105–6, 119, 228–30